THE RA MATERIAL

The Law of One
BOOK I

The Law of One
Book I

AN ANCIENT ASTRONAUT SPEAKS

DON ELKINS ⚘ CARLA RUECKERT
JAMES ALLEN McCARTY

REDFeather
MIND | BODY | SPIRIT

4880 Lower Valley Road, Atglen, PA 19310

First Printing 1981
ISBN: 978-0-89865-260-4

*3,000 copies of *The Law of One* were privately printed by L/L Research, Louisville, KY, before it was printed under the title *The Ra Material*.

Type set in Chaparral Pro

Book I
Softcover ISBN: 978-0-89865-260-4
Hardcover ISBN: 978-0-7643-6554-6
Box Set ISBN (Books I–V): 978-0-7643-6021-3
E-Book ISBN: 978-1-5073-0065-7

Printed in India

Updated Edition
10 9 8 7 6 5 4 3

Published by Red Feather Mind, Body, Spirit
An imprint of Schiffer Publishing, Ltd.
4880 Lower Valley Road
Atglen, PA 19310
Phone: (610) 593-1777; Fax: (610) 593-2002
E-mail: Info@schifferbooks.com
Web: www.redfeathermbs.com

For our complete selection of fine books on this and related subjects, please visit our website at www.schifferbooks.com. You may also write for a free catalog.

—— INTRODUCTION ——

DON ELKINS: This book is an exact transcript from tape recordings of twenty-six sessions of an experiment designed to communicate with an extraterrestrial being. We started the experiment in 1962 and refined the process for nineteen years. In 1981 the experimental results of our efforts changed profoundly in quality and precision. This book is simply a report of the beginning of this latter phase of our work.

Since our experimental work began, and even before we officially formed a research group, there was considerable confusion about the nature of our research. I would like to state that I consider my point of view to be purely scientific. Many readers of this material have used as a basis for its evaluation a previously assumed philosophical bias, which has ranged from what I would call objectively scientific to subjectively theological. It is not the purpose of our research group to attempt to do anything other than make experimental data available. Each reader will undoubtedly reach his own unique conclusion about the meaning of this body of data.

In recent years there has been much controversy about phenomena that were apparently incompatible with accepted methods of scientific research. This included such things as UFOs, mental metal bending, psychic surgery, and many other seemingly miraculous happenings.

To prove or disprove any of these alleged phenomena is certainly not properly the task of the casual observer. However, most of the public opinion that has been generated with respect to these events seems to be the product of quick and superficial investigation. After almost thirty years of research and experimentation in the area of so-called paranormal phenomena, I must recommend extreme caution in reaching a conclusion. If it is possible to make money, gain notoriety, or have fun from perpetrating a hoax, then someone usually does it. Consequently, paranormal or psychic areas are prime targets for the trickster, and the careful researcher usually has to observe copious amounts of "garbage" data in order to find a possible imbedded gem of truth. This is especially true of Philippine psychic surgery and the large area of spirit communication in general.

It seems to me that the presently accepted scientific paradigm is less than adequate. It is my opinion that our present natural philosophy is a very special case of a much more general case yet to be unveiled. It is my hope that our research is in the direction of this discovery. After assimilating several million words of alleged extraterrestrial communication, it is also my opinion that this book and the subsequent volumes of the Ra material contain the most useful information that I have discovered. As a result of all of this delving into the rather confusing subjects of UFOlogy and parapsychology, I, of course, have formed my current opinion of how things "really are." This opinion may change at any time as I become aware of future information. This book is not intended to be a treatise of my opinion, so I will not attempt to defend its validity. The following is the best guess I can make about what we think we are doing. Only time will tell as to the accuracy of this guess.

Our research group uses what I prefer to call "tuned trance telepathy" to communicate with an extraterrestrial race called Ra. We use the English language because it is known by Ra. In fact, Ra knows more of it than I do.

Ra landed on Earth about 11,000 years ago as a sort of extraterrestrial missionary with the objective of helping Earthman with his mental evolution. Failing in this attempt, Ra retreated from the Earth's surface but continued to monitor activities closely on this planet. For this reason, Ra is highly informed about our history, languages, etc.

Probably the most difficult thing to understand about Ra is its nature. Ra is a sixth-density social memory complex. Since Earth is near the end of the third-density cycle of evolution, this means that Ra is three evolutionary cycles ahead of us. In other words, Ra's present state of evolution is millions of years in advance of Earthman's. It is not surprising that Ra had difficulty communicating with Earthman 11,000 years ago. The same problem still exists in our present "enlightened" time.

At this writing we have completed over 100 sessions of experimental communications with Ra. This approximately 300,000 words of information has suggested to me a possibly more adequate scientific paradigm. Only time and future experience will serve to validate and expand this paradigm.

UFOlogy is a large subject. A reasonable amount of background material would swell this introduction to book length. Therefore, the remainder of this introduction does not attempt to cover every portion of this diverse and growing field of study but is instead an accounting of some of the pertinent parts of our research from our beginnings to the present day and the Ra contact. I've asked my longtime research associate, Carla L. Rueckert, to tell our story.

CARLA L. RUECKERT: I first met Don Elkins in **1962**. To me he was a fascinating character, an unusual combination of a college professor and psychic researcher. He had done well over **200** hypnotic age regressions, probing past the birth experience and investigating the possibility that reincarnation might not be just possible but the way things really are.

In 1962, I joined an experiment that Don had created in order to start to test a hypothesis that he had developed with the help of Harold Price, an engineer for Ford Motor Company. Price had acquainted Don with some information that Don found quite interesting. Its source was allegedly extraterrestrial. Its content was largely metaphysical and seemed to be in line with all that Don had learned up to that point. Within this material, instructions were given for creating the means whereby to generate further material from this same source without the necessity of actual physical contact with extraterrestrials.

Don's hypothesis was that this phenomenon might be reproducible, so he invited a dozen of his engineering students to join in an experiment with the objective of achieving some sort of telepathic contact with a source similar to that of the Detroit group's. I was the thirteenth member, having become interested in the project through a friend of mine. In those early days of contact attempts, with Don attempting strenuously to keep the situation controlled, months went by with what seemed to be remarkable but puzzling results. As we sat "meditating," according to the instructions, everyone in the group except me began to make strange noises with their mouths. For my part, my main difficulty during those first six months was keeping a straight face and not laughing as the sessions gradually became a raucous symphony of guttural clicks, slurps, and tongue flops.

The nature of the experiment changed drastically when the group was visited by a contactee from Detroit. The contactee sat down with the group and almost immediately was contacted apparently by telepathic impression, saying: "Why don't you speak the thoughts that are on your minds? We are attempting to use you as instruments of communication, but you are all blocked through fear that you will not be speaking the proper words." Through this instrument, Walter Rogers of Detroit, Michigan, the group was instructed to refrain from analysis, to speak the thoughts and to analyze the communication only after it had been completed.

After that night, a month had not gone by before half the group had begun to produce information. By the time a year had passed, all in the group except me were able to receive transmissions. The speech was slow and difficult at first because each individual wanted a precise impression of each and every word and, in many cases, wanted to be completely controlled for fear of making an error in transmission. Nevertheless, this was an exciting time for the original group of students who began this strange experiment.

In January of 1970, I left my position as school librarian of a thirteen-grade private school here in Louisville and went to work for Don full time. By this time he was convinced that the great mystery of being could best be investigated by research into techniques for contacting extraterrestrial intelligences, and was determined to intensify his efforts in this area.

During this period, Don worked on many peripheral areas of UFO research, always trying to "put the puzzle pieces together." One of the great puzzle pieces for us was the question of how UFOs could materialize and dematerialize. The phenomenon seemed to posit a physics that we had not yet grasped and a being capable of using this physics. Don had gone to many séances by himself before I joined him in his research and had very systematically crossed each name off his list. He was looking for a materialization manifestation, not one he could prove to anyone else, but one that he, himself, could believe. It was his feeling that the materializations that séances manifest were perhaps of the same or similar nature as the materializations of UFOs. Therefore, his reasoning went, viewing personally the mechanism of a materialization and a dematerialization in a séance would enable him to hypothesize more accurately concerning UFOs.

In 1971, after I had been on several fruitless materialization medium searches with Don, we went to a séance held by the Reverend James Tingley of Toledo, a minister of the Spiritualist Church.

We went to see Reverend Tingley's demonstrations four times. Before the first time, Don had casually examined Reverend Tingley's modest meeting place inside and out. It was built of concrete blocks, like a garage. There were no gadgets either inside or outside the building. I did not know that Don was doing this. I merely sat and waited for the demonstration to begin.

This last point is an important one when talking about psychic research of any kind. Don has always said that one of my assets as a research associate is my great gullibility. Almost anyone can play a joke on me because I do not catch on quickly. I have a way of taking things as they come and accepting them at face value and only afterwards analyzing what has occurred. This gullibility is a vital factor in obtaining good results in paranormal research. A desire for proof will inevitably lead to null results and voided experiments. An open mind, one willing to be gullible, leads its possessor to a kind of subjective and personal certainty that does not equal proof, as it cannot be systematically reproduced in others. However, this subjective knowing is a central part of the spiritual evolution to which Ra speaks so compellingly in this volume and that we have researched for many years now.

The séance began, as do all the séances I have attended, with the repetition of the Lord's Prayer and the singing of hymns such as "Rock of Ages" and "I Walked in the Garden." There were approximately twenty-six people in this bare room, sitting on straight chairs in an oval circle. Reverend Tingley had retired behind a simple curtain and was also seated on a folding chair. Of the occurrences of the first séance, perhaps the most interesting to me was the appearance of a rather solid ghost known as "Sister." She wished to speak to me and to thank me for helping Don. Since I had never had a close friend that was a nun, I was quite puzzled. It was not until much later, when Don was flying us home, that he jogged my memory, and I realized that his mother, who had died before I met her, was known in the family as "Sister."

Both in that séance and in the following séance, when Don and I were called up, we could see the ghostlike figures of the materialized spirits quite clearly. I, with impaired night vision, could still make out features, but Don could see even the strands of hair on each entity.

During the second séance, an especially inspiring "Master" appeared suddenly and the room grew very cold. He gave us an inspirational message and then told us that he would touch us so that we would know that he was real. He did so, with enough force to bruise my arm. Then he told us that he would walk through us so that we would know that he was not of this density. This he did, and it is certainly an interesting sensation to watch this occur. Lifting his arms, he blessed all those in the room, walked back through us, and pooled down in a small pool on the floor and was gone.

In 1974, Don decided that it was time for me to become a more serious student of the art of channeling. He argued that twelve years of sitting and listening to inspirational messages were enough, and that it was time for me to take some responsibility for those "cosmic sermonettes," as Brad Steiger has called them, that I so enjoyed. We began a series of daily meetings designed to work intensively on my mental tuning. Many of those who were coming to our meditations on Sunday nights heard about the daily meetings and also came, and within three months we generated about a dozen new telepathic receivers.

During the process of these intensive meditations we instituted our long-standing habit of keeping the tape recorder going whenever we started a session. Using some of the large body of material that our own group had collected, I put together an unpublished manuscript, *Voices of the Gods*, which systematically offered the extraterrestrial viewpoint as recorded by our group meetings. In 1976, when Don and I began to write *Secrets of the UFO* (published by a private printing and available by mail), this unpublished manuscript was of great help.

During this period one other thing occurred that was synchronistic. Don and I, who had officially gone into partnership as L/L Research in 1970, had written an unpublished book titled *The Crucifixion of Esmeralda Sweetwater* in 1968.

In 1974, Andrija Puharich published a book with Doubleday titled *Uri*. The book is the narrative of Dr. Puharich's investigation of Uri Geller and their unexpected communication with extraterrestrial intelligences. The form of contact was quite novel in that, first, some object like an ashtray would levitate, signaling Dr. Puharich to load his cassette tape recorder. The recorder's buttons would then be depressed by some invisible force and the machine would record. On playback, a message from an extraterrestrial source would be present. Don was impressed by the large number of correlations between these messages and our own research.

The book is fascinating in its own right, but it was especially fascinating to us because of the incredible number of distinct and compelling similarities between the characters in the real-life journal of Dr. Puharich's work with Uri and the supposedly fictional characters in our book. We went to New York to meet Andrija after phoning him, sharing our long-standing research with him and comparing notes. As our genial host came out onto his front veranda to welcome us, I stopped, amazed, to look at the house. Even the house in which he lived in the country north of New York City was a dead ringer for the house his fictional counterpart had owned in our book. The identity was so close that I could not help but ask, "Andrija, what happened to your peonies? When I wrote about your house I saw your driveway circled with peony bushes." Puharich laughed, "Oh, those. I had those cut down three years ago."

In 1976, we determined to attempt an introduction to the whole spectrum of paranormal phenomena that are involved in the so-called UFO contactee phenomenon. This phenomenon is not a simple one. Rather, it demands a fairly comprehensive understanding and awareness of several different fields of inquiry. Since *The Ra Material* is a direct outgrowth of our continuous research with "alleged" extraterrestrial entities, it seems appropriate here to review some of the concepts put forward in that book in order that the reader may have the proper introduction to the "mindset," which is most helpful for an understanding of this work.

The first thing to say about the UFO phenomenon is that it is extraordinarily strange. The serious researcher, as he reads more and more and does more and more field research, finds himself less and less able to talk about the UFO phenomenon in a sensible and "down to Earth" way. Well over half the people in the United States have said in nationwide polls that they believe that UFOs are real, and television series and motion pictures reflect the widespread interest in this subject. Yet, there are few researchers who would pretend to be able to understand the phenomenon completely. Dr. J. Allen Hynek has called this quality of the research the "high strangeness" factor and has linked the amount of high strangeness with the probable validity of the case.

Some of the people who see UFOs have the experience of being unable to account for a period of time after the encounter. The UFO is seen and then the witness continues on with his or her daily routine. At some point, it is noticed that a certain amount of time has been lost that cannot be explained. Very often these same people report a type of eye irritation, or conjunctivitis, and sometimes skin problems. In extreme cases, a person who has lost time and seen a UFO will develop a change of personality and find it necessary to contact the aid of a psychologist or a psychiatrist for counseling. Dr. R. Leo Sprinkle, professor of psychology at the University of Wyoming, has been conducting yearly meetings of people who have experienced this type and other types of "Close Encounters."

It was in psychiatric therapy that one of the more famous of the UFO contact cases, that of Betty and Barney Hill, was researched. The Hills had seen a UFO and had lost some time but managed to reduce the significance of these events in their minds enough to get on with their daily lives. However, both of them, over a period of months, began experiencing nightmares and attacks of anxiety.

The psychiatrist to whom they went for help was one who often used regressive hypnosis for therapeutic work. He worked with each of the couple separately and found, to his amazement, that when asked to go back to the source of their distress, both Mr. and Mrs. Hill related the story of being taken onboard a UFO while on a drive, medically examined, and returned to their car.

Don and I have, through the years, investigated quite a few interesting cases, but perhaps a description of one will suffice to show some of the more outstanding strangenesses that are quite commonly associated with what Dr. Hynek calls "Close Encounters of the Third Kind." In January 1977, merely eighteen or so hours after our witness's UFO experience, we were called by a friend of ours, hypnotist Lawrence Allison. Lawrence had been contacted by the witness's mother, who was extraordinarily concerned about her boy. We made an appointment with the witness, a nineteen-year-old high school graduate employed as a truck driver.

He had seen a craft about 40 feet long and 10 feet tall, which was the color of the setting sun, at very low altitude, approximately 100 to 150 feet. The craft was so bright that it hurt his eyes, yet he could not remove his gaze from it. He experienced a good deal of fear and lost all sense of actually driving his car. When he was directly underneath the UFO, it suddenly sped away and disappeared. When the boy arrived home, his mother was alarmed because his eyes were entirely bloodshot. He was able to pinpoint his time loss since he had left precisely when a television program ended and since he noticed the time of his arrival home. He had lost thirty-eight minutes of his life.

The young man wished to try regressive hypnosis to "find" his lost time. We agreed, and after a fairly lengthy hypnotic induction, the proper state of concentration was achieved and the witness was moved back to the point at which he was directly underneath the UFO. Suddenly he was inside the ship in a circular room, which seemed at least twice as high as the entire ship had seemed from the outside. He saw three objects, none of which looked human. One was black, one was red, and one was white. All looked like some sort of machine. Each entity seemed to have a personality, although none spoke to the boy, and he endured a kind of physical examination. After the examination was finished, the machines merged into one and then disappeared. The ship bounced and rocked briefly, and then the witness was back in his car.

If you are interested in reading a full account of this case, it was published in the *A.P.R.O. Bulletin*, in *Flying Saucer Review*, in the *International UFO Reporter*, and in the *MUFON UFO News*.

One of the most familiar aspects of close encounters is the experience that our witness had of seemingly understanding what aliens were thinking and feeling without any speech having taken place. Telepathic communication has long been the subject of much experimentation, and, although there is much interesting research, there has never been a definitive study proving good telepathic communication. Consequently, the field of research into telepathy is still definitely a fringe area of psychic research. However, anyone who has ever known that the phone was going to ring, or has experienced the knowledge of what someone was going to say before it was said, has experienced at least a mild example of telepathy. Don states that telepathic experiments between himself and Uri Geller have been totally successful. However, since they were deliberately not performed under rigorous scientific control, they could not be included in any orthodox report. It is, in fact, our opinion that the rigorous controls have a dampening effect on the outcome of any experiment of this type.

L/L Research, which, since 1980, has been a subsidiary of the Rock Creek Research and Development Labs, to this day holds weekly meetings open to anyone who has read our books. We still tend to insert the word "alleged" before the words "telepathic communications from extraterrestrials" because we know full well that there is no way of proving this basic concept. However, the phenomenon certainly exists—millions of words in our own files and many millions of words in other groups' files attest to this fact.

Regardless of the more than occasional frustrations involved in paranormal research, the serious researcher of the UFO phenomenon needs to be persistent in his investigation of related phenomena, such as mental metal bending. The physics that Ra discusses, having to do with the true nature of reality, posits the possibility of action at a distance as a function of mind, specifically the will. Uri Geller has been tested in several places around the world, including the Stanford Research Laboratories, and an impressive list of publications concerning the results of those tests exists, most notably *The Geller Papers* and, as an offshoot of this metal-bending phenomenon, *The Iceland Papers*.

One example that shows the close connection between UFOs and mental metal bending happened to us in July of 1977, after our book, *Secrets of the UFO*, was published. We had been interviewed on a local program, and a woman in a nearby town had heard the broadcast and was very interested in what we had to say, since her son, a normal fourteen-year-old boy, had had a UFO encounter. He had been awakened by a whistling sound, went to the door, and saw a light so bright that it temporarily blinded him. Again, as is often the case, it was the same night that people nearby also saw lights in the sky. The woman wrote us a letter, and Don immediately called and asked her permission to speak to her son. After questioning the young man to Don's satisfaction, Don asked him to take a piece of silverware and tell it to bend without touching it in any firm or forceful way. The fourteen-year-old picked up a fork and did as Don suggested, and the fork immediately bent nearly double.

The boy was so startled that he would not come back to the phone, and his mother was unable to convince him that there was any value in going further with the experiments. She had enough foresight to realize that in the small town in which he lived, any publicity that might come to him on the subject of metal bending would be to his detriment, since the people of his small town would react in a most predictable way.

Nevertheless, the link is there quite plainly. John Taylor, professor of mathematics at Kings College, London, offered his book *Superminds* to make his careful experimentations on metal bending available to the world. Taylor used only children, about fifty of them, and for a great portion of his experiment he used metal and plastic objects sealed in glass cylinders that had been closed by a glass blower, so that the children could not actually touch the objects without breaking the glass.

Under this controlled circumstance the children were still able to bend and break multitudinous objects. As you read *The Ra Material* you will begin to discover why it is mostly children that are able to do these things, and what the ability to do this has to do with the rest of the UFO message.

Since I am not a scientist, at this point I will turn the narrative back to Don, whose background is more suited to this discussion.

DON: A persistent question when considering psychic demonstrations is: how does the paranormal event happen? The answer may well lie in the area of occult theory, which is concerned with the existence of various "planes."

After death, an individual finds himself at one of these levels of existence spoken of in connection with occult philosophy, the level of being dependent on the spiritual nature or development of the person at the time of his death. The cliché that covers this theory is a heavenly "birds of a feather flock together." When a ghost materializes into our reality, it is from one of these levels that he usually comes for his Earthly visit. In general, it is theorized that a planet is a sort of spiritual distillery, with reincarnation taking place into the physical world until the individual is sufficiently developed in the spiritual sense that he can reach the higher planes of existence and is no longer in need of this planet's developmental lessons.

Most of this theory was developed as a result of reported contact and communication with the inhabitants of these supposedly separate realities. I have come to believe that these levels interpenetrate with our physical space and mutually coexist, though with very little awareness of each other. A simple analogy, to which I've referred before, is to consider the actors in two different TV shows, both receivable on the same set, but each show being exclusive of the other. This seems to be what we experience in our daily lives: one channel or density of existence being totally unaware of the myriad entities occupying other frequencies of our physical space. The point of all this is that our reality is not ultimate or singular; it is, in fact, our reality only at the present.

Many of the UFO reports display ample evidence that the object sighted has its origin in one of these other realities or densities, just as do the materialized ghosts. I would like to emphasize that this does not in any way imply their unreality; rather, it displaces the UFOs' reality from ours. I'm saying the equivalent of: channel 4 on the TV is equivalent to but displaced from channel 3 on the same TV.

If you were told to build a scale model of any atom, using something the size of a pea for the nucleus, it would be necessary to have an area the size of a football stadium to contain even the innermost orbital electrons. If the pea were placed at the center of the 50-yard line, a small cotton ball on the uppermost seat in the stands could represent an electron of the atom. There is very little actual matter in physical matter. When you look at the stars in the night sky, you would probably see something quite similar to what you would see if you could stand on the nucleus of any atom of "solid" material and look outward toward our environment. To demonstrate an electron to you, a physicist will probably show you a curved trace of one on a photographic plate. What he probably does not tell you is that this is secondhand evidence. The electron itself has never been seen; only its effect on a dense medium can be recorded. It is possible, of course, to make accurate mathematical calculations about what we call an electron. For such work we must know some data on magnetic field strength, electron charge, and velocity. But since a magnetic field is caused by moving charges, which in turn are empirically observed phenomena, we find that the entire mathematical camouflage obscures the fact that all we really know is that charged particles have effects on each other. We still don't know what charged particles are, or why they create an action-at-a-distance effect.

Senior scientists would be the first to agree that there is no such thing as an absolute scientific explanation of anything. Science is, rather, a method or tool of prediction, relating one or more observations to each other. In physics, this is usually done through the language of mathematics. Our scientific learning is a learning by observation and analysis of this observation. In the sense of penetrating the fundamental essences of things, we really do not understand anything at all.

A magnetic field is nothing but a mathematical method of expressing the relative motion between electrical fields. Electrical fields are complex mathematical interpretations of a totally empirical observation stated as Coulomb's law. In other words, our forest of scientific knowledge and explanations is made up of trees about which we understand nothing except their effect, their existence.

To a person unfamiliar with the inner workings of modern science, it may seem that modern man has his environment nicely under control and totally figured out. Nothing could be further from the truth. The leaders of science who are researching the frontiers of modern theory argue among themselves continually. As soon as a theory begins to receive wide acceptance as being a valid representation of physical laws, someone finds a discrepancy, and the theory has to be either modified or abandoned entirely. Perhaps the most well-known example of this is Newton's "F=MA." This attained the status of a physical law before being found to be in error. It is not that this equation has not proven extremely useful: we have used it to design everything from a moon rocket to the television picture tube, but its accuracy fails when applied to atomic particle accelerators like the cyclotron. To make accurate predictions of particle trajectories, it is necessary to make the relativistic correction formulated by Einstein. It is interesting to note that this correction is based on the fact that the speed of light is totally independent of the speed of its source.

If Newton had penetrated more deeply into the laws of motion, he might have made this relativistic correction himself and then stated that the velocity correction would always be of no consequence, since the velocity of light was so much greater than any speed attainable by man. This was very true in Newton's day but is definitely not the case now. We still tend to think of the velocity of light as a fantastic and unattainable speed, but with the advent of space flight, a new order of velocities has arrived. We have to change our thinking from our normal terrestrial concepts of velocities. Instead of thinking of the speed of light in terms of miles per second, think of it in terms of Earth diameters per second. The almost unimaginable 186,000 miles per second becomes an entirely thinkable twenty-three Earth diameters per second, or we could think of the speed of light in terms of our solar system's diameter and say that light would speed at about two diameters per day.

Einstein's assertion that everything is relative is so apt that it has become a cliché of our culture. Let us continue being relativistic in considering the size of natural phenomena by considering the size of our galaxy. If you look up at the sky on a clear night, nearly all of the visible stars are in our own galaxy. Each of these stars is a sun like our own. A calculation of the ratio of the number of suns in our galaxy to the number of people on planet Earth discovers that there are sixty suns for each living person on Earth today. It takes light over four years to get from Earth to even the nearest of these stars. To reach the most distant star in our own galaxy would take 100,000 light years.

These calculations are made using the assumption that light has a speed. This may be an erroneous assumption in the face of new theory, but its apparent speed is a useful measuring tool, so we use it anyway.

So we have a creation in which we find ourselves that is so big that at a speed of twenty-three Earth diameters a second we must travel 100,000 years to cross our immediate backyard. That is a big backyard, and it would seem ample for even the most ambitious of celestial architects, but in truth this entire galaxy of over 200 billion stars is just one grain of sand on a very big beach. There are uncounted trillions of galaxies like ours, each with its own billions of stars, spread throughout what seems to be infinite space.

When you think of the mind-boggling expanse of our creation and the infantile state of our knowledge in relation to it, you begin to see the necessity for considering the strong probability that our present scientific approach to investigating these expanses is as primitive as the dugout canoe.

The most perplexing problem of science has always been finding a satisfactory explanation of what is called action at a distance. In other words, everyone knows that if you drop something it will fall, but no one knows precisely why. Many people know that electric charges push or pull on each other even if separated in a vacuum, but again no one knows why. Although the phenomena are quite different, the equations that describe the force of interaction are quite similar:

For gravitation: F=GmmVr2. For electrostatic interaction: F=KqqVr2. The attractive force between our planet and our sun is described by the gravitational equation. The attractive force between orbiting electrons and the atomic nucleus is described by the electrostatic interaction equation. Now each of these equations was determined experimentally. They are not apparently related in any way, and yet they both describe a situation in which attractive force falls off with the square of the distance of separation.

A mathematical representation of an action-at-a-distance effect is called a field, such as a gravitational or electric field. It was Albert Einstein's foremost hope to find a single relation that would express the effect of both electric and gravitational phenomena; in fact, a theory that would unify the whole of physics, a unified field theory. Einstein believed that this was a creation of total order and that all physical phenomena were evolved from a single source.

This unified field theory, describing matter as pure field, has been accomplished now. It seems that the entire situation was analogous to the solution of a ponderously complex Chinese puzzle. If you can find that the right key turns among so many wrong ones, the puzzle easily falls apart. Dewey B. Larson found the solution to this problem, and the puzzle not only fell apart but revealed an elegantly adequate unified field theory rich in practical results; like a good Chinese puzzle, the solution was not complex, just unexpected. Instead of assuming five dimensions, Larson assumed six, and properly labeled them as the three dimensions of space and the three dimensions of time. He assumed that there is a three-dimensional coordinate time analogous to our observed three-dimensional space.

The result of this approach is that one can now calculate from the basic postulate of Larson's theory any physical value within our physical universe, from subatomic to stellar. This long-sought-after unified field theory is different because we are accustomed to thinking of time as one dimensional, as a stream moving in one direction. Yet once you get the hang of it, coordinate time is mathematically a more comfortable concept with which to deal. Professor Frank Meyer of the Department of Physics at the University of Wisconsin currently distributes a quarterly newsletter to scientists interested in Larson's new theory, which explores perplexing questions in physical theory by using Larson's approach. I was interested in testing Larson's theory and made extensive calculations using his postulate. I became convinced that his theory is indeed a workable unified field theory.

I had been pondering several interesting statements communicated through contactees by the alleged UFO source prior to discovering Larson's work in the early sixties. Although the people who had received these communications knew nothing of the problems of modern physics, they were getting information that apparently was quite central to physical theory: first, they suggested that the problem with our science was that it did not recognize enough dimensions. Second, they stated that light does not move; light is. Larson's theory posits six dimensions instead of the customary four and finds the pure field, which Einstein believed would represent matter, to move outward from all points in space at unit velocity, or the velocity of light. Photons are created due to a vibratory displacement in space-time, the fabric of the field. Furthermore, the contactees were saying that consciousness creates vibration, this vibration being light. The vibratory displacements of space-time in Larson's theory are the first physical manifestation, which is the photon or light. According to the UFO contactees, the UFOs lower their vibrations in order to enter our skies. The entire physical universe postulated by Larson is dependent on the rate of vibration and quantized rotations of the pure field of space-time.

The contactees were suggesting that time was not what we think it is. Larson suggests the same thing. The UFOs were said to move in time as we move in space. This would be entirely normal in Larson's time/space portion of the universe.

Lastly, and perhaps most importantly, the contactees were receiving the message that the creation is simple, all one thing. Larson's theory is a mathematical statement of this unity.

For more information about Larsonian physics, contact the International Society of Unified Science, a group of scientists and philosophers currently promoting Larson's theory. Their address is: International Society of Unified Science, Frank H. Meyer, President, 1103 15th Ave., SE, Minneapolis, MN 55414.

What physicists have never before considered worth investigating is now increasing at a very rapid rate. Action at a distance, apparently as a result of some type of mental activity, seems repeatedly the observed effect. When Uri Geller performs on TV, mentally bending metal and fixing clocks, there are often many kids who try to duplicate Uri's "tricks." Sometimes the kids succeed. The number of children that can cause bends and breaks in metal and other materials just by wanting the break or bend to occur is increasing daily. As previously mentioned, John

Taylor, professor of mathematics at Kings College, reports in his excellent book *Superminds* on the extensive tests run in England on several of these gifted children. If the Gellerizing children continue to increase in numbers and ability, the 1980s will see such fantasies of TV as *My Favorite Martian*, *I Dream of Jeannie*, and *Bewitched* becoming a part of reality.

With controlled, repeatable experiments like those conducted by Taylor and by the Stanford Research Institute in the United States, we begin to have good solid data available for study. Gradually we are moving into a position from which we can begin to create a science of "magic," for that which has been called magic through the ages is now being performed at an ever-increasing rate, primarily by children. In the future, we may even find this "magic" added to the curriculum of the sciences at universities. In point of fact, the present disciplines of chemistry, physics, etc., are still basically "magic" to us, since we are still in the position of having no ultimate explanation of causality.

CARLA: One of the concepts most central to the system of study that comes out of research into the contactee messages offered by alleged UFO contact is the concept of the immortality of our individual consciousness. There is a long mystical tradition extending back far beyond biblical times, which posits a type of immortal soul. St. Paul in his Epistles has distinguished between the human body and the spiritual body. Long before St. Paul's century, Egyptian priests had the concept of the ka and posited that this ka, or spiritual personality, existed after death and was the true repository of the essence of consciousness of the person who had lived the life. Egyptians, of course, made very elaborate arrangements for life after death.

If life after death is posited as a probability, one may also posit life before birth. Any mother who has more than one child will testify to the undoubted fact that each child comes into his life or incarnation already equipped with a personality that cannot be explained by environment or heredity. After all the factors of both have been accounted for, there remains a unique personality with which the child seems to have been born. Each child has certain fears that are not explainable in terms of the fears of the parents. A child, for instance, may be terrified of a thunderstorm. The rest of the family may be perfectly comfortable during such a storm. Another child may be extraordinarily gifted at the playing of an instrument when neither parent nor any relative as far back as the parents can remember had musical ability.

This brings us back to the serious consideration of reincarnation. According to the alleged UFO contact messages, reincarnation is one of the most important concepts to be grasped, for through it the universe functions in order to advance the evolution of mankind. This evolution is seen to be not only physical but also metaphysical, not only of the body but also of the spirit, and incarnations are seen in this system of philosophy to be opportunities for an individual to continue his evolution through numerous and varied experiences.

Although perhaps two-thirds of the world's population embraces or is familiar with a religious system that posits reincarnation, those of us of the Judeo-Christian culture are not as familiar with this concept. Nevertheless, Don's early investigations seemed to indicate that reincarnation was a probability and that incarnations contained situations, relationships, and lessons that were far more easily understood in the light of knowledge of previous incarnations.

One succinct example of this relationship, which some are fond of calling karma, is that of a young boy (who requests that his name not be used) who in this life had experienced such intense allergies to all living things that he could not cut the grass, smell the flowers, or, during the blooming season, spend much time at all outside. Under hypnotic regression he experienced in detail a long life in England. He had been a solitary man whose nature was such as to avoid contact with any human being. He had inherited a fairly large estate and he spent his life upon it. His one pleasure was the very extensive garden that he maintained. In it he had his gardeners plant all manner of flowers, fruits, and vegetables.

After the life had been discussed, and while the lad was still in trance, hypnotist Lawrence Allison asked the boy, as he often did, to contact what is loosely referred to as his Higher Self. He had the boy ask his Higher Self if the lesson of putting people first and other things second had been learned. The Higher Self said that indeed the lesson had been learned. The hypnotist then had the boy ask the Higher Self if this allergy could be healed, since the lesson had been learned and the allergy was no longer necessary. The Higher Self agreed. The hypnotist then carefully brought the boy out of the hypnotic state and walked over to his piano on which was placed a magnolia. As magnolia blossoms will do, it had dropped its pollen on the polished surface of the piano, and the hypnotist scraped the pollen onto his hand, took it over to the boy, and deliberately blew the pollen directly at the boy's nose. "How could you do that to me!" exclaimed the boy. "You know how allergic I am." "Oh, really?" asked the hypnotist. "I don't hear you sneezing." The boy remained cured of his allergy.

When we attempt to consider our relationship with the universe, we begin to see that there is a great deal more in heaven and earth than has been dreamt of in most philosophies. It is an unbelievably gigantic universe, and if we have a true relationship to it we must, ourselves, be more than, or other than, our daily lives seem to encompass. In *The Ra*

Material a good deal of information is discussed concerning our true relationship with the universe, but it is good to realize that we do have a long tradition of work upon what may perhaps most simply be called the magical personality.

Magic is, of course, a much misused term and is mostly understood as being the art of prestidigitation, or illusion. When one sees a magician, one accepts the fact that one is seeing very skillfully performed illusions.

However, there is a study of the so-called magical personality that suggests that there is a thread that runs through our daily lives that we can grasp, and, using that thread, remove ourselves from time to time into a framework of reference points in which we see reality as being that of the spiritual body, that of the personality that exists from incarnation to incarnation and indeed "since before the world was." By working upon this magical personality, by interiorizing experience, by accepting responsibility for all that occurs, by carefully analyzing our reactions to all that occurs, and by eventually coming to balance our reactions to all that occurs so that our actions in our environment are generated within the self and are no longer simple reactions to outward stimulus, we strengthen the so-called magical personality until we are able to have some small claim to "the art of causing changes in consciousness at will." This is the classic definition of magic. Each time that a person sustains an unfortunate situation and reacts to it by not giving anger for anger or sadness for sadness but instead offering compassion and comfort where none was expected, we strengthen that thread of inner strength within us and we become more and more associated with a life that is closely related to the organic evolution of the universe.

It is some sense of the wholeness or organic nature of the universe that best informs the student of the UFOs' purposes in being here. They have been here, by many accounts, for thousands of years; at least UFOs have been mentioned, along with many other strange sights, in the annals of all early histories, including the Bible.

Modern-day interest in UFOs can probably be fairly accurately dated from Kenneth Arnold's historic sighting over Mt. Rainier in Washington. Another early and historic sighting, also by an extremely reliable witness, is coincidentally connected with Don Elkins, and so I would choose the Mantell case of January 7, 1948, instead of the Kenneth Arnold case of June 24, 1947, for discussion.

Thomas Mantell had trained as a pilot and had flown missions in Africa, in Europe, and, most notably, on D-day. In 1947 he was out of the Air Corps and had started the Elkins-Mantell Flying School on Bowman Field in Louisville, Kentucky. In 1947 Don Elkins was a youthful student in this school.

At about two o'clock in the afternoon on January 7, 1948, the Kentucky State Police called Fort Knox and reported to the MPs there that they had sighted a circular flying object moving rather quickly in their area. The MPs called the commanding officer at Godman Field at Fort Knox, and through due process the flight service checked with Wright Field in Ohio to see if there were any experimental aircraft that could explain the sighting. Wright Field had none flying.

Meanwhile, the tower at Godman Field, Fort Knox, had already sighted this disc-shaped object, both visually and on radar, and had made a report that was relayed quickly to the commanding officer.

As it happened, four F-51s were in the area en route from Marietta, Georgia, near Atlanta, to Louisville, Kentucky. Since they were already airborne, the commanding officer at Godman Field decided to contact the lead pilot and request that he investigate the UFO. The lead pilot was Captain Thomas Mantell.

Mantell was given a radar vector from Godman tower and moved towards the UFO. He sighted the object and stated that it was traveling slower than he was and that he would close to take a look. Then Mantell informed the tower that the object was now above him, that it appeared to be metallic, and that it was tremendous in size.

None of the F-51s, including Mantell's, were equipped with oxygen. The other pilots leveled off at 15,000 feet. Mantell kept climbing. That was the last transmission from Captain Mantell. Minutes later there was a telephone call stating that a plane had crashed. It was Captain Mantell's. His body lay near the wreckage.

I could spend the length of the book attempting to give you a sketchy introduction to the thousands and thousands of sightings like Captain Mantell's that involve irrefutably puzzling and concrete evidence of something highly strange occurring. There are many radar sightings of UFOs. There is one volume, published by the Center for UFO Studies in Evanston, Illinois, that deals solely with the numerous physical traces that UFOs have left behind, either by irradiating the soil, causing other changes in soil composition, or leaving impressions in the ground. A computer set up by this same organization to carry a program of information regarding UFOs contains well over 80,000 reports, and some things become startlingly clear by the use of "UFOCAT," the computer. For instance, it is now possible, if one measures a landing trace from a UFO sighting, to find out from the computer what the probable description of the UFO itself will be. Thus, in a way, the witness is merely confirming what the computer already knows.

However, this is an introduction to a book that consists of transcripts of messages of a very precise nature having to do with metaphysics, philosophy, and the plan of evolution, both physical and spiritual, of man on Earth. Consequently, what I propose to do is share with you some of the research material that our group has collected through the years. Since all of these examples come from the same group, we never describe who the receiver may be, as we feel that it is the information that is important rather than the person who is transmitting.

According to an entity called Hatonn who has spoken with our group and several others for many years, the purpose in being here of at least some of the UFOs that are seen in our skies at this time is much like the purpose that we might have in sending aid to a disaster-stricken or extremely impoverished country. It is a desire to be of service.

We have been contacting people of planet Earth for many, many of your years. We have been contacting at intervals of thousands of years those who sought our aid. It is time for many of the people of this planet to be contacted, for many now have the understanding and the desire to seek something outside the physical illusion that has for so many years involved the thinking of those of this planet. The process we are stimulating is one which is self-generating. As more and more of those who desire our contact receive it and pass it on to others, then those who receive this passed-on information will then themselves be able to reach a state of thinking and understanding sufficiently in tune, shall I say, with our vibrations in order to receive our contact. For this, my friends, is how contacts work. It is first necessary, if the entity is to be able to receive our contact, for him to become of a certain vibration as a result of his thinking. This is greatly speeded by involvement in groups such as this. And then it is finally done through meditation. In other words, the verbal communications given to the entity by the channels such as this one create a system of thought and a desire for spiritual awareness that raises his vibration.

We of the Confederation of Planets in the Service of the Infinite Creator are very sorry that we cannot step upon your soil and teach those of your people who desire our service. But, my friends, as we have said before, this would be a very great disservice to those who do not desire our service at this time, and we are afraid we would have little effect in bringing understanding even to those who desire it, for understanding, my friends, comes from within. We can only guide. We can only suggest. We are attempting to do this in such a way that the seeking of the individual will be stimulated to turning his thinking inward, inward to that single source of love and understanding, the Creator, that is part of us all, part of everything that exists, for everything that exists, my friends, is the Creator.

We are very privileged to have you join with us in this great service at this time in the history of your planet. For this is a very great time, a great transitional period, in which many of the Earth's people will be raised from their state of confusion to a simple understanding: the love of their Creator.

Hatonn speaks of our desire to seek something outside the physical illusion. What he talks about so persuasively is something that is often referred to by members of what Ra calls the Confederation of Planets in the Service of the Infinite Creator as "the original thought." This is another term for our word "love," but implies a great deal more. It implies a unity that is so great that we do not see each other simply as close friends, or brothers and sisters, but, ideally, as the Creator; and, as we see each other and ourselves as the Creator, we see one being. This concept is at the very heart of telepathy, and Hatonn talks about this concept and the original thought in general:

At this time I am in a craft far above your place of dwelling. I am at this time able to monitor your thoughts. This, my friends, might seem to some of your peoples to be an infringement, but I can assure you that it is not. Our capabilities of knowing the thinking of the peoples of this planet Earth are not designed in any way to infringe upon either their thinking or their activities. We do not consider the knowledge of the thoughts of others to be an infringement for we see these thoughts as our own. We see these thoughts as the thoughts of the Creator.

My friends, it may seem to you that a thought of a nature other than one of love and brotherhood might be a thought generated not of our Creator. This is not possible, my friends. All thought that is generated is generated by the Creator. All things that are generated are generated by the Creator. He is all things and is in all places, and all of the consciousness and all of the thought that exists is the thought of our Creator. His infinite number of parts all have free will, and all may generate in any way they choose. All of His parts communicate with all of the creation, in His entire and infinite sense.

We are not attempting to change the thinking of our Creator. We are only attempting to bring His ideas to some of the more isolated parts for their inspection and appraisal. Isolated parts, I say, my friends, and why should we consider these parts to be isolated? We consider them isolated because from our point of view they have chosen to wander far from the concept that we have found to permeate most of the parts of the creation with which we are familiar. We find, my friends, that man upon planet Earth in his experiences and experiments has become isolated in his thinking and has divorced it from that to which we are accustomed in the vast reaches of creation which we have experienced.

I urge you, my friends, to remember what we have brought to you. The next time that you are, shall we say, backed into a corner by the circumstances which prevail within the illusion of your physical existence, remember what you have learned and do not forget what you have worked so hard to obtain. You will choose at any time to alter your needs and desires from within the physical illusion to your being within the creation of the Father. As long as your objectives lie within this physical illusion it will be necessary for you to be subject to the laws which prevail within this illusion. If your desires can be altered by the application of what you are learning and are lifted in the creation of the Infinite One, then, my friends, you may have a great deal more ability to remove yourself from the corners into which the illusion seems to back you.

To some who may read these words, the concepts may seem to be a less than practical and certainly overly idealistic method of discussing what many have called the new age or the Age of Aquarius. It certainly seems unlikely that an entire planet could go so wrong philosophically and that beings supposedly more advanced than we would care enough about us to attempt to help us.

However, as we look for the heart of the "cosmic" system of philosophy, we find much that is clear and simple without being simplistic in the least, much that is ethical without being dogmatic—in short, much that is informative. Here Hatonn speaks of the nature of reality, which, in the main, seems to have escaped the notice of Earth man:

My friends, man on Earth has become very shortsighted in appreciation of the creation. He does not understand the true meaning of the simple and beautiful life that surrounds him. He does not appreciate its generation and regeneration. He learns that the very atmosphere that he breathes is cycled through the plant life to be regenerated to support him and his fellow beings and creatures, and yet this seems to the vast majority of those who dwell upon this planet to be an exercise in technology rather than one in theology. There is no awareness of the Creator's plan to provide for His children, to provide for their every desire and to provide a state of perfection. Man on Earth has lost the awareness that is rightfully his. And why, my friends, has he lost this awareness? He has lost this because he has focused his attention upon devices and inventions of his own. He has become hypnotized by his playthings and his ideas. He is but a child in his mind.

All of this may be very simply remedied, and man can once more return to an appreciation of reality rather than an appreciation of the illusion created by his mind. All that is necessary, my friends, is that he individually avail himself to this appreciation of reality through the process of meditation, for this process stills his active conscious mind which is continually seeking stimulus within the illusion developed over so many centuries of time upon planet Earth. Very rapidly, then, he can return to an appreciation of the reality in the functioning of the real creation.

This, my friends, is what man of Earth must return to if he is to know reality: this simple thought of absolute love, a thought of total unity with all his brothers regardless of how they might express themselves or whom they might be, for this is the original thought of your Creator.

The creation of the Father, then, as Hatonn calls it, has a very simple nature, a nature in which love is the essence of all things and of all their functions.

Yet this "real" creation obviously is not uppermost in most of our minds because we live in a day-to-day atmosphere to which the Confederation has referred quite often as an illusion.

We of the Confederation of Planets in the Service of the Infinite Creator have been, for many of your years, aware of many principles of reality. We are aware of these principles because we have availed ourselves to them just as the people of your planet may do.

It is possible through meditation to totally reduce the illusion that you now experience that creates the separation—an illusory separation—to what it actually is a total illusion. We have been continuing to speak to you about meditation. We have spoken to you many times about reality and about love and about understanding, and yet you do not seem to be able to overcome the illusion.

The reason for the illusion, my friends, is one that man on Earth has generated. He has generated it out of desire. This illusion is useful.

It is very useful for those who would wish to evolve at a very rapid rate by experiencing it and by using it while within it. Many of us who are now circling your planet would desire to have the opportunity that you have, the opportunity to be within the illusion and then, through the generation of understanding, use the potentials of the illusion. This is a way of gaining progress spiritually and has been sought out by many of our brothers.

I cannot over-emphasize the necessity of becoming able to understand the nature of the potentials within your illusion and then, by self-analysis and meditation, reacting to that in a way that will express the thought that generated us: the thought of our Creator. This was done by the teacher whom you know as Jesus. This man recognized his position. He recognized the illusion. He understood the reason for the potentials within the illusion, and his reaction to these potentials and activities within the illusion was a reaction which was expressing the thought of the Creator, a thought of love.

Keep uppermost in your mind that the illusion that you experience is an illusion, that it is surrounding you for the purpose of teaching you. It can only teach you if you become aware of its teachings. It is said that "He worked His wonders in mysterious ways." This way may seem mysterious; however, it is the way of spiritual evolvement. There are many souls experiencing the illusion in which you find yourself; however, there are few using this illusion to grow. They are not doing this other than at a subliminal level because they have not availed themselves through their seeking to a knowledge of the possibility of doing this.

Once an individual has become aware of the possibility of using the illusion in which he finds himself in your physical world for the progression of spiritual growth, it is necessary that he take the next step and use his knowledge to express, regardless of the potentials that affect him, the love and understanding of his Creator.

As you have by now become aware, meditation is always suggested as the best means of attaining understanding, of progressing spiritually, and of understanding the nature of the illusion and the purpose for which you are experiencing it. Each person is involved in an illusion or game in which we may, if we wish, use our consciousness in meditation in such a way as to create a more rapid growth in personal evolution. But how do we bring ourselves to the point at which this process, which often seems very difficult, is grasped and begun?

Desire, my friends, is the key to what you receive. If you desire it, you shall receive it. This was the Creator's plan, a plan in which all of His parts would receive exactly what they desire. My friends, often in the illusion which you now experience it seems that you do not acquire what you desire. In fact, the opposite seems to be the case in many, many instances. It is a paradox, it seems, that such a statement should be made and that such apparent results of desire are manifested, and yet we state, without exception, that man receives exactly what he desires. Perhaps, my friends, you do not understand desire. Perhaps this understanding is not within the intellectual mind. Perhaps it will be necessary to spend time in meditation to become aware of your real desire. For, my friends, there is much, much more of you and of the creation than you presently appreciate with your intellectual abilities in your present illusion.

It is very difficult for the peoples of this planet to give up their illusion, to give up the preconceived knowledge of what they believe to be cause and effect. However, this is not reality. This is illusion, born of illusion. It is a simple product of the complexity that man upon this planet has generated. Join with us in divorcing your thinking from such complexities and become aware of what has created you, everything that you experience, and everything that is thought. Become aware of your Creator. Become aware of His desire, and when you know this desire you will know your own, for you and your Creator are one, and you are one with all of His parts and, therefore, all of your fellow beings throughout all of the creation. When you know His desire you will feel it. There will be no more confusion. There will be no more questions. You will have found what you have sought. You will have found Love, for this is the desire of your Creator: that all of His parts express and experience the Love that created you. This may be found simply, in meditation. No amount of seeking within the intellectual concepts of your people, no amount of careful planning or careful interpretation of the written or spoken word, will lead you to the simple truth.

The Confederation messages concentrate a great deal upon the concept of seeking and of desire, feeling that the will of each entity is absolutely central to each entity's quest for evolution. In fact, they say, free will is at the foundation of the universe. Each entity is conceived not only as being part of one unity but also as being a totally unique part of that unity. Each person's free will is quite paramount, and the Confederation's concern is always to avoid infringement upon the free will of any person. Their method of contacting man on Earth takes its form from a deep concern for this free will:

> We do not wish to impose our understanding of truth upon your peoples, and this would be something that we would do if we contacted them directly. We could not help it, for our very utterance of truth would be accepted by many of your peoples as being valid. We do not wish to be thought of as the ultimate representatives of the Creator's truth. We wish to give this to your peoples in such a way so that they may accept or reject this at their own will. This, as we understand it, is a necessary provision in the spiritual evolvement of all mankind: that he be, at some state of his evolution, in a position to accept or reject what is necessary for his evolution. In this way, and only in this way, can he *know* the truth, the truth of the Creator, that single truth that is the creation, the truth of the love of the creation.

> It must be realized from within. It cannot be impressed from without. We are attempting to stimulate those of your peoples who would be stimulated to seeking this truth that is within them. We have been required by our understanding of our Creator's principle to remain in hiding, for we cannot serve one individual and at the same time do a disservice to his neighbor by proving within his own mind that we exist, for many of those of planet Earth at this time do not desire to believe in or have proof of our existence. For this reason we find it necessary to speak to those who seek through channels such as this one. We find it necessary to give to those who seek that which they seek in such a way that they, for themselves, may appraise its value and accept or reject, on their own terms, those thoughts that we bring, and understand the reality of the creation in which all of us exist.

Once the desire to receive this message has been developed, the messages are indeed available, not just from our group but from many so-called contactee or channeling groups around the world. Indeed, you will find little new in the "cosmic" system of philosophy. Those concepts are basic, profound, and simple. The Confederation has a name for one of the great goals of this system of meditation and study—understanding:

> Many of your peoples are at this time seeking outside their illusion. To those who seek, we offer our understanding. We do not attempt

to say that we have ultimate wisdom. We only suggest that that which we have to offer may be of value, for we have found, in our experience, as we have passed through the same experiences as those of Earth, that there is a most beneficial direction in seeking to serve. We are acting through instruments such as those here tonight to give, to those who seek, an understanding. Our presence is meant to stimulate seeking. Through this process, we hope to contact as many of the peoples of your planet as would desire our contact. We hope in the very near future to be able to contact many more of the peoples of your planet, the peoples who would desire understanding. It is difficult to contact those people of your planet because of this, shall I say, mixture of types, but it is well worth our effort if we are able to contact but one.

We will continue to act as we do now, speaking through instruments such as this one, until a sufficient number of the peoples of your planet have become aware of truth. We are constantly striving to bring, through many channels of communication, the simple message to the peoples of Earth: the simple message that will leave them with a simple understanding of all that there is, and that is love.

But understanding, that understanding that shows us the love of an Infinite Creator, is again and again described as being possible far more easily through the processes of meditation than by any other method:

There are pieces of information that are of importance and there are pieces of information that are not. Wisdom is a rather lonely matter, my friends. You must accept this truth as you acquire the burden of wisdom. That which you know, you are to be careful of, for what you know in the real creation has power, and that which you desire is all of the direction which that power will be aimed at; but have faith, my friends, in what you know and what you are learning. Feed your faith and your understanding through meditation. The further that you go along this path, my friends, the more meaningful you will find this simple statement: meditate. It begins as a simple process and, little by little, it becomes a way in which you live. Observe it as you progress along your own spiritual path.

It is frequently suggested in contactee messages that the state of mind of the seeker has the opportunity of being continuously in a far more pleasant configuration than is the mind of one who is not actively engaged in pursuing a path of self-knowledge and seeking. However, there are other fruits of the path of meditation and seeking that are predictable and that engage the attention of those who channel these messages.

> It is to be remembered, my friends, that service to others is service to one's self. Notice that we do not say that service is like unto service to one's self. There is no similarity between others and ourselves. There is identity. There is completion and unity. Therefore, that which is felt of a negative nature towards a sheep of the flock is felt towards one's self and is felt toward the Creator. This enters the service which you attempt to give to yourself and to the Creator through service to another, and causes a blot or a stain upon the perfect service you would have performed. It must be remembered that each person is a completely free entity whose independence must in no way be shaken and yet whose identity remains one with you.

* * * * *[1]

> There is only one thing of great importance for you to consider at this time. That is your personal preparation for service. You are to serve your fellow man, and, therefore, it is necessary that you prepare yourselves for this service. This of course, my friends, is done in meditation. We cannot overemphasize the importance of meditation. Through this technique you will receive answers to all of your questions. It is difficult to realize this, but this is true. All of your questions can be reduced to an extremely simple concept. This you can become aware of in meditation. Once this has been done you will be ready to serve, just as others have served and are now serving upon your planet. Follow their example; spend time in meditation. Qualify yourself to reach out to your fellow man and lead him from the darkness of confusion that he is experiencing back into the light that he desires.

One service that the Confederation sources greatly appreciate is that provided by vocal channels, which are trained in groups such as the one that we have had in Louisville since 1962. They never suggest in any way that their message is unique or that "salvation" can only be gained by listening to that message. However, they are aware that there are many who seek that message through sources other than orthodox religion and classical philosophy. Consequently, they are here to provide a service of making information available and can perform their service only through vocal channels:

---

1. Asterisks (******) indicate the separation between a quotation from one transcript and a quotation upon the same subject from another transcript.

There are more people upon this planet seeking than there have been in the past. However, many are quite confused in their attempts to seek, and there is a need at this time for many more channels such as this one who can receive directly the thoughts that so many of the people of this planet are seeking. We are attempting at this time to generate greater numbers of proficient vocal channels who can receive our thoughts quite readily. This requires daily meditation. This is all that is required: daily meditation. It is assumed, of course, that as this daily meditation is performed there is a desire for our contact.

As one who has participated in meditation groups for many years, may I suggest that individual meditations not include the attempt to contact Confederation sources. It is best to pursue this attempt only in a group situation, preferably a group that contains at least one experienced receiver. And always, whether meditating alone or in a group, I strongly recommend some means of "tuning" so that the meditation that follows will be at the highest spiritual level possible. This "tuning" can be accomplished in any way preferable to the meditator. The Lord's Prayer, "Aum-ing" or other singing or chanting, the reading of some inspirational writing, or a careful visualization of the "white light" of the Creator, are all useful "tuning" methods.

Reincarnation is very basic to the Confederation message. One of the most highly regarded fruits of the meditation and seeking process is the ability of the seeker to penetrate what Ra calls the "forgetting process," which occurs at the time of our birth into this incarnation so that we might become aware of the lessons that we have to learn during this incarnation. These lessons are always along the lines of how to love better, more fully, more deeply, or with more kindness and understanding. However, each entity has unique lessons:

At the time at which each of you incarnated, my friends, each of you was aware that certain lessons, hitherto unlearned, were to be the goals for achievement in this incarnation. If it seems to you that your entire incarnation within this illusion has been a series of difficulties of one particular type, then you are almost certainly aware in some manner of one of your lessons. As you can see, these lessons are not to be avoided. They are to be learned.

Further, we must point out to you that when a confrontation in such a lesson has been achieved, that which separates you from understanding is most often your own thinking. Your conscious thinking processes are quite capable of being self-destructive in the sense that they may aid you to avoid the lesson that you wish in reality to learn.

Therefore, as you approach a lesson, we suggest that if it is possible to achieve a temporary abeyance of the conscious, analytical processes, then you may return to the problem with a much clearer mentality, ready to learn what you came to this experience to learn, rather than only to avoid what you came to learn.

We know how difficult it is to achieve the meditative state at all times, for we have been where you are and we are aware of that particular type of illusion that you call physical. We urge you, therefore, to depend on meditation of a formal kind, then to attempt a semi-meditative state at all times, and, by this, we mean simply to achieve a state of attention so that your destructive impulses are not free to clog your mind completely and keep you from learning the lessons you came to learn.

Undergirding all of the lessons that we have to learn about love is the basic concept that all things are one:

Meditate upon the complete unity of yourself and all that you see. Do this not once, and not simply in present circumstances, but at all times, and especially in difficult circumstances. For insofar as you love and feel at one with those things which are difficult for you, to that extent will those circumstances be alleviated. This is not due to any laws within our physical illusion but is due to the Law of Love, for that body which is of spirit, which is interpenetrated with the physical body, is higher than your physical body, and those changes which you make by love upon your spiritual body will, of necessity, reflect themselves within the physical illusion.

All is one, my friends. My voice is now the voice of this instrument; my thoughts are her thoughts. Please believe that the vibration we offer to you is not a vibration of personality, but is a vibration of the Creator. We are also channels. There is only one voice. Within this vibration, we are self-consciously aware that this voice is the voice of the Creator. It is simply a matter of lifting vibrations which are not so self-aware of the Creator. All things will eventually come into harmony in relation to your understanding.

Even if the universe for those around you remains disharmonious and difficult, if your mind is stayed upon the unity of the Creator, your own universe will become harmonious, and this is not by your doing but by the simple love of the Creator.

From many sources we have heard that we are in the last days of a particular era of evolution. Popular writers of the Christian faith have taken the writings of the book of Revelation and analyzed them in such a way that it is suggested that the days of Armageddon are near at hand. Scientists have written many books exploring the possibility that unusual planetary configurations such as the Jupiter effect will occur now and in the year 2000, thus enlarging the possibility for Earth changes. Other scientists have examined much evidence indicating that a polar shift by the year 2000 is probable. Prophets such as Edgar Cayce have channeled information having to do with such drastic changes occurring, and in addition, of course, there are our many concerns having strictly to do with the man-made potential for planetary devastation. We also have gathered information in our meetings on the subject of Earth changes:

> There is a season upon your planet which shall be highly traumatic within your physical illusion. The physical reasons for this are varied. Your scientists will spend a great deal of time, while they can, in attempting to catalog and describe each of the conditions which will produce disaster on this physical plane of your planet. That which your scientists speak of is quite so, and will be part of the program which has been predicted by all of those holy works which you have upon the face of the Earth.

> It is not either permissible or possible for us to tell you precisely what events will occur, or when they will occur, due to the fact that the vibration within the mind and heart of the peoples upon your planet is determining and will determine the precise events. There is within the planet Earth a great deal of karma which must be adjusted as the cycle changes, and these things will manifest. Precisely when, and how, we cannot say, nor would we wish to, my friends. For the rain, and the wind, and fire, will destroy only those things which are in what you call the third density of vibration. You may value those things because you cannot imagine what a fourth-density existence will be like. We suggest to you that you spend no time concerning yourselves with the effort of maintaining your third-density existence after the vibration change to fourth density has been completed.

> If, within your spirit, your graduation day has come, those things necessary for your emergence into fourth density will be done for you. All will be accomplished by helpers which you must be aware that you have.

It is extremely possible that damage will occur to those things which you identify with yourself in the third density. If we may speak plainly, you will observe the valley of the shadow of death. These very words, my friends, have been spoken to you before, and yet you cling to that physical body and those physical surroundings as though your spirit were attached quite permanently to them.

May we suggest to you that you can find your spirit neither in your head, nor in your hands, nor in your chest, nor in your legs, nor in your feet, that nowhere can you find your spirit; nowhere can you operate to remove it, nor to aid it. Your spirit resides within a shell. The shell may be removed, but that is no matter. The spirit does not perish.

What is the metaphysical meaning of this suggested physical trauma of our planet? The Confederation suggests that the planet itself is moving into a new vibration, a new portion of space and time, which many have called the New Age, but into which we shall not be able to enter unless we have indeed learned the lessons of love that it has been our choice to learn or not to learn for many incarnations. Therefore, the Confederation suggests that it is very important to choose to follow the positive path or not to follow it:

There is a choice to be made very shortly, and it would be preferable if all of the people of this planet understand the choice that is to be made. It will be difficult for many of the people of this planet to understand what this choice is, because it is a choice that they have not considered. They have been much too involved in their daily activities and their confusion and their desires of a very trivial nature to be concerned with an understanding of the choice that they are very shortly to make. Whether they wish to or not, whether they understand it or not, regardless of any influence, each and every one of the people who dwell upon planet Earth will shortly make a choice. There will be no middle area. There will be those who choose to follow the path of love and light and those who choose otherwise.

This choice will not be made by saying, "I choose the path of love and light," or "I do not choose it." The verbal choice will mean nothing. This choice will be measured by the individual's demonstration of his choice. This demonstration will be very easy for us of the Confederation of Planets in His Service to interpret. This choice is measured by what we term the vibratory rate of the individual. It is necessary, if an individual is to join those who make the choice of love and understanding, for his rate of vibration to be above a certain minimal level. There are many now that are close to this minimum level, but due to continuing conditions of erroneous thought that prevail upon your surface, they are either fluctuating around this point or are even in some cases drifting away from the path of love and understanding. There are many whose vibratory rate at this time is sufficiently high for them to travel with no difficulty into the density of vibration that this planet is shortly to experience.

At some time in the future, then, something that the Confederation has called the harvest will take place. This concept of the Judgment Day differs from the eschatological one in that the one who judges us is not a God apart from us but the God within us. As a result of this harvest some will go on to a new age of love and light and will learn new lessons in a very positive and beautiful density, as the Confederation calls it. Others will have to repeat this particular grade of lessons and relearn the lessons of love. Here the Confederation entity, Hatonn, speaks once again of the harvest and of the Confederation's purpose in speaking through contactee groups:

> There is going to be a Harvest, as you might call it, a harvest of souls that will shortly occur upon your planet. We are attempting to extract the greatest possible harvest from this planet. This is our mission, for we are the Harvesters.

> In order to be most efficient, we are attempting to create first a state of seeking among the people of this planet who desire to seek. This would be those who are close to the acceptable level of vibration. Those above this level are of course not of as great an interest to us since they have, you might say, already made the grade. Those far below this level, unfortunately, cannot be helped by us at this time. We are attempting at this time to increase by a relatively small percentage the number who will be harvested into the path of love and understanding.

> Even a small percentage of those who dwell upon your planet is a vast number, and this is our mission, to act through groups such as this one in order to disseminate information in such a fashion that it may be accepted or rejected, that it may be in a state lacking what the people of your planet choose to call proof.

We offer them no concrete proof, as they have a way of expressing it. We offer them Truth. This is an important function of our mission—to offer Truth without proof. In this way, the motivation will, in each and every case, come from within the individual. In this way, the individual vibratory rate will be increased. An offering of proof or an impressing of this Truth upon an individual in such a way that he would be forced to accept it would have no usable effect upon his vibratory rate.

This, then, my friends, is the mystery of our way of approaching your peoples.

Another concept that has come out of the many communications from alleged UFO entities is that of "Wanderers." They are usually service-oriented people, and, as would be predictable, they often have a great deal of difficulty fitting into the planetary vibrations of Earth. Often they have the feeling that they do not fit in or do not belong, but at the same time, very often, these people are possessed of many gifts, in the arts, in teaching, or in the simple sharing of a cheerful and happy vibration, which certainly does not suggest the normal attitude of a simple malcontent.

This concept is particularly interesting to many people who will be drawn to *The Ra Material* because, according to that material, much of it will be most easily recognized as being useful by Wanderers. There are not just a few Wanderers on Earth today; Ra suggests a figure of approximately sixty-five million. They have left other densities in harmonious environments to take on a kind of job that is most difficult and dangerous, for if a Wanderer cannot at least begin to pierce the forgetting process that occurs at birth into this density during his or her lifetime on planet Earth, and remember the love and the light that the person was intended to share, the Wanderer can conceivably become caught in the third-density illusion, collecting what may loosely be termed as karma, and be delayed in arriving again at the home planet until all that is unbalanced in third density in this lifetime has been balanced.

When Don Elkins and I wrote *Secrets of the UFO* in 1976, we devoted a chapter to the concept of Wanderers and used material gathered in hypnotic regressions of three women who are friends in this lifetime and who, when separately regressed, gave independent and dovetailing stories of their lives on another planet.

After that book went to press, we were able to work with a man whom the women had named as being a part of that experience on another planet. This man, who was then a student working towards his master's degree in chemical engineering, was aware of no detail of our research except that we were involved in doing some hypnosis. On May 10, 1975, Don, along with Lawrence Allison, an accomplished hypnotist with whom we had worked often when he lived in Louisville, sat down with our fourth volunteer and proceeded to explore that other world for a fourth time. The information was especially interesting, since all three previous regressions had been poetic, and beautiful, but scarcely technical. Our fourth subject had a far different background and was able to see things in a far more accurate and explicit manner. This fourth regression fitted perfectly into the story told by the first three subjects.

One of the first things that Don and Larry (the questioning went back and forth) asked about was the clothing.

Q. *How are you dressed?*
A. In white.

Q. *White what?*
A. Loose white clothes.

Q. *OK. What's above the waist now? Above the pants?*
A. Well, it's just like a robe; it's not really a robe but a loose clothing with a sash, like for a belt.

Q. *And what about on the shoulders?*
A. Well, it's just short sleeved. It's warm.

This type of robe suggests a monastic or religious order, and questions were asked to attempt to discover some orthodox religious connection on this planet. No connection was found, so the questioners moved on to the name of this other world since the surroundings were not those of Earth, but the young man, normally incisive in his answers, seemed totally unaware of the concept of naming.

Q. *The name of your planet?*
A. It's just a . . . we live there, and . . . I don't see any mountains, but I see . . . the name?

* * * * *[2]

A. I have a child.
Q. *One child?*

---

2. Asterisks (****) separate two quotations from the same regressive hypnosis session.

A. Yeah. Little boy.

Q. *His name is?*

A. I just don't have a feeling for names. I have, like, you know when you want somebody, and they know when you want them, sort of. I mean, I just don't have a feeling for names.

Not only did their planet seem to lack a proper name, but speech itself seemed to be a far different process, one that we would probably call telepathy.

Q. *All right, if someone calls to you, what do they call you?*

A. I just haven't heard anybody speak. I don't know if you have to speak.

* * * * *

A. It seems, like, kind of a simple life. But there's obviously—well, there was light at my books, so it's obviously mechanized, or perhaps much more than that even. I don't,

I . . . don't recall people speaking to each other, though. I mean, they seem to, you know, everybody knows each question . . . you know what's going on, but I don't really see. It was singing; there was singing, but there wasn't actually people conversing with each other. You just sort of knew, I guess.

* * * * *

A. I'd be sitting on a stone or a bench and they'd be sitting down, and I'm explaining, but I don't really see myself talking to them.

The subject, with his engineer's eye, was able to put together the architecture of the place in the way the women had not. All four agreed that the center of the community and its purpose was something that may conveniently be called the temple.

A. . . . . think it's a stone . . . I guess limestone, but it's whiter, I guess. That's what it's made of.

Q. *What about the perimeter?*

A. Well, there's, from supports from the side are arches up to the ceiling, but . . . it's not a regular dome, it's . . . well, I haven't seen that kind of dome before.

Q. *Take a good guess. How far across is that dome?*

A. Oh, goodness. It looks like it's 200 feet the long way, and maybe more than that, maybe 250. And, oh, maybe 150 feet wide. It's a huge room, very—

Q. *OK. Now, how is it lighted?*
A. Just, [*laughs a little incredulously*] . . . really, it's just a glow from the ceiling. I mean, you know, like the, well, there's, like the area that's light, and then there's darker, like it's been painted, but the paint, that's light. It seems like it's, well, it just doesn't need any light. The room's bright. Maybe it's coming from the windows, but . . . there doesn't seem to be any shadow in the room.

Q. *What you're saying is that it seems as if the atmosphere in the room is glowing there?*
A. Well, yeah, just like it's bright. I don't see any shadows, like if there was a light source.

Q. *Uh huh. Now I want you to listen inside that big room. What kind of sounds do you hear?*
A. Nothing in that room, but they're singing someplace.

Q. *Very quietly, singing off in the distance?*
A. Um hmm.

Q. *All right. It is, ah, some kind of . . .*
A. It's more like, a kind of choir, a little choir, like.

That music, reported by all four subjects, is not like any music we have ever heard. Two of the subjects actually saw the music sparkling in the air, and none could accurately describe it.

A. I just . . . I can't . . . place the words. It's just, you know, like a sort of praise, a sort of, you know, something like you'd hear in a choir.

Q. *Praise to whom?*
A. Well, uh . . .

Q. *To God?*
A. I'm sure that's who it is, you know, that's . . . it's sort of a happy thing to do, when people get together and sing . . .

The subject spoke of growing up studying in large books.

A. I see myself sitting over . . . over a book and just reading.

Q. History?

A. Well, I don't know.
Q. Practical work? Science? What do you study? Art? The arts?

A. Just great books, big books.
Q. Um hum. Do you have supervised study in classes or . . .
A. Well, in the morning there's a teacher, and in the afternoon or in late evening, I study.

Q. Is there an examination?
A. No exams. You just want to learn; you want to learn. You, uh, it's like you can't learn enough.

Who were these people? Did they represent an entire planetary population or were they a portion only of that population? If they were a portion, how were they chosen to do this work? After looking at this material, Don and I generated a term by which to call this particular group of people: the "clan." Here is one of the questioners on this subject.

Q. Nobody has individual homes?
A. Well, no; this big place is their home. This is, this is home.

* * * * *

A. Well, this is one purpose. Like, it's like a school, or a teaching place to teach those that want to learn it in depth, and those that come when they can.

* * * * *

A. But this isn't like a ruling-type people, by any means. Like, you know, this isn't . . . like the people have to come here. It's not a class system or anything.

Meditation played a very large part in the lives of the inhabitants of this other world, or at least those in this clan. There were meditations alone and there were daily group meditations with the entire clan.

A. Well, let's see. I don't see myself there, in different states of consciousness. There are prayerful times, in the morning and at night. You have them in your room, and then you have others before meals, before the morning meal, and then, not, well, briefly before the evening meal, but, when, it was like when the food was brought, but then afterwards there's, it's a . . . in a room, like a private sort of devotional, except that you're not—like in meditation. And there are times when the whole group gets together other than meals, just . . . like the whole place is like a family I would guess. Because, like I said, you don't feel that attached, necessarily, to one person. You feel attached to everybody. They're all, like, in your family.

Another function of the clan was to open their great temple from time to time to all of those of the planet who wished to come for spiritual inspiration. The questioners, in attempting to determine just how these large crowds came to fill the temple, happened upon the description of what seemed to be a very large heliport. We discovered later that the vehicle was not a helicopter. However, that is the term that the questioner used here.

Q. OK. Now, the people that leave at that heliport—you have no idea where they go?
A. When I say these ships come, it's not like hordes of people just rushing off and rushing back on or anything, it's just . . . it's, oh, how should I . . . you know, it lands there, and the doors open, and the people come out, and people come in. They're allowed to go on the grounds, you know. In other words, this is their place too. But they come as a visitor, sort of, to it.

Q. How long do they stay there?
A. A day.

The description of the heliport:

A. There's a place, a flat place, a flat place, like, that's stone, out in front, but I don't see roads coming to it, for . . . it . . . I see . . . uh, like, sort of, like, uh, like, well, a huge helicopter pad, for instance, but . . .
The questioners had to find out what was landing on that large stone area, and so the subject was asked to describe the type of transport that used it.

Q. All right. I want you to describe that ship, and what makes it go.
A. I don't . . . um . . . it's . . . well, it's like . . . it seems it's probably a space ship. But I don't see it coming from space. It sort of, suddenly almost being there, I don't see it like zipping off or coming in, you know, across the horizon or anything.

Q. Just describe what it looks like.
A. Yeah, well, it's a, it's longer than it is wide, and it's not real thick compared to the length dimensions and the width dimension. It's a—it's not like, it's not spinning when it comes down, because it's a little sort of, like oblong or . . . it just sort of appears and sets down, you know; I mean, I don't see it actually coming into view from small and getting larger.

It is interesting to note the apparent description of materialization and dematerialization implicit in the subject's answer to that question.

And so the young man grew in wisdom and in years and told a story of teaching, growing somewhat gray haired, beginning to teach fewer and more advanced students, and in time preparing to end the incarnation. As the questioners brought the subject back through the death experience in the previous incarnation and forward in time to the experience in which he was at that moment living, they paused with the subject in between incarnations to ask about the purpose this particular Wanderer came to Earth to fulfill. The answer that he gave is both provocative and all too scanty. Many of us seek to help this planet of ours in one way or another, and the question is always: How shall we accomplish it?

Q. Why are you on Earth? What is the purpose of this life? What do you intend to do here? What were you assigned to do here?
A. It seems like, to help.

Q. Helping with what? Something in particular?
A. Something . . .

Q. Have you already helped in this field? Or is the problem yet to come that you are to help with?
A. It hasn't happened yet.

Q. What do you anticipate?
A. Just . . . just great needs.

Q. What would happen, to require so much help from you that you know about? [pause] *Spiritual growth? Spiritual development? Physical needs?*
A. Well, not . . . the . . . I get the feeling of some people that are lost, you know?

Q. Can you help them? This is your mission?
A. I feel like that's what I need to do. This . . . Help those people.

Q. Um hum. Which people?
A. The ones that are lost.

Q. Is this a particular group?
A. No.

Q. Just in general.
A. Just people.

The work I did in early 1976 was to be my last. I had had a condition called juvenile rheumatoid arthritis with several complications, one being SLE, commonly known as lupus, since I was thirteen when my kidneys had failed. In 1956, the advanced techniques that are available now to those whose kidneys fail were not available. In fact, it was considered a miracle that I survived, but survive I did with the loss of approximately half of each kidney.

I consider myself very fortunate to have been able to have had a productive and active physical life for so long with the odds going so far against me. Even now, with the help of exercise, diet, friends, and faith, I feel most blessed. But my activities are limited.

The research that Don and I had done up to that point brought us across the knowledge of a highly unusual type of healing, and it was in part my disability that caused us to put ourselves so wholeheartedly into an examination of that type of healing. Psychic surgery bears only a tangential relationship to orthodox surgery and no relationship to orthodox medicine. It is, like all brands of "faith healing," impossible to prove, and the natural and standard response, not only from scientists but from any person who has not done any research into the subject, is an automatic "turn off" and utter disbelief.

This is to be expected. Were it not for many years of research, this would perhaps be our reaction also. However, we, like most who investigate psychic surgery, knew that we had nothing to lose by investigating this possibility. No psychic surgery patient has ever been lost because nothing actually happens to the patient's physical body. It is truly a psychic form of healing. Consequently, we spent some time both in the Philippines and in Mexico taking part in an examination of the possibilities of psychic surgery.

This is an example of what the psychic surgeon creates as a manifestation for the eye: it is a Philippine bedroom; the patient is undressed, retaining those garments that may be needed for personal modesty, and lies down on the bed, which may in some cases be covered with a simple shower curtain, usually that one borrowed from the motel bathroom. The healer, a religious man, and one who has often spent ten or twelve years of his life praying to become a healer "walking in the wilderness" of the volcanic mountains of Luzon in solitude, enters the room. He carries nothing except perhaps a Bible. Often the healer is accompanied by an assistant who functions as interpreter and, to use a term familiar to our culture, surgical assistant; to use a more accurate term, cleanup man.

The healer normally knows very little English. He or she begins by taking the hands and moving them over the body, palms down. We are informed that this is a method of scanning the body just as an x-ray machine would. A site for "surgery" is then selected, and if the healer is right-handed the left hand is pressed firmly against the skin. The skin seems to separate and the interior of the body is seen. This manifestation is very real looking, and anyone who has seen a genuine psychic surgeon at work and has not studied the phenomenon carefully will swear that the body has been opened with the bare hands. The right hand then enters this open site and manipulates within the body.

In the most interesting case in which I took part, the healer was told that I had arthritis. He scanned my body with the help of his assistant. Then he opened the abdominal cavity and with a very liquid-sounding action pulled gently, but firmly, at what seemed to be organs rather than joints. It was not unpleasant but, to me, the patient, it was puzzling, as I had no arthritis in my organs. He then removed what seemed to be three rather small, long pieces of bloody material, at the center of which was a small piece of hard material. This done, he removed his left hand. The "incision" vanished without a scar or trace of any kind. The two men, in this case, mopped up what had become a fairly considerable amount of blood, rinsed their hands, and then took baby oil and worked it over the abdominal skin, massaging in silence.

When I asked what the healer was doing working in the abdominal area, the interpreter relayed my request and relayed back the information that the scanning had produced the knowledge of three cysts upon my right ovary, and the misplacement or dropping of both ovaries, which had occurred through years of very active life. The pulling had been to reposition the ovaries so that I would not be in discomfort during menstruation. The removal of the cysts had had the same purpose.

Although my gynecologist had diagnosed these three small cysts when I was a very young woman, I had never spoken of them to Don Elkins and, indeed, to no one, since such conversation is not fascinating. One other person knew of these cysts, my mother, but she was 12,000 miles away.

Upon returning to the United States I had my gynecologist examine the area, and he confirmed that the three cysts were no longer palpable. They have remained gone, and the comfort level of my menstrual cycle is correspondingly far better.

The massage with baby oil is a very simplified and unostentatious form of magnetic healing in which prayers are offered and a protective light is visualized around the affected area so that healing will be aided.

It is Don's and my belief that the opening of the body for the removal of parts, the closing of the body, and the manifestation of the blood and all other materials are materializations of the same type as the materializations of ghosts and the materialization of UFOs. Therefore, we have never made any attempt to preserve specimens of this psychic surgery. We are aware that this does not fulfill the rigors of the scientific method that exists today, but it is our belief that we would find out nothing by looking at the results of such analysis of manifestation.

It would seem that a person, no matter how great his desire to be healed, would be nervous and apprehensive, since the opening of the body itself, physical or psychic, seems very traumatic. Once the healer's hands are upon you, a distinct emotional and mental attitude change occurs within every individual with whom I have spoken who has experienced this phenomenon. The psychic surgeons call it the presence of the Holy Spirit. It should be considered part of the phenomenon.

In late 1977 and early 1978 we accompanied Dr. Andrija Puharich and his research associates to Mexico City to investigate a Mexican psychic surgeon, a seventy-eight-year-old woman called Pachita, who had been practicing for a great many years. The gift had come to her on the battlefield with Pancho Villa's army, and, as in the Philippines, more of her patients were native than were American. The one difference in her technique was the culture from which she came. In the Philippines, psychic healing came from an extremely literal belief in Christianity as taught by Spanish missionaries for three hundred years. Christianity was the center of almost every Filipino peasant's life. A large percentage went to mass daily, and, as Don and I were there during Holy Week of 1975, we were able to watch evidence of the ruthlessly literal type of Christianity that was practiced there. On Good Friday, for instance, there was a great Catholic parade of the cross through the streets of Manila. What was different about this parade was that there was a human being nailed to that cross. Many had vied for that position. The one who had achieved it, when asked for comment, simply replied that he felt very exalted and hoped that they would choose him again the following year.

In Mexico, if Christianity is present at all, and it often is, it is an overlay to an extremely strong Indian belief that is harsh and brooding. One brings to mind the memories of the Mayan slaughter of innocents on the steep steps of the Mexican pyramids.

Consequently, Pachita used a very dull knife with a 5-inch blade. She passed it around amongst the entire research group watching to see our reactions, especially mine, since I was the guinea pig. Since her "opera-tions" took place with me lying on my stomach, I cannot give a firsthand account of what occurred, but Don informs me that the knife seemed to disappear 4 inches into my back and was then moved rapidly across the spine. This was repeated several times. Pachita was, she said, working on my kidneys. Again we made no attempt to conserve "evidence," as we knew that it would come to nothing. Many have attempted to research psychic surgery by analysis of its products and have found either incon-clusive results or null results, indicating that psychic surgery is a fraud.

In the book *Arigo*, by John Fuller, on Dr. Puharich's early work with the South American healer of that nickname, psychic surgery is carefully examined, and for those interested in this unusual subject that book is a good place to begin. I have never had any success in getting any ortho-dox doctor to test the possible results of this Mexican experience. This is due to the fact that the procedure used to test the kidneys can, if the kidneys are badly enough damaged already, cause the kidneys to go into failure once again, and no orthodox doctor could be expected to take that risk. Dr. Puharich himself was unwilling for me to go through this procedure.

With all of its frustrations, investigation into areas in the very fringe of psychic phenomena are most interesting, informative, and rewarding to the researcher who is patient and whose approach to the subject is simply to gather data rather than attempting to prove, step by step, hypotheses about that which he is doing research. In *The Ra Material*, manifestations of this type of materialization are discussed, and the information is quite interesting.

Back in the United States, although I could no longer work at the typewriter, I was still able to offer the continuing weekly meditations and to take on advanced students for individual work. In 1978 James Allen McCarty heard about our group, first from a number of people who had meditated at our Sunday night meetings and had gone on to form a "light center" and nature preserve in Marion County, Kentucky, and then from a two-hour, call-in radio show that Don and I had done in Lexington, Kentucky. He came up with many people from the Marion County meditation group to experience our meditations. After two med-itations the group as a whole stopped coming, but Jim made the 140-mile round trip almost weekly, beginning in the spring of 1980. Jim had, for many years, been searching for some method of aiding humanity. Born in 1947, and equipped with degrees in business and education, he had studied, in addition, alternative methods for teaching consciousness expansion. Some of this time was spent working with inner-city children, but he began to find a very strong desire to discover a clearer idea of what it was he was seeking.

In 1972, he took a course of study in consciousness expansion called "brain self-control" with a gruff old mountain man who lived in a log cabin at 10,000 feet in the Rocky Mountains of Colorado. During this course he learned, for the first time, of the possibility of communication with advanced civilization from outer space, not through any man-made means like radios, telegraphs, or electronic gadgetry but through the use of the frontal lobes of the human brain.

Since this very central experience was in wilderness country, rocks, pine, and juniper, he decided to search for an equally remote piece of land upon which he could then offer these brain self-control experiences to others. On 132 acres in central Kentucky, with a running creek for an access road, he formed the Rock Creek Research and Development Laboratories and began to work on the subject closest to his heart: the evolution of mankind. He gave several workshops on this subject but found little interest in that area and so returned to a life of homesteading and solitude for the next six and one-half years, growing his own food, meditating, and studying. He was still curious as to what it would be like to be in a clear, two-way communication with advanced intelligent beings, and, thus, he very much enjoyed the meditations with the Louisville group, but he also had previously become interested in work being done in a group in Oregon. In the fall of 1980, he traveled from Kentucky to Oregon to work with this group that was supposedly channeling the same source that Edgar Cayce had channeled in deep trance.

However, the learning that he had received from the Sunday night meetings and from the advanced study that he had with me had spoken to his inner seeking, and, seemingly of its own accord, his mind made itself up for him after only two months in Oregon. He found that he needed to return to Louisville and work with Don and me. On December 23, 1980, he arrived in Louisville, having traveled 5,000 miles from the woods of central Kentucky to Oregon and back to Louisville.

Don and I were endlessly grateful for McCarty's aid. His abilities were extraordinary. He had a grasp of the metaphysical material going back to his college days, and he had read extensively through all the intervening years, so he came to this work very informed of our areas of study. He was able to take up the physical part of the research, filing, making notes, transcribing tapes, and carrying on the correspondence that had sorely lapsed since my disability. Jim, always thorough, sold his land. L/L Research merged with the Rock Creek Research and Development Laboratories, keeping our old partnership name for our publishing arm, purchased a new typewriter—Jim's fingers, strengthened by six and one-half years of homesteading, overmatched my old electric typewriter*—and we settled down to do . . . *what?* We didn't know.

We discussed doing a new book, updating what we had learned in *Secrets of the UFO*, and had blank paper ready to be filled. Jim had begun to do back research in our voluminous files. Three weeks after he came, the Ra contact began.

During all the years that I had been channeling, I had always channeled consciously, using my free will to clothe telepathic concepts in my own language. In 1980, a longtime friend and meditation group member, Elaine Flaherty, died a tragically young death. She had had juvenile diabetes and had died in her thirties. I had sat with her for many days in the hospital before she finally left her body, and she had told me several times that she wanted to make sure that her husband, Tom, was made aware that she was all right after her death, for she knew that she was likely to die. She had told Tom, also a longtime meditation group member, as well.

After her funeral, Tom came to me and asked if I would attempt to get in touch with Elaine. Having been through all too many séances and not having a great deal of personal commitment to the type of communication that one was likely to get from one's physically dead relatives, I was at first reluctant to attempt such "mediumship." However, these were my good friends and I could not say no. Tom, Don, and Elaine and Tom's son, Mike, gathered with me for the first attempt. After some moments of consciously offering myself for the contact with Elaine, I became unaware of the passing of time, and when I awakened, Tom had what sounded like Elaine's voice on tape speaking through me. That was my first experience with trance. I did not know, and to this day do not know, how it occurred. Tom asked once more if I would do this, and again I went into what seemed to be a very deep trance, remembering nothing and hearing what sounded like Elaine's voice on tape after the session. Don stated that if he had heard me from the next room without seeing me, he would have been certain it was Elaine.

This work was extremely draining to me, and I asked Tom to accept the fact that I really did not wish to continue being this type of medium. Tom agreed, saying that he had what Elaine had promised, and was satisfied. However, only a few days later, while working with an advanced meditation student, Leonard Cecil, I received a new contact, one that I had never had before. As I do in all cases, I challenged this entity in the name of Christ, demanding that it leave if it did not come as a messenger of Christ-consciousness. It remained, so I opened myself to its channel. Again I went almost immediately into trance, and the entity, which called itself Ra, began its series of contacts with us. This contact is ongoing, fascinating, and, to me, a source of some disquiet.

The person who decides to become a vocal channel in the first place has already taken a step that is, to some people, quite difficult; that is, the willingness to speak the words of one that is not controlled by the self. In free-will channeling, it is possible to choose to stop channeling. However, it is also possible to utter complete nonsense because the channel never knows in advance what the next concept will be. I hasten to add that this nonsense has never occurred in my experience, and that the channelings have always made a reasonable amount of sense and, in many cases, have been quite inspirational. Nevertheless, in a society where you are taught to measure your words with some care, it seems an irresponsible act to simply blurt out that which comes into your mind.

When, in order for the contact to occur, trance has to be obtained, the disquiet grows into something close to a near panic on my part. I do not know how the procedure for a trance works, and I am always afraid that in this session, nothing will happen, I will remain conscious, and I will receive no contact. Again, this has never happened. Since neither I nor either of the others in our group has any real idea of how to aid me beyond a certain point in achieving a state of "trance," there is nothing to be done but simply to move ahead. Don states that although my state of trance is similar to others he has observed, it is what he would call "telepathic reception in the trance state."

Although I studied literature in my undergraduate days and was a librarian for many years, reading the material almost always offers me the opportunity to learn a new word or two and has certainly stretched my mind in the area of science, which in my education was woefully lacking.

What concerns me perhaps more than anything else is that someone who reads this material will consider this human being that I am to have some sort of wisdom that Ra certainly has, but that I certainly do not. If this work impresses you, I can only ask that you please make a sharp differentiation in your mind between the words and the "medium" through which the words come. You would not, for instance, expect the water pipe to be responsible for the quality of the water that runs through it. Certainly all of us in the research group try, through meditation and daily life, to prepare ourselves as best we can for these sessions. Nevertheless, what comes through our group stands on its own and cannot be said to reflect on the wisdom or so-called spiritual advancement of any of its members. As our popular philosophy has it, "We are all bozos on this bus."

If you have any questions as you read, please feel free to write the Rock Creek group. Its correspondent, Jim, will never ignore a letter, and since he has his own experiences of the sessions themselves to share, he will finish this introduction.

JIM McCARTY: We are beginners when it comes to knowing how the Ra contact occurs, and it has only been through a process of trial and error, session by session, that we have learned more about how to support our instrument, Carla, in the mental, physical, and spiritual senses. We were so excited about the Ra contact when it first began that we had two sessions per day for days at a time, but we have since learned that this procedure was much too wearing on Carla. We average about one session every week to ten days now, which allows us to prepare for each session with the greater degree of care that seems to be required as sessions accumulate.

A great deal of thought goes into the questions that Don asks during each session. Each of us contributes ideas, but the great bulk of the line of questioning is accomplished by Don, since he has the years of experience in investigating the UFO contactee phenomenon necessary to develop the intellectual foundation required in any attempt to fit the diverse pieces of this puzzle together. He also has the intuitive sense that is vital in following the unexpected and profoundly revealing answers that Ra so often gives with further questions, developed on the spur of the moment, to take advantage of the new insights.

With the decision made to hold a session the night before the session is to occur, we arise the morning of the session, have a light breakfast, and begin the series of steps that will best aid us in successfully completing the session. I give Carla a half-hour back massage to loosen her muscles and joints before each session because she will have to remain absolutely motionless for between an hour and an hour and forty-five minutes. Then we meditate so that the harmony we try to produce in our daily lives is intensified, and so that our desires are unified into the single desire to see contact with Ra. We then perform our ritual of protection and cleansing of the room in which the contact will be made, and situate Carla in a prone position on the bed, covering her body with a white blanket, her eyes with a white cloth, and hook up the three tape recorder microphones just below her chin so that we don't miss any of the session if one or two tape recorders malfunction.

By this time, all that is visible of Carla is her hair flowing down both of her shoulders and her nose poking out of the sea of cloth white surrounding it. As she mentally recites the Prayer of St. Francis, Don is aligning the table, which holds the Bible, candle, incense, and chalice of water in a straight line with her head, as recommended by Ra. After Don lights the candle and incense, he and I walk the Circle of One around Carla and repeat the words that begin each contact.

At some point after that, Carla departs her physical body, and Ra then uses it to make the words that form the responses to Don's questions. I meditate and send light to Carla for the duration of the session, only taking time out to flip the tapes over as they finish each side. When the session is over, Don waits a few moments for Carla to return to her usually quite stiff body, calls her name a few times until she responds, helps her to sit up, rubs her neck a bit, and gives her the chalice full of water to drink after he and I have filled it as full of our love vibrations as we can.

Since Carla has no idea of what has occurred during the session, she is always most curious to know how it went. She has to settle for secondhand bits and pieces of information until I can get the session transcribed from the tapes, which is usually very easy since Ra speaks quite slowly and forms each syllable with precise enunciation.

Participating in this communication with Ra has been most inspiring for each of us because of the blend of eloquence and simplicity that characterizes Ra's responses. The information contained in *The Ra Material* has been most helpful to us in increasing our knowledge of the mystery of the creation and our evolution through it. We hope that it might also be useful to you.

L/L Research

DON ELKINS
CARLA L. RUECKERT
JIM MCCARTY

Louisville, Kentucky
July 7, 1983

From the Ra material, Session no. 88, May 29, 1982:

Firstly, if pictures be taken of a working, the visual image must needs be that which is; that is, it is well for you to photograph only an actual working and no sham nor substitution of any material. There shall be no distortions which this group can avoid any more than we would wish distortions in our words.

Secondly, it is inadvisable to photograph the instrument or any portion of the working room while the instrument is in trance. This is a narrow band contact, and we wish to keep electrical and electromagnetic energies constant when their presence is necessary and not present at all otherwise.

Thirdly, once the instrument is aware of the picture taking, whether before or after the working, the instrument shall be required to continuously respond to speech, thus assuring that no trance is imminent.

* * * * *

We ask that any photographs tell the truth, that they be dated and shine with a clarity so that there is no shadow of any but genuine expression which may be offered to those who seek truth.

We come as humble messengers of the Law of One, desiring to decrease distortions. We ask that you, who have been our friends, work with any considerations such as above discussed, not with the thought of quickly removing an unimportant detail, but, as in all ways, regard such as another opportunity to, as the adept must, be yourselves and offer that which is in and with you without pretense of any kind.

RA, Session no. 2, January 20, 1981: "Place at the entity's head a virgin chalice of water. Place to the center the book most closely aligned with the instrument's mental distortions, which are allied most closely with the Law of One—that being the Bible that she touches most frequently. To the other side of the Bible, place a small amount of cense, or incense, in a virgin censer. To the rear of the book symbolizing One, opened to the Gospel of John, Chapter One, place a white candle." June 9, 1982

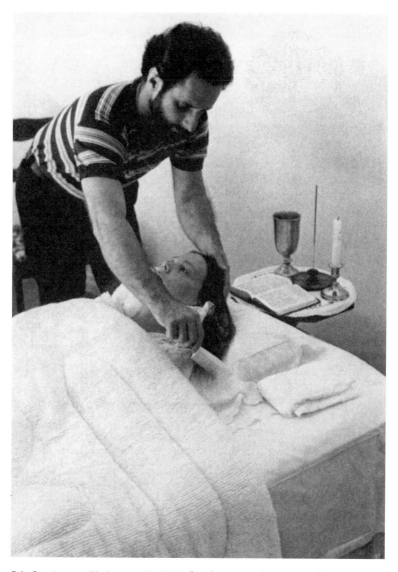

RA, Session no. 69, August 29, 1981: "At this particular working there is some slight interference with the contact due to the hair of the instrument. We may suggest the combing of this antenna-like material into a more orderly configuration prior to the working." June 9, 1982

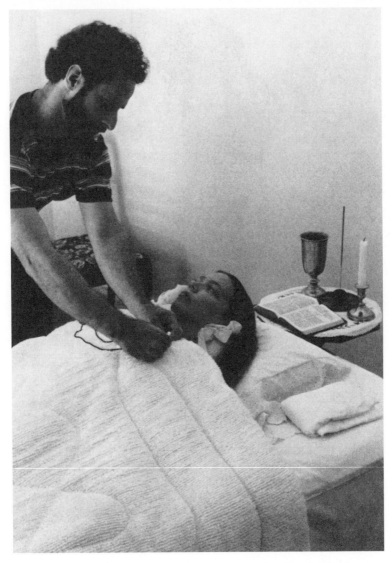

"We hook up three tape recorder microphones just below her chin so that we don't miss any of the session if tape recorder one or two malfunctions, which has happened." From the introduction to *The Ra Material*. June 9, 1982

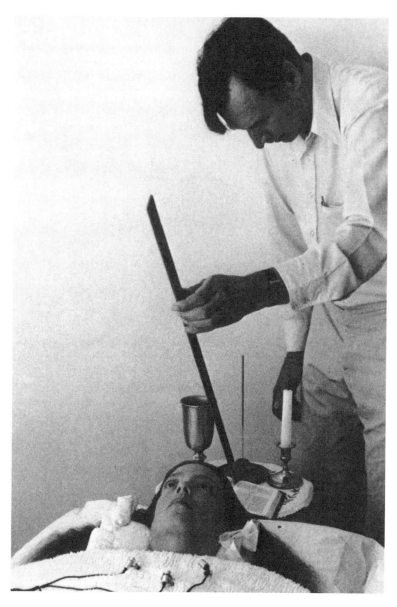

RA, Session no. 2, January 20, 1981: "The proper alignment is with the head pointed 20 degrees north by northeast. This is the direction from which the newer or New Age distortions of love/light, which are less distorted, are emanating, and this instrument will find comfort therein." June 9, 1982

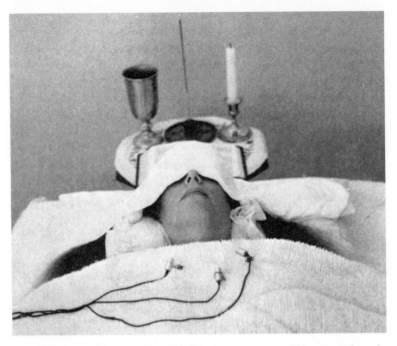

RA, Session no. 2, January 20, 1981: "The instrument would be strengthened by the wearing of a white robe. The instrument shall be covered and prone, the eyes covered." June 9, 1982

From the introduction to *The Ra Material*: "Each of us contributes ideas, but the great bulk of the line of questioning is accomplished by Don, who is the questioner, since he has years of experience in investigating the UFO contactee phenomenon necessary to develop the intellectual foundation which is required in any attempt to fit the diverse pieces of this puzzle together." June 9, 1982

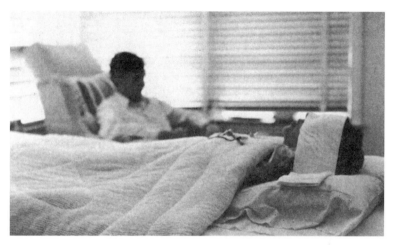

From the introduction to *The Ra Material*: "We average about one session every week or ten days now, which allows us to prepare for each session with the greater degree of care that seems to be required as sessions accumulate. A great deal of thought goes into the questions that Don asks during each session." June 9, 1982

From the introduction to *The Ra Material*: "After Don lights the candle and incense, he and I walk the Circle of One around Carla and repeat the words that begin each contact. At some point after that, Carla departs her physical body, and Ra then uses it to make the words that form the responses to Don's questions. I meditate and send light to Carla for the duration of the session, only taking time out to flip the tapes over as they finish each side."

In this picture, Carla is not channeling Ra but is singing "Amazing Grace" as per Ra's instructions for the instrument to be constantly speaking if her eyes are covered during the picture-taking session. June 9, 1982

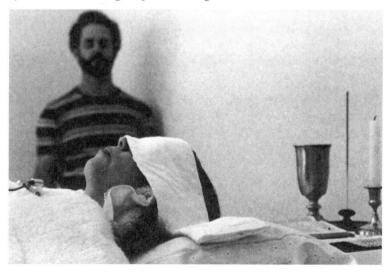

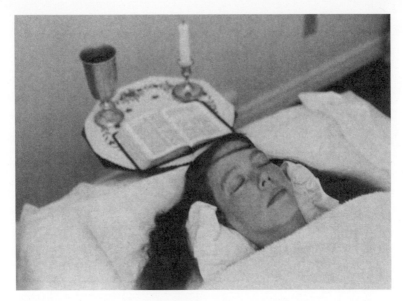

This picture was taken immediately after Carla responded to her name and the eye covering was removed from her face, somewhat mussing her hair. June 9, 1982

From the introduction to *The Ra Material*: "When the session is over, Don waits a few moments for Carla to return to her usually quite stiff body; he calls her name a few times until she responds, helps her to sit up, rubs her neck a bit, and gives her the chalice full of water to drink after he and I have filled it as full of our love vibrations as we can." June 9, 1982

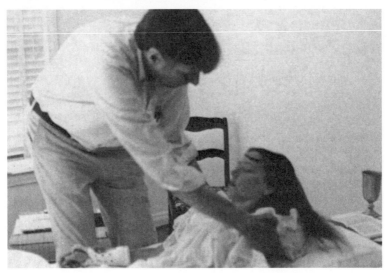

Jim is transcribing Session no. 89 on the afternoon of June 9, 1982, while Chocolate Bar, one of our four cats, observes. June 9, 1982

The exterior of the Ra room: the door and corner windows are part of the outside of the room in which the Ra sessions have taken place since January 1981. June 9, 1982

Carla holding our longtime friend, thirteen-year-old Gandalf. June 26, 1982

Don, in the office, talking to the picture taker, Jim, and attracting a feline audience as well. June 26, 1982

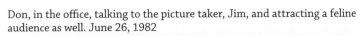

Jim and Carla prepare for the meditation that always precedes a Ra session.
June 26, 1982

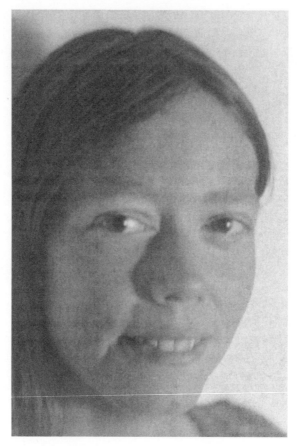

Carla, after Ra session no. 92, July 8, 1982

On January 15, 1981, our research group began receiving a communication from the social memory complex, Ra. From this communication precipitated the Law of One and some of the distortions of the Law of One.

The pages of this book contain an exact transcript, edited only to remove some personal material, of the communications received in the first twenty-six sessions with Ra.

Session 1,
January 15, 1981

RA: I am Ra. I have not spoken through this instrument before. We had to wait until she was precisely tuned, as we send a narrow band vibration. We greet you in the love and in the light of our Infinite Creator.

We have watched your group. We have been called to your group, for you have a need for the diversity of experiences in channeling which go with a more intensive, or as you might call it, advanced approach to the system of studying the pattern of the illusions of your body, your mind, and your spirit, which you call seeking the truth. We hope to offer you a somewhat different slant upon the information which is always and ever the same.

At this time we would be glad to attempt to speak to any subject or question which those entities in the room may have potential use in the requesting.

QUESTIONER: Do you have a specific purpose, and if so, could you tell us something of what your purpose is?

RA: I am Ra. We communicate now. We are those who are of the Law of One. In our vibration the polarities are harmonized; the complexities are simplified; the paradoxes have a solution. We are one. That is our nature and our purpose.

We are old upon your planet and have served with varying degrees of success in transmitting the Law of One, of Unity, of Singleness to your peoples. We have walked your planet. We have seen the faces of your peoples. However, we now feel the great responsibility of staying in the capacity of removing the distortions and powers that have been given to the Law of One. We will continue in this, until, shall we say, your cycle is appropriately ended. If not this one, then the next. We are not a part of time and, thus, are able to be with you in any of your times.

Does this give you enough information from which to extract our purpose, my brother?

QUESTIONER: Yes. Thank you.

RA: I am Ra. We appreciate your vibrations. Is there another query?

QUESTIONER: I've heard of the name "Ra" in connection with the Egyptians. Are you connected with that Ra in any way?

RA: I am Ra. Yes, the connection is congruency. May we elucidate? What do you not understand?

QUESTIONER: Could you give me a little more detail about your role with the Egyptians?

RA: I am Ra. The identity of the vibration Ra is our identity. We as a group, or what you would call a social memory complex, made contact with a race of your planetary kind which you call Egyptians. Others from our density made contact at the same time in South America, and the so-called "lost cities" were their attempts to contribute to the Law of One.

We spoke to one who heard and understood and was in a position to decree the Law of One. However, the priests and peoples of that era quickly distorted our message, robbing it of the, shall we say, compassion with which unity is informed by its very nature. Since it contains all, it cannot abhor any.

When we were no longer able to have appropriate channels through which to enunciate the Law of One, we removed ourselves from the now-hypocritical position which we had allowed ourselves to be placed in. Other myths, shall we say, having more to do with polarity and the things of your vibration that are complex, again took over in that particular society/complex.

Does this form a sufficient amount of information, or could we speak further?

Is there another query?

QUESTIONER: [The question was lost because the questioner was sitting too far from the tape recorder to be recorded.]

RA: I am Ra. Consider, if you will, that the universe is infinite. This has yet to be proven or disproven, but we can assure you that there is no end to your selves, your understanding, what you would call your journey of seeking, or your perceptions of the creation.

That which is infinite cannot be many, for manyness is a finite concept. To have infinity you must identify or define the infinity as unity; otherwise, the term does not have any referent or meaning. In an Infinite Creator there is only unity. You have seen simple examples of unity. You have seen the prism which shows all colors stemming from the sunlight. This is a simplistic example of unity.

In truth there is no right or wrong. There is no polarity, for all will be, as you would say, reconciled at some point in your dance through the mind/body/spirit complex which you amuse yourself by distorting in various ways at this time. This distortion is not in any case necessary. It is chosen by each of you as an alternative to understanding the complete unity of thought which binds all things. You are not speaking of similar or somewhat like entities or things. You are every thing, every being, every emotion, every event, every situation. You are unity. You are infinity. You are love/light, light/love. You are. This is the Law of One.

May we enunciate in more detail?

QUESTIONER: No.

RA: I am Ra. Is there another query at this time?

QUESTIONER: Can you comment on the coming planetary changes in our physical reality?

RA: I am Ra. I preferred to wait till this instrument had again reached a proper state of depth of singleness or one-pointedness before we spoke.

The changes are very, very trivial. We do not concern ourselves with the conditions which bring about harvest.

QUESTIONER: If an individual makes efforts to act as a catalyst in general to increase the awareness of planetary consciousness, is he of any aid in that direction, or is he doing nothing but acting upon himself?

RA: I am Ra. We shall answer your question in two parts, both of which are important equally.

Firstly, you must understand that the distinction between yourself and others is not visible to us. We do not consider that a separation exists between the consciousness-raising efforts of the distortion which you project as a personality and the distortion that you project as another personality. Thus, to learn is the same as to teach unless you are not teaching what you are learning, in which case you have done you/them little good. This understanding should be pondered by your mind/body/spirit complex as it is a distortion which plays a part in your experiences at this nexus.

To turn to the second part of our response, may we state our understanding, limited though it is.

Group-individuated consciousness is that state of sharing understanding with the other distortions of mind/body/spirit complexes, which are within the evident reach of the mind/body/spirit complex individual or group. Thus, we are speaking to you and accepting both our distortions and your own in order to enunciate the laws of creation, more especially the Law of One. We are not available to many of your peoples, for this is not an easily understood way of communication or type of philosophy. However, our very being is hopefully a poignant example of both the necessity and the near hopelessness of attempting to teach.

Each of those in this group is striving to use, digest, and diversify the information which we are sending this instrument into the channels of the mind/body/spirit complex without distortion. The few whom you will illuminate by sharing your light are far more than enough reason for the greatest possible effort. To serve one is to serve all. Therefore, we offer the question back to you to state that indeed it is the only activity worth doing: to learn/teach or teach/learn. There is nothing else which is of aid in demonstrating the original thought except your very being, and the distortions that come from the unexplained, inarticulate, or mystery-clad being are many. Thus, to attempt to discern and weave your way through as many group mind/body/spirit distortions as possible among your peoples in the course of your teaching is a very good effort to make. We can speak no more valiantly of your desire to serve.

May we speak in any other capacity upon this subject?

QUESTIONER: Will you be available for communication? Can we call on you in the future?

RA: I am Ra. We have good contact with this instrument because of her recent experiences with trance. She is to be able to communicate our thoughts in your future. However, we advise care in disturbing the channel for a few moments and then the proper procedure for aiding an instrument who has, to some extent, the need of reentering the mind/body/spirit complex which the instrument has chosen for the life experience of this time/space. Do you understand how to nurture this instrument?

QUESTIONER: No. Could you explain it?

RA: We suggest first a brief period of silence. Then the repetition of the instrument's vibratory complex of sound in your density which you call name. Repeat until an answer is obtained. Then the laying on of the hands at the neck region for a brief period so that the instrument may recharge batteries, which are not, shall we say, full of the essence of this particular field at this time. And finally, a gift of water into which the love of all present has been given. This will restore this entity, for her distortions contain great sensitivity towards the vibrations of love and the charged water will effect comfort. Do you now understand?

QUESTIONER: Not completely.

RA: I am Ra. We search your mind to find the vibration (nickname). It is this vibration from you which contains the largest amount of what you would call love. Others would call this entity (first name). The charging of the water is done by those present placing their hands over the glass and visualizing the power of love entering the water. This will charge that very effective medium with those vibrations.

This instrument is, at this time, quite fatigued. However, her heart is such that she continues to remain open to us and useful as a channel. This is why we have spent the time/space explaining how the distortions of what you may call fatigue may be ameliorated.

Under no circumstances should this instrument be touched until she has responded to her name. I do not wish to take this instrument beyond her capacity for physical energy. It grows low. Therefore, I must leave this instrument. I leave you in the glory and peace of unity. Go forth in peace, rejoicing in the power of the One Creator. I am Ra.

Session 2,
January 20, 1981

RA: I am Ra. I greet you in the love and the light of our Infinite Creator. I am with this mind/body/spirit complex which has offered itself for a channel. I communicate with you.

Queries are in order in your projections of mind distortion at this time/space. Thusly would I assure this group that my own social memory complex has one particular method of communicating with those few who may be able to harmonize their distortions with ours, and that is to respond to queries for information. We are comfortable with this format. May the queries now begin.

QUESTIONER: I'm guessing that there are enough people who would understand what you are saying, who would be interested enough in it, for us to make a book of your communications, and I wondered if you would agree to this?

If so, I was thinking that possibly a bit of historical background of yourself might be in order.

RA: I am Ra. The possibility of communication, as you would call it, from the One to the One, through distortion, acceptable for meaning is the reason we contacted this group. There are few who will grasp, without significant distortion, that which we communicate through this connection with this mind/body/spirit complex. However, if it be your desire to share our communications with others, we have the distortion towards a perception that this would be most helpful in regularizing and crystallizing your own patterns of vibration upon the levels of experience which you call the life. If one is illuminated, are not all illuminated? Therefore, we are oriented towards speaking for you in whatever supply of speakingness you may desire. To teach/learn is the Law of One in one of its most elementary distortions.

QUESTIONER: Could you tell us something of your historical background and your contact with earlier races on this planet? Then we would have something to start with.

RA: I am Ra. We are aware that your mind/body is calculating the proper method of performing the task of creating a teach/learning instrument. We are aware that you find our incarnate, as you call it, state of interest. We waited for a second query so as to emphasize that the time/space of several thousand of your years creates a spurious type of interest. Thus in giving this information, we ask the proper lack of stress be placed upon our experiences in your local space/time. The teach/learning which is our responsibility is philosophical rather than historical. We shall proceed with your request which is harmless if properly evaluated.

We are those of the Confederation who eleven thousand of your years ago came to two of your planetary cultures which were at that time closely in touch with the creation of the One Creator. It was our naive belief that we could teach/learn by direct contact and that the free-will distortions of individual feeling or personality were in no danger. We had no thought of their being disturbed, as these cultures were already closely aligned with an all-embracing belief in the live-ness or consciousness of all. We came and were welcomed by the peoples whom we wished to serve. We attempted to aid them in technical ways having to do with the healing of mind/body/spirit complex distortions through the use of the crystal, appropriate to the distortion, placed within a certain appropriate series of ratios of time/space material. Thus were the pyramids created.

We found that the technology was reserved largely for those with the effectual mind/body distortion of power. This was not intended by the Law of One. We left your peoples. The group that was to work with those in the area of South America, as you call that portion of your sphere, gave up not so easily. They returned. We did not. However, we have never left your vibration due to our responsibility for the changes in consciousness we had first caused and then found distorted in ways not relegated to the Law of One. We attempted to contact the rulers of the land to which we had come, that land which you call Egypt, or in some areas, the Holy Land.

In the Eighteenth Dynasty, as it is known in your records of space/time distortions, we were able to contact a pharaoh, as you would call him. The man was small in life experience on your plane and was a . . . what this instrument would call Wanderer. Thus, this mind/body/spirit complex received our communication distortions and was able to blend his distortions with our own. This young entity had been given a vibratory complex of sound which vibrated in honor of a prosperous god, as this mind/body complex, which we call instrument for convenience, would call "Ammon." The entity decided that this name, being in honor of one among many gods, was not acceptable for inclusion in his vibratory sound complex. Thus, he changed his name to one which honored the sun disc. This distortion, called "Aten," was a close distortion to our reality as we understand our own nature of mind/body/spirit complex distortion. However, it does not come totally into alignment with the intended teach/learning which was sent. This entity, Ikhnaton, became convinced that the vibration of One was the true spiritual vibration and thus decreed the Law of One.

However, this entity's beliefs were accepted by very few. His priests gave lip service only, without the spiritual distortion towards seeking. The peoples continued in their beliefs. When this entity was no longer in this density, again the polarized beliefs in the many gods came into their own and continued so until the one known as Mohammed delivered the peoples into a more intelligible distortion of mind/body/spirit relationships.

Do you have a more detailed interest at this time?

QUESTIONER: We are very interested in the entire story that you have to tell and getting in to the Law of One in quite some detail. There will be several questions that I'll ask as we go along that may or may not be related directly to understanding the Law of One. However, I believe that the proper way of presenting this as a teach/learning vehicle is to investigate different facets of what you tell us. You spoke of crystal healing. (One other thing I want to mention is that when the instrument becomes fatigued, we want to cut off communication and continue questions at a later time when the instrument is recharged.) If the instrument is suitable at this time, we would like a little information about the crystal healing that you mentioned.

RA: I am Ra. The principle of crystal healing is based upon an understanding of the hierarchical nature of the structure of the illusion which is the physical body, as you would call it. There are crystals which work upon the energies coming into the spiritual body; there are crystals which work upon the distortions from spirit to mind; there are crystals which balance the distortions between the mind and the body. All of these crystal healings are charged through purified channels. Without the relative crystallization of the healer working with the crystal, the crystal will not be properly charged. The other ingredient is the proper alignment with the energy fields of the planet upon which you dwell and the holistic or cosmic distortions or streamings which enter the planetary aura in such a manner that an appropriate ratio of shapes and placement within these shapes is of indicated aid in the untangling or balancing process.

To go through the various crystals to be used would be exhaustive to this instrument, although you may ask us if you wish in another session. The delicacy, shall we say, of the choosing of the crystal is very critical and, in truth, a crystalline structure such as a diamond or ruby can be used by a purified channel who is filled with the Love/Light of One, in almost any application.

This, of course, takes initiation, and there never have been many to persevere to the extent of progressing through the various distortion leavings which initiation causes.

May we further inform you in any fairly brief way upon this or another subject?

QUESTIONER: Yes. You mentioned that the pyramids were an outgrowth of this. Could you expand a little on that? Were you responsible for the building of the pyramid, and what was the purpose of the pyramid?
RA: I am Ra. The larger pyramids were built by our ability using the forces of One. The stones are alive. It has not been so understood by the mind/body/spirit distortions of your culture. The purposes of the pyramids were two:

Firstly, to have a properly oriented place of initiation for those who wished to become purified or initiated channels for the Law of One.

Two, we wished then to carefully guide the initiates in developing a healing of the people whom they sought to aid, and of the planet itself. Pyramid after pyramid charged by the crystal and Initiate were designed to balance the incoming energy of the One Creation with the many and multiple distortions of the planetary mind/body/spirit. In this effort we were able to continue work that brothers within the Confederation had effected through building of other crystal-bearing structures and thus complete a ring, if you will, of these about the Earth's, as this instrument would have us vibrate it, surface.

This instrument begins to lose energy. We ask for one more query or subject and then we shall take our leave for this time/space.

QUESTIONER: You might mention that originally there was a capstone on the pyramid at the top: what was it made of and how you moved the heavy blocks to build the pyramid. What technique was used for that?

RA: I am Ra. I request that we be asked this question in our next work-time, as you would term the distortion/sharing that our energies produce.

If you have any questions about the proper use of this mind/body/spirit, we would appreciate your asking them now.

QUESTIONER: Consider them asked. I don't have anything to go on. What is the proper use of this instrument? What should we do? What should we do to maximize her ability and her comfort?

RA: I am Ra. We are pleased that you have asked this question, for it is not our understanding that we have the right/duty to share our perceptions on any subject but philosophy without direct question. However, this mind/body/spirit is not being correctly used and therefore is experiencing unnecessary distortions of body in the area of fatigue.

The vibrations may well be purified by a simple turning to the circle of One and the verbal vibration while doing so of the following dialogue:

Question: "What is the Law?"

Answer: "The Law is One."

Question: "Why are we here?"

Answer: "We seek the Law of One."

Question: "Why do we seek Ra?"

Answer: "Ra is an humble messenger of the Law of One." Both Together: "Rejoice then and purify this place in the Law of One. Let no thought-form enter the circle we have walked about this instrument, for the Law is One."

The instrument at this time should be in trance. The proper alignment is the head pointed 20 degrees north by northeast. This is the direction from which the newer or New Age distortions of love/light, which are less distorted, are emanating, and this instrument will find comfort therein. This is a sensitive instrument, by which we mean the distortions which enter her mind/body/spirit complex come from any of her senses. Thus, it is well to do the following:

Place at the entity's head a virgin chalice of water.

To the center, the book most closely aligned with the instrument's mental distortions which are allied most closely with the Law of One, that being the Bible that she touches most frequently.

To the other side of the Bible, a small amount of cense, or incense, in a virgin censer.

To the rear of the book symbolizing One, opened to the Gospel of John, Chapter One, a white candle.

The instrument would be strengthened by the wearing of a white robe. The instrument shall be covered and prone, the eyes covered.

We feel that, though this is a complex of activity/circumstance and may seem very distorted from a purposeful teach/learning experience, these elaborations on the technique of trance will ease the mind distortions of those about the instrument as they perceive improvement in the instrument's distortions with regard to fatigue. We add only that if these teach/learning sessions are held during time/space during which your sun body does not light your room that it is best to call the instrument before the lighting of the illuminatory mechanism.

I am Ra. I leave you in the glory and the peace of the One Creator. Rejoice in the love/light, and go forth in the power of the One Creator. In joy, we leave you. Adonai.

Session 3,
January 21, 1981

RA: I am Ra. I greet you in love and the light of the One Infinite Creator. I communicate with you now.

QUESTIONER: My first question is, did we correctly perform the ritual for starting the communication?

RA: I am Ra. The placement of the artifacts designated to balance the instrument should be placed at the instrument's head for the least distortion of effect. The remainder of the beginning account of purpose is quite acceptable, for those speaking desire to serve. Otherwise, the attendant emphasis in mind complexities would not have been affected properly. We caution you to guard against those who are not wishing to serve others above all else, from taking part in the beginning or in lending their distortions of mind/body/spirit complex to any session as we should then be unable to properly blend our distortions with those of this instrument.

QUESTIONER: Should I move the Bible, candle, and incense at this time?

RA: I am Ra. This would be appropriate.

QUESTIONER: [*After moving the items*] Is this the proper position?

RA: I am Ra. Please correct the angle of the incense so that it is perpendicular to the plane of 20 degrees north by northeast.

QUESTIONER: [*After making the correction*] Is this satisfactory?

RA: I am Ra. Please check by eye to make fine correction. We will explain the process by which this becomes a significant distortion balancer. The incense acts as energizer to the physical body of this instrument, signifying its humanity. This is, therefore, a necessity that the wafted smoke is perceived from the same relative angle as the instrument perceives the opened Bible balanced by the lighted candle signifying love/light and light/love and, therefore, give the mental and emotional, shall we call it, distortion complex of this instrument the sight of paradise and peace which it seeks. Thus energized from the lower to the higher, the instrument becomes balanced and does not grow fatigued.

We appreciate your concern, for this will enable our teach/learning to proceed more easily.

QUESTIONER: Does everything appear correctly aligned now?

RA: I am Ra. I judge it within limits of acceptability.

QUESTIONER: At the last session we had two questions that we were saving for this session: one having to do with the possible capstone on top of the Great Pyramid at Giza; the other having to do with how you moved the heavy blocks that make up the pyramid. I know these questions are of no importance with respect to the Law of One, but it was my judgment—and please correct me if I am wrong, and make the necessary suggestions—that this would provide an easy entry for those who would read the material that will eventually become a book. We are very grateful for your contact and will certainly take any suggestions as to how we should receive this information.

RA: I am Ra. I will not suggest the proper series of questions. This is your prerogative as free agent of the Law of One having learned/understood that our social memory complex cannot effectually discern the distortions of the societal mind/body/spirit complex of your peoples. We wish now to fulfill our teach/learning honor/responsibility by answering what is asked. This only will suffice for we cannot plumb the depths of the distortion complexes which infect your peoples.

The first question, therefore, is the capstone. We iterate the unimportance of this type of data.

The so-called Great Pyramid had two capstones. One was of our design and was of smaller and carefully contrived pieces of the material upon your planet which you call "granite." This was contrived for crystalline properties and for the proper flow of your atmosphere via a type of what you would call "chimney."

At a time when we as a people had left your density, the original was taken away and a more precious one substituted. It consisted, in part, of a golden material. This did not change the properties of the pyramid, as you call it, at all and was a distortion due to the desire of a few to mandate the use of the structure as a royal place only.

Do you wish to query further upon this first question?

QUESTIONER: What did you mean by chimney? What was its specific purpose?

RA: I am Ra. There is a proper flow of your atmosphere which, though small, freshens the whole of the structure. This was designed by having air-flow ducts, as this instrument might call them, situated so that there was a freshness of atmosphere without any disturbance or draft.

QUESTIONER: How were the blocks moved?

RA: I am Ra. You must picture the activity within all that is created. The energy is, though finite, quite large compared to the understanding/distortion by your peoples. This is an obvious point well known to your people, but little considered.

This energy is intelligent. It is hierarchical. Much as your mind/body/spirit complex dwells within a hierarchy of vehicles and retains, therefore, the shell or shape or field, and the intelligence of each ascendingly intelligent or balanced body, so does each atom of such a material as rock. When one can speak to that intelligence, the finite energy of the physical or chemical rock/body is put into contact with that infinite power which is resident in the more well-tuned bodies, be they human or rock.

With this connection made, a request may be given. The intelligence of infinite rockness communicates to its physical vehicle, and that splitting and moving which is desired is then carried out through the displacement of the energy field of rockness from finity to a dimension which we may conveniently call, simply, infinity.

In this way, that which is required is accomplished due to a cooperation of the infinite understanding of the Creator indwelling in the living rock. This is, of course, the mechanism by which many things are accomplished, which are not subject to your present means of physical analysis of action at a distance.

QUESTIONER: I am reminded of the statement—approximately— that if you had faith to move a mountain, the mountain would move. This seems to be approximately what you were saying. That if you are fully aware of the Law of One, you would be able to do these things. Is that correct?

RA: I am Ra. The vibratory distortion of sound, faith, is perhaps one of the stumbling blocks between those of what we may call the infinite path and those of the finite proving/understanding.

You are precisely correct in your understanding of the congruency of faith and intelligent infinity; however, one is a spiritual term, the other more acceptable perhaps to the conceptual framework distortions of those who seek with measure and pen.

QUESTIONER: Then if an individual is totally informed with respect to the Law of One and lives the Law of One, then such things as the building of the pyramids by direct mental effort would be commonplace. Is that what I am to understand?

RA: I am Ra. You are incorrect in that there is a distinction between the individual power through the Law of One and the combined or societal memory complex mind/body/spirit understanding of the Law of One.

In the first case only the one individual, purified of all flaws, could move a mountain. In the case of mass understanding of unity, each individual may contain an acceptable amount of distortion and yet the mass mind could move mountains. The progress is normally from the understanding which you now seek to a dimension of understanding which is governed by the laws of love, and which seeks the laws of light. Those who are vibrating with the Law of Light seek the Law of One. Those who vibrate with the Law of One seek the Law of Foreverness.

We cannot say what is beyond this dissolution of the unified self with all that there is, for we still seek to become all that there is, and still are we Ra. Thus our paths go onward.

QUESTIONER: Was the pyramid then built by the mutual action of many?

RA: I am Ra. The pyramids which we thought/built were constructed thought-forms created by our social memory complex.

QUESTIONER: Then the rock was created in place rather than moved from someplace else? Is that correct?

RA: I am Ra. We built with everlasting rock the Great Pyramid, as you call it. Other of the pyramids were built with stone moved from one place to another.

QUESTIONER: What is everlasting rock?

RA: I am Ra. If you can understand the concept of thought-forms you will realize that the thought-form is more regular in its distortion than the energy fields created by the materials in the rock which has been created through thought-form from thought to finite energy and being-ness in your, shall we say, distorted reflection of the level of the thought-form.
  May we answer you in any more helpful way?

QUESTIONER: This is rather trivial, but I was wondering why the pyramid was built with many blocks rather than creating the whole thing as one form created at once?

RA: I am Ra. There is a law which we believe to be one of the more significant primal distortions of the Law of One. That is the Law of Confusion. You have called this the Law of Free Will. We wished to make an healing machine, or time/space ratio complex which was as efficacious as possible. However, we did not desire to allow the mystery to be penetrated by the peoples in such a way that we became worshipped as builders of a miraculous pyramid. Thus it appears to be made, not thought.

QUESTIONER: Well, then you speak of the pyramid, the Great Pyramid, I assume, as primarily a healing machine, and also you spoke of it as a device for initiation. Are these one and the same concept?

RA: I am Ra. They are part of one complex of love/light intent/sharing. To use the healing properly it was important to have a purified and dedicated channel, or energizer, for the love/light of the Infinite Creator to flow through; thus the initiatory method was necessary to prepare the mind, the body, and the spirit for service in the Creator's work. The two are integral.

QUESTIONER: Does the shape of the pyramid have a function in the initiation process?

RA: I am Ra. This is a large question. We feel that we shall begin and ask you to reevaluate and ask further at a later session, this somewhat, shall we say, informative point.

To begin. There are two main functions of the pyramid in relation to the initiatory procedures. One has to do with the body. Before the body can be initiated, the mind must be initiated. This is the point at which most adepts of your present cycle find their mind/body/spirit complexes distorted from. When the character and personality that is the true identity of the mind has been discovered, the body then must be known in each and every way. Thus, the various functions of the body need understanding and control with detachment. The first use of the pyramid, then, is the going down into the pyramid for purposes of deprivation of sensory input so that the body may, in a sense, be dead and another life begin.

We advise, at this time, any necessary questions and a fairly rapid ending of this session. Have you any query at this time/space?

QUESTIONER: The only question is, is there anything that we have done wrong, or that we could do to make the instrument more comfortable?

RA: I am Ra. We scan this instrument.

This instrument has been much aided by these precautions. We suggest only some attention to the neck, which seems in this body/distortion to be distorted in the area of strength/weakness. More support, therefore, to the neck area may be an aid.

QUESTIONER: Should we have the instrument drink the water from the chalice behind her head, or should we have her drink from another glass after we charge it with love?

RA: I am Ra. That and only that chalice shall be the most beneficial as the virgin material living in the chalice accepts, retains, and responds to the love vibration activated by your beingness.

I am Ra. I will now leave this group rejoicing in the power and peace of the One Creator. Adonai.

Session 4,
January 22, 1981

RA: I am Ra. I greet you in the love and the light of the Infinite Creator. I communicate with you now.

QUESTIONER: When we finished the last session, I had asked a question that was too long to answer. It had to do with the shape of the pyramid, its relationship to the initiation. Is this the appropriate time to ask this question?

RA: I am Ra. Yes, this is an appropriate time/space to ask that question.

QUESTIONER: Does the shape of the pyramid have an effect upon the initiation?

RA: I am Ra. As we began the last session question, you have already recorded in your individual memory complex the first use of the shape having to do with the body complex initiation. The initiation of spirit was a more carefully designed type of initiation as regards the time/space ratios about which the entity to be initiated found itself.

If you will picture with me the side of the so-called pyramid shape and mentally imagine this triangle cut into four equal triangles, you will find the intersection of the triangle, which is at the first level on each of the four sides, forms a diamond in a plane which is horizontal. The middle of this plane is the appropriate place for the intersection of the energies streaming from the infinite dimensions and the mind/body/spirit complexes of various interwoven energy fields. Thus it was designed that the one to be initiated would, by mind, be able to perceive and then channel this, shall we say, gateway to intelligent infinity. This, then, was the second point of designing this specific shape.

May we provide a further description of any kind to your query?

QUESTIONER: Yes. As I understand it then, the initiate was to be on the centerline of that pyramid, but at an altitude above the base as defined by the intersection of the four triangles made by dividing each side. Is that correct?

RA: I am Ra. This is correct.

QUESTIONER: Then at this point there is a focusing of energy that is extra-dimensional in respect to our dimensions. Am I right?

RA: I am Ra. You may use that vibratory sound complex. However, it is not totally and specifically correct. There are no "extra" dimensions. We would prefer the use of the term "multidimensional."

QUESTIONER: Is the size of the pyramid a function of the effectiveness of the initiation?

RA: I am Ra. Each size pyramid has its own point of streaming in of intelligent infinity. Thus, a tiny pyramid that can be placed below a body or above a body will have specific and various effects depending upon the placement of the body in relationship to the entrance point of intelligent infinity.

For the purposes of initiation, the size needed to be large enough to create the impression of towering size so that the entrance point of multidimensional intelligent infinity would completely pervade and fill the channel, the entire body being able to rest in this focused area. Furthermore, it was necessary for healing purposes that both channel and the one to be healed be able to rest within that focused point.

QUESTIONER: Is the large pyramid at Giza still usable for this purpose, or is it no longer functional?

RA: I am Ra. That, like many other pyramid structures, is like the piano out of tune. It, as this instrument would express it, plays the tune but, oh, so poorly. The disharmony jangles the sensitivity. Only the ghost of the streaming still remains due to the shifting of the streaming points which is in turn due to the shifting electromagnetic field of your planet; due also to the discordant vibratory complexes of those who have used the initiatory and healing place for less compassionate purposes.

QUESTIONER: Would it be possible to build a pyramid and properly align it and use it today from the materials that we have available?

RA: I am Ra. It is quite possible for you to build a pyramid structure. The material used is not critical, merely the ratios of time/space complexes. However, the use of the structure for initiation and healing depends completely upon the inner disciplines of the channels attempting such work.

QUESTIONER: My question then would be, are there individuals incarnate upon the planet today who would have the inner disciplines to, using your instructions, construct and initiate in a pyramid they built? Is this within the limits of what anyone on the planet today can do? Or is there no one available for this?

RA: I am Ra. There are people, as you call them, who are able to take this calling at this nexus. However, we wish to point out once again that the time of the pyramids, as you would call it, is past. It is indeed a timeless structure. However, the streamings from the universe were, at the time we attempted to aid this planet, those which required a certain understanding of purity. This understanding has, as the streamings revolved and all things evolve, changed to a more enlightened view of purity. Thus, there are those among your people at this time whose purity is already one with intelligent infinity. Without the use of structures, healer/patient can gain healing.

May we further speak to some specific point?

QUESTIONER: Is it possible for you to instruct in these healing techniques if we could make available an individual who had the native ability?

RA: I am Ra. It is possible. We must add that many systems of teach/learning the healing/patient nexus are proper given the various mind/body/spirit complexes. We ask your imagination to consider the relative simplicity of the mind in the earlier cycle and the less distorted, but often overly complex, views and thought/spirit processes of the same mind/body/spirit complexes after many incarnations. We also ask your imagination to conceive of those who have chosen the distortion of service and have removed their mind/body/spirit complexes from one dimension to another, thus bringing with them in totally latent form many skills and understandings which more closely match the distortions of the healing/patient processes.

QUESTIONER: I would very much like to continue investigation into the possibility of this healing process, but I'm a little lost as to where to begin. Can you tell me where my first step would be?

RA: I am Ra. I cannot tell you what to ask. I may suggest that you consider the somewhat complex information just given and thus discover several avenues of inquiry. There is one "health," as you call it, in your polarized environment, but there are several significantly various distortions of types of mind/body/spirit complexes. Each type must pursue its own learn/teaching in this area.

QUESTIONER: Would you say, then, that the first step would be to find an individual with ability brought with him into this incarnation? Is this correct?

RA: I am Ra. This is correct.

QUESTIONER: Once I have selected an individual to perform the healing, it would be helpful to receive instruction from you. Is this possible?

RA: I am Ra. This is possible given the distortions of vibratory sound complexes.

QUESTIONER: I'm assuming, then, that the selected individual would be one who was very much in harmony with the Law of One. Even though he may not have any intellectual understanding of it, he should be living the Law of One?

RA: I am Ra. This is both correct and incorrect. The first case, that being correctness, would apply to one such as the questioner himself who has the distortions towards healing, as you call it.

The incorrectness which shall be observed is the healing of those whose activities in your space/time illusion do not reflect the Law of One, but whose ability has found its pathway to intelligent infinity regardless of the plane of existence from which this distortion is found.

QUESTIONER: I'm a little confused. I partially understand you, but I'm not sure that I fully understand you. Could you restate that in another way?

RA: I am Ra. I can restate that in many ways, given this instrument's knowledge of your vibratory sound complexes. I will strive for a shorter distortion at this time.

Two kinds there are who can heal: those such as yourself who, having the innate distortion towards knowledge-giving of the Law of One, can heal but do not; and those who, having the same knowledge, but showing no significant distortions toward the Law of One in mind, body, or spirit, yet, and nevertheless have opened a channel to the same ability.

The point being that there are those who, without proper training, shall we say, nevertheless heal. It is a further item of interest that those whose life does not equal their work may find some difficulty in absorbing the energy of intelligent infinity and thus become quite distorted in such a way as to cause disharmony in themselves and others and perhaps even find it necessary to cease the healing activity. Therefore, those of the first type, those who seek to serve and are willing to be trained in thought, word, and action are those who will be able to comfortably maintain the distortion toward service in the area of healing.

QUESTIONER: Then would it be possible for you to train us in healing awareness?

RA: I am Ra. It is possible.

QUESTIONER: Will you train us?

RA: I am Ra. We will.

QUESTIONER: I have no idea how long this would take. Is it possible for you to give a synopsis of the program of training required? I have no knowledge of what questions to ask at this point.

RA: I am Ra. We consider your request for information, for as you noted, there are a significant number of vibratory sound complexes which can be used in sequence to train the healer.

The synopsis is a very appropriate entry that you might understand what is involved.

Firstly, the mind must be known to itself. This is perhaps the most demanding part of healing work. If the mind knows itself then the most important aspect of healing has occurred. Consciousness is the microcosm of the Law of One.

The second part has to do with the disciplines of the body complexes. In the streamings reaching your planet at this time, these understandings and disciplines have to do with the balance between love and wisdom in the use of the body in its natural functions.

The third area is the spiritual, and in this area the first two disciplines are connected through the attainment of contact with intelligent infinity.

QUESTIONER: I believe I have a little idea of the accomplishment of the first step. Can you elaborate a little bit on the other two steps which I am not at all familiar with.

RA: I am Ra. Imagine the body. Imagine the more dense aspects of the body. Proceed therefrom to the very finest knowledge of energy pathways which revolve and cause the body to be energized. Understand that all natural functions of the body have all aspects from dense to fine and can be transmuted to what you may call sacramental. This is a brief investigation of the second area.

To speak to the third, if you will, imagine the function of the magnet. The magnet has two poles. One reaches up. The other goes down. The function of the spirit is to integrate the up-reaching yearning of the mind/body energy with the downpouring and streaming of infinite intelligence. This is a brief explication of the third area.

QUESTIONER: Then would this training program involve specific things to do, specific instructions and exercises?

RA: I am Ra. We are not at this time incarnate among your peoples; thus, we can guide and attempt to specify, but we cannot, by example, show. This is an handicap. However, there should indeed be fairly specific exercises of mind, body, and spirit during the teach/learning process we offer. It is to be once more iterated that healing is but one distortion of the Law of One. To reach an undistorted understanding of that law, it is not necessary to heal or to show any manifestation but only to exercise the discipline of understanding.

We would ask that one or two more questions be the ending of this session.

QUESTIONER: My objective is primarily to discover more of the Law of One, and it would be very helpful to discover the techniques of healing. I am aware of your problem with respect to free will. Can you state the Law of One and the laws of healing to me?

RA: I am Ra. The Law of One, though beyond the limitation of name, as you call vibratory sound complexes, may be approximated by stating that all things are one, that there is no polarity, no right or wrong, no disharmony, but only identity. All is one, and that one is love/light, light/love, the Infinite Creator.

One of the primal distortions of the Law of One is that of healing. Healing occurs when a mind/body/spirit complex realizes, deep within itself, the Law of One; that is, that there is no disharmony, no imperfection; that all is complete and whole and perfect. Thus, the intelligent infinity within this mind/body/spirit complex reforms the illusion of body, mind, or spirit to a form congruent with the Law of One. The healer acts as energizer or catalyst for this completely individual process.

One item which may be of interest is that a healer asking to learn must take the distortion understood as responsibility for that ask/receiving. This is an honor/duty which must be carefully considered in free will before the asking.

QUESTIONER: I assume that we should continue tomorrow.

RA: I am Ra. Your assumption is correct unless you feel a certain question is necessary. This instrument is nurtured by approximately this length of work.

QUESTIONER: I have one more short question. Is this instrument capable of two of these sessions per day, or should we remain with one?

RA: I am Ra. This instrument is capable of two sessions a day. However, she must be encouraged to keep her bodily complex strong by the ingestion of your foodstuffs to an extent which exceeds this instrument's normal intake of your foodstuffs, this due to the physical material which we use to speak.

Further, this instrument's activities must be monitored to prevent overactivity, for this activity is equivalent to a strenuous working day on the physical level.

If these admonishments are considered, the two sessions would be possible. We do not wish to deplete this instrument.

QUESTIONER: Thank you, Ra.

RA: I am Ra. I leave you in the love and the light of the one Infinite Intelligence which is the Creator. Go forth rejoicing in the power and the peace of the One. Adonai.

Session 5,
January 23, 1981

RA: I am Ra. I greet you in the love and the light of the Infinite Creator. I communicate now.

QUESTIONER: The last time that we communicated we were speaking of the learning of healing. It is my impression from what you gave to us in the earlier session that it is necessary to first purify the self by certain disciplines and exercises. Then in order to heal a patient, it is necessary, by example, and possibly certain exercises, to create the mental configuration in the patient that allows him to heal himself. Am I correct?

RA: I am Ra. Although your learn/understanding distortion is essentially correct, your choice of vibratory/sound complex is not entirely as accurate as this language allows.

It is not by example that the healer does the working. The working exists in and of itself. The healer is only the catalyst, much as this instrument has the catalysis necessary to provide the channel for our words, yet by example or exercise of any kind can take no thought for this working.

The healing/working is congruent in that it is a form of channeling some distortion of the intelligent infinity.

QUESTIONER: We have decided to accept, if offered, the honor/duty of learning/teaching the healing process. I would ask as to the first step which we should accomplish in becoming effective healers.

RA: I am Ra. We shall begin with the first of the three teachings/ learnings.

We begin with the mental learn/teaching necessary for contact with intelligent infinity. The prerequisite of mental work is the ability to retain silence of self at a steady state when required by the self. The mind must be opened like a door. The key is silence.

Within the door lies an hierarchical construction you may liken unto geography and in some ways geometry, for the hierarchy is quite regular, bearing inner relationships.

To begin to master the concept of mental disciplines it is necessary to examine the self. The polarity of your dimension must be internalized. Where you find patience within your mind you must consciously find the corresponding impatience and vice versa. Each thought a being has, has in its turn an antithesis. The disciplines of the mind involve, first of all, identifying both those things of which you approve and those things of which you disapprove within yourself, and then balancing each and every positive and negative charge with its equal. The mind contains all things. Therefore, you must discover this completeness within yourself.

The second mental discipline is acceptance of the completeness within your consciousness. It is not for a being of polarity in the physical consciousness to pick and choose among attributes, thus building the roles that cause blockages and confusions in the already distorted mind complex. Each acceptance smooths part of the many distortions that the faculty you call judgment engenders.

The third discipline of the mind is a repetition of the first but with the gaze outward toward the fellow entities that it meets. In each entity there exists completeness. Thus, the ability to understand each balance is necessary. When you view patience, you are responsible for mirroring in your mental understandings, patience/impatience. When you view impatience, it is necessary for your mental configuration of under-standing to be impatience/patience. We use this as a simple example. Most configurations of mind have many facets, and understanding of either self polarities, or what you would call other-self polarities, can and must be understood as subtle work.

The next step is the acceptance of the other-self polarities, which mirrors the second step. These are the first four steps of learning mental disciplines. The fifth step involves observing the geographical and geometrical relationships and ratios of the mind, the other mind, the mass mind, and the infinite mind.

The second area of learn/teaching is the study/understanding of the body complexes. It is necessary to know your body well. This is a matter of using the mind to examine how the feelings, the biases, what you would call the emotions, affect various portions of the body complex. It shall be necessary to both understand the bodily polarity and to accept them, repeating in a chemical/physical manifestation the work you have done upon the mind bethinking the consciousness.

The body is a creature of the mind's creation. It has its biases. The biological bias must be first completely understood and then the opposite bias allowed to find full expression in understanding. Again, the process of acceptance of the body as a balanced, as well as polarized, individual may then be accomplished. It is then the task to extend this understanding to the bodies of the other-selves whom you will meet.

The simplest example of this is the understanding that each biological male is female; each biological female is male. This is a simple example. However, in almost every case wherein you are attempting the understanding of the body of self or other-self, you will again find that the most subtle discernment is necessary in order to fully grasp the polarity complexes involved.

At this time we would suggest closing the description until the next time of work so that we may devote time to the third area commensurate with its importance.

We can answer a query if it is a short one before we leave this instrument.

QUESTIONER: Is the instrument comfortable? Is there anything that we can do to increase the comfort of the instrument?

RA: I am Ra. The candle could be rotated clockwise approximately 10 degrees each session to improve the flow of spiraled energy through the being's receiving mechanisms. This particular configuration is well otherwise. But we ask that the objects described and used be centered with geometric care and checked from time to time. Also that they not be exposed to that space/time in which work is not of importance.

I am Ra. I leave this instrument in the love and in the light of the One Infinite Creator. Go forth rejoicing in the power and the peace of the One Creator. Adonai.

Session 6,
January 24, 1981

RA: I am Ra. I greet you in the love and the light of the Infinite Creator. I communicate now.

QUESTIONER: We would like to continue the material from yesterday.

RA: I am Ra. This is well with us.

We proceed now with the third part of the teach/learning concerning the development of the energy powers of healing.

The third area is the spiritual complex which embodies the fields of force and consciousness which are the least distorted of your mind/body/spirit complex. The exploration and balancing of the spirit complex is indeed the longest and most subtle part of your learn/teaching. We have considered the mind as a tree. The mind controls the body. With the mind single-pointed, balanced, and aware, the body comfortable in whatever biases and distortions make it appropriately balanced for that instrument, the instrument is then ready to proceed with the greater work.

That is the work of wind and fire. The spiritual body energy field is a pathway, or channel. When body and mind are receptive and open, then the spirit can become a functioning shuttle or communicator from the entity's individual energy/will upwards, and from the streamings of the creative fire and wind downwards.

The healing ability, like all other, what this instrument would call, paranormal abilities, is affected by the opening of a pathway or shuttle into intelligent infinity. There are many upon your plane who have a random hole or gateway in their spirit energy field, sometimes created by the ingestion of chemicals such as what this instrument would call LSD, who are able, randomly and without control, to tap into energy sources. They may or may not be entities who wish to serve. The purpose of carefully and consciously opening this channel is to serve in a more dependable way, in a more commonplace or usual way, as seen by the distortion complex of the healer. To others there may appear to be miracles. To the one who has carefully opened the door to intelligent infinity, this is ordinary; this is commonplace; this is as it should be. The life experience becomes somewhat transformed. The great work goes on.

At this time we feel these exercises suffice for your beginning. We will, at a future time, when you feel you have accomplished that which is set before you, begin to guide you into a more precise understanding of the functions and uses of this gateway in the experience of healing.

QUESTIONER: I think this might be an appropriate time to include a little more background on yourself, possibly information having to do with where you came from prior to your involvement with planet Earth, if this is possible.

RA: I am Ra. I am, with the social memory complex of which I am a part, one of those who voyaged outward from another planet within your own solar system, as this entity would call it. The planetary influence was that you call Venus. We are a race old in your measures. When we were at the sixth dimension our physical beings were what you would call golden. We were tall and somewhat delicate. Our physical body complex covering, which you call the integument, had a golden luster.

In this form we decided to come among your peoples. Your peoples at that time were much unlike us in physical appearance, as you might call it. We, thus, did not mix well with the population and were obviously other than they. Thus, our visit was relatively short, for we found ourselves in the hypocritical position of being acclaimed as other than your other-selves. This was the time during which we built the structures in which you show interest.

QUESTIONER: How did you journey from Venus to this planet?

RA: I am Ra. We used thought.

QUESTIONER: Would it have been possible to have taken one of the people of this planet at that time and placed him on Venus? Would he have survived? Were conditions on Venus hospitable?

RA: I am Ra. The third-density conditions are not hospitable to the life forms of your peoples. The fifth and sixth dimensions of that planetary sphere are quite conducive to growing/learning/teaching.

QUESTIONER: How were you able to make the transition from Venus? Did you have to change your dimension to walk upon the Earth?

RA: I am Ra. You will remember the exercise of the wind. The dissolution into nothingness is the dissolution into unity, for there is no nothingness. From the sixth dimension, we are capable of manipulating, by thought, the intelligent infinity present in each particle of light or distorted light so that we were able to clothe ourselves in a replica visible in the third density of our mind/body/spirit complexes in the sixth density. We were allowed this experiment by the Council which guards this planet.

QUESTIONER: Where is this Council located?

RA: I am Ra. This Council is located in the octave, or eighth dimension, of the planet Saturn, taking its place in an area which you understand in third-dimension terms as the rings.

QUESTIONER: Are there any people such as you find on Earth on any of the other planets in our solar system?

RA: I am Ra. Do you request space/time present information or space/time continuum information?

QUESTIONER: Both.

RA: I am Ra. At one time/space, in what is your past, there was a population of third-density beings upon a planet which dwelt within your solar system. There are various names by which this planet has been named. The vibratory sound complex most usually used by your peoples is Maldek. These entities, destroying their planetary sphere, thus were forced to find room for themselves upon this third density, which is the only one in your solar system at their time/space present which was hospitable and capable of offering the lessons necessary to decrease their mind/body/spirit distortions with respect to the Law of One.

QUESTIONER: How did they come here?

RA: I am Ra. They came through the process of harvest and were incarnated through the processes of incarnation from your higher spheres within this density.

QUESTIONER: How long ago did this happen?

RA: I am Ra. I am having difficulty communicating with this instrument. We must deepen her state.
This occurred approximately 500,000 of your years ago.

QUESTIONER: Is all of the Earth's human population then originally from Maldek?

RA: I am Ra. This is a new line of questioning and deserves a place of its own. The ones who were harvested to your sphere from the sphere known before its dissolution as other names, but to your peoples as

Maldek, incarnated, many within your Earth's surface rather than upon it. The population of your planet contains many various groups harvested from other second-dimension and cycled third-dimension spheres. You are not all one race or background of beginning. The experience you share is unique to this time/space continuum.

QUESTIONER: I think that it would be appropriate to discover how the Law of One acts in this transfer of beings to our planet and the action of harvest?

RA: I am Ra. The Law of One states simply that all things are one, that all beings are one. There are certain behaviors and thought-forms consonant with the understanding and practice of this law. Those who, finishing a cycle of experience, demonstrate grades of distortion of that understanding of thought and action will be separated by their own choice into the vibratory distortion most comfortable to their mind/body/spirit complexes. This process is guarded or watched by those nurturing beings who, being very close to the Law of One in their distortions, nevertheless move towards active service.

Thus, the illusion is created of light, or more properly but less understandably, light/love. This is in varying degrees of intensity. The spirit complex of each harvested entity moves along the line of light until the light grows too glaring, at which time the entity stops. This entity may have barely reached third density or may be very, very close to the ending of the third-density light/love distortion vibratory complex. Nevertheless, those who fall within this octave of intensifying light/love then experience a major cycle during which there are opportunities for the discovery of the distortions which are inherent in each entity and, therefore, the lessening of these distortions.

QUESTIONER: What is the length, in our years, of one of these cycles?

RA: I am Ra. One major cycle is approximately 25,000 of your years. There are three cycles of this nature during which those who have progressed may be harvested at the end of three major cycles. That is, approximately between 75 and 76,000 of your years. All are harvested regardless of their progress, for during that time the planet itself has moved through the useful part of that dimension and begins to cease being useful for the lower levels of vibration within that density.

QUESTIONER: What is the position of this planet with respect to the progression of cycles at this time?

RA: I am Ra. This sphere is at this time in fourth-dimension vibration. Its material is quite confused due to the society memory complexes embedded in its consciousness. It has not made an easy transition to the vibrations which beckon. Therefore, it will be fetched with some inconvenience.

QUESTIONER: Is this inconvenience imminent within a few years?

RA: I am Ra. This inconvenience, or disharmonious vibratory complex, has begun several of your years in your past. It shall continue unabated for a period of approximately thirty of your years.

QUESTIONER: After this period of thirty years I am assuming that this will be a fourth-density planet. Is this correct?

RA: I am Ra. This is so.

QUESTIONER: Is it possible to estimate what percent of the present population will inhabit the fourth-density planet?

RA: I am Ra. The harvesting is not yet; thus, estimation is meaningless.

QUESTIONER: Does the fact that we are in this transition period now have anything to do with the reason that you have made your information available to the population?

RA: I am Ra. We have walked among your people. We remember. We remember sorrow: have seen much. We have searched for an instrument of the proper parameters of distortion in mind/body/spirit complex and supporting and understanding of mind/body/spirit complexes to accept this information with minimal distortion and maximal desire to serve for some of your years. The answer, in short, is yes. However, we wished you to know that in our memory we thank you.

QUESTIONER: The disc-shaped craft that we call UFOs—some have been said to have come from the planet Venus. Would any of these be your craft?

RA: I am Ra. We have used crystals for many purposes. The craft of which you speak have not been used by us in your space/time present memory complex. However, we have used crystals and the bell shape in the past of your illusion.

QUESTIONER: How many years in the past did you use the bell-shaped craft to come to Earth?

RA: I am Ra. We visited your peoples 18,000 of your years ago and did not land; again, 11,000 years ago.

QUESTIONER: Photographs of bell-shaped craft and reports of contact of such from Venus exist from less than thirty years ago. Do you have any knowledge of these reports?

RA: I am Ra. We have knowledge of Oneness with these forays of your time/space present. We are no longer of Venus. However, there are thought-forms created among your peoples from our time of walking among you. The memory and thought-forms created, therefore, are a part of your society-memory complex. This mass consciousness, as you may call it, creates the experience once more for those who request such experience. The present Venus population is no longer sixth density.

QUESTIONER: Do any of the UFOs presently reported at this time come from other planets, or do you have this knowledge?

RA: I am Ra. I am one of the members of the Confederation of Planets in the Service of the Infinite Creator. There are approximately fifty-three civilizations, comprising approximately five hundred planetary consciousness complexes in this Confederation. This Confederation contains those from your own planet who have attained dimensions beyond your third. It contains planetary entities within your solar system, and it contains planetary entities from other galaxies.* It is a true Confederation in that its members are not alike, but allied in service according to the Law of One.

* Ra often uses the word "galaxy" where we would say planetary system. This meaning is listed in the unabridged dictionary but is not in common use.

QUESTIONER: Do any of them come here at this time in spacecraft? In the past, say, thirty years?

RA: I am Ra. We must state that this information is unimportant. If you will understand this, we feel that the information may be acceptably offered. The Law of One is what we are here to express. However, we will speak upon this subject.

Each planetary entity which wishes to appear within your third dimension of space/time distortion requests permission to break quarantine, as you may call it, and appear to your peoples. The reason and purpose for this appearance is understood and either accepted or rejected. There have been as many as fifteen of the Confederation entities in your skies at any one time. The others are available to you through thought.

At present there are seven which are operating with craft in your density. Their purposes are very simple: to allow those entities of your planet to become aware of infinity, which is often best expressed to the uninformed as the mysterious or unknown.

QUESTIONER: I am fully aware that you are primarily interested in disseminating information concerning the Law of One. However, it is my judgment, and I could be wrong, that in order to disseminate this material it will be necessary to include questions such as the one I have just asked. If this is not the objective, then I could limit my questions to the application of the Law of One. But I understand that at this time it is the objective to widely disseminate this material. Is this correct?

RA: I am Ra. This perception is only slightly distorted in your understand/learning. We wish you to proceed as you deem proper. That is your place. We, in giving this information, find our distortion of understanding of our purpose to be that not only of the offering of information, but the weighting of it according to our distorted perceptions of its relative importance. Thus, you will find our statements, at times, to be those which imply that a question is unimportant. This is due to our perception that the given question is unimportant. Nevertheless, unless the question contains the potential for answer giving which may infringe upon free will, we offer our answers.

QUESTIONER: Thank you very much. We do not want to overtire the instrument. We have gone considerably over our normal working time. Could you tell me what condition the instrument is in?

RA: I am Ra. The instrument is balanced due to your care. However, her physical vehicle is growing stiff.

QUESTIONER: In that case perhaps we should continue at a later time.

RA: I am Ra. I leave you in the love and the light of the One Infinite Creator. Go forth rejoicing in the power and the peace of the One Creator. Adonai.

Session 7,
January 25, 1981

RA: I am Ra. I greet you in the love and the light of our Infinite Creator. I communicate now.

QUESTIONER: You mentioned that there were a number of members of the Confederation of Planets. What avenues of service, or types of service, are available to the members of the Confederation?

RA: I am Ra. I am assuming that you intend the service which we of the Confederation can offer, rather than the service which is available to our use.

The service available for our offering to those who call us is equivalent to the square of the distortion/need of that calling divided by, or integrated with, the basic Law of One in its distortion indicating the free will of those who are not aware of the unity of creation.

QUESTIONER: From this, I am assuming that the difficulty that you have in contacting this planet at this time is the mixture of people here, some being aware of the unity, and some not, and for this reason you cannot come openly or give proof of your contact. Is this correct?

RA: I am Ra. As we just repeated through this instrument, we must integrate all of the portions of your social memory complex in its illusory disintegration form. Then the product of this can be seen as the limit of our ability to serve. We are fortunate that the Law of Service squares the desires of those who call. Otherwise, we would have no beingness in this time/space at this present continuum of the illusion. In short, you are basically correct. The thought of not being able is not a part of our basic thought-form complex towards your peoples, but rather it is a maximal consideration of what is possible.

QUESTIONER: By squared, do you mean that if ten people call, you can count that, when comparing it to the planetary ratio, as 100 people, squaring ten and getting 100?

RA: I am Ra. This is incorrect. The square is sequential—one, two, three, four, each squared by the next number.

QUESTIONER: If only ten entities on Earth required your services, how would you compute their calling by using this square method?

RA: I am Ra. We would square one ten sequential times, raising the number to the tenth square.

QUESTIONER: What would be the result of this calculation?

RA: I am Ra. The result is difficult to transmit. It is 1,012, approximately. The entities who call are sometimes not totally unified in their calling and, thus, the squaring slightly less. Thus, there is a statistical loss over a period of call. However, perhaps you may see by this statistically corrected information the squaring mechanism.

QUESTIONER: About how many entities at present on planet Earth are calling for your services?

RA: I am Ra. I am called personally by 352,000. The Confederation, in its entire spectrum of entity complexes, is called by 632,000,000 of your mind/body/spirit complexes. These numbers have been simplified.

QUESTIONER: Can you tell me what the result of the application of the Law of Squares is to those figures?

RA: I am Ra. The number is approximately meaningless in the finite sense as there are many, many digits. It, however, constitutes a great calling which we of all creation feel and hear as if our own entities were distorted towards a great and overwhelming sorrow. It demands our service.

QUESTIONER: At what point would this calling be great enough for you to come openly among the people on Earth? How many entities on Earth would have to call the Confederation?

RA: I am Ra. We do not calculate the possibility of coming among your peoples by the numbers of calling, but by a consensus among an entire societal-memory complex which has become aware of the infinite consciousness of all things. This has been possible among your peoples only in isolated instances.

In the case wherein a social memory complex which is a servant of the Creator sees this situation and has an idea for the appropriate aid which can only be done among your peoples, the social memory complex desiring this project lays it before the Council of Saturn. If it is approved, quarantine is lifted.

QUESTIONER: I have a question about that Council. Who are the members, and how does the Council function?

RA: I am Ra. The members of the Council are representatives from the Confederation and from those vibratory levels of your inner planes bearing responsibility for your third density. The names are not important because there are no names. Your mind/body/spirit complexes request names, and so, in many cases, the vibratory sound complexes which are consonant with the vibratory distortions of each entity are used. However, the name concept is not part of the Council. If names are requested, we will attempt them. However, not all have chosen names.

In number, the Council that sits in constant session, though varying in its members by means of balancing, which takes place what you would call irregularly, is nine. That is the Session Council. To back up this Council, there are twenty-four entities which offer their services as requested. These entities faithfully watch and have been called Guardians.

The Council operates by means of what you would call telepathic contact with the oneness or unity of the nine, the distortions blending harmoniously so that the Law of One prevails with ease. When a need for thought is present, the Council retains the distortion complex of this need, balancing it as described, and then recommends what it considers as appropriate action. This includes: One, the duty of admitting social memory complexes to the Confederation; Two, offering aid to those who are unsure how to aid the social memory complex requesting aid in a way consonant with both the call, the Law, and the number of those calling (that is to say, sometimes the resistance of the call); Three, internal questions in the Council are determined.

These are the prominent duties of the Council. They are, if in any doubt, able to contact the twenty-four, who then offer consensus/judgment/thinking to the Council. The Council then may reconsider any question.

QUESTIONER: You mentioned the nine who sit on the Council. Is this "nine" the same nine as those mentioned in this book? [Questioner gestures to *Uri*]

RA: I am Ra. The Council of Nine has been retained in semi-undistorted form by two main sources, that known in your naming as Mark and that known in your naming as Henry. In one case, the channel became the scribe. In the other, the channel was not the scribe. However, without the aid of the scribe, the energy would not have come to the channel.

QUESTIONER: The names that you spoke of. Were they Mark Probert and Henry Puharich?

RA: I am Ra. This is correct.

QUESTIONER: I am interested in the application of the Law of One as it pertains to free will with respect to what I would call the advertising done by UFO contacts with the planet Earth. The Council seems to have allowed the quarantine to be lifted many times over the past thirty years. This seems to me to be a form of advertising for what we are doing right now, so that more people will be awakened. Am I correct?

RA: I am Ra. It will take a certain amount of untangling of conceptualization of your mental complex to reform your query into an appropriate response. Please bear with us.

The Council of Saturn has not allowed the breaking of quarantine in the time/space continuum you mentioned. There is a certain amount of landing taking place. Some are of the entities known to you as the group of Orion.

Secondly, there is permission granted, not to break quarantine by dwelling among you, but to appear in thought-form capacity for those who have eyes to see.

Thirdly, you are correct in assuming that permission was granted at the time/space in which your first nuclear device was developed and used for Confederation members to minister to your peoples in such a way as to cause mystery to occur. This is what you mean by advertising and is correct. The mystery and unknown quality of the occurrences we are allowed to offer have the hoped-for intention of making your peoples aware of infinite possibility. When your peoples grasp infinity, then and only then can the gateway be opened to the Law of One.

QUESTIONER: You said that Orion was the source of some of these contacts with UFOs. Can you tell me something of that contact, its purpose?

RA: I am Ra. Consider, if you will, a simple example of intentions which are bad/good. This example is Adolf. This is your vibratory sound complex. The intention is to presumably unify by choosing the distortion complex called elite from a social memory complex and then enslaving, by various effects, those who are seen by the distortion as not elite. There is then the concept of taking the social memory complex thus weeded and adding it to a distortion thought of by the so-called Orion group as an empire. The problem facing them is that they face a great deal of random energy released by the concept of separation. This causes them to be vulnerable, as the distortions amongst their own members are not harmonized.

QUESTIONER: What is the density of the Orion group?

RA: I am Ra. Like the Confederation, the densities of the mass consciousnesses which comprise that group are varied. There are a very few third density, a larger number of fourth density, a similarly large number of fifth density, and very few sixth-density entities comprising this organization. Their numbers are perhaps one-tenth ours at any point in the space/time continuum, as the problem of spiritual entropy causes them to experience constant disintegration of their social memory complexes. Their power is the same as ours. The Law of One blinks neither at the light nor the darkness, but is available for service to others and service to self. However, service to others results in service to self, thus preserving and further harmonizing the distortions of those entities seeking intelligent infinity through these disciplines.

Those seeking intelligent infinity through the use of service to self create the same amount of power but, as we said, have constant difficulty because of the concept of separation, which is implicit in the manifestations of the service to self which involve power over others. This weakens and eventually disintegrates the energy collected by such mind/body/spirit complexes who call the Orion group and the social memory complexes which comprise the Orion group.

It should be noted, carefully pondered, and accepted that the Law of One is available to any social memory complex which has decided to strive together for any seeking of purpose, be it service to others or service to self. The laws, which are the primal distortions of the Law of One, then are placed into operation, and the illusion of space/time is used as a medium for the development of the results of those choices freely made. Thus all entities learn, no matter what they seek. All learn the same; some rapidly, some slowly.

QUESTIONER: Using as an example the fifth density concerning the social memory complex of the Orion group, what was their previous density before they became fifth density?

RA: I am Ra. The progress through densities is sequential. A fifth-density social memory complex would be comprised of mind/body/spirit complexes harvested from fourth density. Then the conglomerate or mass mind/body/spirit complex does its melding, and the results are due to the infinitely various possibilities of combinations of distortions.

QUESTIONER: I'm trying to understand how a group such as the Orion group would progress. How it would be possible, if you were in the Orion group and pointed toward self-service, to progress from our third density to the fourth. What learning would be necessary for that?

RA: I am Ra. This is the last question of length for this instrument at this time.

You will recall that we went into some detail as to how those not oriented towards seeking service for others yet, nevertheless, found and could use the gateway to intelligent infinity. This is true at all densities in our octave. We cannot speak for those above us, as you would say, in the next quantum or octave of beingness. This is, however, true of this octave of density. The beings are harvested because they can see and enjoy the light/love of the appropriate density. Those who have found this light/love, love/light without benefit of a desire for service to others nevertheless, by the Law of Free Will, have the right to the use of that light/love for whatever purpose. Also, it may be inserted that there are systems of study which enable the seeker of separation to gain these gateways.

This study is as difficult as the one which we have described to you, but there are those with the perseverance to pursue the study just as you desire to pursue the difficult path of seeking to know in order to serve. The distortion lies in the effect that those who seek to serve the self are seen by the Law of One as precisely the same as those who seek to serve others, for are all not one? To serve yourself and to serve others is a dual method of saying the same thing, if you can understand the essence of the Law of One.

At this time we would answer any brief questions you may have.

QUESTIONER: Is there anything that we can do to make the instrument more comfortable?

RA: I am Ra. There are small adjustments you may make. However, we are now able to use this instrument with minimal distortion and without depleting the instrument to any significant extent.

Do you wish to ask further?

QUESTIONER: We do not wish to tire the instrument. Thank you very much. That was very helpful, and we would like to continue in the next session from this point.

RA: I am Ra. I leave you in the love and the light of the One Infinite Creator. Go forth then rejoicing in the power and the peace of the One Creator. Adonai.

Session 8,
January 26, 1981

RA: I am Ra. I greet you in the love and the light of the Infinite Creator. I communicate now.

QUESTIONER: I have a question regarding what I call the advertising of the Confederation. It has to do with free will. There have been certain contacts allowed, as I understand, by the Confederation, but this is limited because of free will of those who are not oriented in such a way as to want contact. Many people on our planet want this material, but even though we disseminate it, many will not be aware that it is available. Is there any possibility of creating some effect which I would call advertising, or is this against the principle of free will?

RA: I am Ra. Consider, if you will, the path your life-experience complex has taken. Consider the coincidences and odd circumstances by which one thing flowed to the next. Consider this well.

Each entity will receive the opportunity that each needs. This information source beingness does not have uses in the life-experience complex of each of those among your peoples who seek. Thus the advertisement is general and not designed to indicate the searching out of any particular material, but only to suggest the noumenal aspect of the illusion.

QUESTIONER: You said that some of the landings at this time were of the Orion group. Why did the Orion group land here? What is their purpose?

RA: I am Ra. Their purpose is conquest, unlike those of the Confederation who wait for the calling. The so-called Orion group calls itself to conquest. As we have said previously, their objective is to locate certain mind/body/spirit complexes which vibrate in resonance with their own vibrational complex, then to enslave the unelite, as you may call those who are not of the Orion vibration.

QUESTIONER: Was the landing at Pascagoula in 1973 when Charlie Hixson was taken aboard this type of landing?

RA: I am Ra. The landing of which you speak was what you would call an anomaly. It was neither the Orion influence nor our peoples in thought-form, but rather a planetary entity of your own vibration which came through quarantine in all innocence in a random landing.

QUESTIONER: What did they do to Charlie Hixson when they took him onboard?

RA: I am Ra. They used his mind/body/spirit complex's life experience, concentrating upon the experience of the complexes of what you call war.

QUESTIONER: How did they use them?

RA: I am Ra. The use of experience is to learn. Consider a race who watches a movie. It experiences a story and identifies with the feelings, perceptions, and experiences of the hero.

QUESTIONER: Was Charlie Hixson originally of the same social memory complex of the ones who picked him up?

RA: I am Ra. This entity of vibratory sound complex did not have a connection with those who used him.

QUESTIONER: Did those who used him use his war experiences to learn more of the Law of One?

RA: I am Ra. This is correct.

QUESTIONER: Did the entities who picked him up have the normal configuration? His description of them was rather unusual.

RA: I am Ra. The configuration of their beings is their normal configuration. The unusualness is not remarkable. We ourselves, when we chose a mission among your peoples, needed to study your peoples, for had we arrived in no other form than our own, we would have been perceived as light.

QUESTIONER: What density were the entities who picked up Charlie Hixson from?

RA: I am Ra. The entities in whom you show such interest are third-density beings of a fairly advanced order. We should express the understanding to you that these entities would not have used the mind/body/spirit complex, Charlie, except for the resolve of this entity before incarnation to be of service.

QUESTIONER: What was the home or origin of the entities who picked up Charlie?

RA: I am Ra. These entities are of the Sirius galaxy.

QUESTIONER: Would it be possible for any of us to have contact with the Confederation in a more direct way?

RA: I am Ra. In observing the distortions of those who underwent this experiential sequence, we decided to gradually back off, shall I say, from direct contact in thought-form. The least distortion seems to be available in mind-to-mind communication. Therefore, the request to be taken aboard is not one we care to comply with. You are most valuable in your present orientation.

May we ask at this time if you have a needed short query before we end this session?

QUESTIONER: Is there anything that we can do to make the instrument more comfortable?

RA: I am Ra. The instrument is well balanced. It is possible to make small corrections in the configuration of the spine of the instrument that it be straighter. Continue also to continually monitor the placement and orientation of the symbols used. This particular session, the censer is slightly off and, therefore, this instrument will experience a slight discomfort.

QUESTIONER: Is the censer off in respect to angle or in respect to lateral displacement?

RA: I am Ra. There is an approximate 3 degrees' displacement from proper perpendicularity.

I am Ra. I leave you in the love and the light of the One Infinite Creator. Go forth, therefore, rejoicing in the power and the peace of the One Creator. Adonai.

Session 9,
January 27, 1981

RA: I am Ra. I greet you in the love and the light of our Infinite Creator. We communicate now.

QUESTIONER: The healing exercises that you gave us are of such a nature that it is best to concentrate on a particular exercise at a certain time. I would like to ask what exercise that I should concentrate on tonight?

RA: I am Ra. Again, to direct your judgment is an intrusion upon your space/time continuum distortion called future. To speak of past or present within our distortion/judgment limits is acceptable. To guide rather than teach/learn is not acceptable to our distortion in regards to teach/learning. We, instead, can suggest a process whereby each chooses the first of the exercises given in the order in which we gave them, which you, in your discernment, feel is not fully appreciated by your mind/body/spirit complex.

This is the proper choice, building from the foundation, making sure the ground is good for the building. We have assessed for you the intensity of this effort in terms of energy expended. You will take this in mind and be patient for we have not given a short or easy program of consciousness learn/teaching.

QUESTIONER: The way that I understand the process of evolution is that our planetary population has a certain amount of time to progress. This is generally divided into three 25,000-year cycles. At the end of 75,000 years the planet progresses itself. What caused this situation to come about with the preciseness of the years in each cycle?

RA: I am Ra. Visualize, if you will, the particular energy which, outward flowing and inward coagulating, formed the tiny realm of the creation governed by your Council of Saturn. Continue seeing the rhythm of this process. The living flow creates a rhythm which is as inevitable as one of your timepieces. Each of your planetary entities began the first cycle when the energy nexus was able in that environment to support such mind/body experiences. Thus, each of your planetary entities is on a different cyclical schedule, as you might call it. The timing of these cycles is a measurement equal to a portion of intelligent energy.

This intelligent energy offers a type of clock. The cycles move as precisely as a clock strikes your hour. Thus, the gateway from intelligent energy to intelligent infinity opens regardless of circumstance on the striking of the hour.

QUESTIONER: The original, first entities on this planet—what was their origin? Where were they before they were on this planet?

RA: I am Ra. The first entities upon this planet were water, fire, air, and earth.

QUESTIONER: Where did the people who are like us who were the first ones here, where did they come from? From where did they evolve?

RA: I am Ra. You speak of third-density experience. The first of those to come here were brought from another planet in your solar system called by you the Red Planet, Mars. This planet's environment became inhospitable to third-density beings. The first entities, therefore, were of this race, as you may call it, manipulated somewhat by those who were guardians at that time.

QUESTIONER: What race is that, and how did they get from Mars to here?

RA: I am Ra. The race is a combination of the mind/body/spirit complexes of those of your so-called Red Planet and a careful series of genetical adjustments made by the guardians of that time. These entities arrived, or were preserved, for the experience upon your sphere by a type of birthing which is nonreproductive but consists of preparing genetic material for the incarnation of the mind/body/spirit complexes of those entities from the Red Planet.

QUESTIONER: I assume from what you are saying that the guardians transferred the race here after the race had died from the physical as we know it on Mars. Is that correct?

RA: I am Ra. This is correct.

QUESTIONER: The guardians were obviously acting within an understanding of the Law of One in doing this. Can you explain the application of the Law of One in this process?

RA: I am Ra. The Law of One was named by these guardians as the bringing of the wisdom of the guardians in contact with the entities from the Red Planet, thus melding the social memory complex of the guardian race and the Red Planet race. It, however, took an increasing amount of distortion into the application of the Law of One from the viewpoint of other guardians, and it is from this beginning action that the quarantine of this planet was instituted, for it was felt that the free will of those of the Red Planet had been abridged.

QUESTIONER: Were the entities of the Red Planet following the Law of One prior to leaving the Red Planet?

RA: I am Ra. The entities of the Red Planet were attempting to learn the Laws of Love which form one of the primal distortions of the Law of One. However, the tendencies of these people towards bellicose actions caused such difficulties in the atmospheric environment of their planet that it became inhospitable for third-density experience before the end of its cycle. Thus, the Red Planet entities were unharvested and continued in your illusion to attempt to learn the Law of Love.

QUESTIONER: How long ago did this transfer occur from the Red Planet to Earth?

RA: I am Ra. In your time this transfer occurred approximately 75,000 years ago.

QUESTIONER: 75,000 years ago?

RA: I am Ra. This is approximately correct.

QUESTIONER: Were there any entities of the form that I am now—two arms, two legs—on this planet before this transfer occurred?

RA: I am Ra. There have been visitors to your sphere at various times for the last four million of your years, speaking approximately. These visitors do not affect the cycling of the planetary sphere. It was not third density in its environment until the time previously mentioned.

QUESTIONER: Then there were second-density entities here prior to approximately 75,000 years ago. What type of entities were these?

RA: I am Ra. The second density is the density of the higher plant life and animal life which exists without the upward drive towards the infinite. These second-density beings are of an octave of consciousness just as you find various orientations of consciousness among the conscious entities of your vibration.

QUESTIONER: Did any of these second-density entities have shapes like ours—two arms, two legs, head, and walk upright on two feet?

RA: I am Ra. The two higher of the sub-vibrational levels of second-density beings had the configuration of the biped, as you mentioned. However, the erectile movement which you experience was not totally effected in these beings who were tending towards the leaning forward, barely leaving the quadrupedal position.

QUESTIONER: Where did these beings come from? Were they a product of evolution as understood by our scientists? Were they evolved from the original material of the earth that you spoke of?

RA: I am Ra. This is correct.

QUESTIONER: Do these beings then evolve from second density to third density?

RA: I am Ra. This is correct, although no guarantee can be made of the number of cycles it will take an entity to learn the lessons of consciousness of self which are the prerequisite for transition to third density.

QUESTIONER: Is there any particular race of people on our planet now who were incarnated here from second density?

RA: I am Ra. There are no second-density consciousness complexes here on your sphere at this time. However, there are two races which use the second-density form. One is the entities from the planetary sphere you call Maldek. These entities are working their understanding complexes through a series of what you would call karmic restitutions. They dwell within your deeper underground passageways and are known to you as "Bigfoot." The other race is that being offered a dwelling in this density by guardians who wish to give the mind/body/spirit complexes of those who are of this density at this time appropriately engineered physical vehicles, as you would call these chemical complexes, in the event that there is what you call nuclear war.

QUESTIONER: I didn't understand what these vehicles or beings were for that were appropriate in the event of nuclear war.

RA: I am Ra. These are beings which exist as instinctual second-density beings which are being held in reserve to form what you would call a gene pool in case these body complexes are needed. These body complexes are greatly able to withstand the rigors of radiation, which the body complexes you now inhabit could not do.

QUESTIONER: Where are these body complexes located?

RA: I am Ra. These body complexes of the second race dwell in uninhabited deep forest. There are many in various places over the surface of your planet.

QUESTIONER: Are they Bigfoot-type creatures?

RA: I am Ra. This is correct although we would not call these Bigfoot, as they are scarce and are very able to escape detection. The first race is less able to be aware of proximity of other mind/body/spirit complexes, but these beings are very able to escape due to their technological understandings before their incarnations here. These entities of the glowing eyes are those most familiar to your peoples.

QUESTIONER: Then there are two different types of Bigfoot. Correct?

RA: I am Ra. This will be the final question.

There are three types of Bigfoot, if you will accept that vibratory sound complex used for three such different races of mind/body/spirit complexes. The first two we have described. The third is a thought-form.

QUESTIONER: I would like to ask if there is anything that we can do to aid the instrument's comfort.

RA: I am Ra. This instrument will require some adjustment of the tender portions of her body complex. The distortions are due to the energy center blockage you would call pineal.

I leave you in the love and the light of the One Infinite Creator. Go forth, therefore, rejoicing in the power and the peace of the One Creator. Adonai.

Session 10,
January 27, 1981

RA: I am Ra. I greet you in the love and light of the Infinite Creator. I communicate now.

QUESTIONER: I think that it would clarify things for us if we went back to the time just before the transfer of souls from Maldek to see how the Law of One operated with respect to this transfer and why this transfer was necessary. What happened to the people of Maldek that caused them to lose their planet? How long ago did this event occur?

RA: I am Ra. The peoples of Maldek had a civilization somewhat similar to that of the societal complex known to you as Atlantis, in that it gained much technological information and used it without care for the preservation of their sphere following to a majority extent the complex of thought, ideas, and actions which you may associate with your so-called negative polarity or the service to self. This was, however, for the most part, couched in a sincere belief/thought structure which seemed to the perception of the mind/body complexes of this sphere to be positive and of service to others. The devastation that wracked their biosphere and caused its disintegration resulted from what you call war.

The escalation went to the furthest extent of the technology this social complex had at its disposal in the space/time present of the then time. This time was approximately 705,000 of your years ago. The cycles had begun much, much earlier upon this sphere due to its relative ability to support the first-dimensional life forms at an earlier point in the space/time continuum of your solar system. These entities were so traumatized by this occurrence that they were in what you may call a social complex knot or tangle of fear. Some of your time passed. No one could reach them. No beings could aid them.

Approximately 600,000 of your years ago the then-existing members of the Confederation were able to deploy a social memory complex and untie the knot of fear. The entities were then able to recall that they were conscious. This awareness brought them to the point upon what you would call the lower astral planes, where they could be nurtured until each mind/body/spirit complex was able to finally be healed of this trauma to the extent that each entity was able to examine the distortions it had experienced in the previous life/illusion complex.

After this experience of learn/teaching, the group decision was to place upon itself a type of what you may call karma alleviation. For this purpose they came into incarnation within your planetary sphere in what were not acceptable human forms. This then they have been experiencing until the distortions of destruction are replaced by distortions towards the desire for a less distorted vision of service to others. Since this was the conscious decision of the great majority of those beings in the Maldek experience, the transition to this planet began approximately 500,000 of your years ago, and the type of body complex available at that time was used.

QUESTIONER: Was the body complex available at that time what we refer to as the ape body?

RA: I am Ra. That is correct.

QUESTIONER: Have any of the Maldek entities transformed since then? Are they still second density now or are some of them third density?

RA: I am Ra. The consciousness of these entities has always been third density. The alleviation mechanism was designed by the placement of this consciousness in second-dimensional physical chemical complexes which are not able to be dexterous or manipulative to the extent which is appropriate to the working of the third-density distortions of the mind complex.

QUESTIONER: Have any of the entities moved on now, made a graduation at the end of a cycle and made the transition from second-density bodies to third-density bodies?

RA: I am Ra. Many of these entities were able to remove the accumulation of what you call karma, thus being able to accept a third-density cycle within a third-density body. Most of those beings so succeeding have incarnated elsewhere in the creation for the succeeding cycle in third density. As this planet reached third density, some few of these entities became able to join the vibration of this sphere in third-density form. There remain a few who have not yet alleviated through the mind/body/spirit coordination of distortions the previous action taken by them. Therefore, they remain.

QUESTIONER: Are these the Bigfoot that you spoke of?

RA: I am Ra. These are one type of Bigfoot.

QUESTIONER: Then our human race is formed of a few who originally came from Maldek and quite a few who came from Mars. Are there entities here from other places?

RA: I am Ra. There are entities experiencing your time/space continuum who have originated from many, many places, as you would call them, in the creation, for when there is a cycle change, those who must repeat then find a planetary sphere appropriate for this repetition. It is somewhat unusual for a planetary mind/body/spirit complex to contain those from many, many various loci, but this explains much, for, you see, you are experiencing the third-dimension occurrence with a large number of those who must repeat the cycle. The orientation, thus, has been difficult to unify even with the aid of many of your teach/learners.

QUESTIONER: When Maldek was destroyed, did all the people of Maldek have the fear problem or were some advanced enough to transfer to other planets?

RA: I am Ra. In the occurrence of planetary dissolution none escaped, for this is an action which redounds to the social complex of the planetary complex itself. None escaped the knot or tangle.

QUESTIONER: Is there any danger of this happening to Earth at this time?

RA: I am Ra. We feel this evaluation of your planetary mind/body/spirit complexes' so-called future may be less than harmless. We say only the conditions of mind exist for such development of technology and such deployment. It is the distortion of our vision/understanding that the mind and spirit complexes of those of your people need orientation rather than the "toys" needing dismantlement, for are not all things that exist part of the Creator? Therefore, freely to choose is your own duty.

QUESTIONER: When graduation occurs at the end of a cycle, and entities are moved from one planet to another, by what means do they go to a new planet?

RA: I am Ra. In the scheme of the Creator, the first step of the mind/body/spirit/totality/beingness is to place its mind/body/spirit complex distortion in the proper place of love/light. This is done to ensure proper healing of the complex and eventual attunement with the totality/beingness complex. This takes a very variable length of your time/space. After this is accomplished, the experience of the cycle is dissolved and filtered until only the distillation of distortions in its pure form remains. At this time, the harvested mind/body/spirit/totality/beingness evaluates the density needs of its beingness and chooses the more appropriate new environment for either a repetition of the cycle or a moving forward into the next cycle. This is the manner of the harvesting, guarded and watched over by many.

QUESTIONER: When the entity is moved from one planet to the next, is he moved in thought or by a vehicle?

RA: I am Ra. The mind/body/spirit/totality/beingness is one with the Creator. There is no time/space distortion. Therefore, it is a matter of thinking the proper locus in the infinite array of time/spaces.

QUESTIONER: While an entity is incarnate in this third density at this time, he may either learn unconsciously without knowing what he is learning, or he may learn after he is consciously aware that he is learning in the ways of the Law of One. By the second way of learning consciously, it is possible for the entity to greatly accelerate his growth. Is this correct?

RA: I am Ra. This is correct.

QUESTIONER: Then although many entities are not consciously aware of it, what they really desire is to accelerate their growth, and it is their job to discover this while they are incarnate. Is it correct that they can accelerate their growth much more while in the third density than in between incarnations of this density?

RA: I am Ra. This is correct. We shall attempt to speak upon this concept.

The Law of One has as one of its primal distortions the free-will distortion; thus each entity is free to accept, reject, or ignore the mind/body/spirit complexes about it and ignore the creation itself. There are many among your social memory complex distortion who, at this time/space, engage daily, as you would put it, in the working upon the Law of One in one of its primal distortions; that is, the ways of love. However, if this same entity, being biased from the depths of its mind/body/spirit complex towards love/light, were then to accept the responsibility for each moment of the time/space accumulation of present moments available to it, such an entity can empower its progress in much the same way as we described the empowering of the call of your social complex distortion to the Confederation.

QUESTIONER: Could you state this in a little different way . . . how you empower this call?

RA: I am Ra. We understand you to speak now of our previous information. The call begins with one. This call is equal to infinity and is not, as you would say, counted. It is the cornerstone. The second call is added. The third call empowers or doubles the second, and so forth, each additional calling doubling or granting power to all the preceding calls. Thus, the call of many of your peoples is many, many powered and overwhelmingly heard to the infinite reaches of the One Creation.

QUESTIONER: For the general development of the reader of this book, could you state some of the practices or exercises to perform to produce an acceleration toward the Law of One?

RA: I am Ra.

Exercise One. This is the most nearly centered and usable within your illusion complex. The moment contains love. That is the lesson/goal of this illusion or density. The exercise is to consciously see that love in awareness and understanding distortions. The first attempt is the cornerstone. Upon this choosing rests the remainder of the life experience of an entity. The second seeking of love within the moment begins the addition. The third seeking empowers the second, the fourth powering or doubling the third. As with the previous type of empowerment, there will be some loss of power due to flaws within the seeking in the distortion of insincerity. However, the conscious statement of self to self of the desire to seek love is so central an act of will that, as before, the loss of power due to this friction is inconsequential.

Exercise Two. The universe is one being. When a mind/body/spirit complex views another mind/body/spirit complex, see the Creator. This is an helpful exercise.

Exercise Three. Gaze within a mirror. See the Creator.

Exercise Four. Gaze at the creation which lies about the mind/body/spirit complex of each entity. See the Creator.

The foundation or prerequisite of these exercises is a predilection towards what may be called meditation, contemplation, or prayer. With this attitude, these exercises can be processed. Without it, the data will not sink down into the roots of the tree of mind, thus enabling and ennobling the body and touching the spirit.

QUESTIONER: I was wondering about the advent of the civilizations of Atlantis and Lemuria, when these civilizations occurred, and where did they come from?

RA: I am Ra. This is the last question of this working. The civilizations of Atlantis and Lemuria were not one but two. Let us look first at the Mu entities.

They were beings of a somewhat primitive nature, but those who had very advanced spiritual distortions. The civilization was part of this cycle, experienced early within the cycle at a time of approximately 53,000 of your years ago. It was an helpful and harmless place which was washed beneath the ocean during a readjustment of your sphere's tectonic plates through no action of their own. They sent out those who survived and reached many places in what you call Russia, North America, and South America. The Indians of whom you come to feel some sympathy in your social complex distortions are the descendants of these entities. Like the other incarnates of this cycle, they came from elsewhere. However, these particular entities were largely from a second-density planet which had some difficulty, due to the age of its sun, in achieving third-density life conditions. This planet was from the galaxy Deneb.

The Atlantean race was a very conglomerate social complex which began to form approximately 31,000 years in the past of your space/time continuum illusion. It was a slow-growing and very agrarian one until approximately 15,000 of your years ago. It reached quickly a high technological understanding which caused it to be able to use intelligent infinity in an informative manner. We may add that they used intelligent energy as well, manipulating greatly the natural influxes of the indigo or pineal ray from divine or infinite energy. Thus, they were able to create life forms. This they began to do instead of healing and perfecting their own mind/body/spirit complexes, turning their distortions towards what you may call negative.

Approximately 11,000 of your years ago, the first of the, what you call, wars, caused approximately 40 percent of this population to leave the density by means of disintegration of the body. The second and most devastating of the conflicts occurred approximately 10,821 years in the past according to your illusion. This created an Earth-changing configuration, and the large part of Atlantis was no more, having been inundated. Three of the positively oriented of the Atlantean groups left this geographical locus before that devastation, placing themselves in the mountain areas of what you call Tibet, what you call Peru, and what you call Turkey.

Do you have any brief questions before we close this meeting?

QUESTIONER: Only one, other than what we can do to make the instrument more comfortable. I would like to have your definition of galaxy, the word "galaxy" as you have used it.

RA: I am Ra. We use the term known to your people by the sound vibration "galaxy." We accept that some galaxies contain one system of planetary and solar groups. Others contain several. However, the importance of the locus in infinite time/space dimensionality is so little that we accept the distortion implicit in such an ambiguous term.

QUESTIONER: Then the nine planets and sun which we have here in our system, would you refer to that as a galaxy?

RA: I am Ra. We would not.

QUESTIONER: How many stars would be—approximately—in a galaxy?

RA: I am Ra. It depends upon the galactic system. Your own, as you know, contains many, many, millions of planetary entities and star bodies.

QUESTIONER: I was just trying to get to the definition that you were using for galaxy. You mentioned a couple of times the term "galaxy" in reference to what we call a planetary system and it was causing some confusion. Is there any way that we can make the instrument more comfortable?

RA: I am Ra. This instrument could be made somewhat more comfortable if more support were given the body complex. Other than this, we can only repeat the request to carefully align the symbols used to facilitate this instrument's balance. Our contact is narrow banded, and thus the influx brought in with us must be precise.

I am Ra. I leave you in the love and the light of the One Infinite Creator. Go forth, therefore, rejoicing in the power and peace of the One Creator. Adonai.

Session 11,
January 28, 1981

RA: I am Ra. I greet you in the love and the light of the Infinite Creator. I communicate now.

QUESTIONER: Should we include the ritual that you have suggested that we use to call you in the book that will result from these sessions?

RA: I am Ra. This matter is of small importance, for our suggestion was made for the purpose of establishing contact through this instrument with this group.

QUESTIONER: Is it of any assistance to the instrument to have [name] and [name] present during these sessions? Does the number in the group make any difference in these sessions?

RA: I am Ra. The most important of the entities are the questioner and the vibratory sound complex [name]. The two entities additional aid the instrument's comfort by energizing the instrument with their abilities to share the physical energy complex which is a portion of your love vibration.

QUESTIONER: You said yesterday that Maldek was destroyed due to warfare. If Maldek hadn't destroyed itself due to warfare, would it have become a planet that evolved in self-service, and would the entities involved have increased in density and gone on to, say, the fourth density in the negative sense or the sense of self-service?

RA: I am Ra. The planetary social memory complex, Maldek, had in common with your own sphere the situation of a mixture of energy direction. Thus it, though unknown, would most probably have been a mixed harvest—a few moving to fourth density, a few moving towards fourth density in service to self, the great majority repeating third

119

density. This is approximate due to the fact that parallel possibility/probability vortices cease when action occurs and new probability/possibility vortices are begun.

QUESTIONER: Is there a planet opposite our sun, in relation to us, that we do not know about?

RA: I am Ra. There is a sphere in the area opposite your sun of a very, very cold nature, but large enough to skew certain statistical figures. This sphere should not properly be called a planet as it is locked in first density.

QUESTIONER: You say that entities from Maldek might go to fourth density negative. Are there people who go out of our present third density to places in the universe and serve, which are fourth-density self-service negative type of planets?

RA: I am Ra. Your question is unclear. Please restate.

QUESTIONER: As our cycle ends and graduation occurs, is it possible for anyone to go from our third density to a fourth-density planet that is of a self-service or negative type?

RA: I am Ra. We grasp now the specificity of your query. In this harvest the probability/possibility vortex is an harvest, though small, of this type. That is correct.

QUESTIONER: Can you tell us what happened to Adolf [Hitler]?

RA: I am Ra. The mind/body/spirit complex known as Adolf is at this time in an healing process in the middle astral planes of your spherical force field. This entity was greatly confused and, although aware of the circumstance of change in vibratory level associated with the cessation of the chemical body complex, nevertheless needed a great deal of care.

QUESTIONER: Is there anyone in our history who is commonly known who went to a fourth-density self-service or negative type of planet or any who will go there?

RA: I am Ra. The number of entities thus harvested is small. However, a few have penetrated the eighth level, which is only available from the opening up of the seventh through the sixth. Penetration into the eighth or intelligent infinity level allows a mind/body/spirit complex to be harvested if it wishes at any time/space during the cycle.

QUESTIONER: Are any of these people known in the history of our planet by name?

RA: I am Ra. We will mention a few. The one known as Taras Bulba, the one known as Genghis Khan, the one known as Rasputin.

QUESTIONER: How did they accomplish this? What was necessary for them to accomplish this?

RA: I am Ra. All of the aforementioned entities were aware, through memory, of Atlantean understandings having to do with the use of the various centers of mind/body/spirit complex energy influx in attaining the gateway to intelligent infinity.

QUESTIONER: Did this enable them to do what we refer to as magic? Could they do paranormal things while they were incarnate?

RA: I am Ra. This is correct. The first two entities mentioned made little use of these abilities consciously. However, they were bent single-mindedly upon service to self, sparing no efforts in personal discipline to double, redouble, and so empower this gateway. The third was a conscious adept and also spared no effort in the pursuit of service to self.

QUESTIONER: Where are these three entities now?

RA: I am Ra. These entities are in the dimension known to you as fourth. Therefore the space/time continua are not compatible. An approximation of the space/time locus of each would net no actual understanding. Each chose a fourth-density planet which was dedicated to the pursuit of the understanding of the Law of One through service to self, one in what you know as the Orion group, one in what you know as Cassiopeia, one in what you know as Southern Cross; however, these loci are not satisfactory. We do not have vocabulary for the geometric calculations necessary for transfer of this understanding to you.

QUESTIONER: Who went to the Orion group?

RA: I am Ra. The one known as Genghis Khan.

QUESTIONER: What does he presently do there? What is his job or occupation?

RA: I am Ra. This entity serves the Creator in its own way.

QUESTIONER: Is it impossible for you to tell us precisely how he does this service?

RA: I am Ra. It is possible for us to speak to this query. However, we use any chance we may have to reiterate the basic understanding/learning that all beings serve the Creator.

The one you speak of as Genghis Khan, at present, is incarnate in a physical light body which has the work of disseminating material of thought control to those who are what you may call crusaders. He is, as you would term this entity, a shipping clerk.

QUESTIONER: What do the crusaders do?

RA: I am Ra. The crusaders move in their chariots to conquer planetary mind/body/spirit social complexes before they reach the stage of achieving social memory.

QUESTIONER: At what stage does a planet achieve social memory?

RA: I am Ra. A mind/body/spirit social complex becomes a social memory complex when its entire group of entities are of one orientation or seeking. The group memory lost to the individuals in the roots of the tree of mind then becomes known to the social complex, thus creating a social memory complex. The advantages of this complex are the relative lack of distortion in understanding the social beingness and the relative lack of distortion in pursuing the direction of seeking, for all understanding/ distortions are available to the entities of the society.

QUESTIONER: Then we have crusaders from Orion coming to this planet for mind control purposes. How do they do this?

RA: I am Ra. As all, they follow the Law of One observing free will. Contact is made with those who call. Those then upon the planetary sphere act much as do you to disseminate the attitudes and philosophy of their particular understanding of the Law of One which is service to self. These become the elite. Through these, the attempt begins to create a condition whereby the remainder of the planetary entities are enslaved by their free will.

QUESTIONER: Can you name any names that may be known on the planet that are recipients of the crusaders' efforts?

RA: I am Ra. I am desirous of being in nonviolation of the free-will distortion. To name those involved in the future of your space/time is to infringe; thus, we withhold this information. We request your contemplation of the fruits of the actions of those entities whom you may observe enjoying the distortion towards power. In this way you may discern for yourself this information. We shall not interfere with the, shall we say, planetary game. It is not central to the harvest.

QUESTIONER: How do the crusaders pass on their concepts to the individuals on Earth?

RA: I am Ra. There are two main ways, just as there are two main ways of, shall we say, polarizing towards service to others. There are those mind/body/spirit complexes upon your plane who do exercises and perform disciplines in order to seek contact with sources of information and power leading to the opening of the gate to intelligent infinity. There are others whose vibratory complex is such that this gateway is opened, and contact with total service to self with its primal distortion of manipulation of others is then afforded with little or no difficulty, no training, and no control.

QUESTIONER: What type of information is passed on from the crusaders to these people?

RA: I am Ra. The Orion group passes on information concerning the Law of One with the orientation of service to self. The information can become technical just as some in the Confederation, in attempts to aid this planet in service to others, have provided what you would call technical information. The technology provided by this group is in the form of various means of control or manipulation of others to serve the self.

QUESTIONER: Do you mean to say then that some scientists receive technical information, shall we say, telepathically that comes out then as usable gadgetry?

RA: I am Ra. That is correct. However, very positively, as you would call this distortion, oriented scientists have received information intended to unlock peaceful means of progress which redounded unto the last echoes of potential destruction due to further reception of other scientists of a negative orientation/distortion.

QUESTIONER: Is this how we learned of nuclear energy? Was it mixed with both positive and negative orientation?

RA: I am Ra. That is correct. The entities responsible for the gathering of the scientists were of a mixed orientation. The scientists were overwhelmingly positive in their orientation. The scientists who followed their work were of mixed orientation, including one extremely negative entity, as you would term it.

QUESTIONER: Is this extremely negative entity still incarnate on Earth?

RA: I am Ra. This is correct.

QUESTIONER: Then I would assume that you can't name him. So I will ask you where Nikola Tesla got his information?

RA: I am Ra. The one known as Nikola received information from Confederation sources desirous of aiding this extremely, shall we say, angelically positive entity in bettering the existence of its fellow mind/body/spirit complexes. It is unfortunate, shall we say, that like many Wanderers, the vibratory distortions of third-density illusion caused this entity to become extremely distorted in its perceptions of its fellow mind/body/spirit complexes so that its mission was hindered and, in the result, perverted from its purposes.

QUESTIONER: How was Tesla's work supposed to benefit man on Earth, and what were its purposes?

RA: I am Ra. The most desired purpose of the mind/body/spirit complex, Nikola, was the freeing of all planetary entities from the darkness. Thus, it attempted to give to the planet the infinite energy of the planetary sphere for use in lighting and power.

QUESTIONER: By freeing the planetary entities from darkness, precisely what do you mean?

RA: I am Ra. [Most of the following answer was lost due to tape recorder malfunction. The core of the response was as follows.] We spoke of freeing people from darkness in a literal sense.

QUESTIONER: Would this freeing from darkness be commensurate with the Law of One, or does this have any real product?

RA: I am Ra. The product of such a freeing would create two experiences.
Firstly, the experience of no need to find the necessary emolument for payment, in your money, for energy.

Secondly, the leisure afforded, thereby exemplifying the possibility and enhancing the probability of the freedom to then search the self, the beginning of seeking the Law of One.

Few there are working physically from daybreak to darkness, as you name them, upon your plane who can contemplate the Law of One in a conscious fashion.

QUESTIONER: What about the Industrial Revolution in general. Was this planned in any way?

RA: I am Ra. This will be the final question of this session.

That is correct. Wanderers incarnated in several waves, as you may call them, in order to bring into existence the gradual freeing from the demands of the diurnal cycles and lack of freedom of leisure.

QUESTIONER: That was the last question, so I will do as usual and ask if there is anything that we can do to make the instrument more comfortable?

RA: I am Ra. You are doing well. The most important thing is to carefully align the symbols. The adjustment made this particular time/space present will aid this instrument's physical complex in the distortion towards comfort.

May we ask if you have any short questions which we may resolve before closing the session?

QUESTIONER: I don't know if this is a short question or not, so we can save it till next time, but my question is, why do the crusaders from Orion do this? What is their ultimate objective? This is probably too long to answer.

RA: I am Ra. This is not too long to answer. To serve the self is to serve all. The service of the self, when seen in this perspective, requires an ever-expanding use of the energies of others for manipulation to the benefit of the self with distortion towards power.

If there are further queries to further explicate this subject, we shall be with you again.

QUESTIONER: There was one thing that I forgot. Is it possible to have another session later on today?

RA: I am Ra. It is well.

QUESTIONER: Thank you.

RA: I am Ra. I leave you in the love and the light of the One Infinite Creator. Go forth, then, rejoicing in the power and the peace of the One Creator. Adonai.

Session 12,
January 28, 1981

RA: I am Ra. I greet you in the love and the light of the Infinite Creator. I communicate now.

QUESTIONER: In the last session you mentioned that the Orion crusaders came here in chariots. Could you describe the chariots?

RA: I am Ra. The term "chariot" is a term used in warfare among your peoples. That is its significance. The shape of the Orion craft is one of the following: firstly, the elongated, ovoid shape which is of a darker nature than silver but which has a metallic appearance if seen in the light. In the absence of light, it appears to be red or fiery in some manner.

Other craft include disc-shaped objects of a small nature approximately 12 feet in your measurement in diameter, the boxlike shape approximately 40 feet to a side in your measurement. Other craft can take on a desired shape through the use of thought control mechanisms. There are various civilization complexes which work within this group. Some are more able to use intelligent infinity than others. The information is very seldom shared; therefore, the chariots vary greatly in shape and appearance.

QUESTIONER: Is there any effort on the part of the Confederation to stop the Orion chariots from arriving here?

RA: I am Ra. Every effort is made to quarantine this planet. However, the network of guardians, much like any other pattern of patrols on whatever level, does not hinder each and every entity from penetrating quarantine, for if request is made in light/love, the Law of One will be met with acquiescence. If the request is not made, due to the slipping through the net, then there is penetration of this net.

QUESTIONER: Who makes this request?

RA: I am Ra. Your query is unclear. Please restate.

QUESTIONER: I don't understand how the Confederation stops the Orion chariots from coming through the quarantine?

RA: I am Ra. There is contact at the level of light-form or light-body-being depending upon the vibratory level of the guardian. These guardians sweep reaches of your Earth's energy fields to be aware of any entities approaching. An entity which is approaching is hailed in the name of the One Creator. Any entity thus hailed is bathed in love/light and will of free will obey the quarantine due to the power of the Law of One.

QUESTIONER: What would happen to the entity if he did not obey the quarantine after being hailed?

RA: I am Ra. To not obey quarantine after being hailed on the level of which we speak would be equivalent to your not stopping upon walking into a solid brick wall.

QUESTIONER: What would happen to the entity if he did this? What would happen to his chariot?

RA: I am Ra. The Creator is one being. The vibratory level of those able to breach the quarantine boundaries is such that upon seeing the love/light net, it is impossible to break this Law. Therefore, nothing happens. No attempt is made. There is no confrontation. The only beings who are able to penetrate the quarantine are those who discover windows or distortions in the space/time continua surrounding your planet's energy fields. Through these windows they come. These windows are rare and unpredictable.

QUESTIONER: Does this account for what we call "UFO flaps" where a large number of UFOs show up like in 1973?

RA: I am Ra. This is correct.

QUESTIONER: Are most of the UFOs which are seen in our skies from the Orion group?

RA: I am Ra. Many of those seen in your skies are of the Orion group. They send out messages. Some are received by those who are oriented toward service to others. These messages then are altered to be acceptable to those entities while warning of difficulties ahead. This is the most that self-serving entities can do when faced with those whose wish is to serve others. The contacts which the group finds most helpful to their cause are those contacts made with entities whose orientation is towards service to self. There are many thought-form entities in your skies which are of a positive nature and are the projections of the Confederation.

QUESTIONER: You mentioned that the Orion crusaders, when they get through the net, give both technical and nontechnical information. I think I know what you mean by technical information, but what type of nontechnical information do they give? And am I right in assuming that this is done by telepathic contact?

RA: I am Ra. This is correct. Through telepathy the philosophy of the Law of One with the distortion of service to self is promulgated. In advanced groups there are rituals and exercises given, and these have been written down just as the service to others oriented entities have written down the promulgated philosophy of their teachers. The philosophy concerns the service of manipulating others that they may experience service towards the other self, thus through this experience becoming able to appreciate service to self. These entities would become oriented towards service to self and in turn manipulate yet others so that they in turn might experience the service towards the other self.

QUESTIONER: Would this be the origin of what we call black magic?

RA: I am Ra. This is correct in one sense, incorrect in another. The Orion group has aided the so-called negatively oriented among your mind/body/spirit complexes. These same entities would be concerning themselves with service to self in any case, and there are many upon your so-called inner planes which are negatively oriented and thus available as inner teachers or guides and so-called possessors of certain souls who seek this distortion of service to self.

QUESTIONER: Is it possible for an entity here on Earth to be so confused as to call both the Confederation and the Orion group in an alternating way, first one, then the other, and then back to the first again?

RA: I am Ra. It is entirely possible for the untuned channel, as you call that service, to receive both positive and negative communications. If the entity at the base of its confusion is oriented toward service to others, the entity will begin to receive messages of doom. If the entity at the base of the complex of beingness is oriented towards service to self, the crusaders, who in this case do not find it necessary to lie, will simply begin to give the philosophy they are here to give. Many of your so-called contacts among your people have been confused and self-destructive because the channels were oriented towards service to others but, in the desire for proof, were open to the lying information of the crusaders, who then were able to neutralize the effectiveness of the channel.

QUESTIONER: Are most of these crusaders fourth density?

RA: I am Ra. There is a majority of fourth density. That is correct.

QUESTIONER: Is an entity in the fourth density normally invisible to us?

RA: I am Ra. The use of the word "normal" is one which befuddles the meaning of the question. Let us rephrase for clarity. The fourth density is, by choice, not visible to third density. It is possible for fourth density to be visible. However, it is not the choice of the fourth-density entity to be visible due to the necessity for concentration upon a rather difficult vibrational complex which is the third density you experience.

QUESTIONER: Are there any Confederation or Orion entities living upon the Earth and operating visibly among us in our society at this time?

RA: I am Ra. There are no entities of either group walking among you at this time. However, the crusaders of Orion use two types of entities to do their bidding, shall we say. The first type is the thought-form; the second, a kind of robot.

QUESTIONER: Could you describe the robot?

RA: I am Ra. The robot may look like any other being. It is a construct.

QUESTIONER: Is the robot what is normally called the "Men in Black?"

RA: I am Ra. This is incorrect.

QUESTIONER: Who are the Men in Black?

RA: I am Ra. The Men in Black are a thought-form type of entity which have some beingness to their makeup. They have certain physical characteristics given them. However, their true vibrational nature is without third-density vibrational characteristics, and, therefore, they are able to materialize and dematerialize when necessary.

QUESTIONER: Are all of these Men in Black then used by the Orion crusaders?

RA: I am Ra. This is correct.

QUESTIONER: You spoke of Wanderers. Who are Wanderers? Where do they come from?

RA: I am Ra. Imagine, if you will, the sands of your shores. As countless as the grains of sand are the sources of intelligent infinity. When a social memory complex has achieved its complete understanding of its desire, it may conclude that its desire is service to others with the distortion towards reaching their hand, figuratively, to any entities who call for aid. These entities whom you may call the Brothers and Sisters of Sorrow move toward this calling of sorrow. These entities are from all reaches of the infinite creation and are bound together by the desire to serve in this distortion.

QUESTIONER: How many of them are incarnate on Earth now?

RA: I am Ra. The number is approximate due to an heavy influx of those birthed at this time due to an intensive need to lighten the planetary vibration and thus aid in harvest. The number approaches sixty-five million.

QUESTIONER: Are most of these from the fourth density? Or what density do they come from?

RA: I am Ra. Few there are of fourth density. The largest number of Wanderers, as you call them, are of the sixth density. The desire to serve must be distorted towards a great deal of purity of mind and what you may call foolhardiness or bravery, depending upon your distortion complex judgment. The challenge/danger of the Wanderer is that it will forget its mission, become karmically involved, and thus be swept into the maelstrom of which it had incarnated to avert the destruction.

QUESTIONER: What could one of these entities do to become karmically involved? Could you give an example of that?

RA: I am Ra. An entity which acts in a consciously unloving manner in action with other beings can become karmically involved.

QUESTIONER: Do many of these Wanderers have physical ailments in this third-density situation?

RA: I am Ra. Due to the extreme variance between the vibratory distortions of third density and those of the more dense densities, if you will, Wanderers have, as a general rule, some form of handicap, difficulty, or feeling of alienation which is severe. The most common of these difficulties are alienation, the reaction against the planetary vibration by personality disorders, as you would call them, and body complex ailments indicating difficulty in adjustment to the planetary vibrations such as allergies, as you would call them.

QUESTIONER: Thank you. Is there anything that we can do to make the instrument more comfortable?

RA: I am Ra. We ask you to realign the object upon which the symbols sit. It is not a significant distortion for only one session, but you will find upon measuring the entire assemblage that the resting place is 1.4 degrees from the correct alignment, the resting place an additional 0.5 degrees away from proper orientation. Do not concern yourselves with this in the space/time nexus present, but do not allow these distortions to remain over a long period or the contact will be gradually impaired.

I am Ra. I leave you in the love and in the light of the One Infinite Creator. Go forth rejoicing in the power and the peace of the One Creator. Adonai.

Session 13,
January 29, 1981

RA: I am Ra. I greet you in the love and the light of the Infinite Creator. I communicate now.

QUESTIONER: First of all I would like to apologize for asking so many stupid questions while searching for what we should do. I consider what we are doing to be a great honor and privilege to also be humble messengers of the Law of One. I now believe that the way to prepare this book is to start at the beginning of creation and follow through the evolution of man on Earth, investigating at all times how the Law of One was used. I would also like to make as the title of the book *The Law of One*, and I would like to state as the author, Ra. Would you agree to this?

RA: I am Ra. Your query is unclear. Would you please state as separate queries each area of agreement?

QUESTIONER: First, I would like to start at the beginning of creation, as far back as we can go, and follow the development of man to the present time. Is this agreeable?

RA: I am Ra. This is completely your discernment/understanding/decision.

QUESTIONER: Secondly, I would like to title the book *The Law of One*, by Ra. Is this agreeable?

RA: I am Ra. The title of the book is acceptable. The authorship by vibratory sound complex Ra is, in our distortion of understanding, incomplete. We are messengers.

QUESTIONER: Can you state who then should author the book?

RA: I am Ra. I can only request that if your discernment/understanding suggests the use of this vibratory sound complex, Ra, the phrase "An humble messenger of the Law of One" be appended.

QUESTIONER: Thank you. Can you tell me of the first known thing in the creation?

RA: I am Ra. The first known thing in the creation is infinity. The infinity is creation.

QUESTIONER: From this infinity then must come what we experience as creation. What was the next step or the next evolvement?

RA: I am Ra. Infinity became aware. This was the next step.

QUESTIONER: After this, what came next?

RA: I am Ra. Awareness led to the focus of infinity into infinite energy. You have called this by various vibrational sound complexes, the most common to your ears being "Logos" or "Love." The Creator is the focusing of infinity as an aware or conscious principle called by us, as closely as we can create understanding/learning in your language, intelligent infinity.

QUESTIONER: Can you state the next step?

RA: I am Ra. The next step is still at this space/time nexus in your illusion achieving its progression as you may see it in your illusion. The next step is an infinite reaction to the creative principle following the Law of One in one of its primal distortions, freedom of will. Thus many, many dimensions, infinite in number, are possible. The energy moves from the intelligent infinity due first to the outpouring of randomized creative force, this then creating patterns which in holographic style appear as the entire creation no matter which direction or energy is explored. These patterns of energy begin then to regularize their own local, shall we say, rhythms and fields of energy, thus creating dimensions and universes.

QUESTIONER: Then can you tell me how the galaxy and planetary systems were formed?

RA: I am Ra. You must imagine a great leap of thought in this query, for at the last query, the physical, as you call, it, universes were not yet born.

The energies moved in increasingly intelligent patterns until the individualization of various energies emanating from the creative principle of intelligent infinity became such as to be co-Creators. Thus the so-called physical matter began. The concept of light is instrumental in grasping this great leap of thought, as this vibrational distortion of infinity is the building block of that which is known as matter, the light being intelligent and full of energy, thus being the first distortion of intelligent infinity which was called by the creative principle.

This light of love was made to have in its occurrences of being certain characteristics, among them the infinite whole paradoxically described by the straight line, as you would call it. This paradox is responsible for the shape of the various physical illusion entities you call solar systems, galaxies, and planets of revolving and tending towards the lenticular.

QUESTIONER: I think I made an error in getting ahead of the process you were describing. Would it be helpful to fill in that great leap due to the mistake I made?

RA: I am Ra. I attempted to bridge the gap. However, you may question me in any manner you deem appropriate.

QUESTIONER: Taking the question just before the one I asked about the galaxies and planets and tell me what the next step was from there?

RA: I am Ra. The steps, as you call them, are, at the point of question, simultaneous and infinite.

QUESTIONER: Can you tell me how intelligent infinity became, shall we say (I'm having difficulty with the language), how intelligent infinity became individualized from itself?

RA: I am Ra. This is an appropriate question.

The intelligent infinity discerned a concept. This concept was discerned to be freedom of will of awareness. This concept was finity. This was the first and primal paradox or distortion of the Law of One. Thus the one intelligent infinity invested itself in an exploration of manyness. Due to the infinite possibilities of intelligent infinity, there is no ending to manyness. The exploration, thus, is free to continue infinitely in an eternal present.

QUESTIONER: Was the galaxy that we are in created by the infinite intelligence, or was it created by a portion of the infinite intelligence?

RA: I am Ra. The galaxy and all other things of material of which you are aware are products of individualized portions of intelligent infinity. As each exploration began, it, in turn, found its focus and became co-Creator. Using intelligent infinity, each portion created an universe, and allowing the rhythms of free choice to flow, playing with the infinite spectrum of possibilities, each individualized portion channeled the love/light into what you might call intelligent energy, thus creating the so-called Natural Laws of any particular universe.

Each universe, in turn, individualized to a focus becoming, in turn, co-Creator and allowing further diversity, thus creating further intelligent energies regularizing or causing Natural Laws to appear in the vibrational patterns of what you would call a solar system. Thus, each solar system has its own, shall we say, local coordinate system of illusory Natural Laws. It shall be understood that any portion, no matter how small, of any density or illusory pattern contains, as in an holographic picture, the One Creator which is infinity. Thus all begins and ends in mystery.

QUESTIONER: Can you tell me how the individualized infinity created our galaxy and if the same portion created our planetary system, and, if so, how this came about?

RA: I am Ra. We may have misperceived your query. We were under the distortion/impression that we had responded to this particular query. Would you restate the query?

QUESTIONER: I am wondering if the planetary system that we are in now was all created at once, or if our sun was created first and the planets later?

RA: I am Ra. The process is from the larger, in your illusion, to the smaller. Thus the co-Creator, individualizing the galaxy, created energy patterns which then focused in multitudinous focuses of further conscious awareness of intelligent infinity. Thus, the solar system of which you experience inhabitation is of its own patterns, rhythms, and so-called natural laws which are unique to itself. However, the progression is from the galaxy spiraling energy to the solar spiraling energy, to the planetary spiraling energy, to the experiential circumstances of spiraling energy which begin the first density of awareness of consciousness of planetary entities.

QUESTIONER: Could you tell me about this first density of planetary entities?

RA: I am Ra. Each step recapitulates intelligent infinity in its discovery of awareness. In a planetary environment, all begins in what you would call chaos, energy undirected and random in its infinity. Slowly, in your terms of understanding, there forms a focus of self-awareness. Thus the Logos moves. Light comes to form the darkness, according to the co-Creator's patterns and vibratory rhythms, so constructing a certain type of experience. This begins with first density, which is the density of consciousness, the mineral and water life upon the planet learning from fire and wind the awareness of being. This is the first density.

QUESTIONER: How does this first density then progress to greater awareness?

RA: I am Ra. The spiraling energy, which is the characteristic of what you call "light," moves in a straight line spiral, thus giving spirals an inevitable vector upwards to a more comprehensive beingness with regards to intelligent infinity. Thus, first-dimensional beingness strives towards the second-density lessons of a type of awareness which includes growth rather than dissolution or random change.

QUESTIONER: Could you define what you mean by growth?

RA: I am Ra. Picture, if you will, the difference between first-vibrational mineral or water life and the lower second-density beings which begin to move about within and upon its being. This movement is the characteristic of second density, the striving towards light and growth.

QUESTIONER: By striving towards light, what do you mean?

RA: I am Ra. A very simplistic example of second-density growth striving towards light is that of the leaf striving towards the source of light.

QUESTIONER: Is there any physical difference between first and second density? For instance, if I could see both a first- and second-density planet side by side, in my present condition, could I see both of them? Would they both be physical to me?

RA: I am Ra. This is correct. All of the octave of your densities would be clearly visible were not the fourth through the seventh freely choosing not to be visible.

QUESTIONER: Then how does the second density progress to the third?

RA: I am Ra. The second density strives towards the third density, which is the density of self-consciousness or self-awareness. The striving takes place through the higher second density forms who are invested by third-density beings with an identity to the extent that they become self-aware mind/body complexes, thus becoming mind/body/spirit complexes and entering third density, the first density of consciousness of spirit.

QUESTIONER: What is the density level of our planet Earth at this time?

RA: I am Ra. The sphere upon which you dwell is third density in its beingness of mind/body/spirit complexes. It is now in a space/time continuum, fourth density. This is causing a somewhat difficult harvest.

QUESTIONER: How does a third-density planet become a fourth-density planet?

RA: I am Ra. This will be the last full question.

The fourth density is, as we have said, as regularized in its approach as the striking of a clock upon the hour. The space/time of your solar system has enabled this planetary sphere to spiral into space/time of a different vibrational configuration. This causes the planetary sphere to be able to be molded by these new distortions. However, the thought-forms of your people during this transition period are such that the mind/body/spirit complexes of both individual and societies are scattered throughout the spectrum instead of becoming able to grasp the needle, shall we say, and point the compass in one direction.

Thus, the entry into the vibration of love, sometimes called by your people the vibration of understanding, is not effective with your present societal complex. Thus, the harvest shall be such that many will repeat the third-density cycle. The energies of your Wanderers, your teachers, and your adepts at this time are all bent upon increasing the harvest. However, there are few to harvest.

QUESTIONER: I would like to apologize for sometimes asking inappropriate questions. It's difficult sometimes to ask precisely the right question. I don't wish to go over any ground that we've already covered. I notice that this period is slightly shorter than previous work sessions. Is there a reason for this?

RA: I am Ra. This instrument's vital energy is somewhat low.

QUESTIONER: I am assuming from this that it would be a good idea not to have another session today. Is that correct?

RA: I am Ra. It is well to have a session later if it is acceptable that we monitor this instrument and cease using it when it becomes low in the material which we take from it. We do not wish to deplete this instrument.

QUESTIONER: This is always acceptable in any session. I will ask my final question. Is there anything that we can do to make the instrument more comfortable or aid in this communication?

RA: I am Ra. It is well. Each is most conscientious. Continue in the same.
     I am Ra. I leave you in the love and the light of the One Infinite Creator. Go forth, therefore, rejoicing in the power and the peace of the One Creator. Adonai.

Session 14,
January 29, 1981

RA: I am Ra. I greet you in the love and the light of the Infinite Creator. We communicate now.

QUESTIONER: After going over this morning's work, I thought it might be helpful to fill in a few things. You said that the second density strives towards the third density, which is the density of self-consciousness, or self-awareness. The striving takes place through higher second-density forms being invested by third-density beings. Could you explain what you mean by this?

RA: I am Ra. Much as you would put on a vestment, so do your third-density beings invest or clothe some second-density beings with self-awareness. This is often done through the opportunity of what you call pets. It has also been done by various other means of investiture. These include many so-called religious practice complexes which personify and send love to various natural second-density beings in their group form.

QUESTIONER: When this Earth was second density, how did the second-density beings on it become so invested?

RA: I am Ra. There was not this type of investment as spoken, but the simple third-density investment which is the line of spiraling light calling distortion upward from density to density. The process takes longer when there is no investment made by incarnate third-density beings.

QUESTIONER: Then what was the second-density form—what did it look like—that became Earthman in the third density? What did he look like in the second density?

RA: I am Ra. The difference between second- and third-density bodily forms would in many cases have been more like one to the other. In the case of your planetary sphere, the process was interrupted by those who incarnated here from the planetary sphere you call Mars. They were adjusted by genetic changing, and, therefore, there was some difference which was of a very noticeable variety rather than the gradual raising of the bipedal forms upon your second-density level to third-density level. This has nothing to do with the so-called placement of the soul. This has only to do with the circumstances of the influx of those from that culture.

QUESTIONER: I understand from previous material that this occurred 75,000 years ago. It was then that our third-density process of evolution began. Can you tell me the history, hitting only the points of development, shall I say, that occurred within this 75,000 years, any point when contact was made to aid this development?

RA: I am Ra. The first attempt to aid your peoples was at the time 75,000. This attempt 75,000 of your years ago has been previously described by us. The next attempt was approximately 58,000 of your years ago, continuing for a long period in your measurement, with those of Mu as you call this race or mind/body/spirit social complex. The next attempt was long in coming and occurred approximately 13,000 of your years ago when some intelligent information was offered to those of Atlantis, this being of the same type of healing and crystal working of which we have spoken previously. The next attempt was 11,000 of your years ago. These are approximations, as we are not totally able to process your space/time continuum measurement system. This was in what you call Egypt, and of this we have also spoken. The same beings who came with us returned approximately 3,500 years later in order to attempt to aid the South American mind/body/spirit social complex once again. However, the pyramids of those so-called cities were not to be used in the appropriate fashion.

Therefore, this was not pursued further. There was a landing approximately 3,000 of your years ago also in your South America, as you call it. There were a few attempts to aid your peoples approximately 2,300 years ago, this in the area of Egypt. The remaining part of the cycle, we have never been gone from your fifth dimension and have been working in this last minor cycle to prepare for harvest.

QUESTIONER: Was the Egyptian visit of 11,000 years ago the only one where you actually walked the Earth?

RA: I am Ra. I understand your question distorted in the direction of selves rather than other-selves. We of the vibratory sound complex, Ra, have walked among you only at that time.

QUESTIONER: I understood you to say in an earlier session that pyramids were built to ring the Earth. How many pyramids were built?

RA: I am Ra. There are six balancing pyramids and fifty-two others built for additional healing and initiatory work among your mind/body/spirit social complexes.

QUESTIONER: What is a balancing pyramid?

RA: I am Ra. Imagine, if you will, the many force fields of the Earth in their geometrically precise web. Energies stream into the Earth planes, as you would call them, from magnetically determined points. Due to growing thought-form distortions in understanding of the Law of One, the planet itself was seen to have the potential for imbalance. The balancing pyramidal structures were charged with crystals which drew the appropriate balance from the energy forces streaming into the various geometrical centers of electromagnetic energy which surround and shape the planetary sphere.

THE LAW OF ONE

QUESTIONER: Let me make a synopsis and you tell me if I am correct. All of these visits for the last 75,000 years were for the purpose of giving to the people of Earth an understanding of the Law of One, and in this way allowing them to progress upward through the fourth, fifth, and sixth densities. This was to be a service to Earth. The pyramids were used also in giving the Law of One in their own way. The balancing pyramids, I'm not quite sure of. Am I right so far?

RA: I am Ra. You are correct to the limits of the precision allowed by language.

QUESTIONER: Did the balancing pyramid prevent the Earth from changing its axis?

RA: I am Ra. This query is not clear. Please restate.

QUESTIONER: Does the balancing refer to the individual who is initiated in the pyramid, or does it refer to the physical balancing of the Earth on its axis in space?

RA: I am Ra. The balancing pyramidal structures could be and were used for individual initiation. However, the use of these pyramids was also designed for the balancing of the planetary energy web. The other pyramids are not placed correctly for Earth healing but for healing of mind/body/spirit complexes. It came to our attention that your density was distorted towards what is called, by our distortion/understanding of third density on your planetary sphere, more of a time/space continuum in one incarnation pattern in order to have a fuller opportunity to learn/teach the Laws or Ways of the primal distortion of the Law of One which is Love.

QUESTIONER: I want to make this statement and you tell me if I am correct. The balancing pyramids were to do what we call increase the life span of entities here so that they would gain more wisdom of the Law of One while they were in the physical at one time. Is this correct?

RA: I am Ra. This is correct. However, the pyramids not called by us by the vibrational sound complex, balancing pyramids, were more numerous and were used exclusively for the above purpose and the teach/learning of healers to charge and enable these processes.

QUESTIONER: George Van Tassel built a machine in our western desert called an integratron. Will this machine work for that purpose, of increasing the life span?

RA: I am Ra. The machine is incomplete and will not function for the above-mentioned purpose.

QUESTIONER: Who gave George the information on how to build it?

RA: I am Ra. There were two contacts which gave the entity with the vibratory sound complex, George, this information. One was of the Confederation. The second was of the Orion group. The Confederation was caused to find the distortion towards noncontact due to the alteration of the vibrational mind complex patterns of the one called George. Thus, the Orion group used this instrument; however, this instrument, though confused, was a mind/body/spirit complex devoted at the heart to service to others, so the, shall we say, worst that could be done was to discredit this source.

QUESTIONER: Would there be any value to the people of this planet now to complete this machine?

RA: I am Ra. The harvest is now. There is not at this time any reason to include efforts along these distortions toward longevity, but rather to encourage distortions toward seeking the heart of self, for this which resides clearly in the violet-ray energy field will determine the harvesting of each mind/body/spirit complex.

QUESTIONER: Going back to when we started this 75,000-year period, there was a harvest 25,000 years after the start, which would make it 50,000 years ago. Can you tell me how many were harvested at that time?

RA: I am Ra. The harvest was none.

QUESTIONER: There was no harvest? What about 25,000 years ago?

RA: I am Ra. A harvesting began taking place in the latter portion, as you measure time/space, of the second cycle, with individuals finding the gateway to intelligent infinity. The harvest of that time, though extremely small, was those entities of extreme distortion towards service to the entities who were now to repeat the major cycle. These entities, therefore, remained in third density, although they could, at any moment/present nexus, leave this density through use of intelligent infinity.

QUESTIONER: Then in the harvest 25,000 years ago, the entities who could have been harvested into the fourth density chose to remain here in service to this planetary population. Is this correct?

RA: I am Ra. This is correct. Thus, there was no harvest, but there were harvestable entities who shall choose the manner of their entrance into fourth dimension.

QUESTIONER: Then for the last 2,300 years you have been working to create as large a harvest as possible at the end of the total 75,000-year cycle. Can you state with respect to the Law of One why you do this?

RA: I am Ra. I speak for the social memory complex termed Ra. We came among you to aid you. Our efforts in service were perverted. Our desire then is to eliminate as far as possible the distortions caused by those misreading our information and guidance. The general cause of service such as the Confederation offers is that of the primal distortion of the Law of One, which is service. The One Being of the creation is like unto a body, if you will accept this third-density analogy. Would we ignore a pain in the leg? A bruise upon the skin? A cut which is festering? No. There is no ignoring a call. We, the entities of sorrow, chose as our service the attempt to heal the sorrow which we are calling analogous to the pains of a physical body complex/distortion.

QUESTIONER: Of what density level is Ra?

RA: I am Ra. I am sixth density with a strong seeking towards seventh density. The harvest for us will be in only approximately two and one-half million of your years, and it is our desire to be ready for harvest as it approaches in our space/time continuum.

QUESTIONER: And you ready yourselves for this harvest through the service you can provide. Is this correct?

RA: I am Ra. This is correct. We offer the Law of One, the solving of paradoxes, the balancing of love/light and light/love.

QUESTIONER: How long is one of your cycles?

RA: I am Ra. One of our cycles computes to 75 million of your years.

QUESTIONER: 75 million years?

RA: I am Ra. That is correct.

QUESTIONER: In your service in giving the Law of One, do you work with any other planets than Earth at this time, or just Earth?

RA: I am Ra. We work only with this planetary sphere at this time.

QUESTIONER: You stated that you were called by 352,000 Earth entities. Does this mean that it is this number that will understand and accept the Law of One?

RA: I am Ra. We cannot estimate the correctness of your statement, for those who call are not in every case able to understand the answer to their calling. Moreover, those who were not calling previously may, with great trauma, discover the answers to the call nearly simultaneously with their late call. There is no time/space in call. Therefore, we cannot estimate the number of your mind/body/spirit complexes which will, in your space/time continuum/distortion, hear and understand.

QUESTIONER: How do you normally perform your service of giving the Law of One? How have you done this over the last 2,300 years? How have you normally given this to Earth people?

RA: I am Ra. We have used channels such as this one, but in most cases the channels feel inspired by dreams and visions without being aware, consciously, of our identity or existence. This particular group has been accentuatedly trained to recognize such contact. This makes this group able to be aware of a focal or vibrational source of information.

QUESTIONER: When you contact the entities in their dreams and otherwise, these entities first have to be seeking in the direction of the Law of One. Is this correct?

RA: I am Ra. This is correct. For example, the entities of the nation Egypt were in a state of pantheism, as you may call the distortion toward separate worship of various portions of the Creator. We were able to contact one whose orientation was toward the One.

QUESTIONER: I assume that as the cycle ends and inconveniences occur, there will be some entities who start seeking or be catalyzed into seeking because of the trauma and will then hear your words telepathically or in written form such as this book. Is this correct?

RA: I am Ra. You are correct except in understanding that the inconveniences have begun.

QUESTIONER: Can you tell me who was responsible for transmitting the book *Oahspe*?

RA: I am Ra. This was transmitted by one of Confederation social memory complex status whose idea, as offered to the Council, was to use some of the known physical history of the so-called religions or religious distortions of your cycle in order to veil and partially unveil aspects or primal distortions of the Law of One. All names can be taken to be created for their vibrational characteristics. The information buried within has to do with a deeper understanding of love and light, and the attempts of infinite intelligence through many messengers to teach/learn those entities of your sphere.

QUESTIONER: Have there been any other books that you can name that are available for this purpose that have been given by the Confederation?

RA: I am Ra. We cannot share this information, for it would distort your discernment patterns in your future. You may ask about a particular volume.

QUESTIONER: Who transmitted *The Urantia Book*?

RA: I am Ra. This was given by a series of discarnate entities of your own Earth planes, the so-called inner planes. This material is not passed by the Council.

QUESTIONER: Who spoke through Edgar Cayce?

RA: I am Ra. No entity spoke through Edgar Cayce.

QUESTIONER: Where did the information come from that Edgar Cayce channeled?

RA: I am Ra. We have explained before that the intelligent infinity is brought into intelligent energy from eighth density or octave. The one sound vibratory complex called Edgar used this gateway to view the present, which is not the continuum you experience but the potential social memory complex of this planetary sphere. The term your peoples have used for this is the "Akashic Record" or the "Hall of Records." This is the last question which you may now ask.

QUESTIONER: Is there anything that we can do to make the instrument more comfortable or to help during the transmission?

RA: I am Ra. We only reiterate the importance of alignment. This instrument is placed 0.2 degrees away from the direction of the resting place, which is correct. This may be "eyed," shall we say, by sight and the instrument reminded. You are being conscientious. Is there any brief question we may answer before this session is closed?

QUESTIONER: Can you tell me if we are accomplishing our effort reasonably well?

RA: I am Ra. The Law is One. There are no mistakes.

I am Ra. I leave this instrument in the love and the light of the One Infinite Creator. Go forth, therefore, rejoicing in the power and the peace of the One Creator. Adonai.

Session 15,
January 30, 1981

RA: I am Ra. I greet you in the love and the light of the Infinite Creator. I communicate now.

QUESTIONER: I would like to apologize for any past and future stupid questions. They are due to the fact that I am searching for the proper entry into the investigation of the Law of One.

I would like to ask about the use of the instrument, if it is a function of the time we use the instrument or the amount of words or information the instrument gives? In other words, do I have to hurry and ask questions, or can I take my time to ask questions?

RA: I am Ra. There are two portions to your query. Firstly, this instrument's reserve of vital energy, which is a product of body, mind, and spirit distortions in the various complexes, is the key to the length of time which we may expend using this instrument. We searched your group and we contacted you, for each in your group possesses significantly more vital energy of the body complex. However, this instrument was tuned most appropriately by the mind/body/spirit complex distortions of its beingness in this illusion. Therefore, we remained with this instrument.

Secondly, we communicate at a set rate which is dependent upon our careful manipulation of this instrument. We cannot be more, as you would say, quick. Therefore, you may ask questions speedily, but the answers we have to offer are at a set pace given.

QUESTIONER: This isn't exactly what I meant. If it takes me, say, forty-five minutes to ask my questions, does that give the instrument only fifteen minutes to answer, or could the instrument go over an hour, all totaled, with her answers?

RA: I am Ra. The energy required for this contact is entered into this instrument by a function of time. Therefore, the time is the factor, as we understand your query.

QUESTIONER: Then I should ask my questions rapidly so that I do not reduce the time. Is this correct?

RA: I am Ra. You shall do as you deem fit. However, we may suggest that to obtain the answers you require may mean that you invest some of what you experience as time. Although you lose the answer time, you gain thereby in the specificity of the answer. At many times in the past, we have needed clarification of hastily phrased questions.

QUESTIONER: Thank you. The first question is this: Why does rapid aging occur on this planet?

RA: I am Ra. Rapid aging occurs upon this third-density planet due to an ongoing imbalance of receptor web complex in the etheric portion of the energy field of this planet. The thought-form distortions of your peoples have caused the energy streamings to enter the planetary magnetic atmosphere, if you would so term this web of energy patterns, in such a way that the proper streamings are not correctly imbued with balanced vibratory light/love from the, shall we say, cosmic level of this octave of existence.

QUESTIONER: Do I assume correctly that one of your attempts in service to this planet was to help the population more fully understand and practice the Law of One so that this rapid aging could be changed to normal aging?

RA: I am Ra. You assume correctly to a great degree.

QUESTIONER: What is the greatest service that our population on this planet could perform individually?

RA: I am Ra. There is but one service. The Law is One. The offering of self to Creator is the greatest service, the unity, the fountainhead. The entity who seeks the One Creator is with infinite intelligence. From this seeking, from this offering, a great multiplicity of opportunities will evolve depending upon the mind/body/spirit complexes' distortions with regard to the various illusory aspects or energy centers of the various complexes of your illusion.

Thus, some become healers, some workers, some teachers, and so forth.

QUESTIONER: If an entity were perfectly balanced with respect to the Law of One on this planet, would he undergo the aging process?

RA: I am Ra. A perfectly balanced entity would become tired rather than visibly aged. The lessons being learned, the entity would depart. However, this is appropriate and is a form of aging which your peoples do not experience. The understanding comes slowly, the body complex decomposing more rapidly.

QUESTIONER: Can you tell me a little more about the word "balancing," as we are using it?

RA: I am Ra. Picture, if you will, the One Infinite. You have no picture. Thus, the process begins. Love creating light, becoming love/light, streams into the planetary sphere according to the electromagnetic web of points or nexi of entrance. These streamings are then available to the individual who, like the planet, is a web of electromagnetic energy fields with points or nexi of entrance.

In a balanced individual each energy center is balanced and functioning brightly and fully. The blockages of your planetary sphere cause some distortion of intelligent energy. The blockages of the mind/body/spirit complex further distort or unbalance this energy. There is one energy. It may be understood as love/light or light/love or intelligent energy.

QUESTIONER: Am I correct to assume that one of the blockages of the mind/body/spirit complex might be, shall we say, ego, and this could be balanced using a worthiness/unworthiness balance. Am I correct?

RA: I am Ra. This is incorrect.

QUESTIONER: Can you tell me how you balance the ego?

RA: I am Ra. We cannot work with this concept, as it is misapplied and understanding cannot come from it.

QUESTIONER: How does an individual go about balancing himself? What is the first step?

RA: I am Ra. The steps are only one; that is, an understanding of the energy centers which make up the mind/body/spirit complex. This understanding may be briefly summarized as follows. The first balancing is of the Malkuth, or Earth, vibratory energy complex, called the red-ray complex. An understanding and acceptance of this energy is fundamental. The next energy complex which may be blocked is the emotional or personal complex, also known as the orange-ray complex. This blockage will often demonstrate itself as personal eccentricities or distortions with regard to self-conscious understanding or acceptance of self.

The third blockage resembles most closely that which you have called ego. It is the yellow-ray or solar-plexus center. Blockages in this center will often manifest as distortions toward power manipulation and other social behaviors concerning those close and those associated with the mind/body/spirit complex. Those with blockages in these first three energy centers, or nexi, will have continuing difficulties in ability to further their seeking of the Law of One.

The center of heart, or green ray, is the center from which third-density beings may springboard, shall we say, to infinite intelligence. Blockages in this area may manifest as difficulties in expressing what you may call universal love or compassion.

The blue-ray center of energy streaming is the center which, for the first time, is outgoing as well as inpouring. Those blocked in this area may have difficulty in grasping the spirit/mind complexes of its own entity and further difficulty in expressing such understandings of self. Entities blocked in this area may have difficulties in accepting communication from other mind/body/spirit complexes.

The next center is the pineal or indigo-ray center. Those blocked in this center may experience a lessening of the influx of intelligent energy due to manifestations which appear as unworthiness. This is that of which you spoke. As you can see, this is but one of many distortions due to the several points of energy influx into the mind/body/spirit complex. The indigo-ray balancing is quite central to the type of work which revolves about the spirit complex, which has its influx then into the transformation or transmutation of third density to fourth density, it being the energy center receiving the least distorted outpourings of love/light from intelligent energy and also the potential for the key to the gateway of intelligent infinity.

The remaining center of energy influx is simply the total expression of the entity's vibratory complex of mind, body, and spirit. It is as it will be; "balanced" or "imbalanced" has no meaning at this energy level, for it gives and takes in its own balance. Whatever the distortion may be, it cannot be manipulated as can the others and, therefore, has no particular importance in viewing the balancing of an entity.

QUESTIONER: You previously gave us information on what we should do in balancing. Is there any publishable information you can give us now about particular exercises or methods of balancing these energy centers?

RA: I am Ra. The exercises given for publication seen in comparison with the material now given are in total a good beginning. It is important to allow each seeker to enlighten itself rather than for any messenger to attempt in language to teach/learn for the entity, thus being teach/learner and learn/teacher. This is not in balance with your third density. We learn from you. We teach to you. Thus, we teach/learn. If we learned for you, this would cause imbalance in the direction of the distortion of free will. There are other items of information allowable. However, you have not yet reached these items in your line of questioning, and it is our belief/feeling complex that the questioner shall shape this material in such a way that your mind/body/spirit complexes shall have entry to it; thus we answer your queries as they arise in your mind complex.

QUESTIONER: Yesterday you stated that "the harvest is now. There is not at this time any reason to include efforts along this line of longevity, but rather to encourage efforts to seek the heart of self. This which resides clearly in the violet-ray energy field will determine the harvest of the mind/body/spirit complex." Could you tell us the best way to seek the heart of self?

RA: I am Ra. We have given you this information in several wordings. However, we can only say the material for your understanding is the self: the mind/body/spirit complex. You have been given information upon healing, as you call this distortion. This information may be seen in a more general context as ways to understand the self. The understanding, experiencing, accepting, and merging of self with self and other-self, and finally with the Creator, is the path to the heart of self. In each infinitesimal part of your self resides the One in all of Its power. Therefore, we can only encourage these lines of contemplation or prayer as a means of subjectively/objectively using or combining various understandings to enhance the seeking process. Without such a method of reversing the analytical process, one could not integrate into unity the many understandings gained in such seeking.

QUESTIONER: I don't mean to ask the same question twice, but there are some areas that I consider so important that possibly a greater understanding may be obtained if the answer is restated a number of times in other words. I thank you for your patience. Yesterday, you also mentioned that when there was no harvest at the end of the last 25,000-year period, "there were harvestable entities who shall choose the manner of their entrance into the fourth density." Could you tell me what you mean by "they shall choose the manner of their entry into the fourth density"?

RA: I am Ra. These shepherds, or, as some have called them, the "Elder Race," shall choose the time/space of their leaving. They are unlikely to leave until their other-selves are harvestable also.

QUESTIONER: What do you mean by their "other-selves" being harvestable?

RA: I am Ra. The other-selves with whom these beings are concerned are those which did not attain harvest during the second major cycle.

QUESTIONER: Could you tell me just a small amount of the history of what you call the Elder Race?

RA: I am Ra. The question is unclear. Please restate.

QUESTIONER: I ask this question because I have heard of the Elder Race before in a book, *Road in the Sky*, by George Hunt Williamson, and I was wondering if this Elder Race was the same that he talked about?

RA: I am Ra. The question now resolves itself, for we have spoken previously of the manner of decision-making which caused these entities to remain here upon the closing of the second major cycle of your current master cycle. There are some distortions in the descriptions of the one known as Michel; however, these distortions have to do primarily with the fact that these entities are not a social memory complex, but rather a group of mind/body/spirit complexes dedicated to service. These entities work together but are not completely unified; thus, they do not completely see each the other's thoughts, feelings, and motives. However, their desire to serve is the fourth-dimensional type of desire, thus melding them into what you may call a brotherhood.

QUESTIONER: Why do you call them the Elder Race?

RA: I am Ra. We called them thusly to acquaint you, the questioner, with their identity as is understood by your mind complex distortion.

QUESTIONER: Are there any Wanderers with this Elder Race?

RA: I am Ra. These are planetary entities harvested—Wanderers only in the sense that they chose, in fourth-density love, to immediately reincarnate in third density rather than proceeding towards fourth density. This causes them to be Wanderers of a type, Wanderers who have never left the Earth plane because of their free will rather than because of their vibrational level.

QUESTIONER: In yesterday's material you mentioned that the first distortion was the distortion of free will. Is there a sequence, a first, second, and third distortion of the Law of One?

RA: I am Ra. Only up to a very short point. After this point, the manyness of distortions are equal one to another. The first distortion, free will, finds focus. This is the second distortion known to you as Logos, the Creative Principle or Love. This intelligent energy thus creates a distortion known as Light. From these three distortions come many, many hierarchies of distortions, each having its own paradoxes to be synthesized, no one being more important than another.

QUESTIONER: You also said that you offered the Law of One, which is the balancing of love/light with light/love. Is there any difference between light/love and love/light?

RA: I am Ra. This will be the final question of this time/space.

There is the same difference between love/light and light/love as there is between teach/learning and learn/teaching. Love/light is the enabler, the power, the energy giver. Light/love is the manifestation which occurs when light has been impressed with love.

QUESTIONER: Is there anything we can do to make the instrument more comfortable? Can we have two sessions today?

RA: I am Ra. This instrument requires a certain amount of manipulation of the physical or body complex due to a stiffness. Other than this, all is well, the energies being balanced. There is a slight distortion in the mental energy of this instrument due to concern for a loved one, as you call it. This is only slightly lowering the vital energies of the instrument. Given a manipulation, this instrument will be well for another working.

QUESTIONER: By manipulation, do you mean that she should go for a walk or that we should rub her back?

RA: I am Ra. We meant the latter. The understanding must be added that this manipulation be done by one in harmony with the entity.

I am Ra. I leave you in the love and the light of the Infinite Creator. Go forth, then, rejoicing in the power and the peace of the One Infinite Creator. Adonai.

Session 16,
January 31, 1981

RA: I am Ra. I greet you in the love and the light of the Infinite Creator. We communicate now.

QUESTIONER: I would like to ask, considering the free-will distortion of the Law of One, how can the Guardians quarantine the Earth? Is this quarantine within free will?

RA: I am Ra. The Guardians guard the free-will distortion of the mind/body/spirit complexes of third density on this planetary sphere. The events which required activation of quarantine were interfering with the free-will distortion of mind/body/spirit complexes.

QUESTIONER: I may be wrong, but it seems to me that it would be the free will of, say, the Orion group, to interfere. How is this balanced with the information which you just gave?

RA: I am Ra. The balancing is from dimension to dimension. The attempts of the so-called Crusaders to interfere with free will are acceptable upon the dimension of their understanding. However, the mind/body/spirit complexes of this dimension you call third form a dimension of free will which is not able to, shall we say, recognize in full the distortions towards manipulation. Thus, in order to balance the dimensional variances in vibration, a quarantine, this being a balancing situation whereby the free will of the Orion group is not stopped but given a challenge. Meanwhile, the third group is not hindered from free choice.

QUESTIONER: Could these "windows" that occur to let the Orion group come through once in a while have anything to do with this free-will balancing?

RA: I am Ra. This is correct.

QUESTIONER: Could you tell me how that works?

RA: I am Ra. The closest analogy would be a random number generator within certain limits.

QUESTIONER: What is the source of this random number generator? Is it created by the Guardians to balance their guarding? Or is it a source other than the Guardians?

RA: I am Ra. All sources are one. However, we understand your query. The window phenomenon is an other-self phenomenon from the Guardians. It operates from the dimensions beyond space/time in what you may call the area of intelligent energy. Like your cycles, such balancing, such rhythms are as a clock striking. In the case of the windows, no entities have the clock. Therefore, it seems random. It is not random in the dimension which produces this balance. That is why we stated the analogy was within certain limits.

QUESTIONER: Then this window balancing prevents the Guardians from reducing their positive polarization by totally eliminating the Orion contact through shielding. Is this correct?

RA: I am Ra. This is partially correct. In effect, the balancing allows an equal amount of positive and negative influx, this balanced by the mind/body/spirit distortions of the social complex. Thus in your particular planetary sphere, less negative, as you would call it, information or stimulus is necessary than positive due to the somewhat negative orientation of your social complex distortion.

QUESTIONER: In this way, total free will is balanced so that individuals may have an equal opportunity to choose service to others or service to self. Is this correct?

RA: I am Ra. This is correct.

QUESTIONER: This is a profound revelation, I believe, in the Law of Free Will. Thank you.

This is a minor question further to make an example of this principle, but if the Confederation landed on Earth, they would be taken as gods, breaking the Law of Free Will and thus reducing their polarization of service to all. I assume that the same thing would happen if the Orion group landed. How would this affect their polarization of service to self if they were able to land and became known as gods?

RA: I am Ra. In the event of mass landing of the Orion group, the effect of polarization would be strongly toward an increase in the service to self, precisely the opposite of the former opportunity which you mentioned.

QUESTIONER: If the Orion group was able to land, would this increase their polarization? What I am trying to get at is, is it better for them to work behind the scenes to get recruits, shall we say, from our planet, the person from our planet going strictly on his own, using free will, or is it just as good for the Orion group to land on our planet and demonstrate remarkable powers and get people like that?

RA: I am Ra. This first instance is, in the long run, shall we put it, more salubrious for the Orion group in that it does not infringe upon the Law of One by landing and, thus, does its work through those of this planet. In the second circumstance, a mass landing would create a loss of polarization due to the infringement upon the free will of the planet. However, it would be a gamble. If the planet then were conquered and became part of the Empire, the free will would then be reestablished. This is restrained in action due to the desire of the Orion group to progress towards the One Creator. This desire to progress inhibits the group from breaking the Law of Confusion.

QUESTIONER: You mentioned the word "Empire" in relation to the Orion group. I have thought for some time that the movie *Star Wars* was somehow an allegory for what is actually happening. Is this correct?

RA: I am Ra. This is correct in the same way that a simple children's story is an allegory for physical/philosophical/social complex distortion/understanding.

QUESTIONER: Is there a harvest of entities oriented toward service to self like there is a harvest of those oriented toward service to others?

RA: I am Ra. There is one harvest. Those able to enter fourth density through vibrational complex levels may choose the manner of their further seeking of the One Creator.

QUESTIONER: Then as we enter the fourth density there will be a split, shall we say, and part of the individuals who go into the fourth density will go into planets or places where there is service to others, and part will go into places where there is service to self. Is this correct?

RA: I am Ra. This is correct.

QUESTIONER: Can you tell me the origin of the Ten Commandments?

RA: I am Ra. The origin of these commandments follows the law of negative entities impressing information upon positively oriented mind/ body/spirit complexes. The information attempted to copy or ape positivity while retaining negative characteristics.

QUESTIONER: Was this done by the Orion group?

RA: I am Ra. This is correct.

QUESTIONER: What was their purpose in doing this?

RA: I am Ra. The purpose of the Orion group, as mentioned before, is conquest and enslavement. This is done by finding and establishing an elite and causing others to serve the elite through various devices such as the laws you mentioned and others given by this entity.

QUESTIONER: Was the recipient of the commandments positively or negatively oriented?

RA: I am Ra. The recipient was one of extreme positivity, thus accounting for some of the pseudo-positive characteristics of the information received. As with contacts which are not successful, this entity, vibratory complex, Moishe, did not remain a credible influence among those who had first heard the philosophy of One, and this entity was removed from this third-density vibratory level in a lessened or saddened state, having lost, what you may call, the honor and faith with which he had begun the conceptualization of the Law of One and the freeing of those who were of his tribes, as they were called at that time/space.

QUESTIONER: If this entity was positively oriented, how was the Orion group able to contact him?

RA: I am Ra. This was an intensive, shall we say, battleground between positively oriented forces of Confederation origin and negatively oriented sources. The one called Moishe was open to impression and received the Law of One in its most simple form. However, the information became negatively oriented due to his people's pressure to do specific physical things in the third-density planes. This left the entity open for the type of information and philosophy of a self-service nature.

QUESTIONER: It would be wholly unlike an entity fully aware of the knowledge of the Law of One to ever say "Thou shalt not." Is this correct?

RA: I am Ra. This is correct.

QUESTIONER: Can you give me some kind of history of your social memory complex and how you became aware of the Law of One?

RA: I am Ra. The path of our learning is graven in the present moment. There is no history, as we understand your concept. Picture, if you will, a circle of being. We know the alpha and omega as infinite intelligence. The circle never ceases. It is present. The densities we have traversed at various points in the circle correspond to the characteristics of cycles: first, the cycle of awareness; second, the cycle of growth; third, the cycle of self-awareness; fourth, the cycle of love or understanding; fifth, the cycle of light or wisdom; sixth, the cycle of light/love, love/light, or unity; seventh, the gateway cycle; eighth, the octave which moves into a mystery we do not plumb.

QUESTIONER: Thank you very much. In previous material, before we communicated with you, it was stated by the Confederation that there is actually no past or future . . . that all is present. Would this be a good analogy?

RA: I am Ra. There is past, present, and future in third density. In an overview such as an entity may have, removed from the space/time continuum, it may be seen that in the cycle of completion there exists only the present. We, ourselves, seek to learn this understanding. At the seventh level or dimension, we shall, if our humble efforts are sufficient, become one with all, thus having no memory, no identity, no past or future, but existing in the all.

QUESTIONER: Does this mean that you would have awareness of all that is?

RA: I am Ra. This is partially correct. It is our understanding that it would not be our awareness, but simply awareness of the Creator. In the Creator is all that there is. Therefore, this knowledge would be available.

QUESTIONER: I was wondering how many inhabited planets there are in our galaxy, and if they all reach higher density by the Law of One? It doesn't seem that there would be any other way to reach higher density? Is this correct?

RA: I am Ra. Please restate your query.

QUESTIONER: How many inhabited planets are there in our galaxy?

RA: I am Ra. We are assuming that you intend all dimensions of consciousness or densities of awareness in this question. Approximately one-fifth of all planetary entities contain awareness of one or more densities. Some planets are hospitable only for certain densities. Your planet, for instance, is at this time hospitable for densities one, two, three, and four.

QUESTIONER: Roughly how many total planets in this galaxy of stars that we are in are aware regardless of density?

RA: I am Ra. Approximately sixty-seven million.

QUESTIONER: Can you tell me what percentage of those are third, fourth, fifth, sixth, etc. density?

RA: I am Ra. A percentage seventeen for first density, a percentage twenty for second density, a percentage twenty-seven for third density, a percentage sixteen for fourth density, a percentage six for fifth density. The other information must be withheld.

QUESTIONER: Of these first five densities, have all of the planets progressed from the third density by knowledge and application of the Law of One?

RA: I am Ra. This is correct.

QUESTIONER: Then the only way for a planet to get out of the situation that we are in is for the population to become aware of and start practicing the Law of One. Is this correct?

RA: I am Ra. This is correct.

QUESTIONER: Can you tell me what percentage of the third-, fourth-, and fifth-density planets which you have spoken of here are polarized negatively towards service to self?

RA: I am Ra. This is not a query to which we may speak, given the Law of Confusion.
    We may say only that the negatively or self-service-oriented

planetary spheres are much fewer. To give you exact numbers would not be appropriate.

QUESTIONER: I would like to make an analogy as to why there are fewer negatively oriented, and then ask you if the analogy is good. In a positively oriented society with service to others, it would be simple to move a large boulder by getting everyone to help move it. In a society oriented towards service to self, it would be much more difficult to get everyone to work for the good of all to move the boulder; therefore, it is much easier to get things done to create the service to others principle and to grow in positively oriented communities than in negatively oriented communities. Is this correct?

RA: I am Ra. This is correct.

QUESTIONER: Thank you very much.
Can you tell me how the Confederation of Planets was formed and why?

RA: I am Ra. The desire to serve begins, in the dimension of love or understanding, to be an overwhelming goal of the social memory complex. Thus, those percentiles of planetary entities, plus approximately 4 percent more of whose identity we cannot speak, found themselves long, long ago in your time seeking the same thing: service to others. The relationship between these entities as they entered an understanding of other beings, other planetary entities, and other concepts of service was to share and continue together these commonly held goals of service. Thus, each voluntarily placed the social memory complex data in what you may consider a central thought complex available to all. This then created a structure whereby each entity could work in its own service while calling upon any other understanding needed to enhance the service. This is the cause of the formation and the manner of the working of the Confederation.

QUESTIONER: With such a large number of planets in this galaxy, you say that there are approximately five hundred planets in the Confederation. There seems to be a relatively small number of Confederation planets around. Is there a reason for it?

RA: I am Ra. There are many Confederations. This Confederation works with the planetary spheres of seven of your galaxies, if you will, and is responsible for the callings of the densities of these galaxies.

QUESTIONER: Would you define the word "galaxy" as you just used it?

RA: I am Ra. We use that term in this sense as you would use star systems.

QUESTIONER: I'm a little bit confused as to how many total planets the Confederation that you are in serves?

RA: I am Ra. I see the confusion. We have difficulty with your language.

The galaxy term must be split. We call galaxy that vibrational complex that is local. Thus, your sun is what we would call the center of a galaxy. We see you have another meaning for this term.

QUESTIONER: Yes. In our science the term "galaxy" refers to the lenticular star system that contains millions and millions of stars. There was a confusion about this in one of our earlier communications, and I'm glad to get it cleared up.

Using the term "galaxy" in the sense that I just stated, using the lenticular star system that contains millions of stars, do you know of evolution in other galaxies besides this one?

RA: I am Ra. We are aware of life in infinite capacity. You are correct in this assumption.

QUESTIONER: Can you tell me if the progression of life in other galaxies is similar to the progression of life in our galaxy?

RA: I am Ra. The progression is somewhat close to the same, asymptotically approaching congruency throughout infinity. The free choosing of what you would call galactic systems causes variations of an extremely minor nature from one of your galaxies to another.

QUESTIONER: Then the Law of One is truly universal in creating a progression towards the eighth density in all galaxies. Is this correct?

RA: I am Ra. This is correct. There are infinite forms, infinite understandings, but the progression is one.

QUESTIONER: I am assuming that it is not necessary for an individual to understand the Law of One to go from the third to the fourth density. Is this correct?

RA: I am Ra. It is absolutely necessary that an entity consciously realize it does not understand in order for it to be harvestable. Understanding is not of this density.

QUESTIONER: That is a very important point. I used the wrong word. What I meant to say was that I believed that it was not necessary for an entity to be consciously aware of the Law of One to go from the third to the fourth density.

RA: I am Ra. This is correct.

QUESTIONER: At what point in the densities is it necessary for an entity to be consciously aware of the Law of One in order to progress?

RA: I am Ra. The fifth-density harvest is of those whose vibratory distortions consciously accept the honor/duty of the Law of One. This responsibility/honor is the foundation of this vibration.

QUESTIONER: Can you tell me a little more about this honor/responsibility concept?

RA: I am Ra. Each responsibility is an honor; each honor, a responsibility.

QUESTIONER: Thank you. Is it possible for you to give a short description of the conditions in the fourth density?

RA: I am Ra. We ask you to consider as we speak that there are not words for positively describing fourth density. We can only explain what is not and approximate what is. Beyond fourth density our ability grows more limited until we become without words.

That which fourth density is not: it is not of words, unless chosen. It is not of heavy chemical vehicles for body complex activities. It is not of disharmony within self. It is not of disharmony within peoples. It is not within limits of possibility to cause disharmony in any way.

Approximations of positive statements: it is a plane of type of bipedal vehicle which is much denser and more full of life; it is a plane wherein one is aware of the thought of other-selves; it is a plane wherein one is aware of vibrations of other-selves; it is a plane of compassion and understanding of the sorrows of third density; it is a plane striving towards wisdom or light; it is a plane wherein individual differences are pronounced although automatically harmonized by group consensus.

QUESTIONER: Could you define the word "density" as we have been using it?

RA: I am Ra. The term "density" is a, what you call, mathematical one. The closest analogy is that of music, whereby after seven notes on your Western type of scale, if you will, the eighth note begins a new octave. Within your great octave of existence, which we share with you, there are seven octaves or densities. Within each density there are seven sub-densities. Within each sub-density, are seven sub-sub-densities. Within each sub-sub-density, seven sub-sub-sub-densities, and so on infinitely.

QUESTIONER: I noticed that the time of this session has gone slightly over an hour. I would like to ask at this time if we should go on? What is the condition of the instrument?

RA: I am Ra. This instrument is in balance. It is well to continue if you desire.

QUESTIONER: I understand that each density has seven sub-densities which again have seven sub-densities and so on. This is expanding at a really large rate as each is increased by powers of seven. Does this mean that in any density level, anything that you can think of is happening?

RA: I am Ra. From your confusion we select the concept with which you struggle, that being infinity/opportunity. You may consider any possibility/probability complex as having an existence.

QUESTIONER: Do things like daydreams become real in other densities?

RA: I am Ra. This depends upon the nature of the daydream. This is a large subject. Perhaps the simplest thing we can say is if the daydream, as you call it, is one which attracts to self, this then becomes reality to self. If it is a contemplative general daydream, this may enter the infinity of possibility/probability complexes and occur elsewhere, having no particular attachment to the energy fields of the creator.

QUESTIONER: To make this a little more clear, if I were to daydream strongly about building a ship, would this occur in one of these other densities?

RA: I am Ra. This would/would have/or shall occur.

QUESTIONER: Then if an entity daydreams strongly about battling an entity, would this occur?

RA: I am Ra. In this case the entity's fantasy concerns the self and other-self, this binding the thought-form to the possibility/probability complex connected with the self which is the creator of this thought-form. This then would increase the possibility/probability of bringing this into third-density occurrence.

QUESTIONER: Does the Orion group use this principle to create conditions favorable to suit their purpose?

RA: I am Ra. We will answer more specifically than the question. The Orion group uses daydreams of hostile or other negative natures to feed back or strengthen these thought-forms.

QUESTIONER: Are the many Wanderers who have and are coming to our planet subject to the Orion thoughts?

RA: I am Ra. As we have said before, Wanderers become completely the creature of third density in mind/body complex. There is just as much chance of such influence to a Wanderer entity as to a mind/body/spirit complex of this planetary sphere. The only difference occurs in the spirit complex, which, if it wishes, has an armor of light, if you will, which enables it to recognize more clearly that which is not as it would appropriately be desired by the mind/body/spirit complex. This is not more than bias and cannot be called an understanding.

Furthermore, the Wanderer is, in its own mind/body/spirit, less distorted toward the, shall we say, deviousness of third-density positive/negative confusions. Thus, it often does not recognize as easily as a more negative individual the negative nature of thoughts or beings.

QUESTIONER: Then would the Wanderers, as they incarnate here, be high-priority targets of the Orion group?

RA: I am Ra. This is correct.

QUESTIONER: If a Wanderer should be successfully infringed upon, shall I say, by the Orion group, what would happen to this Wanderer when harvest came?

RA: I am Ra. If the Wanderer entity demonstrated through action a negative orientation towards other-selves it would be as we have said before, caught into the planetary vibration and, when harvested, possibly repeat again the master cycle of third density as a planetary entity. This shall be the last full question of this session.

Is there a short question we may answer before we close this session?

QUESTIONER: Can the instrument be made more comfortable?

RA: I am Ra. This instrument is as comfortable as it is possible for you to make it given the weakness distortions of its body complex. You are conscientious.

I am Ra. I leave you in the love and the light of the One Infinite Creator. Go forth, then, rejoicing in the power and the peace. Adonai.

Session 17,
February 3, 1981

RA: I am Ra. I greet you in the love and in the light of the Infinite Creator.

Before we communicate by answer, we shall correct an error which we have discovered in the transmission of our information to you. We have difficulty dealing with your time/space. There may again be errors of this type. Feel free to question us that we may recalculate in your time/space measurements.

The error we have discovered concerns one of the arrivals of both the Orion group into your planetary sphere of influence and the corresponding arrival of emissaries of the Confederation. We gave dates of 2,600 years for the Orion entry, 2,300 for Confederation entry. This is incorrect. The recalculation indicates numbers 3,600 for Orion entry, 3,300 for Confederation entry.

We communicate now.

QUESTIONER: Thank you very much. I would like to say again that we consider it a great honor, privilege, and duty to be able to do this particular work. I would like to reiterate that some of my questions may seem irrelevant at times, but I am trying to ask them in a manner so as to gain a foothold into the application of the Law of One.

We are now in the fourth density. Will the effects of the fourth density increase in the next thirty years? Will we see more changes in our environment and our effect upon our environment?

RA: I am Ra. The fourth density is a vibrational spectrum. Your time/

163

space continuum has spiraled your planetary sphere and your, what we would call galaxy, what you call star, into this vibration. This will cause the planetary sphere itself to electromagnetically realign its vortices of reception of the instreaming of cosmic forces expressing themselves as vibrational webs so that the Earth thus be fourth-density magnetized, as you may call it.

This is going to occur with some inconvenience, as we have said before, due to the energies of the thought-forms of your peoples which disturb the orderly constructs of energy patterns within your Earth spirals of energy, which increases entropy and unusable heat. This will cause your planetary sphere to have some ruptures in its outer garment while making itself appropriately magnetized for fourth density. This is the planetary adjustment.

You will find a sharp increase in the number of people, as you call mind/body/spirit complexes, whose vibrational potentials include the potential for fourth-vibrational distortions. Thus, there will seem to be, shall we say, a new breed. These are those incarnating for fourth-density work.

There will also be a sharp increase in the short run of negatively oriented or polarized mind/body/spirit complexes and social complexes, due to the polarizing conditions of the sharp delineation between fourth-density characteristics and third-density self-service orientation.

Those who remain in fourth density upon this plane will be of the so-called positive orientation. Many will come from elsewhere, for it would appear that with all the best efforts of the Confederation, which includes those from your people's inner planes, inner civilizations, and those from other dimensions, the harvest will still be much less than this planetary sphere is capable of comfortably supporting in service.

QUESTIONER: Is it possible by the use of some technique or other to help an entity to reach fourth-density level in these last days?

RA: I am Ra. It is impossible to help another being directly. It is only possible to make catalyst available in whatever form, the most important being the radiation of realization of oneness with the Creator from the self, less important being information such as we share with you.

We, ourselves, do not feel an urgency for this information to be widely disseminated. It is enough that we have made it available to three, four, or five. This is extremely ample reward, for if one of these obtains fourth-density understanding due to this catalyst, then we shall have fulfilled the Law of One in the distortion of service.

We encourage a dispassionate attempt to share information without concern for numbers or quick growth among others. That you attempt to make this information available is, in your terms, your service. The attempt, if it reaches one, reaches all.

We cannot offer shortcuts to enlightenment. Enlightenment is, of the moment, an opening to intelligent infinity. It can only be accomplished by the self, for the self. Another self cannot teach/learn enlightenment, but only teach/learn information, inspiration, or a sharing of love, of mystery, of the unknown that makes the other-self reach out and begin the seeking process that ends in a moment, but who can know when an entity will open the gate to the present?

QUESTIONER: Thank you. Can you tell me who was the entity, before his incarnation on Earth, known as Jesus of Nazareth?

RA: I am Ra. I have difficulty with this question as it is phrased. Can you discover another form for this query?

QUESTIONER: What I meant to say was can you tell me if Jesus of Nazareth came from the Confederation before incarnation here?

RA: I am Ra. The one known to you as Jesus of Nazareth did not have a name. This entity was a member of fifth density of the highest level of that sub-octave. This entity was desirous of entering this planetary sphere in order to share the love vibration in as pure a manner as possible. Thus, this entity received permission to perform this mission. This entity was then a Wanderer of no name, of Confederation origins, of fifth density, representing the fifth-density understanding of the vibration of understanding or love.

QUESTIONER: Did you say the fifth vibration was that of love?

RA: I am Ra. I have made an error. The fourth-density being is that which we intended to say, the highest level of fourth density going into the fifth. This entity could have gone on to the fifth but chose instead to return to third for this particular mission. This entity was of the highest sub-octave of the vibration of love. This is fourth density.

QUESTIONER: When I am communicating with you as Ra, are you at times individualized as an entity or am I speaking to an entire social memory complex?

RA: I am Ra. You speak with Ra. There is no separation. You would call it social memory complex, thus indicating manyness. To our understanding, you are speaking to an individualized portion of consciousness.

QUESTIONER: Am I always speaking to the same individualized portion of consciousness in each of the sessions?

RA: I am Ra. You speak to the same entity through a channel or instrument. This instrument is at times lower in vital energy. This will sometimes hamper our proceedings. However, this instrument has a great deal of faithfulness to the task and gives whatever it has to this task. Therefore, we may continue even when energy is low. This is why we usually speak to the ending of the session due to our estimation of the instrument's levels of vital energy.

QUESTIONER: I would like to make a point clear now that I am sure of myself. The people of this planet, following any religion or no religion at all, or having no intellectual knowledge at all of the Law of One, can still be harvested into the fourth density if they are of that vibration. Is that not correct?

RA: I am Ra. This is correct. However, you will find few who are harvestable whose radiance does not cause others to be aware of their, what you may call, spirituality, the quality of the mind/body/spirit complex distortion. Thus, it is not particularly probable that an entity would be completely unknown to his immediate acquaintances as an unusually radiant personality, even were this individual not caught up in any of the distortions of your so-called religious systems.

QUESTIONER: When Jesus of Nazareth incarnated, was there an attempt by the Orion group to discredit him in some way?

RA: I am Ra. This is correct.

QUESTIONER: Can you tell me what the Orion group did in order to try to cause his downfall?

RA: I am Ra. We may describe in general what occurred. The technique was that of building upon other negatively oriented information. This information had been given by the one whom your peoples called "Yahweh." This information involved many strictures upon behavior and promised power of the third-density, service to self nature. These two types of distortions were impressed upon those already oriented to think these thought-forms.

This eventually led to many challenges of the entity known as Jesus. It eventually led to one, sound vibration complex "Judas," as you call this entity, who believed that it was doing the appropriate thing in bringing about or forcing upon the one you call Jesus the necessity for bringing in the third-density planetary power distortion of third-density rule over others.

This entity, Judas, felt that if pushed into a corner, the entity you call Jesus would then be able to see the wisdom of using the power of intelligent infinity in order to rule others. The one you call Judas was mistaken in this estimation of the reaction of the entity Jesus, whose teach/learning was not oriented towards this distortion. This resulted in the destruction of the bodily complex of the one known as Jesus.

QUESTIONER: Then if the entity Jesus was fourth density and there are Wanderers on the planet today who came from fifth and sixth density, what was it that Jesus did that enabled him to be such a good healer, and could these fifth- and sixth-density beings here now do the same?

RA: I am Ra. Those who heal may be of any density which has the consciousness of the spirit. This includes third, fourth, fifth, sixth, and seventh. The third density can be one in which healing takes place just as the others. However, there is more illusory material to understand, to balance, to accept, and to move forward from.

The gate to intelligent infinity can only be opened when an understanding of the instreamings of intelligent energy are opened unto the healer. These are the so-called Natural Laws of your local space/time continuum and its web of electromagnetic sources or nexi of instreaming energy.

Know then, first, the mind and the body. Then as the spirit is integrated and synthesized, these are harmonized into a mind/body/spirit complex which can move among the dimensions and can open the gateway to intelligent infinity, thus healing self by light and sharing that light with others.

True healing is simply the radiance of the self causing an environment in which a catalyst may occur which initiates the recognition of self, by self, of the self-healing properties of the self.

QUESTIONER: How did Jesus learn this during his incarnation?

RA: I am Ra. This entity learned the ability by a natural kind of remembering at a very young age. Unfortunately, this entity first discovered his ability to penetrate intelligent infinity by becoming the distortion you call "angry" at a playmate. This entity was touched by the entity known as Jesus and was fatally wounded.

Thus the one known as Jesus became aware that there dwelt in him a terrible potential. This entity determined to discover how to use this energy for the good, not for the negative. This entity was extremely positively polarized and remembered more than most Wanderers do.

QUESTIONER: How did this aggressive action against a playmate affect Jesus in his spiritual growth? Where did he go after his physical death?

RA: I am Ra. The entity you call Jesus was galvanized by this experience and began a lifetime of seeking and searching. This entity studied first day and night in its own religious constructs which you call Judaism and was learned enough to be a rabbi, as you call teach/learners of this particular rhythm or distortion of understanding, at a very young age.

At the age of approximately thirteen and one-half of your years, this entity left the dwelling place of its earthly family, as you would call it, and walked into many other places seeking further information. This went on sporadically until the entity was approximately twenty-five, at which time it returned to its family dwelling and learned and practiced the art of its earthly father.

When the entity had become able to integrate or synthesize all experiences, the entity began to speak to other-selves and teach/learn what it had felt during the preceding years to be of an worthwhile nature. The entity was absolved karmically of the destruction of an other-self when it was in the last portion of lifetime and spoke upon what you would call a cross, saying, "Father, forgive them, for they know not what they do." In forgiveness lies the stoppage of the wheel of action, or what you call karma.

QUESTIONER: What density is the entity known as Jesus in now?

RA: I am Ra. This information is harmless though unimportant. This entity studies now the lessons of the wisdom vibration, the fifth density, also called the light vibration.

QUESTIONER: In our culture there is a saying that he will return. Can you tell me if this is planned?

RA: I am Ra. I will attempt to sort out this question. It is difficult.

This entity became aware that it was not an entity of itself but operated as a messenger of the One Creator, whom this entity saw as love. This entity was aware that this cycle was in its last portion, and spoke to the effect that those of its consciousness would return at the harvest.

The particular mind/body/spirit complex you call Jesus is, as what you would call an entity, not to return except as a member of the Confederation speaking through a channel. However, there are others of the identical congruency of consciousness that will welcome those to the fourth density. This is the meaning of the returning.

QUESTIONER: Can you tell me why you say that the Earth will be fourth density positive instead of fourth density negative, since there seems to be much negativity here now?

RA: I am Ra. The Earth seems to be negative. That is due to the quiet, shall we say, horror which is the common distortion which those good or positively oriented entities have towards the occurrences which are of your time/space present. However, those oriented and harvestable in the ways of service to others greatly outnumber those whose orientation towards service to self has become that of harvestable quality.

QUESTIONER: In other words, there will be fewer negative entities than positive entities harvested into the fourth density. Is this correct?

RA: I am Ra. This is correct. The great majority of your peoples will repeat third density.

QUESTIONER: How did Taras Bulba, Genghis Khan, and Rasputin get harvested prior to the harvest?

RA: I am Ra. It is the right/privilege/duty of those opening consciously the gate to intelligent infinity to choose the manner of their leaving of third density. Those of negative orientation who so achieve this right/duty most often choose to move forward in their learn/teaching of service to self.

QUESTIONER: Am I to understand that the harvest is to occur in the year 2011, or will it be spread out?

RA: I am Ra. This is an approximation. We have stated we have difficulty with your time/space. This is an appropriate probable/possible time/space nexus for harvest. Those who are not in incarnation at this time will be included in the harvest.

QUESTIONER: If an entity wants to be of service to others rather than service to self while he is in this third density, are there "best ways" of being of service to others, or is any way just as good as any other way?

RA: I am Ra. The best way to be of service to others has been explicitly covered in previous material. We will iterate briefly.

The best way of service to others is the constant attempt to seek to share the love of the Creator as it is known to the inner self. This involves self-knowledge and the ability to open the self to the other-self without hesitation. This involves, shall we say, radiating that which is the essence or the heart of the mind/body/spirit complex.

Speaking to the intention of your question, the best way for each seeker in third density to be of service to others is unique to that mind/body/spirit complex. This means that the mind/body/spirit complex must then seek within itself the intelligence of its own discernment as to the way it may best serve other-selves. This will be different for each. There is no best. There is no generalization. Nothing is known.

QUESTIONER: I don't wish to take up extra time asking questions over again. Some areas I consider important enough in relation to the Law of One to ask questions in a different way in order to get another perspective in the answer.

In the book *Oahspe* it states that if an entity goes over 51 percent service to others and is less than 50 percent service to self, then that entity is harvestable. Is this correct?

RA: I am Ra. This is correct if the harvesting is to be for the positive fourth-dimensional level.

QUESTIONER: What is to be the entity's percentage if he is to be harvested for the negative?

RA: I am Ra. The entity who wishes to pursue the path of service to self must attain a grade of five; that is, 5 percent service to others, 95 percent service to self. It must approach totality. The negative path is quite difficult to attain harvestability upon and requires great dedication.

QUESTIONER: Why is the negative path so much more difficult to attain harvestability upon than the positive?

RA: I am Ra. This is due to a distortion of the Law of One which indicates that the gateway to intelligent infinity be a gateway at the end of a straight and narrow path, as you may call it. To attain 51 percent dedication to the welfare of other-selves is as difficult as attaining a grade of 5 percent dedication to other-selves. The, shall we say, sinkhole of indifference is between those two.

QUESTIONER: Then if an entity is harvested into the fourth density with a grade of 51 percent for others and 49 percent for self, what level of the fourth density would he go into? I am assuming that there are different levels of the fourth density.

RA: I am Ra. This is correct. Each enters that sub-density which vibrates in accordance with the entity's understanding.

QUESTIONER: How many levels do we have here in the third density at this time?

RA: I am Ra. The third density has an infinite number of levels.

QUESTIONER: I've heard that there are seven astral and seven devachanic levels. Is this correct?

RA: I am Ra. You speak of some of the more large distinctions in levels in your inner planes. That is correct.

QUESTIONER: Who inhabits the astral and devachanic planes?

RA: I am Ra. Entities inhabit the various planes due to their vibration/nature. The astral plane varies from thought-forms in the lower extremities to enlightened beings who become dedicated to teach/learning in the higher astral planes.

In the devachanic planes, as you call them, are those whose vibrations are even more close to the primal distortions of love/light.

Beyond these planes there are others.

QUESTIONER: Are there seven sub-planes to what we call our physical plane here?

RA: I am Ra. You are correct. This is difficult to understand. There are an infinite number of planes. In your particular space/time continuum distortion, there are seven sub-planes of mind/body/spirit complexes. You will discover the vibrational nature of these seven planes as you pass through your experiential distortions, meeting other-selves of the various levels which correspond to the energy influx centers of the physical vehicle.

The invisible, or inner, third-density planes are inhabited by those who are not of body complex natures such as yours; that is, they do not collect about their spirit/mind complexes a chemical body. Nevertheless these entities are divided in what you may call an artificial dream within a dream into various levels. In the upper levels, desire to communicate knowledge back down to the outer planes of existence becomes less, due to the intensive learn/teaching which occurs upon these levels.

QUESTIONER: Is it necessary to penetrate one level at a time as we move through these planes?

RA: I am Ra. It has been our experience that some penetrate several planes at one time. Others penetrate them slowly. Some in eagerness attempt to penetrate the higher planes before penetrating the energies of the so-called more fundamental planes. This causes energy imbalance.

You will find ill health, as you call this distortion, to frequently be the result of a subtle mismatch of energies in which some of the higher energy levels are being activated by the conscious attempts of the entity while the entity has not penetrated the lower energy centers or sub-densities of this density.

QUESTIONER: Is there a "best way" to meditate?

RA: I am Ra. No.

QUESTIONER: At this time, near the end of the cycle, how are reincarnations into the physical allocated, shall we say, on this planet?

RA: I am Ra. Entities wishing to obtain critically needed experience in order to become harvestable are incarnated with priority over those who will, without too much probable/possible doubt, need to re-experience this density.

QUESTIONER: How long has this type of allocation been going on?

RA: I am Ra. This has been going on since the first individual entity became conscious of its need to learn the lessons of this density. This was the beginning of what you may call a seniority by vibration.

QUESTIONER: Can you explain what you mean by a seniority by vibration?

RA: I am Ra. This will be the final question of this session of working.

The seniority by vibration is the preferential treatment, shall we say, which follows the ways of the Law of One which encourages harvestable individuals, each individual becoming aware of the time of harvest and the need on a self-level to bend mind/body/spirit towards the learn/teaching of these lessons, by giving them priority in order that an entity may have the best possible chance, shall we say, in succeeding in this attempt.

May we ask at this time if there are any brief questions?

QUESTIONER: My only question is, what can we do to make the instrument more comfortable?

RA: I am Ra. This instrument is not wearing the appropriate apparel for this work. As inpourings occur in the regions of the, what you may call, seventh chakra as you speak of these energy centers, filtering through the sixth and so forth, the entity's other or base chakras become somewhat de-energized. Thus, this entity should be more careful in its selection of warm apparel for the part of the body complex you call the feet.

May we answer any other brief questions?

QUESTIONER: Then we want to put heavier clothing on the feet. Is this correct?

RA: I am Ra. This is correct.

I will leave this instrument now. I leave you in the love and the light of the One Infinite Creator. Adonai.

Session 18,
February 4, 1981

RA: I am Ra. I greet you in the love and the light of the Infinite Creator. We communicate now.

QUESTIONER: I was thinking last night that if I were in the place of Ra right now, the first distortion of the Law of One might cause me to mix some erroneous data with the true information that I was transmitting to this group. Do you do this?

RA: I am Ra. We do not intentionally do this. However, there will be confusion. It is not our intent in this particular project to create erroneous information, but to express in this confining ambiance of your language system the feeling of the Infinite Mystery of the One Creation in its infinite and intelligent unity.

QUESTIONER: Thank you. I have a question here that I will read: "Much of the mystic tradition of seeking on Earth holds the belief that the individual self must be erased or obliterated and the material world ignored for the individual to reach 'nirvana,' as it is called, or enlightenment. What is the proper role of the individual self and its worldly activities to aid an individual to grow more into the Law of One?"

RA: I am Ra. The proper role of the entity is in this density to experience all things desired, to then analyze, understand, and accept these experiences, distilling from them the love/light within them. Nothing shall be overcome. That which is not needed falls away.

The orientation develops due to analysis of desire. These desires become more and more distorted towards conscious application of love/light as the entity furnishes itself with distilled experience. We have found it to be inappropriate in the extreme to encourage the overcoming of any desires, except to suggest the imagination rather than the carrying out in the physical plane, as you call it, of those desires not consonant with the Law of One, thus preserving the primal distortion of free will.

The reason it is unwise to overcome is that overcoming is an unbalanced action creating difficulties in balancing in the time/space continuum. Overcoming thus creates the further environment for holding on to that which apparently has been overcome.

All things are acceptable in the proper time for each entity, and in experiencing, in understanding, in accepting, in then sharing with other-selves, the appropriate distortion shall be moving away from distortions of one kind to distortions of another which may be more consonant with the Law of One.

It is, shall we say, a shortcut to simply ignore or overcome any desire. It must instead be understood and accepted. This takes patience and experience which can be analyzed with care, with compassion for self and for other-self.

QUESTIONER: Basically I would say that to infringe upon the free will of another entity would be the basic thing never to do under the Law of One. Can you state any other breaking of the Law of One than this basic rule?

RA: I am Ra. As one proceeds from the primal distortion of free will, one proceeds to the understanding of the focal points of intelligent energy which have created the intelligences or the ways of a particular mind/body/spirit complex in its environment, both what you would call natural and what you would call man-made. Thus, the distortions to be avoided are those which do not take into consideration the distortions of the focus of energy of love/light, or shall we say, the Logos of this particular sphere or density. These include the lack of understanding of the needs of the natural environment, the needs of other-selves' mind/body/spirit complexes. These are many due to the various distortions of man-made complexes in which the intelligence and awareness of entities themselves have chosen a way of using the energies available.

Thus, what would be an improper distortion with one entity is proper with another. We can suggest an attempt to become aware of the other-self as self and thus do that action which is needed by other-self, understanding from the other-self's intelligence and awareness. In many cases this does not involve the breaking of the distortion of free will into a distortion or fragmentation called infringement. However, it is a delicate matter to be of service, and compassion, sensitivity, and an ability to empathize are helpful in avoiding the distortions of man-made intelligence and awareness.

The area or arena called the societal complex is an arena in which there are no particular needs for care, for it is the prerogative/honor/duty of those in the particular planetary sphere to act according to their free will for the attempted aid of the social complex.

Thus, you have two simple directives: awareness of the intelligent energy expressed in nature, awareness of the intelligent energy expressed in self to be shared when it seems appropriate by the entity with the social complex, and you have one infinitely subtle and various set of distortions of which you may be aware; that is, distortions with respect to self and other-selves not concerning free will but concerning harmonious relationships and service to others as other-selves would most benefit.

QUESTIONER: As an entity in this density grows from childhood, he becomes more aware of his responsibilities. Is there an age below which an entity is not responsible for his actions, or is he responsible from the time of his birth?

RA: I am Ra. An entity incarnating upon the Earth plane becomes conscious of self at a varying point in its time/space progress through the continuum. This may have a median, shall we say, of approximately fifteen of your months. Some entities become conscious of self at a period closer to incarnation, some at a period farther from this event. In all cases responsibility becomes retroactive from that point backward in the continuum so that distortions are to be understood by the entity and dissolved as the entity learns.

QUESTIONER: Then an entity four years old would be totally responsible for any actions that were against or inharmonious with the Law of One. Is this correct?

RA: I am Ra. This is correct. It may be noted that it has been arranged by your social complex structures that the newer entities to incarnation are to be provided with guides of a physical mind/body/spirit complex, thus being able to learn quickly what is consonant with the Law of One.

QUESTIONER: Who are these guides?

RA: I am Ra. These guides are what you call parents, teachers, and friends.

QUESTIONER: You stated yesterday that forgiveness is the eradicator of karma. I am assuming that balanced forgiveness for the full eradication of karma would require forgiveness not only of other-selves but also the forgiveness of self. Am I correct?

RA: I am Ra. You are correct. We will briefly expand upon this understanding in order to clarify.

Forgiveness of other-self is forgiveness of self. An understanding of this insists upon full forgiveness upon the conscious level of self and other-self, for they are one. A full forgiveness is thus impossible without the inclusion of self.

QUESTIONER: Thank you—a most important point.

You mentioned that there were a number of Confederations. Do all serve the Infinite Creator in basically the same way, or do some specialize in some particular types of service?

RA: I am Ra. All serve the One Creator. There is nothing else to serve, for the Creator is all that there is. It is impossible not to serve the Creator. There are simply various distortions of this service.

As in the Confederation which works with your peoples, each Confederation is a group of specialized individual social memory complexes, each doing that which it expresses to bring into manifestation.

QUESTIONER: Can you tell me how Yahweh communicated to Earth's people?

RA: I am Ra. This is a somewhat complex question.

The first communication was what you would call genetic. The second communication was the walking among your peoples to produce further genetic changes in consciousness. The third was a series of dialogues with chosen channels.

QUESTIONER: Can you tell me what these genetic changes were and how they were brought about?

RA: I am Ra. Some of these genetic changes were in a form similar to what you call the cloning process. Thus, entities incarnated in the image of the Yahweh entities. The second was a contact of the nature you know as sexual, changing the mind/body/spirit complex through the natural means of the patterns of reproduction devised by the intelligent energy of your physical complex.

QUESTIONER: Can you tell me specifically what they did in this case?

RA: I am Ra. We have answered this question. Please restate for further information.

QUESTIONER: Can you tell me the difference between the sexual programming prior to Yahweh's intervention and after intervention?

RA: I am Ra. This is a question which we can only answer by stating that intervention by genetic means is the same no matter what the source of this change.

QUESTIONER: Can you tell me Yahweh's purpose in making the genetic sexual changes?

RA: I am Ra. The purpose 75,000 years ago, as you measure time, was of one purpose only: that to express in the mind/body complex those characteristics which would lead to further and more speedy development of the spiritual complex.

QUESTIONER: How did these characteristics go about leading to the more spiritual development?

RA: I am Ra. The characteristics which were encouraged included sensitivity of all the physical senses to sharpen the experiences, and the strengthening of the mind complex in order to promote the ability to analyze these experiences.

QUESTIONER: When did Yahweh act to perform the genetic changes?

RA: I am Ra. The Yahweh group worked with those of the planet you call Mars 75,000 years ago in what you would call the cloning process. There are differences, but they lie in the future of your time/space continuum, and we cannot break the free-will Law of Confusion.

The 2,600, approximately, time was the second time—we correct ourselves: 3,600—approximately, the time of attempts by those of the Orion group during this cultural complex; this was a series of encounters in which the ones called Anak were impregnated with the new genetic coding by your physical complex means so that the organisms would be larger and stronger.

QUESTIONER: Why did they want larger and stronger organisms?

RA: I am Ra. The ones of Yahweh were attempting to create an understanding of the Law of One by creating mind/body complexes capable of grasping the Law of One. The experiment was a decided failure from the view of the desired distortions due to the fact that rather than assimilating the Law of One, it was a great temptation to consider the so-called social complex or subcomplex elite or different and better than other-selves, this one of the techniques of service to self.

QUESTIONER: Then the Orion group produced this larger body complex to create an elite so that the Law of One could be applied in what we call the negative sense?

RA: I am Ra. This is incorrect. The entities of Yahweh were responsible for this procedure in isolated cases as experiments in combating the Orion group.

However, the Orion group were able to use this distortion of mind/body complex to inculcate the thoughts of the elite rather than concentrations upon the learning/teaching of oneness.

QUESTIONER: Was Yahweh then of the Confederation?

RA: I am Ra. Yahweh was of the Confederation but was mistaken in its attempts to aid.

QUESTIONER: Then Yahweh's communications did not help or create what Yahweh wished for them to create. Is this correct?

RA: I am Ra. The results of this interaction were quite mixed. Where the entities were of a vibrational sum characteristic which embraced oneness, the manipulations of Yahweh were very useful. Wherein the entities of free will had chosen a less positively oriented configuration of sum total vibratory complex, those of the Orion group were able for the first time to make serious inroads upon the consciousness of the planetary complex.

QUESTIONER: Can you tell me specifically what allowed the most serious of these inroads to be made by the Orion group?

RA: I am Ra. This will be the final full question.
Specifically those who are strong, intelligent, etc., have a temptation to feel different from those who are less intelligent and less strong. This is a distorted perception of oneness with other-selves. It allowed the Orion group to form the concept of the holy war, as you may call it. This is a seriously distorted perception. There were many of these wars of a destructive nature.

QUESTIONER: Thank you very much. As you probably know, I will be working for the next three days, so we will possibly have another session tonight if you think it is possible. The next session after that would not be until four days from now. Do you believe another session tonight is possible?

RA: I am Ra. This instrument is somewhat weak. This is a distortion caused by lack of vital energy. Thus, nurturing the instrument in physical balancing will allow another session. Do you understand?

QUESTIONER: Not completely. What specifically shall we do for physical balancing?

RA: I am Ra. One—take care with the foodstuffs. Two—manipulate the physical complex to alleviate the distortion toward pain. Three—encourage a certain amount of what you would call your exercise. The final injunction: to take special care with the alignments this second session so that the entity may gain as much aid as possible from the various symbols. We suggest you check these symbols most carefully. This entity is slightly misplaced from the proper configuration. Not important at this time. More important when a second session is to be scheduled.
I am Ra. I leave you in the love and the light of the One Infinite Creator. Go forth, therefore, rejoicing in the power and the peace of the One Creator. Adonai.

Session 19,
February 8, 1981

RA: I am Ra. I greet you in the love and the light of the Infinite Creator. We communicate now.

QUESTIONER: We are concerned in this communication with the evolution of mind, body, and spirit. It seems to me that a good place to start would be the transition from the second to the third density, then to investigate in detail the evolution of third-density entities of Earth, paying particular attention to the mechanisms which help or hinder that evolution.

Do all entities make a transition from second to third density, or are there some entities who have never gone through this transition?

RA: I am Ra. Your question presumes the space/time continuum understandings of the intelligent energy which animates your illusion. Within the context of this illusion, we may say that there are some that do not transfer from one particular density to another, for the continuum is finite.

In the understanding which we have of the universe or creation as one infinite being, its heart beating as alive in its own intelligent energy, it merely is one beat of the heart of this intelligence from creation to creation. In this context, each and every entity of consciousness has/is/will experienced/experiencing/experience each and every density.

QUESTIONER: Let's take the point at which an individualized entity of second density is ready for transition to third. Is this second-density being what we would call animal?

RA: I am Ra. There are three types of second-density entities which become, shall we say, enspirited. The first is the animal. This is the most predominant. The second is the vegetable, most especially that which you call, sound vibration complex, "tree." These entities are capable of giving and receiving enough love to become individualized. The third is mineral. Occasionally a certain location/place, as you may call it, becomes energized to individuality through the love it receives and gives in relationship to a third-density entity which is in relationship to it. This is the least common transition.

QUESTIONER: When this transition from second to third density takes place, how does the entity, whether it be animal, [vegetable] tree, or mineral, become enspirited?

RA: I am Ra. Entities do not become enspirited. They become aware of the intelligent energy within each portion, cell, or atom, as you may call it, of its beingness.

This awareness is that which is awareness of that already given. From the infinite come all densities. The self-awareness comes from within, given the catalyst of certain experiences understanding, as we may call this particular energy, the upward spiraling of the cell or atom or consciousness.

You may then see that there is an inevitable pull toward the, what you may call, eventual realization of self.

QUESTIONER: Then after the transition into the third density, am I correct in assuming—we'll take Earth as an example—the entities would then look like us? They would be in human form? Is this correct?

RA: I am Ra. This is correct, taking your planetary sphere as an example.

QUESTIONER: When the first second-density entities became third density on this planet, was this with the help of the transfer of beings from Mars, or were there second-density beings who transferred into third density with no outside influence?

RA: I am Ra. There were some second-density entities which made the graduation into third density with no outside stimulus, but only the efficient use of experience.

Others of your planetary second density joined the third-density cycle due to harvesting efforts by the same sort of sending of vibratory aid as those of the Confederation send you now. This communication was, however, telepathic rather than telepathic/vocal or telepathic/written due to the nature of second-density beings.

QUESTIONER: Who sent the aid to the second-density beings?

RA: I am Ra. We call ourselves the Confederation of Planets in the Service of the Infinite Creator. This is a simplification in order to ease the difficulty of understanding among your people. We hesitate to use the term, sound vibration "understanding," but it is closest to our meaning.

QUESTIONER: Then did this second-density to third-density transition take place 75,000 years ago? Approximately?

RA: I am Ra. This is correct.

QUESTIONER: Where did the second-density beings get physical vehicles of third-density type to incarnate into?

RA: I am Ra. There were among those upon this second-density plane those forms which when exposed to third-density vibrations became the third density, as you would call the sound vibration, human entities.

That is, there was loss of body hair, as you would call it; the clothing of the body to protect it; the changing of the structure of the neck, jaw, and forehead in order to allow the easier vocalization; and the larger cranial development characteristic of third-density needs. This was a normal transfiguration.

QUESTIONER: Over how long a period of time was this transfiguration? It must have been very short.

RA: I am Ra. The assumption is correct, in our terms at least—within a generation and one-half, as you know these things. Those who had been harvested of this planet were able to use the newly created physical complex of chemical elements suitable for third-density lessons.

QUESTIONER: Can you tell me how this newly created physical complex was suited to third-density lessons, and what those lessons were?

RA: I am Ra. There is one necessity for third density. That necessity is self-awareness, or self-consciousness. In order to be capable of such, this chemical complex of body must be capable of abstract thought. Thus, the fundamental necessity is the combination of rational and intuitive thinking. This was transitory in the second-density forms operating largely upon intuition, which proved through practice to yield results.

The third-density mind was capable of processing information in such a way as to think abstractly and in what could be termed "useless" ways, in the sense of survival. This is the primary requisite.

There are other important ingredients: the necessity for a weaker physical vehicle to encourage the use of the mind, the development of the already present awareness of the social complex. These also being necessary: the further development of physical dexterity in the sense of the hand, as you call this portion of your body complex.

QUESTIONER: This seems to be a carefully planned or engineered stage of development. Can you tell me anything of the origin of this plan or its development?

RA: I am Ra. We go back to previous information. Consider and remember the discussion of the Logos. With the primal distortion of free will, each galaxy developed its own Logos. This Logos has complete free will in determining the paths of intelligent energy which promote the lessons of each of the densities given the conditions of the planetary spheres and the sun bodies.

QUESTIONER: I will make a statement then of my understanding and ask you if I am correct. There is a, what I would call, physical catalyst operating at all times upon the entities in third density. I assume this operates approximately the same way in second density. It is a catalyst which acts through what we call pain and emotion. Is the primary reason for the weakening of the physical body and the elimination of body hair etc. so that this catalyst would act more strongly upon the mind and therefore create the evolutionary process?

RA: I am Ra. This is not entirely correct, although closely associated with the distortions of our understanding. Consider, if you will, the tree for instance. It is self-sufficient. Consider, if you will, the third-density entity. It is self-sufficient only through difficulty and deprivation. It is difficult to learn alone, for there is a built-in handicap, at once the great virtue and the great handicap of third density. That is the rational/intuitive mind.

Thus, the weakening of the physical vehicle, as you call it, was designed to distort entities towards a predisposition to deal with each other. Thus, the lessons which approach a knowing of love can be begun.

This catalyst then is shared between peoples as an important part of each self's development as well as the experiences of the self in solitude and the synthesis of all experience through meditation. The quickest way to learn is to deal with other-selves. This is a much greater catalyst than dealing with the self. Dealing with the self without other-selves is akin to living without what you would call mirrors. Thus, the self cannot see the fruits of its beingness. Thus, each may aid each by reflection. This is also a primary reason for the weakening of the physical vehicle, as you call the physical complex.

QUESTIONER: Then we have second-density beings who have primarily motivation towards self and possibly a little motivation towards service to others with respect to their immediate family going into third density and carrying this bias with them but being in a position now where this bias will slowly be modified to one which is aimed toward a social complex and ultimately towards union with the all. Am I correct?

RA: I am Ra. You are correct.

QUESTIONER: Then the newest third-density beings who have just made the transition from second are still strongly biased towards self-service. There must be many other mechanisms to create an awareness of the possibility of service to others.

I am wondering, first, about the mechanism, and I am wondering when the split takes place where the entity is able to continue on the road to service to self that will eventually take him on to fourth density.

I'm assuming that an entity can start, say, in second density with service to self and continue right on through and just stay on what we would call the path of service to self and never be pulled over. Is this correct?

RA: I am Ra. This is incorrect. The second-density concept of serving self includes the serving of those associated with tribe or pack. This is not seen in second density as separation of self and other-self. All is seen as self since in some forms of second-density entities, if the tribe or pack becomes weakened, so does the entity within the tribe or pack.

The new or initial third density has this innocent, shall we say, bias or distortion towards viewing those in the family, the society, as you would call, perhaps, country, as self. Thus, though a distortion not helpful for progress in third density, it is without polarity.

The break becomes apparent when the entity perceives other-selves as other-selves and consciously determines to manipulate other-selves for the benefit of the self. This is the beginning of the road of which you speak.

QUESTIONER: Then, through free will, sometime within the third-density experience, the path splits and the entity consciously chooses—or he probably doesn't consciously choose. Does the entity consciously choose this path of the initial splitting point?

RA: I am Ra. We speak in generalities, which is dangerous for always inaccurate. However, we realize you look for the overview, so we will eliminate anomalies and speak of majorities.

The majority of third-density beings is far along the chosen path before realization of that path is conscious.

QUESTIONER: Can you tell me what bias creates the momentum towards the chosen path of service to self?

RA: I am Ra. We can speak only in metaphor. Some love the light. Some love the darkness. It is a matter of the unique and infinitely various Creator choosing and playing among its experiences as a child upon a picnic. Some enjoy the picnic and find the sun beautiful, the food delicious, the games refreshing, and glow with the joy of creation. Some find the night delicious, their picnic being pain, difficulty, sufferings of others, and the examination of the perversities of nature. These enjoy a different picnic.

All these experiences are available. It is the free will of each entity which chooses the form of play, the form of pleasure.

QUESTIONER: I assume that an entity on either path can decide to change paths at any time and possibly retrace steps, the path-changing being more difficult the farther along the path the change is made. Is this correct?

RA: I am Ra. This is incorrect. The further an entity has, what you would call, polarized, the more easily this entity may change polarity, for the more power and awareness the entity will have.

Those truly helpless are those who have not consciously chosen but who repeat patterns without knowledge of the repetition or the meaning of the pattern.

QUESTIONER: I believe we have a very important point here. It then seems that there is an extreme potential in this polarization, the same as there is in electricity. We have a positive and negative pole. The more you build the charge on either of these, the more the potential difference and the greater the ability to do work, as we call it in the physical.

This would seem to me to be the same analogy that we have in consciousness. Is this correct?

RA: I am Ra. This is precisely correct.

QUESTIONER: Then it would seem that there is a relationship between what we perceive as a physical phenomenon, say the electrical phenomenon, and the phenomenon of consciousness in that they, having stemmed from the One Creator, are practically identical but have different actions. Is this correct?

RA: I am Ra. Again we oversimplify to answer your query.

The physical complex alone is created of many, many energy or electromagnetic fields interacting due to intelligent energy, the mental configurations or distortions of each complex further adding fields of electromagnetic energy and distorting the physical complex patterns of energy, the spiritual aspect serving as a further complexity of fields which is of itself perfect but which can be realized in many distorted and unintegrated ways by the mind and body complexes of energy fields.

Thus, instead of one, shall we say, magnet with one polarity, you have in the body/mind/spirit complex one basic polarity expressed in what you would call violet-ray energy, the sum of the energy fields, but which is affected by thought of all kinds generated by the mind complex, by distortions of the body complex, and by the numerous relationships between the microcosm which is the entity and the macrocosm in many forms which you may represent by viewing the stars, as you call them, each with a contributing energy ray which enters the electromagnetic web of the entity due to its individual distortions.

QUESTIONER: Is this then the root of what we call astrology?

RA: I am Ra. This will be the last full question of this session.

The root of astrology, as you speak it, is one way of perceiving the primal distortions which may be predicted along probability/possibility lines given, shall we say, cosmic orientations and configurations at the time of the entrance into the physical/mental complex of the spirit and at the time of the physical/mental/spiritual complex into the illusion.

This then has the possibility of suggesting basic areas of distortion. There is no more than this. The part astrology plays is likened unto that of one root among many.

QUESTIONER: Is there anything that we can do to make the instrument more comfortable?

RA: I am Ra. This instrument is well aligned. You are being very conscientious. We request you take more care in being assured that this instrument is wearing footwear of what you would call vibratory sound complex "shoes."

I am Ra. I leave you in the love and the light of the One Infinite Creator. Go forth, therefore, rejoicing in the power and the peace of the One Creator. Adonai.

Session 20,
February 9, 1981

RA: I am Ra. I greet you in the love and the light of the Infinite Creator. I communicate now.

QUESTIONER: To go back a bit, what happened to the second-density entities who were unharvestable when the third density began? I assume that there were some that did not make it into third density.

RA: I am Ra. The second density is able to repeat during third density a portion of its cycle.

QUESTIONER: Then the second-density entities who did not get harvested at the beginning of this 75,000-year period, some are still on this planet. Were any of these second-density entities harvested into the third density within the past 75,000 years?

RA: I am Ra. This has been increasingly true.

QUESTIONER: So more and more second-density entities are making it into third density. Can you give me an example of a second-density entity coming into the third density in the recent past?

RA: I am Ra. Perhaps the most common occurrence of second-density graduation during third-density cycle is the so-called pet.

For the animal which is exposed to the individualizing influences of the bond between animal and third-density entity, this individuation causes a sharp rise in the potential of the second-density entity so that upon the cessation of physical complex, the mind/body complex does not return into the undifferentiated consciousness of that species, if you will.

QUESTIONER: Then can you give me an example of an entity in third density that was just previously a second-density entity? What type of entity do they become here?

RA: I am Ra. As a second-density entity returns as third density for the beginning of this process of learning, the entity is equipped with the lowest, if you will so call these vibrational distortions, forms of third-density consciousness; that is, equipped with self-consciousness.

QUESTIONER: This would be a human in our form, then, who would be beginning the understandings of third density. Is this correct?

RA: I am Ra. This is correct.

QUESTIONER: Speaking of the rapid change that occurred in the physical vehicle from second to third density: this occurred, you said, in approximately a generation and a half. Body hair was lost and there were structural changes.

I am aware of the physics of Dewey B. Larson, who states that all is motion or vibration. Am I correct in assuming that the basic vibration that makes up the physical world changes, thus creating a different set of parameters, shall I say, in this short period of time between density changes allowing for the new type of being? Am I correct?

RA: I am Ra. This is correct.

QUESTIONER: Is the physics of Dewey Larson correct?

RA: I am Ra. The physics of sound vibrational complex, Dewey, is a correct system as far as it is able to go. There are those things which are not included in this system. However, those coming after this particular entity, using the basic concepts of vibration and the study of vibrational distortions, will begin to understand that which you know as gravity and those things you consider as "n" dimensions. These things are necessary to be included in a more universal, shall we say, physical theory.

QUESTIONER: Did this entity, Dewey, then bring this material through for use primarily in the fourth density?

RA: I am Ra. This is correct.

QUESTIONER: Yesterday we were talking about the split that occurs when an entity either consciously or unconsciously chooses the path that leads to either service to others or service to self. The philosophical question of why such a split even exists came up. It was my impression that just as it is in electricity, if we have no polarity in electricity we have no electricity; we have no action. Therefore, I am assuming that it is the same in consciousness. If we have no polarity in consciousness, we also have no action or experience. Is this correct?

RA: I am Ra. This is correct. You may use the general term "work."

QUESTIONER: Then the concept of service to self and service to others is mandatory if we wish to have work, whether it be work in consciousness or work of a mechanical nature in the Newtonian concept in the physical. Is this correct?

RA: I am Ra. This is correct with one addendum. The coil, as you may understand this term, is wound, is potential, is ready. The thing that is missing without polarizing is the charge.

QUESTIONER: Then the charge is provided by individualized consciousness. Is this correct?

RA: I am Ra. The charge is provided by the individualized entity using the inpourings and instreamings of energy by the choices of free will.

QUESTIONER: Thank you. As soon as the third density started 75,000 years ago and we have incarnate third-density entities, what was the average human life span at that time?

RA: I am Ra. At the beginning of this particular portion of your space/time continuum, the average life span was approximately nine hundred of your years.

QUESTIONER: Did the average life span grow longer or shorter as we progressed into third-density experience?

RA: I am Ra. There is a particular use for the span of life in this density, and, given the harmonious development of the learning/teachings of this density, the life span of the physical complex would remain the same throughout the cycle. However, your particular planetary sphere developed vibrations by the second major cycle, which shortened the life span dramatically.

QUESTIONER: Assuming a major cycle is 25,000 years, at the end of the first major cycle, what was the life span?

RA: I am Ra. The life span at the end of the first cycle which you call major was approximately seven hundred of your years.

QUESTIONER: Then in 25,000 years we lost two hundred years of life span. Is this correct?

RA: I am Ra. This is correct.

QUESTIONER: Can you tell me the reason for this shortening of life span?

RA: I am Ra. The causes of this shortening are always an ineuphonious or inharmonious relational vibration between other-selves. In the first cycle this was not severe due to the dispersion of peoples, but there was the growing feeling complex/distortion towards separateness from other-selves.

QUESTIONER: I am assuming that at the start of one of these cycles there could have been either a positive polarization that would generally occur over the 25,000 years or a negative polarization. Is the reason for the negative polarization and the shortening of the life span the influx of entities from Mars who had already polarized somewhat negatively?

RA: I am Ra. This is incorrect. There was not a strong negative polarization due to this influx. The lessening of the life span was due primarily to the lack of the building of positive orientation. When there is no progress, those conditions which grant progress are gradually lost. This is one of the difficulties of remaining unpolarized. The chances, shall we say, of progress become steadily less.

QUESTIONER: The way I understand it, at the beginning of this 75,000-year cycle, then, we had a mixture of entities—those who had graduated from second density on Earth to become third density and then a group of entities transferred from the planet Mars to continue third density here. Is this correct?

RA: I am Ra. This is correct. You must remember that those transferred to this sphere were in the middle of their third density, so that this third density was an adaptation rather than a beginning.

QUESTIONER: What percentage of the entities who were here in third density at that time were Martian, and what percentage were harvested from Earth's second density?

RA: I am Ra. There were perhaps one-half of the third-density population being entities from the Red Planet, Mars, as you call it. Perhaps one-quarter from second density of your planetary sphere. Approximately one-quarter from other sources, other planetary spheres whose entities chose this planetary sphere for third-density work.

QUESTIONER: When they incarnated here, did all three of these types mix together in societies or groups or were they separated by groups and society?

RA: I am Ra. They remained largely unmixed.

QUESTIONER: Then did this unmixing lend to a possibility of warlike energy between groups?

RA: I am Ra. This is correct.

QUESTIONER: Did this help to reduce the life span?

RA: I am Ra. This did reduce the life span, as you call it.

QUESTIONER: Can you tell me why 900 years is the optimum life span?

RA: I am Ra. The mind/body/spirit complex of third density has perhaps one hundred times as intensive a program of catalytic action from which to distill distortions and learn/teachings than any other of the densities. Thus the learn/teachings are most confusing to the mind/body/spirit complex, which is, shall we say, inundated by the ocean of experience.

During the first, shall we say, perhaps 150 to 200 of your years as you measure time, a mind/body/spirit complex is going through the process of a spiritual childhood. The mind and the body are not enough in a disciplined configuration to lend clarity to the spiritual influxes. Thus, the remaining time span is given to optimize the understandings which result from experience itself.

QUESTIONER: Then at present it would seem that our current life span is much too short for those who are new to third-density lessons. Is this correct?

RA: I am Ra. This is correct. Those entities which have, in some way, learned/taught themselves the appropriate distortions for rapid growth can now work within the confines of the shorter life span. However, the greater preponderance of your entities find themselves in what may be considered a perpetual childhood.

QUESTIONER: Back in the first 25,000-year period, or major cycle, what type of aid was given by the Confederation to the entities who were in this 25,000-year period so that they would have the opportunity to grow?

RA: I am Ra. The Confederation members which dwell in inner-plane existence within the planetary complex of vibratory densities worked with these entities. There was also the aid of one of the Confederation which worked with those of Mars in making the transition.

For the most part, the participation was limited, as it was appropriate to allow the full travel of the workings of the confusion mechanism to operate in order for the planetary entities to develop that which they wished in, shall we say, freedom within their own thinking.

It is often the case that a third-density planetary cycle will take place in such a way that there need be no outside, shall we say, or other-self aid in the form of information. Rather, the entities themselves are able to work themselves towards the appropriate polarizations and goals of third-density learn/teachings.

QUESTIONER: I make the assumption that if maximum efficiency had been achieved in this 25,000-year period, the entities would have polarized either toward service to self or toward service to others, one or the other. This would have made them harvestable at the end of that 25,000-year period, in which case they would have had to move to another planet because this one would have been third density for 50,000 more years. Is this correct?

RA: I am Ra. Let us untangle your assumption, which is complex and correct in part.

The original desire is that entities seek and become one. If entities can do this in a moment, they may go forward in a moment, and, thus, were this to occur in a major cycle, indeed, the third-density planet would be vacated at the end of that cycle.

It is, however, more towards the median or mean, shall we say, of third-density developments throughout the one infinite universe that there be a small harvest after the first cycle; the remainder having significantly polarized, the second cycle having a much larger harvest; the remainder being even more significantly polarized, the third cycle culminating the process and the harvest being completed.

QUESTIONER: Was the Confederation watching to see and expecting to see a harvest at the end of the 25,000-year period in which a percentage would be harvestable fourth-density positive and a percentage harvestable fourth-density negative?

RA: I am Ra. That is correct. You may see our role in the first major cycle as that of the gardener who, knowing the season, is content to wait for the spring. When the springtime does not occur, the seeds do not sprout; then it is that the gardener must work in the garden.

QUESTIONER: Am I to understand, then, that there was neither a harvest of positive or negative entities at the end of that 25,000 years?

RA: I am Ra. This is correct. Those whom you call the Orion group made one attempt to offer information to those of third density during that cycle. However, the information did not fall upon the ears of any who were concerned to follow this path to polarity.

QUESTIONER: What technique did the Orion group use to give this information?

RA: I am Ra. The technique used was of two kinds: one, the thought transfer or what you may call "telepathy"; two, the arrangement of certain stones in order to suggest strong influences of power, this being those of statues and of rock formations in your Pacific areas, as you now call them, and to an extent in your Central American regions, as you now understand them.

QUESTIONER: Were you speaking in part of the stone heads of Easter Island?

RA: I am Ra. This is correct.

QUESTIONER: How would such stone heads influence the people to take the path of service to self?

RA: I am Ra. Picture, if you will, the entities living in such a way that their mind/body/spirit complexes are at what seems to be the mercy of forces which they cannot control. Given a charged entity such as a statue or a rock formation charged with nothing but power, it is possible for the free will of those viewing this particular structure or formation to ascribe to this power, power over those things which cannot be controlled. This, then, has the potential for the further distortion to power over others.

QUESTIONER: How were these stone heads constructed?

RA: I am Ra. These were constructed by thought after a scanning of the deep mind, the trunk of mind tree, looking at the images most likely to cause the experience of awe in the viewer.

QUESTIONER: Did the Orion entities do this themselves? Did they do this in the physical? Did they land, or did they do it from mental planes?

RA: I am Ra. Nearly all of these structures and formations were constructed at a distance by thought. A very few were created in later times in imitation of original constructs by entities upon your Earth plane/density.

QUESTIONER: What density Orion entity did the construction of these heads?

RA: I am Ra. The fourth density, the density of love or understanding, was the density of the particular entity which offered this possibility to those of your first major cycle.

QUESTIONER: You use the same nomenclature for the fourth-density negative as for the fourth-density positive. Both are called the dimension of love or of understanding. Is this correct?

RA: I am Ra. This is correct. Love and understanding, whether it be of self or of self toward other-self, is one.

QUESTIONER: What was the approximate date in years past of the construction of these heads?

RA: I am Ra. This approximately was 60,000 of your years in the past time/space of your continuum.

QUESTIONER: What structures were built in South America?

RA: I am Ra. In this location were fashioned some characteristic statues, some formations of what you call rock and some formations involving rock and earth.

QUESTIONER: Were the lines at Nazca included in this?

RA: I am Ra. This is correct.

QUESTIONER: Since these can only be seen from an altitude, of what benefit were they?

RA: I am Ra. The formations were of benefit because charged with energy of power.

QUESTIONER: I'm a little confused. These lines at Nazca are hardly understandable for an entity walking on the surface. He cannot see anything but disruption of the surface. However, if you go up to a high altitude you can see the patterns. How was it of benefit to the entities walking on the surface?

RA: I am Ra. At the remove of the amount of time/space which is now your present, it is difficult to perceive that at the time/space 60,000 years ago, the Earth was formed in such a way as to be visibly arranged in powerful structural designs, from the vantage point of distant hills.

QUESTIONER: In other words, at that time there were hills overlooking these lines?

RA: I am Ra. This will be the last full question of this session.

The entire smoothness, as you see this area now, was built up in many places in hills. The time/space continuum has proceeded with wind and weather, as you would say, to erode to a great extent both the somewhat formidable structures of earth designed at that time and the nature of the surrounding countryside.

QUESTIONER: I think I understand then that these lines are just the faint traces of what used to be there?

RA: I am Ra. This is correct.

QUESTIONER: Thank you. We need to know whether or not it is possible to continue with another session today and whether there is anything that we can do to make the instrument more comfortable?

RA: I am Ra. It is possible. We ask that you observe carefully the alignment of the instrument. Otherwise, you are conscientious.

Is there any short query before we close?

QUESTIONER: I intend in the next session to focus upon the development of the positively oriented entities in the first 25,000 years. I know you can't make suggestions. Can you give me any comment on this at all?

RA: I am Ra. The choices are yours according to your discernment.

I am Ra. I leave you in the love and the light of the One Infinite Creator. Adonai.

Session 21,
February 10, 1981

RA: I am Ra. I greet you in the love and the light of the Infinite Creator. I communicate now.

QUESTIONER: I have a couple of questions that I don't want to forget to ask in this period, so I will ask them first.

The first question is: Would the future content of this book be affected in any way if the instrument reads the material that we have already obtained?

RA: I am Ra. The future, as you measure in time/space, communications which we offer through this instrument have no connection with the instrument's mind complex. This is due to two things: first, the fidelity of the instrument in dedicating its will to the service of the Infinite Creator; secondly, the distortion/understanding of our social memory complex that the most efficient way to communicate material with as little distortion as possible, given the necessity of the use of sound vibration complexes, is to remove the conscious mind complex from the spirit/mind/body complex so that we may communicate without reference to any instrument's orientation.

QUESTIONER: Do you use the instrument's vocabulary or your own vocabulary to communicate with us?

RA: I am Ra. We use the vocabulary of the language with which you are familiar. This is not the instrument's vocabulary. However, this particular mind/body/spirit complex retains the use of a sufficiently large number of sound vibration complexes that the distinction is often without any importance.

QUESTIONER: So at the start of this 75,000-year cycle, we know that the quarantine was fully set up. I am assuming then that the Guardians were aware of the infringements on the free will that would occur if they didn't set this up at that time, and therefore did it. Is this correct?

RA: I am Ra. This is partially incorrect. The incorrectness is as follows: those entities whose third-density experience upon your Red Planet was brought to a close prematurely were aided genetically while being transferred to this third density. This, although done in a desire to aid, was seen as infringement upon free will. The light quarantine which consists of the Guardians, or gardeners as you may call them, which would have been in effect was intensified.

QUESTIONER: When the 75,000-year cycle started, the life span was approximately nine hundred years, average. What was the process and scheduling mechanism, shall I say, of reincarnation at that time, and how did the time in between incarnations into third-density physical apply to the growth of the mind/body/spirit complex?

RA: I am Ra. This query is more complex than most. We shall begin. The incarnation pattern of the beginning third-density mind/body/spirit complex begins in darkness, for you may think or consider of your density as one of, as you may say, a sleep and a forgetting. This is the only plane of forgetting. It is necessary for the third-density entity to forget so that the mechanisms of confusion or free will may operate upon the newly individuated consciousness complex.

Thus, the beginning entity is one in all innocence oriented towards animalistic behavior using other-selves only as extensions of self for the preservation of the all-self. The entity becomes slowly aware that it has needs, shall we say, that are not animalistic; that is, that are useless for survival. These needs include the need for companionship, the need for laughter, the need for beauty, the need to know the universe about it. These are the beginning needs.

As the incarnations begin to accumulate, further needs are discovered: the need to trade, the need to love, the need to be loved, the need to elevate animalistic behaviors to a more universal perspective.

During the first portion of third-density cycles, incarnations are automatic and occur rapidly upon the cessation of energy complex of the physical vehicle. There is small need to review or to heal the experiences of the incarnation. As, what you would call, the energy centers begin to be activated to a higher extent, more of the content of experience during incarnation deals with the lessons of love.

Thus the time, as you may understand it, between incarnations is lengthened to give appropriate attention to the review and the healing of experiences of the previous incarnation. At some point in third density, the green-ray energy center becomes activated and at that point incarnation ceases to be automatic.

QUESTIONER: When incarnation ceases to be automatic I am assuming that the entity can decide when he needs to incarnate for the benefit of his own learning. Does he also select his parents?

RA: I am Ra. This is correct.

QUESTIONER: At this time in our cycle, near the end, what percentage of the entities incarnating are making their own choices?

RA: I am Ra. The approximate percentage is 54 percent.

QUESTIONER: Thank you. During this first 25,000-year cycle was there any industrial development at all, any machinery available to the people?

RA: I am Ra. Using the term "machine" to the meaning which you ascribe, the answer is no. However, there were, shall we say, various implements of wood and rock which were used in order to obtain food and for use in aggression.

QUESTIONER: At the end of this first 25,000-year cycle was there any physical change that occurred rapidly like that which occurs at the end of a 75,000-year cycle, or is this just an indexing time for harvesting period?

RA: I am Ra. There was no change except that which according to intelligent energy, or what you may term physical evolution, suited physical complexes to their environment, this being of the color of the skin due to the area of the sphere upon which entities lived; the gradual growth of peoples due to improved intake of foodstuffs.

QUESTIONER: Then, at the end of the first 25,000-year period, I am guessing that the Guardians discovered that there was no harvest of either positively or negatively oriented entities. Tell me then what happened. What action was taken?

RA: I am Ra. There was no action taken except to remain aware of the possibility of a calling for help or understanding among the entities of this density. The Confederation is concerned with the preservation of the conditions conducive to learning. This, for the most part, revolves about the primal distortion of free will.

QUESTIONER: Then the Confederation gardeners did nothing until some of the plants in their garden called them for help. Is this correct?

RA: I am Ra. This is correct.

QUESTIONER: When did the first call occur, and how did it occur?

RA: I am Ra. The first calling was approximately 46,000 of your years ago. This calling was of those of Maldek. These entities were aware of their need for rectifying the consequences of their action and were in some confusion in an incarnate state as to the circumstances of their incarnation; the unconscious being aware, the conscious being quite confused. This created a calling. The Confederation sent love and light to these entities.

QUESTIONER: How did the Confederation send this love and light? What did they do?

RA: I am Ra. There dwell within the Confederation planetary entities who from their planetary spheres do nothing but send love and light as pure streamings to those who call. This is not in the form of conceptual thought but of pure and undifferentiated love.

QUESTIONER: Did the first distortion of the Law of One then require that equal time, shall I say, be given to the self-service-oriented group?

RA: I am Ra. In this case this was not necessary for some of your time due to the orientation of the entities.

QUESTIONER: What was their orientation?

RA: I am Ra. The orientation of these entities was such that the aid of the Confederation was not perceived.

QUESTIONER: Since it was not perceived, it was not necessary to balance this. Is that correct?

RA: I am Ra. This is correct. What is necessary to balance is opportunity. When there is ignorance, there is no opportunity. When there exists a potential, then each opportunity shall be balanced, this balancing caused by not only the positive and negative orientations of those offering aid but also the orientation of those requesting aid.

QUESTIONER: Thank you very much. I apologize in being so stupid in stating my questions, but this has cleared up my understanding nicely.
Then in the second 25,000-year major cycle, was there any great civilization that developed?

RA: I am Ra. In the sense of greatness of technology there were no great societies during this cycle. There was some advancement among those of Deneb who had chosen to incarnate as a body in what you would call China.
There were appropriately positive steps in activating the green-ray energy complex in many portions of your planetary sphere, including the Americas, the continent which you call Africa, the island which you call Australia, and that which you know as India, as well as various scattered peoples.
None of these became what you would name great as the greatness of Lemuria or Atlantis is known to you due to the formation of strong social complexes and, in the case of Atlantis, very great technological understandings.
However, in the South American area of your planetary sphere as

you know it, there grew to be a great vibratory distortion towards love. These entities were harvestable at the end of the second major cycle without ever having formed strong social or technological complexes.

This will be the final question in completion of this session. Is there a query we may answer quickly before we close, as this instrument is somewhat depleted?

QUESTIONER: I would just like to apologize for the confusion on my part in carrying on to this second 25,000 years.

I would like to ask if there is anything that we can do to make the instrument more comfortable? We would like to have a second session today.

RA: I am Ra. You may observe a slight misalignment between book, candle, and perpendicularity of censer. This is not significant, but as we have said, the cumulative effects upon this instrument are not well. You are conscientious. It is well to have a second session given the appropriate exercising and manipulation of this instrument's physical complex.

I am Ra. I leave you in the love and the light of the One Infinite Creator. Go forth, therefore, rejoicing in the power and the peace of the One Creator. Adonai.

Session 22,
February 10, 1981

RA: I am Ra. I greet you in the love and in the light of the One Infinite Creator. I communicate now.

QUESTIONER: I will ask a couple of questions to clear up the end of the second major cycle. Then we will go on to the third and last of the major cycles.

Can you tell me what was the average life span at the end of the second major cycle?

RA: I am Ra. By the end of the second major cycle the life span was as you know it, with certain variations among geographically isolated peoples more in harmony with intelligent energy and less bellicose.

QUESTIONER: Can you tell me the length of the average life span in years at the end of the second major cycle?

RA: I am Ra. The average is perhaps misleading. To be precise, many spent approximately thirty-five to forty of your years in one incarnation, with the possibility not considered abnormal of a life span approaching one hundred of your years.

QUESTIONER: Can I assume then that this drastic drop in average life span from seven hundred years to less than one hundred years in length during this second 25,000 years was caused by an intensification of a lack of service to others?

RA: I am Ra. This is in part correct. By the end of the second cycle, the Law of Responsibility had begun to be effectuated by the increasing ability of entities to grasp those lessons which there are to be learned in this density. Thus, entities had discovered many ways to indicate a bellicose nature, not only as tribes or what you call nations but in personal relationships, each with the other, the concept of barter having given way to the concept of money; also, the concept of ownership having won ascendancy over the concept of nonownership on an individual or group basis.

Each entity then was offered many more subtle ways of demonstrating either service toward others or service to self with the distortion of the manipulation of others. As each lesson was understood, those lessons of sharing, of giving, of receiving in free gratitude—each lesson could be rejected in practice.

Without demonstrating the fruits of such learn/teaching, the life span became greatly reduced, for the ways of honor/duty were not being accepted.

QUESTIONER: Would this shortened life span help the entity in any way in that he would have more time in between incarnations to review his mistakes, or would this shortened life span hinder him?

RA: I am Ra. Both are correct. The shortening of the life span is a distortion of the Law of One which suggests that an entity not receive more experience in more intensity than it may bear. This is only in effect upon an individual level and does not hold sway over planetary or social complexes.

Thus the shortened life span is due to the necessity for removing an entity from the intensity of experience which ensues when wisdom and love are, having been rejected, reflected back into the consciousness of the Creator without being accepted as part of the self, this then causing the entity to have the need for healing and for much evaluation of the incarnation.

The incorrectness lies in the truth that, given appropriate circumstances, a much longer incarnation in your space/time continuum is very helpful for continuing this intensive work until conclusions have been reached through the catalytic process.

QUESTIONER: You spoke of the South American group which was harvestable at the end of the second cycle. How long was their average life span at the end of the second cycle?

RA: I am Ra. This isolated group had achieved life spans stretching upwards towards the 900-year life span appropriate to this density.

QUESTIONER: I am assuming that the planetary action that we are experiencing now, which it seems shortens all life spans here, was not strong enough then to affect them and shorten their life span. Is this correct?

RA: I am Ra. This is correct. It is well to remember that at that nexus in space/time, great isolation was possible.

QUESTIONER: How many people populated the Earth totally at that time; that is, were incarnate in the physical at any one time?

RA: I am Ra. I am assuming that you intend to query regarding the number of incarnate mind/body/spirit complexes at the end of the second major cycle, this number being approximately 345,000 entities.

QUESTIONER: Approximately how many were harvestable out of that total number at the end of the cycle?

RA: I am Ra. There were approximately 150 entities harvestable.

QUESTIONER: Then as the next cycle started, were these the entities who stayed to work on the planet?

RA: I am Ra. These entities were visited by the Confederation and became desirous of remaining in order to aid the planetary consciousness. This is correct.

QUESTIONER: What type of visit did the Confederation make to this group of 150 entities?

RA: I am Ra. A light being appeared bearing that which may be called a shield of light. It spoke of the oneness and infinity of all creation and of those things which await those ready for harvest. It described in golden words the beauties of love as lived. It then allowed a telepathic linkage to progressively show those who were interested the plight of third density when seen as a planetary complex. It then left.

QUESTIONER: Did all of these entities then decide to stay and help during the next 25,000-year cycle?

RA: I am Ra. This is correct. As a group they stayed. There were those peripherally associated with this culture which did not stay. However, they were not able to be harvested either and so, beginning at the very highest, shall we say, of the sub-octaves of third density, repeated this density. Many of those who have been of the loving nature are not Wanderers but those of this particular origin of second cycle.

QUESTIONER: Are all of these entities still with us in this cycle?

RA: I am Ra. The entities repeating the third-density major cycle have, in some few cases, been able to leave. These entities have chosen to join their brothers and sisters, as you would call these entities.

QUESTIONER: Are any of these entities names that we would know from our historical past?

RA: I am Ra. The one known as sound vibration complex, Saint Augustine, is of such a nature. The one known as Saint Teresa of such a nature. The one known as Saint Francis of Assisi of such nature. These entities, being of monastic background, as you would call it, found incarnation in the same type of ambiance appropriate for further learning.

QUESTIONER: As the cycle terminated 25,000 years ago, what was the reaction of the Confederation to the lack of harvest?

RA: I am Ra. We became concerned.

QUESTIONER: Was any action taken immediately, or did you wait for a call?

RA: I am Ra. The Council of Saturn acted only in allowing the entry into third density of other mind/body/spirit complexes of third density, not Wanderers, but those who sought further third-density experience. This was done randomly so that free will would not be violated, for there was not yet a call.

QUESTIONER: Was the next action taken by the Confederation when a call occurred?

RA: I am Ra. This is correct.

QUESTIONER: Who or what group produced this call, and what action was taken by the Confederation?

RA: I am Ra. The calling was that of Atlanteans. This calling was for what you would call understanding with the distortion towards helping oth-er-selves. The action taken is that which you take part in at this time: the impression of information through channels, as you would call them.

QUESTIONER: Was this first calling then at a time before Atlantis became technologically advanced?

RA: I am Ra. This is basically correct.

QUESTIONER: Then did the technological advancement of Atlantis come because of this call? I am assuming that the call was answered to bring them the Law of One, and the Law of Love as a distortion of the Law of One, but did they also then get technological information that caused them to grow into such a highly advanced technological society?

RA: I am Ra. Not at first. At about the same time as we first appeared in the skies over Egypt and continuing thereafter, other entities of the Confederation appeared unto Atlanteans who had reached a level of philosophical understanding, shall we misuse this word, which was con-sonant with communication, to encourage and inspire studies in the mystery of unity.

However, requests being made for healing and other understanding, information was passed having to do with crystals and the building of pyramids as well as temples, as you would call them, which were associ-ated with training.

QUESTIONER: Was this training the same sort of initiatory training that was done with Egyptians?

RA: I am Ra. This training was different in that the social complex was more, shall we say, sophisticated and less contradictory and barbarous in its ways of thinking. Therefore the temples were temples of learning rather than the attempt being made to totally separate and put upon a pedestal the healers.

QUESTIONER: Then were there what we call priests trained in these temples?

RA: I am Ra. You would not call them priests in the sense of celibacy, of obedience, and of poverty. They were priests in the sense of those devoted to learning.

The difficulties became apparent as those trained in this learning began to attempt to use crystal powers for those things other than healing, as they were involved not only with learning but became involved with what you would call the governmental structure.

QUESTIONER: Was all of their information given to them in the same way that we are getting our information now, through an instrument such as this instrument?

RA: I am Ra. There were visitations from time to time, but none of importance in the, shall we say, historical passage of events in your space/time continuum.

QUESTIONER: Was it necessary for them to have a unified social complex for these visitations to occur? What conditions were necessary for these visitations to occur?

RA: I am Ra. The conditions were two: the calling of a group of people whose square overcame the integrated resistance of those unwilling to search or learn; the second requirement, the relative naiveté of those members of the Confederation who felt that direct transfer of information would necessarily be as helpful for Atlanteans as it had been for the Confederation entity.

QUESTIONER: I see, then. What you are saying is that these naive Confederation entities had had the same thing happen to them in the past, so they were doing the same thing for the Atlantean entities. Is this correct?

RA: I am Ra. This is correct. We remind you that we are one of the naive members of that Confederation and are still attempting to recoup the damage for which we feel responsibility. It is our duty as well as honor to continue with your peoples, therefore, until all traces of the distortions of our teach/learnings have been embraced by their opposite distortions, and balance achieved.

QUESTIONER: I see. Then I will state the picture I have of Atlantis, and you tell me if I am correct.

We have a condition where a large enough percentage of the people of Atlantis had started at least going in the direction of the Law of One and living the Law of One for their call to be heard by the Confederation. This call was heard because, using the Law of Squares, it overrode the opposition of the Atlantean entities who were not calling. The Confederation then used channels such as we use now in communication and also made contact directly, but this turned out to be a mistake because it was perverted by the entities of Atlantis. Is this correct?

RA: I am Ra. This is correct with one exception. There is only one law. That is the Law of One. Other so-called laws are distortions of this law, some of them primal and most important for progress to be understood. However, it is well that each so-called law, which we also call "way," be understood as a distortion rather than a law. There is no multiplicity to the Law of One.

This will be the final question in length of this working. Please ask it now.

QUESTIONER: Can you give me the average life span of the Atlantean population?

RA: I am Ra. The average life span, as we have said, is misleading. The Atlanteans were, in the early part of their cultural experience, used to life spans from 70 to 140 years, this being, of course, approximate. Due to increasing desire for power, the lifetime decreased rapidly in the later stages of the civilization, and, thus, the healing and rejuvenating information was requested.

Do you have any brief queries before we close?

QUESTIONER: Is there anything that we can do to make the instrument more comfortable? Is there anything that we can do for her?

RA: I am Ra. The instrument is well. It is somewhat less easy to maintain clear contact during a time when some or one of the entities in the circle of working is or are not fully conscious. We request that entities in the circle be aware that their energy is helpful for increasing the vitality of this contact. We thank you for being conscientious in the asking.

I am Ra. It is a great joy to leave you in the love and the light of the One Infinite Creator. Go forth, therefore, rejoicing in the power and the peace of the One Creator. Adonai.

Session 23,
February 11, 1981

RA: I am Ra. I greet you in the love and the light of the Infinite Creator. We communicate now.

QUESTIONER: You were speaking yesterday of the first contact made by the Confederation which occurred during our third major cycle. You stated that you appeared in the skies over Egypt at approximately the same time that aid was given to Atlantis. Can you tell me why you went to Egypt, and your orientation of attitude and thinking when you first went to Egypt?

RA: I am Ra. At the time of which you speak there were those who chose to worship the hawk-headed sun god, which you know as vibrational sound complex, "Horus." This vibrational sound complex has taken other vibrational sound complexes, the object of worship being the sun disc represented in some distortion.

We were drawn to spend some time, as you would call it, scanning the peoples for a serious interest amounting to a seeking with which we might help without infringement. We found that at that time the social complex was quite self-contradictory in its so-called religious beliefs, and, therefore, there was not an appropriate calling for our vibration. Thus, at that time, which you know of as approximately 18,000 of your years in the past, we departed without taking action.

QUESTIONER: You stated yesterday that you appeared in the skies over Egypt at that time. Were the Egyptian entities able to see you in their skies?

RA: I am Ra. This is correct.

QUESTIONER: What did they see, and how did this affect their attitudes?

RA: I am Ra. They saw what you would speak of as crystal-powered, bell-shaped craft.

This did not affect them due to their firm conviction that many wondrous things occurred as a normal part of a world, as you would call it, in which many, many deities had powerful control over supernatural events.

QUESTIONER: Did you have a reason for being visible to them rather than being invisible?

RA: I am Ra. This is correct.

QUESTIONER: Can you tell me your reason for being visible to them?

RA: I am Ra. We allowed visibility because it did not make any difference.

QUESTIONER: Then at this time you did not contact them. Can you answer the same question that I just asked with respect to your next attempt to contact the Egyptians?

RA: I am Ra. The next attempt was prolonged. It occurred over a period of time. The nexus, or center, of our efforts was a decision upon our parts that there was a sufficient calling to attempt to walk among your peoples as brothers.

We laid this plan before the Council of Saturn, offering ourselves as service-oriented Wanderers of the type which land directly upon the inner planes without incarnative processes. Thus we emerged, or materialized, in physical-chemical complexes representing as closely as possible our natures, this effort being to appear as brothers and spend a limited amount of time as teachers of the Law of One, for there was an ever-stronger interest in the sun body, and this vibrates in concordance with our particular distortions.

We discovered that for each word we could utter, there were thirty impressions we gave by our very being, which confused those entities we had come to serve. After a short period we removed ourselves from these entities and spent much time attempting to understand how best to serve those to whom we had offered ourselves in love/light.

The ones who were in contact with that geographical entity, which you know of as Atlantis, had conceived of the potentials for healing by use of the pyramid-shape entities. In considering this and making adjustments for the difference as in the distortion complexes of the two geographical cultures, as you would call them, we went before the Council again, offering this plan to the Council as an aid to the healing and the longevity of those in the area you know of as Egypt. In this way we hoped to facilitate the learning process as well as offer philosophy articulating the Law of One. Again the Council approved.

Approximately 11,000 of your years ago we entered, by thought-form, your—we correct this instrument. We sometimes have difficulty due to low vitality. Approximately 8,500 years ago, having considered these concepts carefully, we returned, never having left in thought, to the thought-form areas of your vibrational planetary complex and considered for some of your years, as you measure time, how to appropriately build these structures.

The first, the Great Pyramid, was formed approximately 6,000 of your years ago. Then, in sequence, after this performing by thought of the building or architecture of the Great Pyramid using the more, shall we say, local or earthly material rather than thought-form material to build other pyramidal structures.

This continued for approximately 1,500 of your years.

Meanwhile, the information concerning initiation and healing by crystal was being given. The one known as "Ikhnaton" was able to perceive this information without significant distortion and, for a time, moved, shall we say, heaven and earth in order to invoke the Law of One and to order the priesthood of these structures in accordance with the distortions of initiation and true compassionate healing. This was not to be long lasting.

At this entity's physical dissolution from your third-density physical plane, as we have said before, our teachings became quickly perverted; our structures once again went to the use of the so-called "royal" or those with distortions towards power.

QUESTIONER: When you spoke of pyramid healing, I am assuming that the primary healing was for the mind. Is this correct?

RA: I am Ra. This is partially correct. The healing, if it is to be effectuated, must be a funneling without significant distortion of the instreamings through the spiritual complex into the tree of mind. There are parts of this mind which block energies flowing to the body complex. In each case, in each entity, the blockage may well differ.

However, it is necessary to activate the sense of the spiritual channel or shuttle. Then whether the blockage is from spiritual to mental or from mental to physical, or whether it may simply be a random and purely physical trauma, healing may then be carried out.

QUESTIONER: When you started building the pyramid at Giza using thought, were you at that time in contact with incarnate Egyptians and did they observe this building?

RA: I am Ra. At that time we were not in close contact with incarnate entities upon your plane. We were responding to a general calling of sufficient energy in that particular location to merit action. We sent thoughts to all who were seeking our information.

The appearance of the pyramid was a matter of tremendous surprise. However, it was carefully designed to coincide with the incarnation of one known as a great architect. This entity was later made into a deity, in part due to this occurrence.

QUESTIONER: What name did they give this deity?

RA: I am Ra. This deity had the sound vibration complex, "Imhotep."

QUESTIONER: What can you tell me about the overall success of the pyramid? I understand that the pyramids were not successful in producing a rise in consciousness that was hoped for, but there must have been some success that came from them.

RA: I am Ra. We ask you to remember that we are of the Brothers and Sisters of Sorrow. When one has been rescued from that sorrow to a vision of the One Creator, then there is no concept of failure.

Our difficulty lay in the honor/responsibility of correcting the distortions of the Law of One which occurred during our attempts to aid these entities. The distortions are seen as responsibilities rather than failures; the few who were inspired to seek, our only reason for the attempt.

Thus, we would perhaps be in the position of paradox in that as one saw an illumination, we were what you call successful, and as others became more sorrowful and confused, we were failures. These are your terms. We persist in seeking to serve.

QUESTIONER: Can you tell me what happened to Ikhnaton after his physical death?

RA: I am Ra. This entity was then put through the series of healing and review of incarnational experiences which is appropriate for third-density experience. This entity had been somewhat in the distortions of power ameliorated by the great devotion to the Law of One. This entity thus resolved to enter a series of incarnations in which it had no distortions towards power.

QUESTIONER: Can you tell me what the average life span was for the Egyptians at the time of Ikhnaton?

RA: I am Ra. The average life span of these people was approximately thirty-five to fifty of your years. There was much, what you would call, disease of a physical complex nature.

QUESTIONER: Can you tell me of the reasons for the disease? I think I already know, but I think it might be good for the book to state this at this time.

RA: I am Ra. This is, as we have mentioned before, not particularly informative with regard to the Law of One. However, the land you know of as Egypt at that time was highly barbarous in its living conditions, as you would call them. The river which you call Nile was allowed to flood and to recede, thus providing the fertile grounds for the breeding of diseases which may be carried by insects. Also, the preparation of foodstuffs allowed diseases to form. Also, there was difficulty in many cases with sources of water, and water which was taken caused disease due to the organisms therein.

QUESTIONER: I was really questioning about the more basic cause of disease rather than the mechanism of its transmission. I was going back to the root of thought that created the possibility of disease. Could you briefly tell me if I am correct in assuming the general reduction of thought over the long time on planet Earth with respect to the Law of One created a condition whereby what we call disease could develop? Is this correct?

RA: I am Ra. This is correct and perceptive. You, as questioner, begin now to penetrate the outer teachings.
    The root cause in this particular society was not so much a bellicose action, although there were, shall we say, tendencies, but rather the formation of a money system and a very active trading and development of those tendencies towards greed and power; thus, the enslaving of entities by other entities and the misapprehension of the Creator within each entity.

QUESTIONER: I understand, if I am correct, that a South American contact was also made. Can you tell me of the nature of your contact with respect to the attitude about the contact, its ramifications, the plan for the contact, and why the people were contacted in South America?

RA: I am Ra. This will be the final full question of this session.
    The entities who walked among those in your South American continent were called by a similar desire upon the part of the entities therein

to learn of the manifestations of the sun. They worshipped this source of light and life.

Thus, these entities were visited by light beings not unlike ourselves. Instructions were given and they were more accepted and less distorted than ours. The entities themselves began to construct a series of underground and hidden cities including pyramid structures.

These pyramids were somewhat at variance from the design that we had promulgated. However, the original ideas were the same with the addition of a desire or intention of creating places of meditation and rest, a feeling of the presence of the One Creator; these pyramids then being for all people, not only initiates and those to be healed.

They left this density when it was discovered that their plans were solidly in motion and, in fact, had been recorded. During the next approximately 3,500 years these plans became, though somewhat distorted, in a state of near completion in many aspects.

Therefore, as is the case of the breakings of the quarantine, the entity who was helping the South American entities along the South American ways you call in part the Amazon River went before the Council of Saturn to request a second attempt to correct in person the distortions which had occurred in their plans. This having been granted, this entity or social memory complex returned, and the entity chosen as messenger came among the peoples once more to correct the errors.

Again, all was recorded and the entity rejoined its social memory complex and left your skies.

As in our experience, the teachings were, for the most part, greatly and grossly perverted to the extent in later times of actual human sacrifice rather than healing of humans. Thus, this social memory complex is also given the honor/duty of remaining until those distortions are worked out of the distortion complexes of your peoples.

May we ask if there are any questions of a brief nature before we close?

QUESTIONER: Is there anything we can do to make the instrument more comfortable? Since you stated that she seems to be low on energy, is it possible to have another session later on today?

RA: I am Ra. All is well with alignments. However, this instrument would benefit from rest from the trance state for this diurnal period.

I am Ra. I leave this instrument now. I leave each of you in the love and the light of the One Infinite Creator. Go forth, therefore, rejoicing in the power and the peace of the One Creator. Adonai.

Session 24,
February 15, 1981

RA: I am Ra. I greet you in the love and in the light of the Infinite Creator. We communicate now.

QUESTIONER: We are a little concerned about the physical condition of the instrument. She has a slight congestion. If you can tell me of the advisability of the session, I would appreciate it.

RA: I am Ra. This instrument's vital energies of the physical complex are low. The session will be appropriately shortened.

QUESTIONER: In the last session you mentioned that in this last 25,000-year cycle the Atlanteans, Egyptians, and those in South America were contacted and then the Confederation departed. I understand that the Confederation did not come back for some time. Could you tell me of the reasons, consequences, and attitudes with respect to the next contact with those here on planet Earth?

RA: I am Ra. In the case of the Atlanteans, enlargements upon the information given resulted in those activities distorted towards bellicosity, which resulted in the final second Atlantean catastrophe 10,821 of your years in the past, as you measure time.

Many, many were displaced due to societal actions both upon Atlantis and upon those areas of what you would call North African deserts, to which some Atlanteans had gone after the first conflict. Earth changes continued due to these, what you would call, nuclear bombs and other crystal weapons, sinking the last great land masses approximately 9,600 of your years ago.

In the Egyptian and the South American experiments, results, though not as widely devastating, were as far from the original intention of the Confederation. It was clear to not only us but also to the Council and the Guardians that our methods were not appropriate for this particular sphere.

Our attitude thus was one of caution, observation, and continuing attempts to creatively discover methods whereby contact from our entities could be of service with the least distortion and, above all, with the least possibility of becoming perversions or antitheses of our intention in sharing information.

QUESTIONER: Thank you. Then I assume that the Confederation stayed away from Earth for a period of time. What condition created the next contact that the Confederation made?

RA: I am Ra. In approximately 3,600 of your years in the past, as you measure time, there was an influx of those of the Orion group, as you call them. Due to the increasing negative influences upon thinking and acting distortions, they were able to begin working with those whose impression from olden times, as you may say, was that they were special and different.

An entity of the Confederation, many, many thousands of your years in the past, the one you may call "Yahweh," had, by genetic cloning, set up these particular biases among these peoples who had come gradually to dwell in the vicinity of Egypt, as well as in many, many other places, by dispersion after the down-sinking of the land mass Mu. Here the Orion group found fertile soil in which to plant the seeds of negativity, these seeds, as always, being those of the elite, the different, those who manipulate or enslave others.

The one known as Yahweh felt a great responsibility to these entities. However, the Orion group had been able to impress upon the peoples the name Yahweh as the one responsible for this elitism. Yahweh then was able to take what you would call stock of its vibratory patterns and became, in effect, a more eloquently effective sound vibration complex.

In this complex the old Yahweh, now unnamed but meaning "He comes," began to send positively oriented philosophy. This was approximately in your past of 3,300 years. Thus, the intense portion of what has become known as Armageddon was joined.

QUESTIONER: How did the Orion group get through the quarantine 3,600 years ago? The random window effect?

RA: I am Ra. At that time this was not entirely so, as there was a proper calling for this information. When there is a mixed calling, the window effect is much more put into motion by the ways of the densities.

The quarantine in this case was, shall we say, not patrolled so closely, due to the lack of strong polarity, the windows thus needing to be very weak in order for penetration. As your harvest approaches, those forces of what you would call light work according to their call. The ones of Orion have the working only according to their call. This calling is in actuality not nearly as great.

Thus, due to the way of empowering or squares, there is much resistance to penetration. Yet, free will must be maintained and those desiring negatively oriented information, as you would call it, must then be satisfied by those moving through by the window effect.

QUESTIONER: Then Yahweh, in an attempt to correct what I might call a mistake (I know you don't want to call it that), started 3,300 years ago a positive philosophy. Were the Orion and Yahweh philosophies impressed telepathically, or were there other techniques used?

RA: I am Ra. There were two other techniques used: one by the entity no longer called Yahweh, who still felt that if it could raise up entities which were superior to the negative forces, that these superior entities could spread the Law of One. Thus this entity, "Yod-Heh-Shin-Vau-Heh," came among your people in form according to incarnate being and mated in the normal reproductive manner of your physical complexes, thus birthing a generation of much larger beings, these beings called "Anak."

The other method used to greater effect later in the scenario, as you would call it, was the thought-form such as we often use among your peoples to suggest the mysterious or the sublime. You may be familiar with some of these appearances.

QUESTIONER: Could you state some of those?

RA: I am Ra. This is information which you may discover. However, we will briefly point the way by indicating the so-called wheel within a wheel and the cherubim with sleepless eye.

QUESTIONER: Did the Orion group use similar methods for their impression 3,600 years ago?

RA: I am Ra. The group or empire had an emissary in your skies at that time.

QUESTIONER: Can you describe that emissary?

RA: I am Ra. This emissary was of your fiery nature, which was hidden by the nature of cloud in the day. This was to obliterate the questions of those seeing such a vehicle and to make it consonant with these entities' concept of what you may call the Creator.

QUESTIONER: And then how was the information passed on to the entities after they saw this fiery cloud?

RA: I am Ra. By thought transfer and by the causing of fiery phenomena and other events to appear as being miraculous through the use of thought-forms.

QUESTIONER: Then are there any prophets that sprang from this era or soon after it that are recorded?

RA: I am Ra. Those of the empire were not successful in maintaining their presence for long after the approximate three zero, zero, zero date in your history and were, perforce, left with the decision to physically leave the skies. The so-called prophets were often given mixed information, but the worst that the Orion group could do was to cause these prophets to speak of doom, as prophecy in those days was the occupation of those who love their fellow beings and wish only to be of service to them and to the Creator.

QUESTIONER: Are you saying that the Orion group was successful in polluting some of the positively oriented prophets' messages with prophecies of doom?

RA: I am Ra. This is correct. Your next query shall be the last full query for this session.

QUESTIONER: Could you tell me why the Orion group had to leave after what figures to be a 600-year period?

RA: I am Ra. Although the impression that they had given to those who called them was that these entities were an elite group, that which you know as "Diaspora" occurred, causing much dispersion of these peoples so that they became an humbler and more honorable breed, less bellicose and more aware of the loving kindness of the One Creator.

The creation about them tended towards being somewhat bellicose, somewhat oriented towards the enslavement of others, but they themselves, the target of the Orion group by means of their genetic superiority/weakness, became what you may call the underdogs, thereby letting the feelings of gratitude for their neighbors, their family, and their One Creator begin to heal the feelings of elitism which led to the distortions of power over others which had caused their own bellicosity.

Any short queries may be asked now.

QUESTIONER: Is there anything that we can do to make the instrument more comfortable?

RA: I am Ra. You are conscientious. Be careful to adjust this instrument's upper appendages if its upper body is elevated.

I am Ra. All is well. It is our joy to speak with you. We leave in the love and the light of the One Infinite Creator. Go forth, therefore, rejoicing in the power and the peace of the One Creator. Adonai.

Session 25,
February 16, 1981

RA: I am Ra. I greet you in the love and the light of the Infinite Creator. We communicate now.

QUESTIONER: We shall now continue with the material from yesterday. You stated that about 3,000 years ago the Orion group left due to Diaspora. Was the Confederation then able to make any progress after the Orion group left?

RA: I am Ra. For many of your centuries, both the Confederation and the Orion Confederation busied themselves with each other upon planes above your own, shall we say, planes in time/space whereby machinations were conceived and the armor of light girded. Battles have been and are continuing to be fought upon these levels.

Upon the Earth plane, energies had been set in motion which did not cause a great deal of call. There were isolated instances of callings, one such taking place beginning approximately 2,600 of your years in the past in what you would call Greece (at this time) and resulting in writings and understandings of some facets of the Law of One. We especially note the one known as Thales and the one known as Heraclitus, those being of the philosopher career, as you may call it, teaching their students. We also point out the understandings of the one known as Pericles.

At this time there was a limited amount of visionary information which the Confederation was allowed to telepathically impress. However, for the most part, during this time empires died and rose according to the attitudes and energies set in motion long ago, not resulting in strong polarization but rather in that mixture of the positive and the warlike or negative which has been characteristic of this final minor cycle of your beingness.

QUESTIONER: You spoke of an Orion Confederation and of a battle being fought between the Confederation and the Orion Confederation. Is it possible to convey any concept of how this battle is fought?

RA: I am Ra. Picture, if you will, your mind. Picture it then in total unity with all other minds of your society. You are then single-minded, and that which is a weak electrical charge in your physical illusion is now an enormously powerful machine whereby thoughts may be projected as things.

In this endeavor the Orion group charges or attacks the Confederation armed with light. The result, a standoff, as you would call it, both energies being somewhat depleted by this and needing to regroup; the negative depleted through failure to manipulate, the positive depleted through failure to accept that which is given.

QUESTIONER: Could you amplify the meaning of what you mean by the "failure to accept that which is given"?

RA: I am Ra. At the level of time/space at which this takes place in the form of what you may call thought war, the most accepting and loving energy would be to so love those who wished to manipulate that those entities were surrounded and engulfed, transformed by positive energies.

This, however, being a battle of equals, the Confederation is aware that it cannot, on equal footing, allow itself to be manipulated in order to remain purely positive, for then though pure it would not be of any consequence, having been placed by the so-called powers of darkness under the heel, as you may say.

It is thus that those who deal with this thought war must be defensive rather than accepting in order to preserve their usefulness in service to others. Thusly, they cannot accept fully what the Orion Confederation wishes to give, that being enslavement. Thusly, some polarity is lost due to this friction, and both sides, if you will, must then regroup.

It has not been fruitful for either side. The only consequence which has been helpful is a balancing of the energies available to this planet so that these energies have less necessity to be balanced in this space/time, thus lessening the chances of planetary annihilation.

QUESTIONER: Does a portion of the Confederation then engage in this thought battle? What percent engages?

RA: I am Ra. This is the most difficult work of the Confederation. Only four planetary entities at any one time are asked to partake in this conflict.

QUESTIONER: What density are these four planetary entities?

RA: I am Ra. These entities are of the density of love, numbering four.

QUESTIONER: Would an entity of this density be more effective for this work than an entity of density five or six?

RA: I am Ra. The fourth density is the only density besides your own which, lacking the wisdom to refrain from battle, sees the necessity of the battle. Thus it is necessary that fourth-density social memory complexes be used.

QUESTIONER: Am I correct in assuming that both the Confederation and the Orion group utilize only their fourth densities in this battle, and that the fifth and sixth densities of the Orion group do not engage in this?

RA: I am Ra. This will be the last full question, as this entity's energies are low.

It is partially correct. Fifth- and sixth-density entities positive would not take part in this battle. Fifth-density negative would not take part in this battle. Thus, the fourth density of both orientations join in this conflict.

May we ask for a few short questions before we close?

QUESTIONER: I will first ask if there is anything that we can do to make the instrument more comfortable. I would also really like to know the orientation of the fifth-density negative for not participating in this battle.

RA: I am Ra. The fifth density is the density of light or wisdom. The so-called negative service to self entity in this density is at a high level of awareness and wisdom and has ceased activity except by thought. The fifth-density negative is extraordinarily compacted and separated from all else.

QUESTIONER: Thank you very much. We do not wish to deplete the instrument. Is there anything that we can do to make the instrument more comfortable?

RA: I am Ra. You are very conscientious. As we requested previously, it would be well to observe the angles taken by the more upright posture of the entity. It is causing some nerve blockage in the portion of the body complex called the elbows.

I am Ra. I leave you in the love and in the light of the One Infinite Creator. Go forth, then, rejoicing in the power and the peace of the One Creator. Adonai.

Session 26,
February 17, 1981

RA: I am Ra. I greet you in the love and the light of the Infinite Creator. I communicate now.

QUESTIONER: Is any of the changing that we have done here going to affect communication with the instrument in any way?
 Is what we've set up here all right?

RA: I am Ra. This is correct.

QUESTIONER: Do you mean that everything is satisfactory for continued communication?

RA: I am Ra. We meant that the changes affect this communication.

QUESTIONER: Should we discontinue communication because of these changes, or should we continue?

RA: I am Ra. You may do as you wish. However, we would be unable to use this instrument at this space/time nexus without these modifications.

QUESTIONER: Assuming that it is all right to continue, we're down to the last 3,000 years of this present cycle, and I was wondering if the Law of One in its written or spoken form has been made available within this last 3,000 years in any complete way such as we are doing now? Is it available in any other source?

RA: I am Ra. There is no possibility of a complete source of information of the Law of One in this density. However, certain of your writings passed on to you as your so-called holy works have portions of this law.

QUESTIONER: Does the Bible that we know have portions of this law in it?

RA: I am Ra. This is correct.

QUESTIONER: Can you tell me if any of the Old Testament has any of the Law of One?

RA: I am Ra. This is correct.

QUESTIONER: Which has more of the Law of One in it, the Old Testament or the New Testament?

RA: I am Ra. Withdrawing from each of the collections of which you speak the portions having to do with the Law of One, the content is approximately equal. However, the so-called Old Testament has a larger amount of negatively influenced material, as you would call it.

QUESTIONER: Can you tell me about what percentage is of Orion influence in both the Old and New Testaments?

RA: I am Ra. We prefer that this be left to the discretion of those who seek the Law of One. We are not speaking in order to judge. Such statements would be construed by some of those who may read this material as judgmental. We can only suggest a careful reading and inward digestion of the contents. The understandings will become obvious.

QUESTIONER: Thank you. Have you communicated with any of our population in the third-density incarnate state in recent times?

RA: I am Ra. Please restate, specifying "recent times" and the pronoun "you."

QUESTIONER: Has Ra communicated with any of our population in this century, in the last, say, eighty years?

RA: I am Ra. We have not.

QUESTIONER: Has the Law of One been communicated in the last eighty years by any other source to an entity in our population?

RA: I am Ra. The ways of One have seldom been communicated, although there are rare instances in the previous eighty of your years, as you measure time.
There have been many communications from fourth density due to the drawing towards the harvest to fourth density. These are the ways of universal love and understanding. The other teachings are reserved for those whose depth of understanding, if you will excuse this misnomer, recommend and attract such further communication.

QUESTIONER: Then did the Confederation step up its program of helping planet Earth sometime late in this last major cycle? It seems that they did from previous data, especially with the Industrial Revolution. Can you tell me the attitudes and the reasonings behind this?

Is there any reason other than they just wanted to produce more leisure time in the last, say, one hundred years of the cycle? Is this the total reason?

RA: I am Ra. This is not the total reason. Approximately two hundred of your years in the past, as you measure time, there began to be a significant amount of entities who by seniority were incarnating for learn/teaching purposes rather than for the lesser of the learn/teachings of those less aware of the process. This was our signal to enable communication to take place.

The Wanderers which came among you began to make themselves felt at approximately this time, firstly offering ideas or thoughts containing the distortion of free will. This was the prerequisite for further Wanderers which had information of a more specific nature to offer. The thought must precede the action.

QUESTIONER: I was wondering if the one, Abraham Lincoln, could have been a Wanderer?

RA: I am Ra. This is incorrect. This entity was a normal, shall we say, Earth being which chose to leave the vehicle and allow an entity to use it on a permanent basis. This is relatively rare compared to the phenomenon of Wanderers.

You would do better considering the incarnations of Wanderers such as the one known as "Thomas," the one known as "Benjamin."

QUESTIONER: I am assuming that you mean Thomas Edison and Benjamin Franklin?

RA: I am Ra. This is incorrect. We were intending to convey the sound vibration complex, Thomas Jefferson. The other, correct.

QUESTIONER: Thank you. Can you tell me where the entity who used Abraham Lincoln's body—what density he came from and where?

RA: I am Ra. This entity was fourth vibration.

QUESTIONER: I assume positive?

RA: I am Ra. That is correct.

QUESTIONER: Was his assassination in any way influenced by Orion or any other negative force?

RA: I am Ra. This is correct.

QUESTIONER: Thank you. In the recent past of the last thirty to forty years, the UFO phenomena have become known to our population. What was the original reason for the increase in what we call UFO activity in the past forty years?

RA: I am Ra. Information which Confederation sources had offered to your entity, Albert [Einstein], became perverted, and instruments of destruction began to be created, examples of this being the Manhattan Project and its product.

Information offered through Wanderer, sound vibration, Nikola, also was experimented with for potential destruction: example, your so-called Philadelphia Experiment.

Thus, we felt a strong need to involve our thought-forms in whatever way we of the Confederation could be of service in order to balance these distortions of information meant to aid your planetary sphere.

QUESTIONER: Then what you did, I am assuming, is to create an air of mystery with the UFO phenomenon, as we call it, and then by telepathy send many messages which could be accepted or rejected under the Law of One so that the population would start thinking seriously about the consequences of what it was doing. Is this correct?

RA: I am Ra. This is partially correct. There are other services we may perform. Firstly, the integration of souls or spirits, if you will, in the event of use of these nuclear devices in your space/time continuum. This the Confederation has already done.

QUESTIONER: I don't fully understand what you mean by that. Could you expand on that a little bit?

RA: I am Ra. The use of intelligent energy transforming matter into energy is of such a nature among these weapons that the transition from space/time third density to time/space third density or what you may call your heaven worlds is interrupted in many cases.

Therefore, we are offering ourselves as those who continue the integration of soul or spirit complex during transition from space/time to time/space.

QUESTIONER: Could you give us an example from Hiroshima or Nagasaki of how this is done?

RA: I am Ra. Those who were destroyed, not by radiation but by the trauma of the energy release, found not only the body/mind/spirit complex made unviable, but also a disarrangement of that unique vibratory complex you have called the spirit complex, which we understand as a mind/body/spirit complex, to be completely disarranged without possibility of reintegration. This would be the loss to the Creator of part of the Creator, and thus we were given permission not to stop the events, but to ensure the survival of the, shall we say, disembodied mind/body/spirit complex. This we did in those events which you mention, losing no spirit or portion or holograph or microcosm of the macrocosmic Infinite One.

QUESTIONER: Could you tell me just vaguely how you accomplished this?

RA: I am Ra. This is accomplished through our understanding of dimensional fields of energy. The higher or more dense energy field will control the less dense.

QUESTIONER: Then you are saying that in general, you will allow the population of this planet to have a nuclear war and many deaths from that war, but you will be able to create a condition where these deaths will be no more traumatic than entrance to what we call the heaven worlds or the astral world due to death by a bullet or by the normal means of dying by old age. Is this correct?

RA: I am Ra. This is incorrect. It would be more traumatic. However, the entity would remain an entity.

QUESTIONER: Can you tell me the condition of the entities who were killed in Nagasaki and Hiroshima at this time?

RA: I am Ra. They of this trauma have not yet fully begun the healing process. They are being helped as much as is possible.

QUESTIONER: When the healing process is complete with these entities, will this experience of death due to nuclear bomb cause them to be regressed in their climb towards fourth density?

RA: I am Ra. Such actions as nuclear destruction affect the entire planet. There are no differences at this level of destruction, and the planet will need to be healed.

QUESTIONER: I was thinking specifically if an entity was in Hiroshima or Nagasaki at that time, and he was reaching harvestability at the end of our cycle, would this death by nuclear bomb create such trauma that he would not be harvestable at the end of the cycle?

RA: I am Ra. This is incorrect. Once the healing has taken place the harvest may go forth unimpeded. However, the entire planet will undergo healing for this action, no distinction being made betwixt victim and aggressor, this due to damage done to the planet.

QUESTIONER: Can you describe the mechanism of the planetary healing?

RA: I am Ra. Healing is a process of acceptance, forgiveness, and, if possible, restitution. The restitution not being available in time/space, there are many among your peoples now attempting restitution while in the physical.

QUESTIONER: How do these people attempt this restitution in the physical?

RA: I am Ra. These attempt feelings of love towards the planetary sphere and comfort and healing of the scars and the imbalances of these actions.

QUESTIONER: Then as the UFO phenomenon was made obvious to many of the population, many groups of people were reporting contact and telepathic contact with UFO entities and recorded the results of what they considered telepathic communication. Was the Confederation oriented to impressing telepathic communication on groups that were interested in UFOs?

RA: I am Ra. This is correct, although some of our members have removed themselves from the time/space using thought-form projections into your space/time and have chosen, from time to time, with permission of the Council, to appear in your skies without landing.

QUESTIONER: Then are all of the landings that have occurred with the exception of the landing that occurred when [name] was contacted of the Orion group or similar groups?

RA: I am Ra. Except for isolated instances of those of, shall we say, no affiliation, this is correct.

QUESTIONER: Is it necessary in each case of these landings for the entities involved to be calling the Orion group, or do some of these entities come in contact with the Orion group even though they are not calling that group?

RA: I am Ra. You must plumb the depths of fourth-density negative understanding. This is difficult for you. Once having reached third-density space/time continuum through your so-called windows, these crusaders may plunder as they will, the results completely a function of the polarity of the, shall we say, witness/subject or victim.

This is due to the sincere belief of fourth-density negative that to love self is to love all. Each other-self which is thus either taught or enslaved thus has a teacher which teaches love of self. Exposed to this teaching, it is intended there be brought to fruition an harvest of fourth-density negative or self-serving mind/body/spirit complexes.

*3QUESTIONER: Can you tell me of the various techniques used by the service to others positively oriented Confederation contacts with the people of this planet, the various forms and techniques of making contact?

RA: I am Ra. We could.

QUESTIONER: Would you do this, please?

RA: I am Ra. The most efficient mode of contact is that which you experience at this space/time. The infringement upon free will is greatly undesired. Therefore, those entities which are Wanderers upon your plane of illusion will be the only subjects for the thought projections which make up the so-called "Close Encounters" and meetings between positively oriented social memory complexes and Wanderers.

QUESTIONER: Could you give me an example of one of these meetings between a social memory complex and a Wanderer as to what the Wanderer would experience?

RA: I am Ra. One such example of which you are familiar is that of the one known as Morris.**4 In this case the previous contact which other entities in this entity's circle of friends experienced was negatively

---

*3. The following material, from Session 53, May 25, 1981, was added for clarity.
**4. This refers to CASE #1 in Secrets of the UFO by D. T. Elkins with Carla L. Rueckert, Louisville, L/L Research, 1976, pp 10–11

oriented. However, you will recall that the entity, Morris, was impervious to this contact and could not see with the physical optical apparatus, this contact.

However, the inner voice alerted the one known as Morris to go by itself to another place, and there an entity with the thought-form shape and appearance of the other contact appeared and gazed at this entity, thus awakening in it the desire to seek the truth of this occurrence and of the experiences of its incarnation in general.

The feeling of being awakened or activated is the goal of this type of contact. The duration and imagery used varies depending upon the subconscious expectations of the Wanderer which is experiencing this opportunity for activation.

QUESTIONER: In a "Close Encounter" by a Confederation type of craft, I am assuming that this "Close Encounter" is with a thought-form type of craft. Do Wanderers within the past few years have "Close Encounters" with landed thought-form type of craft?

RA: I am Ra. This has occurred, although it is much less common than the Orion type of so-called "Close Encounter."

We may note that in a universe of unending unity, the concept of a "Close Encounter" is humorous, for are not all encounters of a nature of self with self? Therefore, how can any encounter be less than very, very close?

QUESTIONER: Well, talking about this type of encounter of self to self, do any Wanderers of a positive polarization ever have a so-called "Close Encounter" with the Orion or negatively oriented polarization?

RA: I am Ra. This is correct.

QUESTIONER: Why does this occur?

RA: I am Ra. When it occurs it is quite rare and occurs either due to the Orion entities' lack of perception of the depth of positivity to be encountered or due to the Orion entities' desire to, shall we say, attempt to remove this positivity from this plane of existence. Orion tactics normally are those which choose the simple distortions of mind which indicate less mental and spiritual complex activity.

QUESTIONER: I have become aware of a very large variation in the contact with individuals. Could you give me general examples of the methods used by the Confederation to awaken or partially awaken the Wanderers they contact?

RA: I am Ra. The methods used to awaken Wanderers are varied. The center of each approach is the entrance into the conscious and subconscious in such a way as to avoid causing fear and to maximize the potential for an understandable subjective experience which has meaning for the entity. Many such occur in sleep, others in the midst of many activities during the waking hours. The approach is flexible and does not necessarily include the "Close Encounter" syndrome, as you are aware.

QUESTIONER: What about the physical examination syndrome? How does that relate to Wanderers and Confederation and Orion contacts?

RA: I am Ra. The subconscious expectations of entities cause the nature and detail of thought-form experience offered by Confederation thought-form entities. Thus, if a Wanderer expects a physical examination, it will, perforce, be experienced with as little distortion towards alarm or discomfort as is allowable by the nature of the expectations of the subconscious distortions of the Wanderer.

QUESTIONER: Well, are those who are taken on both Confederation and Orion craft then experiencing a seeming physical examination?

RA: I am Ra. Your query indicates incorrect thinking. The Orion group uses the physical examination as a means of terrifying the individual and causing it to feel the feelings of an advanced second-density being such as a laboratory animal. The sexual experiences of some are a subtype of this experience. The intent is to demonstrate the control of the Orion entities over the Terran inhabitant.

The thought-form experiences are subjective and, for the most part, do not occur in this density.

QUESTIONER: Then both Confederation and Orion contacts are being made, and "Close Encounters" are of a dual nature as I understand it. They can either be of the Confederation or of the Orion type of contact. Is this correct?

RA: I am Ra. This is correct, although the preponderance of contacts is Orion oriented.

QUESTIONER: Well, we have a large spectrum of entities on Earth with respect to harvestability, both positively oriented and negatively oriented. Would the Orion group target in on the ends of this spectrum, both positively and negatively oriented, for contact with Earth entities?

RA: I am Ra. This query is somewhat difficult to accurately answer. However, we shall attempt to do so.

The most typical approach of Orion entities is to choose what you might call the weaker-minded entity that it might suggest a greater amount of Orion philosophy to be disseminated.

Some few Orion entities are called by more highly polarized negative entities of your space/time nexus. In this case they share information just as we are now doing. However, this is a risk for the Orion entities due to the frequency with which the harvestable negative planetary entities then attempt to bid and order the Orion contact, just as these entities bid planetary negative contacts. The resulting struggle for mastery, if lost, is damaging to the polarity of the Orion group.

Similarly, a mistaken Orion contact with highly polarized positive entities can wreak havoc with Orion troops unless these crusaders are able to depolarize the entity mistakenly contacted. This occurrence is almost unheard of. Therefore, the Orion group prefers to make physical contact only with the weaker-minded entity.

QUESTIONER: Then in general we could say that if an individual has a "Close Encounter" with a UFO or any other type of experience that seems to be UFO related, he must look to the heart of the encounter and the effect upon him to determine whether it was Orion or Confederation contact. Is this correct?

RA: I am Ra. This is correct. If there is fear and doom, the contact was quite likely of a negative nature. If the result is hope, friendly feelings, and the awakening of a positive feeling of purposeful service to others, the marks of Confederation contact are evident.*5

QUESTIONER: Then I am assuming all of the groups getting telepathic contact from the Confederation are high-priority targets for the Orion crusaders, and I would assume that a large percentage of them are having their messages polluted by the Orion group. Can you tell me what percentage of them had their information polluted by the Orion group, and if any of them were able to remain purely a Confederation channel?

RA: I am Ra. To give you this information would be to infringe upon the free will or confusion of some living. We can only ask each group to consider the relative effect of philosophy and your so-called specific information. It is not the specificity of the information which attracts negative influences. It is the importance placed upon it.

---

*5. End of material from Session 53, May 25, 1981.

This is why we iterate quite often, when asked for specific information, that it pales to insignificance, just as the grass withers and dies while the love and the light of the One Infinite Creator redounds to the very infinite realms of creation forever and ever, creating and creating itself in perpetuity.

Why then be concerned with the grass that blooms, withers, and dies in its season only to grow once again due to the infinite love and light of the One Creator? This is the message we bring. Each entity is only superficially that which blooms and dies. In the deeper sense there is no end to beingness.

QUESTIONER: As you have stated, it is a straight and narrow path. There are many distractions.

We have created an introduction to the Law of One, traveling through and hitting the high points of this 75,000-year cycle. After this introduction, I would like to get directly to the main work, which is an investigation of evolution. I am very appreciative and feel a great honor and privilege to be doing this, and hope that we can accomplish this next phase.

RA: I am Ra. I leave you, my friends, in the love and the light of the One Infinite Creator. Go forth, then, merry and glad and rejoicing in the power and the peace of the One Creator. Adonai.

INDEX

A
Akashic record, 144
Allergies, 22, 131
American Indians, 231
Anak, 178, 215
Armageddon, 36, 214
Astrology, 186
Atlantis, 112, 117–118, 139, 199, 204–208, 213
Augustine, St., 203

B
Balance, 23, 74–75, 77, 87, 90, 119, 139, 147–149, 152–153,
    161, 167, 199, 205, 223
Bible, 23, 47, 53, 77–78, 220
Bigfoot, 111–112, 114
Brothers and sisters of sorrow, 130, 210

C
Cassiopeia, 121
Catalyst, 70, 88–89, 164, 167, 181, 183
Cayce, Edgar, 36, 50, 144
Children, 15, 20–21, 49, 154
China, 199
Confederation of planets in the service of the infinite creator,
    26, 97, 181
Council of Saturn, 100, 102, 108, 203, 208, 212
Crystals, 74–75, 96, 139, 204

D
Death, 16, 21, 45, 51, 168, 210, 224
Deneb, 117, 199

Robot, 129
Russia, 117

S
Saint Teresa, 203
Second coming, the, 168
Seniority by vibration of incarnation, 172
Service, 24–26, 33, 74, 82, 85–86, 95, 97, 99–100, 104, 106,
    122, 125, 128, 140–143, 146, 150, 153, 158, 164–165,
    175–176, 181, 196, 201, 213, 216, 223
Sirius, 107
Social memory complex, 8, 67, 69, 72, 79, 81, 93, 99–103, 109,
    113, 116, 119, 122, 130, 142, 144, 150, 156, 158, 165, 196,
    212, 226
Society, 20, 52, 69, 96, 122, 129, 184, 190, 204, 211, 217
South America, 69, 73, 117, 139, 194, 211, 213
Southern cross, 121
Space, 16, 18–20, 37, 44, 50, 71–73, 75, 77, 81–84, 86, 91,
    94–97, 99, 102–103, 108, 113–118, 120–121, 123, 125,
    127, 131–132, 136, 139–143, 150–151, 153, 155–156,
    163–164, 167, 169, 171, 174–175, 178, 180, 189, 194–
    196, 201–202, 205, 217–218, 220, 223, 225–226, 228
Spiritual entropy, 103
Star Wars, 154

T
Taras bulba, 121, 169
Teaching, 39, 43, 45, 49, 70–71, 85, 90–93, 108, 113, 151, 169,
    171–172, 178, 201, 217, 221, 226
Telepathy, 8, 14, 26, 41, 120, 193, 223
Ten Commandments, The, 155
Tesla, Nikola, 124
Thales, 217
Thought-form, 81, 99, 102, 107, 112, 128–129, 139, 146, 162,
    208–209, 215, 225–228
Tibet, 118
Time, 8–11, 13–14, 16, 19–20, 22–23, 25, 34, 37–40, 44–46,
    49–51, 53–54, 68–79, 81–89, 91–99, 102–105, 107–118,
    120–121, 123, 125, 127, 129–132, 136–143, 145–146,
    148–151, 153–158, 161, 163, 167–175, 177–180, 182,
    185–186, 188–191, 194–199, 201–202, 204–211, 213–
    215, 217–218, 220–226, 228

ABOUT THE AUTHORS

DON ELKINS was born in Louisville, Kentucky, in 1930. He held a BS and MS in mechanical engineering from the University of Louisville, as well as an MS in general engineering from Speed Scientific School. He was professor of physics and engineering at the University of Louisville for twelve years from 1953 to 1965. In 1965 he left his tenured position and became a Boeing 727 pilot for a major airline to devote himself more fully to UFO and paranormal research. He also served with distinction in the US Army as a master sergeant during the Korean War.

Don Elkins began his research into the paranormal in 1955. In 1962, Don started an experiment in channeling, using the protocols he had learned from a contactee group in Detroit, Michigan. That experiment blossomed into a channeling practice that led eventually to the Law of One material 19 years later. Don passed away on November 7, 1984.

CARLA L. RUECKERT (McCarty) was born in 1943 in Lake Forest, Illinois. She completed undergraduate studies in English literature at the University of Louisville in 1966 and earned her master's degree in library service in 1971.

Carla became partners with Don in 1968. In 1970, they formed L/L Research. In 1974, she began channeling and continued in that effort until she was stopped in 2011 by a spinal fusion surgery. During four of those thirty-seven years of channeling (1981–1984), Carla served as the instrument for the Law of One material.

In 1987, she married Jim McCarty, and together they continued the mission of L/L Research. Carla passed into larger life on April 1, 2015.

JAMES MCCARTY was born in 1947 in Kearney, Nebraska. After receiving an undergraduate degrees from the University of Nebraska at Kearney and a master of science in early childhood education from the University of Florida, Jim moved to a piece of wilderness in Marion County, Kentucky, in 1974 to build his own log cabin in the woods, and to develop a self-sufficient lifestyle. For the next six years, he was in almost complete retreat.

He founded the Rock Creek Research and Development Laboratories in 1977 to further his teaching efforts. After experimenting, Jim decided that he preferred the methods and directions he had found in studying with L/L Research in 1978. In 1980, he joined his research with Don's and Carla's.

Jim and Carla were married in 1987. Jim has a wide L/L correspondence and creates wonderful gardens and stonework. He enjoys beauty, nature, dance, and silence.

NOTE: The Ra contact continued until session number 106. There are five volumes total in The Law of One series, Book I–Book V. There is also other material available from our research group on our archive website, www.llre- search.org.

You may reach us by email at contact@llresearch.org, or by mail at: L/L Research, P.O. Box 5195, Louisville, KY 40255-0195

NOTES

THE RA MATERIAL

The Law of One
Book II

The Law of One
Book II

DON ELKINS ⚐ CARLA RUECKERT
JAMES ALLEN McCARTY

REDFeather™
MIND | BODY | SPIRIT
4880 Lower Valley Road, Atglen, PA 19310

Type set in Chaparral Pro

Book II
Softcover ISBN: 978-0-924608-09-4
Hardcover ISBN: 978-0-7643-6555-3
Box Set ISBN (Books I–V): 978-0-7643-6021-3
E-Book ISBN: 978-1-5073-0120-3

Printed in India

Updated Edition
10 9 8 7 6 5 4 3

Published by Red Feather Mind, Body, Spirit
An imprint of Schiffer Publishing, Ltd.
4880 Lower Valley Road
Atglen, PA 19310
Phone: (610) 593-1777; Fax: (610) 593-2002
E-mail: Info@schifferbooks.com
Web: www.redfeathermbs.com

For our complete selection of fine books on this and related subjects, please visit our
website at www.schifferbooks.com. You may also write for a free catalog.

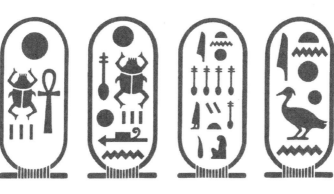

FOREWORD

On January 15, 1981, our research group started receiving a communication from the social memory complex, Ra. From this communication precipitated the Law of One and some of the distortions of the Law of One.

The pages of this book contain an exact transcript, edited only to remove some personal material, of the communications received in Sessions 27 through 50 with Ra.

This material presupposes a point of view which we have developed in the course of many years' study of the UFO phenomenon. If you are not familiar with our previous work, a reading of our book, *Secrets of the UFO*, might prove helpful in understanding the present material. Book II of *The Law of One* builds very carefully on concepts received during the first 26 sessions with Ra, which were published as *The Law of One*. We encourage you to read *The Law of One* first if possible. Both books are available from us by mail.

Book II of *The Law of One* concentrates on the metaphysical principles which govern our spiritual evolution as we seek to understand and use the catalyst of our daily experiences. A more thorough examination of the energy centers of the body, and the connections between mind, body, and spirit, is carried out, building upon information received in the first 26 sessions. We learn more about Wanderers, the various densities, healing, and the many energy exchanges and blockages native to our illusion relating to experiences such as sex, illness, and meditation.

The first three sessions of Book II (27–29) may be difficult and confusing to anyone not familiar with the system of physics authored by Dewey B. Larson. Don't be discouraged, since Larsonian physics is far from well known. Just keep reading and by Session 30, you will be back on firm metaphysical ground. When you've finished Book II, go back and take another look at the first sessions. They'll seem a lot clearer. For those who may wish to study Larsonian physics, *The Structure of the Physical Universe* is a good book with which to begin.

On page 52, the questioner asks about an equation and does not use the classically correct form: in the physics of special relativity, the "c^2" term does not appear. Dr. Andrija Puharich received this form of the equation in his communication with The Nine and, therefore, we felt it appropriate to present it in this form, with the c^2 term included precisely as it had been received by Dr. Puharich.

The Ra contact continued for 106 sessions which were printed into four books in *The Law of One* series. They are available at your local bookstore, from Schiffer Publishing, or from us. If you wish to receive our quarterly newsletter, in which the best of our current channeling is published, please request that you be put on our mailing list.

L/L Research

DON ELKINS
CARLA L. RUECKERT
JIM MCCARTY

Louisville, Kentucky
March 17, 1982

Session 27,
February 21, 1981

RA: I am Ra. I greet you in the love and the light of the One Infinite Creator. I communicate now.

QUESTIONER: This session I thought we would start Book II of *The Law Of One*, which will focus on what we consider to be the only important aspect of our being. This, I assume, will be a much more difficult task than the first book. We want to focus on things that are not transient, and as questioner I may have difficulty at times.

When I do have this difficulty I may fall back on some transient questions simply because I will not be able to formulate what I really need, and I apologize for this. I will try my best to stay on the track and eliminate things of no value from the book if they do occur during my questioning.

The statement I will make to begin with is: In this density we tend to focus our minds on some transient condition or activity with little regard to its value or use as an aid or a tool for growth and understanding of the true and undistorted essence of the creation of which we are an integral part.

I will attempt, by starting at the beginning of creation, to establish an overview of ourselves in the creation, thereby arriving at a more informed viewpoint of what we consider to be reality. It is hoped that this will allow us to participate more effectively in the process of evolution.

I would like to start with definitions of words that we have been using that possibly we have not—and possibly cannot—understand totally, but since the first words that we use are intelligent infinity, I would like for you to define each of these words and give the definition of their combination.

RA: I am Ra. Your vibrations of mind complex indicate a query. However, your vibrational sound complex indicate a preference. Please restate.

QUESTIONER: Would you define the word intelligent in the context of intelligent infinity?

RA: I am Ra. We shall address the entire spectrum of this question before defining as requested. Your language, using vibrational sound complexes, can be at best an approximation of that which is closer to an understanding, if you will, of the nature of conscious thought.

Perceptions are not the same as sound vibration complexes and the attempt to define will therefore be a frustrating one for you, although we are happy to aid you within the limits of your sound vibration complexes.

To define intelligent apart from infinity is difficult, for these two vibration complexes equal one concept. It is much like attempting to divide your sound vibration concept, faith, into two parts. We shall attempt to aid you however.

QUESTIONER: It is not necessary to divide it. The definition of intelligent infinity is sufficient. Could you define that please?

RA: I am Ra. This is exponentially simpler and less confusing. There is unity. This unity is all that there is. This unity has a potential and kinetic. The potential is intelligent infinity. Tapping this potential will yield work. This work has been called by us, intelligent energy.

The nature of this work is dependent upon the particular distortion of free will which in turn is the nature of a particular intelligent energy of kinetic focus of the potential of unity or that which is all.

QUESTIONER: I would like to expand a little on the concept of work. In Newtonian physics the concept of work is the product of force and distance. I am assuming that the work of which you speak is a much broader term including possibly work in consciousness. Am I correct?

RA: I am Ra. As we use this term it is universal in application. Intelligent infinity has a rhythm or flow as of a giant heart beginning with the central sun as you would think or conceive of this, the presence of the flow inevitable as a tide of beingness without polarity, without finity; the vast and silent all beating outward, outward, focusing outward and inward until the focuses are complete. The intelligence or consciousness of foci have reached a state where their, shall we say, spiritual nature or mass calls them inward, inward, inward until all is coalesced. This is the rhythm of reality as you spoke.

QUESTIONER: Then I think I have extracted an important point from this in that in intelligent infinity we have work without polarity, or a potential difference does not have to exist. Is this correct?

RA: I am Ra. There is no difference, potential or kinetic, in unity.

The basic rhythms of intelligent infinity are totally without distortion of any kind. The rhythms are clothed in mystery, for they are being itself. From this undistorted unity, however, appears a potential in relation to intelligent energy.

In this way you may observe the term to be somewhat two-sided, one use of the term, that being as the undistorted unity, being without any kinetic or potential side. The other application of this term, which we use undifferentiatedly for lack of other terms in the sense of the vast potential tapped into by foci or focuses of energy, we call intelligent energy.

QUESTIONER: I understand that the first distortion of intelligent infinity is the distortion of what we call free will. Can you give me a definition of this distortion?

RA: I am Ra. In this distortion of the Law of One it is recognized that the Creator will know Itself.

QUESTIONER: Then am I correct in assuming that the Creator then grants for this knowing the concept of total freedom of choice in the ways of knowing? Am I correct?

RA: I am Ra. This is quite correct.

QUESTIONER: This then being the first distortion of the Law of One, which I am assuming is the Law of Intelligent Infinity, all other distortions which are the total experience of the creation spring from this. Is this correct?

RA: I am Ra. This is both correct and incorrect. In your illusion all experience springs from the Law of Free Will or the Way of Confusion. In another sense, which we are learning, the experiences are this distortion.

QUESTIONER: I will have to think about that and ask questions on it in the next session, so I will go on now to what you have given me as the second distortion which is the distortion of love.

Is this correct?

RA: I am Ra. This is correct.

QUESTIONER: I would like for you to define love in its sense as the second distortion.

RA: I am Ra. This must be defined against the background of

intelligent infinity or unity or the One Creator with the primal distortion of free will. The term Love then may be seen as the focus, the choice of attack, the type of energy of an extremely, shall we say, high order which causes intelligent energy to be formed from the potential of intelligent infinity in just such and such a way. This then may be seen to be an object rather than an activity by some of your peoples, and the principle of this extremely strong energy focus being worshipped as the Creator instead of unity or oneness from which all Loves emanate.

QUESTIONER: Is there a manifestation of love that we could call vibration?

RA: I am Ra. Again we reach semantic difficulties. The vibration or density of love or understanding is not a term used in the same sense as the second distortion, Love; the distortion Love being the great activator and primal co-Creator of various creations using intelligent infinity; the vibration love being that density in which those who have learned to do an activity called "loving" without significant distortion, then seek the ways of light or wisdom. Thus in vibratory sense love comes into light in the sense of the activity of unity in its free will. Love uses light and has the power to direct light in its distortions. Thus vibratory complexes recapitulate in reverse the creation in its unity, thus showing the rhythm or flow of the great heartbeat, if you will use this analogy.

QUESTIONER: I will make a statement that I have extracted from the physics of Dewey Larson which may or may not be close to what we are trying to explain. Larson says that all is motion which we can take as vibration, and that vibration is pure vibration and is not physical in any way or in any form or density, and the first product of that vibration is what we call the photon or particle of light. I am trying to make an analogy between this physical solution and the concept of love and light. Is this close to the concept of Love creating light?

RA: I am Ra. You are correct.

QUESTIONER: Then I will expand a bit more on this concept. We have the infinite vibration of Love which can occur, I am assuming, at varying frequencies.

I would assume that it begins at one basic frequency. Does this have any meaning?

RA: I am Ra. Each Love, as you term the prime movers, comes from one frequency, if you wish to use this term. This frequency is unity. We would perhaps liken it rather to a strength than a frequency, this strength being infinite, the finite qualities being chosen by the particular nature of this primal movement.

QUESTIONER: Then this vibration which is, for lack of better understanding, pure motion; it is pure love; it is nothing that is yet condensed, shall we say, to form any type of density of illusion. This Love then creates by this process of vibration a photon, as we call it, which is the basic particle of light. This photon then, by added vibrations and rotation, further condenses into particles of the densities we experience. Is this correct?

RA: I am Ra. This is correct.

QUESTIONER: Then this light which forms the densities has what we call color. This color is divided into seven categories. Can you tell me if there is a reason or explanation for these categories of color?

RA: I am Ra. This will be the last complete question of this session as this instrument is low on vital energy. We will answer briefly and then you may question further in subsequent sessions.

The nature of the vibratory patterns of your universe is dependent upon the configurations placed upon the original material or light by the focus or Love using Its intelligent energy to create a certain pattern of illusions or densities in order to satisfy Its own intelligent estimate of a method of knowing Itself. Thus the colors, as you call them, are as strait, or narrow, or necessary as is possible to express, given the will of Love.

There is further information which we shall be happy to share by answering your questions. However, we do not wish to deplete this instrument. Is there a short query necessary before we leave?

QUESTIONER: The only thing I need to know is if there is anything that we can do to make the instrument more comfortable or to help her or this contact?

RA: I am Ra. This instrument is slightly uncomfortable. Perhaps a simpler configuration of the body would be appropriate given the instrument's improving physical complex condition.

I am Ra. You are conscientious in your endeavors. We shall be with you. We leave you now in the love and in the light of the One

Infinite Creator. Rejoice, therefore, in the power and the peace of the One Infinite Creator. Adonai.

Session 28,
February 22, 1981

RA: I am Ra. I greet you in the love and the light of the Infinite Creator. I communicate now.

QUESTIONER: I may be backtracking a little today because I think that possibly we are at the most important part of what we are doing in trying to make it apparent how everything is one, how it comes from one intelligent infinity. This is difficult, so please bear with my errors in questioning.

The concept that I have right now of the process, using both what you have told me and some of Dewey Larson's material having to do with the physics of the process, is that intelligent infinity expands outward from all locations everywhere. It expands outward uniformly like the surface of a bubble or a balloon expanding outward from every point everywhere. It expands outward at what is called unit velocity or the velocity of light. This is Larson's idea of the progression of what he calls space/time. Is this concept correct?

RA: I am Ra. This concept is incorrect as is any concept of the one intelligent infinity. This concept is correct in the context of one particular Logos, or Love, or focus of this Creator which has chosen Its, shall we say, natural laws and ways of expressing them mathematically and otherwise.

The one undifferentiated intelligent infinity, unpolarized, full and whole, is the macrocosm of the mystery-clad being. We are messengers of the Law of One. Unity, at this approximation of understanding, cannot be specified by any physics but only become activated or potentiated intelligent infinity due to the catalyst of free will. This may be difficult to accept. However, the understandings we have to share begin and end in mystery.

QUESTIONER: Yesterday we had arrived at a point where we were considering colors of light. You said: "The nature of the vibratory patterns of your universe is dependent upon the configurations placed upon the original material or light by the focus or Love using Its intelligent energy to create a certain pattern of illusions or densities in order to satisfy Its own intelligent estimate of a method of knowing Itself." Then after this you said that there was more material that you would be happy to share, but we ran out of time. Could you give us further information on that?

RA: I am Ra. In discussing this information we then, shall we say, snap back into the particular methods of understanding or seeing that which the one, sound vibration complex, Dewey, offers; this being correct for the second meaning of intelligent infinity: the potential which then through catalyst forms the kinetic.

This information is a natural progression of inspection of the kinetic shape of your environment. You may understand each color or ray as being, as we had said, a very specific and accurate portion of intelligent energy's representation of intelligent infinity, each ray having been previously inspected in other regards .

This information may be of aid here. We speak now nonspecifically to increase the depth of your conceptualization of the nature of what is. The universe in which you live is recapitulation in each part of intelligent infinity. Thus you will see the same patterns repeated in physical and metaphysical areas; the rays or portions of light being, as you surmise, those areas of what you may call the physical illusion which rotate, vibrate, or are of a nature that may be, shall we say, counted or categorized in rotation manner in space/time as described by the one known as Dewey; some substances having various of the rays in a physical manifestation visible to the eye, this being apparent in the nature of your crystallized minerals which you count as precious, the ruby being red and so forth.

QUESTIONER: This light occurred as a consequence of vibration which is a consequence of Love. I am going to ask if that statement is correct?

RA: I am Ra. This statement is correct.

QUESTIONER: This light then can condense into material as we know it into our density, into all of our chemical elements because of rotations of the vibration at quantized units or intervals of angular velocity. Is this correct?

RA: I am Ra. This is quite correct.

QUESTIONER: Thank you. I am wondering, what is the catalyst or the activator of the rotation? What causes the rotation so that light condenses into our physical or chemical elements?

RA: I am Ra. It is necessary to consider the enabling function of the focus known as Love. This energy is of an ordering nature. It orders in a cumulative way from greater to lesser so that when Its universe, as you may call it, is complete, the manner of development of each detail is inherent in the living light and thus will develop in such and such a way; your own universe having been well studied in an empirical fashion by those you call your scientists and having been understood or visualized, shall we say, with greater accuracy by the understandings or visualizations of the one known as Dewey.

QUESTIONER: When does the individualization or the individualized portion of consciousness come into play? At what point does individualized consciousness take over working on the basic light?

RA: I am Ra. You remain carefully in the area of creation itself. In this process we must further confuse you by stating that the process by which free will acts upon potential intelligent infinity to become focused intelligent energy takes place without the space/time of which you are so aware as it is your continuum experience.

The experience or existence of space/time comes into being after the individuation process of Logos or Love has been completed and the physical universe, as you would call it, has coalesced or begun to draw inward while moving outward to the extent that that which you call your sun bodies have in their turn created timeless chaos coalescing into what you call planets, these vortices of intelligent energy spending a large amount of what you would call first density in a timeless state, the space/time realization being one of the learn/teachings of this density of beingness.

Thus we have difficulty answering your questions with regard to time and space and their relationship to the, what you would call, original creation which is not a part of space/time as you can understand it.

QUESTIONER: Thank you. Does a unit of consciousness, an individualized unit of consciousness, create a unit of the creation? I will give an example.

One individualized consciousness creates one galaxy of stars, the type that has many millions of stars in it. Does this happen?

RA: I am Ra. This can happen. The possibilities are infinite. Thus a Logos may create what you call a star system or it may be the Logos creating billions of star systems. This is the cause of the confusion in the term galaxy, for there are many different Logos entities or creations and we would call each, using your sound vibration complexes, a galaxy.

QUESTIONER: Let's take as an example the planet that we are on now and tell me how much of the creation was created by the same Logos that created this planet?

RA: I am Ra. This planetary Logos is a strong Logos creating approximately 250 billion of your star systems for Its creation. The, shall we say, laws or physical ways of this creation will remain, therefore, constant.

QUESTIONER: Then what you are saying is that the lenticular star system which we call a galaxy that we find ourselves in with approximately 250 billion other suns like our own was created by a single Logos. Is this correct?

RA: I am Ra. This is correct.

QUESTIONER: Since there are many individualized portions of consciousness in this lenticular galaxy, did this Logos then subdivide into more individualization of consciousness to create these consciousnesses?

RA: I am Ra. You are perceptive. This is also correct although an apparent paradox.

QUESTIONER: Could you tell me what you mean by an apparent paradox?

RA: I am Ra. It would seem that if one Logos creates the intelligent energy ways for a large system there would not be the necessity or possibility of the further sub-Logos differentiation. However, within limits, this is precisely the case, and it is perceptive that this has been seen.

QUESTIONER: Thank you. I'll call the lenticular galaxy that we are in the major galaxy just so we will not get mixed up in our terms. Does all the consciousness in individualized form that goes into what we are calling the major galaxy start out and go through all of the densities in order, one-two-three-four-five-six-seven and into the eighth, or are there some who start up higher in the rank so that there is always a mixture of intelligent consciousness in the galaxy?

RA: I am Ra. The latter is more nearly correct. In each beginning there is the beginning from infinite strength. Free will acts as a catalyst. Beings begin to form the universes. Consciousness then begins to have the potential to experience. The potentials of experience are created as a part of intelligent energy and are fixed before experience begins.

However, there is always, due to free will acting infinitely upon the creation, a great variation in initial responses to intelligent energy's potential. Thus almost immediately the foundations of the, shall we call it, hierarchical nature of beings begins to manifest as some portions of consciousness or awareness learn through experience in a much more efficient manner.

QUESTIONER: Is there any reason for some portions being much more efficient in learning?

RA: I am Ra. Is there any reason for some to learn more quickly than others? Look, if you wish, to the function of the will . . . the, shall we say, attraction to the upward spiraling line of light.

QUESTIONER: I am assuming that there are eight densities created when this major galaxy was created. Is this correct?

RA: I am Ra. This is basically correct. However, it is well to perceive that the eighth density functions also as the beginning density or first density, in its latter stages, of the next octave of densities.

QUESTIONER: Are you saying then that there are an infinite number of octaves of densities one through eight?

RA: I am Ra. We wish to establish that we are truly humble messengers of the Law of One. We can speak to you of our experiences and our understandings and teach/learn in limited ways. However, we cannot speak in firm knowledge of all the creations. We know only that they are infinite. We assume an infinite number of octaves.

However, it has been impressed upon us by our own teachers that there is a mystery-clad unity of creation in which all consciousness periodically coalesces and again begins. Thus we can only say we assume an infinite progression though we understand it to be cyclical in nature and, as we have said, clad in mystery.

QUESTIONER: Thank you. When this major galaxy is formed by the Logos, polarity then exists in a sense that we have electrical polarity. We do have electrical polarity existing at that time. Is that correct?

RA: I am Ra. I accept this as correct with the stipulation that what you term electrical be understood as not only the one, Larson, stipulated its meaning but also in what you would call the metaphysical sense.

QUESTIONER: Are you saying then that we have not only a polarity of electrical charge but also a polarity in consciousness at that time?

RA: I am Ra. This is correct. All is potentially available from the beginning of your physical space/time; it then being the function of consciousness complexes to begin to use the physical materials to gain experience to then polarize in a metaphysical sense. The potentials for this are not created by the experiencer but by intelligent energy.

This will be the last full question of this session due to our desire to foster this instrument as it slowly regains physical complex energy. May we ask if you have one or two questions we may answer shortly before we close?

QUESTIONER: I am assuming that the process of creation, after the original creation of the major galaxy, is continued by the further individualization of the consciousness of the Logos so that there are many, many portions of the individualized consciousness creating further items for experience all over the galaxy. Is this correct?

RA: I am Ra. This is correct, for within the, shall we say, guidelines or ways of the Logos, the sub-Logos may find various means of differentiating experiences without removing or adding to these ways.

QUESTIONER: Thank you. And since we are out of time I will ask if there is anything that we can do to make the instrument more comfortable or to help the contact?

RA: I am Ra. This instrument is well adjusted. You are conscientious.

I am Ra. I leave you, my friends, in the love and the light of the One Infinite Creator. Go forth then rejoicing in the power and the peace of the One Creator. Adonai.

Session 29,
February 23, 1981

RA: I am Ra. I greet you in the love and the light of the Infinite Creator. I communicate now.

QUESTIONER: Is our sun a sub-Logos or the physical manifestation of a sub-Logos?

RA: I am Ra. This is correct.

QUESTIONER: Then I am assuming that this sub-Logos created this planetary system in all of its densities. Is this correct?

RA: I am Ra. This is incorrect. The sub-Logos of your solar entity differentiated some experiential components within the patterns of intelligent energy set in motion by the Logos which created the basic conditions and vibratory rates consistent throughout your, what you have called, major galaxy.

QUESTIONER: Then is this sub-Logos which is our sun the same sub-Logos just manifesting in different parts through the galaxy, or is it all the stars in the galaxy?

RA: I am Ra. Please restate.

QUESTIONER: What I'm saying is that there are roughly 250 billion stars somewhat like ours in this major galaxy. Are they all part of the same sub-Logos?

RA: I am Ra. They are all part of the same Logos. Your solar system, as you would call it, is a manifestation somewhat and slightly different due to the presence of a sub-Logos.

QUESTIONER: Let me be sure I'm right then. Our sun is a sub-Logos of the Logos of the major galaxy?

RA: I am Ra. This is correct.

QUESTIONER: Are there any sub-sub-Logoi that are found in our planetary system that are "sub" to our sun?

RA: I am Ra. This is correct.

QUESTIONER: Would you give me an example of what I will call a sub-sub-Logos?

RA: I am Ra. One example is your mind/body/spirit complex.

QUESTIONER: Then every entity that exists would be some type of sub or sub-sub-Logos. Is that correct?

RA: I am Ra. This is correct down to the limits of any observation, for the entire creation is alive.

QUESTIONER: Then the planet which we walk upon here would be some form of sub-sub-Logos. Is this correct?

RA: I am Ra. A planetary entity is so named only as Logos if It is working in harmonic fashion with entities or mind/body complexes upon Its surface or within Its electromagnetic field.

QUESTIONER: Do the sub-Logoi such as our sun have a metaphysical polarity positive or negative as we have been using the term?

RA: I am Ra. As you use the term, this is not so. Entities through the level of planetary have the strength of intelligent infinity through the use of free will, going through the actions of beingness. The polarity is not thusly as you understand polarity. It is only when the planetary sphere begins harmonically interacting with mind/body complexes, and more especially mind/body/spirit complexes, that planetary spheres take on distortions due to the thought complexes of entities interacting with the planetary entity. The creation of the One Infinite Creator does not have the polarity you speak of.

QUESTIONER: Thank you. Yesterday you stated that planets in first density are in a timeless state to begin with. Can you tell me how the effect that we appreciate as time comes into being?

RA: I am Ra. We have just described to you the state of beingness of each Logos. The process by which space/time comes into continuum form is a function of the careful building, shall we say, of an entire or whole plan of vibratory rates, densities, and potentials. When this plan has coalesced in the thought complexes of Love, then the physical manifestations begin to appear; this first manifestation stage being awareness or consciousness.

At the point at which this coalescence is at the livingness or beingness point, the point or fountainhead of beginning, space/time then begins to unroll its scroll of livingness.

QUESTIONER: I believe that Love creates the vibration in space/time in order to form the photon. Is this correct?

RA: I am Ra. This is essentially correct.

QUESTIONER: Then the continued application of Love—I will assume that this is directed by a sub-Logos or a sub-sub-Logos— creates rotations of these vibrations which are in discrete units of angular velocity. This then creates chemical elements in our physical illusion and I will assume the elements in the nonphysical or other densities in the illusion. Is this correct?

RA: I am Ra. The Logos creates all densities. Your question was unclear. However, we shall state the Logos does create both the space/time densities and the accompanying time/space densities.

QUESTIONER: What I am assuming is that quantized incremental rotations of the vibrations show up as a material of these densities. Is this correct?

RA: I am Ra. This is essentially correct.

QUESTIONER: Then because of these rotations there is an inward motion of these particles which is opposite the direction of space/time progression as I understand it, and this inward progression then is seen by us as what we call gravity. Is this correct?

RA: I am Ra. This is incorrect.

QUESTIONER: Can you tell me how the gravity comes about?

RA: I am Ra. This that you speak of as gravity may be seen as the pressing towards the inner light/love, the seeking towards the spiral line of light which progresses towards the Creator. This is a manifestation of a spiritual event or condition of livingness.

QUESTIONER: The gravity that we know of on our moon is less than it is on our planet. Is there a metaphysical principle behind this that you could explain?

RA: I am Ra. The metaphysical and physical are inseparable. Thus that of which you spoke which attempts to explain this phenomenon is able to, shall we say, calculate the gravitational force of most objects due to the various physical aspects such as what you know of as mass. However, we felt it was necessary to indicate the corresponding and equally important metaphysical nature of gravity.

QUESTIONER: I sometimes have difficulty in getting a foothold into what I am looking for. I am trying to seek out the metaphysical principles, you might say, behind our physical illusion.

Could you give me an example of the amount of gravity in the third density conditions at the surface of the planet Venus? Would it be greater or less than Earth's?

RA: I am Ra. The gravity, shall we say, the attractive force which we also describe as the pressing outward force towards the Creator is greater spiritually upon the entity you call Venus due to the greater degree of success, shall we say, at seeking the Creator.

This point only becomes important when you consider that when all of creation in its infinity has reached a spiritual gravitational mass of sufficient nature, the entire creation infinitely coalesces; the light seeking and finding its source and thusly ending the creation and beginning a new creation much as you consider the black hole, as you call it, with its conditions of infinitely great mass at the zero point from which no light may be seen as it has been absorbed.

QUESTIONER: Then the black hole would be a point at which the environmental material has succeeded in uniting with unity or with the Creator? Is this correct?

RA: I am Ra. The black hole which manifests third density is the physical complex manifestation of this spiritual or metaphysical state. This is correct.

QUESTIONER: Then when our planet is fully into fourth density, will there be a greater gravity?

RA: I am Ra. There will be a greater spiritual gravity thus causing a denser illusion.

QUESTIONER: This denser illusion then I would assume increases gravitational acceleration above the 32 feet per second squared that we experience. Is this correct?

RA: I am Ra. Your entities do not have the instrumentation to measure spiritual gravity but only to observe a few of its extreme manifestations.

QUESTIONER: This I know, that we can't measure spiritual gravity, but I was just wondering if the physical effect could be measured as an increase in the gravitational constant? That was my question.

RA: I am Ra. The increase measurable by existing instrumentation would and will be statistical in nature only and not significant.

QUESTIONER: OK. As the creation is formed, as the atoms form as rotations of the vibration which is light, they coalesce in a certain manner sometimes. They produce a lattice structure which we call crystalline. I am guessing that because of the formation from intelligent energy of the precise crystalline structure that it is possible by some technique to tap intelligent energy and bring it into the physical illusion by working through the crystalline structure. Is this correct?

RA: I am Ra. This is correct only in so far as the crystalline physical structure is charged by a correspondingly crystallized or regularized or balanced mind/body/spirit complex.

QUESTIONER: I don't wish to get off on subjects of no importance, but it is difficult sometimes to see precisely in what direction to go. I would like to investigate a little bit more this idea of crystals, how they are used. I am assuming then from what you said that in order to use the crystal to tap intelligent energy, it is necessary to have a partially undistorted mind/body/spirit complex. Is this correct?

RA: I am Ra. This is specifically correct.

QUESTIONER: There must be a point at which the removal of distortion reaches the minimum for use of the crystal in tapping intelligent energy. Is this correct?

RA: I am Ra. This is correct only if it is understood, shall we say, that each mind/body/spirit complex has an unique such point.

QUESTIONER: Can you tell me why each mind/body/spirit complex has this unique point of distortion-ridding?

RA: I am Ra. Each mind/body/spirit complex is an unique portion of the One Creator.

QUESTIONER: Then you are saying that there is no single level of purity required to tap intelligent energy through crystals but there can be a wide variation in the amount of distortion that an entity may have, but each entity has to reach his particular point of what I might call energizing the ability. Is this right?

RA: I am Ra. This is incorrect. The necessity is for the mind/body/spirit complex to be of a certain balance, this balance thus enabling it to reach a set level of lack of distortion. The critical difficulties are unique for each mind/body/spirit complex due to the experiential distillations which in total are the, shall we say, violet-ray beingness of each such entity.

This balance is what is necessary for work to be done in seeking the gateway to intelligent infinity through the use of crystals or through any other use. No two mind/body/spirit crystallized natures are the same. The distortion requirements, vibrationally speaking, are set.

QUESTIONER: I see. Then if you are able to read the violet ray of an entity, to see that ray, is it possible to immediately determine whether the entity could use crystals to tap intelligent energy?

RA: I am Ra. It is possible for one of fifth density or above to do this.

QUESTIONER: Is it possible for you to tell me how an entity who has satisfactorily achieved the necessary violet ray qualification should use the crystal?

RA: I am Ra. The gateway to intelligent infinity is born of, shall we say, the sympathetic vibration in balanced state accompanying the will to serve, the will to seek.

QUESTIONER: Can you tell me precisely what the entity would do with the crystal to use it for the purpose of seeking the intelligent infinity?

RA: I am Ra. The use of the crystal in physical manifestation is that use wherein the entity of crystalline nature charges the regularized physical crystal with this seeking, thus enabling it to vibrate harmonically and also become the catalyst or gateway whereby intelligent infinity may thus become intelligent energy, this crystal serving as an analog of the violet ray of the mind/body/spirit in relatively undistorted form.

QUESTIONER: Is it possible for you to instruct us in the specific uses of crystals?

RA: I am Ra. It is possible. There are, we consider, things which are not efficacious to tell you due to possible infringement upon your free will. Entities of the Confederation have done this in the past. The uses of the crystal, as you know, include the uses for healing, for power, and even for the development of lifeforms. We feel that it is unwise to offer instruction at this time as your peoples have shown a tendency to use peaceful sources of power for disharmonious reasons.

QUESTIONER: Is it possible for you to give me an example of various planetary developments in what I would call a metaphysical sense having to do with the development of consciousness and its polarities throughout the galaxy? In other words I believe that some of these planets develop quite rapidly into higher density planets and some take longer times. Can you give me some idea of that development?

RA: I am Ra. This will be the final full query of this session.

The particular Logos of your major galaxy has used a large portion of Its coalesced material to reflect the beingness of the Creator. In this way there is much of your galactic system which does not have the progression of which you speak but dwells spiritually as a portion of the Logos. Of those entities upon which consciousness dwells there is, as you surmise, a variety of time/space periods during which the higher densities of experience are attained by consciousness.

Is there any short query further before we close?

QUESTIONER: Is there anything that we can do to make the instrument more comfortable or to improve the contact?

RA: I am Ra. You are conscientious. The entity is well aligned.

I am Ra. I leave you now in the love and the light of the One Infinite Creator. Go forth, therefore, rejoicing in the power and the peace of the One Infinite Creator. Adonai.

Session 30,
February 24, 1981

RA: I am Ra. I greet you in the love and in the light of the One Infinite Creator. We communicate now.

QUESTIONER: I am going to make a statement and then let you correct it if I have made any errors. This is the statement: Creation is a single entity or unity. If only a single entity exists, then the only concept of service is the concept of service to self. If this single entity subdivides, then the concept of service of one of its parts to one of its other parts is born. From this springs the equality of service to self or to others. It would seem that as the Logos subdivided, parts would select each orientation. As individualized entities emerge in space/time then I would assume that they have polarity. Is this statement correct?

RA: I am Ra. This statement is quite perceptive and correct until the final phrase in which we note that the polarities begin to be explored only at the point when a third density entity becomes aware of the possibility of choice between the concept or distortion of service to self or service to others. This marks the end of what you may call the unself-conscious or innocent phase of conscious awareness.

QUESTIONER: Thank you. Would you define mind, body, and spirit separately?

RA: I am Ra. These terms are all simplistic descriptive terms which equal a complex of energy focuses; the body, as you call it, being the material of the density which you experience at a given space/time or time/space; this complex of materials being available for distortions of what you would call physical manifestation.

The mind is a complex which reflects the inpourings of the spirit and the up-pourings of the body complex. It contains what you know as feelings, emotions, and intellectual thoughts in its more conscious complexities. Moving further down the tree of mind we see the intuition which is of the nature of the mind more in contact or in tune with the total beingness complex. Moving down to the roots of mind we find the progression of consciousness which gradually turns from the personal to the racial memory, to the cosmic influxes, and thus becomes a direct contactor of that shuttle which we call the spirit complex.

This spirit complex is the channel whereby the inpourings from all of the various universal, planetary, and personal inpourings may be funneled into the roots of consciousness and whereby consciousness may be funneled to the gateway of intelligent infinity through the balanced intelligent energy of body and mind.

You will see by this series of definitive statements that mind, body, and spirit are inextricably intertwined and cannot continue, one without the other. Thus we refer to the mind/body/spirit complex rather than attempting to deal with them separately, for the work, shall we say, that you do during your experiences is done through the interaction of these three components, not through any one.

QUESTIONER: Upon our physical death, as we call it, from this particular density and this particular incarnative experience, we lose this chemical body. Immediately after the loss of this chemical body do we maintain a different type of body? Is there still a mind/body/spirit complex at that point?

RA: I am Ra. This is correct. The mind/body/spirit complex is quite intact; the physical body complex you now associate with the term body being but manifestation of a more dense and intelligently informed and powerful body complex.

QUESTIONER: Is there any loss to the mind or spirit after this transition which we call death or any impairment of either because of the loss of this chemical body which we now have?

RA: I am Ra. In your terms there is a great loss of mind complex due to the fact that much of the activity of the mental nature of which you are aware during the experience of this space/time continuum is as much of a surface illusion as is the chemical body complex.

In other terms nothing whatever of importance is lost; the character or, shall we say, pure distillation of emotions and biases or distortions and wisdoms, if you will, becoming obvious for the first time, shall we say; these pure emotions and wisdoms and bias/distortions being, for the most part, either ignored or underestimated during physical life experience.

In terms of the spiritual, this channel is then much opened due to the lack of necessity for the forgetting characteristic of third density.

QUESTIONER: I would like to know how the mind/body/spirit

complexes originate, going as far back as necessary. How does the origination occur? Do they originate by spirit forming mind and mind forming body? Can you tell me this?

RA: I am Ra. We ask you to consider that you are attempting to trace evolution. This evolution is as we have previously described, the consciousness being first, in first density, without movement, a random thing. Whether you may call this mind or body complex is a semantic problem. We call it mind/body complex recognizing always that in the simplest iota of this complex exists in its entirety the One Infinite Creator; this mind/body complex then in second density discovering the growing and turning towards the light, thus awakening what you may call the spirit complex, that which intensifies the upward spiraling towards the love and light of the Infinite Creator.

The addition of this spirit complex, though apparent rather than real, it having existed potentially from the beginning of space/time, perfects itself by graduation into third density. When the mind/body/spirit complex becomes aware of the possibility of service to self or other-self, then the mind/body/spirit complex is activated.

QUESTIONER: Thank you. I don't wish to cover ground that we have covered before but it sometimes is helpful to restate these concepts for complete clarity since words are a poor tool for what we do.

Just as a passing point, I was wondering—on this planet during the second density, I believe there was habitation during the same space/time of bipedal entities and what we call the dinosaurs. Is this correct?

RA: I am Ra. This is correct.

QUESTIONER: These two types of entities seemed to be very incompatible, you might say, with each other. I don't know, but can you tell me the reason for both types of entities inhabiting the same space/time?

RA: I am Ra. Consider the workings of free will as applied to evolution. There are paths that the mind/body complex follows in an attempt to survive, to reproduce, and to seek in its fashion that which is unconsciously felt as the potential for growth; these two arenas or paths of development being two among many.

QUESTIONER: In second density the concept of bisexual reproduction first originates. Is this correct?

RA: I am Ra. This is correct.

QUESTIONER: Can you tell me the philosophy behind this method of propagation of the bodily complex?

RA: I am Ra. The second density is one in which the groundwork is being laid for third density work. In this way it may be seen that the basic mechanism of reproduction capitulates into a vast potential in third density for service to other-self and to self; this being not only by the functions of energy transfer, but also by the various services performed due to the close contact of those who are, shall we say, magnetically attracted, one to the other; these entities thus having the opportunities for many types of service which would be unavailable to the independent entity.

QUESTIONER: Was the basic reason for this to increase the opportunity of the experience of the One Creator?

RA: I am Ra. This is not merely correct but is the key to that which occurs in all densities.

QUESTIONER: Does the process of bisexual reproduction or the philosophy of it play a part in the spiritual growth of second density entities?

RA: I am Ra. In isolated instances this is so due to efficient perceptions upon the part of entities or species. For the greater part, by far, this is not the case in second density, the spiritual potentials being those of third density.

QUESTIONER: Thank you. Can you give me a brief history of the metaphysical principles of the development of each of our planets that surround our sun, their function with respect to the evolution of beings?

RA: I am Ra. We shall give you a metaphysical description only of those planets upon which individual mind/body/spirit complexes have been, are, or shall be experienced. You may understand the other spheres to be a part of the Logos.
　　We take the one known as Venus. This planetary sphere was one of rapid evolution. It is our native earth and the rapidity of the progress of the mind/body/spirit complexes upon its surface was due to harmonious interaction.

Upon the entity known to you as Mars, as you have already discussed, this entity was stopped in mid-third density, thus being unable to continue in progression due to the lack of hospitable conditions upon the surface. This planet shall be undergoing healing for some of your space/time millennia.

The planet which you dwell upon has a metaphysical history well known to you and you may ask about it if you wish. However, we have spoken to a great degree upon this subject.

The planet known as Saturn has a great affinity for the infinite intelligence and thus it has been dwelled upon in its magnetic fields of time/space by those who wish to protect your system.

The planetary entity known to you as Uranus is slowly moving through the first density and has the potential of moving through all densities.

QUESTIONER: Thank you. You stated yesterday that much of this major galactic system dwells spiritually as a part of the Logos. Do you mean that near the center of this major galactic system that the stars there do not have planetary systems? Is this correct?

RA: I am Ra. This is incorrect. The Logos has distributed Itself throughout your galactic system. However, the time/space continua of some of your more central sun systems are much further advanced.

QUESTIONER: Well then, could you generally say that as you get closer to the center of this major system that there is a greater spiritual density or spiritual quality in that area?

RA: I am Ra. This will be the last full question of this session as this instrument is somewhat uncomfortable. We do not wish to deplete the instrument.

The spiritual density or mass of those more towards the center of your galaxy is known. However, this is due simply to the varying timelessness states during which the planetary spheres may coalesce, this process of space/time beginnings occurring earlier, shall we say, as you approach the center of the galactic spiral.

QUESTIONER: Is there anything that we can do to make the instrument more comfortable or to improve the contact?

RA: This instrument is well balanced and the contact is as it should be. This instrument has certain difficulties of a distortion you would call the muscular spasm, thus making the motionless position uncomfortable. Thus we leave the instrument.

I am Ra. You are doing well, my friends. I leave you in the love and the light of the One Infinite Creator. Go forth, then, rejoicing in the power and the peace of the One Creator. Adonai.

Session 31,
February 25, 1981

RA: I am Ra. I greet you in the love and in the light of the One Infinite Creator. We communicate now.

QUESTIONER: I have a question that the instrument has asked me to ask. It reads: You speak of various types of energy blockages and transfers, positive and negative, that may take place due to participation in our sexual reproductive complex of actions. Could you please explain these blockages and energy transfers with emphasis upon what an individual who is seeking to be in accordance with the Law of One may positively do in this area? Is it possible for you to answer this question?

RA: I am Ra. It is partially possible, given the background we have laid. This is properly a more advanced question. Due to the specificity of the question we may give a general answer.

The first energy transfer is red ray. It is a random transfer having to do only with your reproductive system.

The orange- and the yellow-ray attempts to have sexual intercourse create, firstly, a blockage if only one entity vibrates in this area, thus causing the entity vibrating sexually in this area to have a never-ending appetite for this activity. What these vibratory levels are seeking is green ray activity. There is the possibility of orange or yellow ray energy transfer; this being polarizing towards the negative: one being seen as object rather than other-self; the other seeing itself as plunderer or master of the situation.

In green ray there are two possibilities. Firstly, if both vibrate in green ray there will be a mutually strengthening energy transfer, the negative or female, as you call it, drawing the energy from the roots of the beingness through the energy centers, thus being physically revitalized; the positive, or male polarity, as it is deemed in your illusion, finding in its energy transfer an inspiration which satisfies and feeds the spirit portion of the body/mind/spirit complex, thus both being polarized and releasing the excess of that which each has in abundance by nature of intelligent energy, that is, negative/intuitive, positive/physical energies as you may call them; this energy transfer being blocked only if one or both entities have fear of possession or of being possessed, of desiring possession or desiring being possessed.

The other green-ray possibility is that of one entity offering green-ray energy, the other not offering energy of the universal love energy, this resulting in a blockage of energy for the one not green ray thus increasing frustration or appetite; the green ray being polarizing slightly towards service to others.

The blue ray energy transfer is somewhat rare among your people at this time but is of great aid due to energy transfers involved in becoming able to express the self without reservation or fear.

The indigo-ray transfer is extremely rare among your people. This is the sacramental portion of the body complex whereby contact may be made through violet ray with intelligent infinity. No blockages may occur at these latter two levels due to the fact that if both entities are not ready for this energy it is not visible and neither transfer nor blockage may take place. It is as though the distributor were removed from a powerful engine.

QUESTIONER: Could you define sexual energy transfer and expand upon its meaning, please?

RA: I am Ra. Energy transfer implies the release of potential energies across, shall we say, a potentiated space. The sexual energy transfers occur due to the polarizations of two mind/body/spirit complexes, each of which have some potential difference one to the other. The nature of the transfer of energy or of the blockage of this energy is then a function of the interaction of these two potentials. In the cases where transfer takes place, you may liken this to a circuit being closed. You may also see this activity, as all experiential activities, as the Creator experiencing Itself.

QUESTIONER: Could this then be the primal mechanism for the Creator to experience Itself?

RA: I am Ra. This is not a proper term. Perhaps the adjectives would be "one appropriate" way of the Creator knowing Itself, for in each interaction, no matter what the distortion, the Creator is experiencing Itself. The bisexual knowing of the Creator by Itself has the potential for two advantages.

Firstly, in the green-ray-activated being there is the potential for a direct and simple analog of what you may call joy, the spiritual or metaphysical nature which exists in intelligent energy. This is a great

33

aid to comprehension of a truer nature of beingness. The other potential advantage of bisexual reproductive acts is the possibility of a sacramental understanding or connection, shall we say, with the gateway to intelligent infinity, for with appropriate preparation, work in what you may call magic may be done and experiences of intelligent infinity may be had.

The positively oriented individuals concentrating upon this method of reaching intelligent infinity, then, through the seeking or the act of will, are able to direct this infinite intelligence to the work these entities desire to do, whether it be knowledge of service or ability to heal or whatever service to others is desired.

These are two advantages of this particular method of the Creator experiencing Itself. As we have said before, the corollary of the strength of this particular energy transfer is that it opens the door, shall we say, to the individual mind/body/spirit complexes' desire to serve in an infinite number of ways an other-self, thus polarizing towards positive.

QUESTIONER: Can you expand somewhat on the concept that this action not only allows the Creator to know Itself better but also creates, in our density, an offspring or makes available the pathway for another entity to enter this density?

RA: I am Ra. As we have previously said, the sexual energy transfers include the red-ray transfer which is random and which is a function of the second-density attempt to grow, to survive, shall we say. This is a proper function of the sexual interaction. The offspring, as you call the incarnated entity, takes on the mind/body complex opportunity offered by this random act or event called the fertilization of egg by seed which causes an entity to have the opportunity to then enter this density as an incarnate entity.

This gives the two who were engaged in this bisexual reproductive energy transfer the potential for great service in this area of the nurturing of the small-experienced entity as it gains in experience.

It shall be of interest at this point to note that there is always the possibility of using these opportunities to polarize towards the negative, and this has been aided by the gradual building up over many thousands of your years of social complex distortions which create a tendency towards confusion, shall we say, or baffling of the service-to-others aspect of this energy transfer and subsequent opportunities for service to other selves.

QUESTIONER: If a sexual energy transfer occurs in green ray—and

I am assuming in this case that there is no red ray energy transfer—does this mean it is impossible for this particular transfer to include fertilization and the birthing of an entity?

RA: I am Ra. This is incorrect. There is always the red-ray energy transfer due to the nature of the body complex. The random result of this energy transfer will be as it will be, as a function of the possibility of fertilization at a given time in a given pairing of entities each entity being undistorted in any vital sense by the yellow or orange ray energies; thus the gift, shall we say, being given freely, no payment being requested either of the body, of the mind, or of the spirit. The green ray is one of complete universality of love. This is a giving without expectation of return.

QUESTIONER: I was wondering if there was some principle behind the fact that a sexual union does not necessarily lead to fertilization. I'm not interested in the chemical or physical principles of it. I'm interested in whether or not there is some metaphysical principle that leads to the couple having a child or not, or is it purely random?

RA: I am Ra. This is random within certain limits. If an entity has reached the seniority whereby it chooses the basic structure of the life experience, this entity may then choose to incarnate in a physical complex which is not capable of reproduction. Thus we find some entities which have chosen to be unfertile. Other entities, through free will, make use of various devices to insure nonfertility. Except for these conditions, the condition is random.

QUESTIONER: Thank you. In the previous material you mentioned "magnetic attraction." Would you define and expand upon that term?

RA: I am Ra. We used the term to indicate that in your bisexual natures there is that which is of polarity. This polarity may be seen to be variable according to the, shall we say, male/female polarization of each entity, be each entity biologically male or female. Thus you may see the magnetism which two entities with the appropriate balance, male/female versus female/male polarity, meeting and thus feeling the attraction which polarized forces will exert, one upon the other.

This is the strength of the bisexual mechanism. It does not take an act of will to decide to feel attraction for one who is oppositely polarized sexually. It will occur in an inevitable sense, giving the free flow of energy a proper, shall we say, avenue. This avenue may be blocked by some distortion toward a belief/condition stating to the entity that this attraction is not desired. However, the basic mechanism functions as simply as would, shall we say, the magnet and the iron.

QUESTIONER: We have what seems to be an increasing number of entities incarnate here now who have what is called a homosexual orientation. Could you explain and expand upon that concept?

RA: I am Ra. Entities of this condition experience a great deal of distortion due to the fact that they have experienced many incarnations as biological male and as biological female. This would not suggest what you call homosexuality in an active phase were it not for the difficult vibratory condition of your planetary sphere. There is what you may call great aura infringement among your crowded urban areas in your more populous countries, as you call portions of your planetary surface. Under these conditions the confusions will occur.

QUESTIONER: Why does density of population create these confusions?

RA: I am Ra. The bisexual reproductive urge has as its goal, not only the simple reproductive function, but more especially the desire to serve others being awakened by this activity.

In an over-crowded situation where each mind/body/spirit complex is under constant bombardment from other-selves it is understandable that those who are especially sensitive would not feel the desire to be of service to other-selves. This would also increase the probability of a lack of desire or a blockage of the red ray reproductive energy.

In an uncrowded atmosphere this same entity would, through the stimulus of feeling the solitude about it, then have much more desire to seek out someone to whom it may be of service, thus regularizing the sexual reproductive function.

QUESTIONER: Roughly how many previous incarnations would a male entity in this incarnation have had to have had in the past as a female to have a highly homosexual orientation in this incarnation?

RA: I am Ra. If an entity has had roughly 65 percent of its incarnations in the sexual/biological body complex, the opposite polarity to its present body complex, this entity is vulnerable to infringement of your urban areas and may perhaps become of what you call an homosexual nature.

It is to be noted at this juncture that although it is much more difficult, it is possible in this type of association for an entity to be of great service to another in fidelity and sincere green ray love of a nonsexual nature thus adjusting or lessening the distortions of its sexual impairment.

QUESTIONER: Is there an imprint occurring on the DNA coding of an entity so that sexual biases are imprinted due to early sexual experiences?

RA: I am Ra. This is partially correct. Due to the nature of solitary sexual experiences, it is in most cases unlikely that what you call masturbation has an imprinting effect upon later experiences.

This is similarly true with some of the encounters which might be seen as homosexual among those of this age group. These are often, instead, innocent exercises in curiosity.

However, it is quite accurate that the first experience in which the mind/body/spirit complex is intensely involved will indeed imprint upon the entity for that life experience a set of preferences.

QUESTIONER: Does the Orion group use this as a gateway to impress upon entities preferences which could be of a negative polarization?

RA: I am Ra. Just as we of the Confederation attempt to beam our love and light whenever given the opportunity, including sexual opportunities, so the Orion group will use an opportunity if it is negatively oriented or if the individual is negatively oriented.

QUESTIONER: Is there any emotional bias that has nothing to do with male/female sexual polarity that can create sexual energy buildup in an entity?

RA: I am Ra. The sexual energy buildup is extremely unlikely to occur without sexual bias upon the part of the entity. Perhaps we did not understand your question, but it seems obvious that it would take an entity with the potential for sexual activity to experience a sexual energy buildup.

QUESTIONER: I was thinking more of the possibility of the Orion group influencing certain members of the Third Reich who I have read reports of having sexual gratification from the observation of the gassing and killing of entities in the gas chambers.

RA: I am Ra. We shall repeat these entities had the potential for sexual energy buildup. The choice of stimulus is certainly the choice of the entity. In the case of which you speak, these entities were strongly polarized orange ray, thus finding the energy blockage of power over others, the putting to death being the ultimate power over others; this then being expressed in a sexual manner, though solitary.

In this case the desire would continue unabated and be virtually unquenchable.

You will find, if you observe the entire spectrum of sexual practices among your peoples, that there are those who experience such gratification from domination over others either from rape or from other means of domination. In each case this is an example of energy blockage which is sexual in its nature.

QUESTIONER: Would the Orion group be able, then, to impress on entities this orange ray effect? Is this the way that this came about? If we go back to the beginning of third density there must be a primal cause of this.

RA: I am Ra. The cause of this is not Orion. It is the free choice of your peoples. This is somewhat difficult to explain. We shall attempt.

The sexual energy transfers and blockages are more a manifestation or example of that which is more fundamental than the other way about. Therefore, as your peoples became open to the concepts of bellicosity and the greed of ownership, these various distortions then began to filter down through the tree of mind into body complex expressions, the sexual expression being basic to that complex. Thus these sexual energy blockages, though Orion influenced and intensified, are basically the product of the beingness chosen freely by your peoples.

This will be the final question unless we may speak further upon this question to clarify, or answer any short queries before we close.

QUESTIONER: I just need to know then if this works through the racial memory and infects the entire population in some way?

RA: I am Ra. The racial memory contains all that has been

experienced. Thus there is some, shall we say, contamination even of the sexual, this showing mostly in your own culture as the various predispositions to adversary relationships, or, as you call them, marriages, rather than the free giving one to another in the love and the light of the Infinite Creator.

QUESTIONER: That was precisely the point that I was trying to make. Thank you very much. I do not wish to overtire the instrument, so I will just ask if there is anything that we can do to make the instrument more comfortable or to improve the contact?

RA: I am Ra. Please be aware that this instrument is somewhat fatigued. The channel is very clear. However, we find the vital energy low. We do not wish to deplete the instrument. However, there is, shall we say, an energy exchange that we feel an honor/duty to offer when this instrument opens itself. Therefore, counsel we this instrument to attempt to assess the vital energies carefully before offering itself as open channel.

All is well. You are conscientious.

I am Ra. I leave this instrument and you in the love and in the light of the One Infinite Creator. Go forth, then, rejoicing in the power and the peace of the One Creator. Adonai.

Session 32, February 27, 1981

RA: I am Ra. I greet you in the love and the light of the One Infinite Creator. We communicate now.

QUESTIONER: We will now continue with the material from the day before yesterday. The subject is how sexual polarity acts as a catalyst in evolution and how to best make use of this catalyst. Going back to that material, I will fill in a few gaps that we possibly do not understand too well at this point.

Can you tell me the difference between orange- and yellow-ray activation? I am going to work up from the red ray right on through the violet. We have covered red ray, so I would like to ask now what the difference is between yellow- and orange-ray activation?

RA: I am Ra. The orange ray is that influence or vibratory pattern wherein the mind/body/spirit expresses its power on an individual basis. Thus power over individuals may be seen to be orange ray. This ray has been quite intense among your peoples on an individual basis. You may see in this ray the treating of other-selves as non-entities, slaves, or chattel, thus giving other-selves no status whatever.

The yellow ray is a focal and very powerful ray and concerns the entity in relation to, shall we say, groups, societies, or large numbers of mind/body/spirit complexes. This orange—we correct ourselves—this yellow-ray vibration is at the heart of bellicose actions in which one group of entities feels the necessity and right of dominating other groups of entities and bending their wills to the wills of the masters. The negative path, as you would call it, uses a combination of the yellow ray and the orange ray in its polarization patterns. These rays, used in a dedicated fashion, will bring about a contact with intelligent infinity. The usual nature of sexual interaction, if one is yellow or orange in primary vibratory patterns, is one of blockage and then insatiable hunger due to the blockage. When there are two selves vibrating in this area the potential for polarization through the sexual interaction is begun, one entity experiencing the pleasure of humiliation and slavery or bondage, the other experiencing the pleasure of mastery and control over another entity. This way a sexual energy transfer of a negative polarity is experienced.

QUESTIONER: From the material that you transmitted February 17th you stated: "In third ray there are two possibilities. Firstly, if both vibrate in third ray there will be a mutually strengthening energy transfer." What color is third ray in this material?

RA: I am Ra. The ray we were speaking of in that material should be properly the green ray or fourth ray.

QUESTIONER: So I should change that third to fourth or green?

RA: This is correct. Please continue to scan for errors having to do with numbering, as you call them, as this concept is foreign to us and we must translate, if you will, when using numbers. This is an ongoing weakness of this contact due to the difference between our ways and yours. Your aid is appreciated.

QUESTIONER: Thank you. I believe for the time being we have amply covered green ray, so I am going to skip over green ray and go to blue ray. Could you tell me the difference that occurs between green ray and blue ray with the emphasis on blue ray?

RA: I am Ra. With the green ray transfer of energy you now come to the great turning point sexually as well as in each other mode of experience. The green ray may then be turned outward, the entity then giving rather than receiving. The first giving beyond green ray is the giving of acceptance or freedom, thus allowing the recipient of blue ray energy transfer the opportunity for a feeling of being accepted, thus freeing that other-self to express itself to the giver of this ray. It will be noted that once green ray energy transfer has been achieved by two mind/body/spirits in mating, the further rays are available without both entities having the necessity to progress equally. Thus a blue-ray-vibrating entity or indigo-ray-vibrating entity whose other ray vibrations are clear may share that energy with the green-ray other-self, thus acting as catalyst for the continued learn/teaching of the other-self. Until an other-self reaches green ray, such energy transfer through the rays is not possible.

QUESTIONER: What is the difference between indigo and blue ray transfer?

RA: I am Ra. The indigo ray is the ray of, shall we say, awareness of the Creator as self; thus one whose indigo ray vibrations have been activated can offer the energy transfer of Creator to Creator. This is the beginning of the sacramental nature of what you call your bisexual reproductive act. It is unique in bearing the allness, the wholeness, the unity in its offering to other-self.

QUESTIONER: What is the difference between violet ray and the others?

RA: I am Ra. The violet ray, just as the red ray, is constant in the sexual experience. Its experience by other-self may be distorted or completely ignored or not apprehended by other-self. However, the violet ray, being the sum and substance of the mind/body/spirit complex, surrounds and informs any action by a mind/body/spirit complex.

QUESTIONER: Do the energy transfers of this nature occur in the fifth, sixth, and seventh density—all the rays?

RA: I am Ra. The rays, as you understand them, have such a different meaning in the next density and the next and so forth that we must answer your query in the negative. Energy transfers only take place in fourth, fifth, and sixth densities. These are still of what you would call a polarized nature. However, due to the ability of these densities to see the harmonies between individuals, these entities choose those mates which are harmonious, thus allowing constant transfer of energy and the propagation of the body complexes which each density uses. The process is different in the fifth and the sixth density than you may understand it. However, it is in these cases still based upon polarity. In the seventh density there is not this particular energy exchange as it is unnecessary to recycle body complexes.

QUESTIONER: I am assuming we have on Earth today and have had in the past fourth-, fifth-, and sixth-density Wanderers. As they come into incarnation in the physical of this density for a period as a Wanderer, what types of polarizations with respect to these various rays do they find affecting them?

RA: I am Ra. I believe I grasp the thrust of your query. Please ask further if this answer is not sufficient.

Fourth-density Wanderers, of which there are not many, will tend to choose those entities which seem to be full of love or in need of love. There is the great possibility/probability of entities making errors in judgment due to the compassion with which other-selves are viewed.

The fifth-density Wanderer is one who is not tremendously affected by the stimulus of the various rays of other-self, and in its own way offers itself when a need is seen. Such entities are not likely to engage in the, shall we say, custom of your peoples called marriage and are very likely to feel an aversion to childbearing and child raising due to the awareness of the impropriety of the planetary vibrations relative to the harmonious vibrations of the density of light.

The sixth density, whose means of propagation you may liken to what you call fusion, is likely to refrain, to a great extent, from the bisexual reproductive programming of the bodily complex and instead seek out those with whom the sexual energy transfer is of the complete fusion nature insofar as this is possible in manifestation in third density.

QUESTIONER: Can you expand a little bit on what you mean by "complete fusion nature"?

RA: I am Ra. The entire creation is of the One Creator. Thus the division of sexual activity into simply that of the bodily complex is an artificial division, all things thusly being seen as sexual equally, the mind, the body, and the spirit; all of which are part of the polarity of the entity. Thus sexual fusion may be seen with or without what you may call sexual intercourse to be the complete melding of the mind, the body, and the spirit in what feels to be a constant orgasm, shall we say, of joy and delight each in the other's beingness.

QUESTIONER: Would many Wanderers of these densities have considerable problems with respect to incarnation in the third density because of this different orientation?

RA: I am Ra. The possibility/probability of such problems, as you call them, due to sixth density incarnating in third is rather large. It is not necessarily a problem if you would call it thusly. It depends upon the unique orientation of each mind/body/spirit complex having this situation or placement of vibratory relativities.

QUESTIONER: Can you give me an idea how the different colors . . . This is a difficult question to ask. I'm having trouble finding any words. What I'm trying to get at is how the different colors originate as the functions for the different expressions in consciousness? I don't know if this question is sufficient.

RA: I am Ra. This question is sufficiently clear for us to attempt explanation of what, as you have observed, is not easily grasped material for the intellectual mind. The nature of vibration is such that it may be seen as having mathematically strait or narrow steps. These steps may be seen as having boundaries. Within each boundary there are infinite gradations of vibration or color. However, as one approaches a boundary, an effort must be made to cross that boundary. These colors are a simplistic way of expressing the boundary divisions of your density. There is also the time/space analogy which may be seen as the color itself in a modified aspect.

QUESTIONER: Thank you. Is it possible for an entity in third-density physical to vary across the entire band of colors or is the entity pretty well zeroed in on one color?

RA: I am Ra. This will be the last full question of this working. Please restate for clarity.

QUESTIONER: I meant was it possible for a green-ray person who is primarily of green-ray activation to vary on both sides of the green ray in a large or a small amount in regards to energy activation, or is he primarily green ray?

RA: I am Ra. We grasp the newness of material requested by you. It was unclear, for we thought we had covered this material. The portion covered is this: the green-ray activation is always vulnerable to the yellow or orange ray of possession, this being largely yellow ray but often coming into orange ray. Fear of possession, desire for possession, fear of being possessed, desire to be possessed: these are the distortions which will cause the deactivation of green-ray energy transfer.

The new material is this: once the green ray has been achieved, the ability of the entity to enter blue ray is immediate and is only awaiting the efforts of the individual. The indigo ray is opened only through considerable discipline and practice largely having to do with acceptance of self, not only as the polarized and balanced self but as the Creator, as an entity of infinite worth. This will begin to activate the indigo ray.

QUESTIONER: Thank you.

RA: I am Ra. Do you have any brief queries before we close?

QUESTIONER: I think that anything I have would be too long, so I will just ask if there is anything that we can do to make the instrument more comfortable or to make the contact better?

RA: I am Ra. All is well. We caution not only this instrument but each to look well to the vital energies necessary for nondepletion of the instrument and the contact level. You are most conscientious, my friends. We shall be with you. I leave you now in the love and in the light of the One Infinite Creator. Go forth, then, rejoicing in the power and the peace of the One Infinite Creator. Adonai.

Session 33,
March 1, 1981

RA: I am Ra. I greet you in the love and in the light of the One Infinite Creator. I communicate now.

QUESTIONER: In our last session you said that each of us in these sessions should look well to the vital energies necessary for nondepletion of the instrument and the contact level. Did that mean that we should look at the instrument's vital energies or be careful of our own vital energies?

RA: I am Ra. Each entity is responsible for itself. The mechanics of this process taking place involve firstly, the use of the physical bodily complex of third density with its accompanying physical material in order to voice these words. Thus this instrument needs to watch its vital energies carefully, for we do not wish to deplete this instrument. Secondly, the function of the supporting group may be seen to be firstly, that of protection for this contact; secondly, that of energizing the instrument and intensifying its vital energies.

This supporting group has always, due to an underlying harmony, been of a very stable nature as regards protection in love and light, thus ensuring the continuation of this narrow band contact. However, the vital energies of either of the supporting members being depleted, the instrument must then use a larger portion of its vital energies, thus depleting itself more than would be profitable on a long-term basis.

Please understand that we ask your apology for this infringement upon your free will. However, it is our distortion/understanding that you would prefer this information rather than, being left totally to your own dedication/distortion, deplete the instrument or deplete the group to the point where the contact cannot be sustained.

QUESTIONER: Can you give us advice on how to maintain the best possible condition for maintaining contact?

RA: I am Ra. We have given information concerning the proper nurturing of this channel. We, therefore, repeat ourselves only in two ways in general. Firstly, we suggest that rather than being, shall we say, brave and ignoring a physical complex weakness/distortion it is good to share this distortion with the group and thus perhaps, shall we say, remove one opportunity for contact which is very wearying for the instrument, in order that another opportunity might come about in which the instrument is properly supported.

Secondly, the work begun in harmony may continue in harmony, thanksgiving and praise of opportunities and of the Creator. These are your protections. These are our suggestions. We cannot be specific for your free will is of the essence in this contact. As we said, we only speak to this subject because of our grasp of your orientation towards long-term maintenance of this contact. This is acceptable to us.

QUESTIONER: Thank you very much. We have a device for so-called color therapy, and since we were on the concept of the different colors in the last session I was wondering if this would in some way apply to the principle of color therapy in the shining of particular colors on the physical body. Does this create a beneficial effect and can you tell me something about it?

RA: I am Ra. This therapy, as you call it, is a somewhat clumsy and variably useful tool for instigating in an entity's mind/body/spirit complex an intensification of energies or vibrations which may be of aid to the entity. The variableness of this device is due firstly to the lack of true colors used, secondly, to the extreme variation in sensitivity to vibration among your peoples.

QUESTIONER: I would think that you could achieve a true color by passing light through a crystal of the particular color. Is this correct?

RA: I am Ra. This would be one way of approaching accuracy in color. It is a matter of what you would call quality control that the celluloid used is of a varying color. This is not of a great or even visible variation, however, it does make some difference given specific applications.

QUESTIONER: Possibly you could use a prism breaking white light into its spectrum and screening off all parts of the spectrum except that which you wish to use by passing it through a slit. Would this be true?

RA: I am Ra. This is correct.

QUESTIONER: I was wondering if there is a programming of experiences that causes an individual to get certain catalysts in his daily life. For instance, as we go through our daily life there are many things which we can experience. We can look at these experiences as occurring by pure chance or by a conscious design of our own such as making appointments or going places. I was wondering if there was a behind-the-scenes, as you might call it, programming of catalyst to create the necessary experiences for more rapid growth in the case of some entities. Does this happen?

RA: I am Ra. We believe we grasp the heart of your query. Please request further information if we are not correct.

The incarnating entity which has become conscious of the incarnative process and thus programs its own experience may choose the amount of catalyst or, to phrase this differently, the number of lessons which it will undertake to experience and to learn from in one incarnation. This does not mean that all is predestined, but rather that there are invisible guidelines shaping events which will function according to this programming. Thus if one opportunity is missed another will appear until the, shall we say, student of the life experience grasps that a lesson is being offered and undertakes to learn it.

QUESTIONER: Then these lessons would be reprogrammed, you might say, as the life experience continues. Let's say that an entity develops the bias that he actually didn't choose to develop prior to incarnation. It is then possible to program experiences so that he will have an opportunity to alleviate this bias through balancing. Is this correct?

RA: I am Ra. This is precisely correct.

QUESTIONER: Thank you. From this I would extrapolate to the con- jecture that the orientation in mind of the entity is the only thing that is of any consequence at all. The physical catalyst that he expe- riences, regardless of what is happening about him, will be a function strictly of his orientation in mind. I will use as an example (example deleted) this being a statement of the orientation in mind governing the catalyst. Is this correct?

RA: I am Ra. We prefer not to use any well-known examples, sayings, or adages in our communications to you due to the tremendous amount of distortion which any well-known saying has undergone. Therefore, we may answer the first part of your query asking that you delete the example. It is completely true to the best of our knowl- edge that the orientation or polarization of the mind/body/spirit complex is the cause of the perceptions generated by each entity. Thus a scene may be observed in your grocery store. The entity ahead of self may be without sufficient funds. One entity may then take this opportunity to steal. Another may take this opportunity to feel itself a failure. Another may unconcernedly remove the least neces- sary items, pay for what it can, and go about its business. The one behind the self, observing, may feel compassion, may feel an insult because of standing next to a poverty-stricken person, may feel gen- erosity, may feel indifference.

Do you now see the analogies in a more appropriate manner?

QUESTIONER: I think that I do. Then from this I will extrapolate the concept which is somewhat more difficult because as you have explained before, even fourth-density positive has the concept of defensive action, but above the level of fourth density the concept of defensive action is not in use. The concept of defensive action and offensive action are very much in use in our present density.

I am assuming that if an entity is polarized strongly enough in his thought in a positive sense that defensive action is not going to be necessary for him because the opportunity to apply defensive action will never originate for him. Is this correct?

RA: I am Ra. This is unknowable. In each case, as we have said, an entity able to program experiences may choose the number and the intensity of lessons to be learned. It is possible that an extremely positively oriented entity might program for itself situations testing the ability of self to refrain from defensive action even to the point of the physical death of self or other-self. This is an intensive lesson and it is not known, shall we say, what entities have programmed. We may, if we desire, read this programming. However, this is an infringement and we choose not to do so.

QUESTIONER: I will ask you if you are familiar with a motion picture called *The Ninth Configuration*. Are you familiar with this?

RA: I am Ra. We scan your mind and see this configuration called *The Ninth Configuration*.

QUESTIONER: This motion picture brought out the point about which we have been talking. The Colonel had to make a decision. I was wondering about his polarization. He could have knuckled under, you might say, to the negative forces, but he chose to defend his friend instead. Is it possible for you to estimate which is more positively polarizing: to defend the positively oriented entity, or to allow suppression by the negatively oriented entities?

RA: I am Ra. This question takes in the scope of fourth density as well as your own and its answer may best be seen by the action of the entity called Jehoshuah, which you call Jesus. This entity was to be defended by its friends. The entity reminded its friends to put away the sword. This entity then delivered itself to be put to the physical death. The impulse to protect the loved other-self is one which persists through the fourth density, a density abounding in compassion. More than this we cannot and need not say.

QUESTIONER: Thank you. As we near the end of this master cycle there may be an increasing amount of catalyst for entities. I am wondering if, as the planetary vibrations mismatch somewhat with the fourth-density vibrations and catalyst is increased, if this will create more polarization thereby getting a slightly greater harvest?

RA: I am Ra. The question must be answered in two parts. Firstly, the planetary catastrophes, as you may call them, are a symptom of the difficult harvest rather than a consciously programmed catalyst for harvest. Thus we do not concern ourselves with it, for it is random in respect to conscious catalyst such as we may make available.

The second portion is this: the results of the random catalyst of what you call the Earth changes are also random. Thus we may see probability/possibility vortices going towards positive and negative. However, it will be as it will be. The true opportunities for conscious catalyst are not a function of the Earth changes but of the result of the seniority system of incarnations which at the time of the harvest has placed in incarnation those whose chances of using life experiences to become harvestable are the best.

QUESTIONER: Is this seniority system also used in the service-to-self side for becoming harvestable on that side?

RA: I am Ra. This is correct. You may ask one more full question at this time.

QUESTIONER: What I would like for you to do is list all the major mechanisms designed to provide catalytic experience that do not include interaction with other-self. That is the first part.

RA: I am Ra. We grasp from this question that you realize that the primary mechanism for catalytic experience in third density is other-self. The list of other catalytic influences: firstly, the Creator's universe; secondly, the self.

QUESTIONER: Can you list any sub-headings under self or ways the self is acted upon catalytically which would produce experience?

RA: I am Ra. Firstly, the self unmanifested. Secondly, the self in relation to the societal self created by self and other-self. Thirdly, the interaction between self and the gadgets, toys, and amusements of the self, other-self invention. Fourthly, the self-relationship with those attributes which you may call war and rumors of war.

QUESTIONER: I was thinking possibly of the catalyst of physical pain. Does this go under this heading?

RA: I am Ra. This is correct, it going under the heading of the unmanifested self; that is, the self which does not need other-self in order to manifest or act.

QUESTIONER: Do we have enough time left to ask the second part of this question which is to list all major mechanisms designed to provide the catalyst that include action with other-self?

RA: I am Ra. You have much time for this, for we may express this list in one of two ways. We could speak infinitely, or we could simply state that any interaction betwixt self and other-self has whatever potential for catalyst that there exists in the potential difference between self and other-self, this moderated and undergirded by the constant fact of the Creator as self and as other-self. You may ask to this question further if you wish specific information.

QUESTIONER: I believe that this is sufficient for the time being.

RA: I am Ra. Do you have a brief query or two before we close this working?

QUESTIONER: Yes, here is one question. Is there any difference in violet-ray activity or brightness between entities who are at entrance level both positive and negative to fourth density?

RA: I am Ra. This correct. The violet ray of the positive fourth density will be tinged with the green, blue, indigo triad of energies. This tinge may be seen as a portion of a rainbow or prism, as you know it, the rays being quite distinct.
The violet ray of fourth-density negative has in its aura, shall we say, the tinge of red, orange, yellow, these rays being muddied rather than distinct.

QUESTIONER: What would the rays of fifth and sixth density look like?

RA: I am Ra. We may speak only approximately. However, we hope you understand, shall we say, that there is a distinctive difference in the color structure of each density.

Fifth density is perhaps best described as extremely white in vibration.

The sixth density of a whiteness which contains a golden quality as you would perceive it; these colors having to do with the blending into wisdom of the compassion learned in fourth density, then in sixth the blending of wisdom back into an unified understanding of compassion viewed with wisdom. This golden color is not of your spectrum but is what you would call alive.

You may ask one more question briefly.

QUESTIONER: Then I will ask if there is anything that we can do to make the instrument more comfortable or to improve the contact?

RA: I am Ra. This working is well. You are attempting to be conscientious. We thank you. May we say we enjoyed your vision of our social memory complex drinking one of your liquids while speaking through this instrument.

I am Ra. I leave you in the love and in the light of the One Infinite Creator. Go forth, then, rejoicing in the power and the peace of the One Infinite Creator. Adonai.

Session 34,
March 4, 1981

RA: I am Ra. I greet you in the love and in the light of the One Infinite Creator. We communicate now.

QUESTIONER: You stated at an earlier time that penetration of the eighth level or intelligent infinity allows a mind/body/spirit complex to be harvested if it wishes at any time/space during the cycle. When this penetration of the eighth level occurs what does the entity who penetrates it experience?

RA: I am Ra. The experience of each entity is unique in its perception of intelligent infinity. Perceptions range from a limitless joy to a strong dedication to service to others while in the incarnated state. The entity which reaches intelligent infinity most often will perceive this experience as one of unspeakable profundity. However, it is not usual for the entity to immediately desire the cessation of the incarnation. Rather the desire to communicate or use this experience to aid others is extremely strong.

QUESTIONER: Thank you. Would you define karma?

RA: I am Ra. Our understanding of karma is that which may be called inertia. Those actions which are put into motion will continue using the ways of balancing until such time as the controlling or higher principle which you may liken unto your braking or stopping is invoked. This stoppage of the inertia of action may be called forgiveness. These two concepts are inseparable.

QUESTIONER: If an entity develops what is called karma in an incarnation, is there then programming that sometimes occurs so that he will experience catalysts that will enable him to get to a point of forgiveness thereby alleviating the karma?

RA: I am Ra. This is, in general, correct. However, both self and any involved other-self may, at any time through the process of understanding, acceptance, and forgiveness, ameliorate these patterns. This is true at any point in an incarnative pattern. Thus one who has set in motion an action may forgive itself and never again make that error. This also brakes or stops what you call karma.

QUESTIONER: Thank you. Can you give me examples of catalytic action from the last session beginning with the self unmanifested producing learning catalyst?

RA: I am Ra. We observed your interest in the catalyst of pain. This experience is most common among your entities. The pain may be of the physical complex. More often it is of the mental and emotional complex. In some few cases the pain is spiritual in complex nature. This creates a potential for learning. The lessons to be learned vary. Almost always these lessons include patience, tolerance, and the ability for the light touch.

Very often the catalyst for emotional pain, whether it be the death of the physical complex of one other-self which is loved or other seeming loss, will simply result in the opposite, in a bitterness and impatience, a souring. This is catalyst which has gone awry. In these cases then there will be additional catalyst provided to offer the unmanifested self further opportunities for discovering the self as all-sufficient Creator containing all that there is and full of joy.

QUESTIONER: Do what we call contagious diseases play any part in this process with respect to the unmanifested self?

RA: I am Ra. These so-called contagious diseases are those entities of second density which offer an opportunity for this type of catalyst. If this catalyst is unneeded, then these second-density creatures, as you would call them, do not have an effect. In each of these generalizations you may please note that there are anomalies so that we cannot speak to every circumstance but only to the general run or way of things as you experience them.

QUESTIONER: What part do what we call birth defects play in this process?

RA: I am Ra. This is a portion of the programming of the mind/body/spirit complex totality manifested in the mind/body/spirit of third density. These defects are planned as limitations which are part of the experience intended by the entity's totality complex. This includes genetic predispositions, as you may call them.

QUESTIONER: Thank you. Can you give me the same type of information about the self in relation to the societal self?

RA: I am Ra. The unmanifested self may find its lessons those which develop any of the energy influx centers of the mind/body/spirit complex. The societal and self interactions most often concentrate upon the second and third energy centers. Thus those most active in attempting to remake or alter the society are those working from feelings of being correct personally or of having answers which will put power in a more correct configuration. This may be seen to be of a full travel from negative to positive in orientation. Either will activate these energy ray centers.

There are some few whose desires to aid society are of a green-ray nature or above. These entities, however, are few due to the understanding, may we say, of fourth ray that universal love freely given is more to be desired than principalities or even the rearrangement of peoples or political structures.

QUESTIONER: If an entity were to be strongly biased toward positive societal effects, what would this do to his yellow ray in the aura as opposed to an entity who wanted to create an empire of society and govern it with an iron fist?

RA: I am Ra. Let us take two such positively oriented active souls no longer in your physical time/space. The one known as Albert went into a strange and, to it, a barbaric society in order that it might heal.

This entity was able to mobilize great amounts of energy and what you call money. This entity spent much green-ray energy both as a healer and as a lover of your instrument known as the organ. This entity's yellow ray was bright and crystallized by the efforts needed to procure the funds to promulgate its efforts. However, the green and blue rays were of a toweringly brilliant nature as well. The higher levels, as you may call them, being activated, the lower, as you may call them, energy points remaining in a balance, being quite, quite bright.

The other example is the entity, Martin. This entity dealt in a great degree with rather negative orange-ray and yellow-ray vibratory patterns. However, this entity was able to keep open the green-ray energy and due to the severity of its testing, if anything, this entity may be seen to have polarized more towards the positive due to its fidelity to service to others in the face of great catalyst.

QUESTIONER: Could you give me the last names of Albert and Martin?

RA: I am Ra. These entities are known to you as Albert Schweitzer and Martin Luther King.

QUESTIONER: I thought that that was correct, but I wasn't sure. Can you give me the same type of information that we have been getting here with respect to the unmanifested interacting between self and gadgets and toys and inventions?

RA: I am Ra. In this particular instance we again concentrate for the most part in the orange and in the yellow energy centers. In a negative sense many of the gadgets among your peoples, that is what you call your communication devices and other distractions such as the less competitive games, may be seen to have the distortion of keeping the mind/body/spirit complex unactivated so that yellow- and orange-ray activity is much weakened thus carefully decreasing the possibility of eventual green-ray activation.

Others of your gadgets may be seen to be tools whereby the entity explores the capabilities of its physical or mental complexes and in some few cases, the spiritual complex, thus activating the orange ray in what you call your team sports and in other gadgets such as your modes of transport. These may be seen to be ways of investigating the feelings of power; more especially, power over others or a group power over another group of other-selves.

QUESTIONER: What is the general overall effect of television on our society with respect to this catalyst?

RA: I am Ra. Without ignoring the green-ray attempts of many to communicate via this medium such information of truth and beauty as may be helpful, we must suggest that the sum effect of this gadget is that of distraction and sleep.

QUESTIONER: Can you give me the same type of information that we are working on now with respect to war and rumors of war?

RA: I am Ra. You may see this in relationship to your gadgets. This war and self relationship is a fundamental perception of the maturing entity. There is a great chance to accelerate in whatever direction is desired. One may polarize negatively by assuming bellicose attitudes for whatever reason. One may find oneself in the situation of war and polarize somewhat towards the positive activating orange, yellow, and then green rays by heroic, if you may call them this, actions taken to preserve the mind/body/spirit complexes of other-selves.

Finally, one may polarize very strongly third ray by expressing the principle of universal love at the total expense of any distortion towards involvement in bellicose actions. In this way the entity may become a conscious being in a very brief span of your time/space. This may be seen to be what you would call a traumatic progression. It is to be noted that among your entities a large percentage of all progression has as catalyst, trauma.

QUESTIONER: You just used the term third ray in that statement. Was that the term you meant to use?

RA: I am Ra. We intended the green ray. Our difficulty lies in our perception of red ray and violet ray as fixed; thus the inner rays are those which are varying and are to be observed as those indications of seniority in the attempts to form an harvest.

QUESTIONER: Would the red ray, an intense red ray, then be used as an index for seniority in incarnation as well as an intense violet ray?

RA: I am Ra. This is partially correct. In the graduation or harvesting to fourth-density positive, the red ray is seen only as that, which being activated, is the basis for all that occurs in vibratory levels, the sum of this being violet-ray energy.

This violet ray is the only consideration for fourth-density positive. In assessing the harvestable fourth-density negative, the intensity of the red as well as the orange and the yellow rays is looked upon quite carefully as a great deal of stamina and energy of this type is necessary for the negative progression, it being extremely difficult to open the gateway to intelligent infinity from the solar plexus center. This is necessary for harvest in fourth-density negative.

QUESTIONER: Is it possible for you to use as an example our General Patton and tell me the effect that war had on him in his development?

RA: I am Ra. This will be the last full question of this working.

The one of whom you speak, known as George, was one in whom the programming of previous incarnations had created a pattern or inertia which was irresistible in its incarnation in your time/space. This entity was of a strong yellow-ray activation with frequent green-ray openings and occasional blue-ray openings. However, it did not find itself able to break the mold of previous traumatic experiences of a bellicose nature.

This entity polarized somewhat towards the positive in its incarnation due to its singleness of belief in truth and beauty. This entity was quite sensitive. It felt a great honor/duty to the preservation of that which was felt by the entity to be true, beautiful, and in need of defense. This entity perceived itself a gallant figure. It polarized somewhat towards the negative in its lack of understanding the green ray it carried with it, rejecting the forgiveness principle which is implicit in universal love.

The sum total of this incarnation vibrationally was a slight increase in positive polarity but a decrease in harvestability due to the rejection of the Law or Way of Responsibility; that is, seeing universal love, yet still it fought on.

QUESTIONER: Do we have enough time for me to ask if the death, almost immediately after the cessation of war, of this entity could have been so that it could have immediately been reincarnated so that it could make harvest?

RA: I am Ra. This is precisely correct.

QUESTIONER: Thank you. Then I will just ask if there is anything that we can do to make the instrument more comfortable or to improve the contact?

RA: I am Ra. All is well. We leave you, my friends, in the love and the light of the One which is All in All. I leave you in an ever-lasting peace. Go forth, therefore, rejoicing in the power and the peace of the One Infinite Creator. Adonai.

Session 35,
March 6, 1981

RA: I am Ra. I greet you in the love and in the light of the One Infinite Creator. We communicate now.

QUESTIONER: I would like to say that we consider it a great privilege to be doing this work, and we hope that we will be questioning in the direction that will be of value to the readers of this material. I thought that in this session it might be helpful to inspect the effect of the rays of different well-known figures in history to aid in understanding how the catalyst of the illusion creates spiritual growth. I was making a list that I thought we might use to hit the high points on the workings of the catalysts on these individuals starting with the one we know as Franklin D. Roosevelt. Could you say something about that entity?

RA: I am Ra. It is to be noted that in discussing those who are well known among your peoples there is the possibility that information may be seen to be specific to one entity whereas in actuality the great design of experience is much the same for each entity. It is with this in mind that we would discuss the experiential forces which offered catalyst to an individual.

It is further to be noted that in the case of those entities lately incarnate much distortion may have taken place in regard to misinformation and misinterpretation of an entity's thoughts or behaviors.

We shall now proceed to, shall we say, speak of the basic parameters of the one known as Franklin. When any entity comes into third-density incarnation, each of its energy centers is potentiated but must be activated by the self using experience.

The one known as Franklin developed very quickly up through red, orange, yellow, and green and began to work in the blue-ray energy center at a tender age, as you would say. This rapid growth was due, firstly, to previous achievements in the activation of the rays, secondly, to the relative comfort and leisure of its early existence, thirdly, due to the strong desire upon the part of the entity to progress. This entity mated with an entity whose blue ray vibrations were of a strength more than equal to its own thus acquiring catalyst for further growth in that area that was to persist throughout the incarnation.

This entity had some difficulty with continued green-ray activity due to the excessive energy which was put into the activities regarding other-selves in the distortion towards acquiring power. This was to have its toll upon the physical vehicle, as you may call it. The limitation of the nonmovement of a portion of the physical vehicle opened once again, for this entity, the opportunity for concentration upon the more, shall we say, universal or idealistic aspects of power; that is, the nonabusive use of power. Thus at the outset of a bellicose action this entity had lost some positive polarity due to excessive use of the orange- and yellow-ray energies at the expense of green- and blue-ray energies, then had regained the polarity due to the catalytic effects of a painful limitation upon the physical complex.

This entity was not of a bellicose nature but rather during the conflict continued to vibrate in green ray working with the blue-ray energies. The entity who was the one known as Franklin's teacher also functioned greatly during this period as blue-ray activator, not only for its mate but also in a more universal expression. This entity polarized continuously in a positive fashion in the universal sense while, in a less universal sense, developing a pattern of what may be called karma; this karma having to do with inharmonious relationship distortions with the mate/teacher.

QUESTIONER: Two things I would like to clear up. First, then Franklin's teacher was his wife? Is this correct?

RA: I am Ra. This is correct.

QUESTIONER: Secondly, did Franklin place the physical limitation on his body himself?

RA: I am Ra. This is partially correct. The basic guidelines for the lessons and purposes of incarnation had been carefully set forth before incarnation by the mind/body/spirit complex totality. If the one known as Franklin had avoided the excessive enjoyment of or attachment to the competitiveness which may be seen to be inherent in the processes of its occupation, this entity would not have had the limitation.

However, the desire to serve and to grow was strong in this programming and when the opportunities began to cease due to these distortions towards love of power the entity's limiting factor was activated.

QUESTIONER: I would now like to ask for the same type of information with respect to Adolf Hitler. You have given a little of this already. It is not necessary for you to recover what you have already given. Could you complete that information?

RA: I am Ra. In speaking of the one you call Adolf we have some difficulty due to the intense amount of confusion present in this entity's life patterns as well as the great confusion which greets any discussion of this entity.

Here we see an example of one who, in attempting activation of the highest rays of energy while lacking the green-ray key, canceled itself out as far as polarization either towards positive or negative. This entity was basically negative. However, its confusion was such that the personality disintegrated, thus leaving the mind/body/spirit complex unharvestable and much in need of healing.

This entity followed the pattern of negative polarization which suggests the elite and the enslaved, this being seen by the entity to be of an helpful nature for the societal structure. However, in drifting from the conscious polarization into what you may call a twilight world where dream took the place of events in your space/time continuum, this entity failed in its attempt to serve the Creator in an harvestable degree along the path of service to self. Thus we see the so-called insanity which may often arise when an entity attempts to polarize more quickly than experience may be integrated.

We have advised and suggested caution and patience in previous communications and do so again, using this entity as an example of the over-hasty opening of polarization without due attention to the synthesized and integrated mind/body/spirit complex. To know your self is to have the foundation upon firm ground.

QUESTIONER: Thank you. That is an important example I believe. I was wondering if any of those who were subordinate to Adolf at that time were able to polarize in a harvestable nature on the negative path?

RA: I am Ra. We can speak only of two entities who may be harvestable in a negative sense, others still being in the physical incarnation: one known to you as Hermann; the other known, as it preferred to be called, Himmler.

QUESTIONER: Thank you. Earlier we discussed Abraham Lincoln as a rather unique case. Is it possible for you to tell us why the fourth-density being used Abraham Lincoln's body, what its orientation was, and when this took place with respect to the activities that were occurring in our society at that time?

RA: I am Ra. This is possible.

QUESTIONER: Would it be of value for the reader to know this in your estimation?

RA: I am Ra. You must shape your queries according to your discernment.

QUESTIONER: Well in that case I would like to know the motivation for this use of Abraham Lincoln's body at that time?

RA: I am Ra. This shall be the last full query of this session as we find the instrument quite low in vital energies.

The one known as Abraham had an extreme difficulty in many ways and, due to physical, mental, and spiritual pain, was weary of life but without the orientation to self-destruction. In your time, 1853, this entity was contacted in sleep by a fourth-density being. This being was concerned with the battles between the forces of light and the forces of darkness which have been waged in fourth density for many of your years.

This entity accepted the honor/duty of completing the one known as Abraham's karmic patterns and the one known as Abraham discovered that this entity would attempt those things which the one known as Abraham desired to do but felt it could not. Thus the exchange was made.

The entity, Abraham, was taken to a plane of suspension until the cessation of its physical vehicle much as though we of Ra would arrange with this instrument to remain in the vehicle, come out of the trance state, and function as this instrument, leaving this instrument's mind and spirit complex in its suspended state.

The planetary energies at this time were at what seemed to this entity to be at a critical point, for that which you know as freedom had gained in acceptance as a possibility among many peoples. This entity saw the work done by those beginning the democratic concept of freedom, as you call it, in danger of being abridged or abrogated by the rising belief and use of the principle of the enslavement of entities. This is a negative concept of a fairly serious nature in your density. This entity, therefore, went forward into what it saw as the battle for the light, for healing of a rupture in the concept of freedom.

This entity did not gain or lose karma by these activities due to its detachment from any outcome. Its attitude throughout was one of service to others, more especially to the downtrodden or enslaved. The polarity of the individual was somewhat, but not severely, lessened by the cumulative feelings and thought-forms which were created due to large numbers of entities leaving the physical plane due to trauma of battle.

May we ask if this is the information you requested or if we may supply any further information?

QUESTIONER: I will ask any further questions during the next working period which should occur in about four days. We do not want to overtire the instrument. I will only ask if there is anything that we can do to make the instrument more comfortable or to improve the contact?

RA: I am Ra. All is well. I leave you, my friends, in the love and the light of the One Infinite Creator. Go forth, therefore rejoicing in the power and the peace of the One Creator. Adonai.

Session 36,
March 10, 1981

RA: I am Ra. I greet you in the love and the light of the One Infinite Creator. We communicate now.

QUESTIONER: In previous communications you have spoken of the mind/body/spirit complex totality. Would you please give us a definition of the mind/body/spirit complex totality?

RA: I am Ra. There is a dimension in which time does not have sway. In this dimension, the mind/body/spirit in its eternal dance of the present may be seen in totality, and before the mind/body/spirit complex which then becomes a part of the social memory complex is willingly absorbed into the allness of the One Creator, the entity knows itself in its totality.

This mind/body/spirit complex totality functions as, shall we say, a resource for what you perhaps would call the Higher Self. The Higher Self, in turn, is a resource for examining the distillations of third-density experience and programming further experience. This is also true of densities four, five, and six with the mind/body/spirit complex totality coming into consciousness in the course of seventh density.

QUESTIONER: Then would the mind/body/spirit complex totality be responsible for programming changes in catalyst during a third-density experience of the mind/body/spirit complex so that the proper catalyst would be added, shall we say, as conditions for the complex changed during third-density experience?

RA: I am Ra. This is incorrect. The Higher Self, as you call it, that is, that self which exists with full understanding of the accumulation of experiences of the entity, aids the entity in achieving healing of the experiences which have not been learned properly and assists as you have indicated in further life experience programming, as you may call it.

The mind/body/spirit complex totality is that which may be called upon by the Higher Self aspect just as the mind/body/spirit complex calls upon the Higher Self. In the one case you have a structured situation within the space/time continuum with the Higher Self having available to it the totality of experiences which have been collected by an entity and a very firm grasp of the lessons to be learned in this density.

The mind/body/spirit complex totality is as the shifting sands and is in some part a collection of parallel developments of the same entity. This information is made available to the Higher Self aspect. This aspect may then use these projected probability/possibility vortices in order to better aid in what you would call future life programming.

QUESTIONER: Out of the Seth Material we have a statement in which Seth says that each entity here on Earth is one part of or aspect of a Higher Self or Oversoul which has many aspects or parts in many dimensions all of which learn lessons which allow the Higher Self to progress in a balanced manner. Am I to understand from this that there are many experiences similar to the one which we experience in the third density which are governed by a single Higher Self?

RA: I am Ra. The correctness of this statement is variable. The more in balance an entity becomes, the less the possibility/probability vortices may need to be explored in parallel experiences.

QUESTIONER: Do I understand from this then that the Higher Self or Oversoul may break down into numerous units if the experience is required to what we would call simultaneously experience different types of catalysts and then oversee these experiences?

RA: I am Ra. This is a statement we cannot say to be correct or incorrect due to the confusions of what you call time. True simultaneity is available only when all things are seen to be occurring at once. This overshadows the concept of which you speak. The concept of various parts of the being living experiences of varying natures simultaneously is not precisely accurate due to your understanding that this would indicate that this was occurring with true simultaneity. This is not the case.

The case is from universe to universe and parallel existences can then be programmed by the Higher Self, given the information available from the mind/body/spirit complex totality regarding the probability/possibility vortices at any crux.

QUESTIONER: Could you give an example of how this programming by the Higher Self would then bring about education through parallel experiences?

RA: I am Ra. Perhaps the simplest example of this apparent simultaneity of existence of two selves, which are in truth one self at the same time/space, is this: the Oversoul, as you call it, or Higher Self, seems to exist simultaneously with the mind/body/spirit complex which it aids. This is not actually simultaneous, for the Higher Self is moving to the mind/body/spirit complex as needed from a position in development of the entity which would be considered in the future of this entity.

QUESTIONER: Then the Higher Self operates from the future as we understand things. In other words my Higher Self would operate from what I consider to be my future? Is this correct?

RA: I am Ra. From the standpoint of your space/time, this is correct.

QUESTIONER: In that case my Higher Self would have a very large advantage in knowing what was needed since it would know, as far as I am concerned, what was going to happen. Is this correct?

RA: I am Ra. This is incorrect, in that this would be an abrogation of free will. The Higher Self aspect is aware of the lessons learned through the sixth density. The progress rate is fairly well understood. The choices which must be made to achieve the Higher Self as it is are in the provenance of the mind/body/spirit complex itself.

Thus the Higher Self is like the map in which the destination is known; the roads are very well known, these roads being designed by intelligent infinity working through intelligent energy. However, the Higher Self aspect can program only for the lessons and certain predisposing limitations if it wishes. The remainder is completely the free choice of each entity. There is the perfect balance between the known and the unknown.

QUESTIONER: I'm sorry for having so much trouble with these concepts, but they are very difficult I am sure to translate into our understanding and language. Some of my questions may be rather ridiculous, but does this Higher Self have some type of vehicle like our physical vehicle? Does it have a bodily complex?

RA: I am Ra. This is correct. The Higher Self is of a certain advancement within sixth density going into the seventh. After the seventh has been well entered the mind/body/spirit complex becomes so totally a mind/body/spirit complex totality that it begins to gather spiritual mass and approach the octave density. Thus the looking backwards is finished at that point.

QUESTIONER: Is the Higher Self of every entity of a sixth-density nature?

RA: I am Ra. This is correct. This is an honor/duty of self to self as one approaches seventh density.

QUESTIONER: Let me be sure that I understand this then. We have spoken of certain particular individuals. For instance we were speaking of George Patton in a previous communication. Then his Higher Self at the time of his incarnation here as George Patton about forty years ago was of sixth density? Is this correct?

RA: I am Ra. This is correct. We make note at this time that each entity has several beings upon which to call for inner support. Any of these may be taken by an entity to be the mind/body/spirit complex totality. However, this is not the case. The mind/body/spirit complex totality is a nebulous collection of all that may occur held in understanding; the Higher Self itself a projection or manifestation of mind/body/spirit complex totality which then may communicate with the mind/body/spirit during the discarnate part of a cycle of rebirth or during the incarnation; may communicate if the proper pathways or channels through the roots of mind are opened.

QUESTIONER: These channels would then be opened by meditation and I am assuming that the intense polarization would help in this. Is this correct?

RA: I am Ra. This is partially correct. Intense polarization does not necessarily develop, in the mind/body/spirit complex, the will or need to contact the Oversoul. Each path of life experience is unique. However, given the polarization, the will is greatly enhanced and vice versa.

QUESTIONER: Let me take as an example the one that you said was called Himmler. We are assuming from this that his Higher Self was of the sixth density and it was stated that Himmler had selected the negative path. Would his Higher Self then dwell in a sixth-density negative type of situation? Can you expand on this concept?

RA: I am Ra. There are no negative beings which have attained the Oversoul manifestation, which is the honor/duty of the mind/body/spirit complex totality, of late sixth density as you would term it in your time measurements. These negatively oriented mind/body/spirit complexes have a difficulty which to our knowledge has never been overcome, for after fifth-density graduation wisdom is available but must be matched with an equal amount of love. This love/light is very, very difficult to achieve in unity when following the negative path and during the earlier part of the sixth density, society complexes of the negative orientation will choose to release the potential and leap into the sixth-density positive.

Therefore, the Oversoul which makes its understanding available to all who are ready for such aid is towards the positive. However, the free will of the individual is paramount, and any guidance given by the Higher Self may be seen in either the positive or negative polarity depending upon the choice of a mind/body/spirit complex.

QUESTIONER: Then using Himmler as an example, was his Higher Self at the time he was incarnate in the 1940s a sixth-density positively oriented Higher Self?

RA: I am Ra. This is correct.

QUESTIONER: Was Himmler in any way in contact with his Higher Self at that time when he was incarnate during the 1940s?

RA: I am Ra. We remind you that the negative path is one of separation. What is the first separation: the self from the self. The one known as Himmler did not choose to use its abilities of will and polarization to seek guidance from any source but its conscious drives, self-chosen in the life experience and nourished by previous biases created in other life experiences.

QUESTIONER: Well then let's say that when Himmler reaches sixth-density negative, would he realize that his Higher Self was positively oriented and for that reason make the jump from negative to positive orientation?

RA: I am Ra. This is incorrect. The sixth-density negative entity is extremely wise. It observes the spiritual entropy occurring due to the lack of ability to express the unity of sixth density. Thus, loving the Creator and realizing at some point that the Creator is not only self but other-self as self, this entity consciously chooses an instantaneous energy reorientation so that it may continue its evolution.

QUESTIONER: Then the sixth-density entity who has reached that point in positive orientation may choose to become what we call a Wanderer and move back. I am wondering if this ever occurs with a negatively oriented sixth-density entity? Do any ever move back as Wanderers?

RA: I am Ra. Once the negatively polarized entity has reached a certain point in the wisdom density it becomes extremely unlikely that it will choose to risk the forgetting, for this polarization is not selfless but selfish and with wisdom realizes the jeopardy of such "Wandering." Occasionally a sixth-density negative becomes a Wanderer in an effort to continue to polarize towards the negative. This is extremely unusual.

QUESTIONER: Then what is the mechanism that this unusual sixth-density entity would wish to gain to polarize more negatively through Wandering?

RA: I am Ra. The Wanderer has the potential of greatly accelerating the density whence it comes in its progress in evolution. This is due to the intensive life experiences and opportunities of the third density. Thusly the positively oriented Wanderer chooses to hazard the danger of the forgetting in order to be of service to others by radiating love of others. If the forgetting is penetrated the amount of catalyst in third density will polarize the Wanderer with much greater efficiency than shall be expected in the higher and more harmonious densities.

Similarly, the negatively oriented Wanderer dares to hazard the forgetting in order that it might accelerate its progress in evolution in its own density by serving itself in third density by offering to other-selves the opportunity to hear the information having to do with negative polarization.

QUESTIONER: Are there any examples of sixth-density negatively polarized Wanderers in our historical past?

RA: I am Ra. This information could be harmful. We withhold it. Please attempt to view the entities about you as part of the Creator. We can explain no further.

QUESTIONER: It is very difficult at times for us to get more than a small percentage of understanding of some of these concepts because of our limitation of awareness, but I think that some meditation on the information from today will help us in formulating some questions about these concepts.

RA: I am Ra. May we ask for any brief queries before we leave this instrument?

QUESTIONER: I'll just ask one short one before we close. Can you tell me what percentage of the Wanderers on Earth today have been successful in penetrating the memory block and have become aware of who they are, and finally, is there anything that we can do to make the instrument more comfortable or to improve the contact?

RA: I am Ra. We can approximate the percentage of those penetrating intelligently their status. This is between eight and one-half and nine and three-quarters percent. There is a larger percentile group of those who have a fairly well defined, shall we say, symptomology indicating to them that they are not of this, shall we say, "insanity." This amounts to a bit over fifty percent of the remainder. Nearly one-third of the remainder are aware that something about them is different, so you see there are many gradations of awakening to the knowledge of being a Wanderer. We may add that it is to the middle and first of these groups that this information will, shall we say, make sense.

This instrument is well. The resting place is somewhat deleterious in its effect upon the comfort of the dorsal side of this instrument's physical vehicle. We have mentioned this before.

You are conscientious. We leave you now, my friends.

I am Ra. I leave you in the love and in the light of the Infinite Creator. Go forth, then, rejoicing merrily in the power and the peace of the One Creator. Adonai.

Session 37,
March 12, 1981

RA: I am Ra. I greet you in the love and in the light of the One Infinite Creator. We communicate now.

QUESTIONER: You said that each third-density entity has an Higher Self in the sixth density which is moving to the mind/body/spirit complex of the entity as needed. Does this Higher Self also evolve in growth through the densities beginning with the first density, and does each Higher Self have a corresponding Higher Self advanced in densities beyond it?

RA: I am Ra. To simplify this concept is our intent. The Higher Self is a manifestation given to the late sixth-density mind/body/spirit complex as a gift from its future selfness. The mid-seventh density's last action before turning towards the allness of the Creator and gaining spiritual mass is to give this resource to the sixth-density self, moving as you measure time in the stream of time.

This self, the mind/body/spirit complex of late sixth density, has then the honor/duty of using both the experiences of its total living bank of memory of experience, thoughts, and actions, and using the resource of the mind/body/spirit complex totality left behind as a type of infinitely complex thought-form.

In this way you may see your self, your Higher Self or Oversoul, and your mind/body/spirit complex totality as three points in a circle. The only distinction is that of your time/space continuum. All are the same being.

QUESTIONER: Does each entity have an individual mind/body/spirit complex totality or do a number of entities share the same mind/body/spirit complex totality?

RA: I am Ra. Both of these statements are correct given the appropriate time/space conditions. Each entity has its totality and at the point at which a planetary entity becomes a social memory complex the totality of this union of entities also has its Oversoul and its social memory complex totality as resource. As always, the sum, spiritually speaking, is greater than the sum of its parts so that the Oversoul of a social memory complex is not the sum of the Oversouls of its member entities but operates upon the way of what we have called squares and what we grasp you prefer to call doubling.

QUESTIONER: Thank you. And thank you for that explanation of the mathematics too. Could you define spiritual mass?

RA: I am Ra. This will be the last full question of this session.
Spiritual mass is that which begins to attract the out-moving and ongoing vibratory oscillations of beingness into the gravity, speaking in a spiritual sense, well of the great central sun, core, or Creator of the infinite universes.

QUESTIONER: Since we don't want to tire the instrument I will just ask if there is anything that we can do to make the instrument more comfortable or to improve the contact?

RA: I am Ra. All is well. We leave you now in the love and the light of the One Infinite Creator. Go forth, then, rejoicing in the power and the peace of the One Infinite Creator. Adonai.

Session 38,
March 13, 1981

RA: I am Ra. I greet you in the love and in the light of the One Infinite Creator. We communicate now.

QUESTIONER: Backtracking just a little bit today I would like to know if the reason nuclear energy was brought into this density forty or so years ago had anything to do with giving the entities who were here who had caused the destruction of Maldek another chance to use nuclear energy peacefully rather than destructively?

RA: I am Ra. This is incorrect in that it places cart before horse, as your people say. The desire for this type of information attracted this data to your people. It was not given for a reason from outside influences; rather it was desired by your peoples. From this point forward your reasoning is correct in that entities had desired the second chance which you mentioned.

QUESTIONER: What was the mechanism for fulfilling the desire for the information regarding nuclear energy?

RA: I am Ra. As we understand your query the mechanism was what you may call inspiration.

QUESTIONER: Would this inspiration be an entity impressing the person desiring the information with thoughts? Would this be the mechanism of inspiration?

RA: I am Ra. The mechanism of inspiration involves an extraordinary faculty of desire or will to know or to receive in a certain area accompanied by the ability to open to and trust in what you may call intuition.

QUESTIONER: Could you tell me how each of the rays, red through violet, would appear in a perfectly balanced and undistorted entity?

RA: I am Ra. We cannot tell you this for each balance is perfect and each unique. We do not mean to be obscure.

Let us offer an example. In a particular entity, let us use as an example a Wanderer; the rays may be viewed as extremely even, red, orange, yellow. The green ray is extremely bright. This is, shall we say, balanced by a dimmer indigo. Between these two the point of balance resides, the blue ray of the communicator sparkling in strength above the ordinary. In the violet ray we see this unique spectrograph, if you will, and at the same time the pure violet surrounding the whole; this in turn, surrounded by that which mixes the red and violet ray, indicating the integration of mind, body, and spirit; this surrounded in turn by the vibratory pattern of this entity's true density.

This description may be seen to be both unbalanced and in perfect balance. The latter understanding is extremely helpful in dealing with other-selves. The ability to feel blockages is useful only to the healer. There is not properly a tiny fraction of judgment when viewing a balance in colors. Of course when we see many of the energy plexi weakened and blocked, we may understand that an entity has not yet grasped the baton and begun the race. However, the potentials are always there. All the rays fully balanced are there in waiting to be activated.

Perhaps another way to address your query is this: In the fully potentiated entity the rays mount one upon the other with equal vibratory brilliance and scintillating sheen until the surrounding color is white. This is what you may call potentiated balance in third density.

QUESTIONER: Is it possible for a third-density planet to form a social memory complex which operates in third density?

RA: I am Ra. It is possible only in the latter or seventh portion of such a density when entities are harmoniously readying for graduation.

QUESTIONER: Could you give me an example of a planet of this nature, both a third-density service-to-others type and a third-density service-to-self type at this level of attainment?

RA: I am Ra. As far as we are aware there are no negatively oriented third-density social memory complexes. Positively oriented social memory complexes of third density are not unheard of but quite rare. However, an entity from the star Sirius's planetary body has approached this planetary body twice. This entity is late third density and is part of a third-density social memory complex. This has been referred to in the previous material. The social memory complex is properly a fourth-density phenomenon.

QUESTIONER: I was wondering if that particular social memory complex from the Sirius star evolved from trees?

RA: I am Ra. This approaches correctness. Those second-density vegetation forms which graduated into third density upon this planet bearing the name of Dog were close to the tree as you know it.

QUESTIONER: I was also wondering, since action of a bellicose nature is impossible as far as I understand vegetation, would they not have the advantage as they move into third density from second to not carry a racial memory of a bellicose nature and therefore develop a more harmonious society and accelerate their evolution in this nature?

RA: I am Ra. This is correct. However, to become balanced and begin to polarize properly it is then necessary to investigate movements of all kinds, especially bellicosity.

QUESTIONER: I am assuming, then, that their investigations of bellicosity were primarily of the type that they extracted from Hixson's memory rather than warfare among themselves?

RA: I am Ra. This is correct. Entities of this heritage would find it nearly impossible to fight. Indeed, their studies of movements of all kinds is their form of meditation due to the fact that their activity is upon the level of what you would call meditation and thus must be balanced, just as your entities need constant moments of meditation to balance your activities.

QUESTIONER: I believe that this is an important point for us in understanding the balancing aspect of meditation since we have here its antithesis in another type of evolution. These entities moved, we are told by Charlie Hixson, without moving their legs. I am assuming that they used a principle that is somewhat similar to the principle of movement of your crystal bells in the movement of their physical vehicles. Is this correct?

RA: I am Ra. This is partially incorrect.

QUESTIONER: I am assuming that their method of movement is not a function of mechanical leverage such as ours, but a direct function of the mind somehow connected with the magnetic action of a planet. Is this right?

RA: I am Ra. This is largely correct. It is an electromagnetic phenomenon which is controlled by thought impulses of a weak electrical nature.

QUESTIONER: Would their craft have been visible to anyone on our planet in that area at that time? Is it of a third-density material like this chair?

RA: I am Ra. This is correct. Please ask one more full question before we close as this instrument has low vital energy at this space/time.

QUESTIONER: Could you give me some idea of what conditions are like on a fourth-density negative or service-to-self planet?

RA: I am Ra. The graduation into fourth-density negative is achieved by those beings who have consciously contacted intelligent infinity through the use of red, orange, and yellow rays of energy. Therefore, the planetary conditions of fourth-density negative include the constant alignment and realignment of entities in efforts to form dominant patterns of combined energy.

The early fourth density is one of the most intensive struggle. When the order of authority has been established and all have fought until convinced that each is in the proper placement for power structure, the social memory complex begins. Always the fourth-density effect of telepathy and the transparency of thought are attempted to be used for the sake of those at the apex of the power structure.

This, as you may see, is often quite damaging to the further polarization of fourth-density negative entities, for the further negative polarization can come about only through group effort. As the fourth-density entities manage to combine, they then polarize through such services to self as those offered by the crusaders of Orion.

You may ask more specific questions in the next session of working. Are there any brief queries before we leave this instrument?

QUESTIONER: I would just ask if there is anything that we can do to make the instrument more comfortable or to improve the contact?

RA: I am Ra. All is well. We leave you in the love and light of the One Infinite Creator. Go forth rejoicing in the power and in the peace of the one Creator. Adonai.

Session 39,
March 16, 1981

RA: I am Ra. I greet you in the love and in the light of the One Infinite Creator. We communicate now.

QUESTIONER: I noticed that most of the basic things seemed to be divided into units which total seven. In looking at a transcript by Henry Puharich of "The Nine" I found a statement by The Nine where they say, "If we get seven times the electrical equivalent of the human body then it would result in sevenon of the mass of electricity." Could you explain this?

RA: I am Ra. To explain this is beyond the abilities of your language. We shall, however, make an attempt to address this concept.

As you are aware, in the beginning of the creations set up by each Logos, there are created the complete potentials, both electrical, in the sense the one you call Larson intends, and metaphysical. This metaphysical electricity is as important in the understanding, shall we say, of this statement as is the concept of electricity.

This concept, as you are aware, deals with potentiated energy. The electron has been said to have no mass but only a field. Others claim a mass of infinitesimal measure. Both are correct. The true mass of the potentiated energy is the strength of the field. This is also true metaphysically.

However, in your present physical system of knowledge it is useful to take the mass number of the electron in order to do work that you may find solutions to other questions about the physical universe. In such a way, you may conveniently consider each density of being to have a greater and greater spiritual mass. The mass increases, shall we say, significantly but not greatly until the gateway density. In this density the summing up, the looking backwards—in short—all the useful functions of polarity have been used. Therefore, the metaphysical electrical nature of the individual grows greater and greater in spiritual mass.

For an analog one may observe the work of the one known as Albert who posits the growing to infinity of mass as this mass approaches the speed of light. Thus the seventh-density being, the completed being, the Creator who knows Itself, accumulates mass and compacts into the One Creator once again.

QUESTIONER: Then in the equation here I am assuming Mi is spiritual mass.

$$Mi = \frac{m_0 C^2}{\sqrt{1 - v^2/c^2}}$$

RA: I am Ra. This is correct.

QUESTIONER: Thank you. Can you tell me what this transmission from "The Nine" means? "CH is a principle which is the revealing principle of knowledge and of law"? Can you tell me what that principle is?

RA: I am Ra. The principle so veiled in that statement is but the simple principle of the constant or Creator and the transient or the incarnate being and the yearning existing between the two, one for the other, in love and light amidst the distortions of free will acting upon the illusion-bound entity.

QUESTIONER: Was the reason "The Nine" transmitted this principle in this form the first distortion?

RA: I am Ra. This is incorrect.

QUESTIONER: Can you tell me why they gave the principle in such a veiled form then?

RA: I am Ra. The scribe is most interested in puzzles and equations.

QUESTIONER: I see. "The Nine" describe themselves as the "nine principals of God." Can you tell me what they mean by that?

RA: I am Ra. This is also a veiled statement. The attempt is made to indicate that the nine who sit upon the Council are those representing the Creator, the One Creator, just as there may be nine witnesses in a courtroom testifying for one defendant. The term "principal" has this meaning also.

The desire of the scribe may be seen in much of this material to have affected the manner of its presentation just as the abilities and preferences of this group determine the nature of this contact. The difference lies in the fact that we are as we are. Thus we may either speak as we will or not speak at all. This demands a very tuned, shall we say, group.

QUESTIONER: I sense that there is fruitful ground for investigation of our development in tracing the evolution of the bodily energy centers because these seven centers seem to be linked with all of the sevens that I spoke of previously, and these seem to be central to our own development. Could you describe the process of evolution of these bodily energy centers starting with the most primitive form of life to have them?

RA: I am Ra. This material has been covered previously to some extent. Therefore, we shall not repeat information upon which rays dwell in first and second density and the wherefores of this, but rather attempt to enlarge upon this information.

The basic pivotal points of each level of development; that is, each density beyond second, may be seen to be as follows: Firstly, the basic energy of so-called red ray. This ray may be understood to be the basic strengthening ray for each density. It shall never be condescended to as less important or productive of spiritual evolution, for it is the foundation ray.

The next foundation ray is yellow. This is the great stepping-stone ray. At this ray the mind/body potentiates to its fullest balance. The strong red/orange/yellow triad springboards the entity into the center ray of green. This is again a basic ray but not a primary ray.

This is the resource for spiritual work. When green ray has been activated we find the third primary ray being able to begin potentiation. This is the first true spiritual ray in that all transfers are of an integrated mind/body/spirit nature. The blue ray seats the learnings/ teachings of the spirit in each density within the mind/body complex animating the whole, communicating to others this entirety of beingness.

The indigo ray, though precious, is that ray worked upon only by the adept, as you would call it. It is the gateway to intelligent infinity bringing intelligent energy through. This is the energy center worked upon in those teachings considered inner, hidden, and occult, for this ray is that which is infinite in its possibilities. As you are aware, those who heal, teach, and work for the Creator in any way which may be seen to be both radiant and balanced are those activities which are indigo ray.

As you are aware, the violet ray is constant and does not figure into a discussion of the functions of ray activation in that it is the mark, the register, the identity, the true vibration of an entity.

QUESTIONER: In order to clarify a little bit I would like to ask this question: If we have a highly polarized entity polarized towards service to others and a highly polarized entity polarized towards service to self, what would be the difference in the red ray of these two entities?

RA: I am Ra. This shall be the last full question of this working.

There is no difference in equally strongly polarized positive and negative entities as regards red ray.

QUESTIONER: Is this also true of all of the other rays?

RA: I am Ra. We shall answer briefly. You may question further at another working.

The negative ray pattern is the red/orange/yellow moving directly to the blue, this only being used in order to contact intelligent infinity.

In positively oriented entities the configuration is even, crystallinely clear, and of the seven ray description.

Are there any short queries before we leave this instrument?

QUESTIONER: I would just ask if there is anything that we can do to make the instrument more comfortable and to improve the contact?

RA: I am Ra. You are most conscientious. All is well. I leave you, my friends, in the love and in the light of the One Infinite Creator. Go forth therefore rejoicing in the power and in the peace of the One Creator. Adonai.

Session 40,
March 18, 1981

RA: I am Ra. I greet you in the love and in the light of the Infinite Creator. We communicate now.

QUESTIONER: I thought that I would make a statement and let you correct it. I'm trying to make a simple model of the portion of the universe that we find ourselves in. Starting with the sub-Logos, our sun, we have white light emanating from this which is made up of the frequencies ranging from the red to the violet. I am assuming that this white light then contains the experiences through all of the densities and as we go into the eighth density we go into a black hole which becomes, on the other side, another Logos or sun and starts another octave of experience. Can you comment on this part of my statement?

RA: I am Ra. We can comment upon this statement to an extent. The concept of the white light of the sub-Logos being prismatically separated and later, at the final chapter, being absorbed again is basically correct. However, there are subtleties involved which are more than semantic.

The white light which emanates and forms the articulated sub-Logos has its beginning in what may be metaphysically seen as darkness. The light comes into that darkness and transfigures it, causing the chaos to organize and become reflective or radiant. Thus the dimensions come into being.

Conversely, the blackness of the black hole, metaphysically speaking, is a concentration of white light being systematically absorbed once again into the One Creator. Finally, this absorption into the One Creator continues until all the infinity of creations have attained sufficient spiritual mass in order that all form once again the great central sun, if you would so imagine it, of the intelligent infinity awaiting potentiation by free will. Thus the transition of the octave is a process which may be seen to enter into timelessness of unimaginable nature. To attempt to measure it by your time measures would be useless.

Therefore, the concept of moving through the black hole of the ultimate spiritual gravity well and coming immediately into the next octave misses the subconcept or corollary of the portion of this process which is timeless.

QUESTIONER: Our astronomers have noticed that light from spiral galaxies is approximately seventy times less than it should be, considering the calculated mass of the galaxy. I was wondering if that was due to the increase of spiritual mass in the galaxy in what we call white dwarf stars?

RA: I am Ra. This is basically correct and is a portion of the way or process of creation's cycle.

QUESTIONER: Thank you. I was also wondering if the first density corresponded somehow to the color red, the second to the color orange, the third to the color yellow and so on through the densities corresponding to the colors in perhaps a way so that the basic vibration which forms the photon that forms the core of all atomic particles would have a relationship to the color in the density and that that vibration would step up for second, third, and fourth density corresponding to the increase in the vibration of the colors. Is any of this correct?

RA: I am Ra. This is more correct than you have stated. Firstly, you are correct in positing a quantum, if you will, as the nature of each density and further correct in assuming that these quanta may be seen to be of vibratory natures corresponding to color as you grasp this word. However, it is also true, as you have suspected but not asked, that each density is of the metaphysical characteristic complex of its ray. Thus in first density the red ray is the foundation for all that is to come. In second density the orange ray is that of movement and growth of the individual, this ray striving towards the yellow ray of self-conscious manifestations of a social nature as well as individual; third density being the equivalent, and so forth, each density being primarily its ray plus the attractions of the following ray pulling it forward in evolution and to some extent coloring or shading the chief color of that density.

QUESTIONER: Then bodily energy centers for an individual, assuming that the individual evolves in a straight line from first through to eighth density, would then be activated to completion if everything worked as it should? Would each chakra be activated to completion and greatest intensity by the end of the experience in each density?

RA: I am Ra. Hypothetically speaking, this is correct. However, the fully activated being is rare. Much emphasis is laid upon the harmonies and balances of individuals. It is necessary for graduation across densities for the primary energy centers to be functioning in such a way as to communicate with intelligent infinity and to appreciate and bask in this light in all of its purity. However, to fully activate each energy center is the mastery of few, for each center has a variable speed of rotation or activity. The important observation to be made once all necessary centers are activated to the minimal necessary degree is the harmony and balance between these energy centers.

QUESTIONER: Thank you. Taking as an example the transition between second and third density, when this transition takes place, does the frequency of vibration which forms the photon (the core of all the particles of the density) increase from a frequency corresponding to second density or the color orange to the frequency that we measure as the color yellow? What I am getting at is, do all the vibrations that form the density, the basic vibrations of the photon, increase in a quantum fashion over a relatively short period of time?

RA: I am Ra. This is correct. Then you see within each density the gradual upgrading of vibratory levels.

QUESTIONER: This is a guess. Would the frequency going from second to third increase from the middle orange or average orange frequency to the middle or average yellow frequency?

RA: I am Ra. This query is indeterminate. We shall attempt to be of aid. However, the frequency that is the basis of each density is what may be called a true color. This term is impossible to define given your system of sensibilities and scientific measurements, for color has vibratory characteristics both in space/time and in time/space. The true color is then overlaid and tinged by the rainbow of the various vibratory levels within that density and the attraction vibrations of the next true color density.

QUESTIONER: How long was the time of transition from second to third density? A generation and a half I believe you said. Is that correct?

RA: I am Ra. This is correct, the time measured in your years being approximately 1,350.

QUESTIONER: Then what will be the time of transition on this planet from third to fourth density?

RA: I am Ra. This is difficult to estimate due to the uncharacteristic anomalies of this transition. There are at this space/time nexus beings incarnate which have begun fourth-density work. However, the third-density climate of planetary consciousness is retarding the process. At this particular nexus the possibility/probability vortices indicate somewhere between 100 and 700 of your years as transition period. This cannot be accurate due to the volatility of your peoples at this space/time.

QUESTIONER: Has the vibration of the photon increased in frequency already?

RA: I am Ra. This is correct. It is this influence which has begun to cause thoughts to become things. As an example you may observe the thoughts of anger becoming those cells of the physical bodily complex going out of control to become what you call the cancer.

QUESTIONER: I am assuming that this vibratory increase began about twenty to thirty years ago. Is this correct?

RA: I am Ra. The first harbingers of this were approximately forty-five of your years ago, the energies vibrating more intensely through the forty-year period preceding the final movement of vibratory matter, shall we say, through the quantum leap, as you would call it.

QUESTIONER: Starting then, forty-five years ago, and taking the entire increase of vibration that we will experience in this density change, approximately what percentage through this increase in vibrational change are we right now?

RA: I am Ra. The vibratory nature of your environment is true color, green. This is at this time heavily over-woven with the orange ray of planetary consciousness. However, the nature of quanta is such that the movement over the boundary is that of discrete placement of vibratory level.

QUESTIONER: You mentioned that the thoughts of anger now are causing cancer. Can you expand on this mechanism as it acts as a catalyst or its complete purpose?

RA: I am Ra. The fourth density is one of revealed information. Selves are not hidden to self or other-selves. The imbalances or distortions which are of a destructive nature show, therefore, in more obvious ways, the vehicle of the mind/body/spirit complex thus acting as a teaching resource for self-revelation. These illnesses such as cancer are correspondingly very amenable to self-healing once the mechanism of the destructive influence has been grasped by the individual.

QUESTIONER: Then you are saying that cancer is quite easily healed mentally and is a good teaching tool because it is easily healed mentally and once the entity forgives the other-self at whom he is angry, the cancer will disappear. Is this correct?

RA: I am Ra. This is partially correct. The other portion of healing has to do with forgiveness of self and a greatly heightened respect for the self. This may conveniently be expressed by taking care in dietary matters. This is quite frequently a part of the healing and forgiving process. Your basic premise is correct.

QUESTIONER: In dietary matters, what would be the foods that one would include and what would be the foods that one would exclude in a general way for the greatest care of one's bodily complex?

RA: I am Ra. Firstly, we underline and emphasize that this information is not to be understood literally but as a link or psychological nudge for the body and the mind and spirit. Thus it is the care and respect for the self that is the true thing of importance. In this light we may iterate the basic information given for this instrument's diet. The vegetables, the fruits, the grains, and to the extent necessary for the individual metabolism, the animal products. These are those substances showing respect for the self. In addition, though this has not been mentioned for this instrument is not in need of purification, those entities in need of purging the self of a poison thought-form or emotion complex do well to take care in following a program of careful fasting until the destructive thought-form has been purged analogously with the by-products of ridding the physical vehicle of excess material. Again you see the value not to the body complex but used as a link for the mind and spirit. Thus self reveals self to self.

QUESTIONER: Thank you. A very important concept. Does the fact that the basic vibration that we experience now is green true color or fourth density account for the fact that there are many mental effects upon material objects that are now observable for the first time in a mass way such as the bending of metal by mind?

RA: I am Ra. This shall be the final query in total of this working.

This is not only correct but we suggest you take this concept further and understand the great number of entities with the so-called mental diseases being due to the effect of this green-ray true color upon the mental configurations of those unready mentally to face the self for the first time.

Are there any brief queries before we close?

QUESTIONER: Just two. With respect to what you just said, would then people incarnating here by seniority of vibration who incarnate in the service-to-self path be ones who would have extreme difficulty mentally with this green-ray vibration?

RA: I am Ra. This is incorrect. It is rather the numbers who have distracted themselves and failed to prepare for this transition yet who are somewhat susceptible to its influence who may be affected.

QUESTIONER: Thank you. Is there anything that we can do to make the instrument more comfortable or to improve the contact?

RA: This instrument is well. You are conscientious. The appurtenances cause this instrument greater comfort in the distortion of the warmth of the body complex. I am Ra. I leave you, my friends, in the love and in the light of the One Infinite Creator. Go forth then rejoicing in the power and in the peace of the One Infinite Creator. Adonai.

Session 41,
March 20, 1981

RA: I am Ra. I greet you in the love and in the light of the One Infinite Creator. We communicate now.

QUESTIONER: I have one question of logistics to start with. I know that it is a dumb question, but I have to ask it to be sure. There is a possibility that we may have to move from this location. Will this have any effect at all on our contact with Ra?

RA: I am Ra. This is not a foolish question. The location is meaningless, for are we not in the creation? However, the place of the working shall be either carefully adjudged by your selves to be of the appropriate vibratory levels or it shall be suggested that the purification of the place be enacted and dedication made through meditation before initial working. This might entail such seemingly mundane chores as the cleansing or painting of surfaces which you may deem to be inappropriately marred.

QUESTIONER: I am familiar with the Banishing Ritual of the Lesser Pentagram. I was wondering if this ritual was of use in preparing a place for this type of working?

RA: I am Ra. This is correct.

QUESTIONER: In trying to build an understanding from the start, you might say, starting with intelligent infinity and getting to our present condition of being I think that I should go back and investigate our sun since it is the sub-Logos that creates all that we experience in this particular planetary system.

Will you give me a description of our sun?

RA: I am Ra. This is a query which is not easily answered in your language, for the sun has various aspects in relation to intelligent infinity, to intelligent energy, and to each density of each planet, as you call these spheres. Moreover, these differences extend into the metaphysical or time/space part of your creation.

In relationship to intelligent infinity, the sun body is, equally with all parts of the infinite creation, part of that infinity.

In relation to the potentiated intelligent infinity which makes use of intelligent energy, it is the offspring, shall we say, of the Logos for a much larger number of sub-Logoi. The relationship is hierarchical in that the sub-Logos uses the intelligent energy in ways set forth by the Logos and uses its free will to co-create the, shall we say, full nuances of your densities as you experience them.

In relationship to the densities, the sun body may physically, as you would say, be seen to be a large body of gaseous elements undergoing the processes of fusion and radiating heat and light.

Metaphysically, the sun achieves a meaning to fourth through seventh density according to the growing abilities of entities in these densities to grasp the living creation and co-entity, or other-self, nature of this sun body. Thus by the sixth density the sun may be visited and inhabited by those dwelling in time/space and may even be partially created from moment to moment by the processes of sixth-density entities in their evolution.

QUESTIONER: In your last statement did you mean that the sixth-density entities are actually creating manifestations of the sun in their density? Could you explain what you meant by that?

RA: I am Ra. In this density some entities whose means of reproduction is fusion may choose to perform this portion of experience as part of the beingness of the sun body. Thus you may think of portions of the light that you receive as offspring of the generative expression of sixth-density love.

QUESTIONER: Then could you say that sixth-density entities are using that mechanism to be more closely co-Creators with the Infinite Creator?

RA: I am Ra. This is precisely correct as seen in the latter portions of sixth density seeking the experiences of the gateway density.

QUESTIONER: Thank you. What I want to do now is investigate, as the first density is formed, what happens and how energy centers are first formed in beings. Does it make any sense to ask you if the sun itself has a density, or is it all densities?

RA: I am Ra. The sub-Logos is of the entire octave and is not that entity which experiences the learning/teachings of entities such as yourselves.

QUESTIONER: I am going to make a statement of my understanding and ask you to correct me. I intuitively see the first-density being formed by an energy center which is a vortex. This vortex then causes these spinning motions that I have mentioned before of vibration which is light which then starts to condense into materials of the first density. Is this correct?

RA: I am Ra. This is correct as far as your reasoning has taken you. However, it is well to point out that the Logos has the plan of all the densities of the octave in potential completion before entering the space/time continuum in first density. Thus the energy centers exist before they are manifest.

QUESTIONER: Then what is the simplest being that is manifested?

I am supposing that it might be a single cell or something like that. How does it function with respect to energy centers?

RA: I am Ra. The simplest manifest being is light or what you have called the photon. In relationship to energy centers it may be seen to be the center or foundation of all articulated energy fields.

QUESTIONER: When first density is formed we have fire, air, earth, and water. There is at some time the first movement or individuation of life into a portion of consciousness that is self-mobile. Could you describe the process of the creation of this and what type of energy center it has?

RA: I am Ra. The first or red-ray density, though attracted towards growth, is not in the proper vibration for those conditions conducive to what you may call the spark of awareness. As the vibratory energies move from red to orange, the vibratory environment is such as to stimulate those chemical substances which lately had been inert to combine in such a fashion that love and light begin the function of growth.

The supposition which you had earlier made concerning single-celled entities such as the polymorphous dinoflagellate is correct. The mechanism is one of the attraction of upward spiraling light. There is nothing random about this or any portion of evolution.

QUESTIONER: As I remember, the polymorphous dinoflagellate has an iron- rather than a copper-based cell. Could you comment on that?

RA: I am Ra. This information is not central. The base of any metabolism, shall we say, is that which may be found in the chemical substances of the neighborhood of origin.

QUESTIONER: I was just commenting on this because it has the motion of our animal life with copper-based cells, yet it has the iron-based cell of plant life indicating a transition from possibly plant to animal life. Am I wrong? My memory is a little fuzzy on this.

RA: I am Ra. It is not that you are incorrect but that no conclusions should be drawn from such information. There are several different types of bases for conscious entities not only upon this planetary sphere but to a much greater extent in the forms found on planetary spheres of other sub-Logoi. The chemical vehicle is that which most conveniently houses the consciousness. The functioning of consciousness is the item of interest rather than the chemical makeup of a physical vehicle.

We have observed that those whom you call scientists have puzzled over the various differences and possible interrelationships of various stages, types, and conditions of lifeforms. This is not fruitful material as it is that which is of a moment's choice by your sub-Logos.

QUESTIONER: I didn't mean to waste time with that question but you just happened to mention that particular single cell. Does this polymorphous dinoflagellate have an orange energy center?

RA: I am Ra. This is correct.

QUESTIONER: Is this energy center, then, on a very small scale related to the orange energy center in man?

RA: I am Ra. The true color is precisely the same. However, the consciousness of the second-density beginning is primitive and the use of orange ray limited to the expression of self which may be seen to be movement and survival.

In third density, at this time, those clinging to orange ray have a much more complex system of distortions through which orange ray is manifested. This is somewhat complicated. We shall endeavor to simplify.

The appropriate true color for third density is, as you have ascertained, yellow. However, the influences of the true color, green, acting upon yellow ray entities have caused many entities to revert to the consideration of self rather than the stepping forward into consideration of other-self or green ray. This may not be seen to be of a negatively polarized nature, as the negatively polarized entity is working very intensively with the deepest manifestations of yellow-ray group energies, especially the manipulations of other-self for service to self. Those reverting to orange ray, and we may add these are many upon your plane at this time, are those who feel the vibrations of true color green and, therefore, respond by rejecting governmental and societal activities as such and seek once more the self.

However, not having developed the yellow ray properly so that it balances the personal vibratory rates of the entity, the entity then is faced with the task of further activation and balancing of the self in relation to the self, thus the orange-ray manifestations at this space/time nexus.

Thus true color orange is that which it is without difference. However, the manifestations of this or any ray may be seen to be most various depending upon the vibratory levels and balances of the mind/body or mind/body/spirit complexes which are expressing these energies.

QUESTIONER: Could you tell me the simplest and first entity to have both orange- and yellow-ray energy centers?

RA: I am Ra. Upon your planetary sphere those having the first yellow-ray experiences are those of animal and vegetable natures which find the necessity for reproduction by bisexual techniques or who find it necessary to depend in some way upon other-selves for survival and growth.

QUESTIONER: And then what entity would be the simplest that would have red, orange, yellow, and green rays activated?

RA: I am Ra. This information has been covered in a previous session. To perhaps simplify your asking, each center may be seen to be activated potentially in third density, the late second-density entities having the capability, if efficient use is made of experience, of vibrating and activating the green ray energy center.

The third-density being, having the potential for complete self-awareness, thus has the potential for the minimal activation of all energy centers. The fourth, fifth, and sixth densities are those refining the higher energy centers. The seventh density is a density of completion and the turning towards timelessness or foreverness.

QUESTIONER: Then would an animal in second density have all of the energy centers in some way in its being but just not activated?

RA: I am Ra. This is precisely correct.

QUESTIONER: Then the animal in second density is composed of light as are all things. What I am trying to get at is the relationship between the light that the various bodies of the animal are created of and the relationship of this to the energy centers which are active and the ones which are not active and how this is linked with the Logos. It is a difficult question to ask. Can you give me some kind of answer?

RA: I am Ra. The answer is to redirect your thought processes from any mechanical view of evolution. The will of the Logos posits the potentials available to the evolving entity. The will of the entity as it evolves is the single measure of the rate and fastidiousness of the activation and balancing of the various energy centers.

QUESTIONER: Thank you. In the session from the day before yesterday you mentioned variable speed of rotation or activity of energy centers. What did you mean by that?

RA: I am Ra. Each energy center has a wide range of rotational speed or as you may see it more clearly in relation to color, brilliance. The more strongly the will of the entity concentrates upon and refines or purifies each energy center, the more brilliant or rotationally active each energy center will be. It is not necessary for the energy centers to be activated in order in the case of the self-aware entity. Thusly entities may have extremely brilliant energy centers while being quite unbalanced in their violet-ray aspect due to lack of attention paid to the totality of experience of the entity.

The key to balance may then be seen in the unstudied, spontaneous, and honest response of entities toward experiences, thus using experience to the utmost, then applying the balancing exercises and achieving the proper attitude for the most purified spectrum of energy center manifestation in violet ray. This is why the brilliance or rotational speed of the energy centers is not considered above the balanced aspect or violet-ray manifestation of an entity in regarding harvestability; for those entities which are unbalanced, especially as to the primary rays, will not be capable of sustaining the impact of the love and light of intelligent infinity to the extent necessary for harvest.

QUESTIONER: Could you tell me the difference between space/time and time/space?

RA: I am Ra. Using your words, the difference is that between the visible and invisible or the physical and metaphysical. Using mathematical terms, as does the one you call Larson, the difference is that between s/t and t/s.

QUESTIONER: You mentioned in the last session the concept of fasting for removing unwanted thought-forms. Can you expand on this process and explain a little bit more about how this works?

RA: I am Ra. This, as all healing techniques, must be used by a conscious being; that is, a being conscious that the ridding of excess and unwanted material from the body complex is the analogy to the ridding of mind or spirit of excess or unwanted material. Thus the one discipline or denial of the unwanted portion as an appropriate part of the self is taken through the tree of mind down through the trunk to subconscious levels where the connection is made and thus the body, mind, and spirit, then in unison, express denial of the excess or unwanted spiritual or mental material as part of the entity.

All then falls away and the entity, while understanding, if you will, and appreciating the nature of the rejected material as part of the greater self, nevertheless, through the action of the will purifies and refines the mind/body/spirit complex, bringing into manifestation the desired mind complex or spirit complex attitude.

QUESTIONER: Then would this be like a conscious reprogramming of catalyst? For instance, for some entities catalyst is programmed by the Higher Self to create experiences so that the entity can release itself from unwanted biases. Would this be analogous then to the entity consciously programming this release and using fasting as the method of communication to itself?

RA: I am Ra. This is not only correct but may be taken further. The self, if conscious to a great enough extent of the workings of this catalyst and the techniques of programming, may through concentration of the will and the faculty of faith alone cause reprogramming without the analogy of the fasting, the diet, or other analogous body complex disciplines.

QUESTIONER: I have a book, *Initiation*, in which the woman describes initiation. Are you familiar with the contents of this book?

RA: I am Ra. This is correct. We scan your mind.

QUESTIONER: I have only read part of it, but I was wondering if the teachings in the book with respect to balancing were Ra's teachings?

RA: I am Ra. This is basically correct with distortions that may be seen when this material is collated with the material we have offered.

QUESTIONER: Why are the red, yellow, and blue energy centers called primary centers? I think from previous material I understand this, but is there some tracing of these primary colors back to intelligent infinity more profound than what you have given us?

RA: I am Ra. We cannot say what may seem profound to an entity. The red, yellow, and blue rays are primary because they signify activity of a primary nature.

Red ray is the foundation; orange ray the movement towards yellow ray which is the ray of self-awareness and interaction. Green ray is the movement through various experiences of energy exchanges having to do with compassion and all-forgiving love to the primary blue ray which is the first ray of radiation of self regardless of any actions from another.

The green-ray entity is ineffectual in the face of blockage from other-selves. The blue-ray entity is a co-Creator. This may perhaps simply be a restatement of previous activity, but if you consider the function of the Logos as representative of the Infinite Creator in effectuating the knowing of the Creator by the Creator you may perhaps see the steps by which this may be accomplished.

May we ask for one final full question before we leave this working?

QUESTIONER: This may be too long a question for this working, but I will ask it and if it is too long we can continue it at a later time. Could you tell me of the development of the social memory complex Ra, from its first beginnings and what catalysts it used to get to where it is now in activation of rays?

RA: I am Ra. The question does not demand a long answer, for we who experienced the vibratory densities upon that planetary sphere which you call Venus were fortunate in being able to move in harmony with the planetary vibrations with an harmonious graduation to second, to third, and to fourth, and a greatly accelerated fourth-density experience.

We spent much time/space, if you will, in fifth density balancing the intense compassion we had gained in fourth density. The graduation again was harmonious and our social memory complex which had become most firmly cemented in fourth density remained of a very strong and helpful nature.

Our sixth-density work was also accelerated because of the harmony of our social memory complex so that we were able to set out as members of the Confederation to even more swiftly approach graduation to seventh density. Our harmony, however, has been a grievous source of naiveté as regards working with your planet. Is there a brief query before we leave this instrument?

QUESTIONER: Is there anything that we can do to make the instrument more comfortable or to improve the contact?

RA: I am Ra. All is well. I leave you, my friends, in the love and in the light of the One Infinite Creator. Go forth, therefore, rejoicing in the power and the peace of the One Infinite Creator. Adonai.

Session 42,
March 22, 1981

RA: I am Ra. I greet you in the love and in the light of the One Infinite Creator. We communicate now.

QUESTIONER: I am going to make a statement and ask you to comment on its degree of accuracy. I am assuming that the balanced entity would not be swayed either towards positive or negative emotions by any situation which he might confront. By remaining unemotional in any situation, the balanced entity may clearly discern the appropriate and necessary responses in harmony with the Law of One for each situation. Is this correct?

RA: I am Ra. This is an incorrect application of the balancing which we have discussed. The exercise of first experiencing feelings and then consciously discovering their antitheses within the being has as its objective not the smooth flow of feelings both positive and negative while remaining unswayed but rather the objective of becoming unswayed. This is a simpler result and takes much practice, shall we say.

The catalyst of experience works in order for the learn/teachings of this density to occur. However, if there is seen in the being a response, even if it is simply observed, the entity is still using the catalyst for learn/teaching. The end result is that the catalyst is no longer needed. Thus this density is no longer needed. This is not indifference or objectivity but a finely tuned compassion and love which sees all things as love. This seeing elicits no response due to catalytic reactions. Thus the entity is now able to become co-Creator of experiential occurrences. This is the truer balance.

QUESTIONER: I will attempt to make an analogy. If an animal, shall I say, a bull, in a pen attacks you because you have wandered into his pen, you get out of his way rapidly but you do not blame him. You do not have much of an emotional response other than the response that he might damage you. However, if you encounter another self in his territory and he attacks you, your response may be more of an emotional nature creating physical bodily responses. Am I correct in assuming that when your response to the animal and to the other-self is that of seeing both as Creator and loving both and understanding their action in attacking you is the action of their free will then you have balanced yourself correctly in this area? Is this correct?

RA: I am Ra. This is basically correct. However, the balanced entity will see in the seeming attack of an other-self the causes of this action which are, in most cases, of a more complex nature than the cause of the attack of the second-density bull as was your example. Thus this balanced entity would be open to many more opportunities for service to a third-density other-self.

QUESTIONER: Would a perfectly balanced entity feel any emotional response in being attacked by the other-self?

RA: I am Ra. This is correct. The response is love.

QUESTIONER: In the illusion that we now experience it is difficult to maintain this response especially if the attack results in physical pain, but I assume that this response should be maintained even through physical pain or loss of life. Is this correct?

RA: I am Ra. This is correct and further is of a major or principle importance in understanding, shall we say, the principle of balance. Balance is not indifference but rather the observer not blinded by any feelings of separation but rather fully imbued with love.

QUESTIONER: In the last session you made the statement that "We, that is Ra, spent much time/space in the fifth density balancing the intense compassion that we had gained in the fourth density." Could you expand on this concept with respect to the material you just discussed?

RA: I am Ra. The fourth density, as we have said, abounds in compassion. This compassion is folly when seen through the eyes of wisdom. It is the salvation of third density but creates a mismatch in the ultimate balance of the entity.

Thus we, as a social memory complex of fourth density, had the tendency towards compassion even to martyrdom in aid of other-selves. When the fifth-density harvest was achieved we found that in this vibratory level flaws could be seen in the efficacy of such unrelieved compassion. We spent much time/space in contemplation of those ways of the Creator which imbue love with wisdom.

QUESTIONER: I would like to try to make an analogy for third density of this concept. Many entities here feel great compassion for relieving the physical problems of third-density other-selves by administering to them in many ways, with food if there is hunger as there is now in the African nations, by bringing them medicine if they feel that there is a need to minister to them medically, and being selfless in all of these services to a very great extent.

This is creating a vibration that is in harmony with green ray or fourth density but it is not balanced with the understanding of fifth density that these entities are experiencing catalysts and a more balanced administration to their needs would be to provide them with the learning necessary to reach the state of awareness of fourth density than it would be to minister to their physical needs at this time. Is this correct?

RA: I am Ra. This is incorrect. To a mind/body/spirit complex which is starving, the appropriate response is the feeding of the body. You may extrapolate from this.

On the other hand, however, you are correct in your assumption that the green-ray response is not as refined as that which has been imbued with wisdom. This wisdom enables the entity to appreciate its contributions to the planetary consciousness by the quality of its being without regard to activity or behavior which expects results upon visible planes.

QUESTIONER: Then why do we have the extreme starvation problem in, generally, the area of Africa at this time? Is there any metaphysical reason for this, or is it purely random?

RA: I am Ra. Your previous assumption was correct as to the catalytic action of this starvation and ill health. However, it is within the free will of an entity to respond to this plight of other-selves, and the offering of the needed foodstuffs and substances is an appropriate response within the framework of your learn/teachings at this time which involve the growing sense of love for and service to other-selves.

QUESTIONER: What is the difference in terms of energy center activation between a person who represses emotional responses to emotionally charged situations and the person who is balanced and, therefore, truly unswayed by emotionally charged situations?

RA: I am Ra. This query contains an incorrect assumption. To the truly balanced entity no situation would be emotionally charged. With this understood, we may say the following: The repression of emotions depolarizes the entity insofar as it then chooses not to use the catalytic action of the space/time present in a spontaneous manner, thus dimming the energy centers. There is, however, some polarization towards positive if the cause of this repression is consideration for other-selves. The entity which has worked long enough with the catalyst to be able to feel the catalyst but not find it necessary to express reactions is not yet balanced but suffers no depolarization due to the transparency of its experiential continuum. Thus the gradual increase in the ability to observe one's reaction and to know the self will bring the self ever closer to a true balance. Patience is requested and suggested, for the catalyst is intense upon your plane and its use must be appreciated over a period of consistent learn/teaching.

QUESTIONER: How can a person know when he is unswayed by an emotionally charged situation or if he is repressing the flow of emotions, or if he is in balance and truly unswayed?

RA: I am Ra. We have spoken to this point. Therefore, we shall briefly iterate that to the balanced entity no situation has an emotional charge but is simply a situation like any other in which the entity may or may not observe an opportunity to be of service. The closer an entity comes to this attitude the closer an entity is to balance. You may note that it is not our recommendation that reactions to catalyst be repressed or suppressed unless such reactions would be a stumbling block not consonant with the Law of One to an other-self. It is far, far better to allow the experience to express itself in order that the entity may then make fuller use of this catalyst.

QUESTIONER: How can an individual assess what energy centers within its being are activated and in no immediate need of attention and which energy centers are not activated and are in need of immediate attention?

RA: I am Ra. The thoughts of an entity, its feelings or emotions, and least of all its behavior are the signposts for the teaching/learning of self by self. In the analysis of one's experiences of a diurnal cycle an entity may assess what it considers to be inappropriate thoughts, behaviors, feelings, and emotions.

In examining these inappropriate activities of mind, body, and spirit complexes the entity may then place these distortions in the proper vibrational ray and thus see where work is needed.

QUESTIONER: In the last session you said, "that when the self is conscious to a great enough extent of the workings of the catalyst of fasting, and the techniques of programming, it then may through concentration of the will and the faculty of faith alone cause reprogramming without the analogy of fasting, diet, or other analogous bodily complex disciplines." What are the techniques of programming which the Higher Self uses to insure that the desired lessons are learned or attempted by the third-density self?

RA: I am Ra. There is but one technique for this growing or nurturing of will and faith, and that is the focusing of the attention. The attention span of those you call children is considered short. The spiritual attention span of most of your peoples is that of the child. Thus it is a matter of wishing to become able to collect one's attention and hold it upon the desired programming.

This, when continued, strengthens the will. The entire activity can only occur when there exists faith that an outcome of this discipline is possible.

QUESTIONER: Can you mention some exercises for helping to increase the attention span?

RA: I am Ra. Such exercises are common among the many mystical traditions of your entities. The visualization of a shape and color which is of personal inspirational quality to the meditator is the heart of what you would call the religious aspects of this sort of visualization.

The visualization of simple shapes and colors which have no innate inspirational quality to the entity form the basis for what you may call your magical traditions.

Whether you image the rose or the circle is not important. However, it is suggested that one or the other path towards visualization be chosen in order to exercise this faculty. This is due to the careful arrangement of shapes and colors which have been described as visualizations by those steeped in the magical tradition.

QUESTIONER: As a youth I was trained in the engineering sciences which include the necessity for three-dimensional visualization for the processes of design. Would this be helpful as a foundation for the type of visualization which you are speaking of, or would it be of no value?

RA: I am Ra. To you, the questioner, this experience was valuable. To a less sensitized entity it would not gain the proper increase of concentrative energy.

QUESTIONER: Then the less sensitized entity should use . . . What should he use for the proper energy?

RA: I am Ra. In the less sensitized individual the choosing of personally inspirational images is appropriate whether this inspiration be the rose which is of perfect beauty, the cross which is of perfect sacrifice, the Buddha which is the All-Being in One, or whatever else may inspire the individual.

QUESTIONER: Using the teach/learning relationship of parent to child, what type of actions would demonstrate the activation of the energy centers in sequence from red to violet?

RA: I am Ra. This shall be the last full query of this working.

The entity, child or adult, as you call it, is not an instrument to be played. The appropriate teach/learning device of parent to child is the open-hearted beingness of the parent and the total acceptance of the beingness of the child. This will encompass whatever material the child entity has brought into the life experience in this plane.

There are two things especially important in this relationship other than the basic acceptance of the child by the parent. Firstly, the experience of whatever means the parent uses to worship and give thanksgiving to the One Infinite Creator, should if possible be shared with the child entity upon a daily basis, as you would say. Secondly, the compassion of parent to child may well be tempered by the understanding that the child entity shall learn the biases of service-to-others or service-to-self from the parental other-self. This is the reason that some discipline is appropriate in the teach/learning. This does not apply to the activation of any one energy center for each entity is unique and each relationship with self and other-self doubly unique. The guidelines given are only general for this reason.

Is there a brief query before we leave this instrument?

QUESTIONER: Is there anything that we can do to make the instrument more comfortable or to improve the contact?

RA: I am Ra. The instrument is well. I leave you, my friends, in the love and the light of the Infinite Creator. Go forth, then, rejoicing in the power and the peace of the One Infinite Creator. Adonai.

Session 43,
March 24, 1981

RA: I am Ra. I greet you in the love and in the light of the One Infinite Creator.

Before we communicate may we request the adjustment, without the touching of this instrument's physical body complex, of the item which presses upon the instrument's head. This is causing some interference with our contact.

QUESTIONER: Is that the pillow or something else? Do you speak of the pillow under the neck?

RA: I am Ra. There is a line of interference crossing the crown of the head.

QUESTIONER: Is it this? (A two inch fold in the sheet is located three inches from the crown of the instrument's head and is laid flat on the bed.) Is that it?

RA: I am Ra. This is correct. Please increase the distance from the crown of the head.

QUESTIONER: (Ruffles in the sheet are smoothed all along the length of the sheet next to the instrument's head.) Is this satisfactory?

RA: I am Ra. Yes.

QUESTIONER: I am sorry that we failed to notice that.

RA: We communicate now.

QUESTIONER: I don't know if it is of any importance, but it occurred to me that the parts removed from the cattle mutilations are the same every time, and I wondered if this is related to the energy centers and why they were important if that was so?

RA: I am Ra. This is basically correct if you may understand that there is a link between energy centers and various thought-forms. Thus the fears of the mass consciousness create the climate for the concentration upon the removal of bodily parts which symbolize areas of concern or fear in the mass consciousness.

QUESTIONER: Are you saying, then, that these parts that are removed are related to the mass consciousness of the third-density human form and that this fear is being used in some way by the thought-form entities in these mutilations?

RA: I am Ra. This is correct. The thought-form entities feed upon fear; thus they are able to do precise damage according to systems of symbology. The other second-density types of which you speak need the, what you call, blood.

QUESTIONER: These other second-density types need the blood to remain in the physical? Do they come in and out of our physical from one of the lower astral planes?

RA: I am Ra. These entities are, shall we say, creatures of the Orion group. They do not exist in astral planes as do the thought-forms but wait within the Earth's surface. We, as always, remind you that it is our impression that this type of information is unimportant.

QUESTIONER: I agree with you wholeheartedly, but I sometimes am at a loss before investigation into an area as to whether it is going to lead to a better understanding. This just seemed to be related somehow to the energy centers which we had been speaking of.

I am going to make a statement and have you comment on it for its correctness. The statement is: When the Creator's light is split or divided into colors and energy centers for experience, then in order to reunite with the Creator the energy centers must be balanced exactly the same as the split light was as it originated from the Creator. Is this correct?

RA: I am Ra. To give this query a simple answer would be nearly impossible.

We shall simplify by concentrating upon what we consider to be the central idea towards which you are striving. We have, many times now, spoken about the relative importance of balancing as opposed to the relative unimportance of maximal activation of each energy center. The reason is as you have correctly surmised. Thusly the entity is concerned, if it be upon the path of positive harvestability, with the regularizing of the various energies of experience. Thus the most fragile entity may be more balanced than one with extreme energy and activity in service-to-others due to the fastidiousness with which the will is focused upon the use of experience in knowing the self. The densities beyond your own give the minimally balanced individual much time/space and space/time with which to continue to refine these inner balances.

QUESTIONER: In the next density, the fourth density, is the catalyst of physical pain used as a mechanism for experiential balancing?

RA: I am Ra. The use of physical pain is minimal, having only to do with the end of the fourth-density incarnation. This physical pain would not be considered severe enough to treat, shall we say, in third density. The catalysts of mental and spiritual pain are used in fourth density.

QUESTIONER: Why is physical pain a part of the end of fourth density?

RA: I am Ra. You would call this variety of pain weariness.

QUESTIONER: Can you state the average lifespan in the fourth density of space/time incarnation?

RA: I am Ra. The space/time incarnation typical of harmonious fourth density is approximately 90,000 of your years as you measure time.

QUESTIONER: Are there multiple incarnations in fourth density with time/space experiences in between incarnations?

RA: I am Ra. This is correct.

QUESTIONER: How long is a cycle of experience in fourth density in our years?

RA: The cycle of experience is approximately 30 million of your years if the entities are not capable of being harvested sooner. There is in this density a harvest which is completely the function of the readiness of the social memory complex. It is not structured as is your own, for it deals with a more transparent distortion of the One Infinite Creator.

QUESTIONER: Then the big difference in harvestability between third and fourth density is that at the end of the third density the individual is harvested as a function of individual violet ray, but it is the violet ray for the entire social memory complex that must be of a harvestable nature to graduate to the fifth density. Is this correct?

RA: I am Ra. This is correct, although in fifth density entities may choose to learn as a social memory complex or as mind/body/spirit complexes and may graduate to sixth density under these conditions, for the wisdom density is an extremely free density whereas the lessons of compassion leading to wisdom necessarily have to do with other-selves.

QUESTIONER: Then is sixth-density harvest strictly of a social memory complex nature because again we have wisdom and compassion blended back using wisdom?

RA: I am Ra. This is quite correct.

QUESTIONER: The physical vehicle that is used in fourth-density space/time is, I am assuming, quite similar to the one that is now used in third density. Is this correct?

RA: I am Ra. The chemical elements used are not the same. However, the appearance is similar.

QUESTIONER: Is it necessary to eat food in fourth density?

RA: I am Ra. This is correct.

QUESTIONER: The mechanism of, shall we say, social catalyst due to a necessity for feeding the body then is active in fourth density. Is this correct?

RA: I am Ra. This is incorrect. The fourth-density being desires to serve and the preparation of foodstuffs is extremely simple due to increased communion between entity and living foodstuff. Therefore, this is not a significant catalyst but rather a simple precondition of the space/time experience. The catalyst involved is the necessity for the ingestion of foodstuffs. This is not considered to be of importance by fourth-density entities and it, therefore, aids in the teach/learning of patience.

QUESTIONER: Could you expand a little bit on how that aids in the teach/learning of patience?

RA: I am Ra. To stop the functioning of service-to-others long enough to ingest foodstuffs is to invoke patience.

QUESTIONER: I'm guessing that it is not necessary to ingest food-stuffs in fifth density. Is this correct?

RA: I am Ra. This is incorrect. However, the vehicle needs food which may be prepared by thought.

QUESTIONER: What type of food would this be?

RA: I am Ra. You would call this type of food, nectar or ambrosia, or a light broth of golden white hue.

QUESTIONER: What is the purpose of ingesting food in fifth density?

RA: I am Ra. This is a somewhat central point. The purpose of space/time is the increase in catalytic action appropriate to the density. One of the preconditions for space/time existence is some form of body complex. Such a body complex must be fueled in some way.

QUESTIONER: In third density the fueling of our bodily complex is not only simply fueling of the bodily complex but gives us opportunities to learn service. In fourth density it not only fuels the complex but gives us opportunities to learn patience. In fifth density it fuels the complex but does it teach?

RA: I am Ra. In fifth density it is comfort for those of like mind gathered together to share in this broth, thus becoming one in light and wisdom while joining hearts and hands in physical activity. Thus in this density it becomes a solace rather than a catalyst for learning.

QUESTIONER: I am simply trying to trace the evolution of this catalyst that then, as you say, changes in fifth density. I might as well complete this and ask if there is any ingestion of food in sixth density?

RA: I am Ra. This is correct. However, the nature of this food is that of light and is impossible to describe to you in any meaningful way as regards the thrust of your query.

QUESTIONER: On this planet after the harvest is complete, will fourth-density beings be incarnate on the surface as we know it now?

RA: I am Ra. The probability/possibility vortices indicate this to be most likely.

QUESTIONER: Then will there be at that time any fifth-density or sixth-density beings on the surface of the planet?

RA: I am Ra. Not for a fairly long measure of your time as fourth-density beings need to spend their learn/teaching space/time with their own density's entities.

QUESTIONER: Then basically what you are saying is that at that point the teachings of fifth- or sixth-density beings would not be too well understood by the new fourth-density beings?

RA: I am Ra. Do you wish to query us upon this point?

QUESTIONER: I guess I didn't state that correctly. Would the new fourth-density beings then need to evolve in their thinking to reach a point where fifth-density lessons would be of value?

RA: I am Ra. We grasp the thrust of your query. Although it is true that as fourth-density beings progress they have more and more need for other density teachings, it is also true that just as we speak to you due to the calling, so the information called is always available. It is simply that fifth-density beings will not live upon the surface of the planetary sphere until the planet reaches fifth-density vibratory level.

QUESTIONER: I was wondering, then, if the mechanism of teach/learning was the same relatively then in fourth density. From what you say, it is necessary first for a call to exist for the teach/learning of fifth density to be given to fourth just as a call must exist here before fourth-density lessons are given to third density. Is this correct?

RA: I am Ra. This query is misguided, for experience in fourth density is emphatically not the same as third-density experience. However, it is correct that the same mechanism of calling predisposes the information received in a way consonant with free will.

You may ask one more full question at this working.

QUESTIONER: You stated that the key to strengthening the will is concentration. Can you tell me the relative importance of the following aids to concentration? I have listed: silence, temperature control, comfort of body, screening as a Faraday cage would screen electromagnetic radiation, visible light screening, and a constant smell such as the use of incense. In other words, an isolation-type of situation. You mentioned that this was one of the functions of the pyramid.

RA: I am Ra. The analogies of body complex to mind and spirit complex activities have been discussed previously. You may consider all of these aforementioned aids as those helpful to the stimulation of that which in actuality aids concentration, that being the will of the entity. This free will may be focused at any object or goal.

QUESTIONER: I was really trying to get at whether it would be of great importance to construct a better place for our meditations. We have distractions here of the types which I mentioned, and I know that it is a function of our total free will as to whether we construct this or not, but I was trying to get at the principles behind and the relative importance of the Faraday cage. It would be quite a construction and I was wondering if it would be of any real value?

RA: I am Ra. Without infringing upon free will we feel it possible to state that the Faraday cage and the isolation tank are gadgets.

The surrounding of self in a sylvan atmosphere, apart from distractions, in a place of working used for no other purpose, in which you and your associates agree to lay aside all goals but that of the meditative seeking of the Infinite Creator is, shall we say, not gadgetry but the making use of the creation of the Father in second-density love, and in the love and support of other-selves. Are there any brief queries before this working is at an end?

QUESTIONER: Is there anything that we can do to make the instrument more comfortable or to improve the contact?

RA: I am Ra. All is well. I leave you in the love and the light of the One Infinite Creator. Go forth, therefore, rejoicing in the power and the peace of the One Infinite Creator. Adonai.

SESSION 44, MARCH 28,1981, AND SESSION 45, APRIL 6, 1981, CONTAIN ONLY PERSONAL MATERIAL AND WERE, FOR THAT REASON, REMOVED.

Session 46,
April 15, 1981

RA: I am Ra. I greet you in the love and in the light of the One Infinite Creator. We communicate now.

QUESTIONER: If an entity polarizes toward the service-to-self path, would anger have the same physical effect that it would have on the entity polarizing on the service-to-others path? Would it also cause cancer, or is it just a catalytic effect working in the positively polarizing entity?

RA: I am Ra. The catalytic mechanisms are dependent, not upon the chosen polarity of a mind/body/spirit complex, but upon the use or purpose to which this catalyst is put. Thus the entity which uses the experience of anger to polarize consciously positively or negatively does not experience the bodily catalyst but rather uses the catalyst in mental configuration.

QUESTIONER: I am not sure that I understand that. Let's take some examples: an entity polarizing toward the negative path becomes angry. Let's take the condition where he develops a cancer. What is the principle that is at work for him?

RA I am Ra. We see the thrust of your query and will respond at variance with the specific query if that meets with your approval.

QUESTIONER: Certainly.

RA: The entity polarizing positively perceives the anger. This entity, if using this catalyst mentally, blesses and loves this anger in itself. It then intensifies this anger consciously in mind alone until the folly of this red-ray energy is perceived not as folly in itself but as energy subject to spiritual entropy due to the randomness of energy being used.

Positive orientation then provides the will and faith to continue this mentally intense experience of letting the anger be understood, accepted, and integrated with the mind/body/spirit complex. The other-self which is the object of anger is thus transformed into an object of acceptance, understanding, and accommodation, all being reintegrated using the great energy which anger began.

The negatively oriented mind/body/spirit complex will use this anger in a similarly conscious fashion, refusing to accept the undirected or random energy of anger and instead, through will and faith, funneling this energy into a practical means of venting the negative aspect of this emotion so as to obtain control over other-self, or otherwise control the situation causing anger.

Control is the key to negatively polarized use of catalyst. Acceptance is the key to positively polarized use of catalyst. Between these polarities lies the potential for this random and undirected energy creating a bodily complex analog of what you call the cancerous growth of tissue.

QUESTIONER: Then as I understand it you are saying that if the positively polarizing entity fails to accept the other-self or if the negatively polarizing entity fails to control the other-self, either of these conditions will cause cancer, possibly. Is this correct?

RA: I am Ra. This is partially correct. The first acceptance, or control depending upon polarity, is of the self. Anger is one of many things to be accepted and loved as a part of self or controlled as a part of self, if the entity is to do work.

QUESTIONER: Then are you saying that if a negatively polarizing entity is unable to control his own anger or unable to control himself in anger that he may cause cancer? Is this correct?

RA: I am Ra. This is quite correct. The negative polarization contains a great requirement for control and repression.

QUESTIONER: A repression of what?

RA: I am Ra. Any mind complex distortion which you may call emotional which is of itself disorganized, needs, in order to be useful to the negatively oriented entity, to be repressed and then brought to the surface in an organized use. Thus you may find for instance, negatively polarized entities controlling and repressing such basic bodily complex needs as the sexual desire in order that in the practice thereof the will may be used to enforce itself upon the other-self with greater efficiency when the sexual behavior is allowed.

QUESTIONER: Then the positively oriented entity, rather than attempting repression of emotion, would balance the emotion as stated in an earlier contact. Is this correct?

RA: I am Ra. This is correct and illustrates the path of unity.

QUESTIONER: Then cancer is a training catalyst operating for both polarities in approximately the same way but creating or attempting to create polarization in both directions, positive and negative, depending upon the orientation of the entity experiencing the catalyst. Is this correct?

RA: I am Ra. This is incorrect in that catalyst is unconscious and does not work with intelligence but rather is part of the, shall we say, mechanism of learn/teaching set up by the sub-Logos before the beginning of your space/time.

QUESTIONER: How does cancer do this learn/teaching when the entity developing cancer has no conscious idea of what is happening to him when he develops cancer?

RA: I am Ra. In many cases catalyst is not used.

QUESTIONER: What is the plan for use of the catalyst of cancer?

RA: I am Ra. The catalyst, and all catalyst, is designed to offer experience. This experience in your density may be loved and accepted or it may be controlled. These are the two paths. When neither path is chosen the catalyst fails in its design and the entity proceeds until catalyst strikes it which causes it to form a bias towards acceptance and love or separation and control. There is no lack of space/time in which this catalyst may work.

QUESTIONER: I am assuming that the plan of the Logos is for positively and negatively polarized social memory complexes in fourth density and above. Can you tell me the purpose of the plan for these two types of social memory complexes with respect to Coulomb's Law or negative and positive electrical polarity, or in any way that you can?

RA: I am Ra. This instrument grows weary. We shall speak with you again. We may indicate the possibility, without further harm to this instrument, of approximately two sessions per your weekly period until these weeks of potential for attack and presence of very low physical energy are passed. May we say it is good to be with this group. We appreciate your fidelity. Are there any brief queries before the end of this work time?

QUESTIONER: Only is there anything that we can do to make the instrument more comfortable or to improve the contact?

RA: I am Ra. Each is supporting the instrument well and the instrument remains steady in its purpose. You are conscientious. All is well. We ward you ware of any laxity regarding the arrangement and orientation of appurtenances.

I am Ra. I leave you, my friends, in the love and in the light of the One Infinite Creator. Go forth, therefore, rejoicing in the power and the peace of the One Infinite Creator. Adonai.

Session 47,
April 18, 1981

RA: I am Ra. I greet you in the love and in the light of the One Infinite Creator. We communicate now.

QUESTIONER: Could you first give us an indication of the condition of the instrument?

RA: I am Ra. It is as previously stated.

QUESTIONER: The question that I was trying to ask at the end of the last session was: Of what value to evolution or experience with respect to the Creator knowing Itself are the positive and negative social memory complexes that form starting in fourth density, and why was this planned by the Logos?

RA: I am Ra. There are inherent incorrectness in your query. However, we may answer the main point of it.

The incorrectness lies in the consideration that social memory complexes were planned by the Logos or sub-Logos. This is incorrect, as the unity of the Creator exists within the smallest portion of any material created by Love, much less in a self-aware being.

However, the distortion of free will causes the social memory complex to appear as a possibility at a certain stage of evolution of mind. The purpose, or consideration which causes entities to form such complexes, of these social memory complexes, is a very simple extension of the basic distortion towards the Creator's knowing of Itself, for when a group of mind/body/spirits becomes able to form a social memory complex, all experience of each entity is available to the whole of the complex. Thus the Creator knows more of Its creation in each entity partaking of this communion of entities.

QUESTIONER: You gave the values of better than 50 percent

service-to-others for fourth-density positive and better than 95 percent service-to-self for fourth-density negative social memory complexes. Do these two values correspond to the same rate, shall I say, of vibration?

RA: I am Ra. I perceive you have difficulty in expressing your query. We shall respond in an attempt to clarify your query.

The vibratory rates are not to be understood as the same in positive and negative orientations. They are to be understood as having the power to accept and work with intelligent infinity to a certain degree or intensity. Due to the fact that the primary color, shall we say, or energy blue is missing from the negatively oriented system of power, the green/blue vibratory energies are not seen in the vibratory schedules or patterns of negative fourth and fifth rates of vibration.

The positive on the other hand, shall we say, has the full spectrum of true color time/space vibratory patterns and thus contains a variant vibratory pattern or schedule. Each is capable of doing fourth-density work. This is the criterion for harvest.

QUESTIONER: Did you say that blue was missing from fourth-density negative?

RA: I am Ra. Let us clarify further. As we have previously stated, all beings have the potential for all possible vibratory rates. Thus the potential of the green and blue energy center activation is, of course, precisely where it must be in a creation of Love. However, the negatively polarized entity will have achieved harvest due to extremely efficient use of red and yellow/orange, moving directly to the gateway indigo bringing through this intelligent energy channel the instreamings of intelligent infinity.

QUESTIONER: Then at fourth-density graduation into fifth is there anything like that which you gave as the percentages necessary for third-density graduation into fourth in polarization?

RA: I am Ra. There are, in your modes of thinking, responses we can make, which we shall make. However, the important point is that the graduations from density to density do occur. The positive/negative polarity is a thing which will, at the sixth level, simply become history. Therefore, we speak in an illusory time continuum when we discuss statistics of positive versus negative harvest into fifth. A large percentage of fourth-density negative entities continue the negative path from fourth to fifth-density experience, for without wisdom the compassion and desire to aid other-self is not extremely well informed. Thus though one loses approximately two percent moving from negative to positive during the fourth-density experience we find approximately eight percent of graduations into fifth density those of the negative.

QUESTIONER: What I was actually asking was if 50 percent is required for graduation from third to fourth in the positive sense and 95 percent was required for graduation in the negative sense, does this have to more closely approach 100 percent for graduation in both cases for graduation from fourth to fifth density? Does an entity have to be 99 percent polarized for negative and maybe 80 percent polarized positive for graduation?

RA: I am Ra. We perceive the query now.

To give this in your terms is misleading for there are, shall we say, visual aids or training aids available in fourth density which automatically aid the entity in polarization while cutting down extremely upon the quick effect of catalyst. Thus the density above yours must take up more space/time.

The percentage of service-to-others of positively oriented entities will harmoniously approach 98 percent in intention. The qualifications for fifth density, however, involve understanding. This then, becomes the primary qualification for graduation from fourth to fifth density. To achieve this graduation the entity must be able to understand the actions, the movements, and the dance. There is no percentage describable which measures this understanding. It is a measure of efficiency of perception. It may be measured by light. The ability to love, accept, and use a certain intensity of light thus creates the requirement for both positive and negative fourth to fifth harvesting.

QUESTIONER: Can you define what you mean by a "crystallized entity"?

RA: I am Ra. We have used this particular term because it has a fairly precise meaning in your language. When a crystalline structure is formed of your physical material the elements present in each molecule are bonded in a regularized fashion with elements in each other molecule. Thus the structure is regular and, when fully and perfectly crystallized, has certain properties. It will not splinter or break; it is very strong without effort; and it is radiant, traducing light into a beautiful refraction giving pleasure of the eye to many.

QUESTIONER: In our esoteric literature numerous bodies are listed. I have listed here the physical body, the etheric, the emotional, the astral. Can you tell me if this listing is the proper number, and can you tell me the uses and purposes and effects etc., of each of these and any other bodies that may be in our mind/body/spirit complex?

RA: I am Ra. To answer your query fully would be the work of many sessions such as this one, for the interrelationships of the various bodies and each body's effects in various situations is an enormous study. However, we shall begin by referring your minds back to the spectrum of true colors and the usage of this understanding in grasping the various densities of your octave.

We have the number seven repeated from the macrocosm to the microcosm in structure and experience. Therefore, it would only be expected that there would be seven basic bodies which we would perhaps be most lucid by stating as red-ray body, etc. However, we are aware that you wish to correspond these bodies mentioned with the color rays. This will be confusing, for various teachers have offered their teach/learning understanding in various terms. Thus one may name a subtle body one thing and another find a different name.

The red-ray body is your chemical body. However, it is not the body which you have as clothing in the physical. It is the unconstructed material of the body, the elemental body without form. This basic unformed material body is important to understand for there are healings which may be carried out by the simple understanding of the elements present in the physical vehicle.

The orange-ray body is the physical body complex. This body complex is still not the body you inhabit but rather the body formed without self-awareness, the body in the womb before the spirit/mind complex enters. This body may live without the inhabitation of the mind and spirit complexes. However, it seldom does so.

The yellow-ray body is your physical vehicle which you know of at this time and in which you experience catalyst. This body has the mind/body/spirit characteristics and is equal to the physical illusion, as you have called it.

The green-ray body is that body which may be seen in séance when what you call ectoplasm is furnished. This is a lighter body packed more densely with life. You may call this the astral body following some other teachings. Others have called this same body the etheric body. However, this is not correct in the sense that the etheric body is that body of gateway wherein intelligent energy is able to mold the mind/body/spirit complex.

The light body or blue-ray body may be called the devachanic body. There are many other names for this body especially in your so-called Indian Sutras or writings, for there are those among these peoples which have explored these regions and understand the various types of devachanic bodies. There are many, many types of bodies in each density, much like your own.

The indigo-ray body which we choose to call the etheric body is, as we have said, the gateway body. In this body form is substance and you may only see this body as that of light as it may mold itself as it desires.

The violet-ray body may perhaps be understood as what you might call the Buddha body or that body which is complete.

Each of these bodies has an effect upon your mind/body/spirit complex in your life beingness. The interrelationships, as we have said, are many and complex.

Perhaps one suggestion that may be indicated is this: The indigo-ray body may be used by the healer once the healer becomes able to place its consciousness in this etheric state. The violet-ray or Buddhic body is of equal efficacy to the healer for within it lies a sense of wholeness which is extremely close to unity with all that there is. These bodies are part of each entity and the proper use of them and understanding of them is, though far advanced from the standpoint of third-density harvest, nevertheless useful to the adept.

QUESTIONER: Which bodies do we have immediately after physical death from this yellow-ray body that I now am in?

RA: I am Ra. You have all bodies in potentiation.

QUESTIONER: Then the yellow-ray body in potentiation is used to create this chemical arrangement that I have as a physical body now. Is this correct?

RA: I am Ra. This is incorrect only in that in your present incarnation the yellow-ray body is not in potentiation but in activation, it being that body which is manifest.

QUESTIONER: Then after death from this incarnation we still have the yellow-ray body in potentiation, but then in the general case of our planetary population after death, would they then normally have the green-ray body manifested?

RA: I am Ra. Not immediately. The first body which activates itself upon death is the "form-maker" or the indigo-ray body. This body remains—you have called it the "ka"—until etherea has been penetrated and understanding has been gained by the mind/body/spirit totality. Once this is achieved, if the proper body to be activated is green ray, then this will occur.

QUESTIONER: Let me make a statement and you tell me if I am correct. After death then, if an entity is unaware, he may become what is called an earthbound spirit until he is able to achieve the required awareness for activation of one of his bodies. Would it be possible then to activate any of the bodies from red through violet?

RA: I am Ra. Given the proper stimulus, this is correct.

QUESTIONER: What stimulus would create what we call an earthbound spirit or a lingering ghost?

RA: I am Ra. The stimulus for this is the faculty of the will. If the will of yellow-ray mind/body/spirit is that which is stronger than the progressive impetus of the physical death towards realization of that which comes, that is, if the will is concentrated enough upon the previous experience, the entity's shell of yellow ray, though no longer activated, cannot either be completely deactivated and, until the will is released, the mind/body/spirit complex is caught. This often occurs, as we see you are aware, in the case of sudden death as well as in the case of extreme concern for a thing or an other-self.

QUESTIONER: Well then, does orange-ray activation after death occur very frequently with this planet?

RA: I am Ra. Quite infrequently, due to the fact that this particular manifestation is without will. Occasionally an other-self will so demand the form of the one passing through the physical death that some semblance of the being will remain. This is orange ray. This is rare, for normally if one entity desires another enough to call it, the entity will have the corresponding desire to be called. Thus the manifestation would be the shell of yellow ray.

QUESTIONER: What does the large percentage of the Earth's population, as they pass through the physical, activate?

RA: I am Ra. This shall be the last full query of this working.

The normal procedure, given an harmonious passage from yellow-ray bodily manifestation, is for the mind and spirit complex to rest in the etheric or indigo body until such time as the entity begins its preparation for experience in an incarnated place which has a manifestation formed by the etheric energy molding it into activation and manifestation. This indigo body, being intelligent energy, is able to offer the newly dead, as you would term it, soul a perspective and a place from which to view the experience most recently manifested. Is there a short query we may answer at this time?

QUESTIONER: I will only ask if there is anything that we may do to make the instrument more comfortable or to improve the contact?

RA: I am Ra. The appurtenances are conscientiously measured by eye and spirit. You are conscientious. All is well. Observe this instrument to ensure continued building of the vital energies. It will have to work upon its own physical energies for this weakness was brought about by free will of the self.

I am Ra. We leave you now in the love and in the light of the One Infinite Creator. Go forth, therefore, rejoicing in the power and in the peace of the One Infinite Creator. Adonai.

Session 48,
April 22, 1981

RA: I am Ra. I greet you in the love and in the light of the One Infinite Creator. We communicate now.

QUESTIONER: Could you tell us of the instrument's condition and if she is improving with time?

RA: I am Ra. This instrument's vital energies are improving with time, as you measure it. This instrument's physical energies are less than your previous asking.

QUESTIONER: Thank you. If you, Ra, as an individualized entity were incarnate on Earth now with full awareness and memory of what you know now, what would be your objective at this time on Earth as far as activities are concerned?

RA: I am Ra. The query suggests that which has been learned to be impractical. However, were we to again be naive enough to think that our physical presence was any more effective than that love/light we send your peoples and the treasure of this contact, we would do as we did do. We would be, and we would offer our selves as teach/learners.

QUESTIONER: My lecture yesterday was attended by only a few. If this had occurred during a UFO flap many more would have attended. Since Orion entities cause the flaps, what is Orion's reward for visibility in that they actually create greater opportunities for the dissemination of information such as this information at those times?

RA: I am Ra. This assumption is incorrect. The flaps cause many fears among your peoples, many speakings, understandings concerning plots, cover-ups, mutilations, killings, and other negative impressions. Even those supposedly positive reports which gain public awareness speak of doom. You may understand yourself as one who will be in the minority due to the understandings which you wish to share, if we may use that misnomer.

We perceive there is a further point we may posit at this time. The audience brought about by Orion-type publicity is not seeded by seniority of vibration to a great extent. The audiences receiving teach/learnings without stimulus from publicity will be more greatly oriented towards illumination. Therefore, forget you the counting.

QUESTIONER: Thank you. That clears up that point very well.

Can you tell me how positive and negative polarizations in fourth and fifth density are used to cause working in consciousness?

RA: I am Ra. There is very little work in consciousness in fourth and in fifth densities compared to the work done in third density. The work that is accomplished in positive fourth is that work whereby the positive social memory complex, having, through slow stages, harmoniously integrated itself, goes forth to aid those of less positive orientation which seek their aid. Thus their service is their work and through this dynamic between the societal self and the other-self, which is the object of love, greater and greater intensities of understanding or compassion are attained. This intensity continues until the appropriate intensity of the light may be welcomed. This is fourth-density harvest.

Within fourth-density positive there are minor amounts of catalyst of a spiritual and mental complex distortion. This occurs during the process of harmonizing to the extent of forming the social memory complex. This causes some small catalyst and work to occur, but the great work of fourth density lies in the contact betwixt the societal self and less polarized other-self.

In fourth-density negative much work is accomplished during the fighting for position which precedes the period of the social memory complex. There are opportunities to polarize negatively by control of other-selves. During the social memory complex period of fourth-density negative the situation is the same. The work takes place through the societal reaching out to less polarized other-self in order to aid in negative polarization.

In fifth-density positive and negative the concept of work done through a potential difference is not particularly helpful as fifth-density entities are, again, intensifying rather than potentiating.

In positive, the fifth-density complex uses sixth-density teach/learners to study the more illuminated understandings of unity thus becoming more and more wise. Fifth-density positive social memory complexes will choose to divide their service to others in two ways: first, the beaming of light to creation; second, the sending of groups to be of aid as instruments of light such as those whom you are familiar with through channels.

In fifth-density negative, service to self has become extremely intense and the self has shrunk or compacted so that the dialogues with the teach/learners are used exclusively in order to intensify wisdom. There are very, very few fifth-density negative Wanderers for they fear the forgetting. There are very, very few fifth-density Orion members for they do not any longer perceive any virtue in other-selves.

QUESTIONER: Thank you. I would like to take as an example an entity, starting before birth, who is roughly high on the seniority list for positive polarization and possible harvestability at the end of this cycle and follow a full cycle of his experience starting before his incarnation—which body is activated, the process of becoming incarnate, the activation of the third-density physical body, the process as the body moves through this density and is acted upon by catalysts, the process of death, and the activation of the various bodies so that we make a full circuit from a point prior to incarnation back around through incarnation and death; you might say one cycle of incarnation in this density. Could you do that for me?

RA: I am Ra. Your query is most distorted for it assumes that creations are alike. Each mind/body/spirit complex has its own patterns of activation and its own rhythms of awakening. The important thing for harvest is the harmonious balance between the various energy centers of the mind/body/spirit complex. This is to be noted as of relative import. We grasp the thrust of your query and will make a most general answer stressing the unimportance of such arbitrary generalizations.

The entity, before incarnation, dwells in the appropriate, shall we say, place in time/space. The true color type of this location will be dependent upon the entity's needs. Those entities for instance which, being Wanderers, have the green, blue, or indigo true color core of mind/body/spirit complex will have rested therein.

Entrance into incarnation requires the investment or activation of the indigo ray or etheric body for this is the "form-maker." The young or small physical mind/body/spirit complex has the seven energy centers potentiated before the birthing process. There are also analogs in time/space of these energy centers corresponding to the seven energy centers in each of the seven true color densities. Thus in the microcosm exists all the experience that is prepared. It is as though the infant contains the universe.

The patterns of activation of an entity of high seniority will undoubtedly move with some rapidity to the green-ray level which is the springboard to primary blue. There is always some difficulty in penetrating blue primary energy for it requires that which your people have in great paucity; that is, honesty. Blue ray is the ray of free communication with self and with other-self. Having accepted that an harvestable or nearly harvestable entity will be working from this green-ray springboard one may then posit that the experiences in the remainder of the incarnation will be focused upon activation of the primary blue ray of freely given communication, of indigo ray, that of freely shared intelligent energy, and if possible, moving through this gateway, the penetration of violet-ray intelligent infinity. This may be seen to be manifested by a sense of the consecrate or hallowed nature of everyday creations and activities.

Upon the bodily complex death, as you call this transition, the entity will immediately, upon realization of its state, return to the indigo form-maker body and rest therein until the proper future placement is made.

Here we have the anomaly of harvest. In harvest the entity will then transfer its indigo body into violet-ray manifestation as seen in true color yellow. This is for the purpose of gauging the harvestability of the entity. After this anomalous activity has been carefully completed, the entity will move into indigo body again and be placed in the correct true color locus in space/time and time/space at which time the healings and learn/teachings necessary shall be completed and further incarnation needs determined.

QUESTIONER: Who supervises the determination of further incarnation needs and sets up the seniority list for incarnation?

RA: I am Ra. This is a query with two answers.

Firstly, there are those directly under the Guardians who are responsible for the incarnation patterns of those incarnating automatically, that is, without conscious self-awareness of the process of spiritual evolution. You may call these beings angelic if you prefer. They are, shall we say, "local" or of your planetary sphere.

The seniority of vibration is to be likened unto placing various grades of liquids in the same glass. Some will rise to the top; others will sink to the bottom. Layers and layers of entities will ensue. As harvest draws near, those filled with the most light and love will naturally, and without supervision, be in line, shall we say, for the experience of incarnation.

When the entity becomes aware in its mind/body/spirit complex totality of the mechanism for spiritual evolution it, itself, will arrange and place those lessons and entities necessary for maximum growth and expression of polarity in the incarnative experience before the forgetting process occurs. The only disadvantage of this total free will of those senior entities choosing the manner of incarnation experiences is that some entities attempt to learn so much during one incarnative experience that the intensity of catalyst disarranges the polarized entity and the experience thus is not maximally useful as intended.

QUESTIONER: An analogy to that would be a student in college signing up for more courses than he could possibly assimilate in the time they were given. Is this correct?

RA: I am Ra. This is correct.

QUESTIONER: Could you tell me how the various bodies, red through violet, are linked to the energy centers, red through violet? Are they linked in some way?

RA: I am Ra. This shall be the last full query of this working.

As we have noted, each of the true color densities has the seven energy centers and each entity contains all this in potentiation. The activation, while in yellow ray, of violet-ray intelligent infinity is a passport to the next octave of experience. There are adepts who have penetrated many, many of the energy centers and several of the true colors. This must be done with utmost care while in the physical body for as we noted when speaking of the dangers of linking red/orange/yellow circuitry with true color blue circuitry the potential for disarrangement of the mind/body/spirit complex is great. However, the entity who penetrates intelligent infinity is basically capable of walking the universe with unfettered tread.

Is there any brief query before we leave this instrument?

QUESTIONER: Just if there is anything that we can do to make the instrument more comfortable or to improve the contact?

RA: I am Ra. All is well. As we have said, this instrument is weak physically and continued work times will lengthen this weakness. The continued contact also aids in the continued climb in vital energy of the instrument as well as the integration and vital energy of the group as an unit. The choice is yours. We are pleased. All is well. You are conscientious. Continue so.

I am Ra. I leave you in the love and in the light of the One Infinite Creator. Go forth, then, my friends, rejoicing in the power and in the peace of the One Infinite Creator. Adonai.

Session 49,
April 27, 1981

RA: I am Ra. I greet you in the love and in the light of the One Infinite Creator. We communicate now.

QUESTIONER: Would you please give us a reading on the instrument's condition?

RA: I am Ra. It is as previously stated.

QUESTIONER: I was wondering; in a previous session you had mentioned the left and right ear tones, the left and the right brain somehow being related to the polarities of service-to-self and service-to-others. Could you comment on this?

RA: I am Ra. We may comment on this.

QUESTIONER: Will you go ahead and comment on this?

RA: I am Ra. The lobes of your physical complex brain are alike in their use of weak electrical energy. The entity ruled by intuition and impulse is equal to the entity governed by rational analysis when polarity is considered. The lobes may both be used for service to self or service-to-others. It may seem that the rational or analytical mind might have more of a possibility of successfully pursuing the negative orientation due to the fact that in our understanding too much order is by its essence negative. However, this same ability to structure abstract concepts and to analyze experiential data may be the key to rapid positive polarization. It may be said that those whose analytical capacities are predominant have somewhat more to work with in polarizing.

The function of intuition is to inform intelligence. In your illusion the unbridled predominance of intuition will tend to keep an entity from the greater polarizations due to the vagaries of intuitive perception. As you may see, these two types of brain structure need to be balanced in order that the net sum of experiential catalyst will be polarization and illumination, for without the acceptance by the rational mind of the worth of the intuitive faculty the creative aspects which aid in illumination will be stifled.

There is one correspondence between right and left and positive and negative. The web of energy which surrounds your bodies contains somewhat complex polarizations. The left area of the head and upper shoulder is most generally seen to be of a negative polarization whereas the right is of positive polarization, magnetically speaking. This is the cause of the tone's meaning for you.

QUESTIONER: Will you expand on the positive and negative polarizations in general and how they apply to individuals and planets, etc.? I think there is a correlation here, but I'm not sure.

RA: I am Ra. It is correct that there is a correlation between the energy field of an entity of your nature and planetary bodies, for all material is constructed by means of the dynamic tension of the magnetic field. The lines of force in both cases may be seen to be much like the interweaving spirals of the braided hair. Thus positive and negative wind and interweave forming geometric relationships in the energy fields of both persons, as you would call a mind/body/spirit complex, and planets.

The negative pole is the south pole or the lower pole. The north or upper pole is positive. The crisscrossing of these spiraling energies form primary, secondary, and tertiary energy centers. You are familiar with the primary energy centers of the physical, mental, and spiritual body complex. Secondary points of the crisscrossing of positive and negative center orientation revolve about several of your centers. The yellow-ray center may be seen to have secondary energy centers in elbow, in knee, and in the subtle bodies at a slight spacing from the physical vehicle at points describing diamonds about the entity's navel area surrounding the body.

One may examine each of the energy centers for such secondary centers. Some of your peoples work with these energy centers, and you call this acupuncture. However, it is to be noted that there are most often anomalies in the placement of the energy centers so that the scientific precision of this practice is brought into question. Like most scientific attempts at precision, it fails to take into account the unique qualities of each creation.

The most important concept to grasp about the energy field is that the lower or negative pole will draw the universal energy into itself from the cosmos. Therefrom it will move upward to be met and reacted to by the positive spiraling energy moving downward from within. The measure of an entity's level of ray activity is the locus wherein the south pole outer energy has been met by the inner spiraling positive energy.

As an entity grows more polarized this locus will move upwards. This phenomenon has been called by your peoples the kundalini. However, it may better be thought of as the meeting place of cosmic and inner, shall we say, vibratory understanding. To attempt to raise the locus of this meeting without realizing the metaphysical principles of magnetism upon which this depends is to invite great imbalance.

QUESTIONER: What process would be the recommended process for correctly awakening the kundalini and of what value would that be?

RA: I am Ra. The metaphor of the coiled serpent being called upwards is vastly appropriate for consideration by your peoples. This is what you are attempting when you seek. There are, as we have stated, great misapprehensions concerning this metaphor and the nature of pursuing its goal. We must generalize and ask that you grasp the fact that this in effect renders far less useful that which we share. However, as each entity is unique, generalities are our lot when communicating for your possible edification.

We have two types of energy. We are attempting then, as entities in any true color of this octave, to move the meeting place of inner and outer natures further and further along or upward along the energy centers. The two methods of approaching this with sensible method are first, the seating within one's self of those experiences which are attracted to the entity through the south pole. Each experience will need to be observed, experienced, balanced, accepted, and seated within the individual. As the entity grows in self-acceptance and awareness of catalyst the location of the comfortable seating of these experiences will rise to the new true color entity. The experience, whatever it may be, will be seated in red ray and considered as to its survival content and so forth.

Each experience will be sequentially understood by the growing and seeking mind/body/spirit complex in terms of survival, then in terms of personal identity, then in terms of social relations, then in terms of universal love, then in terms of how the experience may beget free communication, then in terms of how the experience may be linked to universal energies, and finally in terms of the sacramental nature of each experience.

Meanwhile the Creator lies within. In the north pole the crown is already upon the head and the entity is potentially a god. This energy is brought into being by the humble and trusting acceptance of this energy through meditation and contemplation of the self and of the Creator.

Where these energies meet is where the serpent will have achieved its height. When this uncoiled energy approaches universal love and radiant being the entity is in a state whereby the harvestability of the entity comes nigh.

QUESTIONER: Will you recommend a technique of meditation?

RA: I am Ra. No.

QUESTIONER: Is it better, or shall I say, does it produce more usable results in meditation to leave the mind as blank as possible and let it run down, so to speak, or is it better to focus in meditation on some object or some thing for concentration?

RA: I am Ra. This shall be the last full query of this work time.

Each of the two types of meditation is useful for a particular reason. The passive meditation involving the clearing of the mind, the emptying of the mental jumble which is characteristic of mind complex activity among your peoples, is efficacious for those whose goal is to achieve an inner silence as a base from which to listen to the Creator. This is an useful and helpful tool and is by far the most generally useful type of meditation as opposed to contemplation or prayer.

The type of meditation which may be called visualization has as its goal not that which is contained in the meditation itself. Visualization is the tool of the adept. Those who learn to hold visual images in mind are developing an inner concentrative power that can transcend boredom and discomfort. When this ability has become crystallized in an adept the adept may then do polarizing in consciousness without external action which can effect the planetary consciousness. This is the reason for the existence of the so-called White Magician. Only those wishing to pursue the conscious raising of planetary vibration will find visualization to be a particularly satisfying type of meditation.

Contemplation or the consideration in a meditative state of an inspiring image or text is extremely useful also among your peoples, and the faculty of will called praying is also of a potentially helpful nature. Whether it is indeed an helpful activity depends quite totally upon the intentions and objects of the one who prays.

May we ask if there are any brief queries at this time?

QUESTIONER: I will just ask if there is anything that we may do to make the instrument more comfortable or to improve the contact and if the two periods per week are still appropriate?

RA: I am Ra. We request your care in the placement of the neck support for this entity as it is too often careless. You are conscientious and your alignments are well. The timing, if we may use that expression, of the sessions is basically correct. However, you are to be commended for observing fatigue in the circle and refraining from a working until all were in love, harmony, and vital energy as one being. This is, and will continue to be, most helpful.

I am Ra. I leave you in the love and in the light of the One Infinite Creator. Go forth, therefore, rejoicing in the power and in the peace of the One Infinite Creator. Adonai.

Session 50,
May 6, 1981

RA: I am Ra. I greet you in the love and in the light of the One Infinite Creator. We communicate now.

QUESTIONER: Could you please give me an indication of the instrument's condition now?

RA: I am Ra. It is as previously stated.

QUESTIONER: In the last session you made the statement that experiences are attracted into the entity through the south pole. Could you expand on that and give us a definition of what you mean?

RA: I am Ra. It takes some consideration to accomplish the proper perspective for grasping the sense of the above information. The south or negative pole is one which attracts. It pulls unto itself those things magnetized to it. So with the mind/body/spirit complex. The in-flow of experience is of the south pole influx. You may consider this a simplistic statement.

The only specific part of this correctness is that the red ray or foundation energy center, being the lowest or root energy center of the physical vehicle, will have the first opportunity to react to any experience. In this way only, you may see a physical locus of the south pole being identified with the root energy center. In every facet of mind and body the root or foundation will be given the opportunity to function first.

What is this opportunity but survival? This is the root possibility of response and may be found to be characteristic of the basic functions of both mind and body. You will find this instinct the strongest, and once this is balanced much is open to the seeker. The south pole then ceases blocking the experiential data and higher energy centers of mind and body become availed of the opportunity to use the experience drawn to it.

QUESTIONER: Why do you say the experience is drawn to or attracted to the entity?

RA: I am Ra. We say this due to our understanding that this is the nature of the phenomenon of experiential catalyst and its entry into the mind/body/spirit complex's awareness.

QUESTIONER: Could you give an example of how an entity sets up a condition for attracting a particular experiential catalyst and how that catalyst then is provided or is learned.

RA: I am Ra. Such an example may be given.

QUESTIONER: Will you give that?

RA: I am Ra. We paused to scan (name's) consciousness to use its experiential catalyst as example. We may proceed.

This is one instance and extrapolation may be made to other entities which are aware of the process of evolution. This entity chose, before incarnation, the means whereby catalyst had great probability of being obtained. This entity desired the process of expressing love and light without expecting any return. This entity programmed also to endeavor to accomplish spiritual work and to comfort itself with companionship in the doing of this work.

Agreements were made prior to incarnation; the first, with the so-called parents and siblings of this entity. This provided the experiential catalyst for the situation of offering radiance of being without expectation of return. The second program involved agreements with several entities. These agreements provided and will provide, in your time/space and space/time continuum, opportunities for the experiential catalyst of work and comradeship.

There are events which were part of a program for this entity only in that they were possibility/probability vortices having to do with your societal culture. These events include the nature of the living or standard of living, the type of relationships entered into in your legal framework, and the social climate during the incarnation. The incarnation was understood to be one which would take place at harvest.

These givens, shall we say, apply to millions of your peoples. Those aware of evolution and desirous in the very extreme of attaining the heart of love and the radiance which gives understanding no matter what the lessons programmed: they have to do with other-selves, not with events; they have to do with giving, not receiving, for the lessons of love are of this nature both for positive and negative. Those negatively harvestable will be found at this time endeavoring to share their love of self.

There are those whose lessons are more random due to their present inability to comprehend the nature and mechanism of the evolution of mind, body, and spirit. Of these we may say that the process is guarded by those who never cease their watchful expectation of being of service. There is no entity without help, either through self-awareness of the unity of creation or through guardians of the self which protect the less sophisticated mind/body/spirit from any permanent separation from unity while the lessons of your density continue.

QUESTIONER: Could you give an example of negative polarization sharing love of self? It would seem to me that that would deplete negative polarization. Could you expand on the concept?

RA: I am Ra. We may not use examples of known beings due to the infringement this would cause. Thus we must be general.

The negatively oriented being will be one who feels that it has found power that gives meaning to its existence precisely as the positive polarization does feel. This negative entity will strive to offer these understandings to other-selves, most usually by the process of forming the elite, the disciples, and teaching the need and rightness of the enslavement of other-selves for their own good. These other-selves are conceived to be dependent upon the self and in need of the guidance and the wisdom of the self.

QUESTIONER: Thank you. How does the ability to hold visual images in mind allow the adept to do polarization in consciousness without external action?

RA: I am Ra. This is not a simple query, for the adept is one which will go beyond the green ray which signals entry into harvestability. The adept will not simply be tapping into intelligent energy as a means of readiness for harvest but tapping into both intelligent energy and intelligent infinity for the purpose of transmuting planetary harvestability and consciousness.

The means of this working lie within. The key is first, silence, and secondly, singleness of thought. Thusly a visualization which can be held steady to the inward eye for several of your minutes, as you measure time, will signal the adept's increase in singleness of thought. This singleness of thought then can be used by the positive adept to work in group ritual visualizations for the raising of positive energy, by negative adepts for the increase in personal power.

QUESTIONER: Can you tell me what the adept, after being able to hold the image for several minutes, does to affect planetary consciousness or affect positive polarity?

RA: I am Ra. When the positive adept touches intelligent infinity from within, this is the most powerful of connections for it is the connection of the whole mind/body/spirit complex microcosm with the macrocosm. This connection enables the, shall we say, green-ray true color in time/space to manifest in your space/time. In green ray thoughts are beings. In your illusion this is normally not so.

The adepts then become living channels for love and light and are able to channel this radiance directly into the planetary web of energy nexi. The ritual will always end by the grounding of this energy in praise and thanksgiving and the release of this energy into the planetary whole.

QUESTIONER: Could you give me more information on the energy fields of the body as related to the right and left brain and if this is somehow related to the pyramid shape as far as energy focusing goes?

I am at a loss as to how to get into this line of questioning, so I will ask that question.

RA: I am Ra. We are similarly at a loss at this line of answering. We may say that the pyramid shape is but one which focuses the instreamings of energy for use by entities which may become aware of these instreamings. We may say further that the shape of your physical brain is not significant as a shape for concentrating instreamings of energy. Please ask more specifically if you may that which you seek.

QUESTIONER: Each of us feels, in meditation, energy upon the head in various places. Could you tell me what this is, what it signifies, and what the various places in which we feel it signify?

RA: I am Ra. Forgetting the pyramid will be of aid to you in the study of these experiences.

The instreamings of energy are felt by the energy centers which need, and are prepared for, activation. Thus those who feel the stimulation at violet-ray level are getting just that. Those feeling it within the forehead between the brows are experiencing indigo ray and so forth. Those experiencing tingling and visual images are having some blockage in the energy center being activated and thus the electrical body spreads this energy out and its effect is diffused.

Those not truly sincerely requesting this energy may yet feel it if the entities are not well trained in psychic defense. Those not desirous of experiencing these sensations and activations and changes even upon the subconscious level will not experience anything due to their abilities at defense and armoring against change.

QUESTIONER: Is it normal to get two simultaneous stimulations at once?

RA: I am Ra. The most normal for the adept is the following: the indigo stimulation activating that great gateway into healing, magical work, prayerful attention, and the radiance of being; and the stimulation of the violet ray which is the spiritual giving and taking from and to Creator, from Creator to Creator.

This is a desirable configuration.

Please ask one more full query at this working.

QUESTIONER: Can you expand on the concept which is that it is necessary for an entity, during incarnation in the physical as we know it, to become polarized or interact properly with other entities and why this isn't possible in between incarnations when the entity is aware of what he wants to do. Why must he come into an incarnation and lose conscious memory of what he wants to do and then act in a way in which he hopes to act?

RA: I am Ra. Let us give the example of the man who sees all the poker hands. He then knows the game. It is but child's play to gamble, for it is no risk. The other hands are known. The possibilities are known and the hand will be played correctly but with no interest.

In time/space and in the true color green density, the hands of all are open to the eye. The thoughts, the feelings, the troubles, all these may be seen. There is no deception and no desire for deception. Thus much may be accomplished in harmony but the mind/body/ spirit gains little polarity from this interaction.

Let us re-examine this metaphor and multiply it into the longest poker game you can imagine, a lifetime. The cards are love, dislike, limitation, unhappiness, pleasure, etc. They are dealt and re-dealt and re-dealt continuously. You may, during this incarnation begin— and we stress begin—to know your own cards. You may begin to find the love within you. You may begin to balance your pleasure, your limitations, etc. However, your only indication of other-selves' cards is to look into the eyes.

You cannot remember your hand, their hands, perhaps even the rules of this game. This game can only be won by those who lose their cards in the melting influence of love, can only be won by those who lay their pleasures, their limitations, their all upon the table face up and say inwardly: "All, all of you players, each other-self, whatever your hand, I love you." This is the game: to know, to accept, to forgive, to balance, and to open the self in love. This cannot be done without the forgetting, for it would carry no weight in the life of the mind/ body/spirit beingness totality.

Is there a brief query before we leave this instrument?

QUESTIONER: Is there anything that we can do to make the instrument more comfortable or to improve the contact?

RA: I am Ra. You are conscientious and your alignments are careful. It would be well to take care that this instrument's neck is placed carefully upon its support.

I am Ra. I leave you, my friends, in the love and the light of the One Infinite Creator. Go forth, then, rejoicing in the power and in the peace of the One Infinite Creator. Adonai.

INDEX

V

Venus, 23, 30, 90

Vibration, 10, 12–13, 15, 17, 22, 24–25, 40, 43, 46, 51, 76, 78–80, 82, 84–85, 93, 108, 114, 117, 122

W

Wanderers, 7, 42–43, 66–67, 115–116

War, 49, 55–56

Will, 7, 9–19, 21–26, 28–29, 31–32, 34–45, 47–53, 56–57, 61, 64–67, 69–70, 74–75, 77–78, 80–83, 88–96, 98, 102–105, 107–110, 112–127

Wisdom, 12, 51, 65–66, 92–93, 100–101, 109, 115, 125

ABOUT THE AUTHORS

DON ELKINS was born in Louisville, Kentucky, in 1930. He held a BS and MS in mechanical engineering from the University of Louisville, as well as an MS in general engineering from Speed Scientific School. He was professor of physics and engineering at the University of Louisville for twelve years from 1953 to 1965. In 1965 he left his tenured position and became a Boeing 727 pilot for a major airline to devote himself more fully to UFO and paranormal research. He also served with distinction in the US Army as a master sergeant during the Korean War.

Don Elkins began his research into the paranormal in 1955. In 1962, Don started an experiment in channeling, using the protocols he had learned from a contactee group in Detroit, Michigan. That experiment blossomed into a channeling practice that led eventually to the Law of One material 19 years later. Don passed away on November 7, 1984.

CARLA L. RUECKERT (McCarty) was born in 1943 in Lake Forest, Illinois. She completed undergraduate studies in English literature at the University of Louisville in 1966 and earned her master's degree in library service in 1971.

Carla became partners with Don in 1968. In 1970, they formed L/L Research. In 1974, she began channeling and continued in that effort until she was stopped in 2011 by a spinal fusion surgery. During four of those thirty-seven years of channeling (1981–1984), Carla served as the instrument for the Law of One material.

In 1987, she married Jim McCarty, and together they continued the mission of L/L Research. Carla passed into larger life on April 1, 2015.

JAMES MCCARTY was born in 1947 in Kearney, Nebraska. After receiving an undergraduate degrees from the University of Nebraska at Kearney and a master of science in early childhood education from the University of Florida, Jim moved to a piece of wilderness in Marion County, Kentucky, in 1974 to build his own log cabin in the woods, and to develop a self-sufficient lifestyle. For the next six years, he was in almost complete retreat.

He founded the Rock Creek Research and Development Laboratories in 1977 to further his teaching efforts. After experimenting, Jim decided that he preferred the methods and directions he had found in studying with L/L Research in 1978. In 1980, he joined his research with Don's and Carla's.

Jim and Carla were married in 1987. Jim has a wide L/L correspondence and creates wonderful gardens and stonework. He enjoys beauty, nature, dance, and silence.

NOTE: The Ra contact continued until session number 106. There are five volumes total in The Law of One series, Book I–Book V. There is also other material available from our research group on our archive website, www.llresearch.org.

You may reach us by email at contact@llresearch.org, or by mail at: L/L Research, P.O. Box 5195, Louisville, KY 40255-0195

THE RA MATERIAL

The Law of One
Book III

The Law of One
Book III

DON ELKINS ⚸ CARLA RUECKERT
JAMES ALLEN McCARTY

REDFeather™
MIND | BODY | SPIRIT

4880 Lower Valley Road, Atglen, PA 19310

Type set in Chaparral Pro

Book III
Softcover ISBN: 978-0-924608-08-7
Hardcover ISBN: 978-0-7643-6556-0
Box Set ISBN (Books I–V): 978-0-7643-6021-3
E-Book ISBN: 978-1-5073-0117-3

Printed in India

Updated Edition
10 9 8 7 6 5 4 3

Published by Red Feather Mind, Body, Spirit
An imprint of Schiffer Publishing, Ltd.
4880 Lower Valley Road
Atglen, PA 19310
Phone: (610) 593–1777; Fax: (610) 593–2002
E–mail: Info@schifferbooks.com
Web: www.redfeathermbs.com

For our complete selection of fine books on this and related subjects, please visit our website at www.schifferbooks.com. You may also write for a free catalog.

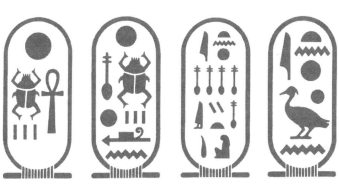

FOREWORD

On January 15, 1981, our research group started receiving a communication from the social memory complex Ra. From this communication precipitated the Law of One and some of the distortions of the Law of One.

The pages of this book contain an exact transcript, edited only to remove some personal material, of the communications received in Sessions 51 through 75 with Ra.

This material presupposes a point of view that we have developed in the course of many years' study of the UFO phenomenon. If you are not familiar with our previous work, a reading of our book *Secrets of the UFO* might prove helpful in understanding the present material. Also, as you can see from this book's title, there are 50 previous sessions with Ra that were collected in *The Law of One* and Book II of *The Law of One*. If at all possible, it is good to begin with the beginning with this material, since concepts build upon previous concepts. The Ra contact continued for 106 sessions, which were printed into four books in *The Law of One* series. They are available at your local bookstore, from Schiffer Publishing, or from us. If you wish to receive our quarterly newsletter, in which the best of our current channeling is published, please request that you be put on our mailing list.

Book III of *The Law of One* is an intensive study of the techniques of balancing of the energy centers and efficient polarization as our planet makes ready for harvest into fourth density. The nature of time/space and space/time is examined, and some of the ramifications of meditation and magic are discussed. A good deal of material about psychic attack and the Orion group is included, and the volume ends with a beginning glance into the archetypical mind.

L/L Research
Louisville, Kentucky
March 17, 1982

Session 51,
May 13, 1981

RA: I am Ra. I greet you in the love and in the light of the One Infinite Creator. We communicate now.

QUESTIONER: As we begin Book III of *The Law of One*, there are a couple of questions of fairly nontransient importance that I have, and one that I consider to be of a transient nature that I feel obligated to ask.

The first is clearing up the final point about harvest. I was wondering if there is a supervision over the harvest, and if so, why this supervision is necessary and how it works since an entity's harvestability is determined by the violet ray? Is it necessary for entities to supervise the harvest, or is it automatic?

RA: I am Ra. In time of harvest there are always harvesters. The fruit is formed as it will be, but there is some supervision necessary to ensure that this bounty is placed as it should be without the bruise or the blemish.

There are those of three levels watching over harvest.

The first level is planetary and that which may be called angelic. This type of guardian includes the mind/body/spirit complex totality or Higher Self of an entity and those inner plane entities which have been attracted to this entity through its inner seeking.

The second class of those who ward this process are those of the Confederation who have the honor/duty of standing in the small places at the edge of the steps of light/love so that those entities being harvested will not, no matter how confused or unable to make contact with their Higher Self, stumble and fall away for any reason other than the strength of the light. These Confederation entities catch those who stumble and set them aright so that they may continue into the light.

The third group watching over this process is that group you call the Guardians. This group is from the octave above our own and serves in this manner as light bringers. These Guardians provide the precise emissions of light/love in exquisitely fastidious disseminations of discrimination so that the precise light/love vibration of each entity may be ascertained.

Thus the harvest is automatic in that those harvested will respond according to that which is unchangeable during harvest. That is the violet-ray emanation. However, these helpers are around to ensure a proper harvesting so that each entity may have the fullest opportunity to express its violet-ray selfhood.

QUESTIONER: This next question I feel to be a transient type of question; however, it has been asked me by one whom I have communicated with who has been involved intensely in the UFO portion of the phenomenon. If you deem it too transient or unimportant, we'll skip it, but I have been asked how it is possible for the craft of the fourth density to get here since it seems that as you approach the velocity of light, the mass approaches infinity. My question would be why craft would be necessary at all?

RA: I am Ra. You have asked several questions. We shall respond in turn.

Firstly, we agree that this material is transient.

Secondly, those for the most part coming from distant points, as you term them, do not need craft as you know them. The query itself requires understanding which you do not possess. We shall attempt to state what may be stated.

Firstly, there are a few third-density entities who have learned how to use craft to travel between star systems while experiencing the limitations you now understand. However, such entities have learned to use hydrogen in a way different from your understanding now. These entities still take quite long durations of time, as you measure it, to move about. However, these entities are able to use hypothermia to slow the physical and mental complex processes in order to withstand the duration of flight. Those such as are from Sirius are of this type. There are two other types.

One is the type which, coming from fourth, fifth, or sixth density in your own galaxy, has access to a type of energy system which uses the speed of light as a slingshot and thus arrives where it wishes without any perceptible time elapsed in your view.

The other type of experience is that of fourth, fifth, and sixth densities of other galaxies and some within your own galaxy which have learned the necessary disciplines of personality to view the universe as one being and, therefore, are able to proceed from locus to locus by thought alone, materializing the necessary craft, if you will, to enclose the light body of the entity.

QUESTIONER: I assume that that latter type is the type we experience with the landings of the Orion group. Is this correct?

RA: I am Ra. The Orion group is mixed between the penultimate and the latter groups.

QUESTIONER: Why is a vehicle necessary for this transition? When you, as Ra, went to Egypt earlier you used bell-shaped craft, but you did this by thought. Can you tell me why you used a vehicle rather than just materializing the body?

RA: I am Ra. The vehicle or craft is that thought-form upon which our concentration may function as motivator. We would not choose to use our mind/body/spirit complexes as the focus for such a working.

QUESTIONER: Thank you. It seems to me, and you can tell me where I am going wrong with this statement, that we have seven bodies each corresponding to one of the seven colors of the spectrum and that energy that creates these seven bodies is a universal type of energy that streams into our planetary environment and comes in through the seven energy centers that we have called chakras to develop and perfect these bodies. Each of these bodies is somehow related to the mental configuration that we have, and the perfection of these bodies and the total instreaming of this energy is a function of this mental configuration, and through this mental configuration we may block, to some extent, the instreamings of energy that created these seven bodies. Could you comment on where I am wrong, and correct that which I have stated?

RA: I am Ra. Your statement is substantially correct. To use the term "mental configuration" is to oversimplify the manners of blockage of instreaming which occur in your density. The mind complex has a relationship to the spirit and body complexes which is not fixed. Thus blockages may occur betwixt spirit and mind, or body and mind, upon many different levels. We reiterate that each energy center has seven sub-colors, let us say, for convenience. Thus spiritual/mental blockages combined with mental/bodily blockages may affect each of the energy centers in several differing ways. Thus you may see the subtle nature of the balancing and evolutionary process.

QUESTIONER: I am unsure as to whether this will provide an avenue of questioning that will be fruitful, but I will ask this question since it seems to me that there is a connection here.

On the back of the book *Secrets of the Great Pyramid*, there are several reproductions of Egyptian drawings or works, some showing birds flying over horizontal entities. Could you tell me what this is and if it has any relationship to Ra?

RA: I am Ra. These drawings of which you speak are some of many

which distort the teaching of our perception of death as the gateway
to further experience. The distortions concern those considerations
of specific nature as to processes of the so-called "dead" mind/body/
spirit complex. This may be termed, in your philosophy, the distortion of Gnosticism: that is, the belief that one may achieve knowledge
and a proper position by means of carefully perceived and accentuated movements, concepts, and symbols. In fact, the process of the
physical death is as we have described before: one in which there is
aid available, and the only need at death is the releasing of that entity
from its body by those around it and the praising of the process by
those who grieve. By these means may the mind/body/spirit which
has experienced physical death be aided, not by the various perceptions of careful and repeated rituals.

QUESTIONER: You spoke at an earlier time of rotational speeds of
energy centers. Am I correct in assuming that this is a function of
the blockage of the energy center, so that when it is less blocked, the
speed of rotation is higher and the energy instreaming is greater?

RA: I am Ra. You are partially correct. In the first three energy centers
a full unblocking of this energy will create speeds of rotation. As the
entity develops the higher energy centers, however, these centers will
then begin to express their nature by forming crystal structures. This
is the higher or more balanced form of activation of energy centers
as the space/time nature of this energy is transmuted to the time/
space nature of regularization and balance.

QUESTIONER: What do you mean by crystal structures?

RA: I am Ra. Each of the energy centers of the physical complex may
be seen to have a distinctive crystalline structure in the more developed entity. Each will be somewhat different; just as in your world,
no two snowflakes are alike. However, each is regular. The red energy
center often is in the shape of the spoked wheel. The orange energy
center in the flower shape containing three petals.
    The yellow center again in a rounded shape, many faceted, as a
star.
    The green energy center sometimes called the lotus shape, the
number of points of crystalline structure dependent upon the
strength of this center.
    The blue energy center capable of having perhaps one hundred
facets and capable of great flashing brilliance.
    The indigo center a more quiet center which has the basic

triangular or three-petalled shape in many, although some adepts who have balanced the lower energies may create more faceted forms.

The violet energy center is the least variable and is sometimes described in your philosophy as thousand petaled, as it is the sum of the mind/body/spirit complex distortion totality.

QUESTIONER: Right now I feel a feeling at the indigo center. If this center were totally activated and not blocked at all, would I then feel nothing there?

RA: I am Ra. This query, if answered, would infringe upon the Law of Confusion.

QUESTIONER: Immediately after the death of the physical body you have stated that the primary activated body is the indigo, and you stated that it is the form-maker. Why is this so?

RA: I am Ra. This will be the last full query of this session of working.

The indigo body may be seen to be an analog for intelligent energy. It is, in microcosm, the Logos. The intelligent energy of the mind/body/spirit complex totality draws its existence from intelligent infinity or the Creator. This Creator is to be understood, both in macrocosm and microcosm, to have, as we have said, two natures: the unpotentiated infinity which is intelligent; this is all that there is.

Free will has potentiated, both the Creator of us all and our selves, as co-Creators with intelligent infinity which has will. This will may be drawn upon by the indigo or form-making body, and its wisdom used to then choose the appropriate locus and type of experience which this co-Creator or sub-sub-Logos you call so carelessly a person will take.

I am Ra. This is the time for any brief queries.

QUESTIONER: Is there anything that we can do to make the instrument more comfortable or to improve the contact?

RA: I am Ra. All is well. You are conscientious. I leave you now, my brothers, in the love and in the light of the One Infinite Creator. Go forth, then, rejoicing in the power and the peace of the One Infinite Creator. Adonai.

Session 52,
May 19, 1981

RA: I am Ra. I greet you in the love and in the light of the One Infinite Creator. We communicate now.

QUESTIONER: In the previous session you stated: "The other type of experience is the fourth, fifth, and sixth densities of other galaxies, and some within your own galaxy which have learned necessary disciplines of personality to view the universe as one being are able to proceed from locus to locus by thought alone, materializing the necessary craft." I would like to ask you when you say fourth, fifth, and sixth densities of other galaxies, some within your own galaxy, are you stating here that more of the entities in other galaxies have developed the abilities of personality than have those in this galaxy for this type of travel? I am using the term "galaxy" with respect to the lenticular shape of billions of stars.

RA: I am Ra. We have once again used a meaning for this term, galaxy, that does not lie within your vocabulary at this time, if you will call it so. We referred to your star system.

It is incorrect to assume that other star systems are more able to manipulate the dimensions than your own. It is merely that there are many other systems besides your own.

QUESTIONER: Thank you. I think that possibly I am on an important point here because it seems to me that the great work in evolution is the discipline of personality, and it seems that we have two types of entities moving around the universe, one stemming from disciplines of personality, and the other stemming from what you call the slingshot effect. I won't even get into the sub-light speeds because I don't consider that too important. I only consider this material important because of the fact that we are considering disciplines of the personality.

Is the use of the slingshot effect for travel what you might call an intellectual or a left-brain type of involvement of understanding rather than a right brain type?

RA: I am Ra. Your perception on this point is extensive. You penetrate the outer teaching. We prefer not to utilize the terminology of right and left brain due to the inaccuracies of this terminology. Some functions are repetitive or redundant in both lobes, and further, to some entities the functions of the right and left are reversed. However, the heart of the query is worth some consideration.

The technology of which you, as a social complex, are so enamored at this time is but the birthing of the manipulation of the intelligent energy of the sub-Logos which, when carried much further, may evolve into technology capable of using the gravitic effects of which we spoke.

We note that this term is not accurate, but there is no closer term. Therefore, the use of technology to manipulate that outside the self is far, far less of an aid to personal evolution than the disciplines of the mind/body/spirit complex resulting in the whole knowledge of the self in the microcosm and macrocosm.

To the disciplined entity, all things are open and free. The discipline which opens the universes opens also the gateways to evolution. The difference is that of choosing either to hitchhike to a place where beauty may be seen, or to walk, step by step, independent and free in this independence to praise the strength to walk and the opportunity for the awareness of beauty.

The hitchhiker, instead, is distracted by conversation and the vagaries of the road and, dependent upon the whims of others, is concerned to make the appointment in time. The hitchhiker sees the same beauty but has not prepared itself for the establishment, in the roots of mind, of the experience.

QUESTIONER: I would ask this question in order to understand the mental disciplines and how they evolve. Does fourth-, fifth-, and sixth-density positive or service-to-others orientation of social memory complexes use both the slingshot and the personality disciplines type of effect for travel, or do they use only one?

RA: I am Ra. The positively oriented social memory complex will be attempting to learn the disciplines of mind, body, and spirit. However, there are some which, having the technology available to use intelligent energy forces to accomplish travel, do so while learning the more appropriate disciplines.

QUESTIONER: Then I am assuming that in the more positively oriented social memory complexes, a much higher percentage of them use the personality disciplines for this travel. Is this correct?

RA: I am Ra. This is correct. As positive fifth density moves into sixth there are virtually no entities which any longer use outer technology for travel or communication.

QUESTIONER: Could you give me the same information on the negatively oriented social memory complexes as to the ratios and as to how they use the slingshot effect or the disciplines of the personality for travel?

RA: I am Ra. The fourth-density negative uses the slingshot gravitic light effect, perhaps 80 percent of its membership being unable to master the disciplines necessary for alternate methods of travel. In fifth-density negative, approximately 50 percent at some point gain the necessary discipline to use thought to accomplish travel. As the sixth density approaches, the negative orientation is thrown into confusion and little travel is attempted. What travel is done is perhaps 73 percent of light/thought.

QUESTIONER: Is there any difference close to the end of fifth density in the disciplines of personality between positive and negative orientation?

RA: I am Ra. There are patent differences between the polarities but no difference whatsoever in the completion of the knowledge of the self necessary to accomplish this discipline.

QUESTIONER: Am I correct, then, in assuming that discipline of the personality, knowledge of self, and control in strengthening of the will would be what any fifth-density entity would see as those things of importance?

RA: I am Ra. In actuality these things are of importance in third through early seventh densities. The only correction in nuance that we would make is your use of the word "control." It is paramount that it be understood that it is not desirable or helpful to the growth of the understanding, may we say, of an entity by itself to control thought processes or impulses except where they may result in actions not consonant with the Law of One. Control may seem to be a shortcut to discipline, peace, and illumination. However, this very control potentiates and necessitates the further incarnative experience in order to balance this control or repression of that self which is perfect.

Instead, we appreciate and recommend the use of your second verb in regard to the use of the will. Acceptance of self, forgiveness of self, and the direction of the will; this is the path towards the disciplined personality. Your faculty of will is that which is powerful within you as co-Creator. You cannot ascribe to this faculty too much importance. Thus it must be carefully used and directed in service to others for those upon the positively oriented path.

There is great danger in the use of the will as the personality becomes stronger, for it may be used even subconsciously in ways reducing the polarity of the entity.

QUESTIONER: I sense, possibly, a connection between what you just said and why so many Wanderers have selected the harvest time on this planet to incarnate. Am I correct?

RA: I am Ra. It is correct that in the chance to remember that which has been lost in the forgetting, there is a nimiety of opportunity for positive polarization. We believe this is the specific thrust of your query. Please ask further if it is not.

QUESTIONER: I would just include the question as to why the time of harvest is selected by so many Wanderers as time for incarnation?

RA: I am Ra. There are several reasons for incarnation during harvest. They may be divided by the terms "self" and "other-self."

The overriding reason for the offering of these Brothers and Sisters of Sorrow in incarnative states is the possibility of aiding other-selves by the lightening of the planetary consciousness distortions and the probability of offering catalyst to other-selves which will increase the harvest.

There are two other reasons for choosing this service which have to do with the self.

The Wanderer, if it remembers and dedicates itself to service, will polarize much more rapidly than is possible in the far more etiolated realms of higher-density catalyst.

The final reason is within the mind/body/spirit totality or the social memory complex totality which may judge that an entity or members of a societal entity can make use of third-density catalyst to recapitulate a learning/teaching which is adjudged to be less than perfect. This especially applies to those entering into and proceeding through sixth density, wherein the balance between compassion and wisdom is perfected.

QUESTIONER: Thank you. Just as something that I am a little inquisitive about, but which is not of much importance, I would like to make a statement that I intuitively hunch. I may be wrong.

You were speaking of the slingshot effect, and that term has puzzled me.

The only thing that I can see is that you must put energy into a craft until it approaches the velocity of light, and this of course requires more and more energy. The time dilation occurs, and it seems to me that it would be possible to, by moving at 90° to the direction of travel, somehow change this stored energy in its application of direction or sense so that you move out of space/time into time/space with a 90° deflection. Then the energy would be taken out in time/space and you would reenter space/time at the end of this energy burst. Am I in any way correct on this?

RA: I am Ra. You are quite correct as far as your language may take you and, due to your training, more able than we to express the concept. Our only correction, if you will, would be to suggest that the 90° of which you speak are an angle which may best be understood as a portion of a tesseract.

QUESTIONER: Thank you. Just a little point that was bothering me, of no real importance.

Is there then, from the point of view of an individual who wishes to follow the service-to-others path, anything of importance other than disciplines of personality, knowledge of self, and strengthening of will?

RA: I am Ra. This is technique. This is not the heart. Let us examine the heart of evolution.

Let us remember that we are all one. This is the great learning/teaching. In this unity lies love. This is a great learn/teaching. In this unity lies light. This is the fundamental teaching of all planes of existence in materialization. Unity, love, light, and joy; this is the heart of evolution of the spirit.

The second-ranking lessons are learn/taught in meditation and in service. At some point the mind/body/spirit complex is so smoothly activated and balanced by these central thoughts or distortions that the techniques you have mentioned become quite significant. However, the universe, its mystery unbroken, is one. Always begin and end in the Creator, not in technique.

QUESTIONER: In the previous session you mentioned the light bringers from the octave. Am I to understand that those who provide the light for the graduation are of an octave above the one we experience? Could you tell me more about these light bringers, who they are, etc.?

RA: I am Ra. This will be the last full query of this working.

This octave density of which we have spoken is both omega and alpha, the spiritual mass of the infinite universes becoming one central sun or Creator once again. Then is born a new universe, a new infinity, a new Logos which incorporates all that the Creator has experienced of Itself. In this new octave there are also those who wander. We know very little across the boundary of octave except that these beings come to aid our octave in its Logos completion. Is there any brief query which you have at this time?

QUESTIONER: Only is there anything that we can do to make the instrument more comfortable or to improve the contact?

RA: I am Ra. This instrument has some distortion in the area of the lungs which has been well compensated for by the position of the physical complex.

All is well.

We leave you, my friends, in the love and in the light of the One Infinite Creator. Go forth, therefore, rejoicing in the power and in the peace of the One Infinite Creator. Adonai.

Session 53,
May 25, 1981

RA: I am Ra. I greet you in the love and in the light of the One Infinite Creator. We communicate now.

QUESTIONER: I would first like to ask what is the instrument's condition, and then ask two questions for her. She would like to know if she can now do one exercise period per day, and also is the pain she feels prior to doing a session due to an Orion attack?

RA: I am Ra. The instrument's condition is as previously stated. In answer to the question of exercise, now that the intensive period is over, this instrument may, if it chooses, exercise one period rather than two. In scanning this instrument's physical complex distortions, we find the current period of exercise at the limit of this instrument's strength. This is well in the long run due to a cumulative building up of the vital energies. In the short run it is wearying to this entity. Thus we suggest the entity be aware of our previous admonitions regarding other aids to appropriate bodily distortions. In answer to the second query, we may say that the physical complex difficulties prior to contact with our social memory complex are due to the action of the subconscious will of the instrument. This will is extremely strong and requires the mind/body/spirit complex to reserve all available physical and vital energies for the contact. Thus the discomforts are experienced due to the dramatic distortion towards physical weakness while this energy is diverted. The entity is, it may be noted, also under psychic attack, and this intensifies preexisting conditions and is responsible for the cramping and the dizziness as well as mind complex distortions.

QUESTIONER: Thank you. I would like to know if [name] may attend one of these sessions in the very near future?

RA: I am Ra. The mind/body/spirit complex, [name], belongs with this group in the spirit and is welcome. You may request that special meditative periods be set aside until the entity sits with this working. We might suggest that a photograph of the one known as [name] be sent to this entity with his writing upon it indicating love and light. This held while meditating will bring the entity into peaceful harmony with each of you so that there be no extraneous waste of energy while greetings are exchanged between two entities, both of whom have a distortion towards solitude and shyness, as you would call it. The same might be done with a photograph of the entity, [name], for the one known as [name].

QUESTIONER: Thank you. During my trip to Laramie, certain things became apparent to me with respect to dissemination of the first book of the Law of One to those who have had experiences with UFOs and other Wanderers, and I will have to ask some questions now that I may have to include in Book I to eliminate a misunderstanding that I am perceiving as a possibility in Book I. Therefore, these questions, although for the most part transient, are aimed at eliminating certain distortions with respect to the understanding of the material in Book I. I hope that I am using the correct approach here. You may not be able to answer some of them, but that's all right. We'll just go on to others then if you can't answer the ones I ask.

Can you tell me of the various techniques used by the service-to-others positively oriented Confederation contacts with the people of this planet, the various forms and techniques of making contact?

RA: I am Ra. We could.

QUESTIONER: Would you do this please?

RA: I am Ra. The most efficient mode of contact is that which you experience at this space/time. The infringement upon free will is greatly undesired. Therefore, those entities which are Wanderers upon your plane of illusion will be the only subjects for the thought projections which make up the so-called Close Encounters and meetings between positively oriented social memory complexes and Wanderers.

QUESTIONER: Could you give me an example of one of these meetings between a social memory complex and a Wanderer as to what the Wanderer would experience?

RA: I am Ra. One such example of which you are familiar is that of the one known as Morris.*[1] In this case the previous contact which other entities in this entity's circle of friends experienced was negatively oriented. However, you will recall that the entity, Morris, was impervious to this contact and could not see, with the physical optical apparatus, this contact.

However, the inner voice alerted the one known as Morris to go by itself to another place, and there an entity with the thought-form shape and appearance of the other contact appeared and gazed at this entity, thus awakening in it the desire to seek the truth of this occurrence and of the experiences of its incarnation in general.

The feeling of being awakened or activated is the goal of this type of contact. The duration and imagery used varies depending upon the subconscious expectations of the Wanderer which is experiencing this opportunity for activation.

QUESTIONER: In a "Close Encounter" by a Confederation type of craft, I am assuming that this "Close Encounter" is with a thought-form type of craft. Have Wanderers within the past few years had "Close Encounters" with landed thought-form type of craft?

RA: I am Ra. This has occurred, although it is much less common than the Orion type of so-called Close Encounter. We may note that in a universe of unending unity, the concept of a "Close Encounter" is humorous, for are not all encounters of a nature of self with self? Therefore, how can any encounter be less than very, very close?

---

*1. This refers to Case #1 in *Secrets of the UFO* by D. T. Elkins with Carla L. Rueckert (Louisville, KY: L/L Research, 1976), pp. 10–11.

QUESTIONER: Well, talking about this type of encounter of self to self, have any Wanderers of a positive polarization ever had a so-called Close Encounter with the Orion or negatively oriented polarization?

RA: I am Ra. This is correct.

QUESTIONER: Why does this occur?

RA: I am Ra. When it occurs it is quite rare and occurs either due to the Orion entities' lack of perception of the depth of positivity to be encountered or due to the Orion entities' desire to, shall we say, attempt to remove this positivity from this plane of existence. Orion tactics normally are those which choose the simple distortions of mind which indicate less mental and spiritual complex activity.

QUESTIONER: I have become aware of a very large variation in the contact with individuals. Could you give me general examples of the methods used by the Confederation to awaken or partially awaken the Wanderers they contact?

RA: I am Ra. The methods used to awaken Wanderers are varied. The center of each approach is the entrance into the conscious and sub-conscious in such a way as to avoid causing fear and to maximize the potential for an understandable subjective experience which has meaning for the entity. Many such occur in sleep; others in the midst of many activities during the waking hours. The approach is flexible and does not necessarily include the "Close Encounter" syndrome as you are aware.

QUESTIONER: What about the physical examination syndrome. How does that relate to Wanderers and Confederation and Orion contacts?

RA: I am Ra. The subconscious expectations of entities cause the nature and detail of thought-form experience offered by Confederation thought-form entities. Thus if a Wanderer expects a physical examination, it will perforce be experienced with as little distortion towards alarm or discomfort as is allowable by the nature of the expectations of the subconscious distortions of the Wanderer.

QUESTIONER: Well, are those who are taken on both Confederation and Orion craft then experiencing a seeming physical examination?

RA: I am Ra. Your query indicates incorrect thinking. The Orion group uses the physical examination as a means of terrifying the individual and causing it to feel the feelings of an advanced second-density being such as a laboratory animal. The sexual experiences of some are a subtype of this experience. The intent is to demonstrate the control of the Orion entities over the Terran inhabitant.

The thought-form experiences are subjective and, for the most part, do not occur in this density.

QUESTIONER: Well, we have a large spectrum of entities on Earth with respect to harvestability, both positively oriented and negatively oriented. Would the Orion group target in on the ends of this spectrum, both positively and negatively oriented, for contact with Earth entities?

RA: I am Ra. This query is somewhat difficult to accurately answer. However, we shall attempt to do so.

The most typical approach of Orion entities is to choose what you might call the weaker-minded entity that it might suggest a greater amount of Orion philosophy to be disseminated.

Some few Orion entities are called by more highly polarized negative entities of your space/time nexus. In this case they share information just as we are now doing. However, this is a risk for the Orion entities due to the frequency with which the harvestable negative planetary entities then attempt to bid and order the Orion contact just as these entities bid planetary negative contacts. The resulting struggle for mastery, if lost, is damaging to the polarity of the Orion group.

Similarly, a mistaken Orion contact with highly polarized positive entities can wreak havoc with Orion troops unless these Crusaders are able to depolarize the entity mistakenly contacted. This occurrence is almost unheard of. Therefore, the Orion group prefers to make physical contact only with the weaker-minded entity.

QUESTIONER: Then in general we could say that if an individual has a "Close Encounter" with a UFO or any other type of experience that seems to be UFO related, he must look to the heart of the encounter and the effect upon him to determine whether it was Orion or Confederation contact. Is this correct?

RA: I am Ra. This is correct. If there is fear and doom, the contact was quite likely of a negative nature. If the result is hope, friendly feelings, and the awakening of a positive feeling of purposeful service to others, the marks of Confederation contact are evident.

QUESTIONER: Thank you. I did not wish to create the wrong impression with the material that we are including in Book I. I may find it necessary to add some of this material. As I say, I know that it is transient, but I believe it is necessary for a full understanding or, shall I say, a correct approach to the material.

I'll ask a few questions here, but if you do not care to answer them, we'll save them. I would like to ask, however, if you can tell me what, for the most part, the Confederation entities look like?

RA: I am Ra. The fourth-density Confederation entity looks variously depending upon the, shall we say, derivation of its physical vehicle.

QUESTIONER: Do some of them look just like us? Could they pass for Earth people?

RA: I am Ra. Those of this nature are most often fifth density.

QUESTIONER: I assume that the same answer would apply to the Orion group. Is this correct?

RA: I am Ra. This is correct.
Is there any other query of a brief nature we may answer?

QUESTIONER: I apologize for asking many transient questions during this session. I felt it necessary to include some of this material so that those Wanderers and others reading the first book of *The Law of One* would not get the wrong impression with respect to their experiences in contacts. I am sorry for any problems that I might have caused.

I will just ask if there is anything that we can do to aid the contact or to aid the instrument?

RA: I am Ra. The instrument is well. Please guard your alignments carefully. We leave you now, my friends, in the love and in the light of the One Infinite Creator. Go forth, therefore, rejoicing in the power and the peace of the Infinite Creator. Adonai.

Session 54,
May 29, 1981

RA: I am Ra. I greet you in the love and in the light of the One Infinite Creator. We communicate now.

QUESTIONER: I would like to trace the energy that I assume comes from the Logos. I will make a statement and let you correct me and expand on my concept.

From the Logos comes all frequencies of radiation of light. These frequencies of radiation make up all of the densities of experience that are created by that Logos. I am assuming that the planetary system of our sun, in all of its densities, is the total of the experience created by our sun as a Logos. Is this correct?

RA: I am Ra. This is correct.

QUESTIONER: I am assuming that the different frequencies are separated, as we have said, into the seven colors, and I am assuming that each of these colors may be the basic frequency for a sub-Logos of our sun Logos and that a sub-Logos or, shall we say, an individual may activate any one of these basic frequencies or colors and use the body that is generated from the activation of the frequency or color. Is this correct?

RA: I am Ra. If we grasp your query correctly, this is not correct in that the sub-sub-Logos resides not in dimensionalities, but only in co-Creators, or mind/body/spirit complexes.

QUESTIONER: What I meant was that a mind/body/spirit complex can then have any body activated that is one of the seven rays. Is this correct?

RA: I am Ra. This is correct in the same sense as it is correct to state that anyone may play a complex instrument which develops an euphonious harmonic vibration complex such as your piano and can play this so well that it might offer concerts to the public, as you would say. In other words, although it is true that each true color vehicle is available, potentially there is skill and discipline needed in order to avail the self of the more advanced or lighter vehicles.

QUESTIONER: I have made these statements to get to the basic question which I wish to ask. It is a difficult question to ask.

We have, coming from the sub-Logos we call our sun, intelligent energy. This intelligent energy is somehow modulated or distorted so that it ends up as a mind/body/spirit complex with certain distortions of personality which are necessary for the mind/body/spirit complex or mental portion of that complex to undistort in order to conform once more with the original intelligent energy.

First, I want to know if my statement on that is correct, and, secondly, I want to know why this is the way that it is and if there is any answer other than the first distortion of the Law of One for this?

RA: I am Ra. This statement is substantially correct. If you will penetrate the nature of the first distortion in its application of self knowing self, you may begin to distinguish the hallmark of an Infinite Creator, variety. Were there no potentials for misunderstanding and, therefore, understanding, there would be no experience.

QUESTIONER: OK. Once a mind/body/spirit complex becomes aware of this process, it then decides that in order to have the full abilities of the Creator it is necessary to reharmonize its thinking with the Original Creative Thought in precise vibration or frequency of vibration. In order to do this, it is necessary to discipline the personality so that it precisely conforms to the Original Thought, and this is broken into seven areas of discipline, each corresponding to one of the colors of the spectrum. Is this correct?

RA: I am Ra. This statement, though correct, bears great potential for being misunderstood. The precision with which each energy center matches the Original Thought lies not in the systematic placement of each energy nexus, but rather in the fluid and plastic placement of the balanced blending of these energy centers in such a way that intelligent energy is able to channel itself with minimal distortion.

The mind/body/spirit complex is not a machine. It is rather what you might call a tone poem.

QUESTIONER: Do all mind/body/spirit complexes in the entire creation have seven energy centers?

RA: I am Ra. These energy centers are in potential in macrocosm from the beginning of creation by the Logos. Coming out of timelessness, all is prepared. This is so of the infinite creation.

QUESTIONER: Then I will assume that the Creator in its intelligent appraisal of the ways of knowing Itself created the concept of the seven areas of knowing. Is this correct?

RA: I am Ra. This is partially incorrect. The Logos creates light. The nature of this light thus creates the nature of the catalytic and energetic levels of experience in the creation. Thus it is that the highest of all honor/duties, that given to those of the next octave, is the supervision of light in its manifestations during the experiential times, if you will, of your cycles.

QUESTIONER: I will make another statement. The mind/body/spirit complex may choose, because of the first distortion, the mental configuration that is sufficiently displaced from the configuration of the intelligent energy in a particular frequency or color of instreaming energy so as to block a portion of instreaming energy in that particular frequency or color. Is this correct?

RA: I am Ra. Yes.

QUESTIONER: Can you give me an idea of the maximum percentage of this energy it is possible to block in any one color?

RA: I am Ra. There may be, in an entity's pattern of instreaming energy, a complete blockage in any energy or color or combination of energies or colors.

QUESTIONER: OK. Then I assume that the first distortion is the motivator or what allows this blockage. Is this correct?

RA: I am Ra. We wish no quibbling but prefer to avoid the use of terms such as the verb "to allow." Free will does not allow, nor would predetermination disallow, experiential distortions. Rather the Law of Confusion offers a free reach for the energies of each mind/body/spirit complex. The verb "to allow" would be considered pejorative in that it suggests a polarity between right and wrong or allowed and not allowed. This may seem a minuscule point. However, to our best way of thinking it bears some weight.

QUESTIONER: Thank you. It bears weight to my own way of thinking also. I appreciate what you have told me.

Now, I would like to then consider the origin of catalyst. First we have the condition of mind/body/spirit complex, which, as a function of the first distortion, has reached a condition of blockage or partial blockage of one or more energy centers. I will assume that catalyst is necessary only if there is at least partial blockage of one energy center. Is this correct?

RA: I am Ra. No.

QUESTIONER: Could you tell me why?

RA: I am Ra. While it is a primary priority to activate or unblock each energy center, it is also a primary priority at that point to begin to refine the balances between the energies so that each tone of the chord of total vibratory beingness resonates in clarity, tune, and harmony with each other energy. This balancing, tuning, and harmonizing of the self is most central to the more advanced or adept mind/body/ spirit complex. Each energy may be activated without the beauty that is possible through the disciplines and appreciations of personal energies or what you might call the deeper personality or soul identity.

QUESTIONER: Let me make an analogy that I have just thought of. A seven-stringed musical instrument may be played by deflecting each string a full deflection and releasing it, producing notes. Instead of producing the notes this way, the individual creative personality could deflect each string the proper amount in the proper sequence, producing music. Is this correct?

RA: I am Ra. This is correct. In the balanced individual the energies lie waiting for the hand of the Creator to pluck harmony.

QUESTIONER: I would like then to trace the evolution of catalyst upon the mind/body/spirit complexes and how it comes into use and is fully used to create this tuning. I assume that the sub-Logos that formed our tiny part of the creation, using the intelligence of the Logos of which it is a part, provides the base catalyst that will act upon mind/body complexes and mind/body/spirit complexes before they have reached a state of development where they can begin to program their own catalyst. Is this correct?

RA: I am Ra. This is partially correct. The sub-Logos offers the catalyst at the lower levels of energy, the first triad; these have to do with the survival of the physical complex. The higher centers gain catalyst from the biases of the mind/body/spirit complex itself in response to all random and directed experiences.

Thus the less developed entity will perceive the catalyst about it in terms of survival of the physical complex with the distortions which are preferred. The more conscious entity, being conscious of the cat-alytic process, will begin to transform the catalyst offered by the sub-Logos into catalyst which may act upon the higher-energy nexi. Thus the sub-Logos can offer only a basic skeleton, shall we say, of catalyst. The muscles and flesh having to do with the, shall we say, survival of wisdom, love, compassion, and service are brought about by the action of the mind/body/spirit complex on basic catalyst so as to create a more complex catalyst which may in turn be used to form distortions within these higher energy centers.

The more advanced the entity, the more tenuous the connection between the sub-Logos and the perceived catalyst, until, finally, all catalyst is chosen, generated, and manufactured by the self, for the self.

QUESTIONER: Which entities incarnate at this time on this planet would be in that category of manufacturing all of their catalyst?

RA: I am Ra. We find your query indeterminate but can respond that the number of those which have mastered outer catalyst completely is quite small.

Most of those harvestable at this space/time nexus have partial control over the outer illusion and are using the outer catalyst to work upon some bias which is not yet in balance.

QUESTIONER: In the case of service-to-self polarization, what type of catalyst would entities following this path program when they reach the level of programming their own catalyst?

RA: I am Ra. The negatively oriented entity will program for maximal separation from and control over all those things and conscious enti-ties which it perceives as being other than the self.

QUESTIONER: A positively oriented entity may select a certain narrow path of thinking and activities during an incarnation and pro-gram conditions that would create physical pain if this were not followed. Is this correct?

RA: I am Ra. This is correct.

QUESTIONER: Would a negatively oriented entity do anything like this? Could you give me an example?

RA: I am Ra. A negatively oriented individual mind/body/spirit complex will ordinarily program for wealth, ease of existence, and the utmost opportunity for power. Thus many negative entities burst with the physical complex distortion you call health.

However, a negatively oriented entity may choose a painful condition in order to improve the distortion toward the so-called negative emotive mentations such as anger, hatred, and frustration. Such an entity may use an entire incarnative experience honing a blunt edge of hatred or anger so that it may polarize more towards the negative or separated pole.

QUESTIONER: Prior to incarnation, as an entity becomes more aware of the process of evolution and has selected a path whether it be positive or negative, at some point the entity becomes aware of what it wants to do with respect to unblocking and balancing its energy centers. At that point it is able to program for the life experience those catalytic experiences that will aid it in its process of unblocking and balancing. Is that correct?

RA: I am Ra. That is correct.

QUESTIONER: The purpose, then, of what we call the incarnate physical state seems to be wholly or almost wholly that of experiencing the programmed catalyst and then evolving as a function of that catalyst. Is that correct?

RA: I am Ra. We shall restate for clarity the purpose of incarnative existence is evolution of mind, body, and spirit. In order to do this, it is not strictly necessary to have catalyst. However, without catalyst the desire to evolve and the faith in the process do not normally manifest, and thus evolution occurs not. Therefore, catalyst is programmed and the program is designed for the mind/body/spirit complex for its unique requirements. Thus it is desirable that a mind/body/spirit complex be aware of and hearken to the voice of its experiential catalyst, gleaning from it that which it incarnated to glean.

QUESTIONER: Then it seems that those upon the positive path as opposed to those on the negative path would have precisely the reciprocal objective in the first three rays; red, orange, and yellow. Each path would be attempting to utilize the rays in precisely the opposite manners. Is this correct?

RA: I am Ra. It is partially and even substantially correct. There is an energy in each of the centers needed to keep the mind/body/spirit complex, which is the vehicle for experience, in correct conformation and composition. Both negative and positive entities do well to reserve this small portion of each center for the maintenance of the integrity of the mind/body/spirit complex. After this point, however, it is correct that the negative will use the three lower centers for separation from and control over others by sexual means, by personal assertion, and by action in your societies.

Contrary-wise, the positively oriented entity will be transmuting strong red-ray sexual energy into green-ray energy transfers and radiation in blue and indigo and will be similarly transmuting selfhood and place in society into energy transfer situations in which the entity may merge with and serve others and then, finally, radiate unto others without expecting any transfer in return.

QUESTIONER: Can you describe the energy that enters these energy centers? Can you describe its path from its origin, its form, and its effect? I don't know if this is possible.

RA: I am Ra. This is partially possible.

QUESTIONER: Would you please do that?

RA: The origin of all energy is the action of free will upon love. The nature of all energy is light. The means of its ingress into the mind/body/spirit complex is duple.

Firstly, there is the inner light which is Polaris of the self, the guiding star. This is the birthright and true nature of all entities. This energy dwells within.

The second point of ingress is the polar opposite of the North Star, shall we say, and may be seen, if you wish to use the physical body as an analog for the magnetic field, as coming through the feet from the earth and through the lower point of the spine. This point of ingress of the universal light energy is undifferentiated until it begins its filtering process through the energy centers. The requirements of each center and the efficiency with which the individual has learned to tap into the inner light determine the nature of the use made by the entity of these instreamings.

QUESTIONER: Does experiential catalyst follow the same path? This may be a dumb question.

RA: I am Ra. This is not a pointless question, for catalyst and the requirements or distortions of the energy centers are two concepts linked as tightly as two strands of rope.

QUESTIONER: You mentioned in an earlier session that the experiential catalyst was first experienced by the south pole and appraised with respect to its survival value. That's why I asked the question. Would you expand on this concept?

RA: I am Ra. We have addressed the filtering process by which incoming energies are pulled upwards according to the distortions of each energy center and the strength of will or desire emanating from the awareness of inner light. If we may be more specific, please query with specificity.

QUESTIONER: I'll make this statement, which may be somewhat distorted, and then let you correct it. We have, coming through the feet and base of the spine, the total energy that the mind/body/spirit complex will receive in the way of what we call light. Each energy center then filters out and uses a portion of this energy, red through violet. Is this correct?

RA: I am Ra. This is largely correct. The exceptions are as follows: The energy ingress ends with indigo. The violet ray is a thermometer or indicator of the whole.

QUESTIONER: As this energy is absorbed by the energy centers at some point, it is not only absorbed into the being but radiates through the energy center outwardly. I believe this begins at the blue center and also occurs in the indigo and violet? Is this correct?

RA: I am Ra. Firstly, we would state that we had not finished answering the previous query and may thus answer both in part by stating that in the fully activated entity, only that small portion of instreaming light needed to tune the energy center is used, the great remainder being free to be channeled and attracted upwards.

To answer your second question more fully, we may say that it is correct that radiation without the necessity of response begins with blue ray, although the green ray, being the great transitional ray, must be given all careful consideration, for until transfer of energy of all types has been experienced and mastered to a great extent, there will be blockages in the blue and indigo radiations.

Again, the violet emanation is, in this context, a resource from which, through indigo, intelligent infinity may be contacted. The radiation thereof will not be violet ray but rather green, blue, or indigo depending upon the nature of the type of intelligence which infinity has brought through into discernible energy.

The green-ray type of radiation in this case is the healing, the blue ray the communication and inspiration, the indigo that energy of the adept which has its place in faith.

QUESTIONER: What if a mind/body/spirit complex feels a feeling in meditation at the indigo center, what is he feeling?

RA: I am Ra. This will be the last full query of this working.

One who feels this activation is one experiencing instreamings at that energy center to be used either for the unblocking of this center, for its tuning to match the harmonics of its other energy centers, or to activate the gateway to intelligent infinity.

We cannot be specific, for each of these three workings is experienced by the entity which feels this physical complex distortion.

Is there a brief query before we leave this instrument?

QUESTIONER: I just would ask if there is anything that we can do to make the instrument more comfortable or to improve the contact?

RA: I am Ra. Please be aware of the need for the support of the instrument's neck. All is well. I leave you, my friends, in the love and in the light of the One Infinite Creator. Go forth, then, rejoicing in the power and the peace of the One Infinite Creator. Adonai.

Session 55,
June 5, 1981

RA: I am Ra. I greet you in the love and in the light of the One Infinite Creator. I communicate now.

QUESTIONER: I would first like to ask as to the condition of the instrument, please?

RA: I am Ra. This instrument is experiencing physical distortions toward weakness of the bodily complex occurring due to psychic attack. This instrument's vital energies have not been affected, however, due to the aid of those present in healing work. This instrument will apparently be subject to such weakness distortions due to incarnative processes which predispose the body complex towards weakness distortions.

QUESTIONER: Is there any specific thing that we can do that you have already told us or otherwise to alleviate this psychic attack or to help the instrument the most?

RA: I am Ra. We scan this instrument and find its distortion towards appreciation of each entity and each entity's caring, as you may call it. This atmosphere, shall we say, offers the greatest contrast to the discomfort of such psychic attacks, being the reciprocal, that is, the atmosphere of psychic support.

This each of you do as a subconscious function of true attitudinal, mental, emotional, and spiritual distortions towards this instrument. There is no magic greater than honest distortion toward love.

QUESTIONER: Thank you. I want to ask a couple questions about previous material that I didn't understand. I am hoping that this will clear up my understanding somewhat with respect to the mental configurations with which we have been dealing.

In the session before last, you stated, "However, this is a risk for the Orion entities due to the frequency with which the harvestable negative planetary entities attempt to bid and order the Orion contact just as these entities bid planetary negative contacts." Can you explain the mechanisms that affect polarization in consciousness with respect to this statement?

RA: I am Ra. The negative polarization is greatly aided by the subjugation or enslavement of other-selves. The potential between two negatively polarized entities is such that the entity which enslaves the other or bids the other gains in negative polarity.

The entity so bidden or enslaved, in serving an other-self, will necessarily lose negative polarity although it will gain in desire for further negative polarization. This desire will then tend to create opportunities to regain negative polarity.

QUESTIONER: Am I to understand then that just the fact that the third-density entity calls or bids an Orion Crusader is a polarizing type of action that affects both entities?

RA: I am Ra. This is incorrect. The calling mechanism is not congruent in the slightest degree with the bidding mechanism. In the calling, the entity which calls is a suppliant neophyte asking for aid in negative understanding, if you may excuse this misnomer. The Orion response increases its negative polarity as it is disseminating the negative philosophy, thereby enslaving or bidding the entity calling.

There are instances, however, when the contact becomes contest, which is prototypical of negativity. In this contest, the caller will attempt not to ask for aid, but to demand results. Since the third-density negatively oriented harvestable entity has at its disposal an incarnative experiential nexus and since Orion Crusaders are, in a great extent, bound by the first distortion in order to progress, the Orion entity is vulnerable to such bidding if properly done. In this case, the third-density entity becomes master and the Orion Crusader becomes entrapped and can be bid. This is rare. However, when it has occurred, the Orion entity or social memory complex involved has experienced loss of negative polarity in proportion to the strength of the bidding third-density entity.

QUESTIONER: You mentioned that this will work when the bidding is properly done. What did you mean by "when the bidding is properly done"?

RA: I am Ra. To properly bid is to be properly negative. The percentage of thought and behavior involving service to self must approach 99 percent in order for a third-density negative entity to be properly configured for such a contest of bidding.

QUESTIONER: What method of communication with the Orion entity would a bidder of this type use?

RA: I am Ra. The two most usual types of bidding are, one, the use of perversions of sexual magic; two, the use of perversions of ritual magic. In each case the key to success is the purity of the will of the bidder. The concentration upon victory over the servant must be nearly perfect.

QUESTIONER: Can you tell me, in the polarizations in consciousness, if there is any analogy with respect to what you just said in this type of contact with respect to what we are doing right now in communicating with Ra?

RA: I am Ra. There is no relationship between this type of contact and the bidding process. This contact may be characterized as one typical of the Brothers and Sisters of Sorrow, wherein those receiving the contact have attempted to prepare for such contact by sacrificing extraneous, self-oriented distortions in order to be of service.

The Ra social memory complex offers itself also as a function of its desire to serve. Both the caller and the contact are filled with gratitude at the opportunity of serving others.

We may note that this in no way presupposes that either the callers or those of our group in any way approach a perfection or purity such as was described in the bidding process. The calling group may have many distortions and the working with much catalyst, as may those of Ra. The overriding desire to serve others, bonded with the unique harmonics of this group's vibratory complexes, gives us the opportunity to serve as one channel for the One Infinite Creator.

Things come not to those positively oriented but through such beings.

QUESTIONER: Thank you. You have stated in an earlier session that "until transfers of energy of all types have been experienced and mastered to a great extent, there will be blockages in the blue and in the indigo radiations." Could you explain that more fully?

RA: I am Ra. At this space/time we have not covered the appropriate intermediate material. Please requestion at a more appropriate space/time nexus.

QUESTIONER: I'm sort of hunting around here for an entry into some information. I may not be looking in a productive area.

You had stated that "as we (Ra) had been aided by shapes such as the pyramid, so we could aid your people." These shapes have been mentioned many, many times, and you have also stated that the shapes themselves aren't of too much consequence. I see a relation between these shapes and the energies that we have been studying with respect to the body, and I would like to ask a few questions on the pyramids to see if we might get an entry into some of this understanding.

You stated, "You will find the intersection of the triangle which is at the first level on each of the four sides forms a diamond in a plane which is horizontal." Can you tell me what you meant by the word "intersection"?

RA: I am Ra. Your mathematics and arithmetic have a paucity of configurative descriptions which we might use. Without intending to be obscure, we may note that the purpose of the shapes is to work with time/space portions of the mind/body/spirit complex. Therefore, the intersection is both space/time and time/space oriented and thus is expressed in three-dimensional geometry by two intersections which, when projected in both time/space and space/time, form one point.

QUESTIONER: I have calculated this point to be one-sixth of the height of the triangle that forms the side of the pyramid. Is this correct?

RA: I am Ra. Your calculations are substantially correct, and we are pleased at your perspicacity.

QUESTIONER: This would indicate to me that in the Great Pyramid at Giza, the Queen's Chamber, as it is called, would be the chamber used for initiation. Is this correct?

RA: I am Ra. Again, you penetrate the outer teaching.
The Queen's Chamber would not be appropriate or useful for healing work, as that work involves the use of energy in a more synergic configuration rather than the configuration of the centered being.

QUESTIONER: Then would the healing work be done in the King's Chamber?

RA: I am Ra. This is correct. We may note that such terminology is not our own.

QUESTIONER: Yes, I understand that. It is just that it is the common naming of the two chambers of the Great Pyramid. I don't know whether this line of questioning is going to take me to a better understanding of the energies, but until I have explored the concepts, there is nothing much that I can do but to ask a few questions.
There is a chamber below the bottom level of the pyramid, down below ground, that appears to be roughly in line with the King's Chamber. What is that chamber?

RA: I am Ra. We may say that there is information to be gained from this line of querying. The chamber you request to be informed about is a resonating chamber. The bottom of such a structure, in order to cause the appropriate distortions for healing catalyst, shall be open.

QUESTIONER: The book *The Life Force of the Great Pyramid* has related the ankh shape with a resonance in the pyramid. Is this a correct analysis?

RA: I am Ra. We have scanned your mind and find the phrase "working with crayons." This would be applicable. There is only one significance to these shapes such as the crux ansata; that is, the placing in coded form of mathematical relationships.

QUESTIONER: Is the 76° and 18' angle at the apex of the pyramid a critical angle?

RA: I am Ra. For the healing work intended, this angle is appropriate.

QUESTIONER: Why does the King's Chamber have the various small chambers above it?

RA: I am Ra. This will be the last full query of this working.

We must address this query more generally in order to explicate your specific question. The positioning of the entity to be healed is such that the life energies, if you will, are in a position to be briefly interrupted or intersected by light. This light then may, by the catalyst of the healer with the crystal, manipulate the aural forces, as you may call the various energy centers, in such a way that if the entity to be healed wills it so, corrections may take place. Then the entity is reprotected by its own, now less distorted, energy field and is able to go its way.

The process by which this is done involves bringing the entity to be healed to an equilibrium. This involves temperature, barometric pressure, and the electrical-charged atmosphere. The first two requirements are controlled by the system of chimneys.

QUESTIONER: Does this healing work by affecting the energy centers in such a way that they are unblocked so as to perfect the seven bodies that they generate and, therefore, bring the entity to be healed into proper balance?

RA: I am Ra. This entity tires. We must answer in brief and state simply that the distorted configuration of the energy centers is intended to be temporarily interrupted, and the opportunity is then presented to the one to be healed to grasp the baton, to take the balanced route and to walk thence with the distortions towards disease of mind, body, and spirit greatly lessened.

The catalytic effect of the charged atmosphere and the crystal directed by the healer must be taken into consideration as integral portions of this process, for the bringing back of the entity to a configuration of conscious awareness would not be accomplished after the reorganization possibilities are offered without the healer's presence and directed will. Are there any brief queries before we leave this instrument?

QUESTIONER: Only is there anything that we can do to make the instrument more comfortable or to improve this contact?

RA: I am Ra. All is well. You are conscientious. I now leave this working. I am Ra. I leave you, my friends, in the love and in the light of the One Infinite Creator. Go forth, then, rejoicing in the power and in the peace of the One Infinite Creator. Adonai.

Session 56,
June 8, 1981

RA: I am Ra. I greet you in the love and in the light of the One Infinite Creator. We communicate now.

QUESTIONER: Would you first please give me an indication of the instrument's condition?

RA: I am Ra. This instrument is severely distorted towards weakness of the mental and physical complexes at this time and is under psychic attack due to this opportunity.

QUESTIONER: Would it be better to discontinue the contact at this time?

RA: I am Ra. This is entirely at your discretion. This instrument has some energy transferred which is available. However, it is not great due to the effects as previously stated.

We, if you desire to question us further at this working, will as always attempt to safeguard this instrument. We feel that you are aware of the parameters without further elaboration.

QUESTIONER: In that case, I will ask how does the pyramid shape work?

RA: I am Ra. We are assuming that you wish to know the principle of the shapes, angles, and intersections of the pyramid at what you call Giza.

In reality, the pyramid shape does no work. It does not work. It is an arrangement for the centralization as well as the diffraction of the spiraling upward light energy as it is being used by the mind/body/spirit complex.

The spiraling nature of light is such that the magnetic fields of an individual are affected by spiraling energy. Certain shapes offer an echo chamber, shall we say, or an intensifier for spiraling prana, as some have called this all-present, primal distortion of the One Infinite Creator.

If the intent is to intensify the necessity for the entity's own will to call forth the inner light in order to match the intensification of the spiraling light energy, the entity will be placed in what you have called the Queen's Chamber position in this particular shaped object. This is the initiatory place and is the place of resurrection.

The offset place, representing the spiral as it is in motion, is the appropriate position for one to be healed, as in this position an entity's vibratory magnetic nexi are interrupted in their normal flux. Thus a possibility/probability vortex ensues; a new beginning, shall we say, is offered for the entity in which the entity may choose a less distorted, weak, or blocked configuration of energy center magnetic distortions.

The function of the healer and crystal may not be overemphasized, for this power of interruption must needs be controlled, shall we say, with incarnate intelligence; the intelligence being that of one which recognizes energy patterns which, without judging, recognizes blockage, weakness, and other distortion and which is capable of visualizing, through the regularity of self and of crystal, the less distorted other-self to be healed.

Other shapes which are arched, groined, vaulted, conical, or, as your tipis, are also shapes with this type of intensification of spiraling light. Your caves, being rounded, are places of power due to this shaping.

It is to be noted that these shapes are dangerous. We are quite pleased to have the opportunity to enlarge upon the subject of shapes such as the pyramid, for we wish, as part of our honor/duty, to state that there are many wrong uses for these curved shapes; for with improper placement, improper intentions, or lack of the crystallized being functioning as channel for healing, the sensitive entity will be distorted more rather than less in some cases.

It is to be noted that your peoples build, for the most part, the cornered or square habitations, for they do not concentrate power. It is further to be noted that the spiritual seeker has, for many of your time periods of years, sought the rounded, arched, and peaked forms as an expression of the power of the Creator.

QUESTIONER: Is there an apex angle that is the angle for maximum efficiency in the pyramid?

RA: I am Ra. Again, to conserve this instrument's energy, I am assuming that you intend to indicate the most appropriate angle of apex for healing work. If the shape is such that it is large enough to contain an individual mind/body/spirit complex at the appropriate offset position within it, the 76° 18', approximate, angle is useful and appropriate. If the position varies, the angle may vary. Further, if the healer has the ability to perceive distortions with enough discrimination, the position within any pyramid shape may be moved about until results are effected. However, we found this particular angle to be useful. Other social memory complexes, or portions thereof, have determined different apex angles for different uses, not having to do with healing but with learning. When one works with the cone, or shall we say, the silo type of shape, the energy for healing may be found to be in a general circular pattern unique to each shape as a function of its particular height and width and in the cone shape, the angle of apex. In these cases, there are no corner angles. Thus the spiraling energy works in circular motion.

QUESTIONER: I will make a statement which you can correct. I intuitively see the spiraling energy of the Giza pyramid being spread out as it moves through the so-called King's Chamber and refocusing in the so-called Queen's Chamber. I am guessing that the spread of energy in the so-called King's Chamber is seen in the spectrum of colors, red through violet, and that the energy centers of the entity to be healed should be aligned with this spread of the spectrum so that the spectrum matches his various energy centers. Will you correct this statement?

RA: I am Ra. We can correct this statement.

QUESTIONER: Will you please do that?

RA: The spiraling energy is beginning to be diffused at the point where it goes through the King's Chamber position. However, although the spirals continue to intersect, closing and opening in double-spiral fashion through the apex angle, the diffusion or strength of the spiraling energies, red through violet color values, lessens, if we speak of strength, and gains, if we speak of diffusion, until at the peak of the pyramid you have a very weak color resolution useful for healing purposes. Thus the King's Chamber position is chosen as the first spiral after the centered beginning through the Queen's Chamber position. You may visualize the diffusion angle as the opposite of the pyramid angle, but the angle being less wide than the apex angle of the pyramid, being somewhere between 33° and 54°, depending upon the various rhythms of the planet itself.

QUESTIONER: Then I assume that if I start my angle at the bottom of the Queen's Chamber and make a 33° to 54° angle from that point, so that half of that angle falls on the side of the centerline that the King's Chamber is on, that will indicate the diffusion of the spectrum, starting from the point at the bottom of the Queen's Chamber; let's say, if we were using a 40° angle, we would have a 20° diffusion to the left of the centerline, passing through the King's Chamber. Is that correct?

RA: I am Ra. This will be the last full question of this session. It is correct that half of the aforementioned angle passes through the King's Chamber position. It is incorrect to assume that the Queen's Chamber is the foundation of the angle. The angle will begin somewhere between the Queen's Chamber position and thence downward towards the level of the resonating chamber, offset for the healing work.

This variation is dependent upon various magnetic fluxes of the planet. The King's Chamber position is designed to intersect the strongest spiral of the energy flow regardless of where the angle begins. However, as it passes through the Queen's Chamber position, this spiraling energy is always centered and at its strongest point.

May we answer any brief queries at this time?

QUESTIONER: I will just ask if there is anything that we can do to make the instrument more comfortable or to improve the contact?

RA: I am Ra. All is well, my friends. It is well, however, to be conscious of the limitations of this instrument. We feel the alignments are excellent at this time. I am Ra. I leave you in the love and in the light of the One Infinite Creator. Go forth, therefore, rejoicing in the power and in the peace of the One Infinite Creator. Adonai.

Session 57,
June 12, 1981

RA: I am Ra. I greet you in the love and in the light of the One Infinite Creator. We communicate now.

QUESTIONER: First, could you give me an indication of the instrument's condition, please?

RA: I am Ra. This instrument is under a most severe psychic attack. This instrument is bearing up well due to replenished vital energies and a distortion towards a sense of proportion which your peoples call a sense of humor.

This attack is potentially disruptive to this contact for a brief period of your space/time.

QUESTIONER: Is there anything in particular that we can do in addition to what we are doing to alleviate this attack?

RA: I am Ra. There is nothing you can do to alleviate the attack. The understanding of its mechanism might be of aid.

QUESTIONER: Could you tell us its mechanism?

RA: I am Ra. The Orion group cannot interfere directly but only through preexisting distortions of mind/body/spirit complexes.

Thus in this case, this entity reached for an heavy object with one hand, and this miscalculated action caused a deformation or distortion of the skeletal/muscular structure of one of this instrument's appendages.

Your aid may be helpful in supporting this instrument in the proper care of this distortion, which is equivalent to what you call your postoperative state when bones are not firmly knit. This instrument needs to be aware of care necessary to avoid such miscalculated actions, and your support in this state of awareness is noted and encouraged.

QUESTIONER: Is there anything that we can specifically do to alleviate this problem that is already existing?

RA: I am Ra. This information is harmless; thus we share it though it is transient, lacking the principle but only offering a specific transient effect.

The wrist area should be wrapped as in the sprained configuration, as you call this distortion, and what you call a sling may be used on this distorted right side of the body complex for one diurnal period. At that time, symptoms, as you call these distortions, shall be reviewed and such repeated until the distortion is alleviated.

The healing work to which each is apprentice may be used as desired.

It is to be noted that a crystal is available.

QUESTIONER: Which crystal is that?

RA: I am Ra. The flawed but sufficient crystal which rests upon the digit of this instrument's right hand.

QUESTIONER: Would you tell me how to use that crystal for this purpose?

RA: I am Ra. This is a large question.

You first, as a mind/body/spirit complex, balance and polarize the self, connecting the inner light with the upward spiraling inpourings of the universal light. You have done exercises to regularize the processes involved. Look to them for the preparation of the crystallized being.

Take then the crystal and feel your polarized and potentiated balanced energy channeled in green-ray healing through your being, going into and activating the crystalline regularity of frozen light which is the crystal. The crystal will resound with the charged light of incarnative love, and light energy will begin to radiate in specified fashion, beaming, in required light vibrations, healing energy, focused and intensified towards the magnetic field of the mind/body/spirit complex which is to be healed. This entity requesting such healing will then open the armor of the overall violet/red-ray protective vibratory shield. Thus the inner vibratory fields, from center to center in mind, body, and spirit, may be interrupted and adjusted momentarily, thus offering the one to be healed the opportunity to choose a less distorted inner complex of energy fields and vibratory relationships.

QUESTIONER: Should the crystal be held in the right hand of the healer?

RA: I am Ra. This is incorrect. There are two recommended configurations.

The first, the chain about the neck to place the crystal in the physical position of the green-ray energy center. Second, the chain hung from the right hand, outstretched, wound about the hand in such a way that the crystal may be swung so as to affect sensitive adjustments.

We offer this information realizing that much practice is needed to efficiently use these energies of self. However, each has the capability of doing so, and this information is not information which, if followed accurately, can be deleterious.

QUESTIONER: Would an unflawed crystal be considerably more effective than the flawed one that we have now?

RA: I am Ra. Without attempting to deem the priorities you may choose, we may note that the regularized or crystallized entity, in its configuration, is as critical as the perfection of the crystal used.

QUESTIONER: Does the physical size of the crystal have any relationship to the effectiveness in the healing?

RA: I am Ra. In some applications concerning planetary healing, this is a consideration. In working with an individual mind/body/spirit complex, the only requirement is that the crystal be in harmony with the crystallized being. There is perhaps a lower limit to the size of what you may call a faceted crystal, for light coming through this crystal needs to be spread the complete width of the spectrum of the one to be healed.

It may further be noted that water is a type of crystal which is efficacious also, although not as easy to hang from a chain in your density.

QUESTIONER: Placing the end of this pencil on my navel, would the point of it then represent the place where the crystal should hang for proper green ray? Is this position correct?

RA: I am Ra. We attempt your measurements. From 2 to 5.4 centimeters towards your heart is optimal.

QUESTIONER: Using this piece of wood, then, I would determine, from my navel, the position to be at the top of the piece of wood. Is this correct?

RA: I am Ra. This is correct.

QUESTIONER: How does the healing that you just told us about relate to the healing done in the King's Chamber in the Giza pyramid?

RA: I am Ra. There are two advantages to doing this working in such a configuration of shapes and dimensions.

Firstly, the disruption or interruption of the violet/red armoring or protective shell is automatic.

In the second place, the light is configured by the very placement of this position in the seven distinctive color or energy vibratory rates, thus allowing the energy through the crystallized being, focused with the crystal, to manipulate with great ease the undisturbed and, shall we say, carefully delineated palate of energies or colors, both in space/time and in time/space. Thus the unarmored being may be adjusted rapidly. This is desirable in some cases, especially when the armoring is the largest moiety of the possibility of continued function of body complex activity in this density. The trauma of the interruption of this armoring vibration is then seen to be lessened.

We take this opportunity to pursue our honor/duty, as some of those creating the pyramid shape, to note that it is in no way necessary to use this shape in order to achieve healings, for seniority of vibration has caused the vibratory complexes of mind/body/spirit complexes to be healed to be less vulnerable to the trauma of the interrupted armoring.

Furthermore, as we have said, the powerful effect of the pyramid, with its mandatory disruption of the armoring, if used without the crystallized being, used with the wrong intention, or in the wrong configuration, can result in further distortions of entities which are perhaps the equal of some of your chemicals which cause disruptions in the energy fields in like manner.

QUESTIONER: Is there currently any use for the pyramid shape at all that is beneficial?

RA: I am Ra. This is in the affirmative if carefully used.

The pyramid may be used for the improvement of the meditative state as long as the shape is such that the entity is in Queen's Chamber position or entities are in balanced configuration about this central point.

The small pyramid shape, placed beneath a portion of the body complex, may energize this body complex. This should be done for brief periods only, not to exceed thirty of your minutes.

The use of the pyramid to balance planetary energies still functions to a slight extent, but due to earth changes, the pyramids are no longer aligned properly for this work.

QUESTIONER: What is the aid or the mechanism of the aid received for meditation by an entity who would be positioned in the so-called Queen's Chamber position?

RA: I am Ra. Consider the polarity of mind/body/spirit complexes. The inner light is that which is your heart of being. Its strength equals your strength of will to seek the light. The position or balanced position of a group intensifies the amount of this will, the amount of awareness of the inner light necessary to attract the instreaming light upward spiraling from the south magnetic pole of being.

Thus this is the place of the initiate, for many extraneous items or distortions will leave the entity as it intensifies its seeking, so that it may become one with this centralized and purified incoming light.

QUESTIONER: Then if a pyramid shape is used, it would seem to me that it would be necessary to make it large enough so that the Queen's Chamber position would be far enough from the King's Chamber position so that you could use that energy position and not be harmed by the energy position of the King's Chamber position. Is this correct?

RA: I am Ra. In this application a pyramid shape may be smaller if the apex angle is less, thus not allowing the formation of the King's Chamber position. Also efficacious for this application are the following shapes: the silo, the cone, the dome, and the tipi.

QUESTIONER: Do these shapes that you just mentioned have any of the effect of the King's Chamber at all, or do they have only the Queen's Chamber effect?

RA: I am Ra. These shapes have the Queen's Chamber effect. It is to be noted that a strongly crystallized entity is, in effect, a portable King's Chamber position.

QUESTIONER: Then are you saying that there is absolutely no need, use, or good in having the King's Chamber effect at this time in our planetary evolution?

RA: I am Ra. If those who desired to be healers were of a crystallized nature and were all supplicants, those wishing less distortion, the pyramid would be, as always, a carefully designed set of parameters to distribute light and its energy so as to aid in healing catalyst.

However, we found that your peoples are not distorted towards the desire for purity to a great enough extent to be given this powerful and potentially dangerous gift. We, therefore, would suggest it not be used for healing in the traditional, shall we say, King's Chamber configuration which we naively gave to your peoples only to see its use grossly distorted and our teachings lost.

QUESTIONER: What would be an appropriate apex angle for a tipi shape for our uses?

RA: I am Ra. This is at your discretion. The principle of circular, rounded, or peaked shapes is that the center acts as an invisible inductive coil. Thus the energy patterns are spiraling and circular. Thus the choice of the most pleasant configuration is yours. The effect is relatively fixed.

QUESTIONER: Is there any variation in the effect with respect to the material of construction, the thickness of the material? Is it simply the geometry of the shape, or is it related to some other factors?

RA: I am Ra. The geometry, as you call it, or relationships of these shapes in their configuration is the great consideration. It is well to avoid stannous material or that of lead or other baser metals. Wood, plastic, glass, and other materials may all be considered to be appropriate.

QUESTIONER: If a pyramid shape were placed below an entity, how would this be done? Would it be placed beneath the bed? I'm not quite sure about how to energize the entity by "placing it below." Could you tell me how to do that?

RA: I am Ra. Your assumption is correct. If the shape is of appropriate size, it may be placed directly beneath the cushion of the head or the pallet upon which the body complex rests.

We again caution that the third spiral of upward-lining light, that which is emitted from the apex of this shape, is most deleterious to an entity in overdose and should not be used overlong.

QUESTIONER: What would the height be, in centimeters, of one of these pyramids for best functioning?

RA: I am Ra. It matters not. Only the proportion of the height of the pyramid from base to apex to the perimeter of the base is at all important.

QUESTIONER: What should that proportion be?

RA: I am Ra. This proportion should be the 1.16 which you may observe.

QUESTIONER: Do you mean that the sum of the four base sides should be 1.16 of the height of the pyramid?

RA: I am Ra. This is correct.

QUESTIONER: By saying that the Queen's Chamber was the initiatory place, could you tell me what you mean by that?

RA: I am Ra. This question is a large one. We cannot describe initiation in its specific sense due to our distortion towards the belief/understanding that the process which we offered so many of your years ago was not a balanced one.

However, you are aware of the concept of initiation and realize that it demands the centering of the being upon the seeking of the Creator. We have hoped to balance this understanding by enunciating the Law of One; that is, that all things are One Creator. Thus seeking the Creator is done not just in meditation and in the work of an adept but in the experiential nexus of each moment.

The initiation of the Queen's Chamber has to do with the abandoning of self to such desire to know the Creator in full that the purified instreaming light is drawn in balanced fashion through all energy centers, meeting in indigo and opening the gate to intelligent infinity. Thus the entity experiences true life or, as your people call it, resurrection.

QUESTIONER: You also mentioned that the pyramid was used for learning. Was this the same process or is there a difference?

RA: I am Ra. There is a difference.

QUESTIONER: What is the difference?

RA: I am Ra. The difference is the presence of other-selves manifesting in space/time and after some study, in time/space, for the purpose of teach/learning. In the system created by us, schools were apart from the pyramid, the experiences being solitary.

QUESTIONER: I didn't quite understand what you meant by that. Could you tell me more of what you are talking about?

RA: I am Ra. This is a wide subject. Please restate for specificity.

QUESTIONER: Did you mean that teachers from your vibration or density were manifest in the Queen's Chamber to teach those initiates, or did you mean something else?

RA: I am Ra. In our system, experiences in the Queen's Chamber position were solitary. In Atlantis and in South America, teachers shared the pyramid experiences.

QUESTIONER: How did this learning process take place—learning or teaching—in the pyramid?

RA: I am Ra. How does teach/learning and learn/teaching ever take place?

QUESTIONER: The dangerous pyramid shape for use today would be a four-sided pyramid that was large enough to create the King's Chamber effect. Is that statement correct?

RA: I am Ra. This statement is correct with the additional understanding that the 76° apex angle is that characteristic of the powerful shape.

QUESTIONER: Then I am assuming that we should not use a pyramid of 76° at the apex angle under any circumstances. Is that correct?

RA: I am Ra. This is at your discretion.

QUESTIONER: I will restate the question. I am assuming then that it might be dangerous to use a 76° angle pyramid, and I will ask what angle less than 76° would be roughly the first angle that would not produce this dangerous effect?

RA: I am Ra. Your assumption is correct. The lesser angle may be any angle less than 70°.

QUESTIONER: Thank you. I want to go on with more questioning on the pyramid, but I want to ask a question that [name] has here. I'll throw it in at this point. Could you please expand on the concept of space/time and time/space and how to get past this concept, and what density level do these concepts no longer affect the individual?

RA: I am Ra. This will be the last full query of this working. This instrument has some vital energy left. However, we become concerned with the increasing distortions of the body complex towards pain.

The space/time and time/space concepts are those concepts describing as mathematically as possible the relationships of your illusion, that which is seen to that which is unseen. These descriptive terms are clumsy. They, however, suffice for this work.

In the experiences of the mystical search for unity, these need never be considered, for they are but part of an illusory system. The seeker seeks the One. The One is to be sought, as we have said, by the balanced and self-accepting self-aware, both of its apparent distortions and its total perfection. Resting in this balanced awareness, the entity then opens the self to the universe which it is. The light energy of all things may then be attracted by this intense seeking, and wherever the inner seeking meets the attracted cosmic prana, realization of the One takes place.

The purpose of clearing each energy center is to allow that meeting place to occur at the indigo-ray vibration, thus making contact with intelligent infinity and dissolving all illusions. Service to others is automatic at the released energy generated by this state of consciousness.

The space/time and time/space distinctions, as you understand them, do not hold sway except in third density. However, fourth, fifth, and, to some extent, sixth work within some system of polarized space/time and time/space.

The calculation necessary to move from one system to another through the dimensions are somewhat difficult. Therefore, we have the most difficulty sharing numerical concepts with you and take this opportunity to repeat our request that you monitor our numbers and query any that seem questionable.

Is there a brief query that we may answer before we leave this instrument?

QUESTIONER: Is there anything that we can do to make the instrument more comfortable or to improve the contact?

RA: I am Ra. All is harmonious. We greet you all in joy. The adjustments are satisfactory.

I am Ra. I leave you in the love and in the light of the One Infinite Creator. Go forth, therefore, rejoicing in the power and in the peace of the One Infinite Creator. Adonai.

Session 58,
June 16, 1981

RA: I am Ra. I greet you in the love and in the light of the One Infinite Creator. We communicate now.

QUESTIONER: Would you please give me an indication of the instrument's condition?

RA: I am Ra. This condition is as previously noted, except that the physical distortions mentioned have somewhat increased.

QUESTIONER: Could you tell me the cause of the increase of the physical distortions.

RA: I am Ra. Physical distortions of this nature are begun, as we have said, due to overactivity of weak, as you call this distortion, portions of the body complex. The worsening is due to the nature of the distortion itself, which you call arthritis. Once begun, the distortion will unpredictably remain and unpredictably worsen or lessen.

QUESTIONER: We have tried healing with the diamond crystal. I have tried both using the crystal around my neck and dangling it from a chain held in my right hand. I think that possibly that to do the best work on the wrist I should dangle the crystal just below my right hand from a distance of just a centimeter or two, holding it directly above the wrist. Is this correct?

RA: I am Ra. This would be appropriate if you were practiced at your healing art. To work with a powerful crystal such as you have, while unable to perceive the magnetic flux of the subtle bodies, is perhaps the same as recommending that the beginner, with saw and nail, create the Vatican.

There is great art in the use of the swung crystal. At this point in your development, you would do well to work with the unpowerful crystals in ascertaining not only the physical major energy centers, but also the physical secondary and tertiary energy centers and then begin to find the corresponding subtle body energy centers. In this way, you may activate your own inner vision.

QUESTIONER: What type of crystal should be used for that?

RA: I am Ra. You may use any dangling weight of symmetrical form, for your purpose is not to disturb or manipulate these energy centers but merely to locate them and become aware of what they feel like when in a balanced state and when in an unbalanced or blocked state.

QUESTIONER: Am I correct in assuming that what I am to do is to dangle a weight approximately 2 feet below my hand and place it over the body, and when the weight starts moving in a clockwise rotational direction, it would indicate an unblocked energy center. Is this correct?

RA: I am Ra. The measurement from hand to weight is unimportant and at your discretion. The circular motion shows an unblocked energy center. However, some entities are polarized the reverse of others, and, therefore, it is well to test the form of normal energy spirals before beginning the procedure.

QUESTIONER: How would you test?

RA: I am Ra. Test is done by first holding the weight over your own hand and observing your particular configuration. Then, using the other-self's hand, repeat the procedure.

QUESTIONER: In the case of the instrument, we are concerned with the healing of the wrists and hands. Would I then test the energy center of the instrument's wrist area? Is this correct?

RA: I am Ra. We have given you general information regarding this form of healing and have explicated the instrument's condition. There is a line beyond which information is an intrusion upon the Law of Confusion.

QUESTIONER: I would like to trace the energy patterns and what is actually happening in these patterns and flow of energy in a couple of instances. I would first take the pyramid shape and trace the energy that is focused somehow by this shape. I will make a statement and let you correct it.

I think that the pyramid can be in any orientation and provide some focusing of spiraling energy, but the greatest focusing of it occurs when one side of it is precisely parallel to magnetic north. Is this correct?

RA: I am Ra. This is substantially correct with one addition. If one corner is oriented to the magnetic north, the energy will be enhanced in its focus also.

QUESTIONER: Do you mean that if I drew a line through two opposite corners of the pyramid at the base and aimed that at magnetic north—that would be precisely 45° out of the orientation of one side aimed at magnetic north—that it would work just as well? Is that what you are saying?

RA: I am Ra. It would work much better than if the pyramid shape were quite unaligned. It would not work quite as efficiently as the aforementioned configuration.

QUESTIONER: Would the pyramid shape work just as well right side up as upside down with respect to the surface of the Earth, assuming the magnetic alignment was the same in both cases?

RA: I am Ra. We do not penetrate your query. The reversed shape of the pyramid reverses the effects of the pyramid. Further, it is difficult to build such a structure, point down. Perhaps we have misinterpreted your query.

QUESTIONER: I used this question only to understand the way the pyramid focuses light, not for the purpose of using one. I was just saying if we did build a pyramid point down, would it focus at the Queen's Chamber position or just below it the same way as if it were point up?

RA: I am Ra. It would only work thusly if an entity's polarity were, for some reason, reversed.

QUESTIONER: Then the lines of spiraling light energy—do they originate from a position towards the center of the Earth and radiate outward from that point?

RA: I am Ra. The pyramid shape is a collector which draws the instreaming energy from what you would term the bottom or base, and allows this energy to spiral upward in a line with the apex of this shape. This is also true if a pyramid shape is upended. The energy is not Earth energy, as we understand your question, but is light energy, which is omnipresent.

QUESTIONER: Does it matter if the pyramid is solid or is made of four thin sides, or is there a difference in effect between those two makes?

RA: I am Ra. As an energy collector, the shape itself is the only requirement. From the standpoint of the practical needs of your body complexes, if one is to house one's self in such a shape, it is well that this shape be solid sided in order to avoid being inundated by outer stimuli.

QUESTIONER: Then if I just used a wire frame that was four pieces of wire joined at the apex running down to the base, and the pyramid were totally open, this would do the same thing to the spiraling light energy? Is this correct?

RA: I am Ra. The concept of the frame as equal to the solid form is correct. However, there are many metals not recommended for use in pyramid shapes designed to aid the meditative process. Those that are recommended are, in your system of barter, what you call expensive. The wood, or other natural materials, or the man-made plastic rods will also be of service.

QUESTIONER: Why is the spiraling light focused by something as open and simple as four wooden rods joined at an apex angle?

RA: I am Ra. If you pictured light in the metaphysical sense, as water, and the pyramid shape as a funnel, this concept might become self-evident.

QUESTIONER: Thank you. I do not wish to get into subject matter of no importance. I had assumed that questions about the pyramid were desired by you due to the fact that some danger was involved to some who had misused the pyramid, etc.

I am trying to understand the way light works and am trying to get a grasp of how everything works together, and I was hoping that questions on the pyramid would help me understand the third distortion, which is light. As I understand it, the pyramid shape acts as a funnel increasing the density of energy so that the individual may have a greater intensity of actually the third distortion. Is this correct?

RA: I am Ra. In general, this is correct.

QUESTIONER: Then the pure crystalline shape, such as the diamond, you mentioned as being frozen light—it seems that this third-density physical manifestation of light is somehow a window or focusing mechanism for the third distortion in a general sense. Is this correct?

RA: I am Ra. This is basically correct. However, it may be noted that only the will of the crystallized entity may cause interdimensional light to flow through this material. The more regularized the entity, and the more regularized the crystal, the more profound the effect.

QUESTIONER: There are many people who are now bending metal, doing other things like that by mentally requesting this happen. What is happening in that case?

RA: I am Ra. That which occurs in this instance may be likened to the influence of the second spiral of light in a pyramid being used by an entity. As this second spiral ends at the apex, the light may be likened unto a laser beam in the metaphysical sense and when intelligently directed may cause bending not only in the pyramid, but this is the type of energy which is tapped into by those capable of this focusing of the upward-spiraling light. This is made possible through contact in indigo ray with intelligent energy.

QUESTIONER: Why are these people able to do this? They seem to have no training; they are just able to do it.

RA: I am Ra. They remember the disciplines necessary for this activity, which is merely useful upon other true color vibratory experiential nexi.

QUESTIONER: Then you are saying that this wouldn't be useful in our present density. Will it be useful in fourth density on this planet in the very near future?

RA: I am Ra. The end of such energy focusing is to build, not to destroy, and it does become quite useful as, shall we say, an alternative to third-density building methods.

QUESTIONER: Is it also used for healing?

RA: I am Ra. No.

QUESTIONER: Is there any advantage in attempting to develop these characteristics or in being able to bend metal, etc.? What I am trying to say is, are these characteristics a signpost of the development of an entity, or is it merely something else? For instance, as an entity develops through his indigo, would a signpost of his development be this bending ability?

RA: I am Ra. This will be the last full query of this working.

Let us specify the three spirals of light energy which the pyramid exemplifies. Firstly, the fundamental spiral, which is used for study and for healing. Second, the spiral to the apex, which is used for building. Thirdly, the spiral spreading from the apex, which is used for energizing.

Contact with indigo ray need not necessarily show itself in any certain gift or guidepost, as you have said. There are some whose indigo energy is that of pure being and never is manifested, yet all are aware of such an entity's progress. Others may teach or share in many ways contact with intelligent energy. Others continue in unmanifested form, seeking intelligent infinity.

Thus the manifestation is lesser signpost than that which is sensed or intuited about a mind/body/spirit complex. This violet-ray beingness is far more indicative of true self.

Are there any brief queries or small matters we may clear up, if we can, before we leave this instrument?

QUESTIONER: I did have a question on what you meant by the "third spiral," and if that is too long I would just ask if there is anything that we can do to make the instrument more comfortable or to improve the contact?

RA: I am Ra. We may answer briefly. You may query in more detail if you deem it desirable at another session.

If you picture the candle flame, you may see the third spiral. This instrument is well balanced. The accoutrements are aligned well. You are conscientious.

I am Ra. I leave you, my friends, in the love and in the light of the One Infinite Creator. Go forth, therefore, rejoicing in the power and the peace of the One Infinite Creator. Adonai.

Session 59,
June 25, 1981

RA: I am Ra. I greet you in the love and in the light of the One Infinite Creator. We communicate now.

QUESTIONER: Could you first tell me the instrument's condition and why she feels so tired?

RA: I am Ra. This instrument's condition is as previously stated. We cannot infringe upon your free will by discussing the latter query.

QUESTIONER: Would it be any greater protection for the instrument if [name] changed his sitting position to the other side of the bed?

RA: I am Ra. No.

QUESTIONER: At the end of the second major cycle, there were a few hundred thousand people on Earth. There are over four billion people on Earth today. Were the over four billion people that are incarnate today in the Earth planes and not incarnate at that time, or did they come in from elsewhere during the last 25,000 years?

RA: I am Ra. There were three basic divisions of origin of these entities.

Firstly, and primarily, those of the planetary sphere you call Maldek, having become able to take up third density once again, were gradually loosed from self-imposed limitations of form.

Secondly, there were those of other third-density entrance or neophytes whose vibratory patterns matched the Terran experiential nexus. These then filtered in through incarnative processes.

Thirdly, in the past approximate 200 of your years you have experienced much visiting of the Wanderers. It may be noted that all possible opportunities for incarnation are being taken at this time due to your harvesting process and the opportunities which this offers.

QUESTIONER: Just to clarify that, could you tell me approximately how many mind/body/spirit complexes were transferred to Earth at the beginning of this last 75,000-year period?

RA: I am Ra. The transfer, as you call it, has been gradual. Over two billion souls are those of Maldek which have successfully made the transition.

Approximately 1.9 billion souls have, from many portions of the creation, entered into this experience at various times. The remainder are those who have experienced the first two cycles upon this sphere or who have come in at some point as Wanderers; some Wanderers having been in this sphere for many thousands of your years; others having come far more recently.

QUESTIONER: I'm trying to understand the three spirals of light in the pyramid shape. I would like to question on each.

The first spiral starts below the Queen's Chamber and ends in the Queen's Chamber? Is that correct?

RA: I am Ra. This is incorrect. The first notion of upward-spiraling light is as that of the scoop, the light energy being scooped in through the attraction of the pyramid shape through the bottom or base. Thus the first configuration is a semi-spiral.

QUESTIONER: Would this be similar to the vortex you get when you release water from a bathtub?

RA: I am Ra. This is correct except that in the case of this action, the cause is gravitic, whereas in the case of the pyramid, the vortex is that of upward-spiraling light being attracted by the electromagnetic fields engendered by the shape of the pyramid.

QUESTIONER: Then the first spiral after this semispiral is the spiral used for study and healing. Relative to the Queen's Chamber position, where does this first spiral begin and end?

RA: I am Ra. The spiral which is used for study and healing begins at or slightly below the Queen's Chamber position, depending upon your Earth and cosmic rhythms. It moves through the King's Chamber position in a sharply delineated form and ends at the point whereby the top approximate third of the pyramid may be seen to be intensifying the energy.

QUESTIONER: The first spiral is obviously different somehow from the second and third spirals, since they have different uses and different properties. The second spiral then starts at the end of the first spiral and goes up to the apex. Is that correct?

RA: I am Ra. This is partially correct. The large spiral is drawn into the vortex of the apex of the pyramid. However, some light energy which is of the more intense nature of the red, shall we say, end of the spectrum is spiraled once again, causing an enormous strengthening and focusing of energy which is then of use for building.

QUESTIONER: And then the third spiral radiates from the top of the pyramid. Is this correct?

RA: I am Ra. The third complete spiral does so. This is correct. It is well to reckon with the foundation semi-spiral which supplies the prana for all that may be affected by the three following upward spirals of light.

QUESTIONER: Now I am trying to understand what happens in this process. I'll call the first semi-spiral zero position, and the other three spirals 1, 2, and 3, the first spiral being a study in healing. What change takes place in light from zero position to the first spiral that makes that first spiral available for healing?

RA: I am Ra. The prana scooped in by the pyramid shape gains coherence of energetic direction. The term "upward-spiraling light" is an indication not of your up-and-down concept, but an indication of the concept of that which reaches towards the source of love and light.

Thus, all light or prana is upward spiraling, but its direction, as you understand this term, is unregimented and not useful for work.

QUESTIONER: Could I assume then that from all points in space, light radiates in our illusion outward in a 360° solid angle, and this scoop shape with the pyramid then creates the coherence to this radiation as a focusing mechanism? Is this correct?

RA: I am Ra. This is precisely correct.

QUESTIONER: Then the first spiral has a different factor of cohesion, you might say, than the second. What is the difference between this first and second spiral?

RA: I am Ra. As the light is funneled into what you term the zero position, it reaches the point of turning. This acts as a compression of the light, multiplying tremendously its coherence and organization.

QUESTIONER: Then is the coherence and organization multiplied once more at the start of the second spiral? Is there just a doubling effect or an increasing effect?

RA: I am Ra. This is difficult to discuss in your language. There is no doubling effect but a transformation across boundaries of dimension, so that light which was working for those using it in space/time-time/space configuration becomes light working in what you might consider an interdimensional time/space-space/time configuration. This causes an apparent diffusion and weakness of the spiraling energy. However, in position 2, as you have called it, much work may be done interdimensionally.

QUESTIONER: In the Giza pyramid there was no chamber at position 2. Do you ever make use of position 2 by putting a chamber in that position on other planets or in other pyramids?

RA: I am Ra. This position is useful only to those whose abilities are such that they are capable of serving as conductors of this type of focused spiral. One would not wish to attempt to train third-density entities in such disciplines.

QUESTIONER: Then the third spiral radiating from the top of the pyramid you say is used for energizing. Can you tell me what you mean by "energizing"?

RA: I am Ra. The third spiral is extremely full of the positive effects of directed prana, and that which is placed over such a shape will receive shocks energizing the electromagnetic fields. This can be most stimulating in third-density applications of mental and bodily configurations. However, if allowed to be in place overlong, such shocks may traumatize the entity.

QUESTIONER: Are there any other effects of the pyramid shape beside the spirals that we have just discussed?

RA: I am Ra. There are several. However, their uses are limited. The use of the resonating chamber position is one which challenges the ability of an adept to face the self. This is one type of mental test which may be used. It is powerful and quite dangerous.

The outer shell of the pyramid shape contains small vortices of light energy which, in the hands of capable crystallized beings, are useful for various subtle workings upon the healing of invisible bodies affecting the physical body.

Other of these places are those wherein perfect sleep may be obtained and age reversed. These characteristics are not important.

QUESTIONER: What position would be the age reversal position?

RA: I am Ra. Approximately 5° to 10° above and below the Queen's Chamber position in ovoid shapes on each face of the four-sided pyramid, extending into the solid shape approximately one-quarter of the way to the Queen's Chamber position.

QUESTIONER: In other words, if I went just inside the wall of the pyramid a quarter of the way but still remained three-quarters of the way from the center at approximately the level above the base of the Queen's Chamber, I would find that position?

RA: I am Ra. This is approximately so. You must picture the double teardrop extending in both the plane of the pyramid face and in half towards the Queen's Chamber, extending above and below it. You may see this as the position where the light has been scooped into the spiral and then is expanding again. This position is what you may call a prana vacuum.

QUESTIONER: Why would this reverse aging?

RA: I am Ra. Aging is a function of the effects of various electromagnetic fields upon the electromagnetic fields of the mind/body/spirit complex. In this position there is no input or disturbance of the fields, nor is any activity within the electromagnetic field complex of the mind/body/spirit complex allowed full sway. The vacuum sucks any such disturbance away. Thus the entity feels nothing and is suspended.

QUESTIONER: Is the pyramid shape constructed in our yard functioning properly? Is it aligned properly and built properly?

RA: I am Ra. It is built within good tolerances, though not perfect. However, its alignment should be as this resting place for maximum efficacy.

QUESTIONER: Do you mean that one of the base sides should be aligned 20° east of north?

RA: I am Ra. That alignment would be efficacious.

QUESTIONER: Previously you stated that one of the base sides should be aligned with magnetic north. Which is better, to align with magnetic north or to align with 20° east of magnetic north?

RA: I am Ra. This is at your discretion. The proper alignment for you of this sphere at this time is magnetic north. However, in your query you asked specifically about a structure which has been used by specific entities whose energy vortices are more consonant with the, shall we say, true color green orientation. This would be the 20° east of north.

There are advantages to each orientation. The effect is stronger at magnetic north and can be felt more clearly. The energy, though weak, coming from the now-distant but soon to be paramount direction is more helpful.

The choice is yours. It is the choice between quantity and quality or wide-band and narrow-band aid in meditation.

QUESTIONER: When the planetary axis realigns, will it realign 20° east of north to conform to the green vibration?

RA: I am Ra. We fear this shall be the last question, as this entity rapidly increases its distortion towards what you call pain of the body complex.

There is every indication that this will occur. We cannot speak of certainties but are aware that the grosser or less dense materials will be pulled into conformation with the denser and lighter energies which give your Logos its proceedings through the realms of experience.

May we answer any brief queries at this time?

QUESTIONER: Only if there is anything that we can do to make the instrument more comfortable or to improve the contact?

RA: I am Ra. All is well. We are aware that you experience difficulties at this time, but they are not due to your lack of conscientiousness or dedication. I am Ra. I leave you in the love and in the light of the One Infinite Creator. Go forth, then, rejoicing in the power and the peace of the One Infinite Creator. Adonai.

Session 60,
July 1, 1981

RA: I am Ra. I greet you in the love and in the light of the One Infinite Creator. We communicate now.

QUESTIONER: When you spoke in the last session of "energizing shocks" coming from the top of the pyramid, did you mean that these came at intervals rather than steadily?

RA: I am Ra. These energizing shocks come at discrete intervals but come very, very close together in a properly functioning pyramid shape. In one whose dimensions have gone awry, the energy will not be released with regularity or in quanta, as you may perhaps better understand our meaning.

QUESTIONER: The next statement that I will make may or may not be enlightening to me in my investigation of the pyramid energy, but it has occurred to me that the effect of the so-called Bermuda Triangle could be possibly due to a large pyramid beneath the water which releases this third spiral in discrete and varying intervals. Entities or craft that are in the vicinity may change their space/time continuum in some way. Is this correct?

RA: I am Ra. Yes.

QUESTIONER: Then this third spiral has an energizing effect that, if strong enough, will actually change the space/time continuum. Is there a use or value to this type of change?

RA: I am Ra. In the hands of one of fifth density or above, this particular energy may be tapped in order to communicate information, love, or light across what you would consider vast distances, but which with this energy may be considered transdimensional leaps. Also, there is the possibility of travel using this formation of energy.

QUESTIONER: Would this travel be the instantaneous type used primarily by sixth-density entities, or is it the slingshot effect that you are talking about?

RA: I am Ra. The former effect is that of which we speak. You may note that as one learns the, shall we say, understandings or disciplines of the personality, each of these configurations of prana is available to the entity without the aid of this shape. One may view the pyramid at Giza as metaphysical training wheels.

QUESTIONER: Then is the large underwater pyramid off the Florida coast one of the balancing pyramids that Ra constructed, or did some other social memory complex construct it, and, if so, which one?

RA: I am Ra. That pyramid of which you speak was one whose construction was aided by sixth-density entities of a social memory complex working with Atlanteans prior to our working with the, as you call them, Egyptians.

QUESTIONER: You mentioned working with one other group other than the Egyptians. Who were they?

RA: I am Ra. These entities were those of South America. We divided our forces to work within these two cultures.

QUESTIONER: The pyramid shape then, as I understand it, was deemed by your social memory complex to be at that time of paramount importance as the physical-training aid for spiritual development. At this particular time in the evolution of our planet, it seems that you place little or no emphasis on this shape. Is this correct?

RA: I am Ra. This is correct. It is our honor/duty to attempt to remove the distortions that the use of this shape has caused in the thinking of your peoples and in the activities of some of your entities. We do not deny that such shapes are efficacious, nor do we withhold the general gist of this efficacy. However, we wish to offer our understanding, limited though it is, that contrary to our naive beliefs many thousands of your years ago, the optimum shape for initiation does not exist.

Let us expand upon this point. When we were aided by sixth-density entities during our own third-density experiences, we, being less bellicose in the extreme, found this teaching to be of help. In our naiveté in third density, we had not developed the interrelationships of your barter or money system and power. We were, in fact, a more philosophical third-density planet than your own, and our choices of polarity were much more centered about the, shall we say, understanding of sexual energy transfers and the appropriate relationships between self and other-self.

We spent a much larger portion of our space/time working with the unmanifested being. In this less complex atmosphere, it was quite instructive to have this learn/teaching device, and we benefited without the distortions we found occurring among your peoples.

We have recorded these differences meticulously in the Great Record of Creation that such naiveté shall not be necessary again.

At this space/time we may best serve you, we believe, by stating that the pyramid for meditation along with other rounded and arched or pointed circular shapes is of help to you. However, it is our observation that due to the complexity of influences upon the unmanifested being at this space/time nexus among your planetary peoples, it is best that the progress of the mind/body/spirit complex take place without, as you call them, training aids, because when using a training aid, an entity then takes upon itself the Law of Responsibility for the quickened or increased rate of learn/teaching. If this greater understanding, if we may use this misnomer, is not put into practice in the moment-by-moment experience of the entity, then the usefulness of the training aid becomes negative.

QUESTIONER: Thank you. I don't know if this question will result in any useful information, but I feel that I must ask it. What was the Ark of the Covenant, and what was its use?

RA: I am Ra. The Ark of the Covenant was that place wherein those things most holy, according to the understanding of the one called Moishe, were placed. The article placed therein has been called by your peoples two tablets called the Ten Commandments. There were not two tablets. There was one writing in scroll. This was placed along with the most carefully written accounts by various entities of their beliefs concerning the creation by the One Creator.

This ark was designed to constitute the place wherefrom the priests, as you call those distorted towards the desire to serve their brothers, could draw their power and feel the presence of the One Creator. However, it is to be noted that this entire arrangement was designed not by the one known to the Confederation as Yahweh but rather was designed by negative entities preferring this method of creating an elite called the Sons of Levi.

QUESTIONER: Was this a device for communication then? You also said that they drew power from it. What sort of power? How did this work?

RA: I am Ra. This was charged by means of the materials with which it was built, being given an electromagnetic field. It became an object of power in this way, and, to those whose faith became that untarnished by unrighteousness or separation, this power designed for negativity became positive and is so, to those truly in harmony with the experience of service, to this day. Thus the negative forces were partially successful, but the positively oriented Moishe, as this entity was called, gave to your planetary peoples the possibility of a path to the One Infinite Creator which is completely positive.

This is in common with each of your orthodox religious systems, which have all become somewhat mixed in orientation yet offer a pure path to the One Creator which is seen by the pure seeker.

QUESTIONER: Where is the Ark of the Covenant now? Where is it located?

RA: I am Ra. We refrain from answering this query due to the fact that it does still exist and is not that which we would infringe upon your peoples by locating.

QUESTIONER: In trying to understand the creative energies, it has occurred to me that I really do not understand why unusable heat is generated as our Earth moves from third into fourth density. I know it has to do with disharmony between the vibrations of third and fourth density, but why this would show up as a physical heating within the Earth is beyond me. Can you enlighten me on that?

RA: I am Ra. The concepts are somewhat difficult to penetrate in your language. However, we shall attempt to speak to the subject. If an entity is not in harmony with its circumstances, it feels a burning within. The temperature of the physical vehicle does not yet rise, only the heat of the temper or the tears, as we may describe this disharmony. However, if an entity persists for a long period of your space/time in feeling this emotive heat and disharmony, the entire body complex will begin to resonate to this disharmony, and the disharmony will then show up as the cancer or other degenerative distortions from what you call health.

When an entire planetary system of peoples and cultures repeatedly experiences disharmony on a great scale, the earth under the feet of these entities shall begin to resonate with this disharmony. Due to the nature of the physical vehicle, disharmony shows up as a blockage of growth or an uncontrolled growth, since the primary function of a mind/body/spirit complex's bodily complex is growth and maintenance. In the case of your planet, the purpose of the planet is the maintenance of orbit and the proper location or orientation with regards to other cosmic influences. In order to have this occurring properly, the interior of your sphere is hot in your physical terms. Thus instead of uncontrolled growth you begin to experience uncontrolled heat and its expansive consequences.

QUESTIONER: Is the Earth solid all the way through from one side to the other?

RA: I am Ra. You may say that your sphere is of an honeycomb nature. The center is, however, solid if you would so call that which is molten.

QUESTIONER: Are there third-density entities living in the honeycomb areas? Is this correct?

RA: I am Ra. This was at one time correct. This is not correct at this present space/time.

QUESTIONER: Are there any inner civilizations or entities living in these areas other than physically incarnate who do come and materialize on the Earth's surface at some times?

RA: I am Ra. As we have noted, there are some which do as you say. Further, there are some inner-plane entities of this planet which prefer to do some materialization into third density visible in these areas. There are also bases, shall we say, in these areas of those from elsewhere, both positive and negative. There are abandoned cities.

QUESTIONER: What are these bases used for by those from elsewhere?

RA: I am Ra. These bases are used for the work of materialization of needed equipment for communication with third-density entities and for resting places for some equipment which you might call small craft. These are used for surveillance when it is requested by entities.

Thus some of the, shall we say, teachers of the Confederation speak partially through these surveillance instruments along computerized lines, and when information is desired and those requesting it are of the proper vibratory level, the Confederation entity itself will then speak.

QUESTIONER: I understand then that the Confederation entity needs communication equipment and craft to communicate with the third-density incarnate entity requesting the information?

RA: I am Ra. This is incorrect. However, many of your peoples request the same basic information in enormous repetition, and for a social memory complex to speak ad infinitum about the need to meditate is a waste of the considerable abilities of such social memory complexes.

Thus some entities have had approved by the Council of Saturn the placement and maintenance of these message givers for those whose needs are simple, thus reserving the abilities of the Confederation members for those already meditating and absorbing information which are then ready for additional information.

QUESTIONER: There has been, for the past thirty years, a lot of information and a lot of confusion, and in fact, I would say that the Law of Confusion has been working overtime—to make a small joke—in bringing information for spiritual catalysis to groups requesting it, and we know that both the positively and the negatively oriented social memory complexes have been adding to this information as they can. This has led to a condition of apathy in a lot of cases with respect to the information. Many who are truly seeking have been thwarted by what I might call spiritual entropy in this information. Can you comment on this and the mechanisms of alleviating these problems?

RA: I am Ra. We can comment on this.

QUESTIONER: Only if you deem it of importance would I request a comment.

If you deem it of no importance, we'll skip it.

RA: I am Ra. This information is significant to some degree, as it bears upon our own mission at this time.

We of the Confederation are at the call of those upon your planet. If the call, though sincere, is fairly low in consciousness of the, shall we say, system whereby spiritual evolution may be precipitated, then we may only offer that information useful to that particular caller. This is the basic difficulty. Entities receive the basic information about the Original Thought and the means—that is, meditation and service to others—whereby this Original Thought may be obtained.

Please note that as Confederation members we are speaking for positively oriented entities. We believe the Orion group has precisely the same difficulty.

Once this basic information is received, it is not put into practice in the heart and in the life experience but instead rattles about within the mind complex distortions as would a building block which has lost its place and simply rolls from side to side uselessly, yet still the entity calls. Therefore, the same basic information is repeated. Ultimately the entity decides that it is weary of this repetitive information. However, if an entity puts into practice that which it is given, it will not find repetition except when needed.

QUESTIONER: Thank you. Are the chakras or bodily energy centers related to or do they operate like the pyramid energy funnel?

RA: I am Ra. No.

QUESTIONER: Was there a purpose for mummification having to do with anything other than bodily burial?

RA: I am Ra. Much as we would like to speak to you of this distortion of our designs in constructing the pyramid, we can say very little, for the intent was quite mixed and the uses, though many felt them to be positive, were of a nonpositive order of generation. We cannot speak upon this subject without infringement upon some basic energy balances between the positive and negative forces upon your planet. It may be said that those offering themselves felt they were offering themselves in service to others.

QUESTIONER: What civilization was it that helped Ra using the pyramid shape while Ra was in third density?

RA: I am Ra. Your people have a fondness for the naming. These entities have begun their travel back to the Creator and are no longer experiencing time.

QUESTIONER: The instrument wished to know, when using the pendulum in discovering energy centers, what the back-and-forth motion meant instead of the circular motion?

RA: I am Ra. This shall have to be the final question, although this entity is still providing us with energy. It is experiencing the distortion towards pain.

The rotations having been discussed, we shall simply say that the weak back-and-forth motion indicates a partial blockage, although not a complete blockage. The strong back-and-forth motion indicates the reverse of blockage, which is over-stimulation of a chakra or energy center, which is occurring in order to attempt to balance some difficulty in body or mind complex activity. This condition is not helpful to the entity, as it is unbalanced. Are there any brief queries before we leave this instrument?

QUESTIONER: Only is there anything that we can do to make the instrument more comfortable or to improve the contact?

RA: I am Ra. Be merry, my friends. All is well and your conscientiousness is to be recommended. We leave you in the love and the light of the One Infinite Creator. Rejoice, then, and go forth in the peace and in the glory of the One Infinite Creator. I am Ra. Adonai.

Session 61,
July 8, 1981

RA: I am Ra. I greet you, my friends, in the love and in the light of the Infinite Creator. We communicate now.

QUESTIONER: Could you give me an indication of the instrument's condition?

RA: I am Ra. This instrument's vital energies are improving. The physical complex distortions are quite marked at this space/time, and there is a decrease in physical complex energies.

QUESTIONER: Is there anything in particular that the instrument could do to improve the physical condition?

RA: I am Ra. This instrument has two factors affecting its bodily distortions. This is in common with all those which by seniority of vibration have reached the green-ray level of vibratory consciousness complexes.

The first is the given instreamings, which vary from cycle to cycle in predictable manner. In this particular entity the cyclical complexes at this space/time nexus are not favorable for the physical energy levels.

The second ramification of condition is that which we might call the degree of mental efficiency in use of catalyst provided for the learning of programmed lessons in particular and the lessons of love in general.

This instrument, unlike some entities, has some further distortion due to the use of pre-incarnative conditions.

QUESTIONER: Can you expand on what you meant by the "cycling instreamings of energy"?

RA: I am Ra. There are four types of cycles which are those given in the moment of entry into incarnation. There are in addition more cosmic and less regularized inpourings which, from time to time, affect a sensitized mind/body/spirit complex. The four rhythms are, to some extent, known among your peoples and are called biorhythms.

There is a fourth cycle which we may call the cycle of gateway of magic of the adept or of the spirit. This is a cycle which is completed in approximately eighteen of your diurnal cycles.

The cosmic patterns are also a function of the moment of incarnative entrance and have to do with your satellite you call the moon, your planets of this galaxy, the galactic sun, and in some cases the instreamings from the major galactic points of energy flow.

QUESTIONER: Would it be helpful to plot these cycles for the instrument and attempt to have these sessions at the most favorable points with respect to the cycles?

RA: I am Ra. To that specific query we have no response.

It may be noted that the three in this triad bring in this energy pattern which is Ra. Thus each energy input of the triad is of note.

We may say that while these information systems are interesting, they are in sway only insofar as the entity or entities involved have not made totally efficient use of catalyst, and, therefore, instead of accepting the, shall we say, negative or retrograde moments or periods without undue notice, have the distortion towards the retaining of these distortions in order to work out the unused catalyst.

It is to be noted that psychic attack continues upon this entity, although it is only effective at this time in physical distortions towards discomfort.

We may suggest that it is always of some interest to observe the roadmap, both of the cycles and of the planetary and other cosmic influences, in that one may see certain wide roads or possibilities. However, we remind that this group is an unit.

QUESTIONER: Is there some way that we could, as a unit, then, do something to reduce the effect of the psychic attack on the instrument and optimize the communicative opportunity?

RA: I am Ra. We have given you the information concerning that which aids this particular mind/body/spirit complex. We can speak no further. It is our opinion, which we humbly offer, that each is in remarkable harmony with each for this particular third-density illusion at this space/time nexus.

QUESTIONER: I would like to ask questions about healing exercises. The first is, in the healing exercises concerning the body, what do you mean by the disciplines of the body having to do with the balance between love and wisdom in the use of the body in its natural functions?

RA: I am Ra. We shall speak more briefly than usual due to this instrument's use of the transferred energy. We, therefore, request further queries if our reply is not sufficient.

The body complex has natural functions. Many of these have to do with the unmanifested self and are normally not subject to the need for balancing. There are natural functions which have to do with other-self. Among these are touching, loving, the sexual life, and those times when the company of another is craved to combat the type of loneliness which is the natural function of the body, as opposed to those types of loneliness which are of the mind/emotion complex or of the spirit.

When these natural functions may be observed in the daily life, they may be examined in order that the love of self and love of other-self versus the wisdom regarding the use of natural functions may be observed. There are many fantasies and stray thoughts which may be examined in most of your peoples in this balancing process.

Equally to be balanced is the withdrawal from the need for these natural functions with regard to other-self. On the one hand there is an excess of love. It must be determined whether this is love of self or other-self or both. On the other hand there is an overbalance towards wisdom.

It is well to know the body complex so that it is an ally, balanced and ready to be clearly used as a tool, for each bodily function may be used in higher and higher, if you will, complexes of energy with other-self. No matter what the behavior, the important balancing is the understanding of each interaction on this level with other-selves, so that whether the balance may be love/wisdom or wisdom/love, the other-self is seen by the self in a balanced configuration, and the self is thus freed for further work.

QUESTIONER: Then the second question is, could you give an example of how feelings affect portions of the body and the sensations of the body?

RA: I am Ra. It is nearly impossible to speak generally of these mechanisms, for each entity of proper seniority has its own programming. Of the less aware entities we may say that the connection will often seem random, as the Higher Self continues producing catalyst until a bias occurs. In each programmed individual the sensitivities are far more active, and, as we have said, that catalyst not used fully by the mind and spirit is given to the body.

Thus you may see in this entity the numbing of the arms and the hands, signifying this entity's failure to surrender to the loss of control over the life. Thus this drama is enacted in the physical distortion complex.

In the questioner we may see the desire not to be carrying the load it carries given as physical manifestation of the soreness of those muscles for carrying used. That which is truly needed to be carried is a pre-incarnative responsibility, which seems highly inconvenient.

In the case of the scribe we see a weariness and numbness of feelings ensuing from lack of using catalyst designed to sensitize this entity to quite significant influxes of unfamiliar distortion complexes of the mental, emotional, and spiritual level. As the numbness removes itself from the higher or more responsive complexes, the bodily complex distortions will vanish. This is true also of the other examples.

We would note at this time that the totally efficient use of catalyst upon your plane is extremely rare.

QUESTIONER: Could you tell me how you are able to give us information like this with respect to the first distortion or Law of Confusion?

RA: I am Ra. Each of those is already aware of this information. Any other reader may extract the heart of meaning from this discussion without interest as to the examples' sources. If each was not fully aware of these answers, we could not speak.

It is interesting that in many of your queries you ask for confirmation rather than information. This is acceptable to us.

QUESTIONER: This brings out the point of the purpose of the physical incarnation, I believe. And that is to reach a conviction through your own thought processes as to a solution to problems and understandings in a totally free situation with no proof at all or anything that you would consider proof, proof being a very poor word in itself. Can you expand on my concept?

RA: I am Ra. Your opinion is an eloquent one, although somewhat confused in its connections between the freedom expressed by subjective knowing and the freedom expressed by subjective acceptance. There is a significant distinction between the two.

This is not a dimension of knowing, even subjectively, due to the lack of overview of cosmic and other inpourings which affect each and every situation which produces catalyst. The subjective acceptance of that which is at the moment and the finding of love within that moment is the greater freedom.

That known as the subjective knowing without proof is, in some degree, a poor friend, for there will be anomalies no matter how much information is garnered due to the distortions which form third density.

QUESTIONER: The third question that I have here is, could you give examples of bodily polarity?

RA: I am Ra. Within the body there are many polarities which relate to the balancing of the energy centers of the various bodies of the unmanifested entity. It is well to explore these polarities for work in healing.

Each entity is, of course, a potential polarized portion of another-self.

QUESTIONER: The last question here says that it would seem the proper balancing exercises for all the sensations of the body would be some sort of inactivity such as meditation or contemplation. Is this correct?

RA: I am Ra. This is largely incorrect. The balancing requires a meditative state in order for the work to be done. However, the balancing of sensation has to do with an analysis of the sensation with especial respect to any unbalanced leaning between the love and the wisdom or the positive and the negative. Then whatever is lacking in the balanced sensation is, as in all balancing, allowed to come into the being after the sensation is remembered and recalled in such detail as to overwhelm the senses.

QUESTIONER: Could you tell me why it is important for the appurtenances and other things to be so carefully aligned with respect to the instrument, and why just a small ruffle in the sheet by the instrument causes a problem with the reception of Ra?

RA: I am Ra. We may attempt an explanation. This contact is narrow band. The instrument is highly sensitive. Thus we have good entry into it and can use it to an increasingly satisfactory level.

However, the trance condition is, shall we say, not one which is without toll upon this instrument. Therefore, the area above the entrance into the physical complex of this instrument must be kept clear to avoid discomfort to the instrument, especially as it reenters the body complex. The appurtenances give to the instrument's sensory input mental visualizations which aid in the trance beginning. The careful alignment of these is important for the energizing group in that it is a reminder to that support group that it is time for a working. The ritualistic behaviors are triggers for many energies of the support group. You may have noticed more energy being used in workings as the number has increased due to the long-term, shall we say, effect of such ritualistic actions.

This would not aid another group, as it was designed for this particular system of mind/body/spirit complexes and especially the instrument.

There is enough energy transferred for one more long query. We do not wish to deplete this instrument.

QUESTIONER: Then I will ask this question. Could you tell us the purpose of the frontal lobes of the brain and the conditions necessary for their activation?

RA: I am Ra. The frontal lobes of the brain will, shall we say, have much more use in fourth density.

The primary mental/emotive condition of this large area of the so-called brain is joy or love in its creative sense. Thus the energies which we have discussed in relationship to the pyramids: all of the healing, the learning, the building, and the energizing are to be found in this area. This is the area tapped by the adept. This is the area which, working through the trunk and root of mind, makes contact with intelligent energy and, through this gateway, intelligent infinity.

Are there any queries before we leave this instrument?

QUESTIONER: Only is there anything that we can do to make the instrument more comfortable or to improve the contact?

RA: I am Ra. This instrument is somewhat distorted but each is doing well. You are conscientious. We thank you for continuing to observe the alignments and request that on each level you continue to be this fastidious, as this will maintain the contact.

I am Ra. I leave you in the love and the light of the One Infinite Creator. Go forth, my friends, rejoicing in the power and the peace of the One Infinite Creator. Adonai.

Session 62,
July 13, 1981

RA: I am Ra. I greet you in the love and in the light of the One Infinite Creator.

Before we begin, may we request that a circle be walked about this instrument and that then each of the supporting group expel breath forcibly, approximately two and one-half feet above the instrument's head, the circle then again being walked about the instrument.

[This was done as directed.]

RA: I am Ra. We appreciate your kind cooperation. Please recheck the alignment of perpendicularity and we will begin.

[This was done as directed.]

RA: I am Ra. We communicate now.

QUESTIONER: Could you tell me what was wrong or what caused the necessity for the rewalking of the circle and the purpose for the expelling of the breath?

RA: I am Ra. This instrument was under specific psychic attack at the time of the beginning of the working. There was a slight irregularity in the words verbalized by your sound complex vibratory mechanisms in the protective walking of the circle. Into this opening came this entity and began to work upon the instrument now in trance state, as you would call it. This instrument was being quite adversely affected in physical complex distortions.

Thus the circle was properly walked. The breath of righteousness expelled the thought-form, and the circle again was walked.

QUESTIONER: What was the nature of the thought-form or its affiliation?

RA: I am Ra. This thought-form was of Orion affiliation.

QUESTIONER: Was the attack successful in creating any further distortion in the instrument's physical complex?

RA: I am Ra. This is correct.

QUESTIONER: What is the nature of this distortion?

RA: This thought-form sought to put an end to this instrument's incarnation by working with the renal distortions which, although corrected upon time/space, are vulnerable to one which knows the way to separate time/space molding and space/time distortions which are being unmolded, vulnerable as before the, shall we say, healing.

QUESTIONER: What detrimental effect has been done?

RA: I am Ra. There will be some discomfort. However, we were fortunate in that this instrument was very open to us and well tuned. Had we not been able to reach this instrument and instruct you, the instrument's physical vehicle would soon be unviable.

QUESTIONER: Will there be any lasting effect from this attack as far as the instrument's physical vehicle is concerned?

RA: I am Ra. This is difficult to say. We are of the opinion that no lasting harm or distortion will occur.

The healer was strong and the bonds taking effect in the remolding of these renal distortions were effective. It is at this point a question of two forms of the leavings of what you may call a spell or a magic working; the healer's distortions versus the attempt at Orion distortions; the healer's distortions full of love; the Orion distortions also pure in separation. It seems that all is well except for some possible discomfort which shall be attended if persistent.

QUESTIONER: Was the opening that was made in the protective circle planned to be made by the Orion entity? Was it a specific planned attempt to make an opening, or was this just something that happened by accident?

RA: I am Ra. This entity was, as your people put it, looking for a target of opportunity. The missed word was a chance occurrence and not a planned one.

We might suggest in the, shall we say, future, as you measure space/time, as you begin a working be aware that this instrument is likely being watched for any opportunity. Thus if the circle is walked with some imperfection, it is well to immediately repeat. The expelling of breath is also appropriate, always to the left.

QUESTIONER: Would you expand on what you just said on the expelling of the breath? I'm not quite sure of what you mean.

RA: I am Ra. The repetition of that performed well at this working is advisable if the circle is walked in less than the appropriate configuration.

QUESTIONER: But you mentioned the expelling of the breath to the left, I believe. Would you tell me what you meant by that?

RA: I am Ra. It is as you have just accomplished, the breath being sent above the instrument's head from its right side to its left.

QUESTIONER: Is there anything that we can do for the instrument after she comes out of the trance to help her recover from this attack?

RA: I am Ra. There is little to be done. You may watch to see if distortions persist, and see that the appropriate healers are brought into contact with this mind/body/spirit complex in the event that difficulty persists. It may not. This battle is even now being accomplished. Each may counsel the instrument to continue its work as outlined previously.

QUESTIONER: Who would the appropriate healers be, and how would we bring them in contact with the instrument?

RA: I am Ra. There are four. The difficulty being at all noticed as bodily distortion, the one known as [name of spiritual healer] and the one known as [name of spiritual healer] may work upon the instrument's bodily complex by means of the practices which are developing in each entity. Given persistence of distortion, the one known as [name of allopathic healer] shall be seen. Given the continued difficulty past the point of one of your cycles called the fortnight, the one known as [name of allopathic healer] shall be seen.

QUESTIONER: Does the instrument know who these people are, [name] and [name]? I don't know who they are?

RA: I am Ra. This is correct.

QUESTIONER: Is that the sum total of what we can do to aid the instrument?

RA: I am Ra. This is correct. We may note that the harmonies and loving social intercourse which prevails habitually in this group create a favorable environment for each of you to do your work.

QUESTIONER: What priority, shall I say, does the Orion group place on the reduction of effectiveness or elimination of effectiveness of this group with respect to activities on planet Earth at this time? Can you tell me that?

RA: I am Ra. This group, as all positive channels and supporting groups, is a greatly high priority with the Orion group. This instrument's bodily distortions are its most easily unbound or unloosed distortion dissolving the mind/body/spirit complex if the Orion group is successful; this particular group, having learned to be without serious chinks, may we say, in mind and spirit complex vibratory patterns. In other channels, other chinks may be more in evidence.

QUESTIONER: I'll make this statement and you correct it. The Orion group has an objective of the bringing of the service-to-self polarized entities to harvest, as great a harvest as possible. This harvest will build their potential or their ability to do work in consciousness as given by the distortion of the Law of One called the Law of Squares or Doubling. Is this correct?

RA: I am Ra. This is correct.

QUESTIONER: Are there other groups of those who are on the service-to-self path joined with those of the Orion constellation—for instance, those of Southern Cross—presently working for the same type of harvest with respect to Earth?

RA: I am Ra. These you mention of Southern Cross are members of the Orion group. It is not, shall we say, according to understood wording that a group from various galaxies should be named by one. However, those planetary social memory complexes of the so-called Orion constellation have the upper hand and thus rule the other members. You must recall that in negative thinking, there is always the pecking order, shall we say, and the power against power in separation.

QUESTIONER: By creating as large a harvest as possible of negatively oriented entities from Earth, then, the social memory complex of the Orion group gains in strength. Am I correct in assuming that this strength then is in the total strength of the complex, the pecking order remaining approximately the same, and those at the top gaining in strength with respect to the total strength of the social memory complex? Is this correct?

RA: I am Ra. This is correct. To the stronger go the greater shares of polarity.

QUESTIONER: Is this the fourth-density group that we are talking about now?

RA: I am Ra. There are fourth- and a few fifth-density members of the Orion group.

QUESTIONER: Then is the top of the pecking order fifth density?

RA: I am Ra. This is correct.

QUESTIONER: What is the objective; what does the leader, the one at the very top of the pecking order in fifth density of the Orion group, have as an objective? I would like to understand his philosophy with respect to his objectives and plans for what we might call the future or his future?

RA: I am Ra. This thinking will not be so strange to you. Therefore, we may speak through the densities, as your planet has some negatively oriented action in sway at this space/time nexus.

The early fifth-density negative entity, if oriented towards maintaining cohesion as a social memory complex, may in its free will determine that the path to wisdom lies in the manipulation in exquisite propriety of all other-selves. It then, by virtue of its abilities in wisdom, is able to be the leader of fourth-density beings which are upon the road to wisdom by exploring the dimensions of love of self and understanding of self. These fifth-density entities see the creation as that which shall be put in order.

Dealing with a plane such as this third density at this harvesting, it will see the mechanism of the call more clearly and have much less distortion towards plunder or manipulation by thoughts which are given to negatively oriented entities, although in allowing this to occur and sending less wise entities to do this work, any successes redound to the leaders.

The fifth density sees the difficulties posed by the light and in this way directs entities of this vibration to the seeking of targets of opportunity such as this one. If fourth-density temptations, shall we say, towards distortion of ego etc., are not successful, the fifth-density entity then thinks in terms of the removal of light.

QUESTIONER: When the Orion entity who waits us seeking the opportunity to attack is with us here, can you describe his method of coming here, what he looks like, and what his signs are? I know that this isn't too important, but it might give me a little insight into what we are talking about.

RA: I am Ra. Fifth-density entities are very light beings, although they do have the type of physical vehicle which you understand. Fifth-density entities are very fair to look upon in your standard of beauty.

The thought is what is sent for a fifth-density entity is likely to have mastered this technique or discipline. There is little or no means of perceiving such an entity, for unlike fourth-density negative entities, the fifth-density entity walks with light feet.

This instrument was aware of extreme coldness in the past diurnal cycle and spent much more time than your normal attitudes would imagine to be appropriate in what seemed to each of you an extremely warm climate. This was not perceived by the instrument, but the drop in subjective temperature is a sign of presence of a negative or non-positive or draining entity.

This instrument did mention a feeling of discomfort but was nourished by this group and was able to dismiss it. Had it not been for a random mishap, all would have been well, for you have learned to live in love and light and do not neglect to remember the One Infinite Creator.

QUESTIONER: Then it was a fifth-density entity that made this particular attack upon the instrument?

RA: I am Ra. This is correct.

QUESTIONER: Isn't this unusual that a fifth-density entity then would bother to do this rather than sending a fourth-density servant, shall I say?

RA: I am Ra. This is correct. Nearly all positive channels and groups may be lessened in their positivity or rendered quite useless by what we may call the temptations offered by the fourth-density negative thought-forms. They may suggest many distortions towards specific information, towards the aggrandizement of the self, towards the flowering of the organization in some political, social, or fiscal way.

These distortions remove the focus from the One Infinite Source of love and light of which we are all messengers, humble and knowing that we, of ourselves, are but the tiniest portion of the Creator, a small part of a magnificent entirety of infinite intelligence.

QUESTIONER: Is there something that the instrument could do or we could do for the instrument to eliminate the problems that she has, that she continually experiences of the cold feeling of these attacks?

RA: I am Ra. Yes.

QUESTIONER: Would you tell me what we could do?

RA: I am Ra. You could cease in your attempts to be channels for the love and the light of the One Infinite Creator.

QUESTIONER: Have I missed anything now that we can do at all to aid the instrument during, before, or after a session or at any time?

RA: I am Ra. The love and devotion of this group misses nothing. Be at peace. There is some toll for this work. This instrument embraces this or we could not speak. Rest then in that peace and love and do as you will, as you wish, as you feel. Let there be an end to worry when this is accomplished. The great healer of distortions is love.

QUESTIONER: I have a question that I didn't properly answer last night for [name]. It has to do with the vibrations of the densities. I understand that the first density is composed of core atomic vibrations that are in the red spectrum, second in the orange, etc. Am I to understand that the core vibrations of our planet are still in the red and that second-density beings are still in the orange at this space/time right now, and that each density as it exists on our planet right now has a different core vibration, or is this incorrect?

RA: I am Ra. This is precisely correct.

QUESTIONER: Then as the fourth-density vibrations come in, this means that the planet can support entities of fourth-density core vibration. Will the planet then still be first-density core vibration and will there be second-density entities on it with second-density vibrations, and will there be third-density entities on it with third-density vibrations?

RA: I am Ra. This will be the last full query of this working. There is energy, but the distortions of the instrument suggest to us it would be well to shorten this working with your permission.

QUESTIONER: Yes.

RA: You must see the Earth, as you call it, as being seven Earths. There is red, orange, yellow, and there will soon be a completed green-color vibratory locus for fourth-density entities which they will call Earth. During the fourth-density experience, due to the lack of development of fourth-density entities, the third-density planetary sphere is not useful for habitation, since the early fourth-density entity will not know precisely how to maintain the illusion that fourth density cannot be seen or determined from any instrumentation available to any third density.

Thus in fourth density the red, orange, and green energy nexi of your planet will be activated while the yellow is in potentiation along with the blue and the indigo.

May we ask at this time if there be any brief queries?

QUESTIONER: Is there anything that we can do to make the instrument more comfortable or to improve the contact?

RA: All is well. You have been most conscientious.

I am Ra. I leave you, my friends, in the glory of the love and the light of the One Infinite Creator. Go forth, then, rejoicing in the power and the peace of the One Infinite Creator. Adonai.

Session 63,
July 18, 1981

RA: I am Ra. I greet you in the love and in the light of the One Infinite Creator. We communicate now.

QUESTIONER: Could you give me an indication of the condition of the instrument?

RA: I am Ra. This instrument's vital energies are at the distortion which is normal for this mind/body/spirit complex. The body complex is distorted due to psychic attack in the area of the kidneys and urinary tract. There is also distortion continuing due to the distortion called arthritis.

You may expect this psychic attack to be constant, as this instrument has been under observation by negatively oriented force for some time.

QUESTIONER: Is the necessity of the instrument to go to the bathroom several times before a session due to the psychic attack?

RA: I am Ra. In general this is incorrect. The instrument is eliminating from the body complex the distortion leavings of the material which we use for contact. This occurs variably, sometimes beginning before contact, other workings this occurring after the contact.

In this particular working, this entity is experiencing the aforementioned difficulties causing the intensification of that particular distortion/condition.

QUESTIONER: I know that you have already answered this question, but I feel it my duty now to ask it each time in case there is some new development, and that is, is there anything that we can do that we aren't doing to lessen the effectiveness of the psychic attack upon the instrument?

RA: I am Ra. Continue in love and praise and thanksgiving to the Creator. Examine previous material. Love is the great protector.

QUESTIONER: Could you give me a definition of vital energy?

RA: I am Ra. Vital energy is the complex of energy levels of mind, body, and spirit. Unlike physical energy, it requires the integrated complexes vibrating in an useful manner.

The faculty of will can, to a variable extent, replace missing vital energy, and this has occurred in past workings, as you measure time, in this instrument. This is not recommended. At this time, however, the vital energies are well nourished in mind and spirit, although the physical energy level is, in and of itself, low at this time.

QUESTIONER: Would I be correct in guessing that the vital energy is a function of the awareness or bias of the entity with respect to his polarity or general unity with the Creator or creation?

RA: I am Ra. In a nonspecific sense we may affirm the correctness of your statement. The vital energy may be seen to be that deep love of life or life experiences such as the beauty of creation and the appreciation of other-selves and the distortions of your co-Creators' making which are of beauty.

Without this vital energy, the least distorted physical complex will fail and perish. With this love or vital energy or élan, the entity may continue though the physical complex is greatly distorted.

QUESTIONER: I would like to continue with the questions about the fact that in fourth density the red, orange, and green energies will be activated, yellow, blue, etc., being in potentiation. Right now, we have green energies activated. They have been activated for the last forty-five years. I am wondering about the transition through this period so that the green is totally activated and the yellow is in potentiation. What will we lose as the yellow goes from activation into potentiation, and what will we gain as green comes into total activation, and what is the process?

RA: I am Ra. It is misleading to speak of gains and losses when dealing with the subject of the cycle's ending and the green-ray cycle beginning upon your sphere. It is to be kept in the forefront of the faculties of intelligence that there is one creation in which there is no loss. There are progressive cycles for experiential use by entities. We may now address your query.

As the green-ray cycle or the density of love and understanding begins to take shape, the yellow-ray plane or Earth which you now enjoy in your dance will cease to be inhabited for some period of your space/time as the space/time necessary for fourth-density entities to learn their ability to shield their density from that of third is learned. After this period there will come a time when third density may again cycle on the yellow-ray sphere.

Meanwhile there is another sphere, congruent to a great extent with yellow ray, forming. This fourth-density sphere coexists with first, second, and third. It is of a denser nature due to the rotational core atomic aspects of its material. We have discussed this subject with you.

The fourth-density entities which incarnate at this space/time are fourth density in the view of experience but are incarnating in less dense vehicles due to desire to experience and aid in the birth of fourth density upon this plane.

You may note that fourth-density entities have a great abundance of compassion.

QUESTIONER: At present we have, in third-density incarnation on this plane, those third-density entities of the planet Earth who have been here for some number of incarnations who will graduate in the three-way split, either positive polarity remaining for fourth-density experience on this planet, the negative polarity harvestable going to another planet, and the rest unharvestable third density going to another third-density planet. In addition to these entities I am assuming that we have here some entities already harvestable from other third-density planets who have come here and have incarnated in third-density form to make the transition with this planet into fourth density, plus Wanderers.

Is this correct?

RA: I am Ra. This is correct except we may note a small point. The positively oriented harvested entities will remain in this planetary influence, but not upon this plane.

QUESTIONER: I think you said there were sixty million Wanderers, approximately, here now. Am I correct in that memory?

RA: I am Ra. This is approximately correct. There is some excess to that amount.

QUESTIONER: Does that number include the harvestable entities who are coming to this planet for the fourth-density experience?

RA: I am Ra. No.

QUESTIONER: Approximately how many are here now who have come here from other planets who are third-density harvestable for fourth-density experience?

RA: I am Ra. This is a recent, shall we say, phenomenon, and the number is not yet in excess of 35,000 entities.

QUESTIONER: Now these entities incarnate into a third-density vibratory body. I am trying to understand how this transition takes place from third to fourth density. I will take the example of one of these entities of which we are speaking who is now in a third-density body. He will grow older, and then will it be necessary that he die from the third-density physical body and reincarnate in a fourth-density body for that transition?

RA: I am Ra. These entities are those incarnating with what you may call a double body in activation. It will be noted that the entities birthing these fourth-density entities experience a great feeling of, shall we say, the connection and the use of spiritual energies during pregnancy. This is due to the necessity for manifesting the double body.

This transitional body is one which will be, shall we say, able to appreciate fourth-density vibratory complexes as the instreaming increases without the accompanying disruption of the third-density body. If a third-density entity were, shall we say, electrically aware of fourth density in full, the third-density electrical fields would fail due to incompatibility.

To answer your query about death, these entities will die according to third-density necessities.

QUESTIONER: You are saying, then, that for the transition from third to fourth density for one of the entities with doubly activated bodies, in order to make the transition the third-density body will go through the process of what we call death. Is this correct?

RA: I am Ra. The third and fourth, combination, density's body will die according to the necessity of third-density mind/body/spirit complex distortions.

We may respond to the heart of your question by noting that the purpose of such combined activation of mind/body/spirit complexes is that such entities, to some extent, conscientiously are aware of those fourth-density understandings which third density is unable to remember due to the forgetting. Thus fourth-density experience may be begun with the added attraction to an entity oriented toward service to others of dwelling in a troubled third-density environment and offering its love and compassion.

QUESTIONER: Would the purpose in transitioning to Earth prior to the complete changeover then be for the experience to be gained here before the harvesting process?

RA: I am Ra. This is correct. These entities are not Wanderers in the sense that this planetary sphere is their fourth-density home planet. However, the experience of this service is earned only by those harvested third-density entities which have demonstrated a great deal of orientation towards service to others. It is a privilege to be allowed this early an incarnation, as there is much experiential catalyst in service to other-selves at this harvesting.

QUESTIONER: There are many children now who have demonstrated the ability to bend metal mentally, which is a fourth-density phenomenon. Would most of these children, then, be the type of entity of which we speak?

RA: I am Ra. This is correct.

QUESTIONER: Is the reason that they can do this and the fifth-density Wanderers who are here cannot do it, the fact that they have the fourth-density body in activation?

RA: I am Ra. This is correct. Wanderers are third density activated in mind/body/spirit and are subject to the forgetting, which can only be penetrated with disciplined meditation and working.

QUESTIONER: I am assuming that the reason for this is, first, since the entities of harvestable third density who very recently have been coming here are coming here late enough so that they will not affect the polarization through their teachings. They are not infringing upon the first distortion because they are children now, and they won't be old enough to really affect any of the polarization until the transition is well advanced. However, the Wanderers who have come here are older and have a greater ability to affect the polarization. They must do their affecting as a function of their ability to penetrate the forgetting process in order to be within the first distortion. Is this correct?

RA: I am Ra. This is quite correct.

QUESTIONER: It would seem to me that some of the harvestable third-density entities are, however, relatively old, since I know of some individuals who can bend metal who are over fifty years old, and some others over thirty. Would there be other entities who could bend metal for other reasons than having dual-activated bodies?

RA: I am Ra. This is correct. Any entity who, by accident or by careful design, penetrates intelligent energy's gateway may use the shaping powers of this energy.

QUESTIONER: Now as this transition continues into fourth-density activation, in order to inhabit this fourth-density sphere it will be necessary for all third-density physical bodies to go through the process which we refer to as death. Is this correct?

RA: I am Ra. This is correct.

QUESTIONER: Are there any inhabitants at this time of this fourth-density sphere who have already gone through this process? Is it now being populated?

RA: I am Ra. This is correct only in the very, shall we say, recent past.

QUESTIONER: I would assume that this population is from other planets since the harvesting has not yet occurred on this planet. It is from planets where the harvesting has already occurred. Is this correct?

RA: I am Ra. This is correct.

QUESTIONER: Then are these entities visible to us? Could I see one of them? Would he walk upon our surface?

RA: I am Ra. We have discussed this. These entities are in dual bodies at this time.

QUESTIONER: Sorry that I am so stupid on this, but this particular concept is very difficult for me to understand. It is something that I am afraid requires some rather dumb questions on my part to fully understand, and I don't think I will ever fully understand it or even get a good grasp of it.

Then as the fourth-density sphere is activated, there is heat energy being generated. I assume that this heat energy is generated on the third-density sphere only. Is this correct?

RA: I am Ra. This is quite correct. The experiential distortions of each dimension are discrete.

QUESTIONER: Then at some time in the future, the fourth-density sphere will be fully activated. What is the difference between full activation and partial activation for this sphere?

RA: I am Ra. At this time the cosmic influxes are conducive to true color green core particles being formed and material of this nature thus being formed. However, there is a mixture of the yellow-ray and green-ray environments at this time, necessitating the birthing of transitional mind/body/spirit complex types of energy distortions. At full activation of the true color green density of love, the planetary sphere will be solid and inhabitable upon its own, and the birthing that takes place will have been transformed through the process of time, shall we say, to the appropriate type of vehicle to appreciate in full the fourth-density planetary environment. At this nexus the green-ray environment exists to a far greater extent in time/space than in space/time.

QUESTIONER: Could you describe the difference that you are speaking of with respect to time/space and space/time?

RA: I am Ra. For the sake of your understanding, we will use the working definition of inner planes. There is a great deal of subtlety invested in this sound vibration complex, but it, by itself, will perhaps fulfill your present need.

QUESTIONER: I will make this statement and have you correct me. What we have is, as our planet is spiraled by the spiraling action of the entire major galaxy and our planetary system spirals into the new

position, the fourth-density vibrations becoming more and more pronounced. These atomic core vibrations begin to create, more and more
completely, the fourth-density sphere and the fourth-density bodily
complexes for inhabitation of that sphere. Is this correct?

RA: I am Ra. This is partially correct. To be corrected is the concept of
the creation of green-ray-density bodily complexes. This creation will
be gradual and will take place beginning with your third-density type
of physical vehicle and, through the means of bisexual reproduction,
become by evolutionary processes the fourth-density body
complexes.

QUESTIONER: Then are these entities of whom we have spoken the
third-density harvestable who have been transferred, the ones who
then will, by bisexual reproduction, create the fourth-density complexes that are necessary?

RA: I am Ra. The influxes of true color green energy complexes will
more and more create the conditions in which the atomic structure of
cells of bodily complexes is that of the density of love. The mind/body/
spirit complexes inhabiting these physical vehicles will be and, to some
extent, are those of whom you spoke, and, as harvest is completed,
the harvested entities of this planetary influence.

QUESTIONER: Is there a clock-like face, shall I say, associated with
the entire major galaxy so that as it revolves it carries all of these stars
and planetary systems through transitions from density to density?
Is this how it works?

RA: I am Ra. You are perceptive. You may see a three-dimensional
clockface or spiral of endlessness which is planned by the Logos for
this purpose.

QUESTIONER: I understand that the Logos did not plan for the heating effect in our third-density transition into fourth. Is this correct?

RA: I am Ra. This is correct except for the condition of free will, which
is, of course, planned by the Logos as It, Itself, is a creature of free
will. In this climate an infinity of events or conditions may occur. They
cannot be said to be planned by the Logos but can be said to have been
freely allowed.

QUESTIONER: It would seem to me that the heating effect that takes place on the planet is analogous to a disease in the body and would have as a root cause the same or analogous mental configuration. Is this correct?

RA: I am Ra. This is correct except that the spiritual configuration as well as mental biases of your peoples has been responsible for these distortions of the body complex of your planetary sphere.

QUESTIONER: When the third density goes out of activation and into potentiation, that will leave us with a planet that is first, second, and fourth density. At that time there will be no activated third-density vibrations on this planet. Am I correct in assuming that all third-density vibrations on this planet now are those vibrations that compose the bodily complexes of entities such as we are; that that is the sum total of third-density vibrations on this planet at this time?

RA: I am Ra. This will be the last full query of this working. This instrument has energy left due to transfer, but there is discomfort. We do not wish to deplete this instrument. May we say that this instrument seems in better configuration despite attack than previous workings.

To answer your query, this is incorrect only in that in addition to the mind/body/spirit complexes of third density, there are the artifacts, thought-forms, and feelings which these co-Creators have produced. This is third density.

May we answer any brief queries as we leave this instrument?

QUESTIONER: Is there anything that we can do to make the instrument more comfortable or to improve the contact?

RA: I am Ra. You are conscientious. All is well. We leave you now, my friends, in the glory of the love and the light of the One Infinite Creator. Go forth, then, rejoicing in the power and the peace of the Infinite Creator. Adonai.

Session 64,
July 26, 1981

RA: I am Ra. I greet you in the love and in the light of the One Infinite Creator. We communicate now.

QUESTIONER: Could you first tell me the condition of the instrument?

RA: I am Ra. It is as previously stated, with the exception of a transitory distortion lessening the free flow of vital energy.

QUESTIONER: Can you tell me what the transitory distortion is?

RA: I am Ra. This is marginal information.

QUESTIONER: Then we won't question on it.

Could you explain the basic principles behind the ritual which we perform to initiate the contact and what I would call the basic white magical principles of protection?

RA: I am Ra. Due to your avenue of question, we perceive the appropriateness of inclusion of the cause of this instrument's transitory vital energy distortion. The cause is a bias towards the yearning for expression of devotion to the One Creator in group worship.

This entity was yearning for this protection both consciously in that it responds to the accoutrements of this expression, the ritual, the colors, and their meanings as given by the distortion system of what you call the church, the song of praise, and the combined prayers of thanksgiving and, most of all, that which may be seen to be most centrally magical, the intake of that food which is not of this dimension but has been transmuted into metaphysical nourishment in what this distortion of expression calls the holy communion.

The subconscious reason, it being the stronger for this yearning, was the awareness that such expression is, when appreciated by an entity as the transmutation into the presence of the One Creator, a great protection of the entity as it moves in the path of service to others.

The principle behind any ritual of the white magical nature is to so configure the stimuli which reach down into the trunk of mind that this arrangement causes the generation of disciplined and purified emotion or love which then may be both protection and the key to the gateway to intelligent infinity.

QUESTIONER: Can you tell me why the slight error made in the ritual starting this communication two sessions ago allowed the intrusion by an Orion-affiliated entity?

RA: I am Ra. This contact is narrow band and its preconditions precise. The other-self offering its service in the negative path also is possessed of the skill of the swordsman. You deal in this contact with, shall we say, forces of great intensity poured into a vessel as delicate as a snow-flake and as crystalline.

The smallest of lapses may disturb the regularity of this pattern of energies which forms the channel for these transmissions.

We may note for your information that our pause was due to the necessity of being quite sure that the mind/body/spirit complex of the instrument was safely in the proper light configuration or density before we dealt with the situation. Far better would it be to allow the shell to become unviable than to allow the mind/body/spirit complex to be, shall we say, misplaced.

QUESTIONER: Could you describe or tell me of rituals or techniques used by Ra in seeking in the direction of service?

RA: I am Ra. To speak of that which sixth-density social memory complexes labor within in order to advance is at best misprision of plain communication, for much is lost in transmission of concept from density to density, and the discussion of sixth density is inevitably distorted greatly.

However, we shall attempt to speak to your query, for it is a helpful one in that it allows us to express once again the total unity of creation. We seek the Creator upon a level of shared experience to which you are not privy, and rather than surrounding ourselves in light, we have become light. Our understanding is that there is no other material except light. Our rituals, as you may call them, are an infinitely subtle continuation of the balancing processes which you are now beginning to experience.

We seek now without polarity. Thus we do not invoke any power from without, for our search has become internalized as we become light/love and love/light. These are the balances we seek, the balances between compassion and wisdom which more and more allow our understanding of experience to be informed that we may come closer to the unity with the One Creator which we so joyfully seek.

Your rituals at your level of progress contain the concept of polarization, and this is most central at your particular space/time.

We may answer further if you have specific queries.

QUESTIONER: Would it be helpful if Ra were to describe the techniques that Ra used while Ra was third density to evolve in mind, body, and spirit?

RA: I am Ra. This query lies beyond the Law of Confusion.

QUESTIONER: What about fourth-density experience of Ra? Would that also lie beyond the Law of Confusion?

RA: I am Ra. This is correct. Let us express a thought. Ra is not elite. To speak of our specific experiences to a group which honors us is to guide to the point of a specific advising. Our work was that of your people, of experiencing the catalyst of joys and sorrows. Our circumstances were somewhat more harmonious. Let it be said that any entity or group may create the most splendid harmony in any outer atmosphere. Ra's experiences are no more than your own. Yours is the dance at this space/time in third-density harvest.

QUESTIONER: The question was brought up recently having to do with possible records left near, in, or under the Great Pyramid at Giza. I have no idea whether this would be of benefit. I will just ask if there is any benefit in investigating in this area?

RA: I am Ra. We apologize for seeming to be so shy of information. However, any words upon this particular subject create the possibility of infringement upon free will.

QUESTIONER: In a previous session you mentioned the gateway of magic for the adept occurring in eighteen-day cycles. Could you expand on that information, please?

RA: I am Ra. The mind/body/spirit complex is born under a series of influences, both lunar, planetary, cosmic, and in some cases, karmic. The moment of the birthing into this illusion begins the cycles we have mentioned.

The spiritual or adept's cycle is an eighteen-day cycle and operates with the qualities of the sine wave. Thus there are a few excellent days on the positive side of the curve, that being the first nine days of the cycle—precisely the fourth, the fifth, and the sixth—when workings are most appropriately undertaken, given that the entity is still without total conscious control of its mind/body/spirit distortion/reality.

The most interesting portion of this information, like that of each cycle, is the noting of the critical point wherein passing from the ninth to the tenth and from the eighteenth to the first days the adept will experience some difficulty especially when there is a transition occurring in another cycle at the same time. At the nadir of each cycle the adept will be at its least powerful but will not be open to difficulties in nearly the degree that it experiences at critical times.

QUESTIONER: Then to find the cycles we would take the instant of birth and the emerging of the infant from the mother into this density and start the cycle at that instant and continue it through the life. Is this correct?

RA: I am Ra. This is mostly correct. It is not necessary to identify the instant of birthing. The diurnal cycle upon which this event occurs is satisfactory for all but the most fine workings.

QUESTIONER: Am I correct in assuming that whatever magic the adept would perform at this time would be more successful or, shall we say, more to his design than that performed at less opportune times in the cycle?

RA: I am Ra. This cycle is a helpful tool to the adept, but as we said, as the adept becomes more balanced, the workings designed will be dependent less and less upon these cycles of opportunity and more and more even in their efficacy.

QUESTIONER: I have no ability to judge at what point the level of abilities of the adept would be reached to be independent of this cyclical action. Can you give me an indication of what level of "adeptness" that would be necessary in order to be so independent?

RA: I am Ra. We are fettered from speaking specifically due to this group's work, for to speak would seem to be to judge. However, we may say that you may consider this cycle in the same light as the so-called astrological balances within your group; that is, they are interesting but not critical.

QUESTIONER: Thank you. I read that recent research has indicated that the normal sleep cycle for entities on this planet occurs one hour later each diurnal period, so that we have a twenty-five-hour cycle instead of a twenty-four-hour cycle. Is this correct, and if so, why is this?

RA: I am Ra. This is in some cases correct. The planetary influences from which those of Mars experience memory have some effect upon these third-density physical bodily complexes. This race has given its genetic material to many bodies upon your plane.

QUESTIONER: Thank you. Ra mentioned the ones [name] and [name] in a previous session. These are members of what we call our medical profession. What is the value of modern medical techniques in alleviating bodily distortions with respect to the purpose for these distortions and what we might call karma?

RA: I am Ra. This query is convoluted. However, we shall make some observations in lieu of attempting one coherent answer, for that which is allopathic among your healing practices is somewhat two-sided.

Firstly, you must see the possibility/probability that each and every allopathic healer is in fact a healer. Within your cultural nexus, this training is considered the appropriate means of perfecting the healing ability. In the most basic sense, any allopathic healer may be seen to, perhaps, be one whose desire is service to others in alleviation of bodily complex and mental/emotional complex distortions so that the entity to be healed may experience further catalyst over a longer period of what you call the life. This is a great service to others when appropriate due to the accumulation of distortions toward wisdom and love which can be created through the use of the space/time continuum of your illusion.

In observing the allopathic concept of the body complex as a machine, we may note the symptomology of a societal complex seemingly dedicated to the most intransigent desire for the distortions of distraction, anonymity, and sleep. This is the result rather than the cause of societal thinking upon your plane.

In turn this mechanical concept of the body complex has created the continuing proliferation of distortions towards what you would call ill health, due to the strong chemicals used to control and hide bodily distortions. There is a realization among many of your peoples that there are more efficacious systems of healing not excluding the allopathic but also including the many other avenues of healing.

QUESTIONER: Let us assume that a bodily distortion occurs within a particular entity who then has a choice of seeking allopathic aid or experiencing the catalyst of the distortion and not seeking correction of the distortion. Can you comment on the two possibilities for this entity and his analysis of each path?

RA: I am Ra. If the entity is polarized towards service to others, analysis properly proceeds along the lines of consideration of which path offers the most opportunity for service to others.

For the negatively polarized entity, the antithesis is the case.

For the unpolarized entity, the considerations are random and most likely in the direction of the distortion towards comfort.

QUESTIONER: I understand [name] brought a four-toed Bigfoot cast by here the other day. Could you tell me which form of Bigfoot that cast was?

RA: I am Ra. We can.

QUESTIONER: I know that it is totally unimportant, but as a service to [name], I thought that I should ask that.

RA: I am Ra. This entity was one of a small group of thought-forms.

QUESTIONER: He also asked—I know this is also unimportant— why there were no Bigfoot remains found after the entities have died on our surface. Could you also answer this? I know this is of no importance, but as a service to him I ask it.

RA: I am Ra. You may suggest that exploration of the caves which underlie some of the western coastal mountain regions of your continent will one day offer such remains. They will not be generally understood if this culture survives in its present form long enough in your time measurement for this probability/possibility vortex to occur.

There is enough energy for one more full query at this time.

QUESTIONER: In the healing exercises, when you say examine the sensations of the body, do you mean those sensations available to the body via the five senses or in relation to the natural functions of the body such as touching, loving, sexual sharing, and company, or are you speaking of something else altogether?

RA: I am Ra. The questioner may perceive its body complex at this moment. It is experiencing sensations. Most of these sensations or, in this case, nearly all of them are transient and without interest. However, the body is the creature of the mind. Certain sensations carry importance due to the charge or power which is felt by the mind upon the experience of this sensation.

For instance, at this space/time nexus, one sensation is carrying a powerful charge and may be examined. This is the sensation of what you call the distortion towards discomfort due to the cramped position of the body complex during this working. In balancing you would then explore this sensation. Why is this sensation powerful? Because it was chosen in order that the entity might be of service to others in energizing this contact.

Each sensation that leaves the aftertaste of meaning upon the mind, that leaves the taste within the memory, shall be examined. These are the sensations of which we speak.

May we answer any brief queries before we leave this instrument?

QUESTIONER: Is there anything that we could do to make the instrument more comfortable or to improve the contact?

RA: I am Ra. Continue to consider the alignments. You are conscientious and aware of the means of caring for the instrument in its present distortions having to do with the wrists and hands. As always, love is the greatest protection.

I am Ra. I leave you, my friends, in the glorious love and joyful light of the Infinite Creator. Go forth, then, rejoicing in the power and in the peace of the One Infinite Creator. Adonai.

Session 65,
August 8, 1981

RA: I am Ra. I greet you in the love and in the light of the One Infinite Creator. We communicate now.

QUESTIONER: Could you first please give us an indication of the instrument's condition and the level of vital and physical energies?

RA: I am Ra. This instrument's vital energies are as previously stated. The physical energies are greatly distorted towards weakness at this space/time due to the distortion complexes symptomatic of that which you call the arthritic condition. The level of psychic attack is constant but is being dealt with by this instrument in such a way as to eliminate serious difficulties due to its fidelity and that of the support group.

QUESTIONER: I may be recovering a little ground already covered today, but I am trying to get a more clear picture of some things that I don't understand, and possibly develop a plan of my own for activity in the future.

I have the impression that in the near future the seeking will increase by many who now are incarnate in the physical on this planet. Their seeking will increase because they will become more aware of the creation as it is and as it is opposed, I might say, to the creation of man. Their orientation and their thinking will be, by catalyst of a unique nature, reoriented to thinking of more basic concepts, shall I say. Is this correct?

RA: I am Ra. The generalities of expression can never be completely correct. However, we may note that when faced with a hole in the curtain, an entity's eyes may well peer for the first time through the window beyond. This tendency is probable given the possibility/probability vortices active within your space/time and time/space continua at this nexus.

QUESTIONER: I have assumed that the reason that so many Wanderers and those harvested third-density entities who have been transferred here find it a privilege and an exceptionally beneficial time to be incarnate upon this planet is that the effect that I just spoke of gives them the opportunity to be more fully of service because of the increased seeking. Is this, in general, correct?

RA: I am Ra. This is the intention which Wanderers had prior to incarnation. There are many Wanderers whose dysfunction with regard to the planetary ways of your peoples have caused, to some extent, a condition of being caught up in a configuration of mind complex activity which, to the corresponding extent, may prohibit the intended service.

QUESTIONER: I noticed that you are speaking more slowly than usual. Is there a reason for this?

RA: I am Ra. This instrument is somewhat weak and, although strong in vital energy and well able to function at this time, is somewhat more fragile than the usual condition we find. We may note a continuing bearing of the physical distortion called pain, which has a weakening effect upon physical energy. In order to use the considerable store of available energy without harming the instrument, we are attempting to channel even more narrow band than is our wont.

QUESTIONER: Have I properly analyzed the condition that creates the possibility of greater service as follows: Seniority by vibration of incarnation has greatly polarized those upon the surface of the planet now, and the influx of Wanderers has greatly increased the mental configuration toward things of a more spiritual nature. This would be, I assume, one of the factors creating a better atmosphere for service. Is this correct?

RA: I am Ra. This is correct.

QUESTIONER: Would the coming changes as we progress into fourth density, such as changes in the physical third-density planet due to the heating effect and changes such as the ability of people to perform what we term paranormal activities, act as catalyst to create a greater seeking?

RA: I am Ra. This is partially correct. The paranormal events occurring are not designed to increase seeking but are manifestations of those whose vibratory configuration enables these entities to contact the gateway to intelligent infinity. These entities capable of paranormal service may determine to be of such service on a conscious level. This, however, is a function of the entity and its free will and not the paranormal ability.

The correct portion of your statements is the greater opportunity for service due to the many changes which will offer many challenges, difficulties, and seeming distresses within your illusion to many who then will seek to understand, if we may use this misnomer, the reason for the malfunctioning of the physical rhythms of their planet.

Moreover, there exists probability/possibility vortices which spiral towards your bellicose actions. Many of these vortices are not of the nuclear war but of the less annihilatory but more lengthy so-called "conventional" war. This situation, if formed in your illusion, would offer many opportunities for seeking and for service.

QUESTIONER: How would conventional warfare offer the opportunities for seeking and service?

RA: I am Ra. The possibility/probabilities exist for situations in which great portions of your continent and the globe in general might be involved in the type of warfare which you might liken to guerrilla warfare. The ideal of freedom from the so-called invading force of either the controlled fascism or the equally controlled social common ownership of all things would stimulate great quantities of contemplation upon the great polarization implicit in the contrast between freedom and control. In this scenario which is being considered at this time/space nexus, the idea of obliterating valuable sites and personnel would not be considered a useful one. Other weapons would be used which do not destroy as your nuclear arms would. In this ongoing struggle, the light of freedom would burn within the mind/body/spirit complexes capable of such polarization. Lacking the opportunity for overt expression of the love of freedom, the seeking for inner knowledge would take root aided by those of the Brothers and Sisters of Sorrow which remember their calling upon this sphere.

QUESTIONER: We would seem to have dual catalysts operating, and the question is which one is going to act first. The prophecies, I will call them, made by Edgar Cayce indicated many Earth changes, and I am wondering about the mechanics describing the future. Ra, it has been stated, is not a part of time, and yet we concern ourselves with possibility/probability vortices. It is very difficult for me to understand how the mechanism of prophecy operates. What is the value of such a prophecy such as Cayce made with respect to Earth changes and all of these scenarios?

RA: I am Ra. Consider the shopper entering the store to purchase food with which to furnish the table for the time period you call a week. Some stores have some items, others a variant set of offerings. We speak of these possibility/probability vortices when asked with the understanding that such are as a can, jar, or portion of goods in your store.

It is unknown to us as we scan your time/space whether your peoples will shop hither or yon. We can only name some of the items available for the choosing. The, shall we say, record which the one you call Edgar read from is useful in that same manner. There is less knowledge in this material of other possibility/probability vortices and more attention paid to the strongest vortex. We see the same vortex but also see many others. Edgar's material could be likened unto one hundred boxes of your cold cereal, another vortex likened unto three, or six, or fifty of another product which is eaten by your peoples for breakfast. That you will breakfast is close to certain. The menu is your own choosing.

The value of prophecy must be realized to be only that of expressing possibilities. Moreover, it must be, in our humble opinion, carefully taken into consideration that any time/space viewing, whether by one of your time/space or by one such as we who view the time/space from a dimension, shall we say, exterior to it will have a quite difficult time expressing time measurement values. Thus prophecy given in specific terms is more interesting for the content or type of possibility predicted than for the space/time nexus of its supposed occurrence.

QUESTIONER: So we have the distinct possibility of two different types of catalyst creating an atmosphere of seeking that is greater than that which we experience at present. There will be much confusion, especially in the scenario of Earth changes, simply because there have been many predictions of these changes by many groups, giving many and sundry reasons for the changes. Can you comment on the effectiveness of this type of catalyst and the rather wide pre-knowledge of the coming changes but also the wide variation in explanation for these changes?

RA: I am Ra. Given the amount of strength of the possibility/probability vortex which posits the expression by the planet itself of the difficult birthing of the planetary self into fourth density, it would be greatly surprising were not many which have some access to space/time able to perceive this vortex. The amount of this cold cereal in the grocery, to use our previous analogy, is disproportionately large. Each which prophesies does so from a unique level, position, or vibratory configuration. Thus biases and distortions will accompany much prophecy.

QUESTIONER: This entire scenario for the next twenty years seems to be aimed at producing an increase in seeking and an increase in the awareness of the natural creation, but also a terrific amount of confusion. Was it the pre-incarnative objective of many of the Wanderers to attempt to reduce this confusion?

RA: I am Ra. It was the aim of Wanderers to serve the entities of this planet in whatever way was requested, and it was also the aim of Wanderers that their vibratory patterns might lighten the planetary vibration as a whole, thus ameliorating the effects of planetary disharmony and palliating any results of this disharmony.

Specific intentions such as aiding in a situation not yet manifest are not the aim of Wanderers. Light and love go where they are sought and needed, and their direction is not planned aforetimes.

QUESTIONER: Then each of the Wanderers here acts as a function of the biases he has developed in any way he sees fit to communicate or simply be in his polarity to aid the total consciousness of the planet. Is there any physical way in which he aids, perhaps by his vibrations, somehow just adding to the planet just as electrical polarity or charging a battery? Does that also aid the planet, just the physical presence of the Wanderers?

RA: I am Ra. This is correct, and the mechanism is precisely as you state. We intended this meaning in the second portion of our previous answer.

You may, at this time, note that as with any entities, each

Wanderer has its unique abilities, biases, and specialties, so that from each portion of each density represented among the Wanderers come an array of pre-incarnative talents which then may be expressed upon this plane which you now experience, so that each Wanderer, in offering itself before incarnation, has some special service to offer in addition to the doubling effect of planetary love and light and the basic function of serving as beacon or shepherd.

Thus there are those of fifth density whose abilities to express wisdom are great. There are fourth- and sixth-density Wanderers whose ability to serve as, shall we say, passive radiators or broadcasters of love and love/light are immense. There are many others whose talents brought into this density are quite varied.

Thus, Wanderers have three basic functions once the forgetting is penetrated, the first two being basic, the tertiary one being unique to that particular mind/body/spirit complex.

We may note at this point while you ponder the possibility/probability vortices that although you have many, many items which cause distress and thus offer seeking and service opportunities, there is always one container in that store of peace, love, light, and joy. This vortex may be very small, but to turn one's back upon it is to forget the infinite possibilities of the present moment. Could your planet polarize towards harmony in one fine, strong moment of inspiration? Yes, my friends. It is not probable, but it is ever possible.

QUESTIONER: How common in the universe is a mixed harvest from a planet of both positively and negatively oriented mind/body/spirit complexes?

RA: I am Ra. Among planetary harvests which yield a harvest of mind/body/spirit complexes, approximately 10 percent are negative, approximately 60 percent are positive, and approximately 30 percent are mixed, with nearly all harvest being positive. In the event of mixed harvest, it is almost unknown for the majority of the harvest to be negative. When a planet moves strongly towards the negative, there is almost no opportunity for harvestable positive polarization.

QUESTIONER: Can you tell me why there is almost no opportunity in that case?

RA: The ability to polarize positively requires a certain degree of self-determination.

QUESTIONER: Then as these final days of the cycle transpire, if the harvest were to occur now, today, it would have a certain number harvested positively and negatively and a certain number of repeaters. I am going to assume that because of the catalyst that will be experienced between now and the actual harvesting time, these numbers of harvestable entities will increase.

Generally speaking, not particularly with respect to this planet but with respect to general experience in harvesting, how big an increase in harvestable entities can you logically assume will occur because of the catalyst that occurs in the final period such as this one, or am I making a mistake in assuming that other planets have added catalyst at the end of a harvesting period when they have a mixed harvest?

RA: I am Ra. In the event of mixed harvest, there is nearly always disharmony and, therefore, added catalyst in the form of your so-called "Earth changes." In this assumption you are correct.

It is the Confederation's desire to serve those who may indeed seek more intensely because of this added catalyst. We do not choose to attempt to project the success of added numbers to the harvest, for this would not be appropriate. We are servants. If we are called, we shall serve with all our strength. To count the numbers is without virtue.

QUESTIONER: Now the added catalyst at the end of the cycle is a function specifically of the orientation of the consciousness that inhabits the planet. The consciousness has provided the catalyst for itself in orienting its thinking in the way it has oriented it, thus acting upon itself the same as catalyst of bodily pain and disease act upon the single mind/body/spirit complex. I made this analogy once before but reiterate it at this time to clarify my own thinking in seeing the planetary entity as somewhat of a single entity made up of billions of mind/body/spirit complexes. Is my viewpoint correct?

RA: I am Ra. You are quite correct.

QUESTIONER: Then we deal with an entity that has not yet formed a social memory but is yet an entity just as one of us can be called a single entity. Can we continue this observation of the conglomerate entity through the galactic entity, or, shall I say, planetary system type of entity? Let me try to phrase it this way. Could I look at a single sun in its planetary system as an entity and then look at a major galaxy with its billions of stars as an entity? Can I continue this extrapolation in this way?

RA: I am Ra. You can, but not within the framework of third-density space/time.

Let us attempt to speak upon this interesting subject. In your space/time, you and your peoples are the parents of that which is in the womb. The Earth, as you call it, is ready to be born, and the delivery is not going smoothly. When this entity has become born, it will be instinct with the social memory complex of its parents which have become fourth-density positive. In this density there is a broader view.

You may begin to see your relationship to the Logos or sun with which you are most intimately associated. This is not the relationship of parent to child but of Creator, that is Logos, to Creator that is the mind/body/spirit complex, as Logos. When this realization occurs, you may then widen the field of "eyeshot," if you will, infinitely recognizing parts of the Logos throughout the one infinite creation and feeling, with the roots of mind informing the intuition, the parents aiding their planets in evolution in reaches vast and unknown in the creation, for this process occurs many, many times in the evolution of the creation as an whole.

QUESTIONER: The Wanderer goes through a forgetting process. You mentioned that those who have both third- and fourth-density bodies activated now do not have the forgetting that the Wanderer has. I was just wondering if, say, a sixth-density Wanderer were here with a third-density body activated, would he have gone through a forgetting that was in sections, shall I say, a forgetting of fourth, fifth, and sixth densities, and if he were to have his fourth-density body activated, then he would have a partial additional memory and then another partial memory if his fifth-density body were activated and full memory if he had his sixth-density body activated? Does this make any sense?

RA: I am Ra. No.

QUESTIONER: Thank you. The forgetting process was puzzling me because you said that the fourth-density activated people who were here who had been harvested did not have the same forgetting problem. Could you tell me why the Wanderer loses his memory?

RA: I am Ra. The reason is twofold. First, the genetic properties of the connection between the mind/body/spirit complex and the cellular structure of the body is different for third density than for third/fourth density.

Secondly, the free will of third-density entities needs be

preserved. Thus, Wanderers volunteer for third-density genetic or DNA connections to the mind/body/spirit complex. The forgetting process can be penetrated to the extent of the Wanderer remembering what it is and why it is upon the planetary sphere. However, it would be an infringement if Wanderers penetrated the forgetting so far as to activate the more dense bodies and thus be able to live, shall we say, in a godlike manner. This would not be proper for those who have chosen to serve.

The new fourth-density entities which are becoming able to demonstrate various newer abilities are doing so as a result of the present experience, not as a result of memory. There are always a few exceptions, and we ask your forgiveness for constant barrages of over-generalization.

QUESTIONER: I don't know if this question is related to what I am trying to get at or not. I'll ask it and see what results. You mentioned in speaking of the pyramids the resonating chamber was used so that the adept could meet the self. Would you explain what you meant by that?

RA: I am Ra. One meets the self in the center or deeps of the being. The so-called resonating chamber may be likened unto the symbology of the burial and resurrection of the body, wherein the entity dies to self and, through this confrontation of apparent loss and realization of essential gain, is transmuted into a new and risen being.

QUESTIONER: Could I make the analogy of in this apparent death of losing the desires that are the illusory, common desires of third density and gaining desires of total service to others?

RA: I am Ra. You are perceptive. This was the purpose and intent of this chamber, as well as forming a necessary portion of the King's Chamber position's effectiveness.

QUESTIONER: Can you tell me what this chamber did to the entity to create this awareness in him?

RA: I am Ra. This chamber worked upon the mind and the body. The mind was affected by sensory deprivation and the archetypical reactions to being buried alive with no possibility of extricating the self. The body was affected both by the mind configuration and by the electrical and piezoelectrical properties of the materials which were used in the construction of the resonating chamber.

This will be the last full query of this working. May we ask if there are any brief queries at this time?

QUESTIONER: Is there anything that we can do to make the instrument more comfortable or to improve the contact?

RA: I am Ra. We feel that the instrument is well supported and that all is well. We caution each regarding this instrument's distortions towards pain, for it dislikes sharing these expressions, but as support group this instrument subconsciously accepts each entity's aid. All is in alignment. You are conscientious. We thank you for this. I am Ra. I leave you, my friends, rejoicing in the love and the light of the One Infinite Creator. Go forth, therefore, glorying in the power and in the peace of the One Infinite Creator. Adonai.

Session 66,
August 12, 1981

RA: I am Ra. I greet you in the love and in the light of the One Infinite Creator. We communicate now.

QUESTIONER: I would like to investigate the mechanism of healing using the crystallized healer. I am going to make a statement, and I would appreciate it if you would correct my thinking.

It seems to me that once the healer has become properly balanced and unblocked with respect to energy centers, it is possible for him to act in some way as a collector and focuser of light in a way analogous to the way a pyramid works, collecting light through the left hand and emitting it through the right; this then, somehow, penetrating the first and seventh chakras' vibratory envelop of the body and allowing for the realignment of energy centers of the entity to be healed. I'm quite sure that I'm not completely correct on this, and possibly considerably off. Could you rearrange my thinking so that it makes sense?

RA: I am Ra. You are correct in your assumption that the crystallized healer is analogous to the pyramidal action of the King's Chamber position. There are a few adjustments we might suggest.

Firstly, the energy which is used is brought into the field complex of the healer by the outstretched hand used in a polarized sense. However, this energy circulates through the various points of energy to the base of the spine and, to a certain extent, the feet, thus coming through the main energy centers of the healer, spiraling through the feet, turning at the red energy center towards a spiral at the yellow energy center, and passing through the green energy center in a microcosm of the King's Chamber energy configuration of prana; this then continuing for the third spiral through the blue energy center and being sent therefrom through the gateway back to intelligent infinity.

It is from the green center that the healing prana moves into the polarized healing right hand and therefrom to the one to be healed.

We may note that there are some who use the yellow-ray configuration to transfer energy, and this may be done, but the effects are questionable and, with regard to the relationship between the healer, the healing energy, and the seeker, questionable due to the propensity for the seeker to continue requiring such energy transfers without any true healing taking place in the absence of the healer due to the lack of penetration of the armoring shell of which you spoke.

QUESTIONER: A Wanderer who has an origin from fifth or sixth density can attempt such a healing and have little or no results. Can you tell me what the Wanderer has lost and why it is necessary for him to regain certain balances and abilities for him to perfect his healing ability?

RA: I am Ra. You may see the Wanderer as the infant attempting to verbalize the sound complexes of your peoples. The memory of the ability to communicate is within the infant's undeveloped mind complex, but the ability to practice or manifest this, called speech, is not immediately forthcoming due to the limitations of the mind/body/spirit complex it has chosen to be a part of in this experience.

So it is with the Wanderer, which, remembering the ease with which adjustments can be made in the home density, yet still having entered third density, cannot manifest that memory due to the limitation of the chosen experience. The chances of a Wanderer being able to heal in third density are only more than those native to this density because the desire to serve may be stronger and this method of service chosen.

QUESTIONER: What about the ones with the dual type of activated third- and fourth-density bodies, harvested from other third-density planets? Are they able to heal using the techniques that we have discussed?

RA: I am Ra. In many cases this is so, but as beginners of fourth density, the desire may not be present.

QUESTIONER: I'm assuming, then, that we have a Wanderer with the desire attempting to learn the techniques of healing while, shall I say, trapped in third density. He then, it seems to me, is primarily concerned with the balancing and unblocking of the energy centers. Am I correct in this assumption?

RA: I am Ra. This is correct. Only insofar as the healer has become balanced may it be a channel for the balancing of an other-self. The healing is first practiced upon the self, if we may say this, in another way.

QUESTIONER: Now as the healer approaches an other-self to do the healing, we have a situation where the other-self has, through programming of catalyst, possibly created a condition which is viewed as a condition needing healing. What is the situation and what are the ramifications of the healer acting upon the condition of programmed catalyst to bring about healing? Am I correct in assuming that in doing this healing, the programmed catalyst is useful to the one to be healed in that the one to be healed then becomes aware of what it wished to become aware of in programming the catalyst? Is this correct?

RA: I am Ra. Your thinking cannot be said to be completely incorrect but shows a rigidity which is not apparent in the flow of the experiential use of catalyst.

The role of the healer is to offer an opportunity for realignment or aid in realignment of either energy centers or some connection between the energies of mind and body, spirit and mind, or spirit and body. This latter is very rare.

The seeker will then have the reciprocal opportunity to accept a novel view of the self, a variant arrangement of patterns of energy influx. If the entity, at any level, desires to remain in the configuration of distortion which seems to need healing, it will do so. If, upon the other hand, the seeker chooses the novel configuration, it is done through free will.

This is one great difficulty with other forms of energy transfer in that they do not carry through the process of free will, as this process is not native to yellow ray.

QUESTIONER: What is the difference, philosophically, between a mind/body/spirit complex healing itself through mental, shall I say, configuration and it being healed by a healer?

RA: I am Ra. You have a misconception. The healer does not heal. The crystallized healer is a channel for intelligent energy which offers an opportunity to an entity that it might heal itself.

In no case is there another description of healing. Therefore, there is no difference as long as the healer never approaches one whose request for aid has not come to it previously. This is also true of the more conventional healers of your culture, and if these healers could but fully realize that they are responsible only for offering the opportunity of healing, and not for the healing, many of these entities would feel an enormous load of misconceived responsibility fall from them.

QUESTIONER: Then in seeking healing, a mind/body/spirit complex would then be seeking in some cases a source of gathered and focused light energy. This source could be another mind/body/spirit complex sufficiently crystallized for this purpose or the pyramid shape, or possibly something else. Is this correct?

RA: I am Ra. These are some of the ways an entity may seek healing. Yes.

QUESTIONER: Could you tell me the other ways an entity could seek healing?

RA: I am Ra. Perhaps the greatest healer is within the self and may be tapped with continued meditation as we have suggested. The many forms of healing available to your peoples . . . each have virtue and may be deemed appropriate by any seeker who wishes to alter the physical complex distortions or some connection between the various portions of the mind/body/spirit complex thereby.

QUESTIONER: I have observed many activities known as psychic surgery in the area of the Philippine Islands. It was my assumption that these healers are providing what I would call a training aid or a way of creating a reconfiguration of the mind of the patient to be healed as the relatively naive patient observes the action of the healer in seeing the materialized blood etc., and reconfigures the roots of mind to believe, you might say, the healing is done, and, therefore, heals himself. Is this analysis that I have made correct?

RA: I am Ra. This is correct. We may speak slightly further on the type of opportunity.

There are times when the malcondition to be altered is without emotional, mental, or spiritual interest to the entity and is merely that which has, perhaps by chance genetic arrangement, occurred. In these cases, that which is apparently dematerialized will remain dematerialized and may be observed as so by any observer. The malcondition which has an emotional, mental, or spiritual charge is likely not to remain dematerialized in the sense of the showing of the objective referent to an observer. However, if the opportunity has been taken by the seeker, the apparent malcondition of the physical complex will be at variance with the actual health, as you call this distortion, of the seeker and the lack of experiencing the distortions which the objective referent would suggest still held sway.

For instance, in this instrument the removal of three small cysts was the removal of material having no interest to the entity. Thus these growths remained dematerialized after the so-called psychic surgery experience. In other psychic surgery, the kidneys of this instrument were carefully offered a new configuration of beingness which the entity embraced. However, this particular portion of the mind/body/spirit complex carried a great deal of emotional, mental, and spiritual charge due to this distorted functioning being the cause of great illness in a certain configuration of events which culminated in this entity's conscious decision to be of service. Therefore, any objective scanning of this entity's renal complex would indicate the rather extreme dysfunctional aspect which it showed previous to the psychic surgery experience, as you call it.

The key is not in the continuation of the dematerialization of distortion to the eye of the beholder but rather lies in the choosing of the newly materialized configuration which exists in time/space.

QUESTIONER: Would you explain that last comment about the configuration in time/space?

RA: I am Ra. Healing is done in the time/space portion of the mind/body/spirit complex, is adopted by the form-making or etheric body, and is then given to the space/time physical illusion for use in the activated yellow mind/body/spirit complex. It is the adoption of the configuration which you call health by the etheric body in time/space which is the key to what you call health, not any event which occurs in space/time. In the process you may see the transdimensional aspect of what you call will, for it is the will, the seeking, the desire of the entity which causes the indigo body to use the novel configuration and to reform the body which exists in space/time. This is done in an instant and may be said to operate without regard to time. We may note that in the healing of very young children, there is often an apparent healing by the healer in which the young entity has no part. This is never so, for the mind/body/spirit complex in time/space is always capable of willing the distortions it chooses for experience, no matter what the apparent age, as you call it, of the entity.

QUESTIONER: Is this desire and will that operates through to the time/space section a function only of the entity who is healed, or is it also the function of the healer, the crystallized healer?

RA: I am Ra. May we take this opportunity to say that this is the activity of the Creator. To specifically answer your query, the crystallized healer has no will. It offers an opportunity without attachment to the outcome, for it is aware that all is one and that the Creator is knowing Itself.

QUESTIONER: Then the desire must be strong in the mind/body/spirit complex who seeks healing to be healed in order for the healing to occur? Is this correct?

RA: I am Ra. This is correct on one level or another. An entity may not consciously seek healing and yet subconsciously be aware of the need to experience the new set of distortions which result from healing. Similarly, an entity may consciously desire healing greatly but within the being, at some level, find some cause whereby certain configurations which seem quite distorted are, in fact, at that level, considered appropriate.

QUESTIONER: I assume that the reason for assuming the distortions appropriate would be that these distortions would aid the entity in its reaching its ultimate objective, which is a movement along the path of evolution in the desired polarity. Is this correct?

RA: I am Ra. This is correct.

QUESTIONER: Then an entity who becomes aware of his polarization with respect to service to others might find a paradoxical situation in the case where it was unable to fully serve because of distortions chosen to reach the understanding it has reached. At this point it would seem that the entity who was aware of the mechanism might, through meditation, understand the necessary mental configuration for alleviating the physical distortion so that it could be of greater service to others. At this particular nexus, am I correct in this thinking?

RA: I am Ra. You are correct, although we might note that there are often complex reasons for the programming of a distorted physical complex pattern. In any case, meditation is always an aid to knowing the self.

QUESTIONER: Is a vertical positioning of the spine useful or helpful in the meditative procedure?

RA: I am Ra. It is somewhat helpful.

QUESTIONER: Would you please list the polarities within the body which are related to the balancing of the energy centers of the various bodies of the unmanifested entity?

RA: I am Ra. In this question there lies a great deal of thought, which we appreciate. It is possible that the question itself may serve to aid meditations upon this particular subject. Each unmanifested self is unique. The basic polarities have to do with the balanced vibratory rates and relationships between the first three energy centers and, to a lesser extent, each of the other energy centers.

May we answer more specifically?

QUESTIONER: Possibly in the next session we will expand on that.

I would like to ask the second question. What are the structure and contents of the archetypical mind, and how does the archetypical mind function in informing the intuition and conscious mind of an individual mind/body/spirit complex?

RA: I am Ra. You must realize that we offered these concepts to you so that you might grow in your own knowledge of the self through the consideration of them. We would prefer, especially for this latter query, to listen to the observations upon this subject which the student of these exercises may make, and then suggest further avenues of the refinement of these inquiries. We feel we might be of more aid in this way.

QUESTIONER: You mentioned that an energizing spiral is emitted from the top of any pyramid and that you could benefit by placing this under the head for a period of thirty minutes or less. Can you tell me how this third spiral is helpful and what help it gives the entity who is receiving it?

RA: I am Ra. There are substances which you may ingest which cause the physical vehicle to experience distortions towards an increase of energy. These substances are crude, working rather roughly upon the body complex increasing the flow of adrenalin.

The vibration offered by the energizing spiral of the pyramid is such that each cell, both in space/time and in time/space, is charged as if hooked to your electricity. The keenness of mind, the physical and sexual energy of body, and the attunement of will of spirit are all touched by this energizing influence. It may be used in any of these ways. It is possible to overcharge a battery, and this is the cause of our cautioning any who use such pyramidal energies to remove the pyramid after a charge has been received.

QUESTIONER: Is there a best material or an optimal size for this small pyramid to go beneath the head?

RA: I am Ra. Given that the proportions are such as to develop the spirals in the Giza pyramid, the most appropriate size for use beneath the head is an overall height small enough to make placing it under the cushion of the head a comfortable thing.

QUESTIONER: There's no best material?

RA: I am Ra. There are better materials which are, in your system of barter, quite dear. They are not that much better than substances which we have mentioned before. The only incorrect substances would be the baser metals.

QUESTIONER: You mentioned the problems with the action in the King's Chamber of the Giza-type pyramid. I am assuming if we used the same geometrical configuration that is used in the pyramid at Giza, this would be perfectly all right for the pyramid placed beneath the head, since we wouldn't be using the King's Chamber radiations but only the third spiral from the top, and I'm also asking if it would be better to use a 60° apex angle than the larger apex angle? Would it provide a better energy source?

RA: I am Ra. For energy through the apex angle the Giza pyramid offers an excellent model. Simply be sure the pyramid is so small that there is no entity small enough to crawl inside it.

QUESTIONER: I assume that this energy, then, this spiraling light energy, is somehow absorbed by the energy field of the body. Is this somehow connected to the indigo energy center? Am I correct in this guess?

RA: I am Ra. This is incorrect. The properties of this energy are such as to move within the field of the physical complex and irradiate each cell of the space/time body and, as this is done, irradiate also the time/space equivalent which is closely aligned with the space/time yellow-ray body. This is not a function of the etheric body or of free will. This is a radiation much like your sun's rays. Thus it should be used with care.

QUESTIONER: How many applications of thirty minutes or less during a diurnal time period would be appropriate?

RA: I am Ra. In most cases, no more than one. In a few cases, especially where the energy will be used for spiritual work, experimentation with two shorter periods might be possible, but any feeling of sudden weariness would be a sure sign that the entity had been over-radiated.

QUESTIONER: Can this energy help in any way as far as healing of physical distortions?

RA: I am Ra. There is no application for direct healing using this energy, although, if used in conjunction with meditation, it may offer to a certain percentage of entities some aid in meditation. In most cases it is most helpful in alleviating weariness and in the stimulation of physical or sexual activity.

QUESTIONER: In a transition from third to fourth density, we have two other possibilities other than the type that we are experiencing now. We have the possibility of a totally positively polarized harvest and the possibility of a totally negatively polarized harvest that I understand have occurred elsewhere in the universe many times. When there is a totally negatively polarized harvest, the whole planet that has negatively polarized makes the transition from third to fourth density. Does the planet have the experience of the distortion of disease that this planet now experiences prior to that transition?

RA: I am Ra. You are perceptive. The negative harvest is one of intense disharmony, and the planet will express this.

QUESTIONER: The planet has a certain set of conditions in late third density, and then the conditions are different in early fourth density. Could you give me an example of a negatively polarized planet and the conditions in late third density and early fourth density so that I can see how they change?

RA: I am Ra. The vibrations from third to fourth density change on a negatively oriented planet precisely as they do upon a positively oriented planet. With fourth-density negative comes many abilities and possibilities of which you are familiar. The fourth density is more dense, and it is far more difficult to hide the true vibrations of the mind/body/spirit complex. This enables fourth-density negatives, as well as positives, the chance to form social memory complexes. It enables negatively oriented entities the opportunity for a different set of parameters with which to show their power over others and to be of service to the self. The conditions are the same as far as the vibrations are concerned.

QUESTIONER: I was concerned about the amount of physical distortions, disease, and that sort of thing in third-density negative just before harvesting, and in fourth-density negative just after harvesting or in transition. What are the conditions of the physical problems, disease, etc. in late third-density negative?

RA: I am Ra. Each planetary experience is unique. The problems, shall we say, of bellicose actions are more likely to be of pressing concern to late third-density negative entities than the Earth's reactions to negativity of the planetary mind, for it is often by such warlike attitudes on a global scale that the necessary negative polarization is achieved.

As fourth density occurs, there is a new planet and new physical vehicle system gradually expressing itself, and the parameters of bellicose actions become those of thought rather than manifested weapons.

QUESTIONER: Well, then, is physical disease and illness as we know it on this planet rather widespread on a third-density negative planet before harvest into fourth-density negative?

RA: I am Ra. Physical complex distortions of which you speak are likely to be less found as fourth-density negative begins to be a probable choice of harvest due to the extreme interest in the self which characterizes the harvestable third-density negative entity. Much more care is taken of the physical body, as well as much more discipline being offered to the self mentally. This is an orientation of great self-interest and self-discipline. There are still instances of the types of disease which are associated with the mind complex distortions of negative emotions such as anger. However, in a harvestable entity these emotional distortions are much more likely to be used as catalyst in an expressive and destructive sense as regards the object of anger.

QUESTIONER: I am trying to understand the way that disease and bodily distortions are generated with respect to polarities, both positive and negative. It seems that they are generated in some way to create the split of polarization, that they have a function in creating the original polarization that occurs in third density. Is this correct?

RA: I am Ra. This is not precisely correct. Distortions of the bodily or mental complex are those distortions found in beings which have need of experiences which aid in polarization. These polarizations may be those of entities which have already chosen the path or polarization to be followed.

It is more likely for positively oriented individuals to be experiencing distortions within the physical complex due to the lack of consuming interest in the self and the emphasis on service to others. Moreover, in an unpolarized entity, catalyst of the physical distortion nature will be generated at random. The hopeful result is, as you say, the original choice of polarity. Oftentimes this choice is not made but the catalyst continues to be generated. In the negatively oriented individual, the physical body is likely to be more carefully tended and the mind disciplined against physical distortion.

QUESTIONER: This planet, to me, seems to be what I would call a cesspool of distortions. This includes all diseases and malfunctions of the physical body in general. It would seem to me that, on the average, this planet would be very, very high on the list if we just took the overall amount of these problems. Am I correct in this assumption?

RA: I am Ra. We will review previous material.

Catalyst is offered to the entity. If it is not used by the mind complex, it will then filter through to the body complex and manifest as some form of physical distortion. The more efficient the use of catalyst, the less physical distortion to be found.

There are, in the case of those you call Wanderers, not only a congenital difficulty in dealing with the third-density vibratory patterns but also a recollection, however dim, that these distortions are not necessary or usual in the home vibration.

We overgeneralize as always, for there are many cases of pre-incarnative decisions which result in physical or mental limitations and distortions, but we feel that you are addressing the question of widespread distortions towards misery of one form or another. Indeed, on some third-density planetary spheres, catalyst has been used more efficiently. In the case of your planetary sphere, there is much inefficient use of catalyst and, therefore, much physical distortion.

We have enough energy available for one query at this time.

QUESTIONER: Then I will ask if there is anything that we can do to make the instrument more comfortable or to improve the contact?

RA: I am Ra. Continue as always in love. All is well. You are conscientious.

I am Ra. I leave you in the love and in the light of the One Infinite Creator. Go forth rejoicing in the power and the peace of the One Infinite Creator. Adonai.

Session 67,
August 15, 1981

RA: I am Ra and I greet you in the love and in the light of the One Infinite Creator. I communicate now.

QUESTIONER: Could you first give us the instrument's condition, please?

RA: I am Ra. The vital energies are more closely aligned with the amount of distortion normal to this entity than previous asking showed. The physical complex energy levels are somewhat less strong than at the previous asking. The psychic attack component is exceptionally strong at this particular nexus.

QUESTIONER: Can you describe what you call the psychic attack component, and tell me why it is strong at this particular time?

RA: I am Ra. We shall elect not to retrace previously given information but rather elect to note that the psychic attack upon this instrument is at a constant level as long as it continues in this particular service.

Variations towards the distortion of intensity of attack occur due to the opportunities presented by the entity in any weakness. At this particular nexus the entity has been dealing with the distortion which you call pain for some time, as you call this measurement, and this has a cumulatively weakening effect upon physical energy levels. This creates a particularly favorable target of opportunity, and the entity of which we have previously spoken has taken this opportunity to attempt to be of service in its own way. It is fortunate for the ongoing vitality of this contact that the instrument is a strong-willed entity with little tendency towards the distortion, called among your peoples hysteria, since the dizzying effects of this attack have been constant and at times disruptive for several of your diurnal periods.

However, this particular entity is adapting well to the situation without undue distortions towards fear. Thus the psychic attack is not successful but does have some draining influence upon the instrument.

QUESTIONER: I will ask if I am correct in this analysis. We would consider that the entity making this so-called attack is offering its service with respect to its distortion in our polarized condition now so that we may more fully appreciate its polarity, and we are appreciative of the fact and thank this entity for its attempt to serve our One Creator in bringing to us knowledge in, shall I say, a more complete sense. Is this correct?

RA: I am Ra. There is no correctness or incorrectness to your statement. It is an expression of a positively polarized and balanced view of negatively polarized actions which has the effect of debilitating the strength of the negatively polarized actions.

QUESTIONER: We would welcome the services of the entity who uses, and I will use the misnomer "attack," since I do not consider this an attack but an offering of service, and we welcome this offering of service, but we would be able, I believe, to make more full use of the services if they were not physically disabling the instrument in a minor way. For with a greater physical ability she would be able to more appreciate the service. We would greatly appreciate it if the service was carried on in some manner which we could welcome in even greater love than at present. This, I assume, would be some service that would not include the dizzying effect.

I am trying to understand the mechanism of this service of the entity that seems to be constantly with us, and I am trying to understand the origin of this entity and his mechanism of greeting us. I will make a statement that will probably be incorrect but is a function of my extreme limitation in understanding the other densities and how they work. I am guessing that this particular entity is a member of the Orion Confederation and is possibly incarnate in a body of the appropriate density, which I assume is the fifth, and by mental discipline he has been able to project a portion or all of his consciousness to our coordinates, you might say, here, and it is possibly one of the seven bodies that make up his mind/body/spirit complex. Is any of this correct, and can you tell me what is correct or incorrect about this statement?

RA: I am Ra. The statement is substantially correct.

QUESTIONER: Would you rather not give me information as to the specifics of my statement?

RA: I am Ra. We did not perceive a query in further detail. Please requestion.

QUESTIONER: Which body in respect to the colors does the entity use to travel to us?

RA: I am Ra. This query is not particularly simple to answer due to the transdimensional nature, not only of space/time to time/space but from density to density. The time/space light or fifth-density body is used while the space/time fifth-density body remains in fifth density. The assumption that the consciousness is projected thereby is correct. The assumption that this conscious vehicle attached to the space/time fifth-density physical complex is that vehicle which works in this particular service is correct.

QUESTIONER: I undoubtedly will ask several uninformed questions. However, I was trying to understand certain concepts that have to do with the illusion, I shall say, of polarization that seems to exist at certain density levels in the creation and how the mechanism of the interaction of consciousness works. It seems to me that the fifth-density entity is attracted in some way to our group by the polarization of this group, which acts somehow as a beacon to this entity. Am I correct?

RA: I am Ra. This is, in substance, correct, but the efforts of this entity are put forward only reluctantly. The usual attempts upon positively oriented entities or groups of entities are made, as we have said, by minions of the fifth-density Orion leaders; these are fourth density. The normal gambit of such fourth-density attack is the tempting of the entity or group of entities away from total polarization towards service to others and toward the aggrandizement of self or of social organizations with which the self identifies. In the case of this particular group, each was given a full range of temptations to cease being of service to each other and to the One Infinite Creator. Each entity declined these choices and instead continued with no significant deviation from the desire for a purely other-self service orientation. At this point one of the fifth-density entities overseeing such detuning processes determined that it would be necessary to terminate the group by what you might call magical means, as you understand ritual magic. We have previously discussed the potential for the removal of one of this group by such attack and have noted that by far the most vulnerable is the instrument due to its pre-incarnative physical complex distortions.

QUESTIONER: In order for this group to remain fully in service to the Creator, since we recognize this fifth-density entity as the Creator, we must also attempt to serve in any way we can, this entity. Is it possible for you to communicate to us the desires of this entity if there are any in addition to us simply ceasing the reception and dissemination of that which you provide?

RA: I am Ra. This entity has two desires. The first and foremost is to, shall we say, misplace one or more of this group in a negative orientation so that it may choose to be of service along the path of service to self. The objective which must precede this is the termination of the physical complex viability of one of this group while the mind/body/spirit complex is within a controllable configuration. May we say that although we of Ra have limited understanding, it is our belief that sending this entity love and light, which each of the group is doing, is the most helpful catalyst which the group may offer to this entity.

QUESTIONER: We find a—I'm sorry. Please continue.

RA: I am Ra. We were about to note that this entity has been as neutralized as possible in our estimation by this love offering, and thus its continued presence is perhaps the understandable limit for each polarity of the various views of service which each may render to the other.

QUESTIONER: We have a paradoxical situation with respect to serving the Creator. We have requests, from those whom we serve in this density, for Ra's information. However, we have requests from another density not to disseminate this information. We have portions of the Creator requesting two seemingly opposite activities of this group. It would be very helpful if we could reach the condition of full service in such a way that we were by every thought and activity serving the Creator to the very best of our ability. Is it possible for you to solve, or for the fifth-density entity who offers its service to solve, this paradox which I have observed?

RA: I am Ra. It is quite possible.

QUESTIONER: Then how could we solve this paradox?

RA: I am Ra. Consider, if you will, that you have no ability not to serve the Creator since all is the Creator. You do not have merely two opposite requests for information or lack of information from this source if you listen carefully to those whose voices you may hear. This is all one voice to which you resonate upon a certain frequency. This frequency determines your choice of service to the One Creator. As it happens, this group's vibratory patterns and those of Ra are compatible and enable us to speak through this instrument with your support. This is a function of free will.

A portion, seemingly of the Creator, rejoices at your choice to question us regarding the evolution of spirit. A seemingly separate portion would wish for multitudinous answers to a great range of queries of a specific nature. Another seemingly separate group of your peoples would wish this correspondence through this instrument to cease, feeling it to be of a negative nature. Upon the many other planes of existence, there are those whose every fiber rejoices at your service, and those such as the entity of whom you have been speaking which wish only to terminate the life upon the third-density plane of this instrument. All are the Creator. There is one vast panoply of biases and distortions, colors and hues, in an unending pattern. In the case of those with whom you, as entities and as a group, are not in resonance, you wish them love, light, peace, joy, and bid them well. No more than this can you do for your portion of the Creator is as it is, and your experience and offering of experience, to be valuable, needs be more and more a perfect representation of who you truly are. Could you, then, serve a negative entity by offering the instrument's life? It is unlikely that you would find this a true service. Thus you may see in many cases the loving balance being achieved, the love being offered, light being sent, and the service of the service-to-self-oriented entity gratefully acknowledged while being rejected as not being useful in your journey at this time. Thus you serve One Creator without paradox.

QUESTIONER: This particular entity, by his service, is able to create a dizzying effect on the instrument. Could you describe the mechanics of such a service?

RA: I am Ra. This instrument, in the small times of its incarnation, had the distortion in the area of the otic complex of many infections, which caused great difficulties at this small age, as you would call it. The scars of these distortions remain, and indeed that which you call the sinus system remains distorted. Thus the entity works with these distortions to produce a loss of the balance and a slight lack of ability to use the optic apparatus.

QUESTIONER: I was wondering about the magical, shall I say, principles used by the fifth-density entity giving this service and his ability to give it. Why is he able to utilize these particular physical distortions from the philosophical or magical point of view?

RA: I am Ra. This entity is able to, shall we say, penetrate in time/space configuration the field of this particular entity. It has moved through the quarantine without any vehicle and thus has been more able to escape detection by the net of the Guardians.

This is the great virtue of the magical working whereby consciousness is sent forth essentially without vehicle as light. The light would work instantly upon an untuned individual by suggestion; that is, the stepping out in front of the traffic because the suggestion is that there is no traffic. This entity, as each in this group, is enough disciplined in the ways of love and light that it is not suggestible to any great extent. However, there is a predisposition of the physical complex which this entity is making maximal use of as regards the instrument, hoping, for instance, by means of increasing dizziness to cause the instrument to fall or to indeed walk in front of your traffic because of impaired vision.

The magical principles, shall we say, may be loosely translated into your system of magic, whereby symbols are used and traced and visualized in order to develop the power of the light.

QUESTIONER: Do you mean then that this fifth-density entity visualizes certain symbols? I am assuming that these symbols are of a nature where their continued use would have some power or charge. Am I correct?

RA: I am Ra. You are correct. In fifth density, light is as visible a tool as your pencil's writing.

QUESTIONER: Then am I correct in assuming that this entity configures the light into symbology; that is, what we would call a physical presence? Is this correct?

RA: I am Ra. This is incorrect. The light is used to create a sufficient purity of environment for the entity to place its consciousness in a carefully created light vehicle which then uses the tools of light to do its working. The will and presence are those of the entity doing the working.

QUESTIONER: The fifth-density entity you mentioned penetrated the quarantine. Was this done through one of the windows or was this because of his, shall I say, magical ability?

RA: I am Ra. This was done through a very slight window which less magically oriented entities or groups could not have used to advantage.

QUESTIONER: The main point with this line of questioning has to do with the first distortion and the fact that this window exists. Was this a portion of the random effect, and are we experiencing the same type of balancing in receiving the offerings of this entity as the planet in general receives because of the window effect?

RA: I am Ra. This is precisely correct. As the planetary sphere accepts more highly evolved positive entities or groups with information to offer, the same opportunity must be offered to similarly wise negatively oriented entities or groups.

QUESTIONER: Then we experience in this seeming difficulty the wisdom of the first distortion and for that reason must fully accept that which we experience. This is my personal view. Is it congruent with Ra's?

RA: I am Ra. In our view we would perhaps go further in expressing appreciation of this opportunity. This is an intensive opportunity in that it is quite marked in its effects, both actual and potential, and as it affects the instrument's distortions towards pain and other difficulties such as the dizziness, it enables the instrument to continuously choose to serve others and to serve the Creator.

Similarly it offers a continual opportunity for each in the group to express support under more distorted or difficult circumstances of the other-self experiencing the brunt, shall we say, of this attack, thus being able to demonstrate the love and light of the Infinite Creator and, furthermore, choosing working by working to continue to serve as messengers for this information which we attempt to offer and to serve the Creator thereby.

Thus the opportunities are quite noticeable, as well as the distortions caused by this circumstance.

QUESTIONER: Thank you. Is this so-called attack offered to myself and [name] as well as the instrument?

RA: I am Ra. This is correct.

QUESTIONER: I personally have felt no effect that I am aware of. Is it possible for you to tell me how we are offered this service?

RA: I am Ra. The questioner has been offered the service of doubting the self and of becoming disheartened over various distortions of the personal nature. This entity has not chosen to use these opportunities, and the Orion entity has basically ceased to be interested in maintaining constant surveillance of this entity.

The scribe is under constant surveillance and has been offered numerous opportunities for the intensification of the mental/emotional distortions and in some cases the connection matrices between mental/emotional complexes and the physical complex counterpart. As this entity has become aware of these attacks, it has become much less pervious to them. This is the particular cause of the great intensification and constancy of the surveillance of the instrument, for it is the weak link due to factors beyond its control within this incarnation.

QUESTIONER: Is it within the first distortion to tell me why the instrument experienced so many physical distortions during the new times of its physical incarnation?

RA: I am Ra. This is correct.

QUESTIONER: In that case, can you answer me as to why the instrument experienced so much during its early years?

RA: I am Ra. We were affirming the correctness of your assumption that such answers would be breaking the Way of Confusion. It is not appropriate for such answers to be laid out as a table spread for dinner. It is appropriate that the complexes of opportunity involved be contemplated.

QUESTIONER: Then there is no other service at this time that we can offer that fifth-density entity of the Orion group who is constantly with us. As I see it now from your point of view, there is nothing that we can do for him? Is this correct?

RA: I am Ra. This is correct. There is great humor in your attempt to be of polarized service to the opposite polarity. There is a natural difficulty in doing so, since what you consider service is considered by this entity nonservice. As you send this entity love and light and wish it well, it loses its polarity and needs to regroup.

Thus it would not consider your service as such. On the other hand, if you allowed it to be of service by removing this instrument from your midst, you might perhaps perceive this as not being of service. You have here a balanced and polarized view of the Creator; two services offered, mutually rejected, and in a state of equilibrium in which free will is preserved and each allowed to go upon its own path of experiencing the One Infinite Creator.

QUESTIONER: Thank you. In closing that part of the discussion I would just say that if there is anything that we can do that is within our ability—and I understand that there are many things such as the ones that you just mentioned that are not within our ability—that we could do for this particular entity, if you would in the future communicate its requests to us, we will at least consider them because we would like to serve in every respect. Is this agreeable to you?

RA: I am Ra. We perceive that we have not been able to clarify your service versus its desire for service. You need, in our humble opinion, to look at the humor of the situation and relinquish your desire to serve where no service is requested. The magnet will attract or repel. Glory in the strength of your polarization and allow others of opposite polarity to similarly do so, seeing the great humor of this polarity and its complications in view of the unification in sixth density of these two paths.

QUESTIONER: Thank you very much. I have a statement here that I will have you comment on for accuracy or inaccuracy. In general, the archetypical mind is a representation of facets of the One Infinite Creation. The Father archetype corresponds to the male or positive aspect of electromagnetic energy and is active, creative, and radiant, as is our local sun. The Mother archetype corresponds to the female or negative aspect of electromagnetic energy and is receptive or magnetic, as is our Earth as it receives the sun's rays and brings forth life via third-density fertility. The Prodigal Son or the Fool archetype corresponds to every entity who seems to have strayed from unity and seeks to return to the One Infinite Creator. The Devil archetype represents the illusion of the material world and the appearance of evil but is more accurately the provider of catalyst for the growth of each entity within the third-density illusion. The Magician, Saint, Healer, or Adept corresponds to the Higher Self and, because of the balance within its energy centers, pierces the illusion to contact intelligent infinity and thereby demonstrates mastery of the catalyst of third density. The archetype of Death symbolizes the transition of an entity from the yellow-ray body to the green-ray body either temporarily between incarnations or, more permanently, at harvest.

Each archetype presents an aspect of the One Infinite Creation to teach the individual mind/body/spirit complex according to the calling or the electromagnetic configuration of mind of the entity. Teaching is done via the intuition. With the proper seeking or mind configuration, the power of will uses the spirit as a shuttle to contact the appropriate archetypical aspect necessary for the teach/learning. In the same way, each of the other informers of intuition are contacted. They are hierarchical and proceed from the entity's own subconscious mind, to group or planetary mind, to guides, to Higher Self, to archetypical mind, to cosmic mind or intelligent infinity. Each is contacted by the spirit, serving as shuttle according to the harmonized electromagnetic configuration of the seeker's mind and the information sought.

Would you please comment on the accuracy of these observations and correct any errors and fill in any omissions?

RA: I am Ra. The entity has been using transferred energy for most of this session due to its depleted physical levels. We shall begin this rather complex answer, which is interesting, but do not expect to finish it. Those portions which we do not respond to we ask that you requestion us on at a working in your future.

QUESTIONER: Perhaps it would be better to start the next session with the answer to this question. Would that be appropriate, or is the energy already fixed?

RA: I am Ra. The energy is as always allotted. The choice, as always, is yours.

QUESTIONER: In that case, continue.

RA: I am Ra. Perhaps the first item we shall address is the concept of the spirit used as a shuttle between the roots and the trunk of mind. This is a misapprehension, and we shall allow the questioner to consider the function of the spirit further, for in working with the mind we are working within one complex and have not yet attempted to penetrate intelligent infinity. It is well said that archetypes are portions of the One Infinite Creator or aspects of its face. It is, however, far better to realize that the archetypes, while constant in the complex of generative energies offered, do not give the same yield of these complexes to any two seekers. Each seeker will experience each archetype in the characteristics within the complex of the archetype which are most important to it. An example of this would be the observation of the questioner that the Fool is described in such and such a way. One great aspect of this archetype is the aspect of faith, the walking into space without regard for what is to come next. This is, of course, foolish but is part of the characteristic of the spiritual neophyte. That this aspect was not seen may be pondered by the questioner. At this time we shall again request that the query be restated at the next working, and we shall at this time cease using this instrument. Before we leave, may we ask if there may be any short questions?

QUESTIONER: Only if there is anything that we can do to make the instrument more comfortable or to improve the contact?

RA: I am Ra. Continue, my friends, in the strength of harmony, love, and light. All is well. The alignments are appreciated for their careful placement.

I am Ra. I leave you now, my friends, in the glory of the love and the light of the Infinite Creator. Go forth, then, rejoicing in the power and the peace of the One Infinite Creator. Adonai.

Session 68,
August 18, 1981

RA: I am Ra. I greet you in the love and in the light of the One Infinite Creator. We communicate now.

QUESTIONER: The primary reason that we decided to have this session today is that I might not be around for a while, and I had a pressing question about what happened Sunday night when, apparently, the instrument was slipping into a trance state during one of the normal Sunday night meditations, and I would like to question you on this. Can you give me information about what happened?

RA: I am Ra. We can.

QUESTIONER: Would you tell me what happened in that case?

RA: I am Ra. We have instructed this instrument to refrain from calling us unless it is within this set of circumscribed circumstances. In the event of which you speak, this instrument was asked a question which pertained to what you have been calling the Ra Material. This instrument was providing the voice for our brothers and sisters of the wisdom density known to you as Latwii.

This instrument thought to itself, "I do not know this answer. I wish I were channeling Ra." The ones of Latwii found themselves in the position of being approached by the Orion entity which seeks to be of service in its own way. The instrument began to prepare for Ra contact. Latwii knew that if this was completed, the Orion entity would have an opportunity which Latwii wished to avoid.

It is fortunate for this instrument, firstly, that Latwii is of fifth density and able to deal with that particular vibratory complex which the Orion entity was manifesting and, secondly, that there were those in the support group at that time which sent great amounts of support to the instrument in this crux. Thus what occurred was the ones of Latwii never let go of this instrument, although this came perilously close to breaking the Way of Confusion. It continued to hold its connection with the mind/body/spirit complex of the instrument and to generate information through it even as the instrument began to slip out of its physical vehicle.

The act of continued communication caused the entity to be unable to grasp the instrument's mind/body/spirit complex, and after but a small measure of your space/time, Latwii recovered the now completely amalgamated instrument and gave it continued communication to steady it during the transition back into integration.

QUESTIONER: Could you tell me what the plan of the fifth-density negatively oriented entity was, and how it would have accomplished it and what the results would have been if it had worked?

RA: I am Ra. The plan, which is ongoing, was to take the mind/body/ spirit complex while it was separated from its yellow body physical complex shell, to then place this mind/body/spirit complex within the negative portions of your time/space. The shell would then become that of the unknowing, unconscious entity and could be, shall we say, worked upon to cause malfunction which would end in coma and then in what you call the death of the body. At this point the Higher Self of the instrument would have the choice of leaving the mind/body/ spirit complex in negative sp—we correct—time/space or of allowing incarnation in space/time of equivalent vibration and polarity distortions. Thus this entity would become a negatively polarized entity without the advantage of native negative polarization. It would find a long path to the Creator under these circumstances, although the path would inevitably end well.

QUESTIONER: Then you are saying that if this fifth-density negative entity is successful in its attempts to transfer the mind/body/spirit complex when that complex is in what we call the trance state to negatively polarized time/space, then the Higher Self has no choice but to allow incarnation in negatively polarized space/time? Is that correct?

RA: I am Ra. This is incorrect. The Higher Self could allow the mind/ body/spirit complex to remain in time/space. However, it is unlikely that the Higher Self would do so indefinitely, due to its distortion towards the belief that the function of the mind/body/spirit complex is to experience and learn from other-selves, thus experiencing the Creator. A highly polarized positive mind/body/spirit complex surrounded by negative portions of space/time will experience only darkness, for like the magnet, there is no, shall we say, likeness. Thus a barrier is automatically formed.

QUESTIONER: Let me be sure that I understand you. Is that darkness experienced in negative space/time or in negative time/space?

RA: I am Ra. Negative time/space.

QUESTIONER: Incarnation in negative space/time then in a condition like that would result in incarnation into which density level for, let us take as an example, the instrument?

RA: I am Ra. The answer to this query violates the first distortion.

QUESTIONER: OK, then, let's not take the instrument as an example. Let's assume that this was done to a Wanderer of sixth density. If this answer violates the first distortion, don't answer. But let's say a sixth-density Wanderer had this happen and went into negative time/space. Would that be a sixth-density negative time/space, and would he incarnate into sixth-density negative space/time?

RA: I am Ra. Your assumption is correct. The strength of the polarization would be matched as far as possible. In some positive sixth-density Wanderers, the approximation would not quite be complete due to the paucity of negative sixth-density energy fields of the equivalent strength.

QUESTIONER: Is the reason that this could be done the fact that the Wanderer's mind/body/spirit complex extracted in what we call the trance state, leaving the third-density physical; in this state the Wanderer does not have the full capability to magically defend itself. Is this correct?

RA: I am Ra. In the case of this instrument, this is correct. This is also correct when applied almost without exception to those instruments working in trance which have not consciously experienced magical training in time/space in the, shall we say, present incarnation. The entities of your density capable of magical defense in this situation are extremely rare.

QUESTIONER: It would seem to me that since I can't imagine anything worse than this particular result, it would be very advisable to seek the magical training and defense for this situation. Could Ra and would Ra instruct us in this type of magical defense?

RA: I am Ra. This request lies beyond the first distortion. The entity seeking magical ability must do so in a certain manner. We may give instructions of a general nature. This we have already done. The instrument has begun the process of balancing the self. This is a lengthy process.

To take an entity before it is ready and offer it the scepter of magical power is to infringe in an unbalanced manner. We may suggest with some asperity that the instrument never call upon Ra in any way while unprotected by the configuration which is at this time present.

QUESTIONER: I think that it is important for me to investigate the techniques, if they are within the first distortion, of the fifth-density entity who wishes to displace the mind/body/spirit complexes of this group. Am I within the first distortion in asking you to describe how this entity goes about this working?

RA: I am Ra. You are.

QUESTIONER: Well, then, how does this fifth-density entity go about this working from the very start of being alerted to the fact that we exist?

RA: I am Ra. The entity becomes aware of power. This power has the capacity of energizing those which may be available for harvest. This entity is desirous of disabling this power source. It sends its legions. Temptations are offered. They are ignored or rejected. The power source persists and indeed improves its inner connections of harmony and love of service.

The entity determines that it must needs attempt the disabling itself. By means of projection it enters the vicinity of this power source. It assesses the situation. It is bound by the first distortion but may take advantage of any free-will distortion. The free-will, pre-incarnative distortions of the instrument with regard to the physical vehicle seem the most promising target. Any distortion away from service to others is also appropriate.

When the instrument leaves its physical vehicle, it does so freely. Thus the misplacement of the mind/body/spirit complex of the instrument would not be a violation of its free will if it followed the entity freely. This is the process.

We are aware of your pressing desire to know how to become impervious as a group to any influences such as this. The processes which you seek are a matter of your free choice. You are aware of the principles of magical work. We cannot speak to advise but can only suggest, as we have before, that it would be appropriate for this group to embark upon such a path as a group, but not individually, for obvious reasons.

QUESTIONER: I am interested as to how the first distortion applies to the negatively polarized entity misplacing the mind/body/spirit complex. Why is the negatively polarized entity followed to the place of negative time/space? Why would one of us freely follow the entity?

RA: I am Ra. The positive polarity sees love in all things. The negative polarity is clever.

QUESTIONER: Then I am assuming if the negative polarity used any other approach that did not use the free will of the other-self, he would lose polarization and magical power. This is correct, isn't it?

RA: I am Ra. This is correct. The transferred energy grows low. We wish to close. Are there any short queries before we leave this instrument?

QUESTIONER: Only if there is anything that we can do to make the instrument more comfortable or to improve the contact?

RA: I am Ra. You are conscientious. We realize your necessity for these queries. All is well, my friends. We thank you and leave you in the love and in the light of the One Infinite Creator. Go forth, therefore, rejoicing in the power and in the peace of the One Infinite Creator. Adonai.

Session 69,
August 29, 1981

RA: I am Ra; I greet you in the love and in the light of the One Infinite Creator.

Before we proceed, may we make a small request for future workings. At this particular working there is some slight interference with the contact due to the hair of the instrument. We may suggest the combing of this antenna-like material into a more orderly configuration prior to the working.

We communicate now.

QUESTIONER: A question which I didn't get to ask at the previous session and which I will be forced to ask at this time is, Is the trance state the only state in which a mind/body/spirit positive entity may be lured by a negative entity or adept to negative time/space configuration?

RA: I am Ra. This is a misperceived concept. The mind/body/spirit complex which freely leaves the third-density physical complex is vulnerable when the appropriate protection is not at hand. You may perceive carefully that very few entities which choose to leave their physical complexes are doing work of such a nature as to attract the polarized attention of negatively oriented entities. The danger to most in trance state, as you term the physical complex being left, is the touching of the physical complex in such a manner as to attract the mind/body/spirit complex back thereunto or to damage the means by which that which you call ectoplasm is being recalled.

This instrument is an anomaly in that it is well that the instrument not be touched or artificial light thrown upon it while in the trance state. However, the ectoplasmic activity is interiorized. The main difficulty, as you are aware, is then the previously discussed negative removal of the entity under its free will.

That this can happen only in the trance state is not completely certain, but it is highly probable that in another out-of-body experience such as death, the entity here examined would, as most positively polarized entities, have a great deal of protection from comrades, guides, and portions of the self which would be aware of the transfer you call the physical death.

QUESTIONER: Then you are saying that the protective friends, we will call them, would be available in every condition except for what we call the trance state, which seems to be anomalistic with respect to the others. Is this correct?

RA: I am Ra. This is correct.

QUESTIONER: Why is this trance state, as we call it, different? Why are there not entities available in this particular state?

RA: I am Ra. The uniqueness of this situation is not the lack of friends, for this, as all entities, has its guides or angelic presences and, due to polarization, teachers and friends also. The unique characteristic of the workings which the social memory complex Ra and your group have begun is the intent to serve others with the highest attempt at near purity which we as comrades may achieve.

This has alerted a much more determined friend of negative polarity which is interested in removing this particular opportunity.

We may say once again two notes: Firstly, we searched long to find an appropriate channel or instrument and an appropriate support group. If this opportunity is ended, we shall be grateful for that which has been done, but the possibility/probability vortices indicating the location of this configuration again are slight. Secondly, we thank you for we know what you sacrifice in order to do that which you as a group wish to do.

We will not deplete this instrument insofar as we are able. We have attempted to speak of how the instrument may deplete itself through too great a dedication to the working. All these things and all else we have said has been heard. We are thankful. In the present situation we express thanks to the entities who call themselves Latwii.

QUESTIONER: Do I understand, then, that death, whether it is by natural means or accidental means or suicide, that all deaths of this type would create the same after-death condition that would avail the entity to its protection from friends? Is this correct?

RA: I am Ra. We presume you mean to inquire whether in the death experience, no matter what the cause, the negative friends are not able to remove an entity. This is correct largely because the entity without the attachment to the space/time physical complex is far more aware and without the gullibility which is somewhat the hallmark of those who love wholeheartedly.

However, the death, if natural, would undoubtedly be the more harmonious; the death by murder being confused and the entity needing some time/space in which to get its bearings, so to speak; the death by suicide causing the necessity for much healing work and, shall we say, the making of a dedication to the third density for the renewed opportunity of learning the lessons set by the Higher Self.

QUESTIONER: Is this also true of unconscious conditions due to accident, or medical anesthetic, or drugs?

RA: I am Ra. Given that the entity is not attempting to be of service in this particular way which is proceeding now, the entities of negative orientation would not find it possible to remove the mind/body/spirit. The unique characteristic, as we have said, which is, shall we say, dangerous is the willing of the mind/body/spirit complex outward from the physical complex of third density for the purpose of service-to-others. In any other situation this circumstance would not be in effect.

QUESTIONER: Would this be a function of the balancing action of the first distortion?

RA: I am Ra. Your query is somewhat opaque. Please restate for specificity.

QUESTIONER: I was just guessing that since the mind/body/spirit complex's will from the third-density body for a particular duty or service to others would then create a situation primarily with respect to the first distortion where the opportunity for balancing this service by the negative service would be available and, therefore, magically possible for the intrusion of the other polarization. Is this thinking at all correct?

RA: I am Ra. No. The free will of the instrument is indeed a necessary part of the opportunity afforded the Orion group. However, this free will and the first distortion applies only to the instrument. The entire hope of the Orion group is to infringe upon free will without losing polarity. Thus this group, if represented by a wise entity, attempts to be clever.

QUESTIONER: Has a Wanderer ever been so infringed upon by a negative adept and then placed in negative time/space?

RA: I am Ra. This is correct.

QUESTIONER: Can you tell me the situation that the Wanderer finds himself in and the path back, why that path could not be the simple moving back into positive time/space?

RA: I am Ra. The path back revolves, firstly, about the Higher Self's reluctance to enter negative space/time. This may be a significant part of the length of that path. Secondly, when a positively oriented entity incarnates in a thoroughly negative environment, it must needs learn/teach the lessons of the love of self, thus becoming one with its other-selves.

When this has been accomplished, the entity may then choose to release the potential difference and change polarities. However, the process of learning the accumulated lessons of love of self may be quite lengthy. Also the entity, in learning these lessons, may lose much positive orientation during the process, and the choice of reversing polarities may be delayed until the mid-sixth density. All of this is, in your way of measurement, time consuming, although the end result is well.

QUESTIONER: Is it possible to tell me roughly how many Wanderers who have come to this planet during this master cycle have experienced this displacement into a negative time/space?

RA: I am Ra. We can note the number of such occurrences. There has been only one. We cannot, due to the Law of Confusion, discuss the entity.

QUESTIONER: You said that the Higher Self is reluctant to enter negative space/time. Is that correct?

RA: I am Ra. The incarnative process involves being incarnated from time/space to space/time. This is correct.

QUESTIONER: I will make this statement and see if I am correct. When first moved into time/space of a negative polarization, the positive entity experiences nothing but darkness. Then, by incarnation into negative space/time by the Higher Self, it experiences a negative space/time environment with negatively polarized other-selves. Is this correct?

RA: I am Ra. This is correct.

QUESTIONER: It would seem to me that it would be an extremely difficult situation for the positively polarized entity, and the learning process would be extremely traumatic. Is this correct?

RA: I am Ra. Let us say that the positively polarized individual makes a poor student of the love of self and thus spends much more time, if you will, than those native to that pattern of vibrations.

QUESTIONER: I am assuming that this misplacement must be a function of his free will in some way. Is this correct?

RA: I am Ra. This is absolutely correct.

QUESTIONER: This is a point that I find quite confusing to me. It is the function of the free will of the positively oriented entity to move into the negatively polarized time/space. However, it is also a function of his lack of understanding of what he is doing. I am sure that if the entity had full understanding of what he was doing, he would not do it. It is a function of his negatively polarized other-self creating a situation where he is lured to that configuration. What is the principle with respect to the first distortion that allows this to occur, since we have two portions of the Creator, each of equal value or of equal potential but oppositely polarized, and we have this situation resulting. Could you tell me the philosophical principle behind this particular act?

RA: I am Ra. There are two important points in this regard. Firstly, we may note the situation wherein an entity gets a road map which is poorly marked and in fact is quite incorrect. The entity sets out to its destination. It wishes only to reach the point of destination, but, becoming confused by the faulty authority and not knowing the territory through which it drives, it becomes hopelessly lost.

Free will does not mean that there will be no circumstances when calculations will be awry. This is so in all aspects of the life experience. Although there are no mistakes, there are surprises.

Secondly, that which we and you do in workings such as this carries a magical charge, if you would use this much misunderstood term; perhaps we may say a metaphysical power. Those who do work of power are available for communication to and from entities of roughly similar power. It is fortunate that the Orion entity does not have the native power of this group. However, it is quite disciplined, whereas this group lacks the finesse equivalent to its power. Each is working in consciousness, but the group has not begun a work as a group. The individual work is helpful, for the group is mutually an aid, one to another.

QUESTIONER: This instrument performs services that involve channeling other members of the Confederation. We are reluctant to continue this because of the possibility of her slipping into trance and being offered the services of the negatively polarized entity or adept. Are there any safeguards to create a situation whereby she cannot go into trance other than at a protected working such as this one?

RA: I am Ra. There are three. Firstly, the instrument must needs improve the disciplined subconscious taboo against requesting Ra. This would involve daily conscious and serious thought. The second safeguard is the refraining from the opening of the instrument to questions and answers for the present. The third is quite gross in its appearance but suffices to keep the instrument in its physical complex. The hand may be held.

QUESTIONER: Are you saying, then, that just by holding the instrument's hand during the channeling sessions, this would prevent trance?

RA: I am Ra. This would prevent those levels of meditation which necessarily precede trance. Also in the event that, unlikely as it might seem, the entity grew able to leave the physical complex, the auric infringement and tactile pressure would cause the mind/body/spirit complex to refrain from leaving.

We may note that long practice at the art which each intuits here would be helpful. We cannot speak of methodology, for the infringement would be most great. However, to speak of group efforts is, as we scan each, merely confirmation of what is known. Therefore, this we may do.

We have the available energy for one fairly brief query.

QUESTIONER: There are many techniques and ways of practicing so-called white magical arts. Are rituals designed by a particular group for their own particular use just as good or possibly better than those that have been practiced by groups such as the Order of the Golden Dawn and other magical groups?

RA: I am Ra. Although we are unable to speak with precision on this query, we may note some gratification that the questioner has penetrated some of the gist of a formidable system of service and discipline.

I am Ra. May we thank you again, my friends, for your conscientiousness. All is well. We leave you rejoicing in the power and the peace of the One Infinite Creator. Go forth with joy. Adonai.

Session 70,
September 9, 1981

RA: I am Ra. I greet you in the love and in the light of the One Infinite Creator. We communicate now.

QUESTIONER: Could you please give me an indication of the condition of the instrument?

RA: I am Ra. We are gratified to say that it is as previously stated.

QUESTIONER: Why do you say that you are gratified to say that?

RA: I am Ra. We say this due to a sense of gratitude at the elements which have enabled this instrument to maintain, against great odds, its vital energy at normal vibratory strength. As long as this complex of energies is satisfactory, we may use this instrument without depletion regardless of the distortions previously mentioned.

QUESTIONER: The instrument has complained of intensive psychic attack for the past diurnal period, approximately. Is there a reason for the intensification of this psychic attack?

RA: I am Ra. Yes.

QUESTIONER: Can you tell me what this reason is, please?

RA: I am Ra. The cause is that with which you are intimately involved; that is, the cause is the intensive seeking for what you may call enlightenment. This seeking upon your parts has not abated, but intensified.

In the general case, pain, as you call this distortion and the various exaggerations of this distortion by psychic attack, would, after the depletion of physical complex energy, begin the depletion of vital energy. This instrument guards its vital energy due to previous errors upon its part. Its subconscious will, which is preternaturally strong for this density, has put a ward upon this energy complex. Thus the Orion visitor strives with more and more intensity to disturb this vital energy as this group intensifies its dedication to service through enlightenment.

QUESTIONER: I have an extra little question that I want to throw in at this time. Is regressive hypnosis on an individual past birth in this incarnation, to reveal memories to it of previous incarnations, a service or a disservice to it?

RA: I am Ra. We scan your query and find you shall apply the answer to your future. This causes us to be concerned with the first distortion. However, the query is also general and contains an opportunity for us to express a significant point. Therefore, we shall speak.

There is an infinite range of possibility of service/disservice in the situation of time-regression hypnosis, as you term this means of aiding memory. It has nothing to do with the hypnotist. It has only to do with the use which the entity so hypnotized makes of the information so gleaned. If the hypnotist desires to serve and if such a service is performed only upon sincere request, the hypnotist is attempting to be of service.

QUESTIONER: In the last session, Ra stated that "the path back from sixth-density negative time/space revolves, firstly, about the Higher Self's reluctance to enter negative time/space." Could you explain the Higher Self's position with respect to positive and negative time/space, and why it is so reluctant to enter negative time/space that it is necessary for the mind/body/spirit complex to incarnate in negative space/time to find its path back?

RA: I am Ra. In brief, you have answered your own query. Please question further for more precise information.

QUESTIONER: Why is the Higher Self reluctant to enter negative time/space?

RA: I am Ra. The Higher Self is reluctant to allow its mind/body/spirit complex to enter negative time/space for the same basic reason an entity of your societal complex would be reluctant to enter a prison.

QUESTIONER: What I am trying to understand here is more about the Higher Self and its relationship with the mind/body/spirit complex. Does the Higher Self have a sixth-density mind/body/spirit complex that is a separate unit from the mind/body/spirit complex that is, in this case, displaced to negative time/space?

RA: I am Ra. This is correct. The Higher Self is the entity of mid-sixth density, which, turning back, offers this service to its self.

QUESTIONER: I think I have an erroneous concept of the mind/body/spirit complex that, for instance, I represent here in this density and my Higher Self. This probably comes from my concept of space and time. I am going to try to unscramble this. The way I see it right now is that I am existing in two different locations, here and in mid-sixth density, simultaneously. Is this correct?

RA: I am Ra. You are existing at all levels simultaneously. It is specifically correct that your Higher Self is you in mid-sixth density, and, in your way of measuring what you know of as time, your Higher Self is your self in your future.

QUESTIONER: Am I correct in assuming that all of the mind/body/spirit complexes that exist below levels of mid-sixth density have a Higher Self at the level of mid-sixth density? Is this correct?

RA: I am Ra. This is correct.

QUESTIONER: Would an analogy for this situation be that an individual's Higher Self is manipulating to some extent, shall I say, the mind/body/spirit complex that is its analog to move it through the lower densities for the purposes of gaining experience and finally transferring that experience or amalgamating it in mid-sixth density with the Higher Self?

RA: I am Ra. This is incorrect. The Higher Self does not manipulate its past selves. It protects when possible and guides when asked, but the force of free will is paramount. The seeming contradictions of determinism and free will melt when it is accepted that there is such a thing as true simultaneity. The Higher Self is the end result of all the development experienced by the mind/body/spirit complex to that point.

QUESTIONER: Then what we are looking at is a long path of experience through the densities up to mid-sixth density, which is a function totally of free will and results in the awareness of the Higher Self in mid-sixth density, but since time is illusory and there is a, shall I say, unification of time and space or an eradication of what we think of as time, then all of this experience that results in the Higher Self, the cause of evolution through the densities, is existing while the evolution takes place. It is all simultaneous. Is this correct?

RA: I am Ra. We refrain from speaking of correctness due to our understanding of the immense difficulty of absorbing the concepts of metaphysical existence. In time/space, which is precisely as much of your self as is space/time, all times are simultaneous just as, in your geography, your cities and villages are all functioning, bustling, and alive with entities going about their business at once. So it is in time/space with the self.

QUESTIONER: The Higher Self existing in mid-sixth density seems to be at the point where the negative and positive paths of experience merge into one. Is there a reason for this?

RA: I am Ra. We have covered this material previously.

QUESTIONER: Oh yes. Sorry about that. It slipped my mind. Now, if a positive entity is displaced to negative time/space, I understand that the Higher Self is reluctant to enter the negative time/space. For some reason it makes it necessary for the mind/body/spirit complex to incarnate in negative space/time. Why is it necessary for this incarnation in negative space/time?

RA: I am Ra. Firstly, let us remove the concept of reluctance from the equation and then, secondly, address your query more to the point. Each time/space is an analog of a particular sort or vibration of space/time. When a negative time/space is entered by an entity, the next experience will be that of the appropriate space/time. This is normally done by the form-making body of a mind/body/spirit complex which places the entity in the proper time/space for incarnation.

QUESTIONER: I think that to clear up this point, I will ask a few questions that are related that will possibly help me to understand this better, because I am really confused about this and I think it is a very important point in understanding the creation and the Creator in general, you might say. If a Wanderer of fourth, fifth, or sixth density dies from this third-density state in which we presently find ourselves, does he then find himself in the third-density time/space after death?

RA: I am Ra. This will depend upon the plan which has been approved by the Council of Nine. Some Wanderers offer themselves for but one incarnation, while others offer themselves for varying lengths of your time, up to and including the last two cycles of 25,000 years. If the agreed-upon mission is completed, the Wanderer's mind/body/spirit complex will go to the home vibration.

QUESTIONER: Have there been any Wanderers on this planet for the past 50,000 years now?

RA: I am Ra. There have been a few. There have been many more which chose to join this last cycle of 25,000 years, and many, many more which have come for harvest.

QUESTIONER: Now here is the point of my confusion. If, after physical death, a Wanderer would return to his home planet, why cannot the same entity be extracted from negative time/space to the home planet rather than incarnating in negative space/time?

RA: I am Ra. As we stated, the position in negative time/space, of which we previously were speaking, is that position which is pre-incarnative. After the death of the physical complex in yellow-ray activation, the mind/body/spirit complex moves to a far different portion of time/space in which the indigo body will allow much healing and review to take place before any movement is made towards another incarnative experience.

I perceive a basic miscalculation upon your part, in that time/space is no more homogeneous than space/time. It is as complex and complete a system of illusions, dances, and pattern as is space/time, and has as structured a system of what you may call natural laws.

QUESTIONER: I'll ask this question to inform me a little about what you just stated. When you came to this planet in craft 18,000 and 11,000 years ago, these craft have been called bell craft and were photographed by George Adamski. If I am correct, these craft looked somewhat like a bell; they had portholes around them in the upper portions, and they had three hemispheres at 120° apart underneath. Is this correct?

RA: I am Ra. This is correct.

QUESTIONER: Were these constructed in time/space or in space/time?

RA: I am Ra. We ask your persistent patience, for our answer must be complex.

A construct of thought was formed in time/space. This portion of time/space is that which approaches the speed of light. In time/space, at this approach, the conditions are such that time becomes infinite and mass ceases, so that one which is able to skim the, shall we say, boundary strength of this time/space is able to become placed where it will.

When we were where we wished to be, we then clothed the construct of light with that which would appear as the crystal bell. This was formed through the boundary into space/time. Thus there were two constructs: the time/space or immaterial construct, and the space/time or materialized construct.

QUESTIONER: Was there a reason for the particular shape that you chose, in particular a reason for the three hemispheres on the bottom?

RA: I am Ra. It seemed an aesthetically pleasing form and one well suited to those limited uses which we must needs make of your space/time motivating requirements.

QUESTIONER: Was there a principle of motivation contained within the three hemispheres on the bottom, or were they just aesthetic, or were they landing gear?

RA: I am Ra. These were aesthetic and part of a system of propulsion. These hemispheres were not landing gear.

QUESTIONER: I am sorry to ask such stupid questions, but I am trying to determine something about space/time, time/space, and this very difficult area of the mechanism of evolution. I think it is central to the understanding of our evolution. However, I am not sure of this, and I may be wasting my time. Could Ra comment on whether I am wasting my time in this particular investigation or whether it would be fruitful?

RA: I am Ra. Since the concepts of space/time, or physics, and time/space, or metaphysics, are mechanical, they are not central to the spiritual evolution of the mind/body/spirit complex. The study of love and light is far more productive in its motion towards unity in those entities pondering such concepts. However, this material is, shall we say, of some small interest and is harmless.

QUESTIONER: I was asking these questions primarily to understand or to build a base for an attempt to get a little bit of enlightenment on the way that time/space and space/time are related to the evolution of the mind/body/spirit complex, so that I could better understand the techniques of evolution. For instance, you stated, "the potential difference may be released and polarity changed after an entity has learned/taught the lessons of love of self" if the entity is a positive entity that has found itself in negative time/space and has had to incarnate into negative space/time. What I was trying to do was build a base for an attempt to get a slight understanding of what you meant by this statement that potential difference may be released and polarity changed after the above step. I am very interested in knowing, if placed in a negative time/space, why it is necessary to incarnate in negative space/time and learn/teach love of self and develop—I guess—a sixth-density level of polarity before you can release that potential difference. Could you speak on that subject?

RA: I am Ra. This will be the last full query of this working.
  The entity which incarnates into negative space/time will not find it possible to maintain any significant positive polarity, as negativity, when pure, is a type of gravity well, shall we say, pulling all into it. Thus the entity, while remembering its learned and preferred polarity, must needs make use of the catalyst given and recapitulate the lessons of service to self in order to build up enough polarity in order to cause the potential to occur for reversal.
  There is much in this line of questioning which is somewhat muddled. May we, at this point, allow the questioner to rephrase the question or to turn the direction of query more towards that which is the heart of its concern.

QUESTIONER: I will, at the next session, then attempt to turn more toward the heart. I was attempting in this session to get at a point that I thought was central to the evolution of spirit, but I seem to have gone awry. It is sometimes very, very difficult for me to question wisely in these areas.

I will just ask if there is anything that we can do to enhance the contact or to make the instrument more comfortable?

RA: I am Ra. You are most conscientious, and the alignments are especially good. We thank you, my friends, and have been glad to speak with you. We are attempting to be of the greatest aid to you by taking care not to deplete this instrument. Thus, although a reserve remains, we will attempt from this working onward to keep this reserve, for this instrument has arranged its subconscious to accept this configuration.

I am Ra. You are all doing well, my friends. We leave you in the love and in the light of the One Infinite Creator. Go forth, therefore, rejoicing and glorying in the power and in the peace of the One Infinite Creator. Adonai.

Session 71,
September 18, 1981

RA: I am Ra. I greet you in the love and in the light of the One Infinite Creator. We communicate now.

QUESTIONER: Could you first please give me the condition of the instrument?

RA: I am Ra. It is as previously stated, with the exception of a slight improvement in the vital energy distortions. One may note to the support group, without infringement, that it is well to aid the instrument in the reminders that while physical complex distortions remain as they are, it is not advisable to use the increased vital energies for physical complex activities as this will take a somewhat harsh toll.

QUESTIONER: In this session I hope to ask several different questions to establish a point of entry into an investigation that will be fruitful. I would first ask if it is possible to increase polarity without increasing harvestability?

RA: I am Ra. The connection between polarization and harvestability is most important in third-density harvest. In this density an increase in the serving of others or the serving of self will almost inevitably increase the ability of an entity to enjoy a higher intensity of light.

Thus in this density, we may say, it is hardly possible to polarize without increasing in harvestability.

QUESTIONER: This would probably be possible in the higher densities, such as the fifth density. Is this correct?

RA: I am Ra. In fifth-density harvest, polarization has very little to do with harvestability.

QUESTIONER: Would you explain the concept of working with the unmanifested being in third density to accelerate evolution?

RA: I am Ra. This is a many-layered question, and which stria we wish to expose is questionable. Please restate, giving any further depth of information requested, if possible.

QUESTIONER: Define, please, the unmanifested being.

RA: I am Ra. We may see that you wish to pursue the deeper strata of information. We shall, therefore, answer in a certain way which does not exhaust the query but is designed to move beneath the outer teachings somewhat.

The unmanifested being is, as we have said, that being which exists and does its work without reference to or aid from other-selves. To move into this concept, you may see the inevitable connection between the unmanifested self and the metaphysical or time/space analog of the space/time self. The activities of meditation, contemplation, and what may be called the internal balancing of thoughts and reactions are those activities of the unmanifested self more closely aligned with the metaphysical self.

QUESTIONER: As an entity goes through the death process in third density, it finds itself in time/space. It finds itself in a different set of circumstances. Would you please describe the circumstances or properties of time/space and then the process of healing of incarnative experiences that some entities encounter?

RA: I am Ra. Although this query is difficult to answer adequately, due to the limitations of your space/time sound vibration complexes, we shall respond to the best of our ability.

The hallmark of time/space is the inequity between time and space. In your space/time the spatial orientation of material causes a tangible framework for illusion. In time/space the inequity is upon the shoulders of that property known to you as time. This property renders entities and experiences intangible in a relative sense. In your framework, each particle or core vibration moves at a velocity which approaches what you call the speed of light from the direction of supraluminal velocities.

Thus the time/space or metaphysical experience is that which is very finely tuned and, although an analog of space/time, lacking in its tangible characteristics. In these metaphysical planes there is a great deal of what you call time which is used to review and re-review the biases and learn/teachings of a prior, as you would call it, space/time incarnation.

The extreme fluidity of these regions makes it possible for much to be penetrated which must needs be absorbed before the process of healing of an entity may be accomplished. Each entity is located in a somewhat immobile state, much as you are located in space/time in a somewhat immobile state in time. In this immobile space the entity has been placed by the form maker and Higher Self so that it may be in the proper configuration for learn/teaching that which it has received in the space/time incarnation.

Depending upon this time/space locus, there will be certain helpers which assist in this healing process. The process involves seeing in full the experience, seeing it against the backdrop of the mind/body/spirit complex total experience, forgiving the self for all missteps as regards the missed guideposts during the incarnation, and, finally, the careful assessment of the next necessities for learning. This is done entirely by the Higher Self until an entity has become conscious in space/time of the process and means of spiritual evolution, at which time the entity will consciously take part in all decisions.

QUESTIONER: Is the process in positive time/space identical with the process in negative time/space for this healing?

RA: I am Ra. The process in space/time of the forgiveness and acceptance is much like that in time/space, in that the qualities of the process are analogous. However, while in space/time it is not possible to determine the course of events beyond the incarnation, but only to correct present imbalances. In time/space, upon the other hand, it is not possible to correct any unbalanced actions but rather to perceive the imbalances and thusly forgive the self for that which is.

The decisions then are made to set up the possibility/probabilities of correcting these imbalances in what you call future space/time experiences. The advantage of time/space is that of the fluidity of the grand overview. The advantage of space/time is that, working in darkness with a tiny candle, one may correct imbalances.

QUESTIONER: If an entity has chosen the negative polarization, are the processes of healing and review similar for the negative path?

RA: I am Ra. This is correct.

QUESTIONER: Are the processes that we are talking about processes that occur on many planets in our Milky Way Galaxy, or do they occur on all planets, or what percentage?

RA: I am Ra. These processes occur upon all planets which have given birth to sub-Logoi such as yourselves. The percentage of inhabited planets is approximately 10 percent.

QUESTIONER: What percentage of stars, roughly, have planetary systems?

RA: I am Ra. This is unimportant information, but harmless. Approximately 32 percent of stars have planets as you know them, while another 6 percent have some sort of clustering material which upon some densities might be inhabitable.

QUESTIONER: This would tell me that roughly 3 percent of all stars have inhabited planets. This process of evolution is in effect throughout the known universe then. Is this correct?

RA: I am Ra. This octave of infinite knowledge of the One Creator is as it is throughout the One Infinite Creation, with variations programmed by sub-Logoi of what you call major galaxies and minor galaxies. These variations are not significant but may be compared to various regions of geographical location sporting various ways of pronouncing the same sound vibration complex or concept.

QUESTIONER: It seems to me from this that the sub-Logos such as our sun uses free will to modify only slightly a much more general idea of created evolution, so that the general plan of created evolution then seems to be uniform throughout the One Infinite Creation. The process is for the sub-Logoi to grow through the densities and, under the first distortion, find their way back to the original thought. Is this correct?

RA: I am Ra. This is correct.

QUESTIONER: Then each entity is of a path that leads to one destination.

This is like many, many roads that travel through many, many places but eventually merge into one large center. Is this correct?

RA: I am Ra. This is correct but somewhat wanting in depth of description. More applicable would be the thought that each entity contains within it all of the densities and sub-densities of the octave, so that in each entity, no matter whither its choices lead it, its great internal blueprint is one with all others. Thusly its experiences will fall into the patterns of the journey back to the original Logos. This is done through free will, but the materials from which choices can be made are one blueprint.

QUESTIONER: You have made the statement that pure negativity acts as a gravity well, pulling all into it. I was wondering first if pure positivity has precisely the same effect? Could you answer that, please?

RA: I am Ra. This is incorrect. Positivity has a much weaker effect due to the strong element of recognition of free will in any positivity approaching purity. Thus, although the negatively oriented entity may find it difficult to polarize negatively in the midst of such resounding harmony, it will not find it impossible.

Upon the other hand, the negative polarization is one which does not accept the concept of the free will of other-selves. Thusly, in a social complex whose negativity approaches purity, the pull upon other-selves is constant. A positively oriented entity in such a situation would desire for other-selves to have their free will and thusly would find itself removed from its ability to exercise its own free will, for the free will of negatively oriented entities is bent upon conquest.

QUESTIONER: Could you please comment on the accuracy of these statements. I am going to talk in general about the concept of magic and first define it as the ability to create changes in consciousness at will. Is this an acceptable definition?

RA: I am Ra. This definition is acceptable in that it places upon the adept the burden it shall bear. It may be better understood by referring back to an earlier query, in your measurement, within this working having to do with the unmanifested self. In magic, one is working with one's unmanifested self in body, in mind, and in spirit, the mixture depending upon the nature of the working.

These workings are facilitated by the enhancement of the activation of the indigo-ray energy center. The indigo-ray energy center is fed, as are all energy centers, by experience, but far more than the others is fed by what we have called the disciplines of the personality.

QUESTIONER: I will state that the objective of the white magical ritual is to create a change in consciousness of a group. Is this correct?

RA: I am Ra. Not necessarily. It is possible for what you term white magic to be worked for the purpose of altering only the self or the place of working. This is done in the knowledge that to aid the self in polarization towards love and light is to aid the planetary vibration.

QUESTIONER: The change in consciousness should result in a greater distortion towards service to others, towards unity with all, and towards knowing in order to serve. Is this correct, and are there any other desired results?

RA: I am Ra. These are commendable phrases. The heart of white magic is the experience of the joy of union with the Creator. This joy will of necessity radiate throughout the life experience of the positive adept. It is for this reason that sexual magic is not restricted solely to the negatively oriented polarizing adepts but, when most carefully used, has its place in high magic as it, when correctly pursued, joins body, mind, and spirit with the One Infinite Creator.

Any purpose which you may frame should, we suggest, take into consideration this basic union with the One Infinite Creator, for this union will result in service to others of necessity.

QUESTIONER: There are, shall I say, certain rules of white magic. I will read these few, and I would like you to comment on the philosophical content or basis of these and add to this list any of importance that I have neglected. First, a special place of working preferably constructed by the practitioners; second, a special signal or key such as a ring to summon the magical personality; third, special clothing worn only for the workings; fourth, a specific time of day; fifth, a series of ritual sound vibratory complexes designed to create the desired mental distortion; sixth, a group objective for each session. Could you comment on this list, please?

RA: I am Ra. To comment upon this list is to play the mechanic which views the instruments of the orchestra and adjusts and tunes the instruments. You will note these are mechanical details. The art does not lie herein.

The one item of least import is what you call the time of day. This is important in those experiential nexi wherein the entities search for the metaphysical experience without conscious control over the search. The repetition of workings gives this search structure. In this particular group the structure is available without the need for inevitable sameness of times of working. We may note that this regularity is always helpful.

QUESTIONER: You stated in a previous session that Ra searched for some time to find a group such as this one. I would assume that this search was for the purpose of communicating the Law of One. Is this correct?

RA: I am Ra. This is partially correct. We also, as we have said, wished to attempt to make reparation for distortions of this law set in motion by our naive actions of your past.

QUESTIONER: Can you tell me if we have covered the necessary material at this point to, if published, make the necessary reparations for the naive actions?

RA: I am Ra. We mean no disrespect for your service, but we do not expect to make full reparations for these distortions. We may, however, offer our thoughts in the attempt. The attempt is far more important to us than the completeness of the result. The nature of your language is such that what is distorted cannot, to our knowledge, be fully undistorted but only illuminated somewhat. In response to your desire to see the relationship betwixt space/time and time/space, may we say that we conducted this search in time/space, for in this illusion one may quite readily see entities as vibratory complexes and groups as harmonics within vibratory complexes.

QUESTIONER: I see the most important aspect of this communication as being a vehicle of partial enlightenment for those incarnate now who have become aware of their part in their own evolutionary process. Am I correct in this assumption?

RA: I am Ra. You are correct. We may note that this is the goal of all artifacts and experiences which entities may come into contact with, and is not only the property of Ra or this contact.

We find that this instrument has neglected to continue to remind its self of the need for holding some portion of energy back for reserve. This is recommended as a portion of the inner program to be reinstated, as it will lengthen the number of workings we may have. This is acceptable to us. The transferred energy grows quite, quite low. We must leave you shortly. Is there a brief query at this time?

QUESTIONER: Is there anything that we can do to improve the contact or to make the instrument more comfortable?

RA: I am Ra. You are conscientious. Remain most fastidious about the alignments of the appurtenances. We thank you. I am Ra. I leave you in the love and in the glorious light of the Infinite Creator. Go forth, therefore, rejoicing in the power and in the peace of the One Infinite Creator. Adonai.

Session 72,
October 14, 1981

RA: I am Ra. I greet you in the love and in the light of the One Infinite Creator. We communicate now.

QUESTIONER: Could you first give me an indication of the instrument's condition?

RA: I am Ra. This instrument's physical energy distortions are as previously stated. The vital energy level has become distorted from normal levels, somewhat downward, due to the distortion in this instrument's mind complex activity that it has been responsible for the, shall we say, difficulties in achieving the appropriate configuration for this contact.

QUESTIONER: Was the banishing ritual that we performed of any effect in purifying the place of working and the screening of influences that we do not wish?

RA: I am Ra. This is quite correct.

QUESTIONER: Can you tell me what I can do to improve the effectiveness of the ritual?

RA: I am Ra. No.

QUESTIONER: Can you tell me what caused the instrument to become in a condition toward unconsciousness in the last two meditations prior to this one, to such an extent that we discontinued them?

RA: I am Ra. We can.

QUESTIONER: Would you please tell me then?

RA: I am Ra. The entity which greets this instrument from the Orion group first attempted to cause the mind/body/spirit complex, which you may call spirit, to leave the physical complex of yellow ray in the deluded belief that it was preparing for the Ra contact. You are familiar with this tactic and its consequences. The instrument, with no pause, upon feeling this greeting, called for the grounding within the physical complex by requesting that the hand be held. Thus the greatest aim of the Orion entity was not achieved. However, it discovered that those present were not capable of distinguishing between unconsciousness with the mind/body/spirit intact and the trance state in which the mind/body/spirit complex is not present.

Therefore, it applied to the fullest extent the greeting which causes the dizziness and in meditation without protection caused, in this instrument, simple unconsciousness, as in what you would call fainting or vertigo. The Orion entity consequently used this tactic to stop the Ra contact from having the opportunity to be accomplished.

QUESTIONER: The instrument has scheduled an operation on her hand next month. If the general anesthetic is used to produce the unconscious state, will this or any other parameters of the operation allow for any inroads by the Orion entities?

RA: I am Ra. It is extremely improbable due to the necessity for the intention of the mind/body/spirit complex, when departing the yellow-ray physical complex, to be serving the Creator in the most specific fashion. The attitude of one approaching such an experience as you describe would not be approaching the unconscious state with such an attitude.

QUESTIONER: We have here, I believe, a very important principle with respect to the Law of One. You have stated that the attitude of the individual is of paramount importance for the Orion entity to be able to be effective. Would you please explain how this mechanism works with respect to the Law of One, and why the attitude of the entity is of paramount importance and why this allows for action by the Orion entity?

RA: I am Ra. The Law of Confusion or Free Will is utterly paramount in the workings of the infinite creation. That which is intended has as much intensity of attraction to the polar opposite as the intensity of the intention or desire.

Thus, those whose desires are shallow or transitory experience only ephemeral configurations of what might be called the magical circumstance. There is a turning point, a fulcrum which swings as a mind/body/spirit complex tunes its will to service. If this will and desire is for service to others, the corresponding polarity will be activated. In the circumstance of this group, there are three such wills acting as one with the instrument in the, shall we say, central position of fidelity to service. This is as it must be for the balance of the working and the continuance of the contact. Our vibratory complex is one-pointed in these workings also, and our will to serve is also of some degree of purity. This has created the attraction of the polar opposite which you experience.

We may note that such a configuration of free will, one-pointed in service to others, also has the potential for the alerting of a great mass of light strength. This positive light strength, however, operates also under free will and must be invoked. We could not speak to this and shall not guide you, for the nature of this contact is such that the purity of your free will must, above all things, be preserved. Thus you wend your way through experiences, discovering those biases which may be helpful.

QUESTIONER: The negatively oriented entities who contact us and others on this planet are limited by the first distortion. They have obviously been limited by the banishing ritual just performed. Could you describe, with respect to free will, how they limit themselves in order to work within the first distortion and how the banishing ritual itself works?

RA: I am Ra. This query has several portions. Firstly, those of negative polarity do not operate with respect to free will unless it is necessary. They call themselves and will infringe whenever they feel it possible.

Secondly, they are limited by the great Law of Confusion in that, for the most part, they are unable to enter this planetary sphere of influence and are able to use the windows of time/space distortion only insofar as there is some calling to balance the positive calling. Once they are here, their desire is conquest.

Thirdly, in the instance of this instrument's being removed permanently from this space/time, it is necessary to allow the instrument to leave its yellow-ray physical complex of its free will. Thus trickery has been attempted.

The use of the light forms being generated is such as to cause such entities to discover a wall through which they cannot pass. This is due to the energy complexes of the light beings and aspects of the One Infinite Creator invoked and evoked in the building of the wall of light.

QUESTIONER: Everything that we experience with respect to this contact, our distortion toward knowledge in order to serve, the Orion entity's distortion towards reducing the effectiveness of this contact, all of this is a result of the first distortion, as I see it, in creating the totally free atmosphere for the Creator to become more knowledgeable of Itself through the interplay of its portions, one with respect to the other. Is my view correct with respect to what I have just said?

RA: I am Ra. Yes.

QUESTIONER: In the last session you mentioned that if the instrument used any of the increased vital energy that she experiences for physical activity that she would pay a "harsh toll." Could you tell me the nature of that harsh toll and why it would be experienced?

RA: I am Ra. The physical energy level is a measure of the amount of available energy of the body complex of a mind/body/spirit complex. The vital energy measurement is one which expresses the amount of energy of being of the mind/body/spirit complex.

This entity has great distortions in the direction of mind complex activity, spirit complex activity, and that great conduit to the Creator, the will. Therefore, this instrument's vital energy, even in the absence of any physical reserve measurable, is quite substantial. However, the use of this energy of will, mind, and spirit for the things of the physical complex causes a far greater distortion in the lessening of the vital energy than would the use of this energy for those things which are in the deepest desires and will of the mind/body/spirit complex. In this entity these desires are for service to the Creator. This entity sees all service as service to the Creator, and this is why we have cautioned the support group and the instrument itself in this regard. All services are not equal in depth of distortion. The overuse of this vital energy is, to be literal, the rapid removal of life force.

QUESTIONER: You mentioned that the large amount of light that is available. Could this group, by proper ritual, use this for recharging the vital energy of the instrument?

RA: I am Ra. This is correct. However, we caution against any working which raises up any personality; rather it is well to be fastidious in your working.

QUESTIONER: Could you explain what you mean by "raises up any personality"?

RA: I am Ra. Clues, we may offer. Explanation is infringement. We can only ask that you realize that all are One.

QUESTIONER: We have included "Shin" in the banishing ritual, "Yod-Heh-Vau-Heh" to make it "Yod-Heh-Shin-Vau-Heh." Is this helpful?

RA: I am Ra. This is helpful especially to the instrument whose distortions vibrate greatly in congruency with this sound vibration complex.

QUESTIONER: We will in the future have group meditations. I am concerned about protection for the instrument if she is once more a channel in these meditations. Is there an optimum time or limiting amount of time for the banishing ritual to be effective, or if we continued daily to purify the place of working with the banishing ritual, would this carry over for long periods of time, or must the ritual be done immediately prior to the meditations?

RA: I am Ra. Your former assumption is more nearly correct.

QUESTIONER: Is there any danger now, with the precautions that we are taking, of the instrument being led away by the Orion entity?

RA: I am Ra. The opportunities for the Orion entity are completely dependent upon the instrument's condition of awareness and readiness. We would suggest that this instrument is still too much the neophyte to open its self to questions since that is the format used by Ra. As the instrument grows in awareness this precaution may become unnecessary.

QUESTIONER: Why is there no protection at the floor or bottom of the banishing ritual, and should there be?

RA: I am Ra. This will be the last full query of this working.
The development of the psychic greeting is possible only through the energy centers, starting from a station which you might call within the violet ray moving through the adept's energy center and therefrom

towards the target of opportunity. Depending upon the vibratory nature and purpose of greeting, be it positive or negative, the entity will be energized or blocked in the desired way.

We of Ra approach this instrument in narrow-band contact through violet ray. Others might pierce down through this ray to any energy center. We, for instance, make great use of this instrument's blue-ray energy center as we are attempting to communicate our distortion/understandings of the Law of One.

The entity of Orion pierces the same violet ray and moves to two places to attempt most of its nonphysical opportunities. It activates the green-ray energy center while further blocking indigo-ray energy center. This combination causes confusion in the instrument and subsequent over-activity in unwise proportions in physical complex workings. It simply seeks out the distortions pre-incarnatively programmed and developed in incarnative state.

The energies of life itself, being the One Infinite Creator, flow from the south pole of the body seen in its magnetic form. Thus only the Creator may, through the feet, enter the energy shell of the body to any effect. The effects of the adept are those from the upper direction, and thus the building of the wall of light is quite propitious.

May we ask if there are any shorter queries at this time?

QUESTIONER: I would just ask if there is anything that we could do to make the instrument more comfortable or to improve the contact?

RA: I am Ra. This instrument has some increased distortion in the region of the neck. Some attention here might provide greater comfort. All is well, my friends. The forbearance and patience observed by Ra are commendable. Continue in this fastidiousness of purpose and care for the appropriate configurations for contact, and our continuance of contact will continue to be possible. This is acceptable to us.

I am Ra. I leave you, my friends, glorying in the love and the light of the One Infinite Creator. Go forth, then, rejoicing in the power and in the peace of the One Infinite Creator. Adonai.

Session 73,
October 21, 1981

RA: I am Ra. I greet you in the love and in the light of the One Infinite Creator. We communicate now.

QUESTIONER: Could you please give me an indication of the instrument's condition?

RA: I am Ra. It is as previously stated, with the exception of the vital energy level which is distorted more nearly towards that which is normal for this entity.

QUESTIONER: Has the banishing ritual that we have performed been helpful for this contact?

RA: I am Ra. The ritual described has gained with each working in making efficacious the purity of contact needed not only for the Ra contact but for any working of the adept.

QUESTIONER: Thank you. I would like to thank Ra at this time for the opportunity to be of service to those on this sphere who would want to have the information that we gain here.

You stated that free will, one-pointed in service to others, had the potential of alerting a great mass of light strength. I assume that the same holds precisely true for the service-to-self polarity. Is this correct?

RA: I am Ra. This is incorrect but subtly so. In invocation and evocation of what may be termed negative entities or qualities, the expression alerts the positively oriented equivalent. However, those upon the service-to-others path wait to be called and can only send love.

QUESTIONER: What I was trying to get at was that this alerting of light strength is, as I see it, a process that must be totally a function of free will, as you say, and as the desire and will and purity of desire of the adept increases, the alerting of light strength increases. Is this part of it the same for both the positive and negative potentials, and am I correct with this statement?

RA: I am Ra. To avoid confusion we shall simply restate for clarity your correct assumption.

Those who are upon the service-to-others path may call upon the light strength in direct proportion to the strength and purity of their will to serve. Those upon the service-to-self path may call upon the dark strength in direct proportion to the strength and purity of their will to serve.

QUESTIONER: I will undoubtedly make many errors in my statements today because what I am trying to do is guess at how this works, and let you correct me. In considering the exercise of the Middle Pillar, I have thought it might be wrong in that in it the adept sees or visualizes the light moving downward from the crown chakra down to the feet. Ra has stated that the Creator enters from the feet and moves upward, that this spiraling light enters from the feet and moves upward. It seems to me that the adept alerting the light strength, in visualizing the use of this, would visualize it entering the feet and energizing, first, the red energy center and then moving upward through the energy centers in that fashion. Is this correct?

RA: I am Ra. No.

QUESTIONER: Could you tell me where I am wrong in that statement?

RA: I am Ra. Yes.

QUESTIONER: Would you please do that?

RA: I am Ra. There are two concepts with which you deal. The first is the great way of the development of the light in the microcosmic mind/body/spirit. It is assumed that an adept will have its energy centers functioning smoothly and in a balanced manner to its best effort before a magical working. All magical workings are based upon evocation and/or invocation.

The first invocation of any magical working is that invocation of the magical personality as you are familiar with this term. In the working of which you speak, the first station is the beginning of the invocation of this magical personality, which is invoked by the motion of putting on something. Since you do not have an item of apparel or talisman, the gesture which you have made is appropriate.

The second station is the evocation of the great cross of life. This is an extension of the magical personality to become the Creator. Again, all invocations and evocations are drawn through the violet energy center. This may then be continued towards whatever energy centers are desired to be used.

QUESTIONER: Then will you speak of the difference between the spiraling light that enters through the feet and the light invoked through the crown chakra?

RA: I am Ra. The action of the upward-spiraling light drawn by the will to meet the inner light of the One Infinite Creator may be likened to the beating of the heart and the movement of the muscles surrounding the lungs and all the other functions of the parasympathetic nervous system. The calling of the adept may be likened to those nerve and muscle actions over which the mind/body/spirit complex has conscious control.

QUESTIONER: Previously you stated that where the two directions meet, you have a measure of the development of the particular mind/body/spirit complex. Am I correct?

RA: I am Ra. This is correct.

QUESTIONER: It would seem to me that the visualization of the invocation would be dependent upon what the use was to be of the light. The use could be for healing, communication, or for the general awareness of the creation and the Creator. Would you please speak on this process and my correctness in making this assumption?

RA: I am Ra. We shall offer some thoughts, though it is doubtful that we may exhaust this subject. Each visualization, regardless of the point of the working, begins with some work within the indigo ray. As you may be aware, the ritual which you have begun is completely working within the indigo ray. This is well for it is the gateway. From this beginning, light may be invoked for communication or for healing.

You may note that in the ritual which we offered you to properly begin the Ra workings, the first focus is upon the Creator. We would further note a point which is both subtle and of some interest. The upward-spiraling light developed in its path by the will and, ultimately reaching a high place of mating with the inward fire of the One Creator, still is only preparation for the work upon the mind/body/spirit which may be done by the adept. There is some crystallization of the energy centers used during each working, so that the magician becomes more and more that which it seeks.

More importantly, the time/space mind/body/spirit analog, which is evoked as the magical personality, has its only opportunity to gain rapidly from the experience of the catalytic action available to the third-density space/time mind/body/spirit. Thus the adept is aiding the Creator greatly by offering great catalyst to a greater portion of the creation which is identified as the mind/body/spirit totality of an entity.

QUESTIONER: Desire and will are the factors in this process. Is this correct?

RA: I am Ra. We would add one quality. In the magical personality, desire, will, and polarity are the keys.

QUESTIONER: Many so-called evangelists which we have in our society at present have great desire and very great will, and possibly great polarity, but it seems to me that in many cases that there is a lack of awareness that creates a less-than-effective working in the magical sense. Am I correct in this analysis?

RA: I am Ra. You are partially correct. In examining the polarity of a service-to-others working, the free will must be seen as paramount. Those entities of which you speak are attempting to generate positive changes in consciousness while abridging free will. This causes the blockage of the magical nature of the working except in those cases wherein an entity freely desires to accept the working of the evangelist, as you have called it.

QUESTIONER: What was the orientation with respect to this type of communication for the one known as Jesus of Nazareth?

RA: I am Ra. You may have read some of this entity's workings. It offered itself as teacher to those mind/body/spirit complexes which gathered to hear and even then spoke as through a veil so as to leave room for those not wishing to hear. When this entity was asked to heal, it oft times did so, always ending the working with two admonitions: firstly, that the entity healed had been healed by its faith—that is, its ability to allow and accept changes through the violet ray into the gateway of intelligent energy; secondly, saying always, "Tell no one." These are the workings which attempt the maximal quality of free will while maintaining fidelity to the positive purity of the working.

QUESTIONER: An observation of the working itself by another entity would seem to me to partially abridge free will, in that a seemingly magical occurrence had taken place as the result of the working of an adept. This could be extended to any phenomenon which is other than normal or acceptable. Could you speak on this paradox that is immediately the problem of anyone doing healing?

RA: I am Ra. We are humble messengers of the Law of One. To us there are no paradoxes. The workings which seem magical and, therefore, seem to infringe upon free will do not, in themselves, do so, for the distortions of perception are as many as the witnesses, and each witness sees what it desires to see. Infringement upon free will occurs in this circumstance only if the entity doing the working ascribes the authorship of this event to its self or its own skills. He who states that no working comes from it but only through it is not infringing upon free will.

QUESTIONER: The one known as Jesus accumulated twelve disciples. What was his purpose in having these disciples with him?

RA: I am Ra. What is the purpose of teach/learning if there be no learn/teachers? Those drawn to this entity were accepted by this entity without regard for any outcome. This entity accepted the honor/duty placed upon it by its nature and its sense that to speak was its mission.

QUESTIONER: In the exercise of the fire, I assume the healer would be working with the same energy that we spoke of as entering through the crown chakra. Is this correct?

RA: I am Ra. This is correct, with some additional notation necessary for your thought in continuing this line of study. When the magical personality has been seated in the green-ray energy center for healing work, the energy then may be seen to be the crystalline center through which body energy is channeled. Thus this particular form of healing uses both the energy of the adept and the energy of the upward-spiraling light. As the green-ray center becomes more brilliant, and we would note this brilliance does not imply over-activation but rather crystallization, the energy of the green-ray center of the body complex spirals twice; firstly, clockwise from the green-ray energy center to the right shoulder, through the head, the right elbow, down through the solar plexus, and to the left hand. This sweeps all the body complex energy into a channel which then rotates the great circle clockwise again from right—we correct this instrument—from the left to the feet, to the right hand, to the crown, to the left hand, and so forth.

Thus the incoming body energy, crystallized, regularized, and channeled by the adept's personality reaching to the green-ray energy center, may then pour out the combined energies of the adept which is incarnate, thus offering the service of healing to an entity requesting that service. This basic situation is accomplished as well when there is an entity which is working through a channel to heal.

QUESTIONER: Can you tell me how this transfer of light, I believe it would be, would affect the patient to be healed?

RA: I am Ra. The effect is that of polarization. The entity may or may not accept any percentage of this polarized life energy which is being offered. In the occasion of the laying on of hands, this energy is more specifically channeled and the opportunity for acceptance of this energy similarly more specific.

It may be seen that the King's Chamber effect is not attempted in this form of working but rather the addition to one, whose energies are low, of the opportunity for the building up of those energies. Many of your distortions called illnesses may be aided by such means.

QUESTIONER: As a general statement, which you can correct, the overall picture, as I see it, of the healer and patient is that the one to be healed has, because of a blockage in one of the energy centers or more—we will just consider one particular problem—because of this energy center blockage, the upward-spiraling light which creates one of the seven bodies has been blocked from the maintenance of that body, and this has resulted in the distortion from the perfection of that body which we call disease or a bodily anomaly which is other than perfect. The healer, having suitably configured its energy centers, is able to channel light, the downward-pouring light, though its properly configured energy centers to the one to be healed. If the one to be healed has the mental configuration of acceptance of this light, the light then enters the physical complex and reconfigures the distortion that is created by the original blockage. I am sure that I have made some mistakes in all this. Would you please correct them?

RA: I am Ra. Your mistakes were small. We would not, at this time, attempt a great deal of refinement of that statement, as there is preliminary material which will undoubtedly come forward. We may say that there are various forms of healing. In many, only the energy of the adept is used. In the exercise of fire, some physical complex energy is also channeled.

We might note further that when the one wishing to be healed, though sincere, remains unhealed, as you call this distortion, you may consider pre-incarnative choices and your more helpful aid to such an entity may be the suggestion that it meditate upon the affirmative uses of whatever limitations it might experience. We would also note that in these cases, the indigo-ray workings are often of aid.

Other than these notes, we do not wish to further comment upon your statement at this working.

QUESTIONER: It seems to me that the primary thing of importance for those on the service-to-others path is the development of an attitude which I can only describe as a vibration. This attitude would be developed through meditation, ritual, and the developing appreciation for the creation or Creator, which results in a state of mind that can only be expressed by me as an increase in vibration or oneness with all. Could you expand and correct that statement?

RA: I am Ra. We shall not correct this statement but shall expand upon it by suggesting that to those qualities, you may add the living day by day and moment by moment, for the true adept lives more and more as it is.

QUESTIONER: Thank you. Could you tell me of the number of possible energy transfers between two or more mind/body/spirit complexes. Is it very large, or are there few?

RA: I am Ra. The number is infinite, for is not each mind/body/spirit complex unique?

QUESTIONER: Could you define this statement: "energy transfer between two mind/body/spirit complexes"?

RA: I am Ra. This will be the last full query of this working. This entity still has transferred energy available, but we find rapidly increasing distortions towards pain in the neck, the dorsal area, and the wrists and manual appendages.

The physical energy transfer may be done numerous ways. We shall give two examples. Each begins with some sense of the self as Creator or in some way the magical personality being invoked. This may be consciously or unconsciously done. Firstly, that exercise of which we have spoken called the exercise of fire: this is, through physical energy transfer, not that which is deeply involved in the body complex combinations. Thusly the transfer is subtle, and each transfer unique in what is offered and what is accepted. At this point we may note that this is the cause for the infinite array of possible energy transfers.

The second energy transfer of which we would speak is the sexual energy transfer. This takes place upon a nonmagical level by all those entities which vibrate green ray active. It is possible, as in the case of this instrument which dedicates itself to the service of the One Infinite Creator, to further refine this energy transfer. When the other-self also dedicates itself in service to the One Infinite Creator, the transfer is doubled. Then the amount of energy transferred is dependent only upon the amount of polarized sexual energy created and released. There are refinements from this point onward, leading to the realm of the high sexual magic.

In the realm of the mental bodies, there are variations of mental energy transferred. This is, again, dependent upon the knowledge sought and the knowledge offered. The most common mental energy transfer is that of the teacher and the pupil. The amount of energy is dependent upon the quality of this offering upon the part of the teacher and regards the purity of the desire to serve, and the quality of information offered and, upon the part of the student, the purity of the desire to learn and the quality of the mind vibratory complex which receives knowledge.

Another form of mental energy transfer is that of the listener and the speaker. When the speaker is experiencing mental/emotional complex distortions towards anguish, sorrow, or other mental pain, from what we have said before, you may perhaps garner knowledge of the variations possible in this transfer.

The spiritual energy transfers are at the heart of all energy transfers as a knowledge of self and other-self as Creator is paramount, and this is spiritual work. The varieties of spiritual energy transfer include those things of which we have spoken this day as we spoke upon the subject of the adept.

Are there any brief queries before we leave this working?

QUESTIONER: Only if there is anything we can do to improve the comfort of the instrument and the contact, and secondly, is there anything that you wish not published in today's session?

RA: I am Ra. We call your attention to two items. Firstly, it is well that the candle which spirals 10° each working be never allowed to gutter, as this would cause imbalance in the alignment of the appurtenances in their protective role for this instrument. Secondly, we might suggest attention to the neck area so that the cushion upon which it is supported be more comfortable. This difficulty has abbreviated many workings.

We thank you, my friends, for your conscientiousness and your fastidiousness with regard to these appurtenances, which, as our workings proceed, seems to be increasing. Secondly, your decisions are completely your own as to that material which you may wish published from this working.

I am Ra. I leave you glorying in the love and in the light of the One Infinite Creator. Go forth, then, rejoicing in the power and in the peace of the One Infinite Creator. Adonai.

Session 74,
October 28, 1981

RA: I am Ra. I greet you in the love and in the light of the One Infinite Creator. We communicate now.

QUESTIONER: Would you first please give me the condition of the instrument?

RA: I am Ra. It is as previously stated.

QUESTIONER: Before we get to new material, in the last session there seems to be a small error that I corrected then having to do with this statement: "no working comes from it but only through it." Was this an error in the transmission? What caused this?

RA: I am Ra. This instrument, while fully open to our narrow-band contact, at times experiences a sudden strengthening of the distortion which you call pain. This weakens the contact momentarily. This type of increased distortion has been occurring in this instrument's bodily complex with more frequency in the time period which you may term the previous fortnight. Although it is not normally a phenomenon which causes difficulties in transmission, it did so twice in the previous working. Both times it was necessary to correct or rectify the contact.

QUESTIONER: Could you please describe the trance state? I am somewhat confused as to how, in a trance, pain can affect the instrument, since I was of the opinion that there would be no feeling of pain by the bodily complex in the trance state?

RA: I am Ra. This is correct. The instrument has no awareness of this or other sensations. However, we of Ra use the yellow-ray-activated physical complex as a channel through which to speak. As the mind/body/spirit complex of the instrument leaves this physical shell in our keeping, it is finely adjusted to our contact.

However, the distortion which you call pain, when sufficiently severe, mitigates against proper contact and, when the increased distortion is violent, can cause the tuning of the channel to waver. This tuning must then be corrected, which we may do as the instrument offers us this opportunity freely.

QUESTIONER: In a previous session there was a question on the archetypical mind that was not fully answered. I would like to continue with the answer to that question. Could you please continue with that, or will it be necessary for me to read the entire question over again?

RA: I am Ra. As a general practice it is well to vibrate the query at the same space/time as the answer is desired. However, in this case it is acceptable to us that a note be inserted at this point in your recording of these sound vibratory complexes referring to the location of the query in previous workings.

[Note: This question was the last question asked in Session 67.]

The query, though thoughtful, is in some degree falling short of the realization of the nature of the archetypical mind. We may not teach/learn for any other to the extent that we become learn/teachers. Therefore, we shall make some general notations upon this interesting subject and allow the questioner to consider and further refine any queries.

The archetypical mind may be defined as that mind which is peculiar to the Logos of this planetary sphere. Thusly, unlike the great cosmic all-mind, it contains the material which it pleased the Logos to offer as refinements to the great cosmic beingness. The archetypical mind, then, is that which contains all facets which may affect mind or experience.

The Magician was named as a significant archetype. However, it was not recognized that this portion of the archetypical mind represents not a portion of the deep subconscious but the conscious mind and more especially the will. The archetype called by some the High Priestess, then, is the corresponding intuitive or subconscious faculty.

Let us observe the entity as it is in relationship to the archetypical mind. You may consider the possibilities of utilizing the correspondences between the mind/body/spirit in microcosm and the archetypical mind/body/spirit closely approaching the Creator. For instance, in your ritual performed to purify this place, you use the term "Ve Geburah." It is a correct assumption that this is a portion or aspect of the One Infinite Creator. However, there are various correspondences with the archetypical mind which may be more and more refined by the adept. "Ve Geburah" is the correspondence of Michael, of Mars, of the positive, of maleness. "Ve Gedulah" has correspondences to Jupiter, to femaleness, to the negative, to that portion of the Tree of Life concerned with Auriel.

We could go forward with more and more refinements of these two entries into the archetypical mind. We could discuss color correspondences, relationships with other archetypes, and so forth. This is the work of the adept, not the teach/learner. We may only suggest that there are systems of study which may address themselves to the aspects of the archetypical mind, and it is well to choose one and study carefully. It is more nearly well if the adept go beyond whatever has been written and make such correspondences that the archetype can be called upon at will.

QUESTIONER: I have a statement here that I am going to make and let you correct. I see that the disciplines of the personality feed the indigo-ray energy center and affect the power of the white magician by unblocking the lower energy centers, allowing for the free flow of the upward-spiraling light to reach the indigo center. Is this correct?

RA: I am Ra. No.

QUESTIONER: Will you please correct me?

RA: I am Ra. The indigo center is indeed most important for the work of the adept. However, it cannot, no matter how crystallized, correct to any extent whatsoever imbalances or blockages in other energy centers. They must needs be cleared seriatim from red upwards.

QUESTIONER: I'm not sure exactly if I understand this. The question is how do disciplines of the personality feed the indigo-ray energy center and affect the power of the white magician? Does that question make sense?

RA: I am Ra. Yes.

QUESTIONER: Would you answer it please?

RA: I am Ra. We would be happy to answer this query. We understood the previous query as being of other import. The indigo ray is the ray of the adept. There is an identification between the crystallization of that energy center and the improvement of the working of the mind/body/spirit as it begins to transcend space/time balancing and to enter the combined realms of space/time and time/space.

QUESTIONER: Let me see if I have a wrong opinion here of the effect of disciplines of the personality. I was assuming that the discipline of the personality to, shall we say, have a balanced attitude toward a single fellow entity would properly clear and balance, to some extent, the orange-ray energy center. Is this correct?

RA: I am Ra. We cannot say that you speak incorrectly, but merely less than completely. The disciplined personality, when faced with an other-self, has all centers balanced according to its unique balance. Thusly the other-self looks in a mirror seeing its self.

QUESTIONER: The disciplines of the personality are the paramount work of any who have become consciously aware of the process of evolution. Am I correct on that statement?

RA: I am Ra. Quite.

QUESTIONER: What I am trying to get at is how these disciplines affect the energy centers and the power of the white magician. Will you tell me how that works?

RA: I am Ra. The heart of the discipline of the personality is threefold. One, know yourself. Two, accept yourself. Three, become the Creator.
     The third step is that step which, when accomplished, renders one the most humble servant of all, transparent in personality and completely able to know and accept other-selves. In relation to the pursuit of the magical working, the continuing discipline of the personality involves the adept in knowing its self, accepting its self, and thus clearing the path towards the great indigo gateway to the Creator. To become the Creator is to become all that there is. There is, then, no personality in the sense with which the adept begins its learn/teaching. As the consciousness of the indigo ray becomes more crystalline, more work may be done; more may be expressed from intelligent infinity.

QUESTIONER: You stated that a working of service to others has the potential of alerting a great mass of light strength. Could you describe just exactly how this works and what the uses of this would be?

RA: I am Ra. There are sound vibratory complexes which act much like the dialing of your telephone. When they are appropriately vibrated with accompanying will and concentration, it is as though many upon your metaphysical or inner planes received a telephone call. This call they answer by their attention to your working.

QUESTIONER: There are many of these. The ones most obvious in our society are those used in the church rather than those used by the magical adept. What is the difference in the effect in those used in our various churches and those specifically magical incantations used by the adept?

RA: I am Ra. If all in your churches were adepts consciously full of will, of seeking, of concentration, of conscious knowledge of the calling, there would be no difference. The efficacy of the calling is a function of the magical qualities of those who call; that is, their desire to seek the altered state of consciousness desired.

QUESTIONER: In selecting the protective ritual, we finally agreed upon the Banishing Ritual of the Lesser Pentagram. I assume that these sound vibratory complexes are of the type of which you speak for the alerting of those on the inner planes. Is this correct?

RA: I am Ra. This is correct.

QUESTIONER: If we had constructed a ritual of our own with words used for the first time in this sequence of protection, what would have been the relative merit of this with respect to the ritual that we chose?

RA: I am Ra. It would be less. In constructing ritual, it is well to study the body of written work which is available for names of positive or service to others power are available.

QUESTIONER: I will make an analogy to the loudness of the ringing of the telephone in using the ritual as the efficiency of the practitioners using the ritual. I see several things affecting the efficiency of the ritual: first, the desire of the practitioners to serve, their ability to invoke the magical personality, their ability to visualize while performing the ritual, and let me ask you as to the relative importance of those items and how each may be intensified?

RA: I am Ra. This query borders upon over-specificity. It is most important for the adept to feel its own growth as teach/learner.
    We may only say that you correctly surmise the paramount import of the magical personality. This is a study in itself. With the appropriate emotional will, polarity, and purity, work may be done with or without proper sound vibration complexes. However, there is no need for the blunt instrument when the scalpel is available.

QUESTIONER: I assume that the reason that the rituals that have been used previously are of effect is that these words have built a bias in consciousness of those who have worked in these areas, so that those who are of a distortion of mind that we seek will respond to imprint in consciousness of this series of words. Is this correct?

RA: I am Ra. This is, to a great extent, correct. The exception is the sounding of some of what you call your Hebrew and some of what you call your Sanskrit vowels. These sound vibration complexes have power before time and space and represent configurations of light which built all that there is.

QUESTIONER: Why do these sounds have this property?

RA: I am Ra. The correspondence in vibratory complex is mathematical.
At this time, we have enough transferred energy for one full query.

QUESTIONER: How did the users of these sounds, Sanskrit and Hebrew, determine what these sounds were?

RA: I am Ra. In the case of the Hebrew, that entity known as Yahweh aided this knowledge through impression upon the material of genetic coding which became language, as you call it.
In the case of Sanskrit, the sound vibrations are pure due to the lack of previous, what you call, alphabet or letter naming. Thus the sound vibration complexes seemed to fall into place as from the Logos. This was a more, shall we say, natural or unaided situation or process.
We would at this time make note of the incident in the previous working where our contact was incorrectly placed for a short period and was then corrected. In the exercise of the fire you may see the initial spiral clockwise from the green-ray energy center, through the shoulders and head, then through the elbows, then to the left hand. The channel had been corrected before the remainder of this answer was completed.
Is there a brief query at this time?

QUESTIONER: Is there anything that we could do to make the instrument more comfortable or to improve the contact?

RA: I am Ra. All is well. The instrument continues in some pain, as you call this distortion. The neck area remains most distorted, although the changes have been, to a small degree, helpful. The alignments are good.

We would leave you now, my friends, in the love and in the light of the One Infinite Creator. Go forth, then, glorying and rejoicing in the power and in the peace of the One Infinite Creator. Adonai.

Session 75,
October 31, 1981

RA: I am Ra. I greet you in the love and in the light of the One Infinite Creator. We communicate now.

QUESTIONER: The instrument would like to know why twice during the "Benedictus" portion of the music, she sang in a group concert that she experienced what she believes to be a psychic attack?

RA: I am Ra. This is not a minor query.*2 We shall first remove the notations, which are minor. In the vibrating, which you call singing, of the portion of what this instrument hallows as the Mass, which immediately precedes that which is the chink called the "Hosanna," there is an amount of physical exertion required that is exhausting to any entity. This portion of which we speak is termed the "Sanctus." We come now to the matter of interest.

When the entity Jehoshuah*3 decided to return to the location called Jerusalem for the holy days of its people, it turned from work mixing love and wisdom and embraced martyrdom, which is the work of love without wisdom.

The "Hosanna," as it is termed, and the following "Benedictus," is that which is the written summation of what was shouted as Jehoshuah came into the place of its martyrdom. The general acceptance of this shout, "Hosanna to the son of David! Hosanna in the highest! Blessed is he who comes in the name of the Lord!," by that which is called the church has been a misstatement, an occurrence which has been, perhaps, unfortunate for it is more distorted than much of the so-called Mass.

There were two factions present to greet Jehoshuah; firstly, a small group of those which hoped for an earthly king. However, Jehoshuah rode upon an ass stating by its very demeanor that it was no earthly king and wished no fight with Roman or Sadducee.

---

*2. It may seem that there is an excessive amount of personal and rather melodramatic material about psychic attack included here. We considered long and hard before deciding not to delete it. Our reason: Ra seems to suggest that any "light worker" will, if successful in this work, attract some sort of negatively oriented greeting. Therefore, we wish to share our experiences and Ra's discussion of them, in hopes that the information might be helpful.
*3. Ra has previously identified this name as the name of Jesus in biblical times

The greater number were those which had been instructed by rabbi and elder to make jest of this entity, for those of the hierarchy feared this entity who seemed to be one of them, giving respect to their laws and then, in their eyes, betraying those time-honored laws and taking the people with it.

The chink for this instrument is this subtle situation which echoes down through your space/time and, more than this, the place the "Hosanna" holds as the harbinger of that turning to martyrdom. We may speak only generally here. The instrument did not experience the full force of the greeting, which it correctly identified during the "Hosanna," due to the intense concentration necessary to vibrate its portion of that composition. However, the "Benedictus" in this particular rendition of these words is vibrated by one entity. Thus the instrument relaxed its concentration and was immediately open to the fuller greeting.

QUESTIONER: The chink then, as I understand it, was originally created by the decision of Jesus to take the path of martyrdom? Is this correct?

RA: I am Ra. This is, in relation to this instrument, quite correct. It is aware of certain overbalances towards love, even to martyrdom, but has not yet, to any significant degree, balanced these distortions. We do not imply that this course of unbridled compassion has any fault, but affirm its perfection. It is an example of love which has served as beacon to many.

For those who seek further, the consequences of martyrdom must be considered, for in martyrdom lies the end of the opportunity, in the density of the martyr, to offer love and light. Each entity must seek its deepest path.

QUESTIONER: Let me see, then, if I understand how the Orion entity finds a chink in this distortion. The entity identifying in any amount toward martyrdom is then open by its free will to the aid of the Orion group to make it a martyr. Am I correct?

RA: I am Ra. You are correct only in the quite specialized position in which the instrument finds itself; that is, of being involved in and dedicated to work which is magical or extremely polarized in nature. This group entered this work with polarity but virtual innocence as to the magical nature of this polarity. That it is beginning to discover.

QUESTIONER: How was the Orion entity able to act through this linkage of the "Hosanna"? Was this simply because of mental distortions of the instrument at this period of time, because of that suggested by the music, or was it a more physical or metaphysical link from the time of Christ?

RA: I am Ra. Firstly, the latter supposition is false. This entity is not linked with the entity Jehoshuah. Secondly, there is a most unique circumstance. There is an entity which has attracted the attention of an Orion light being. This is extremely rare.

This entity has an intense devotion to the teachings and example of the one it calls Jesus. This entity then vibrates in song a most demanding version, called *The Mass in B Minor* by Bach, of this exemplary votive complex of sound vibrations. The entity is consciously identifying with each part of this Mass. Only thusly was the chink made available. As you can see, it is not an ordinary occurrence and would not have happened had any ingredient been left out: exhaustion, bias in the belief complexes, attention from an Orion entity, and the metaphysical nature of that particular set of words.

QUESTIONER: What was the Orion entity's objective with respect to the entity you spoke of who, in a demanding manner, sings the Mass?

RA: I am Ra. The Orion entity wishes to remove the instrument.

QUESTIONER: Is this a fourth or a fifth density?

RA: I am Ra. This instrument is being greeted by a fifth-density entity which has lost some polarity due to its lack of dictatorship over the disposition of the instrument's mind/body/spirit or its yellow-ray-activated physical complex.

QUESTIONER: You are speaking of this other person now who sang in the Mass? Is this correct?

RA: I am Ra. No.

QUESTIONER: I think there was a little miscommunication here. I was asking about the other person who sings the Mass in creating this chink that was also greeted by an Orion entity, and my question was what density is the Orion entity who greets the other person who sings the Mass?

RA: I am Ra. We did not speak of any entity but the instrument.

QUESTIONER: OK. I misunderstood. I thought you were speaking of someone else in the singing group who had been identified with the singing. The entire time we were speaking we were speaking only of the instrument? Is this correct?

RA: I am Ra. This is correct.

QUESTIONER: I am sorry for my confusion. Sometimes, as you say, sound vibration complexes are not very adequate.

The answer to this next question probably has to do with our distorted view of time, but as I see it, Wanderers in this density who come from the fifth density or sixth density should already be of a relatively high degree of adeptness, and they must follow a slightly different path back to the adeptness that they once had in a higher density and get as close to it as they can in the third density. Is this correct?

RA: I am Ra. Your query is less than perfectly focused. We shall address the subject in general.

There are many Wanderers whom you may call adepts who do no conscious work in the present incarnation. It is a matter of attention. One may be a fine catcher of your game sphere, but if the eye is not turned as this sphere is tossed, then perchance it will pass the entity by. If it turned its eyes upon the sphere, catching would be easy. In the case of Wanderers which seek to recapitulate the degree of adeptness which each had acquired previous to this life experience, we may note that even after the forgetting process has been penetrated, there is still the yellow-activated body which does not respond as does the adept which is of a green- or blue-ray-activated body. Thusly, you may see the inevitability of frustrations and confusion due to the inherent difficulties of manipulating the finer forces of consciousness through the chemical apparatus of the yellow-ray-activated body.

QUESTIONER: You probably can't answer this, but are there any suggestions that you could give with respect to the instrument's coming hospital experience that could be of benefit for her?

RA: I am Ra. We may make one suggestion and leave the remainder with the Creator. It is well for each to realize its self as the Creator. Thusly each may support each, including the support of self by humble love of self as Creator.

QUESTIONER: You spoke in a previous session about certain Hebrew and Sanskrit sound vibratory complexes being powerful because they were mathematically related to that which was the creation. Could you expand on this understanding as to how these are linked?

RA: I am Ra. As we previously stated, the linkage is mathematical or that of the ratio you may consider musical. There are those whose mind complex activities would attempt to resolve this mathematical ratio, but at present the coloration of the intoned vowel is part of the vibration, which cannot be accurately measured. However, it is equivalent to types of rotation of your primary material particles.

QUESTIONER: If these sounds are precisely vibrated, then what effect or use, with respect to the purposes of the adept, would they have?

RA: I am Ra. You may consider the concept of sympathetic resonance. When certain sounds are correctly vibrated, the creation sings.

QUESTIONER: Would these sounds, then, be of a musical nature in that there would be a musical arrangement of many different sound vibrations, or would this apply to just one single note? Which would it apply more to?

RA: I am Ra. This query is not easily answered. In some cases only the intoned vowel has effect. In other cases, most notably Sanskrit combinations, the selection of harmonic intervals is also of resonant nature.

QUESTIONER: Then would the adept use this resonant quality to become more one with the creation and, therefore, attain his objective in that way?

RA: I am Ra. It would be perhaps more accurate to state that in this circumstance, the creation becomes more and more contained within the practitioner. The balance of your query is correct.

QUESTIONER: Could you tell me the musical name of the notes to be intoned that are of this quality?

RA: I am Ra. We may not.

QUESTIONER: I didn't think that you could, but I thought it wouldn't hurt to ask.

Then I assume that these must be sought out and determined by empirical observation of their effect by the seeker. Is this correct?

RA: I am Ra. This is partially correct. As your seeking continues, there will be added to empirical data that acuity of sensibility which continued working in the ways of the adept offers.

QUESTIONER: Is the exercise of the fire best for the instrument, or is there anything better that we could do other than the things that you have already suggested to aid the instrument?

RA: I am Ra. Continue as you are at present. We cannot speak of the future, as we may then affect it, but there is a great probability/possibility if you follow the path which you now tread that more efficacious methods for the entire group will be established.

QUESTIONER: You mentioned in an earlier session that the hair was an antenna. Could you expand on that statement as to how that works?

RA: I am Ra. It is difficult to so do due to the metaphysical nature of this antennae effect. Your physics are concerned with measurements in your physical complex of experience. The metaphysical nature of the contact of those in time/space is such that the hair, as it has significant length, becomes as a type of electrical battery which stays charged and tuned and is then able to aid contact even when there are small anomalies in the contact.

QUESTIONER: Is there an optimum length of hair for this aid?

RA: I am Ra. There is no outer limit on length, but the, shall we say, inner limit is approximately 4 to 4-and-one-half inches depending upon the strength of the contact and the nature of the instrument.

QUESTIONER: May anyone in third density accomplish some degree of healing if they have the proper will, desire, and polarity, or is there a minimal balance of the energy centers of the healer that is also necessary?

RA: I am Ra. Any entity may at any time instantaneously clear and balance its energy centers. Thus, in many cases those normally quite blocked, weakened, and distorted may, through love and strength of will, become healers momentarily. To be a healer by nature, one must indeed train its self in the disciplines of the personality.

QUESTIONER: How does the use of the magical ritual invoking the magical personality aid the mind/body/spirit complex totality? Could you expand on the answer that you gave in the last session with respect to that?

RA: I am Ra. When the magical personality is properly and efficaciously invoked, the self has invoked its Higher Self. Thus a bridge betwixt space/time and time/space is made, and the sixth-density magical personality experiences directly the third-density catalyst for the duration of the working. It is most central to deliberately take off the magical personality after the working in order that the Higher Self resume its appropriate configuration as analog to the space/time mind/body/spirit.

QUESTIONER: Then you are saying that the act, signal, or key for the invoking of the magical personality which is the putting of something on or a gesture should also be as carefully taken off to reverse the gesture perhaps at the end of the invocation. Is this correct?

RA: I am Ra. This is correct. It should be fastidiously accomplished either in mind or by gesture as well if this is of significant aid.

QUESTIONER: Now in the invocation of the magical personality, it is not necessarily effective for the neophyte. Is there a point at which there is a definite quantum change and that then the magical personality does reside in the neophyte, or can it be done in small degrees or percentages of magical personality as the neophyte becomes more adept?

RA: I am Ra. The latter is correct.

QUESTIONER: The three aspects of the magical personality are stated to be power, love, and wisdom. Is this correct, and are these the only primary aspects of the magical personality?

RA: I am Ra. The three aspects of the magical personality, power, love, and wisdom, are so called in order that attention be paid to each aspect in developing the basic tool of the adept; that is, its self. It is by no means a personality of three aspects. It is a being of unity, a being of sixth density, and equivalent to what you call your Higher Self, and at the same time is a personality enormously rich in variety of experience and subtlety of emotion.

The three aspects are given that the neophyte not abuse the tools of its trade but rather approach those tools balanced in the center of love and wisdom and thus seeking power in order to serve.

QUESTIONER: Then is it correct that a good sequence for the developing of the magical personality would be alternate meditations, first on power, and then a meditation on love, and then a meditation on wisdom, and then to continue cycling that way?

RA: I am Ra. This is indeed an appropriate technique. In this particular group there is an additional aid in that each entity manifests one of these qualities in a manner which approaches the archetype. Thusly visualization may be personalized and much love and support within the group generated.

QUESTIONER: You made the statement in a previous session that the true adept lives more and more as it is. Will you explain and expand more upon that statement?

RA: I am Ra. Each entity is the Creator. The entity, as it becomes more and more conscious of its self, gradually comes to the turning point at which it determines to seek either in service to others or in service to self. The seeker becomes the adept when it has balanced with minimal adequacy the energy centers red, orange, yellow, and blue with the addition of the green for the positive, thus moving into indigo work.

The adept then begins to do less of the preliminary or outer work, having to do with function, and begins to effect the inner work, which has to do with being. As the adept becomes a more and more consciously crystallized entity, it gradually manifests more and more of that which it always has been since before time; that is, the One Infinite Creator.

This instrument begins to show rapid distortion towards increase of pain.

We, therefore, would offer time for any brief query before we leave this working.

QUESTIONER: Is there anything that we can do to make the instrument more comfortable or to improve the contact?

RA: I am Ra. You are conscientious. The alignments are well.

I am Ra. I leave you, my friends, in the love and the light of the One Infinite Creator. Go forth, therefore, rejoicing in the power and peace of the One Infinite Creator. Adonai.

INDEX

ABOUT THE AUTHORS

DON ELKINS was born in Louisville, Kentucky, in 1930. He held a BS and MS in mechanical engineering from the University of Louisville, as well as an MS in general engineering from Speed Scientific School. He was professor of physics and engineering at the University of Louisville for twelve years from 1953 to 1965. In 1965 he left his tenured position and became a Boeing 727 pilot for a major airline to devote himself more fully to UFO and paranormal research. He also served with distinction in the US Army as a master sergeant during the Korean War.

Don Elkins began his research into the paranormal in 1955. In 1962, Don started an experiment in channeling, using the protocols he had learned from a contactee group in Detroit, Michigan. That experiment blossomed into a channeling practice that led eventually to the Law of One material 19 years later. Don passed away on November 7, 1984.

CARLA L. RUECKERT (McCarty) was born in 1943 in Lake Forest, Illinois. She completed undergraduate studies in English literature at the University of Louisville in 1966 and earned her master's degree in library service in 1971.

Carla became partners with Don in 1968. In 1970, they formed L/L Research. In 1974, she began channeling and continued in that effort until she was stopped in 2011 by a spinal fusion surgery. During four of those thirty-seven years of channeling (1981–1984), Carla served as the instrument for the Law of One material.

In 1987, she married Jim McCarty, and together they continued the mission of L/L Research. Carla passed into larger life on April 1, 2015.

JAMES MCCARTY was born in 1947 in Kearney, Nebraska. After receiving an undergraduate degrees from the University of Nebraska at Kearney and a master of science in early childhood education from the University of Florida, Jim moved to a piece of wilderness in Marion County, Kentucky, in 1974 to build his own log cabin in the woods, and to develop a self-sufficient lifestyle. For the next six years, he was in almost complete retreat.

He founded the Rock Creek Research and Development Laboratories in 1977 to further his teaching efforts. After experimenting, Jim decided that he preferred the methods and directions he had found in studying with L/L Research in 1978. In 1980, he joined his research with Don's and Carla's.

Jim and Carla were married in 1987. Jim has a wide L/L correspondence and creates wonderful gardens and stonework. He enjoys beauty, nature, dance, and silence.

NOTE: The Ra contact continued until session number 106. There are five volumes total in The Law of One series, Book I–Book V. There is also other material available from our research group on our archive website, www.llresearch.org.

You may reach us by email at contact@llresearch.org, or by mail at: L/L Research, P.O. Box 5195, Louisville, KY 40255–0195

NOTES

NOTES

THE RA MATERIAL

The Law of One
Book IV

The Law of One
Book IV

DON ELKINS CARLA RUECKERT
JAMES ALLEN McCARTY

REDFeather™
MIND | BODY | SPIRIT
4880 Lower Valley Road, Atglen, PA 19310

First Printing 1983
ISBN: 978-0-924608-10-0

*3,000 copies of The Law of One were privately printed by L/L Research, Louisville, KY, before it was printed under the title *The Ra Material*.

Type set in Chaparral Pro

Book IV
Softcover ISBN: 978-0-924608-10-0
Hardcover ISBN: 978-0-7643-6557-7
Box Set ISBN (Books I–V): 978-0-7643-6021-3
E-Book ISBN: 978-1-5073-0118-0

Printed in India

Updated Edition
10 9 8 7 6 5 4 3

Published by Red Feather Mind, Body, Spirit
An imprint of Schiffer Publishing, Ltd.
4880 Lower Valley Road
Atglen, PA 19310
Phone: (610) 593–1777; Fax: (610) 593–2002
E–mail: Info@schifferbooks.com
Web: www.redfeathermbs.com

For our complete selection of fine books on this and related subjects, please visit our website at www.schifferbooks.com. You may also write for a free catalog.

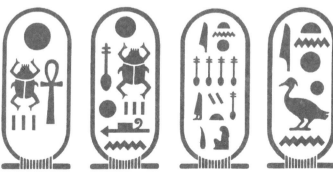

FOREWORD

On January 15, 1981, our research group started receiving a communication from the social memory complex Ra. From this communication precipitated the Law of One and some of the distortions of the Law of One.

The pages of this book contain an exact transcript, edited only to remove some personal material, of the communications received in Sessions 76 through 103 with Ra.

To a certain extent, this material presupposes a point of view that we have developed in the course of many years' study of the UFO phenomenon. If you are not familiar with our previous work, a reading of our book *Secrets of the UFO* might prove helpful in understanding the present material. Also, as you can see from this book's title, there are seventy-five previous sessions with Ra, which were collected in *The Law of One*, Books I, II, and III. If at all possible, it is good to begin with the beginning of this material, as later concepts build upon previous concepts. All these volumes are available from us by mail.

Those who gained familiarity with *The Law of One* through the mass-market publication of that volume under the title, *The Ra Material,* may be assured that the substantial introduction contained in that volume duplicates the subject matter contained in *Secrets of the UFO,* although *Secrets of the UFO* may still be interesting to you.

Book IV of *The Law of One* is a beginning in the examination of the nature and the proper metaphysical use of the archetypical mind. The archetypical mind is the mind of the Logos, the blueprint used to make the creation and the means by which we evolve in mind, body, and spirit. Ra stated that the archetypical mind could best be studied by one of three methods: the Tarot, astrology, or the Tree of Life, which is also known as white ceremonial magic. We decided to investigate the archetypical mind by delving into the Tarot, more especially the twenty-two images of the Major Arcana. In Book IV we work primarily with the first seven cards, which are archetypes for the structure of the mind. An overview of all the Tarot's twenty-two archetypes is also sought.

Any sensible consideration of a contact such as this would yield the conclusion that if the contact were valid, we would at some point begin receiving material the complete basis of which was not familiar to us. This has happened in Book IV. As you may see in the questioning, we scrambled as best we could throughout the entire volume in an attempt to keep up with the information that we were receiving, and to formulate reasonable questions. Even though our session schedule was relaxed, and the intervening time was used for study, we are aware that the questioning in this volume is more scattered than in the first three volumes of Ra sessions. We know of no solution to our own lack of knowledge and are at least confident that we cannot outdistance the reader, for we knew no more than you before we asked each question!

We do feel that it would be helpful if we included some information about the Tarot and its general terminology and compared that with a general outline of the Tarot from Ra's viewpoint, the viewpoint that Ra shared with the Egyptians so many years ago. The following comparison deals only with the twenty-two Major Arcana, since it was only these "concept complexes" that were used by Ra and that were later drawn by Egyptian priests, to describe the process of the evolution of the mind, the body, and the spirit. The Court Arcana and the Minor Arcana were of other influences and were concerned primarily with the astrological approach to this study. Each card is described first by its Arcanum number, then by traditional terminology, and third by Ra's terminology.

The cards upon which we originally questioned were not available for reprinting, so we have reproduced here the Major Arcana of the deck most closely resembling our first deck. These images are to be found in George Fathman's *The Royal Road: A Study in the Egyptian Tarot; Key to Sacred Numbers and Symbols* (Eagle Point, OR: Life Research Foundation, 1951).

As you can see, the first seven cards of the Major Arcana were designed to describe the evolution of the mind; the second seven, the evolution of the body; and the third seven, the evolution of the spirit. Arcanum Number XXII is called The Choice, and the choice spoken of is the central choice each conscious seeker or adept makes as it strives to master the lessons of the third-density experience to seek in service to others or in service to self.

Arcanum Number I
The Magician
MATRIX OF THE MIND

Arcanum Number II
The High Priestess
POTENTIATOR OF THE MIND

Arcanum Number III
The Empress
CATALYST OF THE MIND

Arcanum Number IV
The Emperor
EXPERIENCE OF THE MIND

Arcanum Number V
The Hierophant
SIGNIFICATOR OF THE MIND

Arcanum Number VI
The Lovers or Two Paths
TRANSFORMATION OF THE MIND

Arcanum Number VII
The Chariot
GREAT WAY OF THE MIND

THE
MIND

Arcanum Number VIII

Justice or Balance

MATRIX OF THE BODY

Arcanum Number IX

Wisdom or the Sage

POTENTIATOR OF THE BODY

Arcanum Number X

Wheel of Fortune

CATALYST OF THE BODY

Arcanum Number XI

The Enchantress

EXPERIENCE OF THE BODY

Arcanum Number XII
The Hanged Man or Martyr
SIGNIFICATOR OF THE BODY

Arcanum Number XIII
Death
TRANSFORMATION OF THE BODY

Arcanum Number XIV
The Alchemist
GREAT WAY OF THE BODY

THE
BODY

Arcanum Number XV
The Devil
MATRIX OF THE SPIRIT

Arcanum Number XVI
Lightning Struck Tower
POTENTIATOR OF THE SPIRIT

Arcanum Number XVII
The Star or Hope
CATALYST OF THE SPIRIT

Arcanum Number XVIII
The Moon
EXPERIENCE OF THE SPIRIT

Arcanum Number XIX
The Sun
SIGNIFICATOR OF THE SPIRIT

Arcanum Number XX
Judgment
TRANSFORMATION OF THE SPIRIT

Arcanum Number XXI
The World
GREAT WAY OF THE SPIRIT

THE
SPIRIT

Arcanum Number XXII
The Fool,

THE CHOICE

One of the primary discoveries in Book IV is the concept and purpose of the "veil of forgetting" that exists between the conscious and unconscious minds in our current third-density experience. Third densities closer to the center of our galaxy apparently did not have such a veil and, therefore, did not forget any event in any incarnation. This condition simplified each entity's experience and also the nature of that archetypical mind. Readers, therefore, should be aware that the questioning focuses on both pre-veil and post-veiling experiences and the archetypical minds of both types of experience in order to get a better understanding of our current veiled experience in the third density of this octave of creation.

As a result of our questioning we have drawn our own images, the first seven of which may be found at the back of this volume.

The Ra contact continued for 106 sessions, which were printed into four books in *The Law of One* series. They are available at your local bookstore, from Schiffer Publishing, or from us. If you wish to receive our quarterly newsletter, in which the best of our current channeling is published, please request that you be put on our mailing list.

L/L Research
Don Elkins
Carla L. Rueckert
James A. McCarty

PO Box 5195
Louisville, KY 40255-0195
July 8, 1983

Session 76,
February 3, 1982

RA: I am Ra. I greet you in the love and in the light of the One Infinite Creator. We communicate now.

QUESTIONER: Could you first please give me an indication of the condition of the instrument?

RA: I am Ra. This instrument is in a state of physical-complex bankruptcy, which has existed for some of the measure you call time. The vital energies are normal, with a strong spiritual-complex counterpart and will lending substance to the mind/body/spirit-complex energy levels.

QUESTIONER: Will our continued communication with Ra be deleterious to the physical energies of the instrument?

RA: I am Ra. We may answer in two modes. Firstly, if the instrument were thusly dedicated to this use with no transfer of energy of physical-complex nature, it would begin to call upon the vital energy itself, and this, done in any substantive measure, is actively deleterious to a mind/body/spirit complex if that complex wishes further experience in the illusion which it now distorts.

Secondly, if care is taken, firstly, to monitor the outer parameters of the instrument, then to transfer physical energy by sexual transfer, by magical protection, and, lastly, by the energetic displacements of thought-forms energizing the instrument during contact, there is no difficulty in that there is no worsening of the instrument's mind/body/spirit-complex distortions of strength/weakness.

It is to be noted that the instrument, by dedicating itself to this service, attracts greetings of which you are aware. These are inconvenient but, with care taken, need not be lastingly deleterious either to the instrument or the contact.

QUESTIONER: Of the three things that you mentioned that we could do for the instrument's benefit, would you clarify the last one? I didn't quite understand what you meant.

RA: I am Ra. As the entity which you are allows its being to empathize with any other being, so then it may choose to share with the other-self those energies which may be salubrious to the other-self. The mechanism of these energy transfers is the thought or, more precisely, the thought-form, for any thought is a form or symbol or thing that is an object seen in time/space reference.

QUESTIONER: Has our use of the Banishing Ritual of the Lesser Pentagram been of any value, and what is its effect?

RA: I am Ra. This group's use of the Banishing Ritual of the Lesser Pentagram has been increasingly efficacious. Its effect is purification, cleansing, and protection of the place of working.

The efficacy of this ritual is only beginning to be, shall we say, at the lower limits of the truly magical. In doing the working, those aspiring to adepthood have done the equivalent of beginning the schoolwork, many grades ahead. For the intelligent student this is not to be discouraged; rather to be encouraged is the homework, the reading, the writing, the arithmetic, as you might metaphorically call the elementary steps towards the study of being. It is the being that informs the working, not the working that informs the being. Therefore, we may leave you to the work you have begun.

QUESTIONER: Would it be beneficial for us to perform the banishing ritual more in this room?

RA: I am Ra. It is beneficial to regularly work in this place.

QUESTIONER: I am sorry that we have had such a long delay between the last session and this one. It couldn't be helped, I guess. Could you please tell me the origin of the Tarot?

RA: I am Ra. The origin of this system of study and divination is twofold: firstly, there is that influence which, coming in a distorted fashion from those who were priests attempting to teach the Law of One in Egypt, gave form to the understanding, if you will pardon the misnomer, which they had received. These forms were then made a regular portion of the learn/teachings of an initiate. The second influence is that of those entities in the lands you call Ur, Chaldea, and Mesopotamia, who, from old, had received the, shall we say, data for which they called having to do with the heavens. Thusly we find two methods of divination being melded into one, with uneven results; the, as you call it, astrology and the form being combined to suggest what you might call the correspondences which are typical of the distortions you may see as attempts to view archetypes.

QUESTIONER: Then am I correct in assuming that the priests of

Egypt, in attempting to convert knowledge that they had received initially from Ra into understandable symbology, constructed and initiated the concept of the Tarot? Is this correct?

RA: I am Ra. This is correct, with the addition of the Sumerian influence.

QUESTIONER: Were Ra's teachings focusing on the archetypes for this Logos and the methods of achieving a very close approach to the archetypical configuration? Is this correct?

RA: I am Ra. This is correct without being true. We, of Ra, are humble messengers of the Law of One. We seek to teach/learn this single law. During the space/time of the Egyptian teach/learning, we worked to bring the mind complex, the body complex, and the spirit complex into an initiated state in which the entity could contact intelligent energy and so become teach/learner itself so that healing and the fruits of study could be offered to all. The study of the roots of mind is a portion of the vivification of the mind complex, and, as we have noted, the thorough study of the portion of the roots of mind called archetypical is an interesting and necessary portion of the process as a whole.

QUESTIONER: Is there, in Ra's opinion, any present-day value for the use of the Tarot as an aid in the evolutionary process?

RA: I am Ra. We shall repeat information. It is appropriate to study one form of constructed and organized distortion of the archetypical mind in depth in order to arrive at the position of being able to become and to experience archetypes at will. You have three basic choices. You may choose astrology, the twelve signs, as you call these portions of your planet's energy web, and what has been called the ten planets. You may choose the Tarot with its twenty-two so-called Major Arcana. You may choose the study of the so-called Tree of Life with its ten Sephiroth and the twenty-two relationships between the stations.

It is well to investigate each discipline, not as a dilettante but as one who seeks the touchstone, one who wishes to feel the pull of the magnet. One of these studies will be more attractive to the seeker. Let the seeker, then, investigate the archetypical mind, using, basically, one of these three disciplines. After a period of study, the discipline mastered sufficiently, the seeker may then complete the more important step: that is, the moving beyond the written in order to express in an unique fashion its understanding, if you may again pardon the noun, of the archetypical mind.

QUESTIONER: Would I be correct in saying that the archetypes of this particular Logos are somewhat unique with respect to the rest of the creation? The systems of study that we have just talked about would not translate quickly or easily in other parts of the creation. This is a very difficult question to state. Could you clear that up for me?

RA: I am Ra. We may draw from the welter of statement which you offer the question we believe you ask. Please requestion if we have mistaken your query. The archetypical mind is that mind which is peculiar to the Logos under which influence you are at this space/time distorting your experiences. There is no other Logos the archetypical mind of which would be the same any more than the stars would appear the same from another planet in another galaxy. You may correctly infer that the closer Logoi are indeed closer in archetypes.

QUESTIONER: Since Ra evolved initially on Venus, Ra is of the same archetypical origin as that which we experience here. Is this correct?

RA: I am Ra. This is correct.

QUESTIONER: But I am assuming that the concepts of the Tarot and the magical concepts of the Tree of Life etc. were not in use by Ra. I suspect, possibly, some form of astrology was a previous Ra concept. This is just a guess. Am I correct?

RA: I am Ra. To express Ra's methods of study of the archetypical mind under the system of distortions which we enjoyed would be to skew your own judgment of that which is appropriate for the system of distortions forming the conditions in which you learn/teach. Therefore, we must invoke the Law of Confusion.

QUESTIONER: I am going to ask some questions now that may be a little off the center of what we are trying to do. I'm not sure, because I'm trying to, with these questions, unscramble something that I consider very basic to what we are doing. Please forgive my lack of ability in questioning, since this is a difficult concept for me.
Could you give me an idea of the length of the first and second densities as they occurred for this planet?

RA: I am Ra. There is no method of estimation of the time/space before timelessness gave way in your first density. To the beginnings of your time, the measurement would be vast, and yet this vastness is meaningless. Upon the entry into the constructed space/time, your first density spanned a bridge of space/time and time/space of perhaps two billion of your years.

Second density is more easily estimated and represents your longest density in terms of the span of space/time. We may estimate that time as approximately 4.6 billion years. These approximations are exceedingly rough due to the somewhat uneven development which is characteristic of creations which are built upon the foundation stone of free will.

QUESTIONER: Did you state that second density was 4.6 billion years? B, b-i-l? Is that correct?

RA: I am Ra. This is correct.

QUESTIONER: Then we have a third density that is, comparatively speaking, the twinkling of an eye, the snap of a finger in time compared to the others. Why is the third density cycled so extremely rapidly compared to the first and second?

RA: I am Ra. The third density is a choice.

QUESTIONER: Third density, then, compared to the rest of the densities, all of them, is nothing but a uniquely short period of what we consider to be time, and is for the purpose of this choice.
Is this correct?

RA: I am Ra. This is precisely correct. The prelude to choice must encompass the laying of the foundation, the establishment of the illusion, and the viability of that which can be made spiritually viable. The remainder of the densities is continuous refining of the choice. This also is greatly lengthened, as you would use the term. The choice is, as you put it, the work of a moment but is the axis upon which the creation turns.

QUESTIONER: Is this third-density choice the same throughout all of the creation of which you are aware?

RA: I am Ra. We are aware of creations in which third density is lengthier and more space/time is given to the choosing. However, the proportions remain the same, the dimensions all being somewhat etiolated and weakened by the Logos to have a variant experience of the Creator. This creation is seen by us to be quite vivid.

QUESTIONER: I didn't understand what you meant by what you said "as seen by you to be quite vivid." What did you mean?

RA: I am Ra. This creation is somewhat more condensed by its Logos than some other Logoi have chosen. Thus each experience of the Creator by the Creator in this system of distortions is, relatively speaking, more bright or, as we said, vivid.

QUESTIONER: I am assuming that upon entry into third density, for this planet, disease did not exist in any form. Is this correct?

RA: I am Ra. This is incorrect.

QUESTIONER: What disease or form of disease was there, and why did this exist at the beginning of the third density?

RA: I am Ra. Firstly, that which you speak of as disease is a functional portion of the body complex which offers the body complex the opportunity to cease viability. This is a desirable body complex function. The second portion of the answer has to do with second-density other-selves of a microscopic, as you would call it, size which have in some forms long existed and perform their service by aiding the physical-body complex in its function of ceasing viability at the appropriate space/time.

QUESTIONER: What I am trying to understand is the difference between the plan of the Logos for these second-density entities and the generation of what I would guess to be more or less a runaway array of feedback to create various physical problems to act as catalyst in our present third-density condition. Could you give me an indication of whether my thinking is anywhere near right on that?

RA: I am Ra. This instrument's physical-body complex is becoming more distorted towards pain. We shall, therefore, speak to this subject as our last full query of this working. Your query contains some internal confusion which causes the answer to be perhaps more general than desired. We invite refinements of the query.

The Logos planned for entities of mind/body/spirit complex to gain experience until the amount of experience was sufficient for an incarnation. This varied only slightly from second-density entities, whose mind/body complexes existed for the purpose of experiencing growth and seeking consciousness. As the third density upon your planet proceeded, as has been discussed, the need for the physical-body complex to cease became more rapidly approached due to intensified and more rapidly gained catalyst. This catalyst was not being properly assimilated. Therefore, the, shall we say, lifetimes needed to be shorter that learning might continue to occur with the proper rhythm and increment. Thus, more and more opportunities have been offered as your density has progressed for disease. May we ask if there are further brief queries before we close?

QUESTIONER: I have one question that is possibly of no value. You don't have to expand on it, but there is a crystal skull in the possession of a woman near Toronto. It may be of some value in investigating these communications with Ra, since I think possibly this had some origin from Ra. Can you tell me anything about that, and then is there anything that we can do to improve the contact or to make the instrument more comfortable?

RA: I am Ra. Although your query is one which uncovers interesting material, we cannot answer due to the potential an answer may have for affecting your actions. The appurtenances are carefully placed and requisite care taken. We are appreciative. All is well.

I am Ra. I leave you, my friends, in the love and the light of the One Infinite Creator. Go forth, therefore, glorying and rejoicing in the power and in the peace of the One Infinite Creator. Adonai.

Session 77,
February 10, 1982

RA: I am Ra. I greet you in the love and in the light of the One Infinite Creator. We communicate now.

QUESTIONER: Could you please give me an indication of the condition of the instrument?

RA: I am Ra. It is as previously stated.

QUESTIONER: Was the instrument under attack just prior to this session?

RA: I am Ra. This is correct.

QUESTIONER: Is there anything that we could do to help protect the instrument from these attacks prior to the session?

RA: I am Ra. This is correct.

QUESTIONER: What could we do?

RA: I am Ra. Your group could refrain from continuing this contact.

QUESTIONER: Is that the only thing that we could do?

RA: I am Ra. That is the only thing you could do which you are not already attempting with a whole heart.

QUESTIONER: I have three questions that the instrument asked me to ask, which I will get out of the way first. She wants to know if the preparation for her hospital experience could be improved if she should ever have to repeat it.

RA: I am Ra. All was done well with one exception. The instrument was instructed to spend space/time contemplating itself as the Creator. This, done in a more determined fashion, would be beneficial at times when the mind complex is weakened by severe assaults upon the distortions of the body complex towards pain. There is no necessity for negative thought-forms regardless of pain distortions. The elimination of such creates the lack of possibility for negative elementals and other negative entities to use these thought-forms to create the worsening of the mind-complex deviation from the normal distortions of cheerfulness/anxiety.

QUESTIONER: The instrument would also like to know if what we call tuning could be improved during times when we do not communicate with Ra.

RA: I am Ra. That which has been stated in regard to the latter question will suffice to point the way for the present query.

QUESTIONER: Finally, she wishes to know why several days ago her heart rate went up to 115 per minute, and why she had extreme pain in her stomach. Was that an Orion greeting?

RA: I am Ra. Although this experience was energized by the Orion group, the events mentioned, as well as others more serious, were proximally caused by the ingestion of certain foodstuffs in what you call your tablet form.

QUESTIONER: Can you tell me what these tablets were, specifically?

RA: I am Ra. We examine this query for the Law of Confusion and find ourselves close to the boundary, but acceptably so.

The substance which caused the bodily reaction of the heartbeat was called Pituitone by those which manufacture it. That which caused the difficulty which seemed to be cramping of the lower abdominal musculature but was, in fact, more organic in nature was a substance called Spleentone.

This instrument has a physical-body complex of complicated balances which afford it physical existence. Were the view taken that certain functions and chemicals found in the healthy, as you call it, body complex are lacking in this one and, therefore, simply must be replenished, the intake of the many substances which this instrument began would be appropriate. However, this particular physical vehicle has, for approximately twenty-five of your years, been vital due to the spirit, the mind, and the will being harmoniously dedicated to fulfilling the service it chose to offer.

Therefore, physical healing techniques are inappropriate whereas mental and spiritual healing techniques are beneficial.

QUESTIONER: Is there any technique that we could use that we have not been using that would be beneficial for the instrument in this case?

RA: I am Ra. We might suggest, without facetiousness, two.

Firstly, let the instrument remove the possibility of further ingestion of this group of foodstuffs.

Secondly, each of the group may become aware of the will to a greater extent. We cannot instruct upon this but merely indicate, as we have previously, that it is a vital key to the evolution of the mind/body/spirit complex.

QUESTIONER: Thank you. I would like to go back to the plan of this Logos for Its creation and examine the philosophical basis that is the foundation for what was created in this local creation and the philosophy of the plan for experience. I am assuming that I am correct in stating that the foundation for this, as has been stated many times before, is the first distortion. After that, what was the plan in the philosophical sense?

RA: I am Ra. We cannot reply due to a needed portion of your query which has been omitted; that is, do we speak of this particular Logos?

QUESTIONER: That is correct. I am asking with respect to this particular sub-Logos, our sun.

RA: I am Ra. This query has substance. We shall begin by turning to an observation of a series of concept complexes of which you are familiar as the Tarot.

The philosophy was to create a foundation, first of mind, then of body, and then of spiritual complex. Those concept complexes you call the Tarot lie then in three groups of seven: the mind cycle, one through seven; the physical-complex cycle, eight through fourteen; the spiritual-complex cycle, fifteen through twenty-one. The last concept complex may best be termed The Choice.

Upon the foundation of the transformation of each complex, with free will guided by the root concepts offered in these cycles, the Logos offered this density the basic architecture of a building and the constructing and synthesizing of data culminating in The Choice.

QUESTIONER: Then to condense your statement, I see it meaning that there are seven basic philosophical foundations for mental experience, seven for bodily, seven for spiritual, and that these produce the polarization that we experience sometime during the third-density cycle. Am I correct?

RA: I am Ra. You are correct in that you perceive the content of our prior statement with accuracy. You are incorrect in that you have no mention of the, shall we say, location of all of these concept complexes; that is, they exist within the roots of the mind, and it is from this resource that their guiding influence and leitmotifs[1] may be traced. You may further note that each foundation is itself not single but a complex of concepts. Furthermore, there are relationships betwixt mind, body, and spirit of the same location in octave, for instance: one, eight, fifteen, and relationships within each octave which are helpful in the pursuit of The Choice by the mind/body/spirit complex. The Logos under which these foundations stand is one of free will. Thusly the foundations may be seen to have unique facets and relationships for each mind/body/spirit complex. Only twenty-two, The Choice, is relatively fixed and single.

QUESTIONER: Then I am probably having a problem with the concept of time, since it appears that the Logos was aware of the polarization choice. It seems that this choice for polarization at the end of third

1. Leitmotif—Lit: Leading motive. In Music: A distinguishing theme or melodic phrase representing and recurring with a given character, situation, or emotion in an opera.

density is an important philosophical plan for the experience past third density. Am I correct in assuming that this process is a process to create the proper or desired experience that will take place in the creation after third density is complete?

RA: I am Ra. These philosophical foundations are those of third density. Above this density there remains the recognition of the architecture of the Logos, but without the veils which are so integral a part of the process of making the choice in third density.

QUESTIONER: The specific question that I had was that it seems to me that the choice was planned to create intense polarization past third density so that experience would be intense past third density. Is this correct?

RA: I am Ra. Given that our interpretation of your sound vibration complexes is appropriate, this is incorrect. The intensity of fourth density is that of the refining of the rough-hewn sculpture. This is, indeed, in its own way, quite intense, causing the mind/body/spirit complex to move ever inward and onward in its quest for fuller expression. However, in third density the statue is forged in the fire. This is a type of intensity which is not the property of fourth, fifth, sixth, or seventh densities.

QUESTIONER: What I am really attempting to understand, since all of these twenty-one philosophical bases result in the twenty-second, which is The Choice, is why this choice is so important, why the Logos seems to put so much emphasis on this choice, and what function this choice of polarity has, precisely, in the evolution or the experience of that which is created by the Logos?

RA: I am Ra. The polarization or choosing of each mind/body/spirit is necessary for harvestability from third density. The higher densities do their work due to the polarity gained in this choice.

QUESTIONER: Would it be possible for this work of our density to be performed if all of the sub-Logoi chose the same polarity in any particular expression or evolution of a Logos? Let us make the assumption that our sun created nothing but, through the first distortion, positive polarity. There was no product except positive polarity. Would work then be done in fourth density and higher as a function of only the positive polarization evolving from the original creation of our sub-Logos?

RA: I am Ra. Elements of this query illustrate the reason I was unable to answer your previous question without knowledge of the Logos involved. To turn to your question, there were Logoi which chose to set the plan for the activation of mind/body/spirit complexes through each true color body without recourse to the prior application of free will. It is, to our knowledge, only in an absence of free will that the conditions of which you speak obtain. In such a procession of densities, you find an extraordinarily long, as you measure time, third density; likewise, fourth density. Then, as the entities begin to see the Creator, there is a very rapid, as you measure time, procession towards the eighth density. This is due to the fact that one who knows not, cares not.

Let us illustrate by observing the relative harmony and unchanging quality of existence in one of your, as you call it, primitive tribes. The entities have the concepts of lawful and taboo, but the law is inexorable and all events occur as predestined. There is no concept of right and wrong, good or bad. It is a culture in monochrome. In this context you may see the one you call Lucifer as the true light-bringer in that the knowledge of good and evil both precipitated the mind/body/spirits of this Logos from the Edenic conditions of constant contentment and also provided the impetus to move, to work, and to learn.

Those Logoi whose creations have been set up without free will have not, in the feeling of those Logoi, given the Creator the quality and variety of experience of Itself as have those Logoi which have incorporated free will as paramount. Thusly you find those Logoi moving through the timeless states at what you would see as a later space/time to choose the free-will character when elucidating the foundations of each Logos.

QUESTIONER: I guess, under the first distortion, it was the free will of the Logos to choose to evolve without free will. Is this correct?

RA: I am Ra. This is correct.

QUESTIONER: Do the Logoi that choose this type of evolution choose both the service-to-self and the service-to-others path for different Logoi, or do they choose just one of the paths?

RA: I am Ra. Those, what you would call, early Logoi, which chose lack of free-will foundations, to all extents with no exceptions, founded Logoi of the service-to-others path. The, shall we say, saga of polarity, its consequences and limits, were unimagined until experienced.

QUESTIONER: In other words, you are saying that originally the Logoi that did not choose this free-will path did not choose it simply because they had not conceived of it, and that later Logoi, extending the first distortion farther down through their evolution, experienced it as an outcropping or growth from that extension of the first distortion. Am I correct in saying that?

RA: I am Ra. Yes.

QUESTIONER: Then did this particular Logos that we experience plan for this polarity and know all about it prior to Its plan? I suspect that this is what happened.

RA: I am Ra. This is quite correct.

QUESTIONER: In that case, as a Logos, you would have an advantage of selecting the form of acceleration, you might say, of spiritual evolution by planning what we call the major archetypical philosophical foundations and planning these as a function of the polarity that would be gained in third density. Is this correct?

RA: I am Ra. This is exquisitely correct.

QUESTIONER: In that case, it seems that a thorough knowledge of the precise nature of these philosophical foundations would be of primary importance to the study of evolution of mind, body, and spirit, and I would like to carefully go through each, starting with the mind. Is this agreeable with Ra?

RA: I am Ra. This is agreeable with two requests which must be made. Firstly, that an attempt be made to state the student's grasp of each archetype. We may then comment. We cannot teach/learn to the extent of learn/teaching. Secondly, we request that it be constantly kept before the mind, as the candle before the eye, that each mind/body/spirit complex shall and should and, indeed, must perceive each archetype, if you use this convenient term, in its own way. Therefore, you may see that precision is not the goal; rather, the quality of general-concept complex perception is the goal.

QUESTIONER: Now, there are several general concepts that I would like to be sure that we have clear before going into this process, and I will certainly adhere to the requests that you have just stated.

When our Logos designed this particular evolution of experience, It decided to use a system of which we spoke, allowing for polarization through total free will. How is this different from the Logos that does not do this? I see the Logos creating the possibility of increase in vibration through the densities. How are the densities provided for and set by the Logos, if you can answer this?

RA: I am Ra. This shall be the last full query of this working. The psychic attack upon this instrument has, shall we say, left scars which must be tended, in our own opinion, in order to maintain the instrument.

Let us observe your second density. Many come more rapidly to third density than others, not because of an innate efficiency of catalysis but because of unusual opportunities for investment. In just such a way those of fourth density may invest third, those of fifth density may invest fourth. When fifth density has been obtained, the process takes upon itself a momentum based upon the characteristics of wisdom when applied to circumstance. The Logos Itself, then, in these instances provides investment opportunities, if you wish to use that term. May we inquire if there are any brief queries at this space/time?

QUESTIONER: Is there anything that we can do after this contact to increase the comfort as related to the psychic attack, or is there anything that we can do to make the instrument more comfortable and to improve the contact in the present situation?

RA: I am Ra. The faculties of healing which each has commenced energizing may be used. The entity may be encouraged to remain motionless for a period. As it will not appreciate this, we suggest the proper discussion.

The physical appurtenance called the censer was just a degree off, this having no deeper meaning. We do ask, for reasons having to do with the physical comfort of the instrument, that you continue in your careful efforts at alignment. You are conscientious. All is well.

We leave you, my friends, in the glorious love and light of the One Creator. Go forth, therefore, rejoicing in the power and in the peace of the One Infinite Creator. I am Ra. Adonai.

**Session 78,
February 19, 1982**

RA: I am Ra. I greet you in the love and in the light of the One Infinite Creator. We communicate now.

QUESTIONER: Was there some problem with the ritual we performed that made it necessary to perform the ritual twice?

RA: I am Ra. There was a misstep which created a momentary lapse of concentration. This was not well.

QUESTIONER: What was the misstep?

RA: I am Ra. It was a missed footing.

QUESTIONER: Did this have any detrimental effect on the instrument?

RA: I am Ra. Very little. The instrument felt the presence it has come to associate with cold and spoke. The instrument did the appropriate thing.

QUESTIONER: Could you tell me the condition of the instrument?

RA: I am Ra. The physical complex is as previously stated. There is some slight loss of vital energy. The basic complex distortions are similar to your previous asking.

QUESTIONER: The instrument would like for me to ask if there is any problem with her kidneys.

RA: I am Ra. This query is more complex than its brevity certifies. The physical-complex renal system of this instrument is much damaged. The time/space equivalent which rules the body complex is without flaw. There was a serious question, due to psychic attack, as to whether the spiritual healing of this system would endure. It did so but has the need to be reinforced by affirmation of the ascendancy of the spiritual over the apparent or visible.

When this instrument began ingesting substances designed to heal in a physical sense, among other things, the renal complex, this instrument was ceasing the affirmation of healing. Due to this, again, the healing was weakened. This is of some profound distortion, and it would be well for the instrument to absorb these concepts. We ask your forgiveness for offering information which may abridge free will, but the dedication of the instrument is such that it would persevere regardless of its condition, if possible. Thusly we offer this information that it may persevere with a fuller distortion towards comfort.

QUESTIONER: What was the experience that caused the healing of the time/space kidney?

RA: I am Ra. This experience was the healing of self by self with the catalyst of the spiritual healer whom you call Pachita.

QUESTIONER: Thank you. In utilizing the energetic displacements of thought-forms energizing the instrument during contact most efficiently, what specifically could we do?

RA: I am Ra. Each of the support group has an excess of love and light to offer the instrument during the working. Already each sends to the instrument love, light, and thoughts of strength of the physical, mental, and spiritual configurations. These sendings are forms. You may refine these sendings until the fullest manifestations of love and light are sent into the energy web of this entity which functions as instrument. Your exact sending is, in order to be most potent, the creature of your own making.

QUESTIONER: Thank you. I am going to go back to an earlier time, if you could call it that, in evolution to try to establish a very fundamental base for some of the concepts that seem to be the foundation of everything that we experience so that we can more fully examine the basis of our evolution.

I am guessing that in our Milky Way galaxy (the major galaxy with billions of stars) that the progress of evolution was from the center outward toward the rim, and that in the early evolution of this galaxy, the first distortion was not extended down past the sub-Logos simply because it was not thought of or conceived of, and that this extension of the first distortion, which created polarization, was something that occurred in what we would call a later time as the evolution progressed outward from the center of the galaxy. Am I in any way correct in this statement?

RA: I am Ra. You are correct.

QUESTIONER: We have the first, second, and third distortions of the

Law of One as free will, love, and light. Am I correct in assuming that the central core of this major galaxy began to form with the third distortion? Was that the origin of our Milky Way galaxy?

RA: I am Ra. In the most basic or teleological sense you are incorrect, as the One Infinite Creator is all that there is. In an undistorted seed form, you are correct in seeing the first manifestation visible to the eye of the body complex which you inhabit as the third distortion, light, or to use a technical term, limitless light.

QUESTIONER: I realize that we are on very difficult ground, you might say, for precise terminology. It is totally displaced from our system of coordinates for evaluation in our present system of language.

These early Logoi that formed in the center of the galaxy wished, I assume, to create a system of experience for the One Creator. Did they then start with no previous experience or information about how to do this? This is difficult to ask.

RA: I am Ra. At the beginning of this creation or, as you may call it, octave, there were those things known which were the harvest of the preceding octave. About the preceding creation, we know as little as we do of the octave to come. However, we are aware of those pieces of gathered concept which were the tools which the Creator had in the knowing of the self.

These tools were of three kinds. Firstly, there was an awareness of the efficiency for experience of mind, body, and spirit. Secondly, there was an awareness of the most efficacious nature or, if you will, significator of mind, body, and spirit. Thirdly, there was the awareness of two aspects of mind, of body, and of spirit that the significator could use to balance all catalyst. You may call these two the matrix and the potentiator.

QUESTIONER: Could you elaborate please on the nature and quality of the matrix and the potentiator?

RA: I am Ra. In the mind complex the matrix may be described as consciousness. It has been called the Magician. It is to be noted that of itself, consciousness is unmoved. The potentiator of consciousness is the unconscious. This encompasses a vast realm of potential in the mind.

In the body the matrix may be seen as Balanced Working or Even Functioning. Note that here the matrix is always active, with no means of being inactive. The potentiator of the body complex, then, may be called Wisdom, for it is only through judgment that the unceasing activities and proclivities of the body complex may be experienced in useful modes.

The Matrix of the Spirit is what you may call the Night of the Soul or Primeval Darkness. Again we have that which is not capable of movement or work. The potential power of this extremely receptive matrix is such that the potentiator may be seen as Lightning. In your archetypical system called the Tarot, this has been refined into the concept complex of the Lightning Struck Tower. However, the original potentiator was light in its sudden and fiery form; that is, the lightning itself.

QUESTIONER: Would you elucidate with respect to the significator you spoke of?

RA: I am Ra. The original significators may undifferentiatedly be termed the mind, the body, and the spirit.

QUESTIONER: Then we have, at the beginning of this galactic evolution, an archetypical mind that is the product of the previous octave, which this galaxy then used as and acts upon under the first distortion so as to allow for what we experience as polarity. Was there any concept of polarity carried through from the previous octave in the sense of service-to-others or service-to-self polarity?

RA: I am Ra. There was polarity in the sense of the mover and the moved. There was no polarity in the sense of service to self and service to others.

QUESTIONER: Then the first experiences, as you say, were in monochrome. Was the concept of the seven densities of vibration with the evolutionary process taking place in discrete densities carried through from the previous octave?

RA: I am Ra. To the limits of our knowledge, which are narrow, the ways of the octave are without time; that is, there are seven densities in each creation infinitely.

QUESTIONER: Then I am assuming that the central suns of our galaxy, in starting the evolutionary process in this galaxy, provided for, in their plans, the refinement of consciousness through the densities just as we experience it here. However, they did not conceive of the polarization of consciousness with respect to service to self and service to others. Is this correct?

RA: I am Ra. This is correct.

QUESTIONER: Why do the densities have the qualities that they have? You have named the densities with respect to their qualities, the next density being that of love and so on. Can you tell me why these qualities exist in that form? Is it possible to answer that question?

RA: I am Ra. It is possible.

QUESTIONER: Will you please answer that?

RA: I am Ra. The nature of the vibratory range peculiar to each quantum of the octave is such that the characteristics of it may be described with the same certainty with which you perceive a color with your optical apparatus if it is functioning properly.

QUESTIONER: So the original evolution then was planned by the Logos, but the first distortion was not extended to the product. At some point this first distortion was extended and the first service-to-self polarity emerged. Is this correct, and, if so, could you tell me the history of this process of emergence?

RA: I am Ra. As proem, let me state that the Logoi always conceived of themselves as offering free will to the sub-Logoi in their care. The sub-Logoi had freedom to experience and experiment with consciousness, the experiences of the body, and the illumination of the spirit. That having been said, we shall speak to the point of your query.

The first Logos to instill what you now see as free will, in the full sense, in Its sub-Logoi came to this creation due to contemplation in depth of the concepts or possibilities of conceptualizations of what we have called the significators. The Logos posited the possibility of the mind, the body, and the spirit as being complex. In order for the significator to be what it is not, it then must be granted the free will of the Creator. This set in motion a quite lengthy, in your terms, series of Logos's improving or distilling this seed thought. The key was the significator becoming a complex.

QUESTIONER: Then our particular Logos, when it created Its own particular creation, was at some point far down the evolutionary spiral of the experiment, with the significator becoming what it was not and, therefore, I am assuming, was primarily concerned in designing the archetypes in such a way that they would create the acceleration of this polarization. Is this in any way correct?

RA: I am Ra. We would only comment briefly. It is generally correct. You may fruitfully view each Logos and Its design as the Creator experiencing Itself. The seed concept of the significator being a complex introduces two things: firstly, the Creator against Creator in one sub-Logos in what you may call dynamic tension; secondly, the concept of free will, once having been made fuller by its extension into the sub-Logoi known as mind/body/spirit complexes, creates and re-creates and continues to create as a function of its very nature.

QUESTIONER: You stated previously that The Choice is made in this third density and is the axis upon which the creation turns. Could you expand on your reason for making that statement?

RA: I am Ra. This is a statement of the nature of creation as we speak to you.

QUESTIONER: I did not understand that. Could you say that in a different way?

RA: I am Ra. As you have noted, the creation of which your Logos is a part is a protean entity which grows and learns upon a macrocosmic scale. The Logos is not a part of time. All that is learned from experience in an octave is, therefore, the harvest of that Logos and is further the nature of that Logos.

The original Logos's experience was, viewed in space/time, small; Its experience now, more. Therefore we say, as we now speak to you at this space/time, the nature of creation is as we have described. This does not deny the process by which this nature has been achieved, but merely ratifies the product.

QUESTIONER: After third density, in our experience, social memory complexes are polarized positively and negatively. Is the interaction of social memory complexes of opposite polarity equivalent, but on a magnified scale, to the interaction between mind/body/spirit complexes of opposite polarity? Is this how experience is gained as a function of polarity difference in fourth and fifth densities?

RA: I am Ra. No.

QUESTIONER: This is a hard question to ask, but what is the value experientially of the formation of positive and negative social memory complexes, of the separation of the polarities at that point rather than the allowing for the mixing of mind/body/spirit complexes of opposite polarity in the higher densities?

RA: I am Ra. The purpose of polarity is to develop the potential to do work. This is the great characteristic of those, shall we say, experiments which have evolved since the concept of The Choice was appreciated. Work is done far more efficiently and with greater purity, intensity, and variety by the voluntary searching of mind/body/spirit complexes for the lessons of third and fourth densities. The action of fifth density is viewed in space/time the same with or without polarity. However, viewed in time/space, the experiences of wisdom are greatly enlarged and deepened due, again, to the voluntary nature of polarized mind/body/spirit action.

QUESTIONER: Then you are saying that as a result of the polarization in consciousness, which has occurred later in the galactic evolution, the experiences are much more intense along the two paths. Are these experiences each independent of the other? Must there be action across the potentiated difference between the positive and negative polarity, or is it possible to have this experience simply because of the single polarity? This is difficult to ask.

RA: I am Ra. We would agree. We shall attempt to pluck the gist of your query from the surrounding verbiage.

The fourth and fifth densities are quite independent, the positive polarity functioning with no need of negative and vice versa. It is to be noted that in attempting to sway third-density mind/body/spirit complexes in choosing polarity, there evolves a good bit of interaction between the two polarities. In sixth density, the density of unity, the positive and negative paths must needs take in each other, for all now must be seen as love/light and light/love. This is not difficult for the positive polarity which sends love and light to all other-selves. It is difficult enough for service-to-self polarized entities that at some point the negative polarity is abandoned.

QUESTIONER: The choice of polarity being unique as a circumstance, shall I say, for the archetypical basis for the evolution of consciousness in our particular experience indicates to me that we have arrived, through a long process of the Creator knowing Itself, at a position of present or maximum efficiency for the design of a process of experience. That design for maximum efficiency is in the roots of consciousness and is the archetypical mind and is a product of everything that has gone before. There are, unquestionably, relatively pure archetypical concepts for the seven concepts for mind, body, and spirit. I feel that the language that we have for these is somewhat inadequate.

However, we shall continue to attempt to investigate the foundation for this, and I am hoping that I have laid the foundation with some degree of accuracy in attempting to set a background for the development of the archetypes of our Logos. Have I left out anything or made any errors, or could you make any comments on my attempt to lay the foundation for the construction that our Logos used for the archetypes?

RA: I am Ra. Your queries are thoughtful.

QUESTIONER: Are they accurate, or have I made mistakes?

RA: I am Ra. There are no mistakes.

QUESTIONER: Let me put it this way. Have I made missteps in my analysis of what has led to the construction of the archetypes that we experience?

RA: I am Ra. We may share with you the observation that judgment is no part of interaction between mind/body/spirit complexes. We have attempted to answer each query as fully as your language and the extent of your previous information allow. We may suggest that if, in perusing this present material, you have further queries, refining any concept, these queries may be asked and, again, we shall attempt adequate rejoinders.

QUESTIONER: I understand your limitations in answering that. Thank you.

Could you tell me how, in the first density, wind and fire teach earth and water?

RA: I am Ra. You may see the air and fire of that which is chaos as literally illuminating and forming the formless, for earth and water were, in the timeless state, unformed. As the active principles of fire and air blow and burn incandescently about that which nurtures that which is to come, the water learns to become sea, lake, and river, offering the opportunity for viable life. The earth learns to be shaped, thus offering the opportunity for viable life.

QUESTIONER: Are the seven archetypes for mind a function of or related to the seven densities that are to be experienced in the octave?

RA: I am Ra. The relationship is tangential in that no congruency may be seen. However, the progress through the archetypes has some of the characteristics of the progress through the densities. These relationships may be viewed without being, shall we say, pasted one upon the other.

QUESTIONER: How about the seven bodily energy centers? Are they related to archetypes in some way?

RA: I am Ra. The same may be said of these. It is informative to view the relationships but stifling to insist upon the limitations of congruency. Recall at all times, if you would use this term, that the archetypes are a portion of the resources of the mind complex.

QUESTIONER: Is there any relationship between the archetypes and the planets of our solar system?

RA: I am Ra. This is not a simple query. Properly, the archetypes have some relationship to the planets. However, this relationship is not one which can be expressed in your language. This, however, has not halted those among your people who have become adepts from attempting to name and describe these relationships. To most purely understand, if we may use this misnomer, the archetypes, it is well to view the concepts which make up each archetype and reserve the study of planets and other correspondences for meditation.

QUESTIONER: It just seemed to me that since the planets were an outgrowth of the Logos and since the archetypical mind was the foundation of the experience that the planets of this Logos would be somewhat related. We will certainly follow your suggestion.

I have been trying to get a foothold into an undistorted perception, you might say, of the archetypical mind. It seems to me that everything that I have read having to do with archetypes has been, to some degree or another, distorted by the writers and by the fact that our language is not really capable of description.

You have spoken of the Magician as a basic archetype, and that this seems to have been carried through from the previous octave. Would this be in order—if there is an order—the first archetypical concept for this Logos, the concept that we call the Magician?

RA: I am Ra. We would first respond to your confusion as regards the various writings upon the archetypical mind. You may well consider the very informative difference between a thing in itself and its relationships or functions. There is much study of archetype which is actually the study of functions, relationships, and correspondences. The study of planets, for instance, is an example of archetype seen as function. However, the archetypes are, first and most profoundly, things in themselves, and the pondering of them and their purest relationships with each other should be the most useful foundation for the study of the archetypical mind.

We now address your query as to the archetype which is the Matrix of the Mind. As to its name, the name of Magician is understandable when you consider that consciousness is the great foundation, mystery, and revelation which makes this particular density possible. The self-conscious entity is full of the magic of that which is to come. It may be considered first, for the mind is the first of the complexes to be developed by the student of spiritual evolution.

QUESTIONER: Would the archetype then that has been called the High Priestess, which represents the intuition, be properly the second of the archetypes?

RA: I am Ra. This is correct. You see here the recapitulation of the beginning knowledge of this Logos; that is, matrix and potentiator. The unconscious is indeed what may be poetically described as High Priestess, for it is the Potentiator of the Mind, and as potentiator for the mind is that principle which potentiates all experience.

QUESTIONER: Then for the third archetype, would the Empress be correct and be related to disciplined meditation?

RA: I am Ra. I perceive a mind complex intention of a query but was aware only of sound vibratory statement. Please requestion.

QUESTIONER. I was asking if the third archetype was the Empress, and was it correct to say that this archetype had to do with disciplined meditation?

RA: I am Ra. The third archetype may broadly be grasped as the Catalyst of the Mind. Thus it takes in far more than disciplined meditation. However, it is certainly through this faculty that catalyst is most efficiently used. The Archetype, Three, is perhaps confusedly called

Empress, although the intention of this number is the understanding that it represents the unconscious or female portion of the mind complex, being first, shall we say, used or ennobled by the male or conscious portion of the mind. Thus the noble name.

QUESTIONER: The fourth archetype is called The Emperor and seems to have to do with experience of other-selves and the green-ray energy center with respect to other-selves. Is this correct?

RA: I am Ra. This is perceptive. The broad name for Archetype Four may be the Experience of the Mind. In the Tarot you find the name of Emperor. Again this implies nobility, and in this case we may see the suggestion that it is only through the catalyst which has been processed by the potentiated consciousness that experience may ensue. Thusly is the conscious mind ennobled by the use of the vast resources of the unconscious mind.

This instrument's dorsal side grows stiff, and the instrument tires. We welcome one more query.

QUESTIONER: I would like to ask the reason for this session having been longer than most previous sessions, and also if there is anything that we can do to make the instrument more comfortable or to improve the contact?

RA: I am Ra. This instrument was given far more than the, shall we say, usual amount of transferred energy. There is a limit to the amount of energy of this type which may, with safety, be used when the instrument is, itself, without physical reserves. This is inevitable due to the various distortions such as we mentioned previously in this working having to do with growing dorsal discomfort.

The alignments are fastidious. We appreciate your conscientiousness. In order to enhance the comfort of the instrument, it might be suggested that careful manipulation of the dorsal area be accomplished before a working.

It is also suggested that, due to the attempt at psychic attack, this instrument will require warmth along the right side of the physical complex. There has been some infringement, but it should not be long lasting. It is, however, well to swaddle this instrument sufficiently to ward off any manifestation of this cold in physical form.

I am Ra. I leave you, my friends, in the love and in the light of the One Infinite Creator. Go forth, therefore, merrily rejoicing in the power and in the peace of the One Infinite Creator. Adonai.

Session 79,
February 24, 1982

RA: I am Ra. I greet you in the love and in the light of the One Infinite Creator. We communicate now.

QUESTIONER: Could you first give me the condition of the instrument?

RA: I am Ra. It is as previously stated.

QUESTIONER: The instrument would like to ask if there is any danger in the instrument receiving too much transferred energy in her present condition.

RA: I am Ra. No.

QUESTIONER: She would like to know the function of the energy transfer during the session.

RA: I am Ra. The function of this energy transfer is a most helpful one in that it serves to strengthen the shuttle through which the instreaming contact is received. The contact itself will monitor the condition of the instrument and cease communication when the distortions of the instrument begin to fluctuate towards the distortions of weakness or pain. However, while the contact is ongoing, the strength of the channel through which this contact flows may be aided by the energy transfer of which you spoke.

QUESTIONER: We have been ending our banishing ritual prior to the session by a gesture that relieves us of the magical personality. I was just wondering if we should maintain this personality and omit that gesture while we are walking the Circle of One and then relinquish the magical personality only after the circle is formed or after the session? Which would be more appropriate?

RA: I am Ra. The practice of magical workings demands the most rigorous honesty. If your estimate of your ability is that you can sustain the magical personality throughout this working, it is well. As long as you have some doubt, it is inadvisable. In any case it is appropriate for this instrument to return its magical personality rather than carry this persona into the trance state, for it does not have the requisite magical skill to function in this circumstance and would be far more vulnerable than if the waking personality is offered as channel. This working is indeed magical in nature in the basic sense. However, it is inappropriate to move more quickly than one's feet may walk.

QUESTIONER: I would like to question about the third-density experience of those entities just prior to the original extension of the first distortion to the sub-Logoi to create the split of polarity. Can you describe, in general, the differences between the third-density experience of these mind/body/spirits and the ones who have evolved upon this planet now?

RA: I am Ra. This material has been previously covered. Please query for specific interest.

QUESTIONER: Specifically, in the experience where only the service-to-others polarity in third density evolved, was the veil that was drawn with respect to knowledge of previous incarnations etc. in effect for those entities?

RA: I am Ra. No.

QUESTIONER: Was the reincarnational process like the one that we experience here, in which the third-density body is entered and exited numerous times during the cycle?

RA: I am Ra. This is correct.

QUESTIONER: Is it possible to give a time of incarnation with respect to our years, and would you do so if it is?

RA: I am Ra. The optimal incarnative period is somewhere close to a measure you call a millennium. This is, as you may say, a constant regardless of other factors of the third-density experience.

QUESTIONER: Then prior to the first extension of the first distortion, the veil or loss of awareness did not occur. From this I will make the assumption that this veil or loss of remembering consciously that which occurred before the incarnation was the primary tool for extending the first distortion. Is this correct?

RA: I am Ra. Your correctness is limited. This was the first tool.

QUESTIONER: Then from that statement I assume that the Logos first devised the tool of separating the unconscious from the conscious during what we call physical incarnations to achieve Its objective? Is this correct?

RA: I am Ra. Yes.

QUESTIONER: Then from that statement I would also assume that many other tools were conceived and used after the first tool of the so-called veil. Is this correct?

RA: I am Ra. There have been refinements.

QUESTIONER: The archetypical mind of the Logos prior to this experiment in veiling was what I would consider to be less complex than it is now, possibly containing fewer archetypes. Is this correct?

RA: I am Ra. We must ask your patience. We perceive a sudden flare of the distortion known as pain in this instrument's left arm and manual appendages. Please do not touch this instrument. We shall examine the mind complex and attempt to reposition the limb so that the working may continue. Then please repeat the query.

[Ninety-second pause]

I am Ra. You may proceed.

QUESTIONER: Thank you. Prior to the experiment to extend the first distortion, how many archetypes were there at that time?

RA: I am Ra. There were nine.

QUESTIONER: I will guess that those nine were three of mind, three of body, and three of spirit. Is this correct?

RA: I am Ra. This is correct.

QUESTIONER: I am going to guess that in the system of the Tarot, those archetypes would roughly correspond to, for the mind, The Magician, The Emperor, and The Chariot. Is this correct?

RA: I am Ra. This is incorrect.

QUESTIONER: Could you tell me what they correspond to?

RA: I am Ra. The body, the mind, and the spirit each contained and functioned under the aegis of the matrix, the potentiator, and the significator. The significator of the mind, body, and spirit is not identical to the significator of the mind, body, and spirit complexes.

QUESTIONER: I now understand what you meant in the previous session by saying that to extend free will, the significator must become a complex. It seems that the significator has become the complex that is the third, fourth, fifth, sixth, and seventh of the mind, the tenth on of the body, and the seventeenth on of the spirit. Is this correct?

RA: I am Ra. This is incorrect.

QUESTIONER: Could you tell me what you mean by "the significator must become a complex"?

RA: I am Ra. To be complex is to consist of more than one characteristic element or concept.

QUESTIONER: I would like to try to understand the archetypes of the mind of this Logos prior to the extension of the first distortion. In order to better understand that which we experience now, I believe that this is a logical approach.

We have, as you have stated, the matrix, the potentiator, and the significator. I understand the matrix as being that which is what we call the conscious mind, but since it is also that from which the mind is made, I am at a loss to fully understand these three terms, especially with respect to the time before there was a division in consciousness. Could you expand even more upon the Matrix of the Mind, the Potentiator of the Mind, and the Significator of the Mind, how they differ, and what their relationships are, please?

RA: I am Ra. The Matrix of Mind is that from which all comes. It is unmoving yet is the activator in potentiation of all mind activity. The Potentiator of the Mind is that great resource which may be seen as the sea into which the consciousness dips ever deeper and more thoroughly in order to create, ideate, and become more self-conscious.

The Significator of each mind, body, and spirit may be seen as a simple and unified concept. The Matrix of the Body may be seen to be a reflection in opposites of the mind; that is, unrestricted motion. The Potentiator of the Body then is that which, being informed, regulates activity.

The Matrix of the Spirit is difficult to characterize since the nature of spirit is less motile. The energies and movements of the spirit are, by far, the most profound yet, having more close association with time/space, do not have the characteristics of dynamic motion. Thusly one may see the Matrix as the deepest darkness and the Potentiator of Spirit as the most sudden awakening, illuminating, and generative influence.

This is the description of Archetypes One through Nine before the onset of influence of the co-Creator or sub-Logos's realization of free will.

QUESTIONER: The first change made then for this extension of free will was to make the communication between the Matrix and the Potentiator of the Mind relatively unavailable, one to the other, during the incarnation. Is this correct?

RA: I am Ra. We would perhaps rather term the condition as relatively more mystery filled than relatively unavailable.

QUESTIONER: The idea was then to create some type of veil between the Matrix and the Potentiator of the Mind. Is this correct?

RA: I am Ra. This is correct.

QUESTIONER: This veil then occurs between what we now call the unconscious and conscious minds. Is this correct?

RA: I am Ra. This is correct.

QUESTIONER: It was probably the design of the Logos to allow the conscious mind greater freedom under the first distortion by partitioning, you might say, this from the Potentiator or unconscious, which had a greater communication with the total mind, therefore, allowing for the birth of uneducated, to use a poor term, portions of consciousness. Is this correct?

RA: I am Ra. This is roughly correct.

QUESTIONER: Could you de-roughen it or elucidate a bit on that?

RA: I am Ra. There is intervening material before we may do so.

QUESTIONER: OK. Was then this simple experiment carried out and the product of this experiment observed before greater complexity was attempted?

RA: I am Ra. As we have said, there have been a great number of successive experiments.

QUESTIONER: I was just wondering since this seems to be the crux of the experiment, the large breaking point between no extension of the first distortion and the extension of the first distortion, what the result of this original experiment was with respect to that which was created from it. What was the result of that?

RA: I am Ra. This is previously covered material. The result of these experiments has been a more vivid, varied, and intense experience of Creator by Creator.

QUESTIONER: Well, I was aware of that. I probably didn't state the question correctly. It's a very difficult question to state. I don't know if it's worth attempting to continue with, but what I meant was when this very first experiment with the veiling process occurred, did it result in service-to-self polarization with the first experiment?

RA: I am Ra. The early, if we may use this term, Logoi produced service-to-self and service-to-others mind/body/spirit complexes immediately. The harvestability of these entities was not so immediate, and thus refinements of the archetypes began apace.

QUESTIONER: Now we are getting to what I was trying to determine. Then at this point, were there still only nine archetypes, and the veil had just been drawn between the Matrix and the Potentiator of the Mind?

RA: I am Ra. There were nine archetypes and many shadows.

QUESTIONER: By shadows do you mean the, what I might refer to as, birthing of small archetypical biases?

RA: I am Ra. Rather we would describe these shadows as the inchoate thoughts of helpful structures not yet fully conceived.

QUESTIONER: Would The Choice exist at this point during the creation of the first service-to-self polarity?

RA: I am Ra. Implicit in the veiling or separation of two archetypes is the concept of choice. The refinements to this concept took many experiences.

QUESTIONER: I'm sorry that I have so much difficulty in asking these questions, but this is material that I find somewhat difficult.

I find it interesting that the very first experiment of veiling the Matrix of the Mind from the Potentiator of the Mind and vice versa created service-to-self polarity. This seems to be a very important philosophical point in the development of the creation, and possibly the beginning of a system of what we would call magic not envisioned previously.

Let me ask this question. Prior to the extension of the first distortion, was the magical potential of the higher densities as great as it is now when the greatest potential was achieved in consciousness for each density? This is difficult to ask. What I am asking is that at the end of fourth density, prior to the extension of free will, was what we call magical potential as great as it is now at the end of fourth density?

RA: I am Ra. As you understand, if we may use this misnomer, magic, the magical potential in third and fourth density was then far greater than after the change. However, there was far, far less desire or will to use this potential.

QUESTIONER: Now, to be sure that I understand you: prior to the change and the extension of free will, let's take specifically the end of fourth density, magical potential for the condition when there was only service-to-others polarization was much greater at the end of fourth density than at the end of fourth density immediately after the split of polarization and the extension of free will. Is that correct?

RA: I am Ra. Magical ability is the ability to consciously use the so-called unconscious. Therefore, there was maximal ability prior to the innovation of sub-Logoi's free will.

QUESTIONER: OK. At the present time we are experiencing the effects of a more complex or greater number of archetypes, and I have guessed that the ones we are experiencing now in the mind are as follows: we have the Magician and High Priestess, which correspond to the Matrix and Potentiator with the veil drawn between them, which is the primary creator of the extension of the first distortion. Is that correct?

RA: I am Ra. We are unable to answer this query without intervening material.

QUESTIONER: OK. Sorry about that.

The next archetype, the Empress, is the Catalyst of the Mind, that which acts upon the conscious mind to change it. The fourth archetype is the Emperor, the Experience of the Mind, which is that material stored in the unconscious which creates its continuing bias. Am I correct with those statements?

RA: I am Ra. Though far too rigid in your statements, you perceive correct relationships. There is a great deal of dynamic interrelationship in these first four archetypes.

QUESTIONER: Would the Hierophant then be somewhat of a governor or sorter of these effects so as to create the proper assimilation by the unconscious of that which comes through the conscious?

RA: I am Ra. Although thoughtful, the supposition is incorrect in its heart.

QUESTIONER: What would be the Hierophant?

RA: I am Ra. The Hierophant is the Significator of the Body (Mind)[2] complex, its very nature. We may note that the characteristics of which you speak do have bearing upon the Significator of the Mind complex but are not the heart. The heart of the mind complex is that dynamic entity which absorbs, seeks, and attempts to learn.

QUESTIONER: Then is the Hierophant that link, you might say, between the mind and the body?

RA: I am Ra. There is a strong relationship between the significators of the mind, the body, and the spirit. Your statement is too broad.

QUESTIONER: Let me skip over the Hierophant for a minute, because I am really not understanding that at all and just ask if the Lovers represent a merging of the conscious and the unconscious or the communication of the conscious and unconscious?

RA: I am Ra. Again, without being at all unperceptive, you miss the heart of this particular archetype, which may be more properly called the Transformation of the Mind.

---

2. Ra corrected this error in Session 80. The Hierophant is the Significator of the Mind.

QUESTIONER: Transformation of the mind into what?

RA: I am Ra. As you observe Archetype Six, you may see the student of the mysteries being transformed by the need to choose betwixt the light and the dark in mind.

QUESTIONER: Would the Conqueror or Chariot then represent the culmination of the action of the first six archetypes into a conquering of the mental processes, even possibly removing the veil?

RA: I am Ra. This is most perceptive. The Archetype Seven is one difficult to enunciate. We may call it the Path, the Way, or the Great Way of the Mind. Its foundation is a reflection and substantial summary of Archetypes One through Six.

One may also see the Way of the Mind as showing the kingdom or fruits of appropriate travel through the mind, in that the mind continues to move as majestically through the material it conceives of as a chariot drawn by royal lions or steeds.

At this time we would suggest one more full query, for this instrument is experiencing some distortions towards pain.

QUESTIONER: Then I will just ask about the one of the archetypes which I am the least able to understand at this point, if I can use that word at all. I am still very much in the dark, so to speak, in respect to the Hierophant and precisely what it is. Could you give me some other indication of what that is?

RA: I am Ra. You have been most interested in the Significator, which must needs become complex. The Hierophant is the original archetype of mind, which has been made complex through the subtle movements of the conscious and unconscious. The complexities of mind were evolved rather than the simple melding of experience from Potentiator to Matrix.

The mind itself became an actor possessed of free will and, more especially, will. As the Significator of the mind, The Hierophant has the will to know, but what shall it do with its knowledge, and for what reasons does it seek? The potentials of a complex significator are manifold.

Are there any brief queries at this working?

QUESTIONER: Only is there anything that we can do to make the instrument more comfortable or to improve the contact?

RA: I am Ra. All is well. For some small portion of your future, the instrument would be well advised to wear upon the hands those aids to comfort which it has neglected to use. There has been some trauma to both hands and arms, and, therefore, we have had to somewhat abbreviate this working.

I am Ra. You are conscientious, my friends. We leave you in the love and in the light of the One Infinite Creator. Go forth, therefore, rejoicing in the power and the peace of the One Glorious Infinite Creator. Adonai.

Session 80,
February 27, 1982

RA: I am Ra. We greet you in the love and in the light of the One Infinite Creator.

Before we initiate this working, we would wish to correct an error which we have found in previous material. That Archetype Five, which you have called the Hierophant, is the Significator of the Mind complex.

This instrument is prey to sudden flares towards the distortion known as pain. We are aware of your conscientious attempts to aid the instrument, but know of no other modality available to the support group other than the provision of water therapy upon the erect spinal portion of the physical-body complex, which we have previously mentioned.

This instrument's distortions of body do not ever rule out, shall we say, such flares during these periods of increased distortion of the body complex. Our contact may become momentarily garbled. Therefore, we request that any information which seems garbled be questioned, as we wish this contact to remain as undistorted as the limitations of language, mentality, and sensibility allow.

We communicate now.

QUESTIONER: Thank you. Could you please give me the condition of the instrument?

RA: I am Ra. This instrument is experiencing mild fluctuations of the physical-energy complex, which are causing sudden changes from physical energy deficit to some slight physical energy. This is due to many, what you may call, prayers and affirmations offered to and by the instrument, offset by continual greetings whenever it is feasible by the fifth-density entity of whom you are aware.

In other respects, the instrument is in the previously stated condition.

QUESTIONER: I had to leave the room for a forgotten item after we performed the banishing ritual. Did this have a deleterious effect on the ritual or the working?

RA: I am Ra. Were it the only working, the lapse would have been critical. There is enough residual energy of a protective nature in this place of working that this lapse, though quite unrecommended, does not represent a threat to the protection which the ritual of which you spoke offers.

QUESTIONER: Has our fifth-density visitor been less able to affect the instrument during our more recent workings?

RA: I am Ra. We shall answer in two parts. Firstly, during the workings themselves the entity has been bated to a great extent. Secondly, in the general experiential circumstances of your space/time experience, this fifth-density entity is able to greet this entity with the same effectiveness upon the physical-body complex as always since the inception of its contact with your group. This is due to the several physical-complex distortions of the instrument.

However, the instrument has become more mentally and spiritually able to greet this entity with love, thereby reducing the element of fear, which is an element the entity counts as a great weapon in the attempt to cause cessation, in any degree, of the Ra contact.

QUESTIONER: What is the reason for the fact that the entity is able to act through physical distortions that are already present, as opposed to being unable to act upon an entity who has no physical distortion at all?

RA: I am Ra. The key to this query is the term "distortion." Any distortion, be it physical, mental, or spiritual in complex nature, may be accentuated by the suggestion of one able to work magically; that is, to cause changes in consciousness. This entity has many physical distortions. Each in the group has various mental distortions. Their nature varies. The less balanced the distortion by self-knowledge, the more adeptly the entity may accentuate such a distortion in order to mitigate against the smooth functioning and harmony of the group.

QUESTIONER: As Ra well knows, the information that we accumulate here will be illuminating to a very minor percentage of those who populate this planet, simply because there are very few people who can understand it. However, it seems that our fifth-density visitor is, shall we say, dead set against this communication. Can you tell me why this is so important to him, since it is of such a limited effect, I would guess, upon the harvest of this planet?

RA: I am Ra. Purity does not end with the harvest of third density. The fidelity of Ra towards the attempt to remove distortions is total. This constitutes an acceptance of responsibility for service to others, which is of relative purity. The instrument through which we speak and its support group have a similar fidelity and, disregarding any inconvenience to self, desire to serve others. Due to the nature of the group, the queries made to us by the group have led rapidly into some- what abstruse regions of commentary. This content does not mitigate against the underlying purity of the contact. Such purity is as a light. Such an intensity of light attracts attention.

QUESTIONER: What would our fifth-density visitor hope to gain for himself if he were to be successful in eliminating this contact?

RA: I am Ra. As we have previously stated, the entity hopes to gain a portion of that light; that is, the mind/body/spirit complex of the instrument. Barring this, the entity intends to put out the light.

QUESTIONER: I understand this up to a point, and that point is if the entity were successful in either of these attempts, of what value would this be to him? Would it increase his ability? Would it increase his polarity? By what mechanism would it do whatever it does?

RA: I am Ra. Having attempted for some of your space/time, with no long-lasting result, to do these things, the entity may be asking this question of itself. The gain for triumph is an increase in negative po- larity to the entity, in that it has removed a source of radiance and, thereby, offered to this space/time the opportunity of darkness where there once was light. In the event that it succeeded in enslaving the mind/body/spirit complex of the instrument, it would have enslaved a fairly powerful entity, thus adding to its power.

QUESTIONER: I am sorry for my lack of penetration of these mech- anisms, and I apologize for some rather stupid questions, but I think we have here a point that is somewhat central to what we are presently attempting to understand. Some of my next questions may be almost unacceptably stupid, but I will attempt to try to understand what this power that our visitor seeks is and how he uses it. It seems to me that this is central to the mind and its evolution.

As our visitor increases his power through these works, what is the power that he increases? Can you describe it?

RA: I am Ra. The power of which you speak is a spiritual power. The powers of the mind, as such, do not encompass such works as these. You may, with some fruitfulness, consider the possibilities of moonlight. You are aware that we have described the Matrix of the Spirit as a Night. The moonlight, then, offers either a true picture seen in shadow or chimera and falsity. The power of falsity is deep, as is the power to discern truth from shadow. The shadow of hidden things is an infinite depth in which is stored the power of the One Infinite Creator.

The adept, then, is working with the power of hidden things illuminated by that which can be false or true. To embrace falsity, to know it, and to seek it, and to use it, gives a power that is most great. This is the nature of the power of your visitor and may shed some light upon the power of one who seeks in order to serve others as well, for the missteps in the night are oh! so easy.

QUESTIONER: Are you saying, then, that this power is of the spirit and not of the mind or of the body?

RA: I am Ra. The work of the adept is based upon previous work with the mind and the body; else, work with the spirit would not be possible on a dependable basis. With this comment we may assert the correctness of your assumption.

QUESTIONER: The fifteenth archetype is the Matrix of the Spirit and has been called the Devil. Can you tell me why that is so?

RA: I am Ra. We do not wish to be facile in such a central query, but we may note that the nature of the spirit is so infinitely subtle that the fructifying influence of light upon the great darkness of the spirit is very often not as apparent as the darkness itself. The progress chosen by many adepts becomes a confused path as each adept attempts to use the Catalyst of the Spirit. Few there are which are successful in grasping the light of the sun. By far, the majority of adepts remain groping in the moonlight, and, as we have said, this light can deceive as well as uncover hidden mystery. Therefore, the melody, shall we say, of this matrix often seems to be of a negative and evil, as you would call it, nature.

It is also to be noted that an adept is one which has freed itself more and more from the constraints of the thoughts, opinions, and bonds of other-selves. Whether this is done for service to others or service to self, it is a necessary part of the awakening of the adept. This freedom is seen by those not free as what you would call evil or black. The magic is recognized; the nature is often not.

QUESTIONER: Could I say, then, that implicit in the process of becoming adept is the seeming polarization towards service-to-self, because the adept becomes disassociated with many of his kind?

RA: I am Ra. This is likely to occur. The apparent happening is disassociation, whether the truth is service to self and thus true disassociation from other-selves or service to others, and thus true association with the heart of all other-selves and disassociation only from the illusory husks which prevent the adept from correctly perceiving the self and other-self as one.

QUESTIONER: Then you say that this effect of disassociation on the service-to-others adept is a stumbling block or slowing process in reaching that goal to which he aspires? Is this correct?

RA: I am Ra. This is incorrect. This disassociation from the miasma of illusion and misrepresentation of each and every distortion is a quite necessary portion of an adept's path. It may be seen by others to be unfortunate.

QUESTIONER: Then is this, from the point of view of the fifteenth archetype, somewhat of an excursion into the Matrix of the Spirit in this process? Does that make any sense?

RA: I am Ra. The excursion of which you speak and the process of disassociation is most usually linked with that archetype you call Hope, which we would prefer to call Faith. This archetype is the Catalyst of the Spirit and, because of the illuminations of the Potentiator of the Spirit, will begin to cause these changes in the adept's viewpoint.

QUESTIONER: I didn't intend to get too far ahead of my questioning process here. The positively or negatively polarized adept, then, is building a potential to draw directly on the spirit for power. Is this correct?

RA: I am Ra. It would be more proper to say that the adept is calling directly through the spirit to the universe for its power, for the spirit is a shuttle.

QUESTIONER: The only obvious significant difference, I believe, between the positive and negative adepts in using this shuttle is the way they polarize. Is there a relationship between the archetypes of the spirit and whether the polarization is either positive or negative? Is, for instance, the positive calling through the sixteenth archetype and the negative calling through the fifteenth archetype? I am very confused about this, and I imagine that that question is either poor or meaningless. Can you answer that?

RA: I am Ra. It is a challenge to answer such a query, for there is some confusion in its construction. However, we shall attempt to speak upon the subject.

The adept, whether positive or negative, has the same Matrix. The Potentiator is also identical. Due to the Catalyst of each adept, the adept may begin to pick and choose that into which it shall look further. The Experience of the Spirit, that which you have called the Moon, is then, by far, the more manifest of influences upon the polarity of the adept. Even the most unhappy of experiences, shall we say, which seem to occur in the Catalyst of the adept, seen from the viewpoint of the spirit, may, with the discrimination possible in shadow, be worked with until light equaling the light of brightest noon descends upon the adept, and positive or service-to-others illumination has occurred. The service-to-self adept will satisfy itself with the shadows and, grasping the light of day, will toss back the head in grim laughter, preferring the darkness.

QUESTIONER: I guess the nineteenth archetype of the spirit would be the Significator of the Spirit. Is that correct?

RA: I am Ra. This is correct.

QUESTIONER: How would you describe the Significator of the Spirit?

RA: I am Ra. In answer to the previous query, we set about doing just this. The Significator of the Spirit is that living entity which either radiates or absorbs the love and the light of the One Infinite Creator, radiates it to others or absorbs it for the self.

QUESTIONER: Then would this process of radiation or absorption, since we have what I would call a flux or flux rate, be the measure of the adept?

RA: I am Ra. This may be seen to be a reasonably adequate statement.

QUESTIONER: Then for the twentieth archetype, I'm guessing that this is the Transformation of the Spirit, possibly analogous to the sixth-density merging of the paths. Is this in any way correct?

RA: I am Ra. No.

QUESTIONER: Sorry about that. Can you tell me what the twentieth archetype would be?

RA: I am Ra. That which you call the Sarcophagus in your system may be seen to be the material world, if you will. This material world is transformed by the spirit into that which is infinite and eternal. The infinity of the spirit is an even-greater realization than the infinity of consciousness, for consciousness which has been disciplined by will and faith is that consciousness which may contact intelligent infinity directly. There are many things which fall away in the many, many steps of adepthood. We, of Ra, still walk these steps and praise the One Infinite Creator at each transformation.

QUESTIONER: Then I would guess that the twenty-first archetype would represent contact with intelligent infinity. Is that correct?

RA: I am Ra. This is correct, although one may also see the reflection of this contact as well as the contact with intelligent energy which is the Universe or, as you have called it somewhat provincially, the World.

QUESTIONER: Then by this contact also with intelligent energy, can you give me an example of what this would be for both the contact with intelligent infinity and the contact with intelligent energy? Could you give me an example of what type of experience this would result in, if that is at all possible?

RA: I am Ra. This shall be the last query of this working of full length. We have discussed the possibilities of contact with intelligent energy, for this energy is the energy of the Logos, and thus it is the energy which heals, builds, removes, destroys, and transforms all other-selves as well as the self.

The contact with intelligent infinity is most likely to produce an unspeakable joy in the entity experiencing such contact. If you wish to query in more detail upon this subject, we invite you to do so in another working. Is there a brief query before we close this working?

QUESTIONER: Is there anything that we can do to improve the contact or to make the instrument more comfortable?

RA: I am Ra. The alignments are most conscientious. We are appreciative. The entity which serves as instrument is somewhat distorted towards that condition you call stiffness of the dorsal regions. Manipulation would be helpful.

I am Ra. I leave you, my friends, glorying in the light and the love of the One Infinite Creator. Go forth, therefore, rejoicing in the power and in the peace of the One Infinite Creator. Adonai.

Session 81,
March 22, 1982

RA: I am Ra. I greet you in the love and in the light of the One Infinite Creator. We communicate now.

QUESTIONER: Could you first tell me the condition of the instrument?

RA: I am Ra. The physical-complex energy is in deficit at this particular space/time nexus due to prolonged psychic accentuation of preexisting distortions. The remainder of the energy complex levels are as previously stated.

QUESTIONER: Is this the reason for the instrument's feeling of uninterrupted weariness?

RA: I am Ra. There are portions of your space/time in which this may be said to be symptomatic of the psychic-greeting reaction. However, the continual weariness is not due to psychic greeting but is rather an inevitable consequence of this contact.

QUESTIONER: Why is this an inevitable consequence? What is the mechanism of this contact that creates this weariness?

RA: I am Ra. The mechanism creating weariness is that connection betwixt the density wherein this instrument's mind/body/spirit complex is safely kept during these workings, and the altogether variant density in which the instrument's physical-body complex resides at this space/time. As the instrument takes on more of the coloration of the resting density, the third-density experience seems more heavy and wearisome. This was accepted by the instrument, as it desired to be of service. Therefore, we accept also this effect, about which nothing of which we are aware may be done.

QUESTIONER: Is the effect a function of the number of sessions, and has it reached a peak level or will it continue to increase in effect?

RA: I am Ra. This wearying effect will continue but should not be confused with the physical energy levels, having only to do with the, as you would call it, daily round of experience. In this sphere, those things which are known already to aid this instrument will continue to be of aid. You will, however, notice the gradual increase in transparency, shall we say, of the vibrations of the instrument.

QUESTIONER: I didn't understand what you meant by that last statement. Could you explain it?

RA: I am Ra. Weariness of the time/space nature may be seen to be that reaction of transparent or pure vibrations with impure, confused, or opaque environs.

QUESTIONER: Is there any of this effect upon the other two of us in this group?

RA: I am Ra. This is quite correct.

QUESTIONER: Then we would also experience the uninterrupted weariness as a consequence of the contact. Is this correct?

RA: I am Ra. The instrument, by the very nature of the contact, bears the brunt of this effect. Each of the support group, by offering the love and the light of the One Infinite Creator in unqualified support in these workings and in energy transfers for the purpose of these workings, experiences between 10 and 15 percent, roughly, of this effect. It is cumulative and identical in the continual nature of its manifestation.

QUESTIONER: What could be the result of this continued wearying effect after a long period?

RA: I am Ra. You ask a general query with infinite answers. We shall overgeneralize in order to attempt to reply.

One group might be tempted and thus lose the very contact which caused the difficulty. So the story would end.

Another group might be strong at first but not faithful in the face of difficulty. Thus the story would end.

Another group might choose the path of martyrdom in its completeness and use the instrument until its physical-body complex failed from the harsh toll demanded when all energy was gone.

This particular group, at this particular nexus, is attempting to conserve the vital energy of the instrument. It is attempting to balance love of service and wisdom of service, and it is faithful to the service in the face of difficulty. Temptation has not yet ended this group's story.

We may not know the future, but the probability of this situation continuing over a relatively substantial period of your space/time is large. The significant factor is the will of the instrument and of the group to serve. That is the only cause for balancing the slowly increasing weariness, which will continue to distort your perceptions. Without this will, the contact might be possible but finally seem too much of an effort.

QUESTIONER: The instrument would like to know why she has a feeling of increased vital energy.

RA: I am Ra. We leave this answer to the instrument.

QUESTIONER: She would like to know if she has an increased sensitivity to foods.

RA: I am Ra. This instrument has an increased sensitivity to all stimuli. It is well that it use prudence.

QUESTIONER: Going back to the previous session, picking up on the tenth archetype, which is the Catalyst of the Body, the Wheel of Fortune represents interaction with other-selves. Is this a correct statement?

RA: I am Ra. This may be seen to be a roughly correct statement in that each catalyst is dealing with the nature of those experiences entering the energy web and vibratory perceptions of the mind/body/

spirit complex. The most carefully noted addition would be that the outside stimulus of the Wheel of Fortune is that which offers both positive and negative experience.

QUESTIONER: The eleventh archetype would then be the Experience of the Body, which represents the catalyst which has been processed by the mind/body/spirit complex and is called the Enchantress because it produces further seed for growth. Is this correct?

RA: I am Ra. This is correct.

QUESTIONER: We have already discussed the Significator, so I will skip number thirteen. The Transformation of the Body is called Death, for with death the body is transformed to a higher vibrational body for additional learning. Is this correct?

RA: I am Ra. This is correct and may be seen to be additionally correct in that each moment and certainly each diurnal period of the bodily incarnation offers death and rebirth to one which is attempting to use the catalyst which is offered it.

QUESTIONER: Finally, the fourteenth, the Way of the Body, is called the Alchemist because there is an infinity of time for the various bodies to operate within to learn the lessons necessary for evolution. Is this correct?

RA: I am Ra. This is less than completely correct, as the Great Way of the Body must be seen, as are all the archetypes of the body, to be a mirror image of the thrust of the activity of the mind. The body is the creature of the mind and is the instrument of manifestation for the fruits of mind and spirit. Therefore, you may see the body as providing the athanor[3] through which the Alchemist manifests gold.

QUESTIONER: I have guessed that the way to enter into a better comprehension of the archetypes is to compare what we experience now, after the veil, with what was experienced prior to that time, starting possibly as far back as the beginning of this octave of experience, to see how we got into the condition that we are in now. If this is agreeable, I would like to retreat to the very beginning of this octave of experience to investigate the conditions of mind, body, and spirit as they evolved in this octave. Is this acceptable?

---

3. athanor: an oven; a fire; a digesting furnace, formerly used in alchemy, so constructed as to maintain a uniform and constant heat.

RA: I am Ra. The direction of questions is your provenance.

QUESTIONER: Ra states that it has knowledge of only this octave, but it seems that Ra has complete knowledge of this octave. Can you tell me why this is?

RA: I am Ra. Firstly, we do not have complete knowledge of this octave. There are portions of the seventh density which, although described to us by our teachers, remain mysterious. Secondly, we have experienced a great deal of the available refining catalyst of this octave, and our teachers have worked with us most carefully that we may be one with all, that in turn our eventual returning to the great allness of creation shall be complete.

QUESTIONER: Then Ra has knowledge from the first beginnings of this octave through its present experience and what I might call direct or experiential knowledge through communication with those space/times and time/spaces, but has not yet evolved to or penetrated the seventh level. Is this a roughly correct statement?

RA: I am Ra. Yes.

QUESTIONER: Why does Ra not have any knowledge of that which was prior to the beginning of this octave?

RA: I am Ra. Let us compare octaves to islands. It may be that the inhabitants of an island are not alone upon a planetary sphere, but if an ocean-going vehicle in which one may survive has not been invented, true knowledge of other islands is possible only if an entity comes among the islanders and says, "I am from elsewhere." This is a rough analogy. However, we have evidence of this sort, both of previous creation and creation to be, as we in the stream of space/time and time/space view these apparently non-simultaneous events.

QUESTIONER: We presently find ourselves in the Milky Way galaxy of some 200 or so billion stars, and there are millions and millions of these large galaxies spread out through what we call space. To Ra's knowledge, can I assume that the number of these galaxies is infinite? Is this correct?

RA: I am Ra. This is precisely correct and is a significant point.

QUESTIONER: The point being that we have unity. Is that correct?

RA: I am Ra. You are perceptive.

QUESTIONER: Then what portion of these galaxies is Ra aware of? Has Ra experienced consciousness in many other of these galaxies?

RA: I am Ra. No.

QUESTIONER: Has Ra experienced or does Ra have any knowledge of any of these other galaxies? Has Ra traveled to, in one form or another, any of these other galaxies?

RA: I am Ra. Yes.

QUESTIONER: It's unimportant, but how many other of these galaxies has Ra traveled to?

RA: I am Ra. We have opened our hearts in radiation of love to the entire creation. Approximately 90 percent of the creation is at some level aware of the sending and able to reply. All of the infinite Logoi are one in the consciousness of love. This is the type of contact which we enjoy rather than travel.

QUESTIONER: So that I can just get a little idea of what I am talking about, what are the limits of Ra's travel in the sense of directly experiencing or seeing the activities of various places? Is it solely within this galaxy, and if so, how much of this galaxy? Or does it include some other galaxies?

RA: I am Ra. Although it would be possible for us to move at will throughout the creation within this Logos, that is to say, the Milky Way galaxy, so called, we have moved where we were called to service; these locations being, shall we say, local and including Alpha Centauri, planets of your solar system which you call the Sun, Cepheus, and Zeta Reticuli. To these sub-Logoi we have come, having been called.

QUESTIONER: Was the call in each instance from the third-density beings or was this call from other densities?

RA: I am Ra. In general, the latter supposition is correct. In the particular case of the Sun sub-Logos, third density is the density of calling.

QUESTIONER: Ra then has not moved at any time into one of the other major galaxies. Is this correct?

RA: I am Ra. This is correct.

QUESTIONER: Does Ra have knowledge of any other major galaxy or the consciousness of anything in that galaxy?

RA: I am Ra. We assume you are speaking of the possibility of knowledge of other major galaxies. There are Wanderers from other major galaxies drawn to the specific needs of a single call. There are those among our social memory complex which have become Wanderers in other major galaxies. Thus there has been knowledge of other major galaxies, for to one whose personality or mind/body/spirit complex has been crystallized, the universe is one place and there is no bar upon travel. However, our interpretation of your query was a query concerning the social memory complex traveling to another major galaxy. We have not done this, nor do we contemplate it, for we can reach in love with our hearts.

QUESTIONER: Thank you. In this line of questioning I am trying to establish a basis for understanding the foundation for not only the experience that we have now but how the experience was formed and how it is related to all the rest of the experience through the portion of the octave as we understand it. I am assuming, then, that all of these galaxies, this infinite number of galaxies that we can just begin to become aware of with our telescopes, are all of the same octave. Is this correct?

RA: I am Ra. This is correct.

QUESTIONER: I was wondering if some of the Wanderers from Ra in going to some of the other major galaxies—that is, leaving this system of some 200 billion stars of lenticular shape and going to another cluster of billions of stars and finding their way into some planetary situation there—would encounter the dual polarity that we have here, the service-to-self and the service-to-others polarities?

RA: I am Ra. This is correct.

QUESTIONER: You stated earlier that toward the center of this galaxy is what, to use a poor term, you could call the older portion where you would find no service-to-self polarization. Am I correct in assuming that this is true with the other galaxies with which Wanderers from Ra have experience? At the center of these galaxies, only the service-to-others polarity exists and the experiment started farther out toward the rim of the galaxy?

RA: I am Ra. Various Logoi and sub-Logoi had various methods of arriving at the discovery of the efficiency of free will in intensifying the experience of the Creator by the Creator. However, in each case this has been a pattern.

QUESTIONER: You mean then that the pattern is that the service-to-self polarization appeared farther out from the center of the galactic spiral?

RA: I am Ra. This is correct.

QUESTIONER: From this I will assume that from the beginning of the octave, we had the core of many galactic spirals forming, and I know that this is incorrect in the sense of timelessness, but as the spiral formed, then I am assuming that in this particular octave the experiment of the veiling and the extending of free will must have started, roughly, simultaneously in many, many of the budding or building galactic systems. Am I in any way correct with this assumption?

RA: I am Ra. You are precisely correct. This instrument is unusually fragile at this space/time and has used much of the transferred energy. We would invite one more full query for this working.

QUESTIONER: Actually, I don't have much more on this except to make the assumption that there must have been some type of communication throughout the octave so that, when the first experiment became effective, knowledge of this spread rapidly through the octave and was picked up by other budding galactic spirals, you might say. Is this correct?

RA: I am Ra. This is correct. To be aware of the nature of this communication is to be aware of the nature of the Logos. Much of what you call creation has never separated from the One Logos of this octave and resides within the One Infinite Creator. Communication in such an environment is the communication of cells of the body. That which is learned by one is known to all. The sub-Logoi, then, have been in the position of refining the discoveries of what might be called the earlier sub-Logoi. May we ask if we may answer any brief queries at this working?

QUESTIONER: Only if there is anything that we can do to make the instrument more comfortable or to improve the contact?

RA: I am Ra. It is difficult to determine the energy levels of the instrument and support group. Of this we are aware. It is, however, recommended that every attempt be made to enter each working with the most-desirable configurations of energy possible. All is well, my friends. You are conscientious and the alignments are well.

I am Ra. I leave you in the love and the light of the One Infinite Creator. Go forth, therefore, rejoicing in the power and in the peace of the Infinite Creator. Adonai.

Session 82,
March 27, 1982

RA: I am Ra. I greet you, my friends, in the love and in the light of the One Infinite Creator. We communicate now.

QUESTIONER: Could you first please give me the condition of the instrument?

RA: I am Ra. It is as previously stated.

QUESTIONER: Is there anything at all that we could do that we are not doing—besides eliminating the contact—to increase the physical energy of the instrument?

RA: I am Ra. There is the possibility/probability that the whirling of the water with spine erect would alter, somewhat, the distortion towards what you call pain which this entity experiences in the dorsal region on a continuous level. This in turn could aid in the distortion towards increase of physical energy to some extent.

QUESTIONER: I would like to consider the condition at a time or position just prior to the beginning of this octave of experience. I am assuming that, just prior to the beginning of this octave, intelligent infinity had created and already experienced one or more previous octaves. Is this correct?

RA: I am Ra. You assume correctly. However, the phrase would more informatively read infinite intelligence had experienced previous octaves.

QUESTIONER: Does Ra have any knowledge of the number of previous octaves; if so, how many?

RA: I am Ra. As far as we are aware, we are in an infinite creation. There is no counting.

QUESTIONER: That's what I thought you might say. Am I correct in assuming that at the beginning of this octave, out of what I would call a void of space, seeds of an infinite number of galactic systems such as the Milky Way galaxy appeared and grew in spiral fashion simultaneously?

RA: I am Ra. There are duple areas of potential confusion. Firstly, let us say that the basic concept is reasonably well stated. Now we address the confusions. The nature of true simultaneity is such that, indeed, all is simultaneous. However, in your modes of perception you would perhaps more properly view the seeding of the creation as that of growth from the center or core outward. The second confusion lies in the term "void." We would substitute the noun "plenum."

QUESTIONER: Then, if I were observing the beginning of the octave at that time through a telescope, say from this position, would I see the center of many, many galaxies appearing and each of them then spreading outward in a spiraling fashion over what we would consider billions of years, but the spirals spreading outward in approximately what we would consider the same rate so that all these galaxies began as the first speck of light at the same time and then spread out at roughly the same rate? Is this correct?

RA: I am Ra. The query has confusing elements. There is a center to infinity. From this center, all spreads. Therefore, there are centers to the creation, to the galaxies, to star systems, to planetary systems, and to consciousness. In each case you may see growth from the center outward. Thus you may see your query as being over-general in concept.

QUESTIONER: Considering only our Milky Way galaxy at its beginnings, I will assume that the first occurrence that we could find with our physical apparatus was the appearance of a star of the nature of our sun. Is this correct?

RA: I am Ra. In the case of the galactic systems, the first manifestation of the Logos is a cluster of central systems which generate the outward swirling energies producing, in their turn, further energy centers for the Logos or what you would call stars.

QUESTIONER: Are these central original creations or clusters what we call stars?

RA: I am Ra. This is correct. However, the closer to the, shall we say, beginning of the manifestation of the Logos the star is, the more it partakes in the one original thought.

QUESTIONER: Why does this partaking in the original thought have a gradient radially outward? That's the way I understand your statement.

RA: I am Ra. This is the plan of the One Infinite Creator. The One Original Thought is the harvest of all previous, if you would use this term, experience of the Creator by the Creator. As It decides to know Itself, It generates Itself, into that plenum full of the glory and the power of the One Infinite Creator which is manifested to your perceptions as space or outer space. Each generation of this knowing begets a knowing which has the capacity, through free will, to choose methods of knowing Itself. Therefore, gradually, step by step, the Creator becomes that which may know Itself, and the portions of the Creator partake less purely in the power of the original word or thought. The Creator does not properly create as much as It experiences Itself.

QUESTIONER: What was the form, condition, or experience of the first division of consciousness that occurred at the beginning of this octave at the beginning of this galactic experience?

RA: I am Ra. We touch upon previous material. The harvest of the previous octave was the Creator of Love manifested in mind, body, and spirit. This form of the Creator experiencing Itself may perhaps be said to be the first division.

QUESTIONER: I was interested specifically in how this very first division showed up in this octave. I was interested to know if it made the transition through first, second, third, fourth, etc. densities? I would like to take the first mind/body/spirit complexes and trace their experience from the very start to the present so that I could better understand the condition that we are in now by comparing it with this original growth. Could you please tell me precisely how this came about as to the formation of the planets and growth through the densities, if that is the way it happened, please?

RA: I am Ra. Your queries seem more confused than your basic mental distortions in this area. Let us speak in general and perhaps you may find a less confused and more simple method of eliciting information in this area.

A very great deal of creation was manifested without the use of the concepts involved in consciousness, as you know it. The creation itself is a form of consciousness which is unified, the Logos being the one great heart of creation. The process of evolution through this period, which may be seen to be timeless, is most valuable to take into consideration, for it is against the background of this essential unity of the fabric of creation that we find the ultimate development of the Logoi which chose to use that portion of the harvested consciousness of the Creator to move forward with the process of knowledge of self. As it had been found to be efficient to use the various densities, which are fixed in each octave, in order to create conditions in which self-conscious sub-Logoi could exist, this was carried out throughout the growing flower-strewn field, as your simile suggests, of the one infinite creation.

The first beings of mind, body, and spirit were not complex. The experience of mind/body/spirits at the beginning of this octave of experience was singular. There was no third-density forgetting. There was no veil. The lessons of third density are predestined by the very nature of the vibratory rates experienced during this particular density and by the nature of the quantum jump to the vibratory experiences of fourth density.

QUESTIONER: Am I correct, then, in assuming the first mind/body/spirit experiences, as this galaxy progressed in growth, were those that moved through the densities; that is, the process we have discussed coming out of second density. For instance, let us take a particular planet, one of the very early planets formed near the center of the galaxy. I will assume that the planet solidified during the first density, that life appeared in second density, and that all of the mind/body/spirit complexes of third density progressed out of second density on that planet and evolved in third density. Is this correct?

RA: I am Ra. This is hypothetically correct.

QUESTIONER: Did this in fact happen on some of the planets or on a large percentage of the planets near the center of this galaxy in this way?

RA: I am Ra. Our knowledge is limited. We know of the beginning but cannot asseverate to the precise experiences of those things occurring before us. You know the nature of historical teaching. At our level of learn/teaching we may expect little distortion. However, we cannot, with surety, say there is no distortion as we speak of specific occurrences of which we were not consciously a part. It is our understanding that your supposition is correct. Thus we so hypothesize.

QUESTIONER: Specifically, I am trying to grasp an understanding of the process of experience in third density before the veil so that I can better understand the present process. As I understand it, the mind/body/spirits went through the process of what we call physical incarnation in this density, but there was no forgetting. What was the benefit or purpose of the physical incarnation when there was no forgetting?

RA: I am Ra. The purpose of incarnation in third density is to learn the ways of love.

QUESTIONER: I guess I didn't state that exactly right. What I mean is, since there was no forgetting, since the mind/body/spirits had, in what we call the physical incarnation, their full consciousness, they knew the same thing that they would know while not in the physical incarnation. What was the mechanism of teaching that taught the ways of love in the third-density physical prior to the forgetting process?

RA: I am Ra. We ask your permission to answer this query in an oblique fashion, as we perceive an area in which we might be of aid.

QUESTIONER: Certainly.

RA: I am Ra. Your queries seem to be pursuing the possibility/probability that the mechanisms of experience in third density are different if a mind/body/spirit is attempting them rather than a mind/body/spirit complex. The nature of third density is constant. Its ways are to be learned the same now and ever. Thusly, no matter what form the entity facing these lessons, the lessons and mechanisms are the same. The Creator will learn from Itself. Each entity has unmanifest portions of learning and, most importantly, learning which is involved with other-selves.

QUESTIONER: Then prior to the forgetting process, there was no concept of anything but service-to-others polarization. What sort of societies and experiences in third density were created and evolved in this condition?

RA: I am Ra. It is our perception that such conditions created the situation of a most pallid experiential nexus in which lessons were garnered with the relative speed of the turtle to the cheetah.

QUESTIONER: Did such societies evolve with technologies of a complex nature, or did they remain quite simple? Can you give me a general idea of the evolvement that would be a function of what we would call intellectual activity?

RA: I am Ra. There is infinite diversity in societies under any circumstances. There were many highly technologically advanced societies which grew due to the ease of producing any desired result. When one dwells within what might be seen to be a state of constant potential inspiration, that which even the most highly sophisticated, in your terms, societal structure lacked, given the noncomplex nature of its entities, was what you might call will or, to use a more plebeian term, gusto, or élan vital.

QUESTIONER: Did such technological societies evolve travel through what we call space to other planets or other planetary systems? Did some of them do this?

RA: I am Ra. This is correct.

QUESTIONER: Then even though, from our point of view, there was great evolutionary experience, it was deemed at some point by the evolving Logos that an experiment to create a greater experience was appropriate. Is this correct?

RA: I am Ra. This is correct and may benefit from comment. The Logos is aware of the nature of the third-density requirement for what you have called graduation. All the previous, if you would use this term, experiments, although resulting in many experiences, lacked what was considered the crucial ingredient; that is, polarization. There was little enough tendency for experience to polarize entities that entities repeated habitually the third-density cycles many times over. It was desired that the potential for polarization be made more available.

QUESTIONER: Then since the only possibility at this particular time, as I see it, was a polarization for service-to-others, I must assume from what you said that even though all were aware of this service-to-others necessity, they were unable to achieve it. What was the configuration of mind of the mind/body/spirits at that time? Why did they have such a difficult time serving others to the extent necessary for graduation, since this was the only polarity possible?

RA: I am Ra. Consider, if you will, the tendency of those who are divinely happy, as you call this distortion, to have little urge to alter or better their condition. Such is the result of the mind/body/spirit which is not complex. There is the possibility of love of other-selves and service to other-selves, but there is the overwhelming awareness of the Creator in the self. The connection with the Creator is that of the umbilical cord. The security is total. Therefore, no love is terribly important; no pain terribly frightening; no effort, therefore, is made to serve for love or to benefit from fear.

QUESTIONER: It seems that you might make an analogy in our present illusion of those who are born into extreme wealth and security. Is this correct?

RA: I am Ra. Within the strict bounds of the simile, you are perceptive.

QUESTIONER: We have presently an activity between physical incarnations called the healing and review of the incarnation. Was anything of this nature occurring prior to the veil?

RA: I am Ra. The inchoate structure of this process was always in place, but where there has been no harm there need be no healing. This too may be seen to have been of concern to Logoi, which were aware that without the need to understand, understanding would forever be left undone. We ask your forgiveness for the use of this misnomer, but your language has a paucity of sound vibration complexes for this general concept.

QUESTIONER: I don't grasp too well the condition of incarnation and the time in between incarnations prior to the veil. I do not understand what was the difference other than the manifestation of the third-density, yellow-ray body. Was there any mental difference upon what we call death? I don't see the necessity for what we call the review of the incarnation if the consciousness was uninterrupted. Could you clear up that point for me?

RA: I am Ra. No portion of the Creator audits the course, to use your experiential terms. Each incarnation is intended to be a course in the Creator knowing Itself. A review or, shall we say, to continue the metaphor, each test is an integral portion of the process of the Creator knowing Itself. Each incarnation will end with such a test. This is so that the portion of the Creator may assimilate the experiences in yellow, physical, third density; may evaluate the biases gained; and may then choose, either by means of automatically provided aid or by the self, the conditions of the next incarnation.

QUESTIONER: Before the veil, during the review of the incarnation, were the entities at that time aware that what they were trying to do was sufficiently polarize for graduation?

RA: I am Ra. This is correct.

QUESTIONER: Then I am assuming that this awareness was somehow reduced as they went into the yellow-ray third-density incarnative state even though there was no veil. Is this correct?

RA: I am Ra. This is distinctly incorrect.

QUESTIONER: OK. This is the central important point. It seems to me that if polarization was the obvious thing that more effort would have been put forward to polarize. Let me see if I can state this differently. Before the veil there was an awareness of the need for polarization towards service to others in third density by all entities, whether incarnate in third-density, yellow-ray bodies or in between incarnations. I assume, then, that the condition of which we earlier spoke, one of wealth, you might say, was present through the entire spectrum of experience whether it might be between incarnations or during incarnations, and the entities just simply could not manifest the desire to create this polarization necessary for graduation. Is this correct?

RA: I am Ra. You begin to grasp the situation. Let us continue the metaphor of the schooling but consider the scholar as being an entity in your younger years of the schooling process. The entity is fed, clothed, and protected regardless of whether or not the schoolwork is accomplished. Therefore, the entity does not do the homework but rather enjoys playtime, mealtime, and vacation. It is not until there is a reason to wish to excel that most entities will attempt to excel.

QUESTIONER: You have stated in a much-earlier session that it is necessary to polarize more than 50 percent service to others to be harvestable fourth-density positive. Was this condition the same at the time before the veil?

RA: I am Ra. This shall be the last full query of this working.

The query is not answered easily, for the concept of service to self did not hold sway previous to what we have been calling the veiling process. The necessity for graduation to fourth density is an ability to use, welcome, and enjoy a certain intensity of the white light of the One Infinite Creator. In your own terms at your space/time nexus, this ability may be measured by your previously stated percentages of service.

Prior to the veiling process the measurement would be that of an entity walking up a set of your stairs, each of which was imbued with a certain quality of light. The stair upon which an entity stopped would be either third-density light or fourth-density light. Between the two stairs lies the threshold. To cross that threshold is difficult. There is resistance at the edge, shall we say, of each density. The faculty of faith or will needs to be understood, nourished, and developed in order to have an entity which seeks past the boundary of third density. Those entities which do not do their homework, be they ever so amiable, shall not cross. It was this situation which faced the Logoi prior to the veiling process being introduced into the experiential continuum of third density.

May we ask if there are any brief queries at this working?

QUESTIONER: Is there anything that we can do to improve the contact or make the instrument more comfortable?

RA: I am Ra. All parameters are being met. Remain united in love and thanksgiving. We thank you for your conscientiousness as regards the appurtenances.

I am Ra. I leave you in the love and in the light of the One Infinite Glorious Creator. Go forth, therefore, rejoicing merrily in the power and the peace of the One Creator. Adonai.

Session 83,
April 5, 1982

RA: I am Ra. I greet you in the love and in the light of the One Infinite Creator. I communicate now.

QUESTIONER: Could you first please give me the condition of the instrument?

RA: I am Ra. It is as previously stated.

QUESTIONER: Could you please tell me why the instrument now gains weight after a session instead of losing it?

RA: I am Ra. To assume that the instrument is gaining the weight of the physical bodily complex due to a session or working with Ra is erroneous. The instrument has no longer any physical material which, to any observable extent, must be used in order for this contact to occur. This is due to the determination of the group that the instrument shall not use the vital energy which would be necessary, since the physical-energy-complex level is in deficit. Since the energy, therefore, for these contacts is a product of energy transfer, the instrument must no longer pay this physical price. Therefore, the instrument is not losing the weight.

However, the weight gain, as it occurs, is the product of two factors. One is the increasing sensitivity of this physical vehicle to all that is placed before it, including that towards which it is distorted in ways you would call allergic. The second factor is the energizing of these difficulties.

It is fortunate for the outlook of this contact and the incarnation of this entity that it is not distorted towards the overeating, as the overloading of this much distorted physical complex would override even the most fervent affirmation of health/illness and turn the instrument towards the distortions of illness/health or, in the extreme case, the physical death.

QUESTIONER: Thank you. I'm going to ask a rather long, complex question, and I would request that the answer to each portion of this question be given if there was a significant difference prior to the veil than following the veil, so that I can get an idea of how what we experience now is used for better polarization.

What was the difference before the veil in the following while incarnate in third density: sleep, dreams, physical pain, mental pain, sex, disease, catalyst programming, random catalyst, relationships, and communication with the Higher Self or with the mind/body/spirit totality or any other mind, body, or spirit functions before the veil that would be significant with respect to their difference after the veil?

RA: I am Ra. Firstly, let us establish that both before and after the veil, the same conditions existed in time/space; that is, the veiling process is a space/time phenomenon.

Secondly, the character of experience was altered drastically by the veiling process. In some cases, such as the dreaming and the contact with the Higher Self, the experience was quantitatively different due to the fact that the veiling is a primary cause of the value of dreams and is also the single door against which the Higher Self must stand awaiting entry. Before veiling, dreams were not for the purpose of using the so-called unconscious to further utilize catalyst but were used to learn/teach from teach/learners within the inner planes as well as those of outer origins of higher density. As you deal with each subject of which you spoke, you may observe, during the veiling process, not a quantitative change in the experience but a qualitative one.

Let us, as an example, choose your sexual activities of energy transfer. If you have a desire to treat other subjects in detail, please query forthwith. In the instance of the sexual activity of those not dwelling within the veiling, each activity was a transfer. There were some transfers of strength. Most were rather attenuated in the strength of the transfer due to the lack of veiling.

In the third density, entities are attempting to learn the ways of love. If it can be seen that all are one being, it becomes much more difficult for the undisciplined personality to choose one mate and, thereby, initiate itself into a program of service. It is much more likely that the sexual energy will be dissipated more randomly without either great joy or great sorrow depending from these experiences.

Therefore, the green-ray energy transfer, being almost without exception the case in sexual energy transfer prior to veiling, remains weakened and without significant crystallization. The sexual energy transfers and blockages after veiling have been discussed previously. It may be seen to be a more complex study, but one far more efficient in crystallizing those who seek the green-ray energy center.

QUESTIONER: Let's take, then, since we are on the subject of sex, the relationship before and after the veil of disease, in this particular case venereal disease. Was this type of disease in existence prior to the veil?

RA: I am Ra. There has been that which is called disease, both of this type and others, before and after this great experiment. However, since the venereal disease is in large part a function of the thought-forms of a distorted nature which are associated with sexual energy blockage, the venereal disease is almost entirely the product of mind/body/spirit complexes' interaction after the veiling.

QUESTIONER: You mentioned that it existed in a small way prior to the veil. What was the source of its development prior to the veiling process?

RA: I am Ra. The source was as random as the nature of disease distortions are, at heart, in general. Each portion of the body complex is in a state of growth at all times. The reversal of this is seen as disease and has the benign function of ending an incarnation at the appropriate space/time nexus. This was the nature of disease, including that which you call venereal.

QUESTIONER: I'll make this statement and you can correct me. As I see the nature of the action of disease before the veil, it seems to me that the Logos had decided upon a program where an individual mind/body/spirit would continue to grow in mind, and the body would be the third-density analog of this mind. The growth would be continual unless there was an inability, for some reason, for the mind to continue along the growth patterns. If this growth decelerated or stopped, what we call disease would then act in a way so as to eventually terminate this physical experience so that a new physical experience would be started, after a review of the entire process had taken place between incarnations. Would you clear up my thinking on that, please?

RA: I am Ra. Your thinking is sufficiently clear on this subject.

QUESTIONER: The thing I don't understand is why, if there was no veil, the review of the incarnation after the incarnation would help the process, since it seems to me that the entity should already be aware of what was happening. Possibly this has to do with the nature of space/time and time/space. Could you clear that up, please?

RA: I am Ra. It is true that the nature of time/space is such that a lifetime may be seen whole as a book or record, the pages studied, riffled through, and reread. However, the value of review is that of the testing as opposed to the studying. At the testing, when the test is true, the distillations of all study are made clear. During the process of study, which you may call the incarnation, regardless of an entity's awareness of the process taking place, the material is diffused and overattention is almost inevitably placed upon detail.

The testing upon the cessation of the incarnative state is not that testing which involves the correct memorization of many details. This testing is, rather, the observing of self by self, often with aid as we have said. In this observation one sees the sum of all the detailed study, that being an attitude or complex of attitudes which bias the consciousness of the mind/body/spirit.

QUESTIONER: Now, before the veil an entity would be aware that he was experiencing a disease. As an analogy would you give me, if you are aware of a case, a disease an entity might experience prior to the veil and how he would react to this and think about it and what effect it would have on him?

RA: I am Ra. Inasmuch as the universe is composed of an infinite array of entities, there is also an infinity of response to stimulus. If you will observe your peoples you will discover greatly variant responses to the same distortion towards disease. Consequently, we cannot answer your query with any hope of making any true statements, since the over-generalizations required are too capacious.

QUESTIONER: Was there any uniformity or like functions of societies or social organizations prior to the veil?

RA: I am Ra. The third density is, by its very fiber, a societal one. There are societies wherever there are entities conscious of the self and conscious of other-selves and possessed with intelligence adequate to process information indicating the benefits of communal blending of energies. The structures of society before as after veiling were various. However, the societies before veiling did not depend in any case upon the intentional enslavement of some for the benefit of others, this not being seen to be a possibility when all are seen as one. There was, however, the requisite amount of disharmony to produce various experiments in what you may call governmental or societal structures.

QUESTIONER: In our present illusion we have undoubtedly lost sight of the techniques of enslavement that are used, since we are so far departed from the pre-veil experience. I am sure that many of service-to-others orientation are using techniques of enslavement even though they are not aware that these are techniques of enslavement, simply because they have been evolved over so long a period of time and we are so deep into the illusion. Is this not correct?

RA: I am Ra. This is incorrect.

QUESTIONER: Then you say that there are no cases where those who are of a service-to-others orientation are using techniques of enslavement that have grown as a result of the evolution of our social structures? Is this what you mean?

RA: I am Ra. It was our understanding that your query concerned conditions before the veiling. There was no unconscious slavery, as you call this condition, at that period. At the present space/time the conditions of well-meant and unintentional slavery are so numerous that it beggars our ability to enumerate them.

QUESTIONER: Then for a service-to-others-oriented entity at this time, meditation upon the nature of these little-expected forms of slavery might be productive in polarization, I would think. Am I correct?

RA: I am Ra. You are quite correct.

QUESTIONER: I would say that a very high percentage of the laws and restrictions within what we call our legal system are of a nature of enslavement of which I just spoke. Would you agree with this?

RA: I am Ra. It is a necessary balance to the intention of law, which is to protect, that the result would encompass an equal distortion towards imprisonment. Therefore, we may say that your supposition is correct. This is not to denigrate those who, in green- and blue-ray energies, sought to free a peaceable people from the bonds of chaos, but only to point out the inevitable consequences of codification of response which does not recognize the uniqueness of each and every situation within your experience.

QUESTIONER: Is the veil supposed to be what I would call semipermeable?

RA: I am Ra. The veil is indeed so.

QUESTIONER: What techniques and methods of penetration of the veil were planned, and are there any others that have occurred other that those planned?

RA: I am Ra. There were none planned by the first great experiment. As all experiments, this rested upon the nakedness of hypothesis. The outcome was unknown. It was discovered, experientially and empirically, that there were as many ways to penetrate the veil as the imagination of mind/body/spirit complexes could provide. The desire of mind/body/spirit complexes to know that which was unknown drew to them the dreaming and the gradual opening to the seeker of all of the balancing mechanisms, leading to adepthood and communication with teach/learners which could pierce this veil.

The various unmanifested activities of the self were found to be productive in some degree of penetration of the veil. In general, we may say that by far the most vivid and even extravagant opportunities for the piercing of the veil are a result of the interaction of polarized entities.

QUESTIONER: Could you expand on what you mean by that interaction of polarized entities in piercing the veil?

RA: I am Ra. We shall state two items of note. The first is the extreme potential for polarization in the relationship of two polarized entities which have embarked upon the service-to-others path or, in some few cases, the service-to-self path. Secondly, we would note that effect which we have learned to call the doubling effect. Those of like mind which together seek shall far more surely find.

QUESTIONER: Specifically, by what process would, in the first case, two polarized entities attempt to penetrate the veil, whether they be positively or negatively polarized? By what technique would they penetrate the veil?

RA: I am Ra. The penetration of the veil may be seen to begin to have its roots in the gestation of green-ray activity, that all-compassionate love which demands no return. If this path is followed, the higher energy centers shall be activated and crystallized until the adept is born. Within the adept is the potential for dismantling the veil to a greater or lesser extent that all may be seen again as one. The other-self is primary catalyst in this particular path to the piercing of the veil, if you would call it that.

QUESTIONER: What was the mechanism of the very first veiling process? I don't know if you can answer that. Would you try to answer that?

RA: I am Ra. The mechanism of the veiling between the conscious and unconscious portions of the mind was a declaration that the mind was complex. This, in turn, caused the body and the spirit to become complex.

QUESTIONER: Would you give me an example of a complex activity of the body that we have now, and how it was not complex prior to the veil?

RA: I am Ra. Prior to the great experiment a mind/body/spirit was capable of controlling the pressure of blood in the veins, the beating of the organ you call the heart, the intensity of the sensation known to you as pain, and all the functions now understood to be involuntary or unconscious.

QUESTIONER: When the veiling process originally took place, then, it seems that the Logos must have had a list of those functions that would become unconscious and those that would remain consciously controlled. I am assuming that if this occurred, there was good reason for these divisions. Am I in any way correct on this?

RA: I am Ra. No.

QUESTIONER: Would you correct me, please?

RA: I am Ra. There were many experiments whereby various of the functions or distortions of the body complex were veiled and others not. A large number of these experiments resulted in nonviable body complexes or those only marginally viable. For instance, it is not a survival-oriented mechanism for the nerve receptors to blank out unconsciously any distortions towards pain.

QUESTIONER: Before the veil the mind could blank out pain. I assume, then, that the function of the pain at that time was to signal the body to assume a different configuration so that the source of the pain would leave, and then the pain could be eliminated mentally. Is that correct, and was there another function for the pain prior to the veiling?

RA: I am Ra. Your assumption is correct. The function of pain at that time was as the warning of the fire alarm to those not smelling the smoke.

QUESTIONER: Then let's say that an entity at that time burned its hand due to carelessness. It would immediately remove its hand from the burning object, and then, in order to not feel the pain any more, its mind would cut the pain off until healing had taken place. Is this correct?

RA: I am Ra. This is correct.

QUESTIONER: We would look at this in our present illusion as an elimination of a certain amount of catalyst that would produce an acceleration in our evolution. Is this correct?

RA: I am Ra. The attitude towards pain varies from mind/body/spirit complex to mind/body/spirit complex. Your verbalization of attitude towards the distortion known as pain is one productive of helpful distortions as regards the process of evolution.

QUESTIONER: What I was trying to indicate was that the plan of the Logos in veiling the conscious from the unconscious mind in such a way that pain could not so easily be controlled would have created a system of catalyst that was not previously usable. Is this generally correct?

RA: I am Ra. Yes.

QUESTIONER: In some cases it seems that this use of catalyst is almost in a runaway condition for some entities, in that they are experiencing much more pain than they can make good use of as far as catalytic nature would be considered. Could you comment on that?

RA: I am Ra. This shall be the last query of this working of a full length. You may see, in some cases, an entity which, either by pre-incarnative choice or by constant reprogramming while in incarnation, has developed an esurient program of catalyst. Such an entity is quite desirous of using the catalyst and has determined to its own satisfaction that what you may call the large board needs to be applied to the forehead in order to obtain the attention of the self. In these cases it may indeed seem a great waste of the catalyst of pain and a distortion towards feeling the tragedy of so much pain may be experienced by the other-self. However, it is well to hope that the other-self is grasping that which it has gone to some trouble to offer itself; that is, the catalyst which it desires to use for the purpose of evolution. May we ask if there are any brief queries at this time?

QUESTIONER: I noticed you started this session with "I communicate now," and you usually use "We communicate now." Is there any significance or difference with respect to that, and then is there anything that we can do to make the instrument more comfortable or to improve the contact?

RA: I am Ra. We am Ra. You may see the grammatical difficulties of your linguistic structure in dealing with a social memory complex. There is no distinction between the first-person singular and plural in your language when pertaining to Ra.

We offer the following, not to infringe upon your free will, but because this instrument has specifically requested information as to its maintenance, and the support group does so at this querying. We may suggest that the instrument has two areas of potential distortion, both of which may be aided in the bodily sense by the ingestion of those things which seem to the instrument to be desirable. We do not suggest any hard-and-fast rulings of diet, although we may suggest the virtue of the liquids. The instrument has an increasing ability to sense that which will aid its bodily complex. It is being aided by affirmations and also by the light which is the food of the density of resting.

We may ask the support group to monitor the instrument as always, so that in the case of the desire for the more complex proteins, that which is the least distorted might be offered to the bodily complex which is indeed at this time potentially capable of greatly increased distortion.

I am Ra. We thank you, my friends, for your continued conscientiousness in the fulfilling of your manifestation of desire to serve others. You are conscientious. The appurtenances are quite well aligned.

I am Ra. I leave you, my friends, in the love and in the light of the One Infinite Creator. Go forth, therefore, rejoicing merrily in the power and in the peace of the One Infinite Creator. Adonai.

Session 84,
April 14, 1982

RA: I am Ra. I greet you, my friends, in the love and in the light of the One Infinite Creator. We communicate now.

QUESTIONER: Could you first please give me the condition of the instrument?

RA: I am Ra. The physical-complex energy level of the instrument is in sizable deficit. The vital energies are well.

QUESTIONER: In the last session you mentioned the least distorted complex protein for the instrument since its body complex was capable of greatly increased distortion. Would you define the protein of which you spoke, and in which direction is the increased distortion, towards health or ill health?

RA: I am Ra. We were, in the cautionary statement about complex protein, referring to the distortions of the animal protein which has been slaughtered and preservatives added in order to maintain the acceptability to your peoples of this nonliving, physical material. It is well to attempt to find those items which are fresh and of the best quality possible in order to avoid increasing this particular entity's distortions which may be loosely termed allergic.

We were speaking of the distortion towards disease which is potential at this space/time.

QUESTIONER: The instrument asked the following question: Ra has implied that the instrument is on the path of martyrdom, but since we all die, are we not all martyred to something, and when, if ever, does martyrdom partake of wisdom?

RA: I am Ra. This is a thoughtful query. Let us use as exemplar the one known as Jehoshua. This entity incarnated with the plan of martyrdom. There is no wisdom in this plan, but rather understanding and compassion extended to its fullest perfection. The one known as Jehoshua would have been less than fully understanding of its course had it chosen to follow its will at any space/time during its teachings. Several times, as you call this measure, this entity had the possibility of moving towards the martyr's place which was, for that martyr, Jerusalem. Yet, in meditation this entity stated, time and again, "It is not yet the hour." The entity could also have, when the hour came, walked another path. Its incarnation would then have been prolonged, but the path for which it incarnated somewhat confused. Thusly, one may observe the greatest amount of understanding, of which this entity was indeed capable, taking place as the entity in meditation felt and knew that the hour had come for that to be fulfilled which was its incarnation.

It is indeed so that all mind/body/spirit complexes shall die to the third-density illusion; that is, that each yellow-ray physical-complex body shall cease to be viable. It is a misnomer to, for this reason alone, call each mind/body/spirit complex a martyr, for this term is reserved for those who lay down their lives for the service they may provide to others. We may encourage meditation upon the functions of the will.

QUESTIONER: The instrument asked if the restricted, unpublishable healing information that was given during the first book could be included in Book IV, since readers who have gotten that far will be dedicated somewhat?

RA: I am Ra. This publication of material shall, in time, shall we say, be appropriate. There is intervening material.

QUESTIONER: Going back to the previous session, you stated that each sexual activity was a transfer before the veil. Would you trace the flow of energy that is transferred and tell me if that was the planned activity or a planned transfer by the designing Logos?

RA: I am Ra. The path of energy transfer before the veiling during the sexual intercourse was that of the two entities possessed of green-ray capability. The awareness of all as Creator is that which opens the green energy center. Thusly there was no possibility of blockage due to the sure knowledge of each by each that each was the Creator. The transfers were weak due to the ease with which such transfers could take place between any two polarized entities during sexual intercourse.

QUESTIONER: What I was getting at, precisely, was, for example, when we close an electrical circuit it is easy to trace the path of current. It goes along the conductor. I am trying to determine whether this transfer is between the green energy centers (the heart chakras). I am trying to trace the physical flow of the energy to try to get an idea of blockages after the veil. I may be off on the wrong track here, but if I am wrong we'll just drop it. Can you tell me something about that?

RA: I am Ra. In such a drawing or schematic representation of the circuitry of two mind/body/spirits or mind/body/spirit complexes in sexual or other energy transfer, the circuit opens always at the red or base center and moves as possible through the intervening energy centers. If baffled, it will stop at orange. If not, it shall proceed to yellow. If still unbaffled, it shall proceed to green. It is well to remember in the case of the mind/body/spirit that the chakras or energy centers could well be functioning without crystallization.

QUESTIONER: In other words, they would be functioning, but it would be equivalent in an electrical circuitry to having a high resistance, shall we say, and although the circuit would be complete, red through green, the total quantity of energy transferred would be less. Is this correct?

RA: I am Ra. We might most closely associate your query with the concept of voltage. The uncrystallized, lower centers cannot deliver the higher voltage. The crystallized centers may become quite remarkable in the high-voltage characteristics of the energy transfer as it reaches green ray, and indeed as green ray is crystallized this also applies to the higher energy centers until such energy transfers become an honestation[4] for the Creator.

QUESTIONER: Would you please correct me on this statement. I am guessing that what happens is that when a transfer takes place, the energy is that light energy that comes in through the feet of the entity, and the voltage or potential difference is measured between the red energy center and, in the case of the green-ray transfer, the green energy center and then must leap or flow from the green energy center of one entity to the green energy center of the other, and then something happens to it. Could you clarify my thinking on that?

RA: I am Ra. Yes.

QUESTIONER: Would you please do that?

RA: I am Ra. The energy transfer occurs in one releasing of the potential difference. This does not leap between green and green energy centers but is the sharing of the energies of each from red ray upwards. In this context it may be seen to be at its most efficient when both entities have orgasm simultaneously. However, it functions as transfer if either has the orgasm, and indeed in the case of the physically expressed love between a mated pair which does not have the conclusion you call orgasm, there is, nonetheless, a considerable amount of energy transferred due to the potential difference which has been raised as long as both entities are aware of this potential and release its strength to each other by desire of the will in a mental or mind complex dedication. You may see this practice as being used to generate energy transfers in some of your practices of what you may call other than Christian religious-distortion systems of the Law of One.

QUESTIONER: Could you give me an example of that last statement?

---

4. honestation: n. adornment; grace. [obs.]

RA: I am Ra. We preface this example with the reminder that each system is quite distorted, and its teachings always half lost. However, one such system is that called the tantric yoga.

QUESTIONER: Considering individual A and individual B, if individual A experiences the orgasm, is the energy, then, transferred to individual B in a greater amount? Is that correct?

RA: I am Ra. Your query is incomplete. Please restate.

QUESTIONER: I am trying to determine whether the direction of energy transfer is a function of orgasm. Which entity gets the transferred energy? I know it's a dumb question, but I want to be sure that I have it cleared up.

RA: I am Ra. If both entities are well polarized and vibrating in green-ray love, any orgasm shall offer equal energy to both.

QUESTIONER: I see. Before the veil, can you describe any other physical difference that we haven't talked about yet with respect to the sexual energy transfers or relationships or anything prior to veiling?

RA: I am Ra. Perhaps the most critical difference of the veiling, before and after, was that before the mind, body, and spirit were veiled, entities were aware that each energy transfer and, indeed, very nearly all that proceeds from any intercourse, social or sexual, between two entities has its character and substance in time/space rather than space/time. The energies transferred during the sexual activity are not, properly speaking, of space/time. There is a great component of what you may call metaphysical energy transferred. Indeed, the body complex as a whole is greatly misunderstood due to the post-veiling assumption that the physical manifestation called the body is subject only to physical stimuli. This is emphatically not so.

QUESTIONER: After the veil, in our particular case now, we have, in the circuitry of which we were speaking, what you call blockages. Could you describe what occurs with the first blockage and what its effects are on each of the entities, assuming that one blocks and the other does not, or if both are blocked?

RA: I am Ra. This material has been covered previously. If both entities are blocked, both will have an increased hunger for the same activity, seeking to unblock the baffled flow of energy. If one entity is blocked and the other vibrates in love, the entity baffled will hunger still but have a tendency to attempt to continue the procedure of satiating the increasing hunger with the one vibrating green ray, due to an impression that this entity might prove helpful in this endeavor. The green-ray-active individual shall polarize slightly in the direction of service to others but have only the energy with which it began.

QUESTIONER: I didn't mean to cover previously covered material. What I was actually attempting to do was discover something new in asking the question, so please, if I ask any questions in the future that have already been covered, don't bother to repeat the material. I am just searching the same area for the possibility of greater enlightenment with respect to this particular area, since it seems to be one of the major areas of experience in our present condition of veiling that produces a very large amount of catalyst, and I am trying to understand, to use a poor term, how this veiling process created a greater experience and how this experience evolved. These questions are very difficult to ask.

It occurs to me that many statues or drawings of the one known as Lucifer or the Devil are shown with an erection. Is this a function of orange-ray blockage, and was this known in a minimal way by those who devised these statues and drawings?

RA: I am Ra. There is, of course, much other distortion involved in a discussion of any mythic archetypical form. However, we may answer in the affirmative and note that you are perceptive.

QUESTIONER: With respect to the green, blue, and indigo transfers of energy, how would the mechanism for these transfers differ from the orange-ray mechanism in making them possible or setting the groundwork for them? I know this is very difficult to ask, and I may not be making any sense, but what I am trying to do is gain an understanding of the foundation for the transfers in each of the rays, and the preparations for the transfers or the fundamental requirements or biases and potentials for these transfers. Could you expand on that for me, please? I am sorry for the poor question.

RA: I am Ra. We would take a moment to state in reply to a previous comment that we shall answer each query whether or not it has been previously covered, for not to do so would be to baffle the flow of quite another transfer of energy.

To respond to your query, we firstly wish to agree with your supposition that the subject you now query upon is a large one, for in it lies an entire system of opening the gateway to intelligent infinity. You may see that some information is necessarily shrouded in mystery by our desire to preserve the free will of the adept. The great key to blue, indigo, and, finally, that great capital of the column of sexual energy transfer, violet energy transfers, is the metaphysical bond or distortion which has the name among your peoples of unconditional love. In the blue-ray energy transfer the quality of this love is refined in the fire of honest communication and clarity; this, shall we say, normally speaking in general, takes a substantial portion of your space/time to accomplish, although there are instances of matings so well refined in previous incarnations and so well remembered that the blue ray may be penetrated at once. This energy transfer is of great benefit to the seeker in that all communication from this seeker is, thereby, refined and the eyes of honesty and clarity look upon a new world. Such is the nature of blue-ray energy, and such is one mechanism of potentiating and crystallizing it.

As we approach indigo-ray transfer, we find ourselves in a shadowland. We cannot give you information straight out or plain, for this is seen by us to be an infringement. We cannot speak at all of violet-ray transfer as we do not, again, desire to break the Law of Confusion.

We may say that these jewels, though dearly bought, are beyond price for the seeker and might suggest that just as each awareness is arrived at through a process of analysis, synthesis, and inspiration, so should the seeker approach its mate and evaluate each experience, seeking the jewel.

QUESTIONER: Is there any way to tell which ray the transfer was for an individual after the experience?

RA: I am Ra. There is only a subjective yardstick or measure of such. If the energies have flowed so that love is made whole, green-ray transfer has taken place. If, by the same entities' exchange, greater ease in communication and greater sight has been experienced, the energy has been refined to the blue-ray energy center. If the polarized entities, by this same energy transfer experience, find that the faculties of will and faith have been stimulated, not for a brief while but for a great duration of what you call time, you may perceive the indigo-ray transfer. We may not speak of the violet-ray transfer except to note that it is an opening to the gateway of intelligent infinity. Indeed, the indigo-ray transfer is also this, but, shall we say, the veil has not yet been lifted.

QUESTIONER: Did most Logoi plan, before the veil, to create a system of random sexual activity or the specific pairing of entities for specific periods of time, or did they have an objective in this respect?

RA: I am Ra. This shall be the last full query of this working.

The harvest from the previous creation was that which included the male and female mind/body/spirit. It was the intention of the original Logoi that entities mate with one another in any fashion which caused a greater polarization. It was determined, after observation of the process of many Logoi, that polarization increased manyfold if the mating were not indiscriminate. Consequent Logoi thusly preserved a bias towards the mated relationship which is more characteristic of more-disciplined personalities and of what you may call higher densities. The free will of each entity, however, was always paramount, and a bias only could be offered.

May we ask if there may be any brief queries before we leave this instrument?

QUESTIONER: Is there any way that we can make the instrument more comfortable or to improve the contact?

RA: I am Ra. We would ask that each of the support group be especially vigilant in the, what you would call, immediate future due to this instrument's unbidden but serious potential for increased distortion towards illness/health.

You are most conscientious. We thank you, my friends, and leave you in the glorious light and love of the One Infinite Creator. Go forth, therefore, rejoicing in the power and in the peace of the One Infinite Creator. Adonai.

Session 85,
April 26, 1982

RA: I am Ra. We communicate now.

QUESTIONER: Could you first give me the condition of the instrument?

RA: I am Ra. We ask your permission to preface this answer by the inclusion of the greeting which we use.

QUESTIONER: That is agreeable.

RA: I am Ra. We greet you in the love and in the light of the One Infinite Creator. We were having some difficulty with the channel of energy influx due to pain flare, as you call this distortion of the physical-body complex of this instrument. Therefore, it was necessary to speak as briefly as possible until we had safely transferred the mind/body/spirit complex of this instrument. We beg your kind indulgence for our discourtesy, which was appropriate.

The condition of this instrument is as follows. The necessity for extreme vigilance is less, due to the somewhat lessened physical-complex energy deficit. The potential for distortion remains, and continued watchfulness over the ingestion of helpful foodstuffs continues to be recommended. Although the instrument is experiencing more than the, shall we say, normal, for this mind/body/spirit complex, distortions towards pain at this space/time nexus, the basic condition is less distorted. The vital energies are as previously stated.

We commend the vigilance and care of this group.

QUESTIONER: What is the current situation with respect to our fifth-density, service-to-self polarized companion?

RA: I am Ra. Your companion has never been more closely associated with you than at the present nexus. You may see a kind of crisis occurring upon the so-called magical level at this particular space/time nexus.

QUESTIONER: What is the nature of this crisis?

RA: I am Ra. The nature of this crisis is the determination of the relative polarity of your companion and your selves. You are in the position of being in the third-density illusion and consequently having the conscious collective magical ability of the neophyte, whereas your companion is most adept. However, the faculties of will and faith and the calling to the light have been used by this group to the exclusion of any significant depolarization from the service-to-others path.

If your companion can possibly depolarize this group, it must do so and that quickly, for in this unsuccessful attempt at exploring the wisdom of separation, it is encountering some depolarization. This shall continue. Therefore, the efforts of your companion are pronounced at this space/time and time/space nexus.

QUESTIONER: I am totally aware of the lack of necessity or rational need for naming of entities or things, but I was wondering if this particular entity had a name, just so that we could increase our efficiency of communicating with respect to him. Does he have a name?

RA: I am Ra. Yes.

QUESTIONER: Would it be magically bad for us to know that name, or would it make no difference?

RA: I am Ra. It would make a difference.

QUESTIONER: What would the difference be?

RA: I am Ra. If one wishes to have power over an entity, it is an aid to know that entity's name. If one wishes no power over an entity but wishes to collect that entity into the very heart of one's own being, it is well to forget the naming. Both processes are magically viable. Each is polarized in a specific way. It is your choice.

QUESTIONER: I am assuming that it would be a problem for the instrument to meditate without the hand pressure from the other-self at this time because of the continued greeting. Is this correct?

RA: I am Ra. This is correct if the instrument wishes to remain free from this potential separation of its mind/body/spirit complex from the third density it now experiences.

QUESTIONER: Since our fifth-density companion has been monitoring our communication with Ra, it has been made aware of the veiling process of which we have been speaking. It seems to me that conscious knowledge and acceptance of the fact that this veiling process was used for the purpose for which it was used would make it difficult to maintain high negative polarization. Could you clear up my thinking on that, please?

RA: I am Ra. We are unsure as to our success in realigning your modes of mentation. We may, however, comment.

The polarization process, as it enters fourth density, is one which occurs with full knowledge of the veiling process which has taken place in third density. This veiling process is that which is a portion of the third-density experience. The knowledge and memory of the outcome of this and all portions of the third-density experience informs the higher-density polarized entity. It, however, does not influence the choice which has been made and which is the basis for further work past third density in polarization. Those which have chosen the service-to-others (self)[5] path have simply used the veiling process in order to potentiate that which is not. This is an entirely acceptable method of self-knowledge of and by the Creator.

QUESTIONER: You just stated that those who are on the service-to-others path use the veiling process to potentiate that which is not. I believe that I am correct in repeating what you said. Is that correct?

RA: I am Ra. Yes.

QUESTIONER: Then the service-to-others path has potentiated that which is not. Could you expand that a little bit so that I could understand it a little better?

RA: I am Ra. If you see the energy centers in their various colors completing the spectrum, you may see that the service-to-others (self)[5] choice is one which denies the very center of the spectrum, that being universal love. Therefore, all that is built upon the penetration of the light of harvestable quality by such entities is based upon an omission. This omission shall manifest in fourth density as the love of self; that is, the fullest expression of the orange and yellow energy centers, which then are used to potentiate communication and adepthood.

When fifth-density refinement has been achieved, that which is not is carried further, the wisdom density being explored by entities which have no compassion, no universal love. They experience that which they wish by free choice, being of the earnest opinion that green-ray energy is folly.

That which is not may be seen as a self-imposed darkness in which harmony is turned into an eternal disharmony. However, that which is not cannot endure throughout the octave of third density, and, as darkness eventually calls the light, so does that which is not eventually call that which is.

QUESTIONER: I believe that there were salient errors in the communication that we just completed because of transmission difficulties. Are you aware of these errors?

RA: I am Ra. We are unaware of errors, although this instrument is

---

5. Ra corrects this error in the next two answers.

experiencing flares of pain, as you call this distortion. We welcome and encourage your perceptions in correcting any errors in transmission.

QUESTIONER: I think that the statement that was made when we were speaking about the service-to-others path was incorrect. Would you check that, please?

RA: I am Ra. May we ask that you be apprised of our intention to have spoken of the service-to-self path as the path of that which is not.

QUESTIONER: I am interested in the problem that we sometimes have with the transmission, since the word "others" was used three times in this transmission rather than the word "self." Could you give me an idea of this problem which could create a discrepancy in communication?

RA: I am Ra. Firstly, we may note the clumsiness of language and our unfamiliarity with it in our native, shall we say, experience. Secondly, we may point out that once we have miscalled or misnumbered an event or thing, that referent is quite likely to be reused for some trans-mission time, as you call this measurement, due to our original error having gone undetected by ourselves.

QUESTIONER: Thank you. Do you have use of all the words in the English language and, for that matter, all of the words in all of the languages that are spoken on this planet at this time?

RA: I am Ra. No.

QUESTIONER: I have a question here from [name]. It states: "As we see compassion developing in ourselves, is it more appropriate to bal-ance this compassion with wisdom or to allow the compassion to develop as much as possible without being balanced?"

RA: I am Ra. This query borders upon that type of question to which answers are unavailable due to the free-will prohibitions upon infor-mation from teach/learners.

To the student of the balancing process, we may suggest that the most stringent honesty be applied. As compassion is perceived, it is suggested that, in balancing, this perception be analyzed. It may take many, many essays into compassion before true universal love is the product of the attempted opening and crystallization of this all-important springboard energy center. Thus the student may discover many other components to what may seem to be all-embracing love. Each of these components may be balanced and accepted as part of the self and as transitional material as the entity's seat of learn/teaching moves ever more clearly into the green ray.

When it is perceived that universal love has been achieved, the next balancing may or may not be wisdom. If the adept is balancing manifestations, it is indeed appropriate to balance universal love and wisdom. If the balancing is of mind or spirit, there are many subtleties to which the adept may give careful consideration. Love and wisdom, like love and light, are not black and white, shall we say, but faces of the same coin, if you will. Therefore, it is not, in all cases, that balancing consists of a movement from compassion to wisdom.

We may suggest at all times the constant remembrance of the density from which each adept desires to move. This density learns the lessons of love. In the case of Wanderers, there are half-forgotten overlays of other lessons and other densities. We shall leave these considerations with the questioner and invite observations which we shall then be most happy to respond to in what may seem to be a more effectual manner.

QUESTIONER: What changes of functions of the mind/body/spirits were most effective in producing the evolution desired due to the veiling process?

RA: I am Ra. We are having difficulty retaining clear channel through this instrument. It has a safe margin of transferred energy but is experiencing pain flares. May we ask that you repeat the query, as we have better channel now.

QUESTIONER: After the veiling process, certain veiled functions or activities must have been paramount in creating evolution in the desired polarized directions. I was just wondering which of these had the greatest effect on polarization.

RA: I am Ra. The most effectual veiling was that of the mind.

QUESTIONER: I would like to carry that on to find out what specific functions of the mind were most effectual, and the three or four most effective changes brought about to create the polarization.

RA: I am Ra. This is an interesting query. The primary veiling was of such significance that it may be seen to be analogous to the mantling of the Earth over all the jewels within the Earth's crust, whereas previously, all facets of the Creator were consciously known. After the veiling, almost no facets of the Creator were known to the mind. Almost all was buried beneath the veil.

If one were to attempt to list those functions of mind most significant, in that they might be of aid in polarization, one would need to begin with the faculty of visioning, envisioning, or far-seeing. Without the veil the mind was not caught in your illusory time. With the veil, space/time is the only obvious possibility for experience.

Also upon the list of significant veiled functions of the mind would be that of dreaming. The so-called dreaming contains a great deal which, if made available to the conscious mind and used, shall aid it in polarization to a great extent.

The third function of the mind which is significant and which has been veiled is that of the knowing of the body. The knowledge of and control over the body, having been lost to a great extent in the veiling process, is thusly lost from the experience of the seeker. Its knowledge before the veiling is of small use. Its knowledge after the veiling, and in the face of what is now a dense illusion of separation of body complex from mind complex, is quite significant.

Perhaps the most important and significant function that occurred due to the veiling of the mind from itself is not in itself a function of mind but rather is a product of the potential created by this veiling. This is the faculty of will or pure desire.

We may ask for brief queries at this time. Although there is energy remaining for this working, we are reluctant to continue this contact, experiencing continual variations due to pain flares, as you call this distortion. Although we are unaware of any misgiven material, we are aware that there have been several points during which our channel was less than optimal. This instrument is most faithful, but we do not wish to misuse this instrument. Please query as you will.

QUESTIONER: I will just ask in closing: is an individualized portion or entity of Ra inhabiting the instrument's body for the purpose of communication? Then, is there anything that we could do to improve the contact or to make the instrument more comfortable?

RA: I am Ra. We of Ra communicate through narrow band channel through the violet-ray energy center. We are not, as you would say, physically indwelling in this instrument; rather, the mind/body/spirit complex of this instrument rests with us.

You are diligent and conscientious. The alignments are excellent. We leave you rejoicing in the power and in the peace of the One

Infinite Creator. Go forth, then, my friends, rejoicing in the power and in the peace of the infinite love and the ineffable light of the One Creator. I am Ra. Adonai.

Session 86,
May 4, 1982

RA: I am Ra. I greet you in the love and in the light of the One Infinite Creator. We communicate now.

QUESTIONER: Would you first please give me the condition of the instrument?

RA: I am Ra. The instrument's distortion towards physical-energy-complex deficit has slightly increased since the last asking. The vital energy levels have had significant calls upon them and are somewhat less than the last asking also.

QUESTIONER: What was the nature of the significant calls upon the vital energy?

RA: I am Ra. There are those entities which entertain the thought distortion towards this entity that it shall remove for the other selves all distortions for the other-self. This entity has recently been in close contact with a larger-than-normal number of entities with these thought complex distortions. This entity is of the distortion to provide whatever service is possible and is not consciously aware of the inroads made upon the vital energies.

QUESTIONER: Am I correct in assuming that you are speaking of incarnate third-density entities that were creating the condition of the use of the vital energy?

RA: I am Ra. Yes.

QUESTIONER: What is the present situation with our fifth-density service-to-self polarized companion?

RA: I am Ra. The period which you may call crisis remains.

QUESTIONER: Can you tell me anything of the nature of this crisis?

RA: I am Ra. The polarity of your companion is approaching the critical point at which the entity shall choose either to retreat for the nonce and leave any greetings to fourth-density minions or lose polarity. The only other potential is that in some way this group might lose polarity, in which case your companion could continue its form of greeting.

QUESTIONER: In the last session you had mentioned the properties precipitating from the veiling of the mind, the first being envisioning or far-seeing. Would you explain the meaning of that?

RA: I am Ra. Your language is not overstrewn with non-emotional terms for the functional qualities of what is now termed unconscious mind. The nature of mind is something which we have requested that you ponder. However, it is, shall we say, clear enough to the casual observer that we may share some thoughts with you without infringing upon your free learn/teaching experiences.

The nature of the unconscious is of the nature of concept rather than word. Consequently, before the veiling the use of the deeper mind was that of the use of unspoken concept. You may consider the emotive and connotative aspects of a melody. One could call out, in some stylized fashion, the terms for the notes of the melody. One could say, quarter note A, quarter note A, quarter note A, whole note F. This bears little resemblance to the beginning of the melody of one of your composer's most influential melodies, that known to you as a symbol of victory.

This is the nature of the deeper mind. There are only stylized methods with which to discuss its functions. Thusly our descriptions of this portion of the mind, as well as the same portions of body and spirit, were given terms such as "far-seeing," indicating that the nature of penetration of the veiled portion of the mind may be likened unto the journey too rich and exotic to contemplate adequate describing thereof.

QUESTIONER: You have stated that dreaming, if made available to the conscious mind, will aid greatly in polarization. Could you define dreaming or tell us what it is and how it aids polarization?

RA: I am Ra. Dreaming is an activity of communication through the veil of the unconscious mind and the conscious mind. The nature of this activity is wholly dependent upon the situation regarding the energy center blockages, activations, and crystallizations of a given mind/body/spirit complex.

In one who is blocked at two of the three lower energy centers, dreaming will be of value in the polarization process in that there will be a repetition of those portions of recent catalyst as well as deeper-held blockages, thereby giving the waking mind clues as to the nature of these blockages, and hints as to possible changes in perception which may lead to the unblocking.

This type of dreaming or communication through the veiled portions of the mind occurs also with those mind/body/spirit complexes which are functioning with far less blockage and enjoying the green-ray activation or higher activation at those times at which the mind/body/spirit complex experiences catalyst, momentarily reblocking or baffling or otherwise distorting the flow of energy influx. Therefore, in all cases it is useful to a mind/body/spirit complex to ponder the content and emotive resonance of dreams.

For those whose green-ray energy centers have been activated, as well as for those whose green-ray energy centers are offered an unusual unblockage due to extreme catalyst, such as what is termed the physical death of the self or one which is beloved occurring in what you may call your near future, dreaming takes on another activity. This is what may loosely be termed precognition or a knowing which is prior to that which shall occur in physical manifestation in your yellow-ray, third- density space/time. This property of the mind depends upon its placement, to a great extent, in time/space, so that the terms of present and future and past have no meaning. This will, if made proper use of by the mind/body/spirit complex, enable this entity to enter more fully into the all-compassionate love of each and every circumstance, including those circumstances against which an entity may have a strong distortion towards what you may call unhappiness.

As a mind/body/spirit complex consciously chooses the path of the adept and, with each energy balanced to a minimal degree, begins to open the indigo-ray energy center, the so-called dreaming becomes the most efficient tool for polarization, for, if it is known by the adept that work may be done in consciousness while the so-called conscious mind rests, this adept may call upon those which guide it, those presences which surround it, and, most of all, the magical personality, which is the Higher Self in space/time analog as it moves into the sleeping mode of consciousness. With these affirmations attended to, the activity of dreaming reaches that potential of learn/teaching which is most helpful to increasing the distortions of the adept towards its chosen polarity.

There are other possibilities of the dreaming not so closely aligned with the increase in polarity, which we do not cover at this particular space/time.

QUESTIONER: How is the dream designed or programmed? Is it done by the Higher Self, or who is responsible for this?

RA: I am Ra. In all cases the mind/body/spirit complex makes what use it can of the faculty of the dreaming. It, itself, is responsible for this activity.

QUESTIONER: Then you are saying that the subconscious is responsible for what I will call the design or scriptwriter for the dream. Is this correct?

RA: I am Ra. This is correct.

QUESTIONER: Is the memory that the individual has upon waking from the dream usually reasonably accurate? Is the dream easily remembered?

RA: I am Ra. You must realize that we are overgeneralizing in order to answer your queries, as there are several sorts of dreams. However, in general, it may be noted that it is only for a trained and disciplined observer to have reasonably good recall of the dreaming. This faculty may be learned by virtue of a discipline of the recording immediately upon awakening of each and every detail which can be recalled. This training sharpens one's ability to recall the dream. The most common perception of a mind/body/spirit complex of dreams is muddied, muddled, and quickly lost.

QUESTIONER: In remembering dreams, then, you are saying that the individual can find specific clues to current energy center blockages and may, thereby, reduce or eliminate those blockages. Is this correct?

RA: I am Ra. This is so.

QUESTIONER: Is there any other function of dreaming that is of value in the evolutionary process?

RA: I am Ra. Although there are many which are of some value, we would choose two to note, since these two, though not of value in polarization, may be of value in a more generalized sense.

The activity of dreaming is an activity in which there is made a finely wrought and excellently fashioned bridge from conscious to unconscious. In this state the various distortions which have occurred in the energy web of the body complex, due to the misprision with which energy influxes have been received, are healed. With the proper amount of dreaming comes the healing of these distortions. Continued lack of this possibility can cause seriously distorted mind/body/ spirit complexes.

The other function of the dreaming which is of aid is that type of dream which is visionary and which prophets and mystics have experienced from days of old. Their visions come through the roots of mind and speak to a hungry world. Thus the dream is of service without being of a personally polarizing nature. However, in that mystic or prophet who desires to serve, such service will increase the entity's polarity.

QUESTIONER: There is a portion of sleep that has been called REM. Is this the state of dreaming?

RA: I am Ra. This is correct.

QUESTIONER: It was noticed that this occurs in small units during the night, with gaps in between. Is there any particular reason for this?

RA: I am Ra. Yes.

QUESTIONER: If it is of any value to know that, would you tell me why the dreaming process works like that?

RA: I am Ra. The portions of the dreaming process which are helpful for polarization and also for the vision of the mystic take place in time/space and, consequently, use the bridge from metaphysical to physical for what seems to be a brief period of your space/time. The time/space equivalent is far greater. The bridge remains, however, and traduces each distortion of mind, body, and spirit as it has received the distortions of energy influxes so that healing may take place. This healing process does not occur with the incidence of rapid eye movement but rather occurs largely in the space/time portion of the mind/ body/spirit complex using the bridge to time/space for the process of healing to be enabled.

QUESTIONER: You mentioned the loss of knowledge and control over the body as being a factor that was helpful in the evolutionary process due to veiling. Could you enumerate the important losses of knowledge and control of the body?

RA: I am Ra. This query contains some portions which would be more helpfully answered were some intervening material requested.

QUESTIONER: I'm at a loss to know what to request. Can you give me an idea of what area of intervening material I should work on?

RA: I am Ra. No. However, we shall be happy to answer the original query if it is still desired, if you first perceive that there is information lacking.

QUESTIONER: Perhaps I can question slightly differently here. I might ask why the loss of knowledge and control over the body was helpful?

RA: I am Ra. The knowledge of the potentials of the physical vehicle before the veiling offered the mind/body/spirit a free range of choices with regard to activities and manifestations of the body but offered little in the way of the development of polarity. When the knowledge of these potentials and functions of the physical vehicle is shrouded from the conscious-mind complex, the mind/body/spirit complex is often nearly without knowledge of how to best manifest its beingness. However, this state of lack of knowledge offers an opportunity for a desire to grow within the mind complex. This desire is that which seeks to know the possibilities of the body complex. The ramifications of each possibility and the eventual biases thusly built have within them a force which can only be generated by such a desire or will to know.

QUESTIONER: Perhaps you could give examples of the use of the body prior to veiling and after the veiling in the same aspect, to help us understand the change in knowledge of and control over the body more clearly. Could you do this, please?

RA: I am Ra. We could.

QUESTIONER: Will you do this?

RA: I am Ra. Yes. Let us deal with the sexual energy transfer. Before the veiling, such a transfer was always possible due to there being no shadow upon the grasp of the nature of the body and its relationship to other mind/body/spirits in this particular manifestation. Before the veiling process there was a near-total lack of the use of this sexual energy transfer beyond green ray.

This also was due to the same unshadowed knowledge each had

of each. There was, in third density then, little purpose to be seen in the more intensive relationships of mind, body, and spirit which you may call those of the mating process, since each other-self was seen to be the Creator and no other-self seemed to be more the Creator than another.

After the veiling process it became infinitely more difficult to achieve green-ray energy transfer due to the great areas of mystery and unknowing concerning the body complex and its manifestations. However, also due to the great shadowing of the manifestations of the body from the conscious-mind complex, when such energy transfer was experienced it was likelier to provide catalyst which caused a bonding of self with other-self in a properly polarized configuration.

From this point it was far more likely that higher energy transfers would be sought by this mated pair of mind/body/spirit complexes, thus allowing the Creator to know Itself with great beauty, solemnity, and wonder. Intelligent infinity having been reached by this sacramental use of this function of the body, each mind/body/spirit complex of the mated pair gained greatly in polarization and in ability to serve.

QUESTIONER: Did any of the other aspects of loss of knowledge or control of the body approach, to any degree in efficiency, the description which you have just given?

RA: I am Ra. Each function of the body complex has some potential after the veiling to provide helpful catalyst. We did choose the example of sexual energy transfer due to its central place in the functionary capabilities of the body complex made more useful by means of the veiling process.

This instrument grows somewhat low in energy. We would prefer to retain the maximal portion of reserved energy for which this instrument has given permission. We would, therefore, ask for one more full query at this working.

QUESTIONER: I would assume that the veiling of the sexual aspect was of great efficiency because it is an aspect that has to do totally with a relationship with an other-self. It would seem to me that the bodily veilings having to do with other-self interaction would be more efficient when compared with those only related to self, which would be lower in efficiency in producing either positive or negative polarization. Am I correct in this assumption?

RA: I am Ra. You are correct to a great extent. Perhaps the most notable exception is the attitude of one already strongly polarized negatively towards the appearance of the body complex. There are those entities upon the negative path which take great care in the preservation of the distortion your peoples perceive as fairness/ugliness. This fairness of form is, of course, then used in order to manipulate other-selves. May we ask if there are any brief queries?

QUESTIONER: Is there anything that we can do to make the instrument more comfortable or to improve the contact?

RA: I am Ra. We are pleased that this instrument was more conscientious in preparing itself for contact by means of the careful mental vibrations which you call prayer. This enabled the channel to be free from the distortions which the contact fell prey to during the last working.

We would suggest to the support group some continued care in the regulating of the physical activities of the instrument. However, at this nexus it is well to encourage those activities which feed the vital energies, as this instrument lives in this space/time present almost completely due to the careful adherence to the preservation of those mental and spiritual energies which make up the vital energy complex of this entity. Each is conscientious. The alignments are good.

We would caution the support group as to the physical alignment of the appurtenance known as the censer. There has been some slight difficulty due to variation in the pattern of the effluvium of this incense.

I am Ra. I leave you rejoicing in the power and in the peace of the One Infinite Creator. Go forth, then, rejoicing in the love and in the light of the One Creator. Adonai.

Session 87,
May 12, 1982

RA: I am Ra. I greet you in the love and in the light of the One Infinite Creator. I communicate now.

QUESTIONER: Could you first please give me the condition of the instrument?

RA: I am Ra. The distortions of the physical complex are unchanged. The vital energy levels are greatly enhanced.

QUESTIONER: Thank you. In considering what was mentioned in the last session about the censer, I have thought about the fact that the position of the origin of the smoke changes approximately 6 inches horizontally. Would it be better to have a censer in a single, horizontal smoking position?

RA: I am Ra. This alteration would be an helpful one, given that the censer is virgin.

QUESTIONER: What would be the optimum geometrical arrangement of censer, chalice, and candle with respect to the Bible and table and the positions that we now have them in?

RA: I am Ra. Both chalice and candle occupy the optimal configuration with respect to the book most closely aligned with the Law of One in the distortion complexes of this instrument. It is optimal to have the censer to the rear of this book and centered at the spine of its open configuration.

QUESTIONER: Would a position directly between the chalice and the candle be optimum, then, for the censer?

RA: I am Ra. This is not an exact measurement, since both chalice and candle are irregularly shaped. However, speaking roughly, this is correct.

QUESTIONER: Thank you. What is the present situation with respect to our fifth-density negative companion?

RA: I am Ra. This entity has withdrawn for a period of restoration of its polarity.

QUESTIONER: Would you expand upon the concept of the acquisition of polarity by this particular entity; its use, specifically, of this polarity other than the simple, obvious need for sixth-density harvest, if this is possible, please?

RA: I am Ra. We would. The nature of the densities above your own is that a purpose may be said to be shared by both positive and negative polarities. This purpose is the acquisition of the ability to welcome more and more the less and less distorted love/light and light/love of the One Infinite Creator. Upon the negative path, the wisdom density is one in which power over others has been refined until it is approaching absolute power. Any force such as the force your group and those of Ra offer which cannot be controlled by the power of such a negative fifth-density mind/body/spirit complex then depolarizes the entity which has not controlled other-self.

It is not within your conscious selves to stand against such refined power, but rather it has been through the harmony, the mutual love, and the honest calling for aid from the forces of light which have given you the shield and buckler.

QUESTIONER: What is the environmental situation of this particular fifth-density entity, and how does he work with fourth-density negative entities in order to establish power and control; what is his particular philosophy with respect to himself as Creator and with respect to the use of the first distortion and the extension of the first distortion to the fourth-density negative? I hope that this isn't too complex a question.

RA: I am Ra. The environment of your companion is that of the rock, the cave, the place of barrenness, for this is the density of wisdom, and that which is needed may be thought and received. To this entity, very little is necessary upon the physical, if you will, or space/time complex of distortions.

Such an entity spends its consciousness within the realms of time/space in an attempt to learn the ways of wisdom through the utmost use of the powers and resources of the self. Since the self is the Creator, the wisdom density provides many informative and fascinating experiences for the negatively polarized entity. In some respects, one may see a more lucid early attachment to wisdom from those of negative polarity, as the nexus of positions of consciousness upon which wisdom is laid is simpler.

The relationship of such an entity to fourth-density negative entities is one of the more powerful and the less powerful. The negative path posits slavery of the less powerful as a means of learning the desire to serve the self to the extent that the will is brought to bear. It is in this way that polarity is increased in the negative sense. Thus, fourth-density entities are willing slaves of such a fifth-density entity, there being no doubt whatsoever of the relative power of each.

QUESTIONER: A reflection of this could be seen in our density in many of those leaders who instigate war and have followers who support, in total conviction that the direction of conquest is correct. Is this correct?

RA: I am Ra. Any organization which demands obedience without question upon the basis of relative power is functioning according to the above-described plan.

QUESTIONER: One point that I am not clear on is the understanding and use of the first distortion by fifth- and fourth-density negative entities in manipulating third-density entities. I would like to know how the first distortion affects the attempts to carry out the conquest of third-density entities and the attempt to add them, under the premise of the first distortion, to their social memory complexes. Would you expand on that concept, please?

RA: I am Ra. This latter plan is not one of which fourth-density negative social memory complexes are capable. The fourth-density habit is that of offering temptations and of energizing preexisting distortions. Fourth-density entities lack the subtlety and magical practice which the fifth-density experience offers.

QUESTIONER: It seems, though, that in the case of many UFO contacts that have occurred on this planet that there must be some knowledge of and use of the first distortion. The fourth-density entities have carefully remained aloof and anonymous, you might say, for the most part, so that no proof in a concrete way of their existence is available. How are they oriented with respect to this type of contact?

RA: I am Ra. We misperceived your query, thinking it was directed towards this particular type of contact. The nature of the fourth density's observance of the free-will distortion, while pursuing the seeding of the third-density thought patterns, is material which has already been covered. That which can be offered of the negatively oriented information is offered. It is altered to the extent that the entity receiving such negative information is of positive orientation. Thus many such contacts are of a mixed nature.

QUESTIONER: I'm sorry for getting confused on my question here in not asking it correctly. There is a philosophical point of central importance that I am trying to clear up here. It has to do with the fact that fourth-density negative seems to be aware of the first distortion. They are in a nonveiled condition, and they seem to use this knowledge of the first distortion to maintain the situation that they maintain in contacts with this planet. I am trying to extract their ability to understand the mechanism of the first distortion and the consequences of the veiling process and still remain in a mental configuration of separation on the negative path. I hope that I have made myself clear there. I have had a hard time asking this question.

RA: I am Ra. The answer may still not satisfy the questioner. We ask that you pursue it until you are satisfied. The fourth-density negative entity has made the choice available to each at third-density harvest. It is aware of the full array of possible methods of viewing the universe of the One Creator, and it is convinced that the ignoring and nonuse of the green-ray energy center will be the method most efficient in providing harvestability of fourth density. Its operations among those of third density which have not yet made this choice are designed to offer to each the opportunity to consider the self-serving polarity and its possible attractiveness.

QUESTIONER: It seems to me that this is a service-to-others action in offering the possibility of the self-serving path. What is the relative effect of polarization in this action? I don't understand that.

RA: I am Ra. In your armed bands, a large group marauds and pillages successfully. The success of the privates is claimed by the corporals, the success of corporals by sergeants, then lieutenants, captains, majors, and finally the commanding general. Each successful temptation, each successful harvestable entity, is a strengthener of the power and polarity of the fourth-density social memory complex which has had this success.

QUESTIONER: If one mind/body/spirit complex is harvested from third density to a fourth-density social memory complex, is the total power of the social memory complex before the absorption of this single entity doubled when this entity is absorbed?

RA: I am Ra. No.

QUESTIONER: The Law of Doubling, then, does not work in this way. How much does the power of the social memory complex increase relative to this single entity that is harvested and absorbed into it?

RA: I am Ra. If one entity in the social memory complex is responsible for this addition to its being, that mind/body/spirit complex will absorb, in linear fashion, the power contained in the, shall we say, recruit. If a subgroup is responsible, the power is then this subgroup's. Only very rarely is the social memory complex of negative polarity capable of acting totally as one being. The loss of polarity due to this difficulty, to which we have previously referred as of kind of spiritual entropy, is quite large.

QUESTIONER: Then assuming that a single negatively oriented entity is responsible for the recruiting of a harvested third-density entity and adds its polarity to his negative polarity and power, what type of ability or what type of benefit is this, and how is it used by the entity?

RA: I am Ra. The so-called pecking order is immediately challenged, and the entity with increased power exercises that power to control more other-selves and to advance within the social memory complex structure.

QUESTIONER: How is this power measured? How is it obvious that this entity has gained this additional power?

RA: I am Ra. In some cases there is a kind of battle. This is a battle of wills, and the weapons consist of the light that can be formed by each contender. In most cases where the shift of power has been obvious, it simply is acknowledged, and those seeing benefit from associating with this newly more powerful entity aid it in rising within the structure.

QUESTIONER: Thank you. We noticed a possibility of confusion between the term "mind/body/spirit" and "mind/body/spirit complex" in the last session. Were there a couple of misuses of those terms in shifting one for the other?

RA: I am Ra. There was an error in transmission. The use of the term "mind/body/spirit" should refer to those entities dwelling in third density prior to the veiling process, the term "mind/body/spirit complex" referring to those entities dwelling in third density after the veiling process. We also discover a failure on our part to supply the term "complex" when speaking of body after the veiling. Please correct these errors. Also, we ask that you keep a vigilant watch over these transmissions for any errors, and question without fail, as it is our intention to provide as undistorted a series of sound vibration complexes as is possible.

This entity, though far better cleared of distortions towards the pain flares when prepared by those mental-vibration complexes you call prayer, is still liable to fluctuation due to its pre-incarnative body complex distortions and the energizing of them by those of negative polarity.

QUESTIONER: Thank you. We will make the corrections.[6] In the last session you made the statement that before the veiling, sexual energy transfer was always possible. I would like to know what you meant by "it was always possible" and why it was not always possible after the veiling, just to clear up that point?

RA: I am Ra. We believe that we grasp your query and will use the analogy in your culture of the battery which lights the flashlight bulb. Two working batteries placed in series always offer the potential of the bulb's illumination. After the veiling, to continue this gross analogy, the two batteries being placed not in series would then offer no possible illumination of the bulb. Many mind/body/spirit complexes after the veiling have, through blockages, done the equivalent of reversing the battery.

QUESTIONER: What was the primary source of the blockages that caused the battery reversal?

RA: I am Ra. Please query more specifically as to the mind/body/spirits or mind/body/spirit complexes about which you request information.

QUESTIONER: Before the veil, there was knowledge of the bulb-lighting technique, shall we say. After the veil, some experiments created a bulb lighting; some resulted in no bulb lighting. Other than the fact that information was not available on methods of lighting the bulb, was there some root cause of the experiments that resulted in no bulb lighting?
RA: I am Ra. This is correct.

QUESTIONER: What was this root cause?

RA: I am Ra. The root cause of blockage is the lack of the ability to see the other-self as the Creator, or, to phrase this differently, the lack of love.

QUESTIONER: In our particular illusion the sexual potential for the male seems to peak somewhere prior to the age twenty, and the female's peak is some ten years later. What is the cause of this difference in peaking sexual energy?

---

6. The text was corrected before printing and now reads as it should.

RA: I am Ra. We must make clear distinction between the yellow-ray, third-density, chemical bodily complex and the body complex which is a portion of the mind/body/spirit complex. The male, as you call this polarity, has an extremely active yellow-ray desire at the space/time in its incarnation when its sperm is the most viable and full of the life-giving spermato. Thusly the red ray seeks to reproduce most thickly at the time when this body is most able to fulfill the red-ray requirements.

The yellow-ray, chemical body complex of the female, as you call this polarity, must needs have a continued and increasing desire for the sexual intercourse, for it can only conceive once in one fifteen-to-eighteen-month period, given that it carries the conceived body complex, bears it, and suckles it. This is draining to the physical body of yellow ray. To compensate for this, the desire increases so that the yellow-ray body is predisposed to continue in sexual congress, thus fulfilling its red-ray requirement to reproduce as thickly as possible.

The more, shall we say, integral sexuality or polarity of the body complex, which is a portion of the mind/body/spirit complex, does not concern itself with these yellow-ray manifestations but rather follows the ways of the seeking of energy transfer and the furthering of aid and service to others or to the self.

QUESTIONER: In addition, why is the ratio of male to female orgasms so heavily loaded on the side of the male?

RA: I am Ra. We refer now to the yellow-ray physical body or, if you will, body complex. At this level the distinction is unimportant. The male orgasm, which motivates the sperm forward to meet its ovum, is essential for the completion of the red-ray desire to propagate the species. The female orgasm is unnecessary. Again, as mind/body/spirit complexes begin to use the sexual energy transfer to learn, to serve, and to glorify the One Infinite Creator, the function of the female orgasm becomes more clear.

QUESTIONER: What was this ratio before the veil?

RA: I am Ra. The ratio of male to female orgasms before the veil was closer to one to one by a great deal, as the metaphysical value of the female orgasm was clear and without shadow.

QUESTIONER: Is it meaningful to give this ratio in early fourth density, and, if so, would you do that?

RA: I am Ra. In many ways it is quite meaningless to speak of orgasm of male and female in higher densities, as the character and nature of orgasm becomes more and more naturally a function of the mind/body/spirit complex as an unit. It may be said that the veil in fourth density is lifted and the choice has been made. In positive polarities, true sharing is almost universal. In negative polarities, true blockage so that the conqueror obtains orgasm, the conquered almost never is almost universal. In each case you may see the function of the sexual portion of experience as being a most efficient means of polarization.

QUESTIONER: In our illusion we have physical definitions for possible transfers of energy. We label them as the conversion of potential to kinetic or kinetic to heat and examine this with respect to the increasing entropy. When we speak of sexual energy transfers and other more basic forms of energy, I am always at a loss to properly use, you might say, the terms since I am not understanding—and possibly can't understand—the basic form of energy that we speak of. However, I intuit that this is the energy of pure vibration; that is, at the basic level of our illusion, that vibration between the space and time portion of the space/time continuum and yet somehow is transferred into our illusion in a more basic form than that. Could you expand on this area for me, please?

RA: I am Ra. Yes.

QUESTIONER: Would you do that?

RA: I am Ra. You are correct in assuming that the energy of which we speak in discussing sexual energy transfers is a form of vibratory bridge between space/time and time/space. Although this distinction is not apart from that which follows, that which follows may shed light upon that basic statement.

Due to the veiling process, the energy transferred from male to female is different than that transferred from female to male. Due to the polarity difference of the mind/body/spirit complexes of male and female, the male stores physical energy, the female mental and mental/emotional energy. When third-density sexual energy transfer is completed, the male will have offered the discharge of physical energy. The female is, thereby, refreshed, having far less physical vitality. At the same time, if you will use this term, the female discharges the efflux of its stored mental and mental/emotional energy, thereby offering inspiration, healing, and blessing to the male, which by nature is less vital in this area.

At this time, may we ask for one more full query.

QUESTIONER: Why is the male and the female nature different?

RA: I am Ra. When the veiling process was accomplished, to the male polarity was attracted the Matrix of the Mind, and to the female, the Potentiator of the Mind; to the male, the Potentiator of the Body, to the female, the Matrix of the Body. May we ask if there are any brief queries before we close this working?

QUESTIONER: Is there anything that we can do to make the instrument more comfortable or to improve the contact?

RA: I am Ra. We shall find the suggested readjustment of the censer helpful. The alignments are good. You have been conscientious, my friends. We leave you now in the love and in the light of the One Infinite Creator. Go forth, therefore, rejoicing merrily in the power and in the ineffable peace of the One Infinite Creator. Adonai.

Session 88,
May 29, 1982

RA: I am Ra. I greet you in the love and in the light of the One Infinite Creator. We communicate now.

QUESTIONER: Could you first please give me the condition of the instrument?

RA: I am Ra. The physical-complex energy deficit is considerable at this space/time. There has been also a significant loss of the vital energies. However, these energies are still well within the distortion you may call strength.

QUESTIONER: Of all of the things that you have mentioned before for replenishing these energies, at this particular space/time, which would be most appropriate for the replenishing of both of these energies?

RA: I am Ra. As you note, there are many factors which contribute to the aiding of the strength distortions and the amelioration of distortions towards weakness in this instrument. We suggest to each that those many things which have been learned be conscientiously applied.

We would single out one physical distortion for discussion. The fourth-density negative minions which visit your group at this time are energizing a somewhat severe complex of imbalances in the manual appendages of this instrument and, to a lesser extent, those distortions of the thoracic region. We suggest care be taken to refrain from any unnecessary use of these appendages. As this instrument will not appreciate this suggestion, we suggest the appropriate discussion.

QUESTIONER: I assume from this that our fifth-density negative companion is still on R and R. Is this correct?

RA: I am Ra. Your fifth-density companion is not accompanying you at this time. However, it is not resting.

QUESTIONER: Is the censer that we have provided all right? It does go out prior to the end of the session. Would it be better if it did not go out prior to the end of the session?

RA: I am Ra. The new configuration of the censer is quite helpful to the more subtle patterns of energy surrounding these workings. It would be helpful to have a continuously burning amount of cense. However, the difficulty is in providing this without overpowering this enclosure with the amount of effluvium and physical product of combustion. Having to choose betwixt allowing the censer to finish its burning and having an overabundance of the smoke, we would suggest the former as being more helpful.

QUESTIONER: The instrument has mentioned what she refers to as bleed-through or being aware, during these sessions sometimes, of the communication. Would you comment on this?

RA: I am Ra. We have the mind/body/spirit complex of the instrument with us. As this entity begins to awaken from the metaphorical crib of experiencing light and activity in our density, it is beginning to be aware of the movement of thought. It does not grasp these thoughts any more than your third-density infant may grasp the first words it perceives. The experience should be expected to continue and is an appropriate outgrowth of the nature of these workings and of the method by which this instrument has made itself available to our words.

QUESTIONER: The instrument mentioned a recurrence of the need to go to the bathroom prior to the session. Is this because of the low vital energy?

RA: I am Ra. It is part of the cause of the lowered vital-energy level. This entity has been sustaining a level of the distortion you call pain which few among your peoples experience without significant draining of the energies. Indeed, the stability of the entity is notable. However, the entity has thusly become drained and further has felt other distortions such as those for a variety of experiences accentuated, for this is one means of balancing the inward-looking experience of the physical pain. Due to concern for this entity, such activities have been discouraged. This has further drained the entity.

The will to be of service to the Creator through the means of offering itself as instrument in these workings, therefore, was given an opportunity for the testing of resolve. This entity used some vital energy to fuel and replenish the will. No physical energy has been used by the instrument, but the vital energies were tapped so that this entity might have the opportunity to once again consciously choose to serve the One Infinite Creator.

QUESTIONER: Our publisher requests pictures for the book *The Law of One*, which is going to press at this time. Would you comment on the advisability, the benefit, or detriment, magical or otherwise, of us using pictures of this particular setup, the instrument, and the appurtenances in the book?

RA: I am Ra. The practical advisability of such a project is completely a product of your discrimination. There are magical considerations.

Firstly, if pictures be taken of a working the visual image must needs be that which is; that is, it is well for you to photograph only an actual working, and no sham nor substitution of any material. There shall be no distortions which this group can avoid any more than we would wish distortions in our words.

Secondly, it is inadvisable to photograph the instrument or any portion of the working room while the instrument is in trance. This is a narrow-band contact, and we wish to keep electrical and electromagnetic energies constant when their presence is necessary, and not present at all otherwise.

QUESTIONER: From what you . . . I'm sorry. Go ahead. If you meant to continue, continue. If not, I'll ask a question.

RA: I am Ra. We wished to state, thirdly, that once the instrumental is aware that the picture-taking will be performed, that during the entire picture-taking, whether before or after the working, the instrument be required to continuously respond to speech, thus assuring that no trance is imminent.

QUESTIONER: From what you have told me, then, I have planned the following: We will, after the session is complete and the instrument has been awakened, and before moving the instrument, have the instrument continually talk to us while I take pictures. In addition to this, I will take some other pictures as requested by the publisher. Is this the optimal filling of this requirement?

RA: I am Ra. Yes. We ask that any photographs tell the truth, that they be dated, and shine with a clarity so that there is no shadow of any but genuine expression which may be offered to those which seek truth. We come as humble messengers of the Law of One, desiring to decrease distortions. We ask that you, who have been our friends, work with any considerations such as above discussed, not with the thought of quickly removing an unimportant detail, but, as in all ways, regard such as another opportunity to, as the adept must, be yourselves and offer that which is in and with you without pretense of any kind.

QUESTIONER: Thank you. I would like to ask you as to the initial production of the Tarot—where this concept was first formed and where the Tarot was first recorded.

RA: I am Ra. The concept of the Tarot originated within the planetary influence you call Venus.

QUESTIONER: Was the concept given to or devised for a training tool for those inhabiting Venus at that time, or was it devised by those of Venus as a training tool for those of Earth?

RA: I am Ra. The Tarot was devised by the third-density population of Venus a great measure of your space/time in your past. As we have noted, the third-density experience of those of Venus dealt far more deeply and harmoniously with what you would call relationships with other-selves, sexual-energy-transfer work, and philosophical or metaphysical research. The product of many, many generations of work upon what we conceived to be the archetypical mind produced the Tarot which was used by our peoples as a training aid in developing the magical personality.

QUESTIONER: I'll make a guess that those of Venus of third density who were the initial ones to partially penetrate the veil gleaned information as to the nature of the archetypical mind and the veiling process and from this designed the Tarot as a method of teaching others. Is this correct?

RA: I am Ra. It is so.

QUESTIONER: I will also assume, and I may not be correct, that the present list that I have of twenty-two names of the Tarot cards of the Major Arcana are not in exact agreement with Ra's original generation of the Tarot. Could you describe the original Tarot, first telling me if there were twenty-two archetypes? That must have been the same. Were they the same as the list that I read to you in a previous session, or were there differences?

RA: I am Ra. As we have stated previously, each archetype is a concept complex and may be viewed not only by individuals but by those of the same racial and planetary influences in unique ways. Therefore, it is not informative to reconstruct the rather minor differences in descriptive terms between the Tarot used by us and that used by those of Egypt and the spiritual descendants of those first students of this system of study.

The one great breakthrough which was made after our work in third density was done was the proper emphasis given to the Arcanum Number Twenty-Two, which we have called The Choice. In our own experience we were aware that such an unifying archetype existed, but did not give that archetype the proper complex of concepts in order to most efficaciously use that archetype in order to promote our evolution.

QUESTIONER: I will make this statement as to my understanding of some of the archetypes and let you correct this statement. It seems to me that the Significators of Mind, Body, and Spirit are acted upon in each of these by the catalyst. This produces Experience, which then leads to the Transformation and produces the Great Way. This is the same process for the mind, the body, and spirit. The archetypes are just repeated but act in a different way as catalyst because of the differences of mind, body, and spirit and produce a different type of experience for each because of the difference in the three. The Transformation is slightly different. The Great Way is somewhat different, but the archetypes are all basically doing the same thing. They are just acting on three different portions of the mind/body/spirit complex so that we can say that in making the Significator a complex, basically we have provided a way for Catalyst to create the Transformation more efficiently. Would you correct that statement, please?

RA: I am Ra. In your statement, correctness is so plaited up with tendrils of the most fundamental misunderstanding that correction of your statement is difficult. We shall make comments and from these comments request that you allow a possible realignment of conceptualization to occur.

The archetypical mind is a great and fundamental portion of the mind complex, one of its most basic elements and one of the richest sources of information for the seeker of the One Infinite Creator. To attempt to condense the archetypes is to make an erroneous attempt. Each archetype is a significant *ding an sich,* or thing in itself, with its own complex of concepts. While it is informative to survey the relationships of one archetype to another, it can be said that this line of inquiry is secondary to the discovery of the purest gestalt or vision or melody which each archetype signifies to both the intellectual and intuitive mind.

The Significators of Mind, Body, and Spirit complexes are complex in and of themselves, and the archetypes of Catalyst, Experience, Transformation, and the Great Way are most fruitfully viewed as independent complexes which have their own melodies with which they may inform the mind of its nature.

We ask that you consider that the archetypical mind informs those thoughts which then may have bearing upon the mind, the body, or the spirit. The archetypes do not have a direct linkage to body or spirit. All must be drawn up through the higher levels of the subconscious mind to the conscious mind, and thence they may flee whither they have been bidden to go. When used in a controlled way they are most helpful. Rather than continue beyond the boundaries of your prior statement, we would appreciate the opportunity for your requestioning at this time so that we may answer you more precisely.

QUESTIONER: Did Ra use cards similar to the Tarot cards for training in third density?

RA: I am Ra. No.

QUESTIONER: What did Ra use in third density?

RA: I am Ra. You are aware in your attempts at magical visualization of the mental configuration of sometimes rather complex visualizations. These are mental and drawn with the mind. Another example well known in your culture is the visualization, in your mass, of the distortion of the love of the One Infinite Creator called Christianity, wherein a small portion of your foodstuffs is seen to be a mentally configured but entirely real man, the man known to you as Jehoshuah or, as you call this entity now, Jesus. It was by this method of sustained visualization over a period of training that we worked with these concepts.

These concepts were occasionally drawn. However, the concept of one visualization per card was not thought of by us.

QUESTIONER: How did the teacher relay information to the student in respect to visualization?

RA: I am Ra. The process was cabalistic; that is, of the oral tradition of mouth to ear.

QUESTIONER: Then when Ra attempted to teach the Egyptians the concept of the Tarot, was the same process used, or a different one?

RA: I am Ra. The same process was used. However, those which were teach/learners after us first drew these images to the best of their ability within the place of initiation and later began the use of what you call cards bearing these visualizations' representations.

QUESTIONER: Were the Court Arcana and the Minor Arcana a portion of Ra's teachings, or was this something that came along later?

RA: I am Ra. Those cards of which you speak were the product of the influence of those of Chaldea and Sumer.

QUESTIONER: You mentioned earlier that the Tarot was a method of divination. Would you explain that?

RA: I am Ra. We must first divorce the Tarot as a method of divination from this Major Arcana as representative of twenty-two archetypes of the archetypical mind.

The value of that which you call astrology is significant when used by those initiated entities which understand, if you will pardon the misnomer, the sometimes intricate considerations of the Law of Confusion. As each planetary influence enters the energy web of your sphere, those upon the sphere are moved much as the moon which moves about your sphere moves the waters upon your deeps. Your own nature is water, in that you as mind/body/spirit complexes are easily impressed and moved. Indeed, this is the very fiber and nature of your journey and vigil in this density: to not only be moved but to instruct yourself as to the preferred manner of your movement in mind, body, and spirit.

Therefore, as each entity enters the planetary energy web, each entity experiences two major planetary influxes, that of the conception, which has to do with the physical, yellow-ray manifestation of the incarnation, and that of the moment you call birth, when the breath is first drawn into the body complex of chemical yellow ray. Thus those who know the stars and their configurations and influences are able to see a rather broadly drawn map of the country through which an entity has traveled, is traveling, or may be expected to travel, be it upon the physical, the mental, or the spiritual level. Such an entity will have developed abilities of the initiate which are normally known among your peoples as psychic or paranormal.

When the archetypes are shuffled into the mix of astrologically oriented cards which form the so-called Court Arcana and Minor Arcana, these archetypes become magnetized to the psychic impressions of the one working with the cards, and thusly become instruments of a linkage between the practitioner of the astrological determinations and divinations and the one requesting information. Ofttimes, such archetypical representations will appear in such a manner as to have seemingly interesting results, meaningful in configuration to the questioner. In and of themselves, the Major Arcana have no rightful place in divination but, rather, are tools for the further knowledge of the self by the self for the purpose of entering a more profoundly, acutely realized present moment.

QUESTIONER: Ra must have had, shall we say, a lesson plan or course of training for the twenty-two archetypes to be given either to those of third density of Ra or, later on, to those in Egypt. Could you describe this scenario for the training course?

RA: I am Ra. This shall be the last full query of this working.

We find it more nearly appropriate to discuss our plans in acquainting initiates upon your own planet with this particular version of the archetypes of the archetypical mind. Our first stage was the presentation of the images, one after the other, in the following order: one, eight, fifteen; two, nine, sixteen; three, ten, seventeen; four, eleven, eighteen; five, twelve, nineteen; six, thirteen, twenty; seven, fourteen, twenty-one; twenty-two. In this way the fundamental relationships between mind, body, and spirit could begin to be discovered, for as one sees, for instance, the Matrix of the Mind in comparison to the Matrices of Body and Spirit, one may draw certain tentative conclusions.

When, at length, the student had mastered these visualizations and had considered each of the seven classifications of archetype, looking at the relationships between mind, body, and spirit, we then suggested consideration of archetypes in pairs: one and two; three and four; five; six and seven. You may continue in this form for the body and spirit archetypes. You will note that the consideration of the Significator was left unpaired, for the Significator shall be paired with Archetype Twenty-Two.

At the end of this line of inquiry, the student was beginning to grasp more and more deeply the qualities and resonances of each archetype. At this point, using various other aids to spiritual evolution, we encouraged the initiate to learn to become each archetype and, most importantly, to know as best as possible within your illusion when the adoption of the archetype's persona would be spiritually or metaphysically helpful.

As you can see, much work was done creatively by each initiate. We have no dogma to offer. Each perceives that which is needful and helpful to the self.

May we ask if there are any brief queries before we leave this working?

QUESTIONER: Is there anything that we can do to improve the contact or to make the instrument more comfortable?

RA: I am Ra. We, again, ward you concerning the distortions of the instrument's hands. The fourth-density influence upon them could be inconvenient in that, if allowed to proceed without abatement, what you call your surgery shall be almost immediately necessary.

The alignments are good. You have been fastidious. We leave you, my friends, in the love and in the light of the One Infinite Creator. Go forth, therefore, rejoicing merrily in the power and in the glorious peace of the One Infinite Creator. Adonai.

Session 89,
June 9, 1982

RA: I am Ra. I greet you in the love and in the light of the One Infinite Creator. We communicate now.

QUESTIONER: Could you first please give me the condition of the instrument?

RA: I am Ra. It is as previously stated.

QUESTIONER: I have two questions, the first of which is: during the last intensive meditation here the instrument experienced very strong conditioning from an entity which did not identify itself and which did not leave when she asked it to. Would you tell us what was occurring then?

RA: I am Ra. We find the instrument to have been given the opportunity to become a channel for a previously known friend. This entity was not able to answer the questioning of spirits in the name of Christ as is this instrument's distortion of the means of differentiating betwixt those of positive and those of negative orientation. Therefore, after some resistance, the entity found the need to take its leave.

QUESTIONER: Was this particular entity the fifth-density visitor that we have had quite often previously?

RA: I am Ra. This is correct.

QUESTIONER: Is he back with us at this time?

RA: I am Ra. No. The attempt to speak was due to the vigilant eye of the minions of this entity, which noted what one may call a surge of natural telepathic ability upon the part of the instrument. This ability is cyclical, of the eighteen-diurnal-period cycle, as we have mentioned aforetimes. Thusly, this entity determined to attempt another means of access to the instrument by free will.

QUESTIONER: Was this what I would refer to as an increased ability to receive telepathically over a broader range of basic frequencies so as to include not only the Confederation but also this entity?

RA: I am Ra. This is incorrect. The high point of the cycle sharpens the ability to pick up the signal but does not change the basic nature of the carrier wave. Shall we say, there is greater power in the receiving antennae.

QUESTIONER: This question may be meaningless, but would a

fifth-density entity of the Confederation who was positively polarized transmit on the same frequency as our negatively polarized fifth-density companion?

RA: I am Ra. This is correct and is the reason that the questioning of all contacts is welcomed by the Confederation of Planets in the Service of the Infinite Creator.

QUESTIONER: Question 2: [Name] has also felt some conditioning which was unbidden while channeling Latwii recently and in his personal meditations. Could you also tell us what occurred in these cases?

RA: I am Ra. The entity which has been companion has a vibratory frequency but a small amount lesser than that of the social memory complex known as Latwii. Also, Latwii is the primary Comforter of the Confederation for entities seeking at the vibratory-complex level of the one known as [name]. Therefore, this same companion has been attempting the contact of this instrument also, although this instrument would have great difficulty in distinguishing the actual contact due to the lack of experience of your companion at this type of service. Nevertheless, it is well that this instrument also choose some manner of the challenging of contacts.

QUESTIONER: How many of our years ago was Ra's third density ended?

RA: I am Ra. The calculations necessary for establishing this point are difficult, since so much of what you call time is taken up before and after third density as you see the progress of time from your vantage point. We may say in general that the time of our enjoyment of the choice-making was approximately 2.6 million of your sun-years in your past. However—we correct this instrument. Your term is billion, 2.6 billion of your years in your past. However, this time, as you call it, is not meaningful, for our intervening space/time has been experienced in a manner quite unlike your third-density experience of space/time.

QUESTIONER: It appears that the end of Ra's third density coincided with the beginning of this planet's second density. Is that correct?

RA: I am Ra. This is roughly correct.

QUESTIONER: Did the planet Venus become a fourth-density planet at that time?

RA: I am Ra. This is so.

QUESTIONER: Did it later, then, become a fifth-density planet?

RA: I am Ra. It later became a fourth/fifth-density planet; then, later a fifth-density planet for a large measure of your time. Both fourth- and fifth-density experiences were possible upon the planetary influence of what you call Venus.

QUESTIONER: What is its density at present?

RA: I am Ra. Its core vibrational frequency is sixth density. However we, as a social memory complex, have elected to leave that influence. Therefore, the beings inhabiting this planetary influence at this space/time are fifth-density entities. The planet may be considered a fifth/sixth-density planet.

QUESTIONER: What was your reason for leaving?

RA: I am Ra. We wished to be of service.

QUESTIONER: I have here a deck of twenty-two Tarot cards which have been copied, according to information we have, from the walls of the large pyramid at Giza. If necessary we can duplicate these cards in the book which we are preparing. I would ask Ra if these cards represent an exact replica of that which is in the Great Pyramid.

RA: I am Ra. The resemblance is substantial.

QUESTIONER: In other words, you might say that these were better than 95 percent correct as far as representing what is on the walls of the Great Pyramid?

RA: I am Ra. Yes.

QUESTIONER: The way that I understand this, then, Ra gave these archetypical concepts to the priests of Egypt, who then drew them upon the walls of one of the chambers of the Great Pyramid. What was the technique of transmission of this information to the priests? At this time was Ra walking the surface among the Egyptians, or was this done through some form of channeling?

RA: I am Ra. This was done partially through old teachings and partially through visions.

QUESTIONER: Then at this particular time, Ra had long since vacated the planet as far as walking among the Egyptians. Is this correct?

RA: I am Ra. Yes.

QUESTIONER: I would like to question Ra on each of these cards, in order to better understand the archetypes. Is this agreeable?

RA: I am Ra. As we have previously stated, these archetypical-concept complexes are a tool for learn/teaching. Thusly, if we were to offer information that were not a response to observations of the student, we would be infringing upon the free will of the learn/teacher by being teach/learner and learn/teacher at once.

QUESTIONER: You stated that Ra used the Tarot to develop the magical personality. Was this done to mentally become the essence of each archetype and in this way develop the magical personality?

RA: I am Ra. This is incorrect. The clothing one's self within the archetype is an advanced practice of the adept which has long studied this archetypical system. The concept complexes which together are intended to represent the architecture of a significant and rich portion of the mind are intended to be studied as individual concept complexes as Matrix, Potentiator, etc. in viewing mind/body/spirit connections and in pairs with some concentration upon the polarity of the male and the female. If these are studied, there comes the moment when the deep threnodies and joyful ditties of the deep mind can successfully be brought forward to intensify, articulate, and heighten some aspect of the magical personality.

QUESTIONER: You stated that each archetype is a concept complex. Would you please define what you mean by that statement?

RA: I am Ra. Upon the face of it, such a definition is without merit, being circular. A concept complex is a complex of concepts just as a molecule is a complex structure made up of more than one type of energy nexus or atom. Each atom within a molecule is its unique identity and, by some means, can be removed from the molecule. The molecule of water can, by chemical means, be caused to separate into hydrogen and oxygen. Separately they cannot be construed to equal water. When formed in the molecular structure which exemplifies water, the two are irrefragably water.

Just in this way, each archetype has within it several root atoms of organizational being. Separately the overall structure of the complex cannot be seen. Together the concept complex is irrefragably one thing. However, just as it is most useful in grasping the potentials in your physical systems of the constituted nature of water, so in grasping the nature of an archetype it is useful to have a sense of its component concepts.

QUESTIONER: In Archetype One, represented by Tarot card number 1, the Matrix of the Mind seems to have four basic parts to the complex. Looking at the card, we have, first and most obvious, the Magician and what seems to be an approaching star. A stork or similar bird seems to be in a cage. On top of the cage seems to be something that seems to be very difficult to discern. Am I in any way correct in this analysis?

RA: I am Ra. You are competent at viewing pictures. You have not yet grasped the nature of the Matrix of the Mind as fully as is reliably possible upon contemplation. We would note that the representations drawn by priests were somewhat distorted by acquaintance with and dependence upon the astrologically based teachings of the Chaldees.

QUESTIONER: When Ra originally trained or taught the Egyptians about the Tarot, did Ra act as teach/learners to a degree that Ra became learn/teachers?

RA: I am Ra. This distortion we were spared.

QUESTIONER: Then could you tell me what information you gave to the Egyptian priests who first were contacted or taught with respect to the first archetype? Is this possible for you to do within the limits of the first distortion?

RA: I am Ra. It is possible. Our first step, as we have said, was to present the descriptions in verbal form of three images: one, eight, fifteen; then the questions were asked: "What do you feel that a bird might represent?" "What do you feel that a wand might represent?" "What do you feel that the male represents?" And so forth, until those studying were working upon a system whereby the images used became evocative of a system of concepts. This is slow work when done for the first time.

We may note, with sympathy, that you undoubtedly feel choked by the opposite difficulty, that of a great mass of observation upon this system, all of which has some merit, as each student will experience the archetypical mind and its structure in an unique way useful to that student. We suggest that one or more of this group do that which we have suggested, in order that we may, without infringement, offer observations on this interesting subject which may be of further aid to those inquiring in this area.

We would note at this time that the instrument is having almost continuous pain flares. Therefore, we ask that each of the support group be especially aware of any misinformation in order that we may correct any distortions of information the soonest possible.

QUESTIONER: Now as I understand it, what you suggest as far as the Tarot goes is to study the writings that we have available, and from those formulate questions. Is this correct?

RA: I am Ra. No.

QUESTIONER: I'm sorry that I didn't understand exactly what you meant with respect to this. Would it be appropriate then for me to answer the questions with what I think is the meaning of the three items that you spoke of for Card Number One and then Card Eight, etc.? Is this what you mean?

RA: I am Ra. This is very close to our meaning. It was our intention to suggest that one or more of you go through the plan of study which we have suggested. The queries having to do with the archetypes as found in the Tarot after this point may take the form of observing what seem to be the characteristics of each archetype, relationships between mind, body, and spiritual archetypes of the same ranking such as Matrix, or archetypes as seen in relationship to polarity, especially when observed in the pairings.

Any observations made by a student which have fulfilled the considerations will receive our comment in return. Our great avoidance of interpreting, for the first time, for the learn/teacher various elements of a picture upon a piece of pasteboard is involved both with the Law of Confusion and with the difficulties of the distortions of the pictures upon the pasteboard. Therefore, we may suggest a conscientious review of that which we have already given concerning this subject, as opposed to the major reliance being either upon any rendition of the archetype pictures or any system which has been arranged as a means of studying these pictures.

QUESTIONER: All right; I'll have to do that. Ra stated that a major breakthrough was made when proper emphasis was put on Arcanum Twenty-Two. This didn't happen until Ra had completed third density. I assume from this that Ra, being polarized positively, probably had some of the same difficulty that occurred prior to the veil, in that the negative polarity was not appreciated. That's a guess. Is this correct?

RA: I am Ra. In one way it is precisely correct. Our harvest was overwhelmingly positive, and our appreciation of those which were negative was relatively uninformed. However, we were intending to suggest that in the use of the system known to you as the Tarot, for advancing the spiritual evolution of the self, a proper understanding, if we may use this misnomer, of Archetype Twenty-Two is greatly helpful in sharpening the basic view of the Significator of Mind, Body, and Spirit and, further, throws into starker relief the Transformation and Great Way of Mind, Body, and Spirit complexes.

QUESTIONER: Were some of Ra's population negatively harvested at the end of Ra's third density?

RA: I am Ra. We had no negative harvest as such, although there had been two entities which had harvested themselves during the third density in the negative or service-to-self path. There were, however, those upon the planetary surface during third density whose vibratory patterns were in the negative range but were not harvestable.

QUESTIONER: What was Ra's average total population incarnate on Venus in third density?

RA: I am Ra. We were a small population which dwelt upon what you would consider difficult conditions. Our harvest was approximately six million five hundred thousand mind/body/spirit complexes. There were approximately thirty-two million mind/body/spirit complexes repeating third density elsewhere.

QUESTIONER: What was the attitude prior to harvest of those harvestable entities of Ra with respect to those who were obviously unharvestable?

RA: I am Ra. Those of us which had the gift of polarity felt deep compassion for those who seemed to dwell in darkness. This description is most apt, as ours was a harshly bright planet in the physical sense.

There was every attempt made to reach out with whatever seemed to be needed. However, those upon the positive path have the comfort of companions, and we of Ra spent a great deal of our attention upon the possibilities of achieving spiritual or metaphysical adepthood or work in indigo ray through the means of relationships with other-selves. Consequently, the compassion for those in darkness was balanced by the appreciation of the light.

QUESTIONER: Would Ra have the same attitude toward the unharvestable entities or would it be different at this nexus than at the time of harvest from the third density?

RA: I am Ra. Not substantially. To those who wish to sleep, we could only offer those comforts designed for the sleeping. Service is only possible to the extent it is requested. We were ready to serve in whatever way we could. This still seems satisfactory as a means of dealing with other-selves in third density. It is our feeling that to be each entity which one attempts to serve is to simplify the grasp of what service is necessary or possible.

QUESTIONER: What techniques did the two negatively harvested entities use for negative polarization upon such a positively polarized planet?

RA: I am Ra. The technique of control over others and domination unto the physical death was used in both cases. Upon a planetary influence much unused to slaughter, these entities were able to polarize by this means. Upon your third-density environment at the time of your experiencing, such entities would merely be considered, shall we say, ruthless despots which waged the holy war.

QUESTIONER: Did these two entities evolve from the second density of the planet Venus along with the rest of the population of Venus that became Ra from second density to third?

RA: I am Ra. No.

QUESTIONER: What was the origin of the two entities of which you speak?

RA: I am Ra. These entities were Wanderers from early positive fifth density.

QUESTIONER: And though they had already evolved through a positive fourth density, they, shall we say, switched polarity in the reincarnating in third density. Is this correct?

RA: I am Ra. This is correct.

QUESTIONER: What was the catalyst for their change?

RA: I am Ra. In our peoples there was what may be considered, from the viewpoint of wisdom, an overabundance of love. These entities looked at those still in darkness and saw that those of a neutral or somewhat negative viewpoint found such harmony, shall we say, sickening. The Wanderers felt that a more wisdom-oriented way of seeking love could be more appealing to those in darkness.

First one entity began its work. Quickly the second found the first. These entities had agreed to serve together and so they did, glorifying the One Creator, but not as they intended. About them were soon gathered those who found it easy to believe that a series of specific knowledges and wisdoms would advance one towards the Creator. The end of this was the graduation into fourth-density negative of the Wanderers, which had much power of personality, and some small deepening of the negatively polarized element of those not polarizing positively. There was no negative harvest as such.

QUESTIONER: What was the reason for the wandering of these two Wanderers, and were they male and female?

RA: I am Ra. All Wanderers come to be of assistance in serving the Creator, each in its own way. The Wanderers of which we have been speaking were indeed incarnated male and female, as this is by far the most efficient system of partnership.

QUESTIONER: As a wild guess, one of these entities wouldn't be the one who has been our companion here for some time, would it?

RA: I am Ra. No.

QUESTIONER: Then from what you say, I am guessing that these Wanderers returned or wandered to Ra's third density possibly to seed greater wisdom in what they saw as an overabundance of compassion in the Ra culture. Is this correct?

RA: I am Ra. This is incorrect in the sense that before incarnation, it was the desire of these Wanderers only to aid in service to others. The query has correctness when seen from the viewpoint of the Wanderers within that incarnation.

QUESTIONER: I just can't understand why they would think that a planet that was doing as well as the population of Venus was doing, as far as I can tell, would need Wanderers in order to help with the harvest. Was this at an early point in Ra's third density?

RA: I am Ra. It was in the second cycle of 25,000 years. We had a harvest of six out of thirty, to speak roughly, of millions of mind/body/spirit complexes, less than 20 percent. Wanderers are always drawn to whatever percentage has not yet polarized, and come when there is a call. There was a call from those which were not positively polarized as such but which sought to be positively polarized and sought wisdom, feeling the compassion of other-selves upon Venus as complacent or pitying towards other-selves.

QUESTIONER: What was the attitude of these two entities after they graduated into fourth-density negative and, the veil being removed, realized that they had switched polarities?

RA: I am Ra. They were disconcerted.

QUESTIONER: Then did they continue striving to polarize negatively for a fifth-density harvest in the negative sense, or did they do something else?

RA: I am Ra. They worked with the fourth-density negative for some period until, within this framework, the previously learned patterns of the self had been recaptured and the polarity was, with great effort, reversed. There was a great deal of fourth-density positive work then to be retraced.

QUESTIONER: How is Ra aware of this information? By what means does Ra know the precise orientation of these two entities in fourth-density negative, etc.?

RA: I am Ra. These entities joined Ra in fourth-density positive for a portion of the cycle which we experienced.

QUESTIONER: I assume, then, that they came in late. Is this correct?

RA: I am Ra. Yes.

QUESTIONER: I didn't mean to get so far off the track of my original direction, but I think that some of these excursions are enlightening and will help in understanding the basic mechanisms that we are so interested in, in evolution.

Ra stated that archetypes are helpful when used in a controlled way. Would you give me an example of what you mean by using an archetype in a controlled way?

RA: I am Ra. We speak with some regret in stating that this shall be our last query of length. There is substantial energy left, but this instrument has distortions that rapidly approach the limit of our ability to maintain secure contact.

The controlled use of the archetypes is that which is done within the self for the polarization of the self and to the benefit of the self, if negatively polarized, or others, if positively polarized, upon the most subtle of levels.

Keep in mind at all times that the archetypical mind is a portion of the deep mind and informs thought processes. When the archetype is translated without regard for magical propriety into the manifested daily actions of an individual, the greatest distortions may take place, and great infringement upon the free will of others is possible. This is more nearly acceptable to one negatively polarized. However, the more carefully polarized of negative mind/body/spirit complexes will also prefer to work with a finely tuned instrument. May we ask if there are any brief queries before we leave this working?

QUESTIONER: I'll just make the statement that I perceive that a negative-polarity harvest is possible with less negativity in the environment like Ra's environment than in the environment such as we have at present, and ask if that is correct, and then is there anything that we can do to improve the contact or the comfort of the instrument?

RA: I am Ra. Firstly, the requirements of harvest are set. It is, however, easier to serve the self completely or nearly so if there is little resistance.

In the matter of the nurturing of the instrument, we suggest further manipulation of the dorsal side and appendages of this instrument and the whirling of the waters, if possible. The alignments are conscientious. We ask for your vigilance in alignments and preparations. All is well, my friends.

I am Ra. I leave you in the love and in the light of the One Infinite Creator. Go forth, then, rejoicing in the power and in the peace of the One Infinite Creator. Adonai.

Session 90,
June 19, 1982

RA: I am Ra. I greet you in the love and in the light of the One Infinite Creator. We communicate now.

QUESTIONER: Could you first please give me the condition of the instrument?

RA: I am Ra. The physical-complex energy deficit is somewhat increased by continued distortions towards pain. The vital energy levels are as previously stated, having fluctuated slightly between askings.

QUESTIONER: Could you tell me the situation with respect to our fourth- and fifth-density companions at this time?

RA: I am Ra. The fourth-density league of companions accompanies your group. The fifth-density friend, at this space/time nexus, works within its own density exclusively.

QUESTIONER: By what means do these particular fourth-density entities get from their origin to our position?

RA: I am Ra. The mechanism of calling has been previously explored. When a distortion which may be negatively connotated is effected, this calling occurs. In addition, the light of which we have spoken, emanating from attempts to be of service to others in a fairly clear and lucid sense, is another type of calling in that it represents that which requires balance by temptation. Thirdly, there have been certain avenues into the mind/body/spirit complexes of this group which have been made available by your fifth-density friend.

QUESTIONER: Actually, the question that I intended was, how do they get here? By what means of moving do they get here?

RA: I am Ra. In the mechanism of the calling, the movement is as you would expect; that is, the entities are within your planetary influence and are, having come through the quarantine web, free to answer such calling.

The temptations are offered by those negative entities of what you would call your inner planes. These, shall we say, dark angels have been impressed by the service-to-self path offered by those which have come through quarantine from days of old, and these entities, much like your angelic presences of the positive nature, are ready to move in thought within the inner planes of this planetary influence working from time/space to space/time.

The mechanism of the fifth-density entity is from density to density and is magical in nature. The fourth density, of itself, is not capable of building the highway into the energy web. However, it is capable of using that which has been left intact. These entities are, again, the Orion entities of fourth density.

QUESTIONER: You stated previously that fifth-density entities bear a resemblance to those of us in third density on planet Earth, but fourth density does not. Could you describe the fourth-density entities and tell me why they do not resemble us?

RA: I am Ra. The description must be bated under the Law of Confusion. The cause for a variety of so-called physical vehicles is the remaining variety of heritages from second-density physical vehicular forms. The process of what you call physical evolution continues to hold sway into fourth density. Only when the ways of wisdom have begun to refine the power of what you may loosely call thought is the form of the physical-complex manifestation more nearly under the direction of the consciousness.

QUESTIONER: If the population of this planet presently looks similar to fifth-density entities, I was wondering why this is. If I understand you correctly, the process of evolution would normally be that of third density resembling that from which evolved in second density and refining it in fourth and then again in fifth density, becoming what the population of this looks like in the third density. It seems to me that this planet is ahead of itself by the way that its mind/body/spirit complex or body complex looks. What is the reason for this?

RA: I am Ra. Your query is based upon a misconception. Do you wish us to comment or do you wish to requestion?

QUESTIONER: Please comment on my misconception, if that is possible.

RA: I am Ra. In fifth density the manifestation of the physical complex is more and more under the control of the conscious-mind complex. Therefore, the fifth-density entity may dissolve one manifestation and create another. Consequently, the choice of a fifth-density entity or complex of entities wishing to communicate with your peoples would be to resemble your peoples' physical-complex, chemical, yellow-ray vehicles.

QUESTIONER: I see. Very roughly, if you were to move a third-density entity from some other planet to this planet, what percentage of all of those within the knowledge of Ra would look enough like entities of Earth so that they would go unnoticed in a crowd?

RA: I am Ra. Perhaps 5 percent.

QUESTIONER: Then there is an extreme variation in the form of the physical vehicle in third density in the universe. I assume that this is also true of fourth density. Is this correct?

RA: I am Ra. This is so. We remind you that it is a great theoretical distance between demanding that the creatures of an infinite creation be unnoticeably similar to one's self, and observing those signs which may be called human which denote the third-density characteristics of self-consciousness, the grouping into pairs, societal groups, and races, and the further characteristic means of using self-consciousness to refine and search for the meaning of the milieu.

QUESTIONER: Within Ra's knowledge of the third-density physical forms, what percentage would be similar enough to this planet's physical forms that we would assume the entities to be human even though they were a bit different? This would have to be very rough because of my definition's being very rough.

RA: I am Ra. This percentage is still small; perhaps 13 to 15 percent due to the capabilities of various second-density life forms to carry out each necessary function for third-density work. Thusly to be observed would be behavior indicating self-consciousness and purposeful interaction with a sentient ambiance about the entity, rather than those characteristics which familiarly connote to your peoples the humanity of your third-density form.

QUESTIONER: Now, in this line of questioning, I am trying to link to the creations of various Logoi and their original use of a system of archetypes in their creation, and I apologize for a lack of efficiency in doing this, but I find this somewhat difficult. For this particular Logos in the beginning, prior to Its creation of the first density, did the archetypical system which it had chosen include the forms that would evolve in third density, or was this related to the archetypical concept at all?

RA: I am Ra. The choice of form is prior to the formation of the archetypical mind. As the Logos creates Its plan for evolution, then the chosen form is invested.

QUESTIONER: Was there a reason for choosing the forms that have evolved on this planet, and, if so, what was it?

RA: I am Ra. We are not entirely sure why our Logos and several neighboring Logoi of approximately the same space/time of flowering chose the bipedal, erect form of the second-density apes to invest. It has been our supposition, which we share with you as long as you are aware that this is mere opinion, that our Logos was interested in, shall we say, further intensifying the veiling process by offering to the third-density form the near-complete probability for the development of speech taking complete precedence over concept communication or telepathy. We also have the supposition that the so-called opposable thumb was looked upon as an excellent means of intensifying the veiling process, so that rather than rediscovering the powers of the mind, the third-density entity would, by the form of its physical manifestation, be drawn to the making, holding, and using of physical tools.

QUESTIONER: I will guess that the system of archetypes then was devised to further extend these particular principles. Is this correct?

RA: I am Ra. The phrasing is faulty. However, it is correct that the images of the archetypical mind are the children of the third-density physical manifestations of form of the Logos which has created the particular evolutionary opportunity.

QUESTIONER: Now, as I understand it, the archetypes are the biases of a very fundamental nature that, under free will, generate the experiences of each entity. Is this correct?

RA: I am Ra. The archetypical mind is part of that mind which informs all experience. Please recall the definition of the archetypical mind as the repository of those refinements to the cosmic or all-mind made by this particular Logos and peculiar only to this Logos. Thus it may be seen as one of the roots of mind, not the deepest but certainly the most informative in some ways. The other root of mind to be recalled is that racial or planetary mind which also informs the conceptualizations of each entity to some degree.

QUESTIONER: At what point in the evolutionary process does the archetypical mind first have effect upon the entity?

RA: I am Ra. At the point at which an entity, either by accident or design, reflects an archetype, the archetypical mind resonates. Thusly, random activation of the archetypical resonances begins almost immediately in third-density experience. The disciplined use of this tool of evolution comes far later in this process.

QUESTIONER: What was the ultimate objective of this Logos in designing the archetypical mind as It did?

RA: I am Ra. Each Logos desires to create a more eloquent expression of experience of the Creator by the Creator. The archetypical mind is intended to heighten this ability to express the Creator in patterns more like the fanned peacock's tail, each facet of the Creator vivid, upright, and shining with articulated beauty.

QUESTIONER: Is Ra familiar with the archetypical mind of some other Logos that is not the same as the one we experience?

RA: I am Ra. There are entities of Ra which have served as far Wanderers to those of another Logos. The experience has been one which staggers the intellectual and intuitive capacities, for each Logos sets up an experiment enough at variance from all others that the subtleties of the archetypical mind of another Logos are most murky to the resonating mind, body, and spirit complexes of this Logos.

QUESTIONER: There seems to have been created by this Logos, to me anyway, a large percentage of entities whose distortion was towards warfare. There have been the Maldek and Mars experiences and now Earth. It seems that Venus was the exception to what we could almost call the rule of warfare. Is this correct, and was this envisioned and planned into the construction of the archetypical mind, possibly not with respect to warfare as we have experienced it but as to the extreme action of polarization in consciousness?

RA: I am Ra. It is correct that the Logos designed Its experiment to attempt to achieve the greatest possible opportunities for polarization in third density. It is incorrect that warfare of the types specific to your experiences was planned by the Logos. This form of expression of hostility is an interesting result which is apparently concomitant with the tool-making ability. The choice of the Logos to use the life form with the grasping thumb is the decision to which this type of warfare may be traced.

QUESTIONER: Then did our Logos hope to see generated a positive and negative harvest from each density up to the sixth, starting with the third, as being the most efficient form of generating experience known to It at the time of Its construction of this system of evolution?

RA: I am Ra. Yes.

QUESTIONER: Then built into the basis for the archetypes is possibly the mechanism for creating the polarization in consciousness for service to others and service to self. Is this, in fact, true?

RA: I am Ra. Yes. You will notice the many inborn biases which hint to the possibility of one path's being more efficient than the other. This was the design of the Logos.

QUESTIONER: Then what you are saying is that once the path is recognized, either the positive or the negative polarized entity can find hints along his path as to the efficiency of that path. Is this correct?

RA: I am Ra. That which you say is correct upon its own merits but is not a repetition of our statement. Our suggestion was that within the experiential nexus of each entity within its second-density environment and within the roots of mind, there were placed biases indicating to the watchful eye the more efficient of the two paths. Let us say, for want of a more precise adjective, that this Logos has a bias towards kindness.

QUESTIONER: Then you say that the more efficient of the two paths was suggested in a subliminal way to second density to be the service-to-others path. Am I correct?

RA: I am Ra. We did not state which was the more efficient path. However, you are correct in your assumption, as you are aware from having examined each path in some detail in previous querying.

QUESTIONER: Could this be the reason for the greater positive harvest? I suspect that it isn't, but would there be Logoi that have greater negative-percentage harvests because of this type of biasing?

RA: I am Ra. No. There have been Logoi with greater percentages of negative harvests. However, the biasing mechanisms cannot change the requirements for achieving harvestability either in the positive or in the negative sense. There are Logoi which have offered a neutral background against which to polarize. This Logos chose not to do so but instead to allow more of the love and light of the Infinite Creator to be both inwardly and outwardly visible and available to the sensations and conceptualizations of mind/body/spirit complexes undergoing Its care in experimenting.

QUESTIONER: Were there any other circumstances, biases, consequences, or plans set up by the Logos other than those we have discussed for the evolution of Its parts through the densities?

RA: I am Ra. Yes.

QUESTIONER: What were these?

RA: I am Ra. One more; that is, the permeability of the densities so that there may be communication from density to density and from plane to plane or sub-density to sub-density.

QUESTIONER: Then as I see the plan for the evolution by this Logos, it was planned to create as vivid an experience as possible but also one which was somewhat informed with respect to the Infinite Creator and able to accelerate the progress as a function of will because of the permeability of densities. Have I covered accurately the general plan of this Logos with respect to Its evolution?

RA: I am Ra. Excepting the actions of the unmanifested self and the actions of self with other-self, you have been reasonably thorough.

QUESTIONER: Then, is the major mechanism forming the ways and very essence of the experience that we presently experience here the archetypical mind and the archetypes?

RA: I am Ra. These resources are a part of that which you refer to.

QUESTIONER: What I am really asking is what percentage of a part, roughly, are these responsible for?

RA: I am Ra. We ask once again that you consider that the archetypical mind is a part of the deep mind. There are several portions to this mind. The mind may serve as a resource. To call the archetypical mind the foundation of experience is to oversimplify the activities of the mind/body/spirit complex. To work with your query as to percentages is, therefore, enough misleading in any form of direct answer that we would ask that you requestion.

QUESTIONER: That's OK. I don't think that was too good a question anyway.

When Ra initially planned for helping the Egyptians with their evolution, what was the primary concept, and also secondary and tertiary if you can name those, that Ra wished to impart to the Egyptians? In other words, what was Ra's training plan or schedule for making the Egyptians aware of what was necessary for their evolution?

RA: I am Ra. We came to your peoples to enunciate the Law of One. We wished to impress upon those who wished to learn of unity that in unity, all paradoxes are resolved; all that is broken is healed; all that is forgotten is brought to light. We had no teaching plan, as you have called it, in that our intention when we walked among your peoples was to manifest that which was requested by those learn/teachers to which we had come.

We are aware that this particular line of querying—that is, the nature and architecture of the archetypical mind—has caused the questioner to attempt, to its own mind unsuccessfully, to determine the relative importance of these concepts. We cannot learn/teach for any, nor would we take this opportunity from the questioner. However, we shall comment.

The adept has already worked much, not only within the red, orange, yellow, and green energy centers but also in the opening of blue and indigo. Up through this point the archetypes function as the great base or plinth of a builded structure or statue, keeping the mind complex viable, level, and available as a resource whenever it may be evoked. There is a point at which the adept takes up its work. This is the point at which a clear and conscious consideration of the archetypical mind is useful.

QUESTIONER: I have an observation on Archetype Number One made by [name], and I request comment on it by Ra. I will read it: "The Matrix of the Mind is the conscious mind and is sustained by the power of the spirit as symbolized by the star which flows to it through the subconscious mind. It contains the will, which is signified by the scepter of power in the Magician's hand. All of creation is made through the power of the will directed by the conscious mind of the Magician, and the bird in the cage represents the illusion in which the self seems trapped. The Magician represents maleness or the radiance of being manifested as the creation through which each entity moves."

RA: I am Ra. As this instrument is becoming somewhat weary, we shall not begin this considerable discussion. We would request that this series of observations be repeated at the outset of the next working. We would suggest that each concept be discussed separately, or, if appropriate, a pair of concepts be related one to the other within the concept complex. This is slow work but shall make the eventual building of the concept complexes more smoothly accomplished.

Were we to have answered the observations as read by you at this space/time, as much space/time would have been given to the untangling of various concepts as to the building up of what were very thoughtful perceptions.

May we ask if there are any brief queries at this time?

QUESTIONER: Is there anything that we can do to make the instrument more comfortable or to improve the contact?

RA: I am Ra. It is well that the appliances for the arms were placed upon the instrument. We ask that continued vigilance be accorded these distortions, which are, if anything, more distorted towards disease than at our previous cautionary statement.

All is well, my friends. You are conscientious and faithful in your alignments. We appreciate your fastidiousness.

I am Ra. I leave you now, rejoicing merrily in the love and the light of the One Infinite Creator. Go forth, then, rejoicing in the power and in the peace of the One Infinite Creator. Adonai.

Session 91,
June 26, 1982

RA: I am Ra. I greet you in the love and in the light of the One Infinite Creator. We communicate now.

QUESTIONER: Could you first please give me the condition of the instrument?

RA: I am Ra. It is as previously stated.

QUESTIONER: I have listed the different minds and would like to know if they are applied in this particular aspect: first, we have the cosmic mind, which is, I would think, the same for all sub-Logoi like our sun. Is this correct?

RA: I am Ra. This is correct.

QUESTIONER: A sub-Logos such as our sun, then, in creating Its own particular evolutionary experience, refines the cosmic mind or, shall we say, articulates it by Its own additional bias or biases. Is this the correct observation?

RA: I am Ra. It is a correct observation with the one exception that concerns the use of the term "addition," which suggests the concept of that which is more than the all-mind. Instead, the archetypical mind is a refinement of the all-mind in a pattern peculiar to the sub-Logo's choosing.

QUESTIONER: Then the very next refinement that occurs as the cosmic mind is refined is what we call the archetypical mind. Is this correct?

RA: I am Ra. Yes.

QUESTIONER: Then this creates, I would assume, the planetary or racial mind. Is this correct?

RA: I am Ra. No.

QUESTIONER: What is the origin of the planetary or racial mind?

RA: I am Ra. This racial or planetary mind is, for this Logos, a repository of biases remembered by the mind/body/spirit complexes which have enjoyed the experience of this planetary influence.

QUESTIONER: Now, some entities on this planet evolved from second density into third, and some were transferred from other planets to recycle in third density here. Did the ones who were transferred here to recycle in third density add to the planetary or racial mind?

RA: I am Ra. Not only did each race add to the planetary mind, but also each race possesses a racial mind. Thus we made this distinction in discussing this portion of mind. This portion of mind is formed in the series of seemingly non-simultaneous experiences which are chosen in freedom of will by the mind/body/spirit complexes of the planetary influence. Therefore, although this Akashic, planetary, or racial mind is indeed a root of mind, it may be seen in sharp differentiation from the deeper roots of mind which are not a function of altering memory, if you will.

We must ask your patience at this time. This channel has become somewhat unclear due to the movement of the cover which touches this instrument. We ask that the opening sentences be repeated and the breath expelled.

[The microphones attached to the cover upon the instrument were pulled slightly as a rug was being placed over a noisy tape recorder. The Circle of One was walked, breath was expelled 2 feet above the instrument's head from her right to her left, and the Circle of One was walked again as requested.]

RA: I am Ra. We communicate now.

QUESTIONER: Were we successful in re-establishing clear contact?

RA: I am Ra. There was the mis-step which then needed to be rerepeated. This was done. The communication is once again clear. We enjoyed the humorous aspects of the necessary repetitions.

QUESTIONER: What occurred when the microphone cords were slightly moved?

RA: I am Ra. The link between the instrument's mind/body/spirit complex and its yellow-ray, chemical, physical vehicle was jarred. This caused some maladjustment of the organ you call the lungs, and, if the repair had not been done, would have resulted in a distorted physical-complex condition of this portion of the instrument's physical vehicle.

QUESTIONER: What kind of distortion?

RA: I am Ra. The degree of distortion would depend upon the amount of neglect. The ultimate penalty, shall we say, for the disturbing of the physical vehicle is the death, in this case by what you would call the congestive heart failure. As the support group was prompt, there should be little or no distortion experienced by the instrument.

QUESTIONER: Why does such a very minor effect like the slight movement of the microphone cord result in this situation, not mechanically or chemically, but philosophically, if you can answer this question?

RA: I am Ra. We can only answer mechanically as there is no philosophy to the reflexes of physical vehicular function.

There is what you might call the silver-cord reflex; that is, when the mind/body/spirit complex dwells without the environs of the physical shell and the physical shell is disturbed, the physical shell will reflexively call back the absent enlivener; that is, the mind/body/spirit complex, which is connected with what may be metaphysically seen as what some of your philosophers have called the silver cord. If this is done suddenly, the mind/body/spirit complex will attempt entry into the energy web of the physical vehicle without due care, and the effect is as if one were to stretch one of your elastic bands and let it shrink rapidly. The resulting snap would strike hard at the anchored portion of the elastic band.

The process through which you as a group go in recalling this instrument could be likened unto taking this elastic and gently lessening its degree of tension until it was without perceptible stretch.

QUESTIONER: To get back to what we were talking about, would the different races of this planet be from different planets in our local vicinity or the planets of nearby Logoi which have evolved through their second-density experiences, and would they create the large number of different races that we experience on this planet?

RA: I am Ra. There are correctnesses to your supposition. However, not all races and sub-races are of various planetary origins. We suggest that in looking at planetary origins, one observes not the pigmentation of the integument but the biases concerning interactions with other-selves and definitions regarding the nature of the self.

QUESTIONER: How many different planets have supplied the individuals which now inhabit this planet?

RA: I am Ra. This is perceived by us to be unimportant information, but harmless. There are three major planetary influences upon your planetary sphere, besides those of your own second-density derivation, and thirteen minor planetary groups in addition to the above.

QUESTIONER: Thank you. One more question before we start on the specific questions in regard to archetypes. Do all Logoi evolving after the veil have twenty-two archetypes?

RA: I am Ra. No.

QUESTIONER: Is it common for Logoi to have twenty-two archetypes, or is this relatively unique to our Logos?

RA: I am Ra. The system of sevens is the most articulated system yet discovered by any experiment by any Logos in our octave.

QUESTIONER: What is the largest number of archetypes, to Ra's knowledge, used by a Logos?

RA: I am Ra. The sevens plus The Choice is the greatest number which has been used, by our knowledge, by Logoi. It is the result of many, many previous experiments in articulation of the One Creator.

QUESTIONER: I assume, then, that twenty-two is the greatest number of archetypes. I also ask is it the minimum number presently in use by any Logos, to Ra's knowledge?

RA: I am Ra. The fewest are the two systems of five which are completing the cycles or densities of experience.

You must grasp the idea that the archetypes were not developed at once but step by step, and not in order as you know the order at this space/time but in various orders. Therefore, the two systems of fives were using two separate ways of viewing the archetypical nature of all experience. Each, of course, used the Matrix, the Potentiator, and the Significator, for this is the harvest with which our creation began.

One way or system of experimentation had added to these the Catalyst and the Experience. Another system, if you will, had added Catalyst and Transformation. In one case, the methods whereby experience was processed was further aided, but the fruits of experience less aided. In the second case, the opposite may be seen to be the case.

QUESTIONER: Thank you. We have some observations on the archetypes, which are as follows. First, the Matrix of the Mind is depicted in the Egyptian Tarot by a male, and this we take as creative energy intelligently directed. Will Ra comment on this?

RA: I am Ra. This is an extremely thoughtful perception, seeing as it does the male not specifically as biological male but as a male principle. You will note that there are very definite sexual biases in the images. They are intended to function both as information as to which biological entity or energy will attract which archetype, and also as a more general view which sees polarity as a key to the archetypical mind of third density.

QUESTIONER: The second observation is that we have a wand that has been seen as the power of the will. Will Ra comment?

RA: I am Ra. The concept of will is indeed pouring forth from each facet of the image of the Matrix of the Mind. The wand as the will, however, is, shall we say, an astrological derivative of the outreaching hand forming the, shall we say, magical gesture. The excellent portion of the image which may be seen distinctly as separate from the concept of the wand is that sphere which indicates the spiritual nature of the object of the will of one wishing to do magical acts within the manifestation of your density.

QUESTIONER: The hand downward has been seen as seeking from within and not from without, and the active dominance over the material world. Would Ra comment on that?

RA: I am Ra. Look again, O student. Does the hand reach within? Nay. Without potentiation, the conscious mind has no inwardness. That hand, O student, reaches towards that which, outside its unpotentiated influence, is locked from it.

QUESTIONER: The square cage represents the material illusion and is an unmagical shape. Can Ra comment on that?

RA: I am Ra. The square, wherever seen, is the symbol of the third-density illusion and may be seen either as unmagical or, in the proper configuration, as having been manifested within; that is, the material world given life.

QUESTIONER: The dark area around the square, then, would be the darkness of the subconscious mind. Would Ra comment on that?

RA: I am Ra. There is no further thing to say to the perceptive student.
QUESTIONER: The checkered portion would represent polarity?
RA: I am Ra. This also is satisfactory.

QUESTIONER: The bird is a messenger, which the hand is reaching down to unlock. Can Ra comment on that?

RA: I am Ra. The winged visions or images in this system are to be noted not so much for their distinct kind as for the position of the wings. All birds are indeed intended to suggest that just as the Matrix figure, the Magician, cannot act without reaching its winged spirit, so neither can the spirit fly, lest it be released into conscious manifestation and fructified thereby.

QUESTIONER: The star would represent the potentiating forces of the subconscious mind. Is this correct?

RA: I am Ra. This particular part of this image is best seen in astrological terms. We would comment at this space/time that Ra did not include the astrological portions of these images in the system of images designed to evoke the archetypical leitmotifs.

QUESTIONER: Are there any other additions to Card Number One other than the star that are of other than the basic archetypical aspects?

RA: I am Ra. There are details of each image seen through the cultural eye of the time of inscription. This is to be expected. Therefore, when viewing the, shall we say, Egyptian costumes and systems of mythology used in the images, it is far better to penetrate to the heart of the costumes' significance or the creatures' significance rather than clinging to a culture which is not your own.

In each entity the image will resonate slightly differently. Therefore, there is the desire upon Ra's part to allow for the creative envisioning of each archetype, using general guidelines rather than specific and limiting definitions.

QUESTIONER: The cup represents a mixture of positive and negative passions. Could Ra comment on that?

RA: I am Ra. The otic portions of this instrument's physical vehicle did not perceive a significant portion of your query. Please requery.

QUESTIONER: There is apparently a cup which we have as containing a mixture of positive and negative influences. However, I personally doubt this. Could Ra comment on this, please?

RA: I am Ra. Doubt not the polarity, O student, but release the cup from its stricture. It is indeed a distortion of the original image.

QUESTIONER: What was the original image?

RA: I am Ra. The original image had the checkering as the suggestion of polarity.

QUESTIONER: Then was this a representation of the waiting polarity to be tasted by the Matrix of the Mind?

RA: I am Ra. This is exquisitely perceptive.

QUESTIONER: I have listed here the sword as representing struggle. I am not sure that I even can call anything in this diagram a sword. Would Ra comment on that?

RA: I am Ra. Doubt not the struggle, O student, but release the sword from its stricture. Observe the struggle of a caged bird to fly.

QUESTIONER: I have listed the coin represents work accomplished. I am also in doubt about the existence of the coin in this diagram. Could Ra comment on that please?

RA: I am Ra. Again, doubt not that which the coin is called to represent, for does not the Magus strive to achieve through the manifested world? Yet release the coin from its stricture.

QUESTIONER: And finally, the Magician represents the conscious mind. Is this correct?

RA: I am Ra. We ask the student to consider the concept of the unfed conscious mind, the mind without any resource but consciousness. Do not confuse the unfed conscious mind with that mass of complexities which you as students experience, as you have so many, many times dipped already into the processes of potentiation, catalyst, experience, and transformation.

QUESTIONER: Are these all of the components, then, of this first archetype?

RA: I am Ra. These are all you, the student, see. Thusly the complement is complete for you. Each student may see some other nuance. We, as we have said, did not offer these images with boundaries but only as guidelines intending to aid the adept and to establish the architecture of the deep, or archetypical, portion of the deep mind.

QUESTIONER: How is the knowledge of the facets of the archetypical mind used by the individual to accelerate his evolution?

RA: I am Ra. We shall offer an example based upon this first-explored archetype or concept complex. The conscious mind of the adept may be full to bursting of the most abstruse and unimaginable of ideas, so that further ideation becomes impossible, and work in blue ray or indigo is blocked through over-activation. It is then that the adept would call upon the new mind, untouched and virgin, and dwell within the archetype of the new and unblemished mind without bias, without polarity, full of the magic of the Logos.

QUESTIONER: Then you are saying, if I am correct in understanding what you have just said, that the conscious mind may be filled with an almost infinite number of concepts, but there is a set of basic concepts which are what I would call important simply because they are the foundations for the evolution of consciousness, and will, if carefully applied, accelerate the evolution of consciousness, whereas the vast array of concepts, ideas, and experiences that we meet in our daily lives may have little or no bearing upon the evolution of consciousness except in a very indirect way. In other words, what we are attempting to do here is find the motivators of evolution and utilize them to move through our evolutionary track. Is this correct?

RA: I am Ra. Not entirely. The archetypes are not the foundation for spiritual evolution but rather are the tool for grasping in an undistorted manner the nature of this evolution.

QUESTIONER: So for an individual who wished to consciously augment his own evolution, an ability to recognize and utilize the archetypes would be beneficial in sorting out that which he wishes to seek from that which would be not as efficient a seeking tool. Would this be a good statement?

RA: I am Ra. This is a fairly adequate statement. The term "efficient" might also fruitfully be replaced by the term "undistorted." The archetypical mind, when penetrated lucidly, is a blueprint of the builded structure of all energy expenditures and all seeking without distortion. This, as a resource within the deep mind, is of great potential aid to the adept.

We would ask for one more query at this space/time, as this instrument is experiencing continuous surges of the distortion you call pain, and we wish to take our leave of the working while the instrument still possesses a sufficient amount of transferred energy to ease the transition to the waking state, if you would call it that.

QUESTIONER: Since we are at the end of the Matrix of the Mind, I will just ask if there is anything that we can do to make the instrument more comfortable or to improve the contact.

RA: I am Ra. Each is most conscientious. The instrument might be somewhat more comfortable with the addition of the swirling of the waters with spine erect. All other things which can be performed for the instrument's benefit are most diligently done. We commend the continual fidelity of the group to the ideals of harmony and thanksgiving. This shall be your great protection. All is well, my friends. The appurtenances and alignments are excellent.

I am Ra. I leave you glorying in the love and in the light of the One Infinite Creator. Go forth, then, rejoicing in the power and the peace of the One Infinite Creator. Adonai.

Session 92,
July 8, 1982

RA: I am Ra. I greet you in the love and in the light of the One Infinite Creator. We communicate now.

QUESTIONER: Could you first please give me the condition of the instrument?

RA: I am Ra. The condition of this instrument is slightly more distorted towards weakness in each respect since the previous asking.

QUESTIONER: Is there a specific cause for this, and could you tell us what it is?

RA: I am Ra. The effective cause of the increased physical distortions has to do with the press of continuing substantial levels of the distortion you call pain. Various vehicular distortions other than the specifically arthritic have been accentuated by psychic greeting, and the combined effect has been deleterious.

The continued slight but noticeable loss of the vital energies is due to the necessity for the instrument to call upon this resource in order to clear the, shall we say, way for a carefully purified service-to-others working. The use of the will in the absence of physical and, in this particular case, mental and mental/emotional energies requires vital energies.

QUESTIONER: We have been trying to figure out how to provide the instrument with the swirling waters, and we hope to do that soon. Is there any other thing that we can do to improve this situation?

RA: I am Ra. Continue in peace and harmony. Already the support group does much. There is the need for the instrument to choose the manner of its beingness. It has the distortion, as we have noted, towards the martyrdom. This can be evaluated and choices made only by the entity.

QUESTIONER: What is the present situation with the negative fifth-density visitor?

RA: I am Ra. It is with this group.

QUESTIONER: What prompted it to return?

RA: I am Ra. The promptings were duple. There was the recovery of much negative polarity upon the part of your friend of fifth density, and at the same approximate nexus a temporary lessening of the positive harmony of this group.

QUESTIONER: Is there anything that we can do about the instrument's stomach problem or constipation?

RA: I am Ra. The healing modes of which each is capable are already in use.

QUESTIONER: In the last session we discussed the first Tarot card of the Egyptian type. Are there any distortions in the cards that we have that Ra did not originally intend, or any additions that Ra did intend in this particular Tarot?

RA: The distortions remaining after the removal of astrological material are those having to do with the mythos of the culture to which Ra offered this teach/learning tool. This is why we have suggested approaching the images looking for the heart of the image rather than being involved overmuch by the costumes and creatures of a culture not familiar to your present incarnation. We have no wish to add to an already distorted group of images, feeling that although distortion is inevitable, there is the least amount which can be procured in the present arrangement.

QUESTIONER: Then you are saying that the cards that we have here are the best available cards.

RA: I am Ra. Your statement is correct in that we consider the so-called Egyptian Tarot the most undistorted version of the images which Ra offered. This is not to intimate that other systems may not, in their own way, form an helpful architecture for the adept's consideration of the archetypical mind.

QUESTIONER: I would like to make an analogy of when a baby is first born. I am assuming that the Matrix of the Mind is new and undistorted and veiled from the Potentiator of the Mind and ready for that which it is to experience in the incarnation. Is this correct?

RA: I am Ra. Yes.

QUESTIONER: I will read several statements and ask for Ra's comments. The first is: Until an entity becomes consciously aware of the evolutionary process, the Logos or intelligent energy creates the potentials for an entity to gain the experience necessary for polarization. Would Ra comment on that?

RA: I am Ra. This is so.

QUESTIONER: Then, this occurs because the Potentiator of the Mind is directly connected, through the roots of the tree of mind, to the archetypical mind and to the Logos which created it, and because the veil between the Matrix and Potentiator of the Mind allows for the development of the will. Will Ra comment on that?

RA: I am Ra. Some untangling may be needed. As the mind/body/spirit complex which has not yet reached the point of the conscious awareness of the process of evolution prepares for incarnation, it has programmed for it a less than complete—that is to say, a partially randomized—system of learnings. The amount of randomness of potential catalyst is proportional to the newness of the mind/body/spirit complex to third density. This, then, becomes a portion of that which

151

you may call a potential for incarnational experience. This is indeed carried within that portion of the mind which is of the deep mind, the architecture of which may be envisioned as being represented by that concept complex known as the Potentiator.

It is not in the archetypical mind of an entity that the potential for incarnational experience resides, but in the mind/body/spirit complex's insertion, shall we say, into the energy web of the physical vehicle and the chosen planetary environment. However, to more deeply articulate this portion of the mind/body/spirit complex's beingness, this archetype, the Potentiator of the Mind, may be evoked with profit to the student of its own evolution.

QUESTIONER: Then are you saying that the source of pre-incarnatively programmed catalyst is the Potentiator of the Mind?

RA: I am Ra. No. We are suggesting that the Potentiator of the Mind is an archetype which may aid the adept in grasping the nature of this pre-incarnative and continuingly incarnative series of choices.

QUESTIONER: The third statement: Just as free will taps intelligent infinity, which yields intelligent energy, which then focuses and creates the densities of this octave of experience, the Potentiator of the Mind utilizes its connection with intelligent energy and taps or potentiates the Matrix of the Mind, which yields the Catalyst of the Mind. Is this correct?

RA: I am Ra. This is thoughtful but confused. The Matrix of the Mind is that which reaches just as the kinetic phase of intelligent infinity, through free will, reaches for the Logos, or, in the case of the mind/body/spirit complex, the sub-sub-Logos which is the free-will-potentiated beingness of the mind/body/spirit complex; to intelligent infinity, Love, and all that follows from that Logos; to the Matrix or, shall we say, the conscious, waiting self of each entity, the Love or the sub-sub-Logos spinning through free will all those things which may enrich the experience of the Creator by the Creator.

It is indeed so that the biases of the potentials of a mind/body/spirit complex cause the catalyst of this entity to be unique and to form a coherent pattern that resembles the dance, full of movement, forming a many-figured tapestry of motion.

QUESTIONER: The fourth statement: When the Catalyst of the Mind is processed by the entity, the Experience of the Mind results. Is this correct?

RA: I am Ra. There are subtle misdirections in this simple statement, having to do with the overriding qualities of the Significator. It is so that catalyst yields experience. However, through free will and the faculty of imperfect memory, catalyst is most often only partially used and the experience thus correspondingly skewed.

QUESTIONER: Then, the dynamic process between the Matrix, Potentiator, Catalyst, and Experience of the Mind forms the nature of the mind or the Significator of the Mind. Is this correct?

RA: I am Ra. As our previous response suggests, the Significator of the Mind is both actor and acted upon. With this exception, the statement is largely correct.

QUESTIONER: As the entity becomes consciously aware of this process, it programs this activity itself before the incarnation. Is this correct?

RA: I am Ra. This is correct. Please keep in mind that we are discussing not the archetypical mind, which is a resource available equally to each but unevenly used, but that to which it speaks: the incarnational experiential process of each mind/body/spirit complex. We wish to make this distinction clear, for it is not the archetypes which live the incarnation but the conscious mind/body/spirit complex which may indeed live the incarnation without recourse to the quest for articulation of the processes of potentiation, experience, and transformation.

QUESTIONER: Thank you. And finally, as each energy center becomes activated and balanced, the Transformation of the Mind is called upon more and more frequently. When all of the energy centers are activated and balanced to a minimal degree, contact with intelligent infinity occurs, the veil is removed, and the Great Way of the Mind is called upon. Is this correct?

RA: I am Ra. No. This is a quite eloquent look at some relationships within the archetypical mind. However, it must be seen once again that the archetypical mind does not equal the acting incarnational mind/body/spirit complex's progression or evolution.

Due to the first misperception, we hesitate to speak to the second consideration but shall attempt clarity. While studying the archetypical mind, we may suggest that the student look at the Great Way of the Mind, not as that which is attained after contact with intelligent infinity, but rather as that portion of the archetypical mind which denotes and configures the particular framework within which the Mind, the Body, or the Spirit archetypes move.

QUESTIONER: Turning, then, to my analogy or example of the newborn infant and its undistorted Matrix of the Mind, this newborn infant has its subconscious mind veiled from the Matrix of the Mind. The second archetype, the Potentiator of the Mind, is going to act at some time through the veil—though I hesitate to say through the veil, since I don't think that is a very good way of stating it—but the Potentiator of the Mind will act to create a condition such as the example I mentioned of the infant touching a hot object. The hot object we could take as random catalyst. The infant can either leave its hand on the hot object or rapidly remove it. My question is, is the Potentiator of the Mind involved at all in this experience, and, if so, how?

RA: I am Ra. The Potentiator of Mind and of Body are both involved in the questing of the infant for new experience. The mind/body/spirit complex which is an infant has one highly developed portion which may be best studied by viewing the Significators of Mind and Body. You notice we do not include the spirit. That portion of a mind/body/spirit complex is not reliably developed in each and every mind/body/spirit complex. Thusly the infant's significant self, which is the harvest of biases of all previous incarnational experiences, offers to this infant biases with which to meet new experience.

However, the portion of the infant which may be articulated by the Matrix of the Mind is indeed unfed by experience and has the bias of reaching for this experience through free will, just as intelligent energy in the kinetic phase, through free will, creates the Logos. These sub-sub-Logoi, then, or those portions of the mind/body/spirit complex which may be articulated by consideration of the Potentiators of Mind and Body, through free will, choose to make alterations in their experiential continuum. The results of these experiments in novelty are then recorded in the portion of the mind and body articulated by the Matrices thereof.

QUESTIONER: Are all activities that the entity has from the state of infancy a function of the Potentiator of the Mind?

RA: I am Ra. Firstly, although the functions of the mind are indeed paramount over those of the body, the body being the creature of the mind, certainly not all actions of a mind/body/spirit complex could be seen to be due to the potentiating qualities of the mind complex alone, as the body and in some cases the spirit also potentiates action.

Secondly, as a mind/body/spirit complex becomes aware of the process of spiritual evolution, more and more of the activities of the mind and body which precipitate activity are caused by those portions of the mind/body/spirit complex which are articulated by the archetypes of Transformation.

QUESTIONER: The Matrix of the Mind is depicted as a male on the card, and the Potentiator as female. Could Ra state why this is, and how this affects these two archetypes?

RA: I am Ra. Firstly, as we have said, the Matrix of the Mind is attracted to the biological male, and the Potentiator of the Mind to the biological female. Thusly, in energy transfer the female is able to potentiate that which may be within the conscious mind of the male so that it may feel enspirited.

In a more general sense, that which reaches may be seen as a male principle. That which awaits the reaching may be seen as a female principle. The richness of the male and female system of polarity is interesting and we would not comment further but suggest consideration by the student.

QUESTIONER: In card #2, the Potentiator of the Mind, we see a female seated on a rectangular block. She is veiled and sitting between two pillars, which seem to be identically covered with drawings, but one is much darker than the other. I am assuming that the veil represents the veil between the conscious and subconscious or Matrix and Potentiator of the Mind. Is this correct?

RA: I am Ra. This is quite correct.

QUESTIONER: I am assuming that she sits between the different-colored columns, with the dark one on her left, to indicate at this position an equal opportunity for the potentiation of the mind to be of the negative or positive nature. Would Ra comment on this?

RA: I am Ra. Although this is correct, it is not as perceptive as the notice that the Priestess, as this figure has been called, sits within a structure in which polarity, symbolized as you correctly noted by the light and dark pillars, is an integral and necessary part. The unfed mind has no polarity just as intelligent infinity has none. The nature of the sub-sub-sub-Logos which offers the third-density experience is one of polarity, not by choice but by careful design.

We perceive an unclear statement. The polarity of Potentiator is there not for the Matrix to choose. It is there for the Matrix to accept as given.

QUESTIONER: In other words, this particular illusion has polarity as its foundation, which might be represented by the structural significance of these columns. Is this correct?

RA: I am Ra. This is correct.

QUESTIONER: It seems to me that the drawings on each of these columns are identical, but that the left-hand column—that is, the one on the Priestess's left—has been shaded much darker, indicating that the events and the experiences may be identical in the incarnation but may be approached, viewed, and utilized with either polarity. Is this correct?

RA: I am Ra. This is correct. You will note also, from the symbol denoting spirit in manifestation upon each pillar, that the One Infinite Creator is no respecter of polarity but offers Itself in full to all.

QUESTIONER: There seems to be a book on the Priestess's lap which is half hidden by a robe or material that covers her right shoulder. It would seem that this indicates that knowledge is available if the veil is lifted but is not only hidden by the veil but is hidden partially by her very garment, which she must somehow remove to become aware of the knowledge which she has available. Is this correct?

RA: I am Ra. In that the conceit of the volume was not originated by Ra, we ask that you release the volume from its strictured form. Your perceptions are quite correct.

The very nature of the feminine principle of mind, which, in Ra's suggestion, was related specifically to what may be termed sanctified sexuality, is, itself, without addition, the book which neither the feminine nor the male principle may use until the male principle has reached and penetrated, in a symbolically sexual fashion, the inner secrets of this feminine principle.

All robes, in this case indicating the outer garments of custom, shield these principles. Thusly there is great dynamic tension, if you will, betwixt the Matrix and the Potentiator of the Mind.

QUESTIONER: Are there any other parts of this picture that were not given by Ra?

RA: I am Ra. The astrological symbols offered are not given by Ra.

QUESTIONER: The fact that the Priestess sits atop the rectangular block indicates to me that the Potentiator of the Mind has dominance or is above the material illusion. Is this in any way correct?

RA: I am Ra. Let us say, rather, that this figure is immanent, near at hand, shall we say, within all manifestation. The opportunities for the reaching to the Potentiator are numerous. However, of itself the Potentiator does not enter manifestation.

QUESTIONER: Would the half moon on the crown represent the receptivity of the subconscious mind?

RA: I am Ra. This symbol is not given by Ra, but it is not distasteful, for within your own culture the moon represents the feminine, the sun the masculine. Thusly we accept this portion as a portion of the image, for it seems without significant distortion.

QUESTIONER: Was the symbol on the front of the Priestess's shirt given by Ra?

RA: I am Ra. The crux ansata is the correct symbol. The addition and slight distortion of this symbol thereby is astrological and may be released from its stricture.

QUESTIONER: Would this crux ansata then be indicating the sign of life as the spirit enlivening matter?

RA: I am Ra. This is quite correct. Moreover, it illuminates a concept which is a portion of the archetype which has to do with the continuation of the consciousness which is being potentiated, in incarnation, beyond incarnation.

QUESTIONER: Were the grapes depicted on the cloth over her shoulder of Ra's communication?

RA: I am Ra. Yes.

QUESTIONER: We have those as indicating the fertility of the subconscious mind. Is that correct?

RA: I am Ra. This is correct, O student, but note ye the function of the mantle. There is great protection given by the very character of potentiation. To bear fruit is a protected activity.

QUESTIONER: The protection here seems to be depicted as being on the right-hand side but not the left. Would this indicate that there is protection for the positive path but not for the negative?

RA: I am Ra. You perceive correctly an inborn bias offering to the seeing eye and listing ear information concerning the choice of the more efficient polarity. We would at this time, as you may call it, suggest one more full query.

QUESTIONER: I will attempt an example of the Potentiator of the Mind acting. As the infant gains time in incarnation, would it experience the Potentiator offering both positive and negative potential thoughts, shall I say, for the Matrix to experience, which then begin to accumulate in the Matrix and color it one way or the other in polarity depending upon its continuing choice of that polarity? Is this in any way correct?

RA: I am Ra. Firstly, again may we distinguish between the archetypical mind and the process of incarnational experience of the mind/body/spirit complex.

Secondly, each potentiation which has been reached for by the Matrix is recorded by the Matrix but experienced by the Significator. The experience of the Significator of this potentiated activity is of course dependent upon the acuity of its processes of Catalyst and Experience.

May we ask if there are briefer queries before we leave this instrument?

QUESTIONER: Is there anything that we can do to make the instrument more comfortable or to improve the contact?

RA: I am Ra. The support group is functioning well. The instrument, itself, might ponder some earlier words and consider their implications. We say this because the continued calling upon vital energies, if allowed to proceed to the end of the vital energy, will end this contact. There is not the need for continued calling upon these energies. The instrument must find the key to this riddle or face a growing loss of this particular service at this particular space/time nexus.

All is well. The alignments are exemplary.

I am Ra. I leave you, my friends, in the love and the light of the

One Infinite Creator. Go forth, then, rejoicing in the power and in the peace of the One Infinite Creator. Adonai.

Session 93,
August 18, 1982

RA: I am Ra. I greet you in the love and in the light of the One Infinite Creator. We communicate now.

QUESTIONER: Could you first please give me the condition of the instrument?

RA: I am Ra. The physical complex distortions of this instrument far more closely approach what you might call the zero mark; that is, the instrument, while having no native physical energy, is not nearly so far in physical energy-deficit distortions. The vital-energy distortions are somewhat strengthened since the last asking.

QUESTIONER: What is the position and condition of our fifth-density, negatively oriented visitor?

RA: I am Ra. This entity is with this group but in a quiescent state due to some bafflement as to the appropriate method for enlarging upon its chosen task.

QUESTIONER: Thank you. You have stated previously that the foundation of our present illusion is the concept of polarity. I would like to ask, since we have defined the two polarities as service to others and service to self, is there a more complete or eloquent or enlightening definition of these polarities or any more information that we don't have at this time that you could give on the two ends of the poles that would give us a better insight into the nature of polarity itself?

RA: I am Ra. It is unlikely that there is a more pithy or eloquent description of the polarities of third density than service to others and service to self, due to the nature of the mind/body/spirit complexes' distortions towards perceiving concepts relating to philosophy in terms of ethics or activity. However, we might consider the polarities using slightly variant terms. In this way a possible enrichment of insight might be achieved for some.

One might consider the polarities with the literal nature enjoyed by the physical polarity of the magnet. The negative and positive, with electrical characteristics, may be seen to be just as in the physical sense. It is to be noted in this context that it is quite impossible to judge the polarity of an act or an entity, just as it is impossible to judge the relative goodness of the negative and positive poles of the magnet.

Another method of viewing polarities might involve the concept of radiation/absorption. That which is positive is radiant; that which is negative is absorbent.

QUESTIONER: Now, if I understand correctly, prior to the veiling process the electrical polarities, the polarities of radiation and absorption, all existed in some part of the creation, but the service-to-others/service-to-self polarity with which we are familiar had not evolved and only showed up after the veiling process as an addition to the list of possible polarities in the creation. Is this correct?

RA: I am Ra. No.

QUESTIONER: Would you correct me on that?

RA: I am Ra. The description of polarity as service to self and service to others, from the beginning of our creation, dwelt within the architecture of the primal Logos. Before the veiling process, the impact of actions taken by mind/body/spirits upon their consciousness was not palpable to a significant enough degree to allow the expression of this polarity to be significantly useful. Over the period of what you would call time, this expression of polarity did indeed work to alter the biases of mind/body/spirits so that they might eventually be harvested. The veiling process made the polarity far more effective.

QUESTIONER: I might make the analogy, then, in that when a polarization in the atmosphere occurs to create thunderstorms, lightning, and much activity, this more vivid experience could be likened to the polarization in consciousness which creates the more vivid experience. Would this be appropriate as an analogy?

RA: I am Ra. There is a shallowness to this analogy in that one entity's attention might be focused upon a storm for the duration of the storm. However, the storm-producing conditions are not constant, whereas the polarizing conditions are constant. Given this disclaimer, we may agree with your analogy.

QUESTIONER: With the third Tarot card we come to the first addition of archetypes after the veiling process, as I understand it. I am assuming that this third archetype is, shall I say, loaded in a way so as to create the possible polarization, since that seems to be one of the primary objectives of this particular Logos in the evolutionary process. Am I in any way correct on that?

RA: I am Ra. Before we reply to your query, we ask your patience as we must needs examine the mind complex of this instrument in order that we might attempt to move the left manual appendage of the instrument. If we are not able to effect some relief from pain, we shall take our leave. Please have patience while we do that which is appropriate.

[Thirty-second pause]

I am Ra. There will continue to be pain flares. However, the critical portion of the intense pain has been alleviated by repositioning.

Your supposition is correct.

QUESTIONER: There seems to be no large hint of polarity in this drawing except for the possible coloration of the many cups in the wheel. Part of them are colored black, and part are colored white. Would this indicate that each experience has within it the possible negative or positive use of that experience that is randomly generated by this seeming wheel of fortune?

RA: I am Ra. Your supposition is thoughtful. However, it is based upon an addition to the concept complex which is astrological in origin. Therefore, we request that you retain the concept of polarity but release the cups from their strictured form. The element you deal with is not in motion in its original form but is indeed the abiding sun, which, from the spirit, shines in protection over all catalyst available from the beginning of complexity to the discerning mind/body/spirit complex.

Indeed, you may, rather, find polarity expressed, firstly, by the many opportunities offered in the material illusion which is imaged by the not-white and not-dark square upon which the entity of the image is seated, secondly, upon the position of that seated entity. It does not meet opportunity straight on but glances off to one side or another. In the image you will note a suggestion that the offering of the illusion will often seem to suggest the opportunities lying upon the left-hand path or, as you might refer to it more simply, the service-to-self path. This is a portion of the nature of the Catalyst of the Mind.

QUESTIONER: The feet of the entity seem to be on an unstable platform that is dark to the rear and light to the front. I am guessing that possibly this indicates that the entity standing on this could sway in either direction, to the left- or to the right-hand path. Is this correct?

RA: I am Ra. This is most perceptive.

QUESTIONER: The bird, I am guessing, might be a messenger of the two paths depicted by the position of the wings, bringing catalyst which could be used to polarize on either path. Is this in any way correct?

RA: I am Ra. It is a correct perception that the position of the winged creature is significant. The more correct perception of this entity and its significance is the realization that the mind/body/spirit complex is, having made contact with its potentiated self, now beginning its flight towards that great Logos which is that which is sought by the adept.

Further, the nature of the winged creature is echoed both by the female holding it and the symbol of the female upon which the figure's feet rest; that is, the nature of catalyst is overwhelmingly of an unconsciousness, coming from that which is not of the mind and which has no connection with the intellect, as you call it, which precedes or is concomitant with catalytic action. All uses of catalyst by the mind are those consciously applied to catalyst. Without conscious intent, the use of catalyst is never processed through mediation, ideation, and imagination.

QUESTIONER: I would like, if possible, an example of the activity we call Catalyst of the Mind in a particular individual undergoing this process. Could Ra give an example of that?

RA: I am Ra. All that assaults your senses is catalyst. We, in speaking to this support group through this instrument, offer catalyst. The configurations of each in the group of body offer catalyst through comfort/discomfort. In fact, all that is unprocessed that has come before the notice of a mind/body/spirit complex is catalyst.

QUESTIONER: Then presently we receive catalyst of the mind as we are aware of Ra's communication, and we receive catalyst of the body as our bodies sense all of the inputs to them, but could Ra then describe catalyst of the spirit, and are we at this time receiving that catalyst, and, if not, could Ra give an example of that?

RA: I am Ra. Catalyst being processed by the body is catalyst for the body. Catalyst being processed by the mind is catalyst for the mind. Catalyst being processed by the spirit is catalyst for the spirit. An individual mind/body/spirit complex may use any catalyst which comes before its notice, be it through the body and its senses or through mediation or through any other more highly developed source, in its unique way to form an experience unique to it, with its biases.

QUESTIONER: Would I be correct in saying that the archetype for the Catalyst of the Mind is the Logos's model for its most efficient plan for the activity or use of the catalyst of the mind?

RA: I am Ra. Yes.

QUESTIONER: Then the adept, in becoming familiar with the Logos's archetype in each case, would be able to most efficiently use the Logos's plan for evolution. Is this correct?

RA: I am Ra. In the archetypical mind, one has the resource of not specifically a plan for evolution but rather a blueprint or architecture of the nature of evolution. This may seem to be a small distinction, but it has significance in perceiving more clearly the use of this resource of the deep mind.

QUESTIONER: Then Ra presented the images which we know now as the Tarot, so that the Egyptian adepts of the time could accelerate their personal evolution. Is this correct, and was there any other reason for the presentation of these images by Ra?

RA: I am Ra. You are correct.

QUESTIONER: Are there any other uses at all of Tarot cards other than the one I just named?

RA: I am Ra. To the student, the Tarot images offer a resource for learn/teaching the processes of evolution. To any other entity, these images are pictures and no more.

QUESTIONER: I was specifically thinking of the fact that Ra, in an earlier session, spoke of the Tarot as a system of divination. Would you tell me what you meant by that?

RA: I am Ra. Due to the influence of the Chaldees, the system of archetypical images was incorporated by the priests of that period into a system of astrologically based study, learning, and divination. This was not a purpose for which Ra developed the Tarot.

QUESTIONER: The third card also shows the wand, I am assuming it is, in the right hand. The ball atop the wand is the round magical shape. Am I in any way correct in guessing that the Catalyst of the Mind suggests the possible eventual use of the magic depicted by this wand?

RA: I am Ra. The wand is astrological in its origin and as an image may be released from its stricture. The sphere of spiritual power is an indication indeed that each opportunity is pregnant with the most-extravagant magical possibilities for the far-seeing adept.

QUESTIONER: The fact that the clothing of the entity is transparent indicates the semipermeability of the veil for the catalytic process. Is this correct?

RA: I am Ra. We again must pause.

[Fifteen-second pause]

I am Ra. We continue under somewhat-less-than-optimal conditions. However, due to the nature of this instrument's opening to us, our pathway is quite clear and we shall continue. Because of pain flares, we must ask you to repeat your last query.

QUESTIONER: I was just wondering if the transparency of the garments on the third card indicates the semipermeable nature of the veil between the conscious and unconscious mind.

RA: I am Ra. This is a thoughtful perception and cannot be said to be incorrect. However, the intended suggestion, in general, is an echo of our earlier suggestion that the nature of catalyst is that of the unconscious; that is, outward catalyst comes through the veil.

All that you perceive seems to be consciously perceived. This is not the correct supposition. All that you perceive is perceived as catalyst unconsciously. By the, shall we say, time that the mind begins its appreciation of catalyst, that catalyst has been filtered through the veil, and in some cases much is veiled in the most apparently clear perception.

QUESTIONER: I'm at a loss to know the significance of the serpents that adorn the head of the entity on this drawing. Are they of Ra, and, if so, what do they stand for?

RA: I am Ra. They are cultural in nature. In the culture to which these images were given, the serpent was the symbol of wisdom. Indeed, to the general user of these images, perhaps the most accurate connotation of this portion of the concept complexes might be the realization that the serpent is that which is powerful magically. In the positive sense this means that the serpent will appear at the indigo-ray site upon the body of the image figures. When a negative connotation is intended, one may find the serpent at the solar plexus center.

QUESTIONER: Is there any significance to the serpent? Is there any polarity to the serpent as we experience it in this illusion?

RA: I am Ra. We assume that you question the serpent as used in these images rather than the second-density life form which is a portion of your experience. There is a significance to the serpent form in a culture which coexists with your own but which is not your own; that is, the serpent is symbol of that which some call the kundalini and which we have discussed in previous material.

QUESTIONER: Is there any other aspect of this third card that Ra could comment on at this time?

RA: I am Ra. There may be said to be many aspects which another student might note and ponder in this image. However, it is the nature of teach/learning to avoid trespass into the realms of learn/teaching for the student. We are quite agreed to comment upon all observations that the student may make. We cannot speak further than this for any student.

We would add that it is expected that each student shall naturally have an unique experience of perception dealing with each image. Therefore, it is not expected that the questioner ask comprehensively for all students. It is, rather, expected and accepted that the questioner will ask a moiety of questions which build up a series of concepts concerning each archetype, which then offer to each succeeding student the opportunity for more-informed study of the archetypical mind.

May we ask for one more query at this time. We are pleased to report that this instrument has remembered to request the reserving of some transferred energy to make more comfortable the transition back to the waking state. Therefore, we find that there is sufficient energy for one more query.

QUESTIONER: I am assuming that you mean one full question. I'll make that question in this form. I'd like to know the significance of the shape of the crux ansata, and if that's too much of an answer, I'll just ask if there is anything that we can do to make the instrument more comfortable or to improve the contact?

RA: I am Ra. There are mathematical ratios within this image which may yield informative insights to one fond of riddles. We shall not untangle the riddle. We may indicate that the crux ansata is a part of the concept complexes of the archetypical mind, the circle indicating the magic of the spirit, the cross indicating that nature of manifestation which may only be valued by the losing. Thus the crux ansata is intended to be seen as an image of the eternal in and through manifestation and beyond manifestation through the sacrifice and the transformation of that which is manifest.

The support group functions well. The swirling waters experienced by the instrument since our previous working have substantially aided the instrument in its lessening of the distortion of pain.

All is well. The alignments are well guarded.

We leave you, my friends, in the love and the light of the Infinite One. Go forth, therefore, rejoicing in the power and in the peace of the One Infinite and Glorious Creator. Adonai.

Session 94,
August 26, 1982

RA: I am Ra. I greet you in the love and in the light of the One Infinite Creator. I communicate now.

QUESTIONER: Could you first please give me the condition of the instrument?

RA: I am Ra. There is some small increase in physical-energy deficit. It is not substantial. All else is as at the previous asking.

QUESTIONER: From the previous session the statement was made that much is veiled to the most apparently clear observation. Would Ra expand on what was meant by that statement? I assume that this means the veiling of all that which is outside the limits of what we call our physical perception having to do with the spectrum of light, etc., but I also intuit that there is more than that veiled. Would Ra expand on that concept?

RA: I am Ra. You are perceptive in your supposition. Indeed, we meant not any suggestions that the physical apparatus of your current illusion was limited as part of the veiling process. Your physical limits are as they are.

However, because of the unique biases of each mind/body/spirit complex, there are sometimes quite simple instances of distortion when there is no apparent cause for such distortion. Let us use the example of the virile and immature male who meets and speaks clearly with a young female whose physical form has the appropriate configuration to cause, for this male entity, the activation of the red-ray sexual arousal.

The words spoken may be upon a simple subject such as naming, information as to the occupation, and various other common interchanges of sound vibratory complex. The male entity, however, is using almost all the available consciousness it possesses in registering the desirability of the female. Such may also be true of the female.

Thusly an entire exchange of information may be meaningless because the actual catalyst is of the body. This is unconsciously controlled and is not a conscious decision. This example is simplistic.

QUESTIONER: I have drawn a small diagram in which I simply show an arrow which represents catalyst penetrating a line at right angles to the arrow, which is the veil, depositing in one of two repositories which I would call the right-hand path and the left-hand path, and I have labeled these two repositories the Experience. Would this be a very rough analogy of the way the catalyst is filtered through the veil to become experience?

RA: I am Ra. Again, you are partially correct. The deeper biases of a mind/body/spirit complex pilot the catalyst around the many isles of positivity and negativity as expressed in the archipelago of the deeper mind. However, the analogy is incorrect in that it does not take into account the further polarization which most certainly is available to the conscious mind after it has perceived the partially polarized catalyst from the deeper mind.

QUESTIONER: It seems to me that the Experience of the Mind would act in such a way as to change the nature of the veil so that catalyst would be filtered so as to be acceptable in the bias that is increasingly chosen by the entity. For instance, if he had chosen the right-hand path, the Experience of the Mind would change the permeability of the veil to accept more and more positive catalyst. Also, the other would be true for accepting more negative catalyst if the left-hand path were the one that was chosen. Is this correct?

RA: I am Ra. This is not only correct, but there is a further ramification. As the entity increases in experience, it shall, more and more, choose positive interpretations of catalyst if it is upon the service-to-others path, and negative interpretations of catalyst if its experience has been of the service-to-self path.

QUESTIONER: Then the mechanism designed by the Logos of the action of catalyst resulting in experience was planned to be self-accelerating, in that it would create this process of variable permeability. Is this an adequate statement?

RA: I am Ra. There is no variable permeability involved in the concepts we have just discussed. Except for this, you are quite correct.

QUESTIONER: Now I can understand, to use a poor term again, the necessity for the archetype of Catalyst of the Mind, but what is the reason for having a blueprint or model for the Experience of the Mind other than this simple model of dual repositories for negative and positive catalyst? It seems to me that the first distortion of free will would be better served if no model for experience was made. Could you clear that up for me?

RA: I am Ra. Your question is certainly interesting and your confusion hopefully productive. We cannot learn/teach for the student. We shall simply note, as we have previously, the attraction of various archetypes to male and to female. We suggest that this line of consideration may prove productive.

QUESTIONER: In the fourth archetype the card shows a male whose body faces forward. I assume that this indicates that the Experience of the Mind will reach for catalyst. However, the face is to the left, which indicates to me that in reaching for catalyst, negative catalyst will be more apparent in its power and effect. Would Ra comment on this?

RA: I am Ra. The archetype of Experience of the Mind reaches not, O student, but, with firm authority, grasps what it is given. The remainder of your remarks are perceptive.

QUESTIONER: The Experience is seated upon the square of the material illusion which is colored much darker than in Card Number Three. However, there is a cat inside this square. I am guessing that as experience is gained, the second-density nature of the illusion is understood and the negative and positive aspects separate. Would Ra comment on this?

RA: I am Ra. This interpretation varies markedly from Ra's intention. We direct the attention to the cultural meaning of the great cat which guards. What, O student, does it guard? And with what oriflamme does it lighten that darkness of manifestation? The polarities are, indeed, present; the separation nonexistent except through the sifting which is the result of cumulative experience. Other impressions were intended by this configuration of the seated image with its milk-white leg and its pointed foot.

QUESTIONER: In Card Number Three the feet of the female entity are upon the unstable platform, signifying the dual polarity by its color. In Card Number Four, one foot is pointed so that if the male entity stands on the toe it would be carefully balanced. The other foot is pointed to the left. Would Ra comment on my observation that if the entity stands on this foot, it will be very, very carefully balanced?

RA: I am Ra. This is an important perception, for it is a key to not only this concept complex but to others as well. You may see the T square, which, at times riven as is one foot from secure fundament by the nature of experience yet still by this same nature of experience, is carefully, precisely, and architecturally placed in the foundation of this concept complex and, indeed, in the archetypical mind complex. Experience[7] has the nature of more effectively and poignantly expressing the architecture of experience, both the fragility of structure and the surety of structure.

QUESTIONER: It would seem to me, from the configuration of this male entity in Card Number Four, who looks to the left with the right foot pointed to the left, that this card would indicate you must be in a defensive position with respect to the left-hand path, but there is no need to concern yourself about protection with respect to the right-hand path. Would Ra comment on that?

---

7. i.e., Card Number Four

RA: I am Ra. Again, this is not the suggestion we wished to offer by constructing this image. However, the perception cannot be said to be incorrect.

QUESTIONER: The magical shape is on the right edge of the Card Number Four, which indicates to me that the spiritual experience would be on the right-hand path. Could Ra comment on that?

RA: I am Ra. Yes. The figure is expressing the nature of experience by having its attention caught by what may be termed the left-hand catalyst. Meanwhile, the power, the magic, is available upon the right-hand path.

The nature of experience is such that the attention shall be constantly given varieties of experience. Those that are presumed to be negative, or interpreted as negative, may seem in abundance. It is a great challenge to take catalyst and devise the magical, positive experience. That which is magical in the negative experience is much longer coming, shall we say, in the third density.

QUESTIONER: Both the third and fourth archetypes, as I see it, work together for the sole purpose of creating the polarity in the most efficient manner possible. Is this correct?

RA: I am Ra. This cannot be said to be incorrect. We suggest contemplation of this thought complex.

QUESTIONER: Then prior to the veiling process, that which we call catalyst after the veiling was not catalyst simply because it was not efficiently creating polarity, because this loading process, you might say, that I have diagrammed, of catalyst passing through the veil and becoming polarized experience, was not in effect because the viewing of what we call catalyst by the entity was seen much more clearly as the experience of the One Creator and not something that was a function of other mind/body/spirit complexes. Would Ra comment on that statement?

RA: I am Ra. The concepts discussed seem without significant distortion.

QUESTIONER: Thank you. Then we're expecting, in Card Number Four, to see the result of catalytic action and, therefore, a greater definition between the dark and the light areas. In just glancing at this card, we notice that it is more definitely darkly colored in some areas and more white in others in a general sense than in Card Number Three, indicating to me that the separation along the two biases has occurred and should occur in order to follow the blueprint for experience. Could Ra comment on that?

RA: I am Ra. You are perceptive, O student.

QUESTIONER: The bird in Card Number Three now seems to be internalized in the center of the entity in Card Number Four, in that it has changed from its flight in Card Number Three. The flight has achieved its objective and has become a part, a central part, of the experience. Could Ra comment on that?

RA: I am Ra. This perception is correct, O student, but what shall the student find the bird to signify?

QUESTIONER: I would guess that the bird signifies that a communication that comes as catalyst signified in Card Number Three is accepted by the female and, used, becomes a portion of the experience. I'm not sure of that at all. Am I in any way correct?

RA: I am Ra. That bears little of sense.

QUESTIONER: I'll have to work on that.
        Then I am guessing that the crossed legs of the entity in Card Four have a meaning similar to the crux ansata. Is this correct?

RA: I am Ra. This is correct. The cross formed by the living limbs of the image signifies that which is the nature of mind/body/spirit complexes in manifestation within your illusion. There is no experience which is not purchased by effort of some kind, no act of service to self or others which does not bear a price, to the entity manifesting, commensurate with its purity. All things in manifestation may be seen in one way or another to be offering themselves in order that transformations may take place upon the level appropriate to the action.

QUESTIONER: The bird is within the circle on the front of the entity on Card Four. Would that have the same significance of the circular part of the crux ansata?

RA: I am Ra. It is a specialized form of this meaningful shape. It is specialized in great part due to the nature of the crossed legs of manifestation, which we have previously discussed.

QUESTIONER: The entity on Card Four wears a strangely shaped skirt. Is there a significance to the shape of this skirt?

RA: I am Ra. Yes.

QUESTIONER: The skirt is extended toward the left hand but is somewhat shorter toward the right. There is a black bag hanging from the belt of the entity on the left side. It seems to me that this black bag has a meaning of the acquiring of the material possessions of wealth as a part of the left-hand path. Would Ra comment on that?

RA: I am Ra. Although this meaning was not intended by Ra as part of this complex of concepts, we find the interpretation quite acceptable.

[Thirty-second pause]

I am Ra. As we observe a lull in the questioning, we shall take this opportunity to say that the level of transferred energy dwindles rapidly, and we would offer the opportunity for one more full question at this working, if it is desired.

QUESTIONER: I would just state that this card, being male, would indicate that as experience is gained, the mind becomes the motivator or that which reaches or does more than the simple experiencer it was prior to the gaining of the catalytic action. There is a greater tendency for the mind to direct the mind/body/spirit complex, and other than that, I would just ask if there is anything that we can do to make the instrument more comfortable or to improve the contact.

RA: I am Ra. In the context of your penultimate query, we would suggest that you ponder again the shape of the garment which the image wears. Such habiliment is not natural. The shape is significant and is so along the lines of your query.

The support group cares well for the instrument. We would ask that care be taken, as the instrument has been offered the gift of a distortion towards extreme cold by the fifth-density friend which greets you.

Although you may be less than pleased with the accoutrements, may we say that all was as carefully prepared as each was able. More than that, none can do. Therefore, we thank each for the careful alignments. All is well.

We leave you, my friends, in the love and in the light of the One

Glorious Infinite Creator. Go forth, then, rejoicing in the power and in the peace of the One. Adonai.

Session 95,
September 2, 1982

RA: I am Ra. I greet you, my friends, in the love and in the light of the One Infinite Creator. We communicate now.

QUESTIONER: Could you first please give me the condition of the instrument?

RA: I am Ra. It is as previously stated.

QUESTIONER: Thank you. What is the situation with respect to our fifth-density negative associate?

RA: I am Ra. The aforenamed entity has chosen various means to further its service, and though each is effective in itself, none leads to the lessening of the dedication to service for others or the valuing of harmonious interaction. Therefore, the entity, though not quiet as it has been, is somewhat depolarized on balance.

QUESTIONER: There seems to be an extremely high probability that we will move from this position to another residence. If we move from this residence and cease using this room for workings with Ra, is there a magically appropriate ritual for closing the use of this place of working, or is there anything that we should do with respect to leaving this particular place?

RA: I am Ra. It would be appropriate to remove from this room and, to a lesser extent, from the dwelling, the charging of what you might call the distortion towards sanctity. To remove this charge, it is valuable either to write upon your paper your own working or to use existing rituals for the deconsecration of a sacred place such as one of your churches.

QUESTIONER: Thank you. The new room that we choose for this working will of course be carefully cleaned, and marred surfaces made well. We shall also use the Banishing Ritual of the Lesser Pentagram prior to a working. Is there anything else that Ra could suggest? I would like, also, to know if there is anything in particular that you might suggest with respect to the particular place that has been chosen for our new location.

RA: I am Ra. We scan the recent memory configurations of the questioner. Firstly, there have been some less-than-harmonious interactions within this dwelling. The dynamics of this interaction were potent enough to attract a lesser thought-form. Therefore, we suggest the salting and ritual cleansing by blessed water of all windows and doorways which offer adit into the domicile or any outbuildings thereof.

Further, we suggest the hanging of the cut garlic clove in the portion of the room which has accommodated those whose enjoyment has turned into a darker emotion, centering upon the area we find you call the wet bar, also the room intended for the sleeping which is found near the kitchen area. The appropriate words used to bid farewell to those of the lower astral shall be used in connection with the hanging of the garlic cloves for the period of approximately thirty-six of your hours. We believe that this is equivalent to two of your night periods and one of your lit periods. This should cleanse the house as you find it, to the extent that it is neutral in its vibrations of harmony, love, and thanksgiving which this group shall then, as the incarnational experience proceeds, offer to the domicile.

QUESTIONER: I am assuming that we would prepare the blessed water the same as we prepare the water for the instrument to drink after a session, and would then wipe the windows and doors with this water. This would probably have to be done in a bucket. I would like to know if this is correct, and what was meant by salting the windows and doors?

RA: I am Ra. Firstly, you may bless the water yourselves or may request so-called holy water from any blessed place; that is, blessed by intention. Secondly, the water shall be carefully shaken from the fingers along the sills of all windows and doors as they have been opened. Thirdly, prior to the sprinkling of this cleansing, blessing sacrament of water, the salt shall be trailed along these sills in a line and again allowed to exist in this configuration for thirty-six to forty-eight hours. Then the virgin broom may ritually sweep the salt out of each window and doorway, sweeping with each stroke the less fortunate of the vibrations within the dwelling which might find coexistence with the group difficult.

QUESTIONER: I assume that you mean that we should put the salt only on the outer doorway sills and not on the inner doorway sills in the house. Is that correct?

RA: I am Ra. This is correct. We cannot express the nature of salt and water and garlic with clarity enough to inform you as to the efficacy with which salt absorbs vibrations which have been requested to move into salt when salt has been given water. We cannot express the full magical nature of your water, nor can we express the likeness and attractiveness of the garlic cut to lower astral forms. The attractiveness is negative, and no service-to-self astral form will accept coexistence with the cut garlic.

Therefore, we offer the suggestions. We also request, carefully, that the broom be clean and that the garlic be burned. The virginity of the broom is most efficacious.

QUESTIONER: Let me see if I have the scenario correctly in mind. I'll repeat my version of it. We would hang fresh-cut garlic in the area of the wet bar and in the area of the bedroom that is adjacent to the kitchen area. We would salt all window sills and all outer-wall door sills and then sprinkle blessed water from our fingers on the salted areas. We would then say the appropriate words to bid farewell to lower astrals. Those words I am not sure of. Would Ra comment on the scenario that I have stated?

RA: I am Ra. Your grasp of our suggestions is good. We note that the salt be poured in the straight line with no gaps. There are various ritual words of blessing and farewell to entities such as you are removing. We might suggest the following.

When the salt is laid, you may repeat, "We praise the One Creator which gave to salt the ability to enable those friends, to which we wish to bid farewell, to find a new home."

As the water is sprinkled, you may say, "We give thanks to the One Creator for the gift of water. Over it the Creator moves Its hand and stirs Its will to be done."

The hanging of the cut garlic may be accompanied by the words "We praise the One Creator for the gift of garlic and bless its ability to offer to those friends to whom we wish to bid farewell the arrow which points their way of egress."

When the sweeping is done, you may say, "We praise the One Creator and give thanksgiving for the spiritual cleanliness of this dwelling place."

As the garlic is burned, you may say, "We give thanks to the One Creator for the gift of spiritual cleanliness in our dwelling place and seal the departure of all those who have left by this exit by the consuming of this substance."

QUESTIONER: Is there any place more appropriate than any other to hang the garlic in the room; for instance, over the windows or anything like that? I know that it is supposed to be hung in the area of the bar, but I meant in the bedroom. Is there any more appropriate place than another?

RA: I am Ra. The windows and the doorways are most appropriate, and, in addition, we suggest the salting and sprinkling of any door which may lead elsewhere than out of the dwelling, in order to afford to the entities the understanding that they are not desired elsewhere within the dwelling.

QUESTIONER: I understand that the garlic is to be used at the bar area and the bedroom that is close to the kitchen and has an exit onto the carport. If I am correct, those are the only two places that it is to be used. This is correct, isn't it?

RA: I am Ra. This is correct.

QUESTIONER: We would like to pick the most appropriate room for sanctifying for the Ra contact. Is there any room that would be most appropriate that Ra could name?

RA: I am Ra. When you have finished with your work, the dwelling shall be as a virgin dwelling in the magical sense. You may choose that portion of the dwelling that seems appropriate, and once having chosen it you may then commence with the same sort of preparation of the place with which you have been familiar here in this dwelling place.

QUESTIONER: I am assuming that the newly chosen place meets the parameters for the best contact with Ra on the exterior of the house, and I would like to ask Ra at this time if there are any suggestions with respect to the exterior of the house.

RA: I am Ra. The dwelling seems surrounded with the trees and fields of your countryside. This is acceptable. We suggest the general principle of preparing each part of your environment as it best suits each in the group with the beauty which each may feel to be appropriate. There is much of blessing in the gardening and the care of surroundings, for when this is accomplished in love of the creation, the second-density flowers, plants, and small animals are aware of this service and return it.

QUESTIONER: On one end of the house are four stalls that have been occupied by horses. Would it be appropriate or necessary to modify in any way the condition of that area even though it is outside the living area?

RA: I am Ra. There has been no undesirable negative energy stored in this area. Therefore, it is acceptable if physically cleaned.

QUESTIONER: Is there any other comment about our new location that Ra could make?

RA: I am Ra. We are gratified that this query was offered to us, for there has been a concentration of negative thought patterns at a distance north to 10° of north, approximately 45 of what you call yards extending therefrom to all four directions in a rectangular but irregular shape.

We ask that the garlic be strung approximately 60–70 feet beyond the far verge of this area, which is approximately 57 yards from the dwelling on a bearing north to 10° of north. We suggest that the garlic be hung in the funnel so that the energies are drawn into the south small end of the funnel and traduced northward and away from the dwelling. The procedure of the hanging will be one for testing your ingenuity, but there are several ways to suspend the substance, and it is well to do so.

QUESTIONER: I envision a cardboard funnel approximately 3 feet in length, and then a small cardboard of the same configuration inside of that funnel, the garlic placed between the two cardboard surfaces so that the garlic actually makes a funnel itself, held in place by the two cardboard cones. The smaller end of the cone would be toward the house, and the larger end would be away from the house.

I would also like to know that I am accurately aware of the position that we are talking about. Taking a specific point on the house such as the front door, I suspect that the direction is up toward the road that leads out of the property. An exact measurement from the doorknob to the center of the area of negativity of which we speak would be helpful. Would Ra comment on that?

RA: I am Ra. We were working from the other side of the dwelling. However, the exact distance is not important due to the generalized

nature of the astral leavings. The heading would be approximately 10°
east of north to 5° east of north. This is not a heading in which absolute fastidiousness needs be paramount. The yardage is approximately
as given. As to the hanging of the garlic, it must be able to be blown
by the wind. Therefore, the structure which was envisioned is less than
optimal. We might suggest the stringing between two placed posts on
either side of the funnel of the strung cloves.

QUESTIONER: Would a wire framework such as chicken wire which
has a small inch-square mesh or something like that shaped into a
cone, with the garlic attached to the cone, with the small end toward
the house and the open end away from the house, strung between two
poles, be appropriate?

RA: I am Ra. That is appropriate. You see in this case the center of the
negativity is as described, but there will be a general cleansing of the
dwelling and its acreage by this means. One action you might take in
order to improve the efficacy of the cleansing of the environment is
the walking of the perimeter with the opened clove in hand, swinging
the clove. No words need be said unless each wishes to silently or
verbally speak those words given for garlic previously.

QUESTIONER: Is there any other thing that we can do to prepare this
new place that Ra could mention at this time?

RA: I am Ra. There are no more-specific suggestions for the specific
location you contemplate. In general, the cleanliness is most helpful.
The removal from the mind complex of those thoughts not of harmony
is most helpful, and those practices which increase faith and will that
the spirit may do its work are most helpful.

QUESTIONER: After the suggestions are accomplished with respect
to cleansing of the property, does Ra anticipate our contact with Ra
will be as efficient there as in this particular place?

RA: I am Ra. All places in which this group dwells in love and thanksgiving are acceptable to us.

QUESTIONER: Thank you. A question has been asked which I will ask
at this time. In processing the catalyst of dreams, is there a universal
language of the unconscious mind which may be used to interpret
dreams, or does each entity have a unique language in its own unconscious mind which it may use to interpret the meaning of dreams?

RA: I am Ra. There is what might be called a partial vocabulary of the dreams, due to the common heritage of all mind/body/spirit complexes. Due to each entity's unique incarnational experiences, there is an overlay which grows to be a larger and larger proportion of the dream vocabulary as the entity gains experience.

QUESTIONER: Thank you. In the last session you indicated in the statement about the immature male meeting the immature female that the information exchanged was quite different with respect to what occurred because of the veil. Would you give an example of the information exchange prior to the veil for the same case?

RA: I am Ra. Given this same case—that is, the random red-ray sexual arousal being activated in both male and female—the communication would far more likely have been to the subject of the satisfying of that red-ray sexual impulse. When this had occurred, other information such as the naming could be offered with clear perception. It is to be noted that the catalyst which may be processed by the pre-veil experience is insignificant compared to the catalyst offered to the thoroughly bemused male and female after the veil. The confusion which this situation, simplistic though it is, offers is representative of the efficiency of the enlargement of the catalytic processes occurring after the veiling.

QUESTIONER: For the condition of meeting after the veiling process, either entity will choose, as a function of its previous biases or Card Four, the experience and the way in which it will handle the situation with respect to polarity, therefore probably producing more catalyst for itself along the chosen path of polarization. Would Ra comment on this statement?

RA: I am Ra. This statement is correct.

QUESTIONER: In Card Four, in the last session we spoke of the shape of the skirt, and it has occurred to us that the skirt of the entity representing the archetype of the Experience of the Mind is extended to the left to indicate that other-selves would not be able to get close to this entity if it had chosen the left-hand path. There would be a greater separation between it and other-selves, whereas if it had chosen the right-hand path, there would be much less of a separation. Would Ra comment on that observation?

RA: I am Ra. The student is perceptive.

QUESTIONER: And it seems that the square upon which the entity sits, which is almost totally black, is a representation of the material illusion, and the white cat is guarding the right-hand path, which is now separated in experience from the left. Would Ra comment on that observation?

RA: I am Ra. O student, your sight almost sees that which was intended. However, the polarities need no guardians. What, then, O student, needs the guard?

QUESTIONER: What I meant to say was that the entity is guarded along the right-hand path, once it has chosen this path, from effects of the material illusion that are of the negative polarity. Would Ra comment on that?

RA: I am Ra. This is an accurate perception of our intent, O student. We may note that the great cat guards in direct proportion to the purity of the manifestations of intention and the purity of inner work done along this path.

QUESTIONER: From that statement I interpret the following. If the Experience of the Mind has sufficiently chosen the right-hand path, and as total purity is approached in the choosing of the right-hand path, then total imperviousness from the effect of the left-hand catalyst is also approached. Is this correct?

RA: I am Ra. This is exquisitely perceptive. The seeker which has purely chosen the service-to-others path shall certainly not have a variant apparent incarnational experience. There is no outward shelter in your illusion from the gusts, flurries, and blizzards of quick and cruel catalyst.

However, to the pure, all that is encountered speaks of the love and the light of the One Infinite Creator. The cruelest blow is seen with an ambiance of challenges offered and opportunities to come. Thusly, the great pitch of light is held high above such an one so that all interpretation may be seen to be protected by light.

QUESTIONER: I have often wondered about the action of random and programmed catalyst with respect to the entity with the very strong positive or negative polarization. Would either polarity be free to a great extent from random catalyst such as great natural catastrophes or warfare or something like that which generates a lot of random catalyst in the physical vicinity of a highly polarized entity? Does this great cat, then, have an effect on such random catalyst on the right-hand path?

RA: I am Ra. In two circumstances this is so. Firstly, if there has been the pre-incarnative choice that, for instance, one shall not take life in the service of the cultural group, events shall fall in a protective manner. Secondly, if any entity is able to dwell completely in unity, the only harm that may occur to it is the changing of the outward physical, yellow-ray vehicle into the more light-filled mind/body/spirit complex's vehicle by the process of death. All other suffering and pain is as nothing to one such as this.

We may note that this perfect configuration of the mind, body, and spirit complexes, while within the third-density vehicle, is extraordinarily rare.

QUESTIONER: Am I to understand, then, that there is no protection at all if the Experience of the Mind has chosen the left-hand path and that path is traveled? All random catalyst may affect the negatively polarized individual as a function of the statistical nature of the random catalyst. Is this correct?

RA: I am Ra. This is correct. You may note some of those of your peoples which, at this space/time nexus, seek places of survival. This is due to the lack of protection when service to self is invoked.

QUESTIONER: The possibility of the legs of the entity of Card Four being at right angles was linked with the tesseract,[8] mentioned in a much earlier session by Ra, as the direction of transformation from space/time into time/space, and I was thinking that possibly it was also linked with the crux ansata. Am I in any way correct in this observation?

RA: I am Ra. This shall be the last query of this working, as transferred energy wanes. The observation of the right angles and their transformational meaning is most perceptive, O student. Each of the images leading to the Transformations of Mind, Body, and Spirit and ultimately to the great transformative Choice has the increasing intensity of increasing articulation of concept; that is to say, each image in which you find this angle may increasingly be seen to be a more and more stridently calling voice of opportunity to use each resource, be it experience as you now observe or further images, for the grand work of the adept which builds towards transformation using the spirit's bountiful shuttle to intelligent infinity. Please ask any brief queries at this space/time.

---

8. tesseract: in speculative mathematics, a cube which has developed at least one additional dimension.

QUESTIONER: Is there anything that we can do to make the instrument more comfortable or to improve the contact?

RA: I am Ra. We observe some small worsening of the distortions of the dorsal side. This is due to the nature of the beginning use of the swirling waters. The difficulties are physically accentuated as the swirling waters begin to aid the musculature surrounding the nexi of distortions. We encourage the swirling waters and note that complete immersion in them is somewhat more efficacious than the technique now used.

We ask that the support group attempt to aid the instrument in remembering to preserve the physical energies and not expend them upon movements associated with the packing, as you call this activity, and the movement between geographical locations upon your sphere.

The alignments are excellent. All is well.

We leave you glorying in the love and in the light of the One Infinite Creator. Go forth, therefore, rejoicing in the mighty peace of the One Infinite Creator. Adonai.

Session 96,
September 9, 1982

RA: I am Ra. I greet you in the love and in the light of the One Infinite Creator. We communicate now.

QUESTIONER: Could you first please give me the condition of the instrument?

RA: I am Ra. The physical-energy deficit is significantly greater than the last asking. There has been substantive lessening also of the vital energies, although the perquisite degree of energy for mental/emotional distortions of normalcy are yet available.

QUESTIONER: The instrument asks if the house which is to be our new location is capable of being transformed by painting and cleaning. We don't plan to put down all new carpets. Would cleaning the carpets that are there now be acceptable?

I want to bring this particular house up to acceptable limits so that it is neutral after we do the salting. I have a concern only for the conditions for our work there. The physical location isn't that important. In fact, I don't consider that important at all. Could Ra comment on this?

RA: I am Ra. It is, of course, the preference of this group which is the only consideration in the situation for the contact with Ra. The domicile in question has already been offered a small amount of blessing by this group through its presence, and, as we have previously stated, each of your days spent in love, harmony, and thanksgiving will continue transforming the dwelling.

It is correct, as we have previously stated, that physical cleanliness is most important. Therefore, the efforts shall be made to most thoroughly cleanse the dwelling. In this regard it is to be noted that neither in the dwelling as a whole wherein you now reside or in the chamber of this working is there an absence of your dust, earth, and other detritus which is in toto called dirt. If the intention is to clean, as much as is physically possible, the location, the requirements for physical cleanliness are fulfilled. It is only when a lower astral entity has, shall we say, placed portions of itself in the so-called dirt that care should be taken to remove the sentient being. These instructions we have given.

May we note that just as each entity strives in each moment to become more nearly one with the Creator but falls short, just so is physical spotlessness striven for but not achieved. In each case the purity of intention and thoroughness of manifestation are appreciated. The variance between the attempt and the goal is never noted and may be considered unimportant.

QUESTIONER: The sequence of events that I am considering is first the painting and then the cleaning, then the moving in of the furniture, then the salting and use of garlic. Is this as good as any other sequence, or would another sequence be better?

RA: I am Ra. Any sequence which results in the cleansing is acceptable. It is to be noted that the thresholds are not to be crossed during the cleansing. Since such stricture upon use of the limen may affect your considerations, we make note of this.

QUESTIONER: Would Ra comment on the technique of blessing the water that we will use to sprinkle the salt? I assume that we just sprinkle the water directly off of our finger tips onto the line of salt. How much water, in general, should be sprinkled on the salt? How wet should we get it? I would like to get this done right.

RA: I am Ra. The blessing of the water may be that one we have previously given, or it may be that one which is written within the liturgy of this instrument's distortion of the worship of the One Creator, or it may simply be obtained from what you call your Catholic Church in the form of holy water.

The intention of blessing is the notable feature of blessed water. The water may be sprinkled not so that all salt is soaked but so that a goodly portion has been dampened. This is not a physical working. The substances need to be seen in their ideal state so that water may be seen to be enabling the salt.

QUESTIONER: I have planned to redraw the Tarot cards, omitting the extraneous additions by those who came after Ra, and I would like quickly to go through those things that I intend to eliminate from each card and ask Ra if there is anything else that should be eliminated to make the cards as they were before the astrological and other appendages were added.

I would eliminate all of the letters from the edge of the card, with the possible exception of the number of the card. That would be the case for all of the cards. In Card Number One I would eliminate the star and the wand in the Magician's hand, and I understand that the sphere remains, but I am not really sure where it should be. Would Ra comment on that please?

RA: I am Ra. Firstly, the elimination of letters is acceptable.

Secondly, the elimination of stars is acceptable in all cases.

Thirdly, the elimination of the wand is appropriate.

Fourthly, the sphere may be seen to be held by the thumb and index and second finger.

Fifthly, we would note that it is not possible to offer what you may call a pure deck, if you would use this term, of Tarot due to the fact that when these images were first drawn, there was already distortion in various and sundry ways, mostly cultural.

Sixthly, although it is good to view the images without the astrological additions, it is to be noted that the more general positions, phases, and characteristics of each concept complex are those which are significant. The removal of all distortions is unlikely and, to a great extent, unimportant.

QUESTIONER: I didn't think that we could ever remove all distortions, but it is very difficult to work with or interpret these cards because of the quality of the drawing, and as we go through them we get a better idea of what some of these things are and how they should be drawn. I think that we can improve on the quality of the cards and also remove some of the extraneous material that is misleading.

On the second card we should remove the letters and the stars. At the center of the female form here, she is wearing something that looks some-thing like a crux ansata, and we should change that. Is that correct?

RA: I am Ra. We perceive an incomplete query. Please requestion.

QUESTIONER: I think that I should put a crux ansata in the place of this thing that looks a little like a crux ansata on the front of the female. Is that correct?

RA: I am Ra. This is correct.

QUESTIONER: Then as to the thing that she wears on her head, that, I believe, is a bit confusing. What should it be shaped like?

RA: I am Ra. We shall allow the student to ponder this point. We note that although it is an astrologically based addition to the concept complex, it is not entirely unacceptable when viewed with a certain feeling. Therefore, we suggest, O student, that you choose whether to remove the crown or to name its meaning in such a way as to enhance the concept complex.

QUESTIONER: Would Ra please give me any information possible on the ratios of dimensions, and the shape of the crux ansata as it should be made or drawn?

RA: I am Ra. No.

QUESTIONER: In Card Number Three we will remove all the letters and the stars, and I assume that the little cups around the outside of the rays representing the sun should be removed? Is that correct?

RA: I am Ra. Yes.

QUESTIONER: In Card Number Four we will remove all the letters and the stars, and it seems that again we have a situation of removing the wand and putting the sphere in the hand. Is that correct?

RA: I am Ra. Again, this is a matter of choice. Though astrological in nature, this particular scepter has possibilities of relevance in the originally intended concept complex.

This instrument is experiencing some small lack of that distortion which you call proper breathing due to the experience of your near past, as you perceive it. Therefore, as this instrument has requested a substantial enough amount of transferred energy to be retained that it might effect a comfortable re-entry, we shall at this time ask for one more query, after noting the following.

We did not complete our statement upon the dimensions of the crux ansata. It is given in many places. There are decisions to be made as to which drawing of this image is the appropriate one. We may, of course, suggest viewing the so-called Great Pyramid if the puzzle is desired. We do not wish to work this puzzle. It was designed in order that in its own time it be deciphered. In general, of course, this image has the meaning previously stated.

QUESTIONER: Is there anything that we can do to make the instrument more comfortable or to improve the contact?

RA: I am Ra. Continue in harmony, communication, praise, and thanksgiving.

We would note that this instrument's distortions would be lessened were it to refrain from the speaking to some extent for a diurnal period or perhaps two if the difficulty remains. We would also recommend against the activity such as running, which would cause rapid respiration. This aftereffect of the greeting is not necessarily long-lasting. However, as this instrument has some blood vessels in the forward regions of the skull—that is, the integument covering the skull—which are greatly swollen at this time, and since this instrument has the distortion known as the streptococcal infection, it is best to be full of care for a short period in order that the distortions do not catapult the entity into longer-term aftereffects.

All is well. We find the alignments satisfactory.

I am Ra. I leave you in the love and light of the Infinite One. Go forth, therefore, rejoicing in the power and in the peace of the One Infinite Creator. Adonai.

Session 97,
September 15, 1982

RA: I am Ra. I greet you in the love and in the light of the One Infinite Creator. We communicate now.

QUESTIONER: Could you first please give me the condition of the instrument?

RA: I am Ra. It is as previously stated.

QUESTIONER: What is the situation with our fifth-density negative friend?

RA: I am Ra. It is as previously stated.

QUESTIONER: Are there any items in the first four cards not of Ra's intention that we could remove to present a less confusing card as we make our new drawings?

RA: I am Ra. We find much material in this query which would constitute repetition. May we suggest rephrasing the query?

QUESTIONER: Possibly I didn't phrase that the way I meant to. We had already determined the items that should be removed from the first four cards, and my question was this: Had I missed anything that should be removed that was not of Ra's original intention?

RA: I am Ra. We shall repeat our opinion that there are several concepts which, in each image, are astrologically based. However, these concepts are not without merit within the concept complex intended by Ra, given the perception by the student of these concepts in an appropriate manner.

We wish not to form that which may be considered by any mind/body/spirit complex to be a complete and infallible series of images. There is a substantial point to be made in this regard. We have been, with the questioner's aid, investigating the concept complexes of the great architecture of the archetypical mind. To more clearly grasp the nature, the process, and the purpose of archetypes, Ra provided a series of concept complexes. In no way whatsoever should we, as humble messengers of the One Infinite Creator, wish to place before the consideration of any mind/body/spirit complex which seeks its evolution the palest tint of the idea that these images are anything but a resource for working in the area of the development of the faith and the will.

To put this into perspective, we must gaze then at the stunning mystery of the One Infinite Creator. The archetypical mind does not resolve any paradoxes or bring all into unity. This is not the property of any source which is of the third density. Therefore, may we ask the student to look up from inward working and behold the glory, the might, the majesty, the mystery, and the peace of oneness. Let no consideration of bird or beast, darkness or light, shape or shadow, keep any which seeks from the central consideration of unity.

We are not messengers of the complex. We bring the message of unity. In this perspective only may we affirm the value to the seeker of adepthood of the grasping, articulating, and use of this resource of the deep mind exemplified by the concept complex of the archetypes.

QUESTIONER: Thank you. Card Number Five, the Significator of the Mind, indicates, firstly, as I see it, simply a male within a rectangularly structured form which suggests to me that the Significator of the Mind in third density is well bounded within the illusion, as is also suggested by the fact that the base of the male is a rectangular form showing no ability for movement. Would Ra comment on that?

RA: I am Ra. O student, you have grasped the barest essence of the nature of the Significator's complete envelopment within the rectangle. Consider for the self, O student, whether your thoughts can walk. The abilities of the most finely honed mentality shall not be known without the use of the physical vehicle which you call the body. Through the mouth the mind may speak. Through the limbs the mind may effect action.

QUESTIONER: The entity looks to the left, indicating that the mind has the tendency to notice more easily catalyst of a negative essence. Would Ra comment on that observation?

RA: I am Ra. This is substantially correct.

QUESTIONER: There are two small entities at the bottom, one black and one white. I will first ask Ra if this drawing is correct in the coloring. Is the black one in the proper position with respect to Ra's original drawings?

RA: I am Ra. That which you perceive as black was first red. Other than this difference, the beings in the concept complex are placed correctly.

QUESTIONER: The red coloration is a mystery to me. We had originally decided that these represented the polarization of the mind. Would Ra comment on that?

RA: I am Ra. The indications of polarity are as presumed by the questioner. The symbolism of old for the left-hand path was the russet coloration.

We shall pause at this time if the questioner will be patient. There are fairly serious difficulties with the instrument's throat. We shall attempt to ameliorate the situation and suggest the rewalking of the Circle of One.

[The Circle of One was rewalked, and breath expelled 2 feet above the instrument's head.]

RA: I am Ra. Please continue.

QUESTIONER: What was the nature of the problem?

RA: I am Ra. The fifth-density entity which greets this instrument affected a previous difficulty distorting the throat and chest area of the instrument. Some fraction of this distortion remained unmentioned by the instrument. It is helpful if the instrument speaks as clearly as possible to the support group of any difficulties that more care may be taken.

However, we find very little distortion left in the chest area of the instrument. However, immediately preceding the working, the instrument was offered an extreme activation of what you may call the allergies, and the mucous from the flow which this distortion causes began to cause difficulty to the throat. At this juncture the previous potential for the tightening of the throat was somewhat activated by reflex of the yellow-ray, chemical body, over which we have only gross control.

We would appreciate you reminding us to cause this instrument to cough before or after each query for the remainder of this working. Once conscious, this instrument should have no serious difficulty.

QUESTIONER: I was wondering why the dark entity was on the right side of the card in relation to the Significator. Could Ra comment on that after making the instrument cough?

RA: [Cough] The nature of . . . We pause.

[Ten-second pause]

I am Ra. There was a serious pain flare. We may now continue.

The nature of polarity is interesting in that those experiences offered to the Significator as positive frequently become recorded as productive of biases which may be seen to be negative, whereas the fruit of those experiences apparently negative is frequently found to be helpful in the development of the service-to-others bias. As this is perhaps the guiding characteristic of that which the mind processes and records, these symbols of polarity have thusly been placed.

You may note that the hands of the central image indicate the appropriate bias for right- and left-hand working; that is, the right hand gestures in service to others, offering its light outward. The left hand attempts to absorb the power of the spirit and point it for its use alone.

QUESTIONER: The eight cartouches at the bottom would possibly signify the energy centers and the evolution through those centers with the possibility for positive or negative polarization because of the white and black coloration of the figures. Would Ra comment on that after making the instrument cough?

RA: [Cough] I am Ra. The observations of the student are perceptive. It is informative to continue the study of octaves in association with this concept complex. Many are the octaves of a mind/body/spirit complex's beingness. There is not one that does not profit from being pondered in connection with the considerations of the nature of the development of polarity exemplified by the concept complex of your Card Number Five.

QUESTIONER: Do the symbols on the face of each of these little cartouches such as the birds and the other symbols have a meaning in this card that is of value in considering the archetypes? Could you answer that after making the instrument cough?

RA: [Cough] I am Ra. These symbols are letters and words much as your language would receive such an entablature. They are, to a great extent, enculturated by a people not of your generation. Let us, in the rough, suggest that the information written upon these cartouches be understood to be such as the phrase "And you shall be born again to eternal life."

QUESTIONER: Thank you. I thought that the wings on top of the card might indicate the protection of the spirit over the process of evolution. Would Ra comment on that after having the instrument cough?

RA: [Cough] I am Ra. We shall end this session, for we are having considerable difficulty in using the sympathetic nervous system in order to aid the instrument in providing sufficient of your air for its respiration. Therefore, we prematurely suggest ending this session.

Is there any brief query before we leave this instrument?

QUESTIONER: It's not necessary to answer this if you want to end right now for the instrument's benefit, but is there anything that we can do to improve the contact or make the instrument more comfortable?

RA: I am Ra. All is well. The support group functions well.

It is suggested that the instrument be encouraged to take steps to recover completely from the distortion towards the aching of the throat and, to a lesser extent, the chest. There is no way in which we or you may remove that working which has been done. It simply must be removed by physical recovery of the normal distortion. This is not easy due to this instrument's tendency towards allergy.

The alignments are being carefully considered.

I am Ra. I leave you, my friends, glorying and rejoicing in the love and the light of the Infinite Creator. Go forth, then, in the great dance, empowered by the peace of the One Infinite Creator. Adonai.

Session 98, September 24, 1982, contains only personal material and was, for that reason, removed.

Session 99,
November 18, 1982

RA: I am Ra. I greet you in the love and in the light of the One Infinite Creator. We communicate now.

QUESTIONER: Would you please give me the condition of the instrument?

RA: I am Ra. This instrument's physical deficit continues but has the potential for the lessening due to the removal in your probable future of foodstuffs to which the instrument has significant allergy. The vital energy levels are somewhat lessened than the last asking but remain strong. The change in the mental/emotional energy level is towards the distortion of the weakening of this complex.

QUESTIONER: We now have an additional set of Tarot images. Which of these two sets are closer to Ra's original intention?

RA: I am Ra. The principle which moves in accordance with the dynamics of teach/learning with most efficiency is constancy. We could
explore the archetypical mind, using that set of images produced by
the one known as Fathman, or we could use those which have been
used.

In point of fact, those which are being used have some subtleties
which enrich the questioning. As we have said, this set of images is
not that which we gave. This is not material. We could use any of a
multitude of devised Tarot sets. Although this must be at the discretion of the questioner, we suggest the maintaining of one and only
one set of distorted images to be used for the querying, and note that
the images you now use are good.

QUESTIONER: The wings above Card Five, I am guessing, have to do
with a protection over the Significator of the Mind. I am guessing that
they are a symbol of protection. Is this in any way correct?

RA: I am Ra. Let us say that you are not incorrect but rather less than
correct. The Significator owns a covenant with the spirit which it shall
in some cases manifest through the thought and action of the adept.
If there is protection in a promise, then you have chosen the correct
sound vibration, for the outstretched wings of spirit, high above manifestation, yet draw the caged mind onward.

QUESTIONER: Thank you. In Card Number Six I see the Transformation of the Mind, the male with crossed arms, representing
transformation. The transformation is possible either toward the left-
or the right-hand path. The path is beckoned or led by the female, the
Potentiator. The one on the right has the serpent of wisdom at the
brow and is fully clothed, the one on the left having less clothing and
indicating that the Potentiator is more concerned or attracted to the
physical as the left-hand path is chosen and more concerned and attracted to the mental as the right-hand path is chosen.

The creature above points an arrow at the left-hand path, indicating that if this path is chosen, the chips, shall we say, will fall where
they may, the path being unprotected as far as the activity of catalyst.
The intellectual abilities of the chooser of the left-hand path would be
the main guardian rather than the designed or built-in protection of
the Logos for the right-hand path. The entity firing the arrow seems
to be a second-density entity, which indicates that this catalyst could
be produced by a lesser evolved source, you might say. Would Ra comment on these observations?

RA: I am Ra. We shall speak upon several aspects seriatim.

Firstly, let us examine the crossed arms of the male who is to be transformed. What, O student, do you make of the crossing? What see you in this tangle? There is a creative point to be found in this element which was not discussed overmuch by the questioner.

Let us now observe the evaluation of the two females. The observation that to the left-hand path moves the roughly physical and to the right-hand path the mental has a shallow correctness. There are deeper observations to be made concerning the relationship of the great sea of the unconscious mind to the conscious mind which may fruitfully be pursued. Remember, O student, that these images are not literal. They haunt rather than explicate.

Many use the trunk and roots of mind as if that portion of mind were a badly used, prostituted entity. Then this entity gains from this great storehouse that which is rough, prostituted, and without great virtue. Those who turn to the deep mind, seeing it in the guise of the maiden, go forth to court it. The courtship has nothing of plunder in its semblance and may be protracted, yet the treasure gained by such careful courtship is great. The right-hand and left-hand transformations of the mind may be seen to differ by the attitude of the conscious mind towards its own resources as well as the resources of other-selves.

We now speak of that genie, or elemental, or mythic figure, culturally determined, which sends the arrow to the left-hand transformation. This arrow is not the arrow which kills but rather that which, in its own way, protects. Those who choose separation, that being the quality most indicative of the left-hand path, are protected from other-selves by a strength and sharpness equivalent to the degree of transformation which the mind has experienced in the negative sense. Those upon the right-hand path have no such protection against other-selves, for upon that path the doughty seeker shall find many mirrors for reflection in each other-self it encounters.

QUESTIONER: In the previous session you mentioned the use of the forty-five-minute interval of the tape recorders as a signal for the end of the session. Is this still the appropriate time?

RA: I am Ra. This is, of course, at the discretion of the questioner, for this instrument has some transferred energy and remains open as it has unfailingly done. However, the fragility of the instrument has been more and more appreciated by us. We, in the initial observations, saw the strength of will and overestimated greatly the recuperative abilities of the physical complex of this entity.

Therefore, we may say that ending a working at approximately this amount of energy expenditure—that is, some point soon following upon the sound vibration of which you speak—would be appropriate and, insofar as we may determine, may well extend the incarnational amount of your space/time which this instrument shall be able to offer to this contact.

QUESTIONER: In that case I will just ask this short question as we terminate this session. I want to know if the Logos of this system planned for the mating process as possibly depicted in Card Six—I don't know if this is related to some type of DNA imprinting. In many second-density creatures there seems to be some sort of imprinting that creates a lifetime mating relationship, and I was wondering if this was also carried into third density.

RA: I am Ra. There are some of your second-density fauna which have instinctually imprinted monogamous mating processes. The third-density physical vehicle which is the basic incarnational tool of manifestation upon your planet arose from entities thusly imprinted, all the aforesaid being designed by the Logos.

The free will of third-density entities is far stronger than the rather mild carryover from second-density DNA encoding, and it is not part of the conscious nature of many of your mind/body/spirit complexes to be monogamous due to the exercise of free will. However, as has been noted, there are many signposts in the deep mind indicating to the alert adept the more efficient use of catalyst. As we have said, the Logos of your peoples has a bias towards kindness.

QUESTIONER: Thank you. In closing I will ask if there is anything that we can do to make the instrument more comfortable or to improve the contact?

RA: I am Ra. We note the relative discomfort of this group at this space/time and offer those previous statements made by Ra as possible aids to the regaining of the extraordinary harmony which this group has the capability of experiencing in a stable manner.

We find the addition of the swirling waters to be helpful. The appurtenances are conscientiously aligned.

We encourage the conscious strengthening of those invisible rib-bands which fly from the wrists of those who go forward to seek what you may call the Grail. All is well, my friends. We leave you in hopes that each may find true colors to fly in that great metaphysical quest, and urge each to urge each other in love, praise, and thanksgiving.

I am Ra. We leave you in the love and light of the One Infinite Creator. Go forth rejoicing in the power and in the peace of the One Glorious Infinite Creator. Adonai.

Session 100,
November 29, 1982

RA: I am Ra. I greet you, my friends, in the love and in the light of the One Infinite Creator. We communicate now.

QUESTIONER: Could you first please give me the condition of the instrument?

RA: I am Ra. It is as previously stated with the exception of the vital-energy distortion, which leans more towards strength/weakness than the last asking.

QUESTIONER: Thank you. To continue with the Tarot, I would like to make the additional observation with respect to Card Number Six that with the male's arms being crossed, if the female to his right pulls on his left hand it would turn his entire body, and the same is true for the female on the left pulling on his right hand from the other side. This is my interpretation of what is meant by the tangle of the arms. The transformation, then, occurs by the pull, which tends to turn the entity toward the left- or the right-hand path. Would Ra comment on that observation?

RA: I am Ra. We shall. The concept of the pull towards mental polarity may well be examined in the light of what the student has already accreted concerning the nature of the conscious, exemplified by the male, and the unconscious, exemplified by the female. Indeed, both the prostituted and the virginal of deep mind invite and await the reaching.

In this image of Transformation of Mind, then, each of the females points the way it would go, but is not able to move, nor are the two female entities striving to do so. They are at rest. The conscious entity holds both and will turn itself one way or the other or, potentially, backwards and forwards, rocking first one way then the other and not achieving the transformation. In order for the Transformation of Mind to occur, one principle governing the use of the deep mind must be abandoned.

It is to be noted that the triangular shape formed by the shoulders and crossed elbows of consciousness is a shape to be associated with transformation. Indeed, you may see this shape echoed twice more in the image, each echo having its own riches to add to the impact of this complex of concepts.

QUESTIONER: Thank you. We will probably return to this card in the next session with more observations after we consider Ra's comments. To make efficient use of our time, at this time I will make some notes with respect to Card Seven.

First, the veil between the conscious and unconscious mind is removed. The veil, I assume, is the curtain at the top and is lifted. Even though this veil has been removed, the perception of intelligent infinity is still distorted by the beliefs and means of seeking of the seeker. Would Ra comment on that?

RA: I am Ra. As one observes the veil of the image of the Great Way of Mind, it may be helpful to ideate using the framework of environment. The Great Way of Mind, Body, or Spirit is intended to limn the milieu within which the work of mind, body, or spirit shall be placed.

Thusly, the veil is shown both somewhat lifted and still present, since the work of mind and its transformation involves progressive lifting of the great veil betwixt the conscious and deep minds. The complete success of this attempt is not properly a portion of third-density work and, more especially, third-density mental processes.

QUESTIONER: The fact that the veil is raised higher on the right-hand side indicates to me that the adept choosing the positive polarity would have greater success in penetrating the veil. Would Ra comment?

RA: I am Ra. This is a true statement if it is realized that the questioner speaks of potential success. Indeed, your third-density experience is distorted or skewed so that the positive orientation has more aid than the so-called negative.

QUESTIONER: It would also seem to me that since Ra stated in the last session that the limit of the viewpoint is the source of all distortions,[9] the very nature of the service-to-self distortions that create the left-hand path are a function of the veil. Therefore, they are dependent, you might say, to some degree on at least a partial continued veiling. Does this make any sense?

---

9. Ra made this statement in response to a personal question, which, along with its answer, was removed from the last session.

RA: I am Ra. There is the thread of logic in what you suppose. The polarities are both dependent upon a limited viewpoint. However, the negative polarity depends more heavily upon the illusory separation betwixt the self and all other mind/body/spirit complexes. The positive polarity attempts to see through the illusion to the Creator in each mind/body/spirit complex but for the greater part is concerned with behaviors and thoughts directed towards other-selves in order to be of service. This attitude, in itself, is full of the stuff of your third-density illusion.

QUESTIONER: The crown of three stars, we are guessing, would represent the balancing of the mind, body, and spirit. Is this in any way correct?

RA: I am Ra. This device is astrological in origin, and the interpretation given somewhat confusing. We deal, in this image, with the environment of mind. It is perhaps appropriate to release the starry crown from its stricture.

QUESTIONER: The small black—or russet—and white entities have changed so that they now appear to be sphinxes, which we are assuming means that the catalyst has been mastered. I am also assuming that they act as the power that moves the chariot depicted here, so this mastery enables the mind in its transformation to become mobile, unlike it was prior to this mastery, locked as it was within the illusion. Would Ra comment?

RA: I am Ra. Firstly, we ask that the student consider the Great Way not as the culmination of a series of seven activities or functions but as a far more clearly delineated image of the environment within which the mind, body, or spirit shall function. Therefore, the culturally determined creatures called sphinxes do not indicate mastery over catalyst.

The second supposition, that of placing the creatures as the movers of the chariot of mind, has far more virtue. You may connote the concept of time to the image of the sphinx. The mental and mental/emotional complex ripens and moves and is transformed in time.

QUESTIONER: There is the forty-five-minute signal. Does Ra suggest a termination of this session, taking into consideration the instrument's condition?

RA: I am Ra. Information pertinent to this query has been previously covered. The choice of termination time, as you call it, is solely that of the questioner until the point at which we perceive the instrument beginning to use its vital resources due to the absence of transferred or native physical energy. The instrument remains open, as always.

QUESTIONER: In that case I will ask only one more question, and that will have to do with the sword and the scepter. It seems that the sword would represent the power of the negative adept in controlling other-selves, and the scepter would indicate the power of the positive adept operating in the unity of the mind, body, and spirit. However, they seem to be in the opposite hands than I would have guessed. Would Ra comment on these observations?

RA: I am Ra. These symbols are astrological in origin. The shapes, therefore, may be released from their stricture.

We may note that there is an overriding spiritual environment and protection for the environment of the mind. We may further note that the negatively polarized adept will attempt to fashion that covenant for its own use, whereas the positively polarized entity may hold forth that which is exemplified by the astrological sword; that is, light and truth.

QUESTIONER: Would there be two more appropriate objects or symbols to have the entity in Card Seven holding other than the ones shown?

RA: I am Ra. We leave this consideration to you, O student, and shall comment upon any observation which you may make.

QUESTIONER: Is there anything that we can do to make the instrument more comfortable or to improve the contact?

RA: I am Ra. All is well. The appurtenances are most conscientiously placed. We thank this diligent group. There is much-greater distortion towards harmony at this asking, and we join you in praise and thanksgiving. This is always the greatest boon to improvement of the contact, for it is the harmony of the group which supports this contact.

I am Ra. I leave you in the love and the light of the One. Go forth, therefore, rejoicing in the power and in the peace of the One Infinite Creator. Adonai.

Session 101, December 21, 1982, and Session 102, April 22, 1983, contain only personal material—pertaining to the illnesses of the instrument and the scribe which delayed the Ra contact during the winter—and were, for that reason, removed.

Session 103,
June 10, 1983

RA: I am Ra. I greet you in the love and in the light of the One Infinite Creator. We communicate now.

QUESTIONER: Could you first please give me the condition of the instrument?

RA: I am Ra. The physical distortions of the instrument remain serious. Further, the vital energies of this mind/body/spirit complex are much diminished, although acceptable for the needs of this working. This is to be noted as the lowest or most distorted vital reading of this all-important energy. The mental and mental/emotional distortions are as last seen.

We find the will of the instrument, having been unwisely used, to have encouraged the distortions of vital energy. It is well that the instrument ponder this.

QUESTIONER: What is the situation with respect to the physical problems with the digestive portions of the body that the instrument had previously?

RA: The yellow ray—we must correct ourselves. I am Ra. Please expel breath across this instrument's chest area.

[This was done as directed.]

RA: I am Ra. The channel is now satisfactory. We find the yellow-ray, chemical body of the instrument to be exhausted, but to be attempting the improvement by action such as exercise and diet. We may state that the infection has not completely left the body complex, although it is far less virulent.

QUESTIONER: What is the present situation with respect to our fifth-density, service-to-self-oriented companion?

RA: I am Ra. This entity has, for some period of your space/time, been at rest. However, it has been alerted to the workings taking place, and is soon to be your companion once again.

QUESTIONER: Can Ra recommend anything that the instrument can do, or that we can do, to improve any of the energies of the instrument?

RA: I am Ra. This is previously covered material. We have outlined the path the instrument may take in thought.

QUESTIONER: I didn't mean to cover previously covered material. I was hoping to add to this anything that we could do to specifically focus on at this time, the best possible thing that we or the instrument could do to improve these energies, the salient activity.

RA: I am Ra. Before responding, we ask your vigilance during pain flares, as the channel is acceptable but is being distorted periodically by the severe physical distortions of the yellow-ray, chemical body of the instrument.

Those salient items for the support group are praise and thanksgiving in harmony. These the group has accomplished with such a degree of acceptability that we cavil not at the harmony of the group.

As to the instrument, the journey from worth in action to worth in *esse* is arduous. The entity has denied itself in order to be free of that which it calls addiction.[10] This sort of martyrdom, and here we speak of the small but symbolically great sacrifice of the clothing, causes the entity to frame a selfhood in poorness, which feeds unworthiness unless the poverty is seen to be true richness. In other words, good works for the wrong reasons cause confusion and distortion. We encourage the instrument to value itself and to see that its true requirements are valued by the self. We suggest contemplation of true richness of being.

QUESTIONER: Is there anything else that either we or the instrument could do that would specifically work on the vital energy of the instrument to increase it?

_____

10. The instrument made a New Year's resolution to give up buying clothes for herself for one year.

RA: I am Ra. We have come up against the full stop of free will.

QUESTIONER: In that case, I have a few questions on Card Number Seven in order to finish off our first run-through of the archetypes of the mind. There is a T with two right angles above it on the chest of the entity on Card Seven. We have guessed that the lower T has to do with the possibility of choosing either path in the transformation, and the upper two angles represent the great way of the left and the right-hand paths in the mental transformation that makes the change from space/time into time/space, you might say. This is difficult to express. Is anything correct in this?

RA: I am Ra. Yes.

QUESTIONER: Would Ra comment on that?

RA: I am Ra. The use of the tau[11] and the architect's square is indeed intended to suggest the proximity of the space/time of the Great Way's environment to time/space. We find this observation most perceptive.

The entire mood, shall we say, of the Great Way is indeed dependent upon its notable difference from the Significator. The Significator is the significant self, to a great extent but not entirely influenced by the lowering of the veil.

The Great Way of the Mind, the Body, or the Spirit draws the environment which has been the new architecture caused by the veiling process and, thusly, dipped in the great, limitless current of time/space.

QUESTIONER: I am guessing that the wheels of this chariot indicate the ability of the mind to be able to move in time/space. Is this correct?

RA: I am Ra. We cannot say that the observation is totally incorrect, for there is as much work in time/space as the individual who evokes this complex of concepts has assimilated.

However, it would be more appropriate to draw the attention to the fact that although the chariot is wheeled, it is not harnessed to that which draws it by a physical or visible harness. What then, O Student, links and harnesses the chariot's power of movement to the chariot?

QUESTIONER: I'll have to think about that. I'll come back to that.

---

11. tau: in heraldry, a type of cross called a "tau cross."

We were thinking of replacing the sword in the right hand with the magical sphere and putting a downward-pointing scepter in the left hand, similar to Card Five, the Significator, as symbols more appropriate for this card. Would Ra comment on that, please?

RA: I am Ra. This is quite acceptable, especially if the sphere may be imaged as spherical and effulgent.

QUESTIONER: The bent left leg of the sphinxes indicates a transformation that occurs on the left that doesn't occur on the right, possibly an inability in that position to move. Does this have any merit?

RA: I am Ra. The observation has merit in that it may serve as the obverse of the connotation intended. The position is intended to show two items, one of which is the dual possibilities of the timeful characters there drawn.

The resting is possible in time, as is the progress. If a mixture is attempted, the upright, moving leg will be greatly hampered by the leg that is bent. The other meaning has to do with the same right angle, with its architectural squareness, as the device upon the breast of the actor.

Time/space is close in this concept complex, brought close due to the veiling process and its efficaciousness in producing actors who wish to use the resources of the mind in order to evolve.

QUESTIONER: I am assuming that the skirt is skewed to the left for the same reason that it is in Card Number Four, indicating the distance service-to-self polarized entities keep from others, and I am also assuming that the face is turned to the left for the same reason that it is in Card Number Five, because of the nature of catalyst. Is this roughly correct?

RA: I am Ra. Please expel breath over the breast of the instrument from right to left.

[This was done as directed.]

I am Ra. That is well.

Your previous supposition is indeed roughly correct. We might also note that we, in forming the original images for your peoples, were using the cultural commonplaces of artistic expression of those in Egypt. The face is drawn to the side most often, as are the feet turned. We made use of this and, thus, wish to soften the significance of the sidelong look. In no case thus far in these deliberations, however, has any misinterpretation or unsuitable interpretation been drawn.

QUESTIONER: Our appropriate time limit for this working, I believe, is rapidly approaching, so I would like to ask what was the problem in this session when twice in this session we had to expel breath over the instrument's chest?

RA: I am Ra. This instrument is unaware of the method used to contact Ra. However, its desire was particularly strong, at the outset of this working, for this working to transpire. Thus it inadvertently was somewhat premature in its leaving of the yellow-ray, physical body.

In this state the object was dropped upon the instrument which you call the tie-pin microphone. The unexpected contact caused injury of the chest muscles, and we would advise some care depending from this working to avoid stress so that this injury may heal. There is a metaphysical component to this injury, and, therefore, we wished to be quite sure that all portions of the environment were cleansed. Since this place of working has not its usual level of protection, we used your breath to so cleanse the environment, which was at risk.

QUESTIONER: Is the reason for this lack of protection the fact that it has been a considerable time since we have worked in here?

RA: I am Ra. No.

QUESTIONER: What is the reason?

RA: I am Ra. The lack of regular repetition of the so-called Banishing Ritual is the lack of which we spoke.

QUESTIONER: From this I assume that it would be most appropriate to perform the Banishing Ritual daily in this room. Is this correct?

RA: I am Ra. That is acceptable.

QUESTIONER: I don't want to overtire the instrument. We're running close to time here. I will just ask if there is anything that we can do to improve the contact or to make the instrument more comfortable, and anything else that Ra could state at this time that would aid us?

RA: I am Ra. We find the alignments quite fastidiously observed. You are conscientious. Continue in support, one for the other, and find the praise and thanksgiving that harmony produces. Rest your cares and be merry.

I am Ra. I leave you, glorying in the love and in the light of the One Infinite Creator. Go forth, therefore, rejoicing in the power and in the peace of the One Infinite Creator. Adonai.

NOTE TO OUR READERS: As we look back over the material in Book IV, we find the following statement by Ra from Session 97 to be the key for this beginning of the study of the archetypical mind.

"We wish not to form that which may be considered by any mind/body/spirit complex to be a complete and infallible series of images. There is a substantial point to be made in this regard. We have been, with the questioner's aid, investigating the concept complexes of the great architecture of the archetypical mind. To more clearly grasp the nature, the process, and the purpose of archetypes, Ra provided a series of concept complexes. In no way whatsoever should we, as humble messengers of the One Infinite Creator, wish to place before the consideration of any mind/body/spirit complex, which seeks its evolution, the palest tint of the idea that these images are anything but a resource for working in the area of the development of the faith and the will.

To put this into perspective, we must gaze then at the stunning mystery of the One Infinite Creator. The archetypical mind does not resolve any paradoxes or bring all into unity. This is not the property of any source which is of the third density. Therefore, may we ask the student to look up from inward working and behold the glory, the might, the majesty, the mystery, and the peace of oneness. Let no consideration of bird or beast, darkness or light, shape or shadow, keep any which seeks from the central consideration of unity.

We are not messengers of the complex. We bring the message of unity. In this perspective only may we affirm the value to the seeker of adepthood of the grasping, articulating, and use of this resource of the deep mind exemplified by the concept complex of the archetypes."

EPILOGUE

After 106 sessions, the Ra contact ended with Don Elkin's death on November 7, 1984, after a year of declining health. It was the harmony between the three of us that supported the Ra contact; thus we no longer work with Ra or the trance state but now channel other Confederation sources. If you are interested in our other books, channeling transcripts, interviews, speeches, and more, please visit our archive website at www.llresearch.org. You may reach us by email at contact@ llresearch.org or by "snail-mail" at L/L Research, PO Box 5195, Louisville, KY 40255-0195.

INDEX

T

Tantric yoga, 86
Tarot, 6–7, 17–19, 25, 33, 40, 43, 115–116, 118–119, 123–127, 145, 151, 161, 163–164, 184–185, 192, 195
Tau cross, 201
Telepathy, 135
Thought–form, 16–17, 174
Time/space, 17, 19–20, 30–31, 36, 45, 58, 61, 75–76, 86, 91, 98, 100–101, 105, 112, 133, 182, 201–202
Timelessness, 20, 64
Trance, Ra contact, 41, 115, 205
Tree of life, 6, 18–19

U

UFOs, 6, 106
Unity, 36, 62, 68, 139, 181, 188, 198, 205
Ur, 17

V

Veil of forgetting, 15
Venus, 19, 115–116, 123, 127, 129–130, 137
Vibration, 26, 29, 33, 71, 109, 111, 193–194

W

Wanderers, 63–64, 94, 129–130, 136
War, 106, 128
Water, 37, 50, 65, 119, 125, 174–176, 184
Will, 16–18, 20, 23–27, 29, 31–32, 34–35, 38, 40–45, 47, 49, 52–56, 58–60, 62, 64, 66–73, 75, 77, 82–85, 87–89, 91, 94–96, 98–102, 105–110, 112–117, 119–120, 122, 124, 126–127, 131, 135–138, 140, 142–143, 145, 147–159, 161–162, 165–166, 168–169, 173–180, 183–184, 186, 188–189, 193–196, 198, 200–202, 204–205

Z

Zeta reticuli, 62

ABOUT THE AUTHORS

DON ELKINS was born in Louisville, Kentucky, in 1930. He held a BS and MS in mechanical engineering from the University of Louisville, as well as an MS in general engineering from Speed Scientific School. He was professor of physics and engineering at the University of Louisville for twelve years from 1953 to 1965. In 1965 he left his tenured position and became a Boeing 727 pilot for a major airline to devote himself more fully to UFO and paranormal research. He also served with distinction in the US Army as a master sergeant during the Korean War.

Don Elkins began his research into the paranormal in 1955. In 1962, Don started an experiment in channeling, using the protocols he had learned from a contactee group in Detroit, Michigan. That experiment blossomed into a channeling practice that led eventually to the Law of One material 19 years later. Don passed away on November 7, 1984.

CARLA L. RUECKERT (McCarty) was born in 1943 in Lake Forest, Illinois. She completed undergraduate studies in English literature at the University of Louisville in 1966 and earned her master's degree in library service in 1971.

Carla became partners with Don in 1968. In 1970, they formed L/L Research. In 1974, she began channeling and continued in that effort until she was stopped in 2011 by a spinal fusion surgery. During four of those thirty-seven years of channeling (1981–1984), Carla served as the instrument for the Law of One material.

In 1987, she married Jim McCarty, and together they continued the mission of L/L Research. Carla passed into larger life on April 1, 2015.

JAMES MCCARTY was born in 1947 in Kearney, Nebraska. After receiving an undergraduate degrees from the University of Nebraska at Kearney and a master of science in early childhood education from the University of Florida, Jim moved to a piece of wilderness in Marion County, Kentucky, in 1974 to build his own log cabin in the woods, and to develop a self–sufficient lifestyle. For the next six years, he was in almost complete retreat.

He founded the Rock Creek Research and Development Laboratories in 1977 to further his teaching efforts. After experimenting, Jim decided that he preferred the methods and directions he had found in studying with L/L Research in 1978. In 1980, he joined his research with Don's and Carla's.

Jim and Carla were married in 1987. Jim has a wide L/L correspondence and creates wonderful gardens and stonework. He enjoys beauty, nature, dance, and silence.

NOTE: The Ra contact continued until session number 106. There are five volumes total in The Law of One series, Book I–Book V. There is also other material available from our research group on our archive website, www.llresearch.org.

You may reach us by email at contact@llresearch.org, or by mail at: L/L Research, P.O. Box 5195, Louisville, KY 40255–0195

MATRIX OF THE MIND
Arcanum Number I

THE MAGICIAN

POTENTIATOR OF THE MIND
Arcanum Number II

THE HIGH PRIESTESS

CATALYST OF THE MIND
Arcanum Number III

THE EMPRESS

EXPERIENCE OF THE MIND
Arcanum Number IV

THE EMPEROR

SIGNIFICATOR OF THE MIND
Arcanum Number V

THE HIEROPHANT

TRANSFORMATION OF THE MIND
Arcanum Number VI

THE TWO PATHS OR LOVERS

GREAT WAY OF THE MIND
Arcanum Number VII

THE CHARIOT OR CONQUEROR

THE RA MATERIAL

The Law of One
Book V

The Law of One
Book V

DON ELKINS ☟ CARLA RUECKERT
JAMES ALLEN McCARTY

REDFeather™
MIND | BODY | SPIRIT

4880 Lower Valley Road, Atglen, PA 19310

PERSONAL MATERIAL
Fragments Omitted from the First Four Books

with Commentary by
JIM McCARTY and CARLA L. RUECKERT

CONTENTS

INTRODUCTION

[JIM] The material in this book was originally withheld from publication in the first four books of THE LAW OF ONE series because it is predominantly of a personal or sensitive nature, and it was our feeling that if this material were included, it would be easy for readers to become overly interested in the personalities behind this information, rather than focusing on the information itself. It is now our hope that we may be able to use this same information to illustrate the general application of this material to all seekers of truth. We are certain that this information has general application to people like you because we are people just like you, with the same range of human emotions, the same strengths and weaknesses, and the same desire to know what is loosely called the truth.

The death of Don Elkins, questioner for the Ra contact, in November 1984 marked the end of the Ra contact, because it was the harmony between the three of us that was the primary factor that allowed those of Ra to speak through our group. It is our opinion that in order to be of the most appropriate service, we must simply desire to serve without any conditions put on that desire. It was with that simple desire that we joined as a group at the end of 1980, and within three weeks we were amazed to be part of what developed into the Ra contact. We do not consciously seek a third person with whom to attempt to reestablish contact with those of Ra, because that would not be a full surrender of our will to the Greater Will and would be, rather, the imposition of our lesser and more distorted wills upon what is most appropriate for us as a way of being of service to others. It now feels like the appropriate time to share the last of the information that we have as a fruit of the contact with those of Ra with people who, like us, would like to read whatever Ra might have to say on any subject and use that speaking as catalyst for personal evolution.

Since the personal material comes from many of the 106 sessions that we completed during the Ra contact, it suffers from being quite disjointed. Through our written words we hope to be able to fashion a reasonably coherent fabric of our experiences into which each of the personal segments of the Ra contact may fit. Even the best of what we may write and share with you is mere human opinion. We are quite fallible and do not wish to place any stumbling block in your path, so please disregard any words that do not sound right to you. Use only those that ring true.

[**CARLA**] *Jim has taken the task of describing to you the circumstances in which each fragment was collected. My part is to add my viewpoint on many subjects, but perhaps most importantly on Don and me, which Jim has no way to address, as he did not know either of us until just three years before the contact with those of Ra. I echo Jim's feeling that it is time for the final bits of this contact to be shared. Those who have enjoyed Ra's thoughts will continue to appreciate the bon mots they are so good at giving us. We at L/L can sigh with relief now and say, yes, this is ALL of the material. There ain't no more! And without a doubt, the reader will see from these bits of our lives that we are just as foolish as the rest of humankind and are not to be confused with the source of these channelings. This I have come to count as a valuable thing.*

It has been the greatest privilege and the greatest challenge of my life to have had the care and feeding of Donald Tully Elkins for the last 16 years of his life. Never have two people loved more deeply, yet Don's need to remain aloof was such that none of his feelings were ever displayed to me, and this was my catalyst to work with. I treasured and cherished this dear man the very best I knew how, and honor him as the only truly great man I have ever personally met. It was his driving intellect that first posed the questions that the Ra contact attempted to answer. It was he who had the vision of living as a spiritual family rather than a nuclear one. Jim and I are very fortunate to have had such a man as our leader and ofttimes our teacher. And I have been blessed with a pure and faithful romance with a soulmate who means all to me. As you enjoy this last part of a contact that will likely never come again, just rejoice that Don Elkins lived and served among us wanderers with such devotion and light.

THE FRAGMENTS

Fragment 1

The beginning of Session 1 appears here precisely as it was received. In our first private printing of Book I of *The Law of One* we omitted a portion of this first session because Don felt that compared with the other twenty-five sessions of Book I, it was anomalistic—and perhaps too confusing as such—for first-time readers. That omission was reproduced when the mass market edition was printed by the Donning Company under the title of *The Ra Material*.

This is the only session in which Ra delivered anything close to what Brad Steiger has called a "cosmic sermonette" before beginning with the question-and-answer format that was used exclusively throughout the remainder of the Ra contact. Ra preferred the question-and-answer format because it allowed our free will to decide what information we would seek rather than their determining that choice for us by using the lecture method of teach/learning.

And it was interesting to us that Ra mentioned in this first session that they were not able to offer any "conditioning" to any instrument due to their own transmitting limitations. This conditioning often involves seemingly involuntary movement of some part of the vocal cords, mouth, lip, jaw, or some other physiological sensation that the one serving as instrument identifies with the approach of the contact. This session also marks the last time that Ra ever attempted to speak through any instrument other than Carla.

Since the channeling phenomenon has become so commonplace, we would like to make an additional comment on the conditioning vibration. Many who serve as instruments feel that they recognize the entities who speak through them by the conditioning vibration, and need no other identification to be sure that they are channeling whom they think they are channeling. We have found that this is not always so, because negative entities of the same relative vibration will feel just like the familiar positive entity to the one serving as instrument when the negative entity wishes to call itself by another name and mimic the positive entity as a part of the process of tricking the instrument and then detuning the positive work done by the group receiving its information. This is standard procedure for those of the path of service to self. The fundamental concept involved is that the opportunity for positive entities to speak through instruments and groups must be balanced by the same opportunity being offered to negative entities. This need not be a difficulty for any instrument, however, if it and its support group utilize the twin processes of tuning the group and challenging the contact each time channeling occurs.

Tuning the group is the process whereby each individual in the group refines the desire to serve others and puts it first and foremost in the mind and heart. The group may accomplish this tuning by any method that has meaning to each within the group, whether that be by singing sacred songs, chanting, praying, telling jokes, sharing information, visualizing light surrounding the group, or whatever blends each present into one unified source of seeking.

Then, when the instrument feels the entities that wish to channel through it are present, the challenge is mentally given, again in whatever way that feels appropriate to the instrument and in whatever way that the instrument can get behind with every fiber of its being. The instrument will demand to know if the entities wishing to channel through it come in the name of whatever principle the instrument feels is the highest and best in its own life. One may challenge the entity wishing to speak in the name of Jesus the Christ, the Christ consciousness, the positive polarity, service to others, or in the name of one of the archangels or in whatever represents the center of one's life, that for which the instrument lives and would gladly die. This forms a wall of light through which an entity of negative polarity has as much trouble passing through as you and I would discover with a solid brick wall.

Negative entities stand ready to fill in any lapse of care in this regard with their offering of service in their own way. They mimic the positive contact only as much as necessary to maintain the channel and then give false information whenever possible, usually having to do with dates and descriptions of upcoming cataclysmic earth changes, which, when made public by the group receiving such information, makes the group lose credibility since the dates are never correct. Thus the negative entity takes the spiritual strength of the light that the group had been able to share in service-to-others work.

Carla used this method of challenging Ra for the first two sessions. This was and is her normal method, as she usually does conscious channeling. But in the Ra contact she involuntarily went into trance and could not tune in that way, so we were glad when, at the end of the second session, Ra gave us the ritual of walking the Circle of One to replace the challenging procedure used in telepathic channeling, since in all sessions after the first two, Carla was immediately in the trance state, out of her body, and unaware of any activity whatsoever. None of us ever discovered how she was able to accomplish this trance state and the leaving of her body. It was apparently a pre-incarnatively chosen ability to aid in the contact with Ra. Our meditation before each session was our group process of tuning.

We used what Don called "tuned trance telepathy" to communicate with those of Ra. This is to say that while the contact was ongoing, neither Carla nor those of Ra inhabited Carla's body. Carla's spirit was apparently in the care of those of Ra while Ra used Carla's body from a distance to form the words that responded to Don's questions. Ra mentioned many times that they had only the grossest control over her body and had difficulty, for example, in repositioning her hands when one of them was experiencing pain flares due to her arthritic condition. Carla could not feel these pain flares, but repositioning them was sometimes necessary since the pain was like static on the line. This occurred only occasionally and was always noted in the text.

Don and Carla had been working together for twelve years, channeling, researching, and writing two books in the area of metaphysics before I joined them in December 1980. Unsure of what to do as the first project together, we considered rewriting one of those books, *Secrets of the UFO*, and I had begun background reading and taking notes. Three weeks later the first Ra contact occurred and was totally unexpected. It happened when Carla was conducting a teaching session in which one of the Sunday meditation group members was learning how to channel. Don sat in on the session, but I was out shopping and happened to walk in through the front door loaded with sacks of groceries just as Don was asking about the earth changes that were anticipated at the end of this cycle of growth. At that point Ra requested a moment to deepen Carla's trance state before continuing. Such an interruption never happened again, because after the second session we prepared another room especially for the Ra contact and continued to use the living room for all other meditations and teaching sessions. This first session is one of only four of the total 106 sessions with Ra in which anyone besides Don, Carla, and I attended. Since the three of us lived together, the harmony that we developed between us was very stable and was a critical ingredient in establishing and maintaining the contact.

These days, I am teaching very few people to channel. Through the years, I have seen the kind of havoc that an opened and untuned channel can wreak in the personality of the seeker who channels just for a while, or just for the fun of it. The basic problem with channeling tends to be that the channel needs to be actively attempting to live the message she is receiving. In spiritual work, no one has the luxury of saying, "Do as I say, not as I do." If we do not embody the principles we offer to others, we receive often-dramatic and life-shaking catalyst that points up the divergence of ideals from true intention. I have seen people lose their sanity when carelessly involved with channeling. So I take the responsibility of taking students very, very seriously. For the most part, I now work with people who come to me already channeling, and having difficulties with that. This has involved me with people being moved around the world by signals from Indians, UFO contactees with strange stories, and all manner of diverse folks who are in some way at risk in the "new age" sea of confusion. The phrase "spiritual counselor" has a smug, know-it-all feeling to it, which I hope I do not reflect, but it's pretty much what I am doing these days. Perhaps "spiritual listener" is more accurate. With email there has come a wider opportunity to relate with seekers personally. We welcome anyone's communication here at L/L Research and have never failed to answer any mail sent to us, so please feel free to address questions to us. We're delighted to help in any way we can. Our website address is www.llresearch.org; *our email address is* contact@llresearch.org.

Session 1,
January 15, 1981

RA: I am Ra. I have not spoken through this instrument before. We had to wait until she was precisely tuned as we send a narrow-band vibration. We greet you in the love and in the light of our Infinite Creator.

We have watched your group. We have been called to your group, for you have a need for the diversity of experiences in channeling which go with a more intensive or, as you might call it, advanced approach to the system of studying the pattern of illusions of your body, your mind, and your spirit, which you call seeking the truth. We hope to offer you a somewhat different slant upon the information which is always and ever the same.

The Confederation of Planets in the Service of the Infinite Creator has only one important statement. That statement, my friends, as you know, is that all things, all life, all of the creation is part of one original thought.

We will exercise each channel if we are able to. The reception of our beam is a somewhat more advanced feat than some of the more broad vibration channels opened by other members for more introductory and intermediate work.

Let us for a moment consider thought. What is it, my friends, to take thought? Took you then thought today? What thoughts did you think today? What thoughts were part of the original thought today? In how many of your thoughts did the creation lie? Was love contained? And was service freely given? You are not part of a material universe. You move your body, your mind, and your spirit in somewhat eccentric patterns, for you have not completely grasped the concept that you are part of the original thought.

We would at this time transfer to the instrument known as Don. I am Ra.

[*pause*]

RA: I am Ra. I am again with this instrument. We are close to initiating a contact, but we are having difficulty penetrating a certain mental tension and distraction that are somewhat characteristic of this channel. We will therefore describe the type of vibration which is being sent. The instrument will find us entering the energy field at a slight angle towards the back of the top of the head, in a narrow but strong area of intensity. We are not able to offer any conditioning due to our own transmitting limitations; therefore, if the instrument can feel this particular effect he may then speak our thoughts as they come to him. We will again attempt this contact. I am Ra.

[*pause*]

RA: This instrument is resisting our contact. However, we assure you that we are satisfied that contact with the one known as Don is not preferable to that instrument. We will, therefore, move on to the one known as Leonard. Again we caution the instrument that it is a narrow band of communication which is felt as a vibration entering the aura. We will now transfer this contact. I am Ra.

[*pause*]

RA: I am Ra. We greet you once more in the love and the light of our Infinite Creator. We ask that you be patient with us. We are a difficult channel to receive. We may perhaps add some dimensions to your understanding. At this time we would be glad to attempt to speak to any subject or question which those entities in the room may have potential use in the requesting.

Fragment 2

The following material in Session 6 concerns the basic requirement for the Ra contact; that is, harmony. During the 106 sessions with Ra, there were only three people who ever attended a Ra session besides the three of us, and in each case it was Ra's recommendation that each entity needed not only to have the appropriate attitude in its personal means of seeking, but that each person needed to be in harmony with each of us before attending any session. In Tom's case this was achieved by Don's explaining to Tom the meaning that the Bible, candle, incense, and chalice of water held for us as triggering mechanisms or signals to our subconscious minds that a session was about to take place, and that from all levels of our being we should begin the process of purifying our desires to serve others above all else and to surround ourselves with the joy-filled light of praise and thanksgiving. The harmony that this process produced among our group, then, was much as a musical chord with which those of Ra could blend their vibrations, and upon that harmonious blend of vibrations, information of a metaphysical nature could be transmitted by being drawn to those who sought it.

Tom is one of the members of L/L Research's spiritual family who attended our meditation group's Sunday meetings for some years. It is impossible to say how many "members" have come to our sessions over the years since 1962, when we began. Like many of these dear souls, he has kept in touch, although his personal path has taken him elsewhere. We have always attempted to "tune" our circle before we begin to meditate together, so Tom was perfectly clear on what we needed.

That altar, with its Christian accouterments, may well puzzle some who think that it takes a new-age channel to produce new-age information. Not so for me, unless one counts Jesus Christ as a new-age channel himself! I was a cradle Anglican and have attended Episcopal churches my whole life. That those of Ra worked with these deeply ingrained biases within me is, to me, a signal characteristic of this unique source. I felt loved, accepted, and cherished by having these items placed near me, and that they thought this out was a constant blessing during this contact.

Session 6,
January 24, 1981

QUESTIONER: I would like to ask if it is possible for Tom to attend one of these sessions tomorrow. Are you familiar with the entity Tom?

RA: I am Ra. This mind/body/spirit complex sound vibration "Tom" is acceptable. We caution you to instruct this entity in the frame of mind and various appurtenances which it must understand before it is conducted into the circle.

QUESTIONER: I'm not quite sure what you mean by appurtenances.

RA: I was referring to the symbolic objects which trigger this instrument's distortions towards love/light. The placement and loving acceptance of them by all present is important in the nurturing of this instrument. Therefore, the appurtenances involved must be described and their presence explained in your own words of teach/learning, for you have the proper attitude for the required results.

QUESTIONER: The only question that I have is that I will assume that since Leonard was here when you first made contact that it is suitable for him to be here as well as Tom.

RA: This is correct and completes the number of those at this time able to come who are suitable. Again, remember the instructions given for the preparation of the vibratory sound complex Tom.

Fragment 3

Early in the Ra contact we received answers to our questions that fell into a controversial portion of our third-density illusion. Almost everyone, at some point within the study of the paranormal, spends some time being fascinated by the so-called conspiracy theories, which have generally to do with the supposedly unseen groups and individuals who are said to be the real powers behind governments and their activities in the world today. Such theories usually hold that the news reports that we hear and read concerning politics, economics, the military, and so forth are but the tip of a very large iceberg that has mainly to do with various schemes for world domination and that functions through the secret activities of this small, elite group of human beings and their alien allies.

The following information falls into this category and resulted from a follow-up question Don asked about UFOs and their sources. You will note Don's incredulous attitude throughout this portion of his questioning. It was our decision to remove this information from Book I of *The Law of One* because we felt it to be entirely unimportant and of a transient nature, since knowing it adds nothing to one's ability or desire to seek the truth and the nature of the evolutionary process, whether the information is true or not. In fact, knowing and continuing to seek this kind of information can become a major stumbling block to one's spiritual journey because it removes one's attention from the eternal truths that may serve anyone's journey—at any time—and places it upon that which is only of fleeting interest and of little use spiritually. Concentrating on conspiracy theories and their participants tends to reinforce the illusion of separation and ignores the love that binds all things as One Being. If we had continued to pursue this particular line of questioning, or any other line of questioning of a transient nature, we would soon have lost the contact with those of Ra because, as Ra mentioned in the very first session, Ra communicated with us through a "narrow band" of vibration or wave length.

Through various clues that Ra gave us when Don asked about the alignments at the end of each session, we were able to determine that this "narrow band" meant that only information of the purest and most precise nature concerning the process of the evolution of mind, body, and spirit could be successfully transmitted on a sustainable basis through our instrument. To ask Ra questions of a transient nature would be like trying to run a finely tuned engine on crude petroleum.

Many groups become fascinated with transient information of a specific, mundane nature and have their information polluted by negative entities, who gradually replace the positive entities that began their contact. Pursuing information of this kind is like moving the dial on your radio so that you end up with another station altogether from the one with which you began. This change in desire for the kind of information that the group seeks from its contact is the signal to that contact that what it has to offer is no longer desired, and the Law of Free Will requires that only hints of this detuning process be given to the group so that all choices that the group makes are totally a product of its free will. When a group continues to seek the transient information, the positive contact gives hints here and there that such information is not of importance, but when the group persists in seeking this kind of information, the positive contact, in order to observe the free will of the group, must slowly withdraw and is then eventually replaced by a negative contact, which is only too happy to give this kind of information, but with less desire for accuracy and with maximal desire to remove the group from the ranks of those who serve others. When the group has been discredited by false information—such as dates of future disasters that are publicized by the group and then do not occur—then the negative entities have been successful in removing the power of the group's light and have gathered it for themselves.

We still feel that this information is totally unimportant, and the only reason that we include it now is to show how easy it is for a group to get off the track, shall we say, and to lose the focus of desire for that which is important and that with which the group began: the desire to serve others by gathering information that may aid in the evolution of mind, body, and spirit. Ten thousand years from now, it will not matter one whit who did what to whom on this tiny speck of whirling dust. All that will matter is that love may be found at any time in every person and particle of the one creation, or any illusion thereof. Hopefully information gained through any effort such as the Ra contact will help some other third-density entities to discover more of that truth and to move one step further on their evolutionary journey to the One Creator.

All I can add to this is a plea to all official sources: we do not know anything, we are not in on any conspiracies, and please, please don't tap our telephones . . . again! When Don and I joined Andrija Puharich for a mind link in 1977, we caught the attention of some agency who played havoc with our telephone system. And how utterly without use to listen in to our converse! Mystics seldom plot! We honestly don't care about this stuff and just stumbled into it by accident.

I'd like to point out the way those of Ra seem here somewhat off-balance compared to their usual steady selves. It is subtle, but easy to see—the opening to each answer is normally "I am Ra." Several times in this fragment, however, that signature is missing. The contact was going slightly out of tune here, I think, due to the information's transient nature.

Session 8,
January 26, 1981

QUESTIONER: There was a portion of the material from yesterday that I will read where you say, "There is a certain amount of landing taking place. Some of these landings are of your own people; some are of the group known to you as Orion." My first question is, what did you mean that some of the landings are of your peoples?

RA: I am Ra. Your peoples have, at this time/space present, the technological achievement, if you would call it that, of being able to create and fly the shape and type of craft known to you as unidentified flying objects. Unfortunately for the social memory complex vibratory rate of your peoples, these devices are not intended for the service of mankind, but for potential destructive use. This further muddles the vibratory nexus of your social memory complex, causing a situation where neither those oriented towards serving others nor those oriented towards serving self can gain the energy/power which opens the gates to intelligent infinity for the social memory complex. This in turn causes the harvest to be small.

QUESTIONER: Are these craft that are from our peoples from what we call planes that are not incarnate at this time? Where are they based?

RA: I am Ra. These of which we spoke are of third density and are part of the so-called military complex of various of your peoples' societal divisions or structures.

The bases are varied. There are bases, as you would call them, undersea in your southern waters near the Bahamas, as well as in your Pacific seas in various places close to your Chilean borders on the water. There are bases upon your moon, as you call this satellite, which are at this time being reworked. There are bases which move about your lands. There are bases, if you would call them that, in your skies. These are the bases of your peoples, very numerous and, as we have said, potentially destructive.

QUESTIONER: Where do the people who operate these craft come from? Are they affiliated with any nation on Earth? What is their source?

RA: These people come from the same place as you or I. They come from the Creator.

As you intend the question, in its shallower aspect, these people are those in your and other selves' governments responsible for what you would term national security.

QUESTIONER: Am I to understand then that the United States has these craft in undersea bases?

RA: I am Ra. You are correct.

QUESTIONER: How did the United States learn the technology to build these craft?

RA: I am Ra. There was a mind/body/spirit complex known to your people by the vibratory sound complex Nikola. This entity departed the illusion, and the papers containing the necessary understandings were taken by mind/body/spirit complexes serving your security of national divisional complex. Thus your people became privy to the basic technology. In the case of those mind/body/spirit complexes which you call Russians, the technology was given from one of the Confederation in an attempt, approximately twenty-seven of your years ago, to share information and bring about peace among your peoples. The entities giving this information were in error, but we did many things at the end of this cycle in attempts to aid your harvest, from which we learned the folly of certain types of aid. That is a contributing factor to our more cautious approach at this date, even as the need is power upon power greater, and your peoples' call is greater and greater.

QUESTIONER: I'm puzzled by these craft which have undersea bases. Is this technology sufficient to overshadow all other armaments? Do we have the ability to just fly in these craft, or are they just craft for transport? What is the basic mechanism of their power source? It's really hard to believe is what I'm saying.

RA: I am Ra. The craft are perhaps misnamed in some instances. It would be more appropriate to consider them as weaponry. The energy used is that of the field of electromagnetic energy which polarizes the Earth sphere. The weaponry is of two basic kinds: that which is called by your peoples psychotronic and that which is called by your peoples particle beam. The amount of destruction which is contained in this technology is considerable, and the weapons have been used in many cases to alter weather patterns and to enhance the vibratory change which engulfs your planet at this time.

QUESTIONER: How have they been able to keep this a secret? Why aren't these craft in use for transport?

RA: The governments of each of your societal-division illusions desire to refrain from publicity so that the surprise may be retained in case of hostile action from what your peoples call enemies.

QUESTIONER: How many of these craft does the United States have?

RA: I am Ra. The United States has 573 at this time. They are in the process of adding to this number.

QUESTIONER: What is the maximum speed of one of these craft?

RA: I am Ra. The maximum speed of these craft is equal to the Earth energy squared. This field varies. The limit is approximately one-half the light speed, as you would call it. This is due to imperfections in design.

QUESTIONER: Would this type of craft come close to solving many of the energy problems as far as transport goes?

RA: I am Ra. The technology your peoples possess at this time is capable of resolving each and every limitation which plagues your social memory complex at this present nexus of experience. However, the concerns of some of your beings with distortions towards what you would call powerful energy cause these solutions to be withheld until the solutions are so needed that those with the distortion can then become further distorted in the direction of power.

QUESTIONER: You also said that some of the landings at this time were of the Orion group. Why did the Orion group land here? What is their purpose?

RA: I am Ra. Their purpose is conquest, unlike those of the Confederation who wait for the calling. The so-called Orion group calls itself to conquest.

QUESTIONER: Specifically, what do they do when they land?

RA: There are two types of landings. In the first, entities among your peoples are taken on their craft and programmed for future use. There are two or three levels of programming. First, the level that will be discovered by those who do research. Second, a triggering program. Third, a second and most deep triggering program crystallizing the entity, thereby rendering it lifeless and useful as a kind of beacon. This is a form of landing.
The second form is that of landing beneath the Earth's crust, which is entered from water. Again, in the general area of your South American and Caribbean areas and close to the so-called northern pole. The bases of these people are underground.

QUESTIONER: The most startling information that you have given me, which I must admit that I'm having difficulty believing, is that the United States has 573 craft of the type which you described. How many people of United States designation are aware of these craft, including those who operate them?

RA: I am Ra. The number of your peoples varies, for there are needs to communicate at this particular time/space nexus so that the number is expanding at this time. The approximate number is 1,500. It is only approximate, for as your illusory time/space continuum moves from present to present at this nexus, many are learning.

QUESTIONER: Where are these craft constructed?

RA: These craft are constructed one by one in two locations: in the desert or arid regions of your so-called New Mexico and in the desert or arid regions of your so-called Mexico, both installations being under the ground.

QUESTIONER: Am I to believe that the United States actually has a manufacturing plant in Mexico?

RA: I am Ra. I spoke thusly. May I, at this time, reiterate that this type of information is very shallow and of no particular consequence compared to the study of the Law of One. However, we carefully watch these developments in hopes that your peoples are able to be harvested in peace.

QUESTIONER: I am totally aware that this line of questioning is of totally no consequence at all, but this particular information is so startling to me that it makes me question your validity on this. Up until this point I was in agreement with everything you had said. This is very startling to me. It just does not seem possible to me that this secret could have been kept for twenty-seven years, and that we are operating these craft. I apologize for my attitude, but I thought that I would be very honest. It is unbelievable to me that we would operate a plant in Mexico, outside of the United States, to build these craft. Maybe I'm mistaken. These craft are physical craft built by physical people? Could I go get in one and ride in one? Is that correct?

RA: I am Ra. This is incorrect. You could not ride one. The United States, as you call your society divisional complex, creates these as a type of weapon.

QUESTIONER: There are no occupants then? No pilot, shall I say?

RA: I am Ra. This is correct.

QUESTIONER: How are they controlled?

RA: I am Ra. They are controlled by computer from a remote source of data.

QUESTIONER: Why do we have a plant in Mexico?

RA: I am Ra. The necessity is both for dryness of the ground and for a near-total lack of population. Therefore, your so-called government and the so-called government of your neighboring geographical vicinity arranged for an underground installation. The government officials who agreed did not know the use to which their land would be put, but thought it a governmental research installation for use in what you would call bacteriological warfare.

QUESTIONER: Is this the type of craft that Dan Frye was transported in?

RA: I am Ra. The one known as Daniel was, in thought-form, transported by Confederation thought-form vehicular illusion in order to give this mind/body/spirit complex data so that we might see how this type of contact aided your people in the uncovering of the intelligent infinity behind the illusion of limits.

QUESTIONER: The reason that I have questioned you so much and so carefully about the craft which you say the United States government operates is that if we include this in the book, it will create numerous problems. It is something that I am considering leaving out of the book entirely, or I am going to have to question you in considerable detail about it. It's difficult to even question in this area, but I would like to ask a few more questions about it, with the possible option of leaving it in the book. What is the diameter of the craft which the United States has?

RA: I am Ra. I suggest that this be the last question for this session. We will speak as you deem fit in further sessions, asking you to be guided by your own discernment only.

The approximate diameter, given several model changes, is 23 of your feet, as you measure.

Fragment 4

None of us were ever greatly interested in previous incarnational experiences. Again, it's easy to lose the focus on the present moment's opportunities for growth if one becomes overly interested in one's lives before this one. The one query of this nature that we did ask of Ra elicited an answer that seemed to support our lack of interest in past lives.

I do personally believe that we incarnate many times, and that we fashion, through these cycles of manifestation, complex and meaningful relationships that root deeply within our beings. When Don and I met, he has said he knew for certain that we would be together. Since what immediately thereafter ensued for me was a four-year marriage to a fellow who wished not to be married, I once braced him for not having told me this home truth right then in 1962, and saved me that difficult four years. "What? And have you miss all that good catalyst?" he said.

Both Donald and Jim had a loving and generous regard of me that is amazing unless one introduces the concept of previous connections. I have no doubt that we have served together before, in other lives and other times. An interesting bit of possible past history was expressed years ago to Jim in a psychic reading: it was suggested that in the American great plains frontier of the nineteenth century, Don and Jim were brothers living together as farmers. I was Jim's child, Don's nephew, and I lived only to the age of five, being sickly from birth. This was suggested as being preparation for their taking care of me in this life, as I dealt with disability, limitation, and especially psychic greeting during the time of the Ra contact. It rings true at some level with me. However, I also feel that we do not need to know anything of our past associations in order to learn and serve together at this present moment. We have all we need to meet the present moment. The rest is just details.

Session 9,
January 27, 1981

QUESTIONER: Is it possible for you to tell us anything about our past experiences, our past incarnations before this incarnation?

RA: I am Ra. It is possible. However, such information as this is carefully guarded by your mind/body/spirit being totality so that your present space/time experiences will be undiluted.

Let us scan for harmless material for your beingness. I am, in the distortion of desire for your freedom from preconception, able to speak only generally. There have been several times when this group worked and dwelt together. The relationships varied. There is balanced karma, as you call it; each thus teacher of each. The work has involved healing, understanding the uses of the earth energy, and work in aid of civilizations which called just as your sphere has done and we have come. This ends the material which we consider harmless.

Fragment 5

In the first paragraph of the next section, one can see how easy it is for even the most serious of seekers occasionally to lose the proper attitude for finding the heart of the evolutionary process. Properly attuning one's being for efficient seeking has far less to do with what one does than with how one does it and how one balances it or seats it within one's being with meditation and contemplation. Without the balance of the meditative attitude, the mind tends to become distracted by the mundane repetition of events, and one's lessons tend to orbit the periphery of one's being without becoming seated in the center of the being, there to provide a deeper grasp of the nature of this illusion and a sense of how to navigate one's self through it in a more harmonious fashion. We also see in Ra's next response that it is imperative that all such navigational movements of one's being be a product of one's free will choices, never to be abridged by any other being. That point is echoed again in Ra's response to Don's query about the metaphysical implications of attempting to lock a Man in Black in one's closet, an opportunity that we never had, incidentally!

This is another good example of a line of questioning veering off into transient and unimportant information. Note how Ra ends Session 12 in Book I, also titled *The Ra Material*, with hints that the "correct alignment" and "proper orientation" of the Bible, candle, censer, and water are somewhat askew. It took us twelve sessions to determine that Ra was not actually speaking of the physical placement of the Bible and so forth, but Ra was giving us a hint that our metaphysical alignment was off. Our line of questioning was misplaced from the heart of the evolutionary process. Since our contact with Ra was "narrow band," that meant that Ra could not long respond to questions that were off the target. If we had allowed these distortions to remain over a long period of time, the contact would have been impaired and eventually we would have lost the contact.

The last portion of this session deals with the concept of what is called the Wanderers, and their frequently shared characteristics of exhibiting physical ailments such as allergies and personality disorders, which, in the deeper sense, seem to be a reaction against this planet's vibrational frequency. This is apparently a side effect that is due to such entities having another planetary influence in a higher density as their home vibration. They incarnate on this third-density planet in order to be of service in whatever way is possible to help the population of this planet to become more aware of the evolutionary process and to move in harmony with it. These Wanderers go through the same forgetting process that every other third-density being who incarnates here goes through, and they become completely the third-density being—even as they slowly begin to remember why it is that they have been born here. Apparently, about one in every seventy people on Earth is of such an origin.

It almost seems to be in vogue now to say that one is from this or that planet, this or that higher density, and that one is really this or that exalted being come down to Earth to be a great teacher. It is embarrassing to us to see such a magnificent opportunity for rendering a humble service cheapened to a game of who has the most spiritual sergeant's stripes. We do not hide the possibility that we may be of such origins, but neither do we nor those of Ra feel that such an origin is particularly remarkable. As Don used to say, "You've got to be somewhere doing something. You might as well be here doing this."

I think one thing to keep in mind, if we are Wanderers from elsewhere, is that we came here for a reason: to serve at this time right here in this very shadow world of Earth's third density. Yes, we suffer the results of trying to live in a vibratory range that is difficult for us, and yes, we somehow remember a "better way" to live. With this in mind, it becomes clearer that our main mission here is simply to live, to breathe the air, and to let the love within us flow. Just the simple living of an everyday life is sacramental when the person is living with that consciousness of "all is love" humming its tune beneath our words and thoughts. To live devotionally does not mean, necessarily, that one becomes a hermit or a wandering pilgrim, although if you feel called to it, blessings on your way. To me, at least, the daily things are the most holy: the washing up, the chores, the errands. All moves in rhythm, and we are just part of that symphony of all life that shares energy back and forth.

I know that one of the great hopes a Wanderer has is to find its service. The living of a devotional life, right in the busy midst of everything, is ample and perfect service. It is what we came here to do. As we let love flow through us, others change, and as they open their hearts, the circle of light grows. We are now at a stage where the light sources are beginning to connect . . . do I hear the sound of global mind being born?

The global mind is a very real concept to me, as well, especially since the advent of email and the World Wide Web. With information being exchanged without pen or paper, we are basically working with light, surely one of the purer ways to communicate. As I collect stories of Wanderers' blues, I am struck by how intense and constant is the general desire for a spiritual home, an identity, and a way of service. I encourage all those who experience themselves as Wanderers to link up and "network" with other awakened consciousnesses, to live in the open heart together and allow the light to come through us all into the "world-wide web" of planetary consciousness. As Jim says, there is no greater service than being yourself in this sometimes refractory world.

Don loved Andrija Puharich and was a loyal and generous friend to him for many years. We met Andrija in 1974, after we read the book URI, which he wrote, and identified him as one of the characters in our oddly prophetic novel, The Crucifixion of Esmerelda Sweetwater, *which we had written in 1968 and 1969. We helped with the now-historic "Mind Link" of 1977 and heard from him from far and wide as he dodged bullets and various agents of various governments who thought he was up to something. Puharich was a person of immense hospitality and kindness of character, although quite insensitive to and unaware of the world and its requirements outside his work. This was a guy who got up in the morning and worked steadily, only stopping to grab some food, literally, until time for bed. He rather ran through people, using their talents and donations as they aided the work, and unaware of depleting people's resources or time, because he focused on the work before him, never on making money. This was a born scholar and a brilliant man, and much occurred in his ken. It is a loss to the world of ideas that his carefully kept journals were confiscated at the time of his death and have disappeared. I admit readily to feeling ofttimes that he was "using" Don. I felt he was a man of more energy, but less wisdom, than Don. I felt he should have followed Don's sage council at times. Don himself never felt anything like this. He was glad to help. I celebrate Andrija. What a singular and remarkable fellow, and what a contribution he made in so many ways!*

George Hunt Williamson was a channel we greatly admired; indeed, we used his channeling of Brother Philip in our tape Messages from the UFOs. *We were in telephone contact with him only, and like Andrija, he never made it to our sessions. It's likely he was not too pleased at Ra's request for him to prepare! He is one of the great pioneers in UFO and related metaphysical research, and I think the first to name Wanderers. He called them "apples," quoting the radio-channeled UFO message "To the apples we salt, we shall return."*

Session 12,
January 28, 1981

QUESTIONER: I got a call from Henry Puharich this afternoon, and he will be here next month. I would like to ask if it is permissible for him to join in our circle and ask questions. I would also like to ask if Michel D'Obrenovic, also known as George Hunt Williamson, could join our circle as well.

RA: I am Ra. These entities, at present, are not properly attuned for the particular work due to vibrational distortions, which in turn are due to a recent lack of time/space which you call busyness. It would be requested that the entities spend a brief time/space in each diurnal cycle of your planet in contemplation. At a future time/space in your continuum, you are requested to ask again. This group is highly balanced to this instrument's vibratory distortions due to, firstly, contact with the instrument on a day-to-day basis. Secondly, due to contact with the instrument through meditation periods. Thirdly, through a personal mind/body/spirit complex distortion towards contemplation, which in sum causes this group to be effective.

QUESTIONER: Which group was it that contacted Henry Puharich in Israel around 1972?

RA: I am Ra. We must refrain from answering this query due to the possibility/probability that the one you call Henry will read this answer. This would cause distortions in his future. It is necessary that each being use free and complete discernment from within the all-self which is at the heart of the mind/body/spirit complex.

QUESTIONER: Would that also keep you from answering who it was that the group I was in, in 1962, contacted then?

RA: I am Ra. This query may be answered. The group contacted was the Confederation.

QUESTIONER: Did they have any of their craft in our area at that time?

RA: I am Ra. There was no craft. There was a thought-form.

QUESTIONER: If a Man In Black were to visit me and I locked him in the closet, could I keep him, or would he disappear?

RA: I am Ra. It depends upon which type of entity you grab. You are perhaps able to perceive a construct. The construct might be kept for a brief period, although these constructs also have an ability to disappear. The programming on these constructs, however, makes it more difficult to remotely control them. You would not be able to grapple with a thought-form entity of the Man in Black, as you call it, type.

QUESTIONER: Would this be against the Law of One? Would I be making a mistake by grabbing one of those entities?

RA: I am Ra. There are no mistakes under the Law of One.

QUESTIONER: What I mean to ask is, would I be polarizing more towards self-service or service to others when I did this act of locking up the thought-form or construct?

RA: I am Ra. You may consider that question for yourself. We interpret the Law of One, but not to the extent of advice.

QUESTIONER: Is there a way for these Wanderers to heal themselves of their physical ailments?

RA: I am Ra. This will be the last complete question of this time/space.

The self-healing distortion is effected through realization of the intelligent infinity resting within. This is blocked in some way in these who are not perfectly balanced in bodily complexes. The blockage varies from entity to entity. It requires the conscious awareness of the spiritual nature of reality, if you will, and the corresponding pourings of this reality into the individual mind/body/spirit complex for healing to take place.

Is there a short question before we close this session?

QUESTIONER: Is it possible for you to tell us if any of the three of us are Wanderers?

RA: I am Ra. In scanning each of the mind/body/spirit complexes present, we find an already complete sureness of this occurrence and, therefore, find no harm in recapitulating this occurrence. Each of those present are [*sic*] Wanderers pursuing a mission, if you will.

Fragment 6

However, our curiosity did periodically return. And, once again, we see the importance of maintaining one's free will by not diluting the present incarnational experience with too much information concerning one's previous experiences. Meditations and lives tend to be more efficient if they remain focused upon one point or moment.

We have spent a few moments of our lives thinking about who was fifth density and who was sixth, but it has never been clear, nor have we been much pushed to figure it out!

Session 15,
January 30, 1981

QUESTIONER: Is it possible, since we are Wanderers, for you to tell us anything about which our last density was, which density we came from?

RA: I scan each and find it acceptable to share this information. The Wanderers in this working are of two densities: one the density of five; that is, of light; one the density of love/light, or unity. To express the identity of which came from which density, we observe this to be an infringement upon the free will of each. Therefore, we state simply the two densities, both of which are harmoniously oriented towards work together.

Fragment 7

The following material on "silver flecks" is curious in that these small, shiny pieces of what looked like silver rectangles would occasionally appear on or around us when we were discussing matters of a metaphysical nature. Apparently, if we were on the track of thinking that was felt appropriate by our subconscious minds, we would be given a sign of this correctness in the form of the "silver fleck." There are apparently many, many different ways in which people may receive such subconscious confirmations of the appropriateness of their thoughts or actions. The most common, of course, is that feeling of rightness that wells up from within when one is on the right track or receiving spiritually helpful information.

The awareness of this method of feedback from the winds of destiny is most helpful to one on a spiritual path. The natural world seems very open to the production of synchronicities that are subjectively meaningful. Once the seeker "gets" the presence of these signs and begins consciously to watch for them, she can actually have influence in the creating of more-subjective signs, until there are times when meaningful coincidence seems to take on a constant presence in her life. I certainly have found these signs most comforting and strengthening.

Session 16,
January 31, 1981

QUESTIONER: Can you tell me of the silver flecks that we have found sometimes on our faces or elsewhere?

RA: I am Ra. These of which you speak are a materialization of a subjectively oriented signpost indicating to one mind/body/spirit complex, and no other, a meaning of subjective nature.

QUESTIONER: Who creates these silver flecks?

RA: I am Ra. Picture, if you will, the increasing potential for learn/teaching. At some point a sign will be given indicating the appropriateness or importance of that learn/teaching. The entity itself, in cooperation with the inner planes, creates whatever signpost is most understandable or noticeable to it.

QUESTIONER: I understand then that we ourselves create this?

RA: I am Ra. Entities consciously do not create these. The roots of mind complex, having touched in understanding, intelligent infinity, create them.

Fragment 8

Before each contact with those of Ra, we conducted a meditation that we used as our tuning device; that is, our means of becoming as one in our seeking to be of service to others. Oftentimes during this meditation, Don would get a hunch as to an addition to the line of questioning that we had decided upon the night before. In Session 17, such a hunch came to him concerning a crater in the Tunguska region of Russia, which, it is speculated, was made by either a crashed UFO or a large meteor of some kind in 1908. There is also speculation that some scientists of the Soviet Union first became interested in the possibility of life in other parts of the galaxy and solar system as a result of their investigation of this crater and its possible origin.

After asking about this crater and following it up with questions concerning the development of nuclear energy on Earth, and the odd and rarely reported phenomenon of spontaneous combustion of a human being, Don determined that this line of questioning would yield little of value.

Donald was a scientist, and he never could quite accept that Ra was in no position to chat with us about phenomena that can be measured. The desire that had brought Ra to our group was a true desire for nontransient material, and this desire fueled our sessions. When we departed from that level of information, Ra would remind us to get back on track in a subtle way: by telling us to watch our alignments. We at first took them literally and thought they were referring to the items on the altar, to getting them lined up rightly. Later, we figured out that they were grading our questions, not our Bible and candle placement. It's worth emphasizing that anything measurable is also transient. The human spirit, the force of creative love, the creation's essence: these things are unfindable, noumenal, always sensed, and never penetrated by our fact-finding intellects. But we sense into them through living with an open heart, and by talking about them with sources such as Ra and Q'uo and other "universal" or "outer" energies and essences. The personal guides and other teachers of the inner planes of our planet have much more leeway in offering personal information, whenever their last incarnation. Go to them to get your readings on your health and other specific issues. Go to outer sources such as our confederation sources with questions that transcend space and time. If it will matter less in 10,000 years than it does now, it is probably not a universal question!

Session 17,
February 3, 1981

QUESTIONER: In meditation I got the question about the crater in Russia in the, I believe, Tunguska region. Can you tell me what caused the crater?

RA: I am Ra. The destruction of a fission reactor caused this crater.

QUESTIONER: Whose reactor?

RA: I am Ra. This was what you may call a "drone" sent by Confederation, which malfunctioned. It was moved to an area where its destruction would not cause infringement upon the will of mind/body/spirit complexes. It was then detonated.

QUESTIONER: What was its purpose in coming here?

RA: It was a drone designed to listen to the various signals of your peoples. You were, at that time, beginning work in a more technical sphere. We were interested in determining the extent and the rapidity of your advances. This drone was powered by a simple fission motor or engine, as you would call it. It was not that type which you now know, but was very small. However, it has the same destructive effect upon third-density molecular structures. Thus, as it malfunctioned, we felt it was best to pick a place for its destruction rather than attempt to retrieve it, for the possibility/probability modes for this maneuver looked very, very minute.

QUESTIONER: Was its danger both blast and radiation?

RA: I am Ra. There is very little radiation, as you know of it, in this particular type of device. There is radiation which is localized, but the localization is such that it does not drift with the winds as does the emission of your somewhat primitive weapons.

QUESTIONER: I believe that analysis has detected very little radiation in the trees in this area. Is this low level of radiation a result of what you are speaking of?

RA: I am Ra. This is correct. The amount of radiation is very localized. However, the energy which is released is powerful enough to cause difficulties.

QUESTIONER: Then was the Confederation responsible for the Earth receiving nuclear power?

RA: I am Ra. It is a point which one cannot judge what is cause. The basic equation which preceded this work was an equation brought through by a Wanderer dedicated to service to the planet. That this work should have become the foundation for instruments of destruction was not intended and was not given.

QUESTIONER: Can you tell me who this Wanderer was who brought through the equation?

RA: I am Ra. This information seems harmless, as this entity is no longer of your planetary third density. This entity was named sound vibratory complex Albert.

QUESTIONER: Is this the reason for what we call spontaneous combustion of human beings?

RA: I am Ra. This is not correct.

QUESTIONER: Can you tell me what causes that phenomenon?

RA: I am Ra. Picture, if you will, a forest. One tree is struck by lightning. It burns. Lightning does not strike elsewhere. Elsewhere does not burn. There are random occurrences which do not have to do with the entity, but with the window phenomenon of which we spoke.

QUESTIONER: Are these entities uniquely the same, or are they random entities?

RA: I am Ra. The latter is correct.

Fragment 9

At the beginning of Session 18, in response to a general query from Don concerning the information Ra was transmitting to our group, Ra innocently "told on" Carla. A good friend of hers had offered her the opportunity to experience the effects of LSD, which she had never experienced before. She used it twice in early February 1981 as a programming device to attempt to achieve an experience of unity with the Creator, but she did not wish Don to know about these experiences, since he was very much against the use of any illegal substances at any time and especially during the time during which our group was working with the Ra contact. In a later session it will be suggested by Ra that these two experiences were arranged by the negative entities monitoring our work with those of Ra, in hopes that Carla's ability to serve in the Ra contact might be hindered. As a result of this particular session, it was the determination of the three of us that there would be no further use of any illegal substances for as long as we were privileged to work with the Ra contact, so that no chinks in our "armor of light" that we could eliminate would be present, and so that the Ra contact could never be associated with the use of any such drugs.

The information on Aleister Crowley is self-explanatory and underlines again the caution that each seeker must take in moving carefully through its energy centers in a balanced fashion.

By chance, a few sessions earlier, we had discovered that sexual intercourse was an aid to Carla's vital energies during the trance state and would increase the length of a session if engaged in the night before a session was to be held. Thus, at the end of Session 18, when Don asked how we might avoid further difficulties in the contact, Ra affirmed the aid that we had discovered sexual intercourse provided. We also found that the conscious dedication of the act of love-making to the service of others via the Ra contact increased its beneficial effects.

As a young college woman, I never dated or spent time with anyone who smoked marijuana or took LSD, or any other drugs. People all around me were experimenting, but I never was offered any drugs. It was the day of flower children and high ideals, a wonderful time to be young. The hippies ruled, but I was only an honorary flower child, since I worked steadily throughout that decade. In 1981, I was thirty-eight. When an old friend offered to let me try LSD, I was tickled and eager to try it, for I had long been curious to see what this much-touted substance did to one's head. In the event, I thoroughly enjoyed the experiences—I tried LSD twice—and found that there really was a wonderful increase in the sense of rightness of things under its benign influence on me. Since then, I have heard from many people that my utterly positive experiences with LSD were somewhat atypical, in that most people deal with at least a little hallucination or departure from consensus reality, or even a negatively experienced "high" or bad trip. So I was either lucky or my subconscious mind was more settled in its own skin than some others. I'd bet on luck!

Needless to say, I was not happy to learn that Ra had blithely told my secret to Don. I valued Don's opinion above all things, and he was not pleased with my judgment in taking illegal substances. But I did not, and do not, feel guilty or ashamed for satisfying my curiosity under circumstances as safe as one could make them. I also have tried cigarettes and alcohol, both heavily addictive substances, but rarely drink and never use tobacco. (In cooking, however, I use many different spirits, as they offer such delightful notes when put into the harmony of cooking things.) My curiosity was satisfied and I moved on. The freedom to do this, to know what is out there, is a valuable one, to my mind, if not abused. Moderation seems to me the key.

I have very fond memories of reading Aleister Crowley's autohagiography to Don. He did not like to read, so I frequently read to him. Once we got into this outrageous, brilliant man's work, we were fascinated. Crowley is a fine writer, regardless of what his polarity might have been fumbling around with. Our favorite poem of his is a perfectly ghoulish nursery rhyme he wrote as a precocious toddler. It begins, "In her hospital bed she lay, rotting away, rotting away, rotting by night and rotting by day, rotting and rotting and rotting away." Now that I have told you this, you may perhaps see why this character grew up to become . . . eccentric! But always interesting.

In working to fit myself into Don's requirements for a mate, I became a user of relative ethics, a practice that seems always to offer a challenge eventually. Don wished to be celibate, which became obvious to me within six months of our coming together in 1968. I always said that his inability to resist me for those first few months we lived together was my greatest compliment of all time! I attempted a celibate life, after we had talked this issue through, for a little over two years, before I concluded that celibacy was not for me. Don had also decided that we should not marry. This implied, to me, a relationship based on a commonality in a metaphysical rather than a physical sense. Always logical, I suggested to Don that we make an agreement: I would tell him before I took a lover and when I had ceased seeing him. In between, there was no need to discuss it. This would preclude his hearing about such company from others. As he was gone flying about half the time, I had no difficulty in finding time for the lovers' relationship. My lover for most of the time Don and I spent together, ten of the sixteen years, was a trusted and much-loved buddy of mine ever since high school. We had thought of marriage years before and then decided against it, but we'd remained close. He got the notion to come see me perhaps once a month. I stopped seeing him when he began to wish to take our relationship further, and I was celibate again for some four years before Jim. When Jim began coming to the group, we eventually got together and he became my lover. All of this was done in the good mutual faith between Donald and me. He was genuinely happy for me to have these relationships, and they did not intrude upon our harmony.

However, in time, after Donald's death, it became clear to me that my relationship with Jim, especially the intimately sexual part of it, did bother Don at a level below the threshold of his awareness, or mine, for that matter. I doubt he ever realized or acknowledged the emotion. I certainly never saw any trace of it, and I am a sensitive person, able to pick up nuances of feeling. But he must have felt these things, and it led him, in the end, to lose faith in my allegiance. And that completely misplaced doubt was the weakness in his armor of light that resulted in his dying.

Long are the hours I have spent reflecting upon this matter. On the one hand, if I had been completely chaste and celibate, he would never have doubted me. He would have still been living and with me. But we would not have had the contact with Ra that gave us the Law of One material, because it was the combined energy of us three that contacted Ra, not myself as channel, or any one of us at L/L Research, or even L/L Research as an entity. This is clear from the simple dates: Jim came to L/L permanently on December 23, 1980, and we received our first contact from those of Ra on January 15, 1981, less than three weeks after Jim moved in. And Donald felt from the first session with Ra that this was his life's work, the culmination of all he had been through since the '50s, and his gift to the world. Logic fails in matters like these. One can hew completely and faithfully to the agreements one has made and still err.

If one can move beyond the mythic tragedy of Donald's death, and believe me, one can, after a decade or so, barely, one begins to see the inherent humor in that human, prideful assumption that one can control one's destiny by doing only what is seen as right. One can certainly try to be without error or sin. My pride in myself as being one who always keeps her word blinded me to the suspicions Donald had but kept completely to himself. His lack of faith in any opinion but his own, even when completely healthy of mind, made it more likely that when he became mentally ill, he would experience paranoia. It is a perfect tragedy.

Don wanted always and only my presence. He never asked for anything else, with the exception of the work we did together. He even begrudged me the time to work on his projects when he was at home. I did all the work for the books we wrote together while he was flying. When he was home, my job was to be in the same room he was in. I was delighted to do this. He could never bring himself to express it, but well I knew how devoted he was, and I felt the same. We had little choice in this; we both felt we were destined to be together, that we were truly star-crossed. Loving him was like breathing, and it did not matter how his needs impinged on mine. Indeed, my spiritual adviser said more than once that I was guilty of idolatry. I did not care what had to be lost to achieve his comfort. I knew these losses included marriage, home, and children, things I valued highly and had hoped for. But we were "home" to each other in a way I cannot describe. He rested me, and I, him. I received two compliments from him, in our whole life together. He did not want to spoil me! The lessons were to see through the issues of home, family, and reassurance to the ground of being that we shared, to the sensibility we had in common. I embraced them. He was worth whatever it cost. I look back and know I would not change anything. All our choices were made as well as we could make them.

This was the jigsaw puzzle within which we were living, in the world-drama, soap-opera consensus reality of our everyday lives. Carla and Don worked perfectly, as did Jim and Carla, and Don and Jim, who loved each other like family from the first meeting. These relationships were strong and true. Naught could have come between us except for doubt. It never occurred to me that Donald could mistake my fondness for Jim for any sort of alteration in Don's and my unmarriage version of being wed—and we were indeed truly wed, in spirit. You can imagine my wretchedness when one of his friends told me, long after the funeral, that Don had thought I had fallen out of love with him. I was flabbergasted, completely unaware of these doubts, so it never occurred to me to reassure him. How I wish I had! But I was grieving, for the man I knew was gone, and what took his place was a person in very bad need of help. And I was angry that he would not seek help or follow any medical suggestions. He was my world, and without him, I felt I did not exist. I think most of my grieving was done before his death, in those surrealistic months when he was so very ill, and nothing I did to help was of avail. It took years after he died for me to come to a new sense of myself. That I have now done so is a gift of grace from the Creator and has been greatly aided by Jim's sensitive treatment of me during the long years of confinement with debilitating episodes of arthritis and other troubles in the decade following Don's death, and during my rehab period in 1992. For the first six years after Don died, I actively felt I should kill myself, because I had "caused" his death, inadvertently, but surely. This was my longest walk in the desert until this present moment. I was resigned to having this basic mindset for the rest of my life, and I was not aware that time had begun its healing work until I picked up something I'd written and forgot about. I read it anew, and thought, "You know, I like this person." Six years in the desert! Many were the times I was tempted to lay down my faith, but I could not, would not do that. So I survived and waited for grace. The lesson here is simply that waiting does bring all things to one. Patience cannot be overvalued in the spiritual journey.

This world remains to me a sea of confusion. Knowing well how much I have erred, in what I have done and what I've left undone, and knowing how little I understand, I am well content to remain in the hands of destiny. One of my desires in publishing this personal material is to expose, with utter lack of modesty or fear, the humanness of the three of us. We were not "worthy" of the Ra contact, in the sense of being perfect people. We were three pilgrims who found comfort in each other, and who sought honestly and deeply to serve the light. The material is completely apart from who any of us was or is, and we are not to be confused with Ra, as having some sort of special excellence. This just is not so.

Are relative ethics OK? I still believe they are, and that keeping carefully made agreements is a real key to harmonious living and clear relationships. But it is just the best we can do. That doesn't make it perfect. Further, one cannot expect the universe to bless us with perfect peace just because we are keeping our agreements. We all are blindsided by life itself and continue only by blunder, faith, and a good humor in the face of all. There is an art to cooperating with destiny. And may I say, I am grateful to James Allen McCarty for that selfsame good humor, and for deciding with me, three years after Don's death, to take hold of our friendship and create a marriage between us. He was most ill-suited to such, as I said, and his gallant cheer and courtesy in accommodating himself to this role has been and continues to be remarkable to me. Truly, he has been a good companion through many waters.

One thing is sure: in true love, the star-crossed kind, there is incredible sweetness, but also immense pain. Don was a hard man to love. Not communicative in the usual sense, he never said what he wanted of me, but just waited for me to guess right. I did not mind and still am glad of every bit of pain I went through trying to be what he needed me to be, which was essentially without sexuality or the usual reassurance of words, yet greatly intimate. In the density we came from, we were already one, Ra said. So there was an ultimate satisfaction in being with Don, having to do much more with eternity than any particular time or space. What Jim and I had and have is the devoted love of old friends and lovers, who have an earthly pilgrimage together. Our time together is child's play after Don, as far as my being able to handle whatever happens with us. Jim will communicate until we find every bit of misunderstanding, and so we have an easy time of it, and when we do have catalyst together, it is quickly worked through. Jim's never had that ultimate romance and occasionally misses it. But what we do have is so good to us that we have found a considerable happiness with each other, and the good work we have between us.

We see ourselves as still working for and with Don, keeping L/L's doors open and our hearts as well, and living the devotional life that we have learned about from the Confederation teachings. These teachings are at one with universal wisdom as well as my Christian heritage and have to do simply with living in love. This is such a simple teaching that it escapes many people. But that focus upon Love is one's access to truth, and one's willingness to keep the heart open, which one may call faith, is the energy that brings to us all that was meant for us, both of lessons to learn and of service to offer.

And above all, we may acknowledge, for once and for all, that we are but dust, unless we are living in Love. This helps one to deal with sorrows that inevitably visit our lives. We are not supposed to be in control, or perfect, or any particular thing, but just those who continue to love, through whatever confusion there is. Sheer persistence in faith, regardless of the illusion, is the key to many blessings.

Session 18,
February 4, 1981

QUESTIONER: I was thinking last night that if I was in the place of Ra right now, the first distortion of the Law of One might cause me to mix some erroneous data with the true information that I was transmitting to this group. Do you do this?

RA: I am Ra. We do not intentionally do this. However, there will be confusion. The errors which have occurred have occurred due to the occasional variation in the vibrational complex of this instrument due to its ingestion of a chemical substance. It is not our intent in this particular project to create erroneous information, but to express in the confining ambiance of your language system the feeling of the infinite mystery of the one creation in its infinite and intelligent unity.

QUESTIONER: Can you tell me what the chemical substance is that, when ingested, causes poor contact?

RA: I am Ra. This is not a clear query. Could you please restate.

QUESTIONER: You just stated that you had some problems with the instrument because of the ingestion of some chemical substance by the instrument. Can you tell me what the chemical substance was?

RA: I am Ra. The substance of which we speak is called vibration sound complex LSD. It does not give poor contact if it is used in conjunction with the contact. The difficulty of this particular substance is that there is, shall we say, a very dramatic drop-off of the effect of this substance. In each case this instrument began the session with the distortion towards extreme vital energy which this substance produces. However, this entity was, during the session, at the point where this substance no longer was in sufficient strength to amplify the entity's abilities to express vital energy. Thus, first the phenomenon of, shall we say, a spotty contact and then, as the instrument relies again upon its own vibrational complexes of vital energy, the vital energy in this case being very low, it became necessary to abruptly cut off communication in order to preserve and nurture the instrument. This particular chemical substance is both helpful and unhelpful in these contacts for the causes given.

QUESTIONER: Are there any foods that are helpful or harmful that the instrument might eat?

RA: I am Ra. This instrument has body complex distortion towards ill health in the distortion direction corrected best by ingestion of the foodstuffs of your grains and your vegetables, as you call them. However, this is extremely unimportant when regarded as an aid with equality to other aids such as attitude, which this instrument has in abundance. It, however, aids the vital energies of this instrument, with less distortion towards ill health, to ingest foodstuffs in the above manner, with the occasional ingestion of what you call your meats, due to the instrument's need to lessen the distortion towards low vital energy.

QUESTIONER: The entity Aleister Crowley wrote, "Do what thou wilt is the whole of the law." He was obviously of some understanding of the Law of One. Where is this entity now?

RA: I am Ra. This entity is within your inner planes. This entity is in an healing process.

THE LAW OF ONE

QUESTIONER: Did this entity, then, even though he intellectually understood the Law of One, misuse it and have to go through this healing process?

RA: I am Ra. This entity became, may we use the vibration sound complex, overstimulated with the true nature of things. This overstimulation resulted in behavior that was beyond the conscious control of the entity. The entity thus, in many attempts to go through the process of balancing, as we have described the various centers beginning with the red ray and moving upwards, became somewhat overly impressed or caught up in this process and became alienated from other-selves. This entity was positive. However, its journey was difficult due to the inability to use, synthesize, and harmonize the understandings of the desires of self so that it might have shared, in full compassion, with other-selves. This entity thus became very unhealthy, as you may call it, in a spiritual complex manner, and it is necessary for those with this type of distortion towards inner pain to be nurtured in the inner planes until such an entity is capable of viewing the experiences again with the lack of distortion towards pain.

QUESTIONER: I just have two little questions here at the end. The instrument wanted to ask if there were any other substances, foods, etc., that she should not eat or drink, or things that she should not do because she does not wish to have poor contact for any reason.

RA: I am Ra. There is no activity which this instrument engages in which affects abilities negatively. There is one activity which affects its abilities positively. This is the sexual activity, as you would call it. There are substances ingested which do not aid the individual in the service it has chosen, this being that which you would call the marijuana. This is due to the distortion towards chemical lapses within the mind complex, causing lack of synaptic continuity. This is a chemical reaction of short duration. This instrument, however, has not used this particular substance at any time while performing this service. We believe we have covered the use of such chemical agents as LSD, this being positive to a certain extent due to the energizing or speeding up of the vital forces. However, it is not recommended for this instrument due to the toll it takes upon the vital energies once the substance wears off. This being true of any speeding-up chemical.

Fragment 10

As we were preparing to welcome Dr. Puharich into our circle of working with Ra, we were reminded once again of the prerequisite of the tuning in the personal life that was necessary for all of those involved in the contact.

In the event, Andrija never visited us here in Kentucky. But it is worth noting that Ra frequently did respond to our questions by invoking the law of confusion. Those of Ra felt that the primary importance in personal ethics of allowing people to do their own learning, make their own mistakes, cannot be overemphasized.

Session 21,
February 10, 1981

QUESTIONER: Andrija Puharich will be visiting later this month. Can he read the unpublished healing material?

RA: I am Ra. The entity of whom you speak has a knowledge of this material in its conscious memory in somewhat altered form. Therefore, it is harmless to allow this entity to become acquainted with this material. However, we request the mind/body/spirit complex, Henry, be sufficiently prepared by means of meditation, contemplation, or prayer before entering these workings. At present, as we have said before, this mind/body/spirit complex is not of proper vibrational distortion.

QUESTIONER: I had already determined to exclude him from these workings. I had only determined to let him read the material. The only other thing that I have noticed within the material as it exists now is that there is a certain statement that will allow him to understand who I believe Spectra really was. It seems to be my duty to remove this from his knowledge to preserve the same free will that you attempted to preserve by not naming the origin of the Spectra contact in Israel. Am I correct?

RA: I am Ra. This is a matter for your discretion.

QUESTIONER: That's what I thought you'd say.

Fragment 11

Most of the personal information from Session 22 is self-explanatory. The prayer that Ra speaks of in relation to Carla is the Prayer of St. Francis, which Carla has used as her own personal tuning mechanism since she began channeling in 1974. It further refines the tuning done by the support group and is always prayed mentally before any session, whether telepathic or trance.

The limitations of which Ra speaks in the second answer refer to Carla's rheumatoid arthritis, which was apparently chosen before the incarnation to provide an inner focus for her meditative work rather than to allow the ease of outer expression that might have dissipated the inner orientation. Thus, not all disabilities are meant to yield to even the best efforts of healers, and when such a disability does not respond to any kind of healing effort, one may begin to consider what opportunities for learning and service are opened up by the disability. Ra even mentioned in the last sentence that her acceptance of her disabilities and limitations would ease the amount of pain that she suffered because of them.

It was distinctly odd to be going about and walking into aromas that had no overt origin. It seemed to me throughout this time that I was being more and more sensitized, and less and less vibrating with my humanhood. I feel sure that the constant weight loss added to this Alice in Wonderland feeling. To the present day, I continue to have a very sensitized physical vehicle. However, my formerly tiny body has grown from size preteen 5/8 to its present position athwart 14/16, a weight gain of double the lightest weight reached during the contact. Just for a feel for where "normal" is for me, I used to weigh between 115 and 120, year after year. I looked quite normal at that weight. It's been interesting to feel the different weights I have been, to live with a more or less bulky vehicle. One feels stronger, the heavier one is. I was surprised at this, figuring that lighter weights would make one feel more toned and vital. It makes it easier to understand why we in America so often allow ourselves to eat to the point of obesity. It feels good! One doubts that it is a life-lengthening thing, however!

The pre-incarnative choice that I made to have a body that would limit what I could do is one I have taken a long time to appreciate. It is frustrating at first not to be able to do the work one's trained to do. I loved being a librarian; I enjoyed researching for Don. When I could no longer work in these ways, I was profoundly puzzled and not a little upset. But then, quiet years taught me so much. I learned the open heart although my body was declining; I found hope and faith although the physical picture grew steadily worse. After Donald died, I came close to dying too, and in 1992, when at last I was able to turn the boat around, I felt the grip of death loosen and fall away.

My present experience is of living in a barely working physical vehicle. Taking no less than seven medications, I walk the razor's edge between doing too much and not doing enough. The one thing that has never changed throughout this experience is my dedication to helping the Wanderers of this planet. All the various skills that I have had to give up have their place in my work with people who are having trouble with their spiritual path, and so I feel fully useful at last. And yet I know that we are all most useful, not by what we do or say, but in the quality of our being.

Session 22,
February 10, 1981

QUESTIONER: The instrument would like to ask a couple of questions of you. The instrument would like to know why she smells the incense at various times during the day at various places.

RA: I am Ra. This instrument has spent a lifetime in dedication to service. This has brought this instrument to this nexus in space/time with the conscious and unconscious distortion towards service, with the further conscious distortion towards service by communication. Each time, as you would put it, that we perform this working, our social memory complex vibrational distortion meshes more firmly with this instrument's unconscious distortions towards service. Thus we are becoming a part of this instrument's vibratory complex, and it, a part of ours. This occurs upon the unconscious level, the level whereby the mind has gone down through to the roots of consciousness which you may call cosmic. This instrument is not consciously aware of this slow changing of the meshing vibratory complex. However, as the dedication on both levels continues, and the workings continue, there are signals sent from the unconscious in a symbolic manner. Because this instrument is extremely keen in its sense of smell, this association takes place unconsciously, and the thought-form of this odor is witnessed by the entity.

QUESTIONER: Secondly, she would like to know why she feels more healthy now that she has begun these sessions and feels more healthy as time goes on.

RA: I am Ra. This is a function of the free will of the entity. This entity has, for many of your years, prayed a certain set of sound vibration complexes before opening to communication. Before the trance state was achieved, this prayer remained within the conscious portion of the mind complex and, though helpful, was not as effective as the consequence of this prayer, as you would call this vibrational sound complex, which then goes directly into the unconscious level, thus more critically affecting the communication from the spiritual complex. Also, this entity has begun, due to this working, to accept certain limitations which it placed upon itself in order to set the stage for services such as it now performs. This also is an aid to realigning the distortions of the physical complex with regard to pain.

Fragment 12

Dr. Puharich never did visit us during the Ra contact, so all of our questions about how he should prepare for joining the contact were only for our information. His strong desire to solve riddles and puzzles and his desire to prove spiritual truth would have made it difficult for him to become a part of our circle, since it was supported by the opposite mental attitude, faith.

Once one starts watching for synchronicities, one can find many a book, movie, or any other object or event bringing repeated messages and reminders of our path. So often, Jim and I will be discussing an issue only to find that for the next day or two, we receive confirmations meaningful only to us.

And I do think that many wanderers here are making today's movies and songs. One has only to listen to the wonderful words to current songs, sung by people as diverse as Arlo Guthrie and Donovan, Black Oak Arkansas and Earth, Wind and Fire, the Rolling Stones . . . the list is as long as my legs! We have wonderful company, we who wander here on earth.

Session 23,
February 11, 1981

QUESTIONER: I can't answer this question but I will ask it anyway, since we are in the area that I think that this occurred in. I feel this is somewhat of a duty to ask this question because Henry Puharich will be visiting us here later this month. Was this entity involved in any of these times of which you have just spoken?

RA: I am Ra. You are quite correct in your assumption that we can speak in no way concerning the entity Henry. If you will consider this entity's distortions with regard to what you call "proof," you will understand/grasp our predicament.

QUESTIONER: I had assumed before I asked the question that that would be the answer. I only asked it for his benefit because he wished for me to. This may be a dumb question. There is a movie called *Battle Beyond the Stars*. I don't know if you are familiar with it or not. I guess you are. It just seemed to have what you are telling us included in the script. Is this correct?

RA: I am Ra. This particular creation of your entities had some distortions of the Law of One and its scenario upon your physical plane. This is correct.

Fragment 13

The following information refers to two of the most widely rumored events in ufology in this country. The first refers to the supposed face-to-face meeting between extraterrestrials and then president Dwight D. Eisenhower and some senior military staff at Edwards Air Force Base in California in February 1954. The second incident refers to the supposed crash of a UFO outside Roswell, New Mexico, in which the ufonauts onboard supposedly died. It is further rumored that their bodies were stored in Hangar #18 at Wright-Patterson Air Force Base in Ohio. Once again we encountered the temptation to pursue information that seemed on the surface to be extremely interesting, but which in truth would yield little or no information that might aid in the evolution of mind, body, or spirit. And we would have lost the Ra contact because Ra's "narrow-band contact" was focused only on aiding our evolution and not on revealing the transient intricacies of how groups play games in this illusion.

In 1962, when I joined with Donald to help make up the initial meditation group that grew into L/L Research, there were several rumors being bruited about. Supposedly, the government knew all about UFOs, had had contact. There were alleged conspiracies that various sources warned the public about. To this day, there has continued a steady stream of such prophecies and doomsday warnings of all kinds. Only the dates of Armageddon have changed, usually predicting doom within the next two or three years.

It is not that I do not think UFOs are communicating with our government. They might be. Certainly they are here; the landing-trace cases alone prove that something that makes dents in the ground is visiting us, and the many witnesses and abductees create a comprehensive picture of human-alien contact that is undeniable. It is that I feel that the real treasure the UFO entities have brought us are those of the spirit, not those of this world. Whatever the physical reality of UFOs and governmental doings, they remain part of the transient world picture: part of this heavy illusion. But the messages have a metaphysical content that 10,000 years would not make out of date or less meaningful. So I tend to respond to people's questions about such hijinks as these with a redirection, back from phenomena to metaphysical truth.

Session 24,
February 15, 1981

QUESTIONER: One thing that has been bothering me that I was just reading about is not too important, but I would really be interested in knowing if Dwight Eisenhower met with either the Confederation or the Orion group in the 1950s?

RA: I am Ra. The one of which you speak met with thought-forms which are indistinguishable from third density. This was a test. We, the Confederation, wished to see what would occur if this extremely positively oriented and simple congenial person with no significant distortion towards power happened across peaceful information and the possibilities which might append therefrom. We discovered that this entity did not feel that those under his care could deal with the concepts of other beings and other philosophies. Thus, an agreement reached then allowed him to go his way—ourselves to do likewise—and a very quiet campaign, as we have heard you call it, be continued alerting your peoples to our presence gradually. Events have overtaken this plan. Is there any short query before we close?

QUESTIONER: Another question with that is, was there a crashed spaceship with small bodies now stored in our military installations?

RA: I am Ra. We do not wish to infringe upon your future. Gave we you this information, we might be giving you more than you could appropriately deal with in the space/time nexus of your present somewhat muddled configuration of military and intelligence thought. Therefore, we shall withhold this information.

Fragment 14
The following information gave us some insight into how one's choices can be used in either the positive or the negative sense, even when there is the seeming interference of negative entities in the manner of what many light workers call psychic attack, and what we came to call psychic greetings. We chose the term "greeting" to emphasize that there does not have to be a negative experience on the part of the one

who is greeted, and that the experience that the one who is greeted actually has is in direct proportion to how that entity looks at the situation. If one wishes to see such a greeting as a difficult attack, then that becomes the experience. One can, however, also choose to see the Creator in all entities and events and can praise and seek the light within any situation, and then that will tend to become the experience.

When this latter choice is made, the psychic greeting becomes a great blessing in that it presents to the one who is greeted an intensive opportunity to see the One Creator where it may be more difficult to see, and which, when accomplished, develops a great deal more spiritual strength than may normally be developed without the negative entity's aid in pointing out the weaker areas of our magical personalities. Psychic greetings can only be offered by negative entities enhancing our own free will choices that are distorted toward service-to-self thought and behavior. Our poor choices, usually reflecting a lack of love toward another or the self, get magnified by the negative entity and bleed away our efforts to seek the light and serve others until we are able to balance the situation with love, acceptance, compassion, tolerance, and the light touch. This is why Jesus said to "resist not evil." To resist and fight is to see someone or something as other than the self, as other than the One Creator. That is the negative path. The positive path sees and loves all as the self and as the One.

The work that was perforce mine during this time of psychic greeting was, as Jim pointed out, very helpful in focusing my will and attention. I remember feeling tremendously uplifted and held in safe hands through all of the episodes. The key was the surrender to seeing one's own dark side. I think Dion Fortune's description of how to deal with a vampiric entity, in that case a wolf, still to be the most direct example of the understanding needed to move through such times. This wise soul had a wolf appearing at her bed, during training in white Western ritual magic. The solution was to draw the wolf directly into the breast, loving it and accepting it as self. Against fearless love, the powers of negation and death are helpless and melt away.

I think those of Ra were very careful of our group, compared to some sources, who did not show much concern that they were wearing the instrument out. Advice such as was given for me could well apply to anyone who must husband one's energy.

Session 25,
February 16, 1981

QUESTIONER: What cause or complex of causes has led to the instrument's chest cold, as it is called?

RA: I am Ra. This distortion towards illness was caused by the free will of the instrument in accepting a chemical substance which you call LSD. This was carefully planned by those entities which do not desire this instrument to remain viable. The substance has within it the facility of removing large stores of vital energy from the ingestor. The first hope of the Orion entity which arranged this opportunity was that this instrument would become less polarized towards what you call the positive. Due to conscious efforts upon the part of this instrument, using the substance as a programmer for service to others and for thankfulness, this instrument was spared this distortion and there was no result satisfactory to the Orion group.

The second hope lay in the possible misuse of the most-powerful means of transmission of energy between your peoples in the area of body complex distortions. We have not previously spoken of the various types of energy blockages and transfers, positive and negative, that may take place due to participation in your sexual-reproductive complex of actions. This entity, however, is a very strong entity with very little distortion from universal green-ray love energy. Thus this particular plan was not effected either, as the entity continued to give of itself in this context in an open or green-ray manner rather than attempting to deceive or to manipulate other-self.

The only remaining distortion available, since this entity would not detune and would not cease sharing love universally under this chemical substance, was simply to drain this entity of as much energy as possible. This entity has a strong distortion towards busyness which it has been attempting to overcome for some time, realizing it not to be the appropriate attitude for this work. In this particular area the ingestion of this substance did indeed, shall we say, cause distortions away from viability due to the busyness and the lack of desire to rest; this instrument staying alert for much longer than appropriate. Thus much vital energy was lost, making this instrument unusually susceptible to infections such as it now experiences.

QUESTIONER: The second question that the instrument requested is: How may I best revitalize myself not only now but in the future?

RA: I am Ra. This instrument is aware of the basic needs of its constitution, those being meditation, acceptance of limitations, experiences of joy through association with others, and with the beauty as of the singing, and the exercising with great contact, whenever possible, with the life forces of second density, especially those of trees; this entity also needing to be aware of the moderate but steady intake of foodstuffs, exercise being suggested at a fairly early portion of the day and at a later portion of the day before the resting.

QUESTIONER: The third question that she requested was: How may Don and Jim help to revitalize me?

RA: I am Ra. This is not an appropriate question for full answer. We can say only that these entities are most conscientious. We may add that due to this instrument's distortion towards imbalance in the space/time nexus, it would be well were this entity accompanied during exercise.

Fragment 15

The following information refers again to Carla's two experiences with LSD. We were very thankful that there were only two experiences with which she and we had to deal, for, as you can see, the debilitating effects apparently mount rapidly with each ingestion. The sessions in Book II of *The Law of One* were necessarily shortened in order to conserve the vital energy of the instrument, which had been drained by the LSD.

I can only add the fact that this period of weakness did occur, and so Ra's suggestion not to mix any drugs with channeling seems to me a sound piece of advice that I have followed ever since.

Session 26,
February 17, 1981

QUESTIONER: The instrument asks how long will the debilitating effects that I am experiencing due to the LSD last, and is there anything that we can do to make the instrument more comfortable?

RA: I am Ra. Firstly, the period of weakness of bodily complex is approximately three of your lunar cycles: the first ingestion causing approximately one of your lunar cycles; the second having a cumulative or doubling effect.

Fragment 16

Just before I joined Don and Carla, at the end of 1980, I traveled to the Portland, Oregon, area to work with Paul Shockley and the Aquarian Church of Universal Service. It was a happy experience in itself, and it also provided the catalyst that eventually saw me return to Kentucky and join L/L Research. After two months in Oregon I decided to take a weekend alone to think about an opportunity to earn a great deal of money that had been presented to me by one of the members of the Aquarian Church. Thirty seconds into my first meditation of the weekend, the very clear message to return to Don and Carla flashed across my inner sky. So I said goodbye to my new friends and returned to Louisville. Three weeks later the Ra contact began, and when Paul Shockley was informed of the nature of the contact, he asked that two questions be asked for him of the social memory complex Ra.

The answer to the second query is especially interesting to us because it seems to suggest the means by which some of the pyramids of Egypt were constructed.

In 1986, we were invited to Shockley's "Friendship" conference, and I finally met this channel for a source called "Cosmic Awareness." He was a very sincere and valiant channel, pure in his desire to serve. I feel it unfortunate that the questions put to this channel, over a period of time, pretty much changed and worsened the quality of information received. As always when this occurs, the culprit was a fascination with transient material. I think that it was the questions put to this excellent channel that lessened the metaphysical level of this channeling.

Session 27,
February 21, 1981

QUESTIONER: Jim has felt the obligation to ask two questions that were asked of him by Paul Shockley, and I will ask those two first, in case you are able to answer them before we get started. The first question: Paul Shockley is presently channeling the same source which Edgar Cayce channeled, and he has received information that he took part in the design and construction of the Egyptian pyramids. Can you tell us what his role was in that effort?

RA: I am Ra. This was in your space/time continuum two periods and two lifetimes. The first of a physical nature working with Confederation entities in what you know of as Atlantis, this approximately 13,000 of your years ago. This memory, shall we say, being integrated into the unconscious of the mind/body/spirit complex of this entity due to its extreme desire to remember the service of healing and polarization possible by the mechanisms of the crystal and the charged healer.

The second experience being approximately 1,000 of your years later, during which experience this entity prepared, in some part, the consciousness of the people of what you now call Egypt, that they were able to offer the calling that enabled those of our social memory complex to walk among your peoples. During this life experience, this entity was of a priest and teaching nature and succeeded in remembering in semidistorted form the learn/teachings of the Atlantean pyramidal experiences. Thus, this entity became a builder of the archetypal thought of the Law of One with distortions towards healing, which aided our people in bringing this through into a physical manifestation.

QUESTIONER: The second question is: Paul has also received information that there were other beings aiding in the construction of the pyramids, but that they were not fully materialized in the third density. They were materialized from their waist up to their heads but were not materialized from their waist down to their feet. Did such entities exist and aid in the construction of the pyramids, and who were they?

RA: I am Ra. Consider, if you will, the intelligent infinity present in the absorption of livingness and beingness as it becomes codified into intelligent energy, due to the thought impressions of those assisting the living stone into a new shape of beingness. The release and use of intelligent infinity for a brief period begins to absorb all the consecutive or interlocking dimensions, thus offering brief glimpses of those projecting to the material their thought. These beings thus beginning to materialize but not remaining visible. These beings were the thought-form or third-density visible manifestation of our social memory complex as we offered contact from our intelligent infinity to the intelligent infinity of the stone.

Fragment 17

Ra had advised Carla never to do any kind of physical healing, because she was always very low on physical energy, and such healing would tend to drain her already low reserve in that area.

Since I was a child, I have had some sort of odd ability to sit with someone and, with our hands in contact, be able to clear some of the surface clutter away from the other person's mind or being. I have never investigated what

I am doing or how to do it better, trusting rather in my instinct for the right time to offer this. Perhaps I should, but it has always struck me as a very marginal gift, not one near my central path. I think that if I have any healing ability, it is in my listening. When someone comes to me for private counsel, I think of the time as a "listening session" and see myself as a spiritual listener. There is much healing in a person's talking something through with another in a supportive atmosphere. The listener simply enables the person to listen better to herself. And I have very deep instincts toward doing this. So this is where I have focused my own efforts to become a better healer. Listening is truly an art, and I think it begins with the way we listen to ourselves. There is a tremendous strength in knowing one's full self, the dark side as well as the one that sees the light of everyday behavior.

Once one has finally become able to bear one's own full nature and has gone through the painful process of surrendering the pride that would deny that wretchedness within, one becomes better able to love and forgive oneself. Often I think we feel our failure comes in being unkind to another. But when this occurs, you can be sure the first and proximate cause of this outer ruthlessness lies within, in the self's refusal to reckon with the full-circle self.

Session 29,
February 23, 1981

QUESTIONER: The instrument had a question, if we have time for a short question. I will read it. The instrument does not desire to do physical-healing work. She already does spiritual balancing by hands. Can she read the private healing material without doing physical healing? I am assuming that she means can she read it without creating problems in her life pattern. She does not wish to incur lessening of positive polarity. Can she read the material under these conditions?

RA: I am Ra. We shall speak shortly due to the fact that we are attempting to conserve this instrument's vital energies during the three-month period of which we have spoken.

This entity has an experiential history of healing on levels other than the so-called physical. Thus it is acceptable that this material be read. However, the exercise of fire shall never be practiced by this instrument, as it is used in the stronger form for physical healing.

Fragment 18

A fellow associated with Cosmic Awareness Communications in

Washington State was developing and distributing a machine that was supposed to augment the general health and well-being of a person, and we asked Ra whether it might aid Carla. The response suggested that Carla's magnetic field was somewhat unusual and very likely formed in such an unusual way as to permit contact with those of Ra specifically. This unusual magnetic field has been a source of frequent inconveniences with any electromagnetic equipment that Carla has used on a regular basis. She breaks it—just by touching it periodically. She can't wear any but quartz crystal watches, and we have many, many semifunctional tape recorders lying about different areas of our house.

It makes for a good story, but it can be frustrating to have electronically damaging energy—I am not amused when I break things. The last thing I want to do is destroy the very machines that allow me to communicate. And my tendency to feel various odd energies has at times been an unwelcome gift. I remember a couple of times when my being able to perceive some occult frequency or another put me in the way of very forceful people who decided that I was to work with them. Of course, I have withstood any requests for help that I felt uncomfortable accepting, but I really don't enjoy the process of convincing someone that I won't come out and play!

In all of the things, and there are a million or two, that we've tried to better my physical condition, we have not found anything of that nature that avails. However, the gifts of spirit and faith are far more efficacious. So I have become relatively uninterested in new modalities and gadgets— and rest in prayer and peace, knowing the perfect self within.

Session 30,
February 24, 1981

QUESTIONER: The instrument would like to know if you could tell her whether or not this item which is called Sam Millar's polarizer would help her physical well-being. Could you do that?

RA: I am Ra. As we scan the instrument, we find anomalies of the magnetic field which are distorted towards our abilities to find narrow-band channel into this instrument's mind/body/spirit complex. The polarizer of which you speak, as it is, would not be helpful. A careful reading of this instrument's aura by those gifted in this area, and subsequent alterations of the magnetizing forces of this polarizer, would assist the entity, Sam, in creating such a polarizer that would be of some aid to the instrument. However, we would suggest that no electrical or magnetic equipment not necessary for the recording of our words be brought into these sessions, for we wish no distortions that are not necessary.

Fragment 19

Many people have written to us over the years, telling us of what they call psychic attacks and asking how to protect themselves from them. It seems that one needn't perform any elaborate rituals or call upon any big-league light bearers for assistance. Ra describes the manner in which anyone can provide all the protection that will ever be necessary in any situation. And it is very, very simple.

I will be 54 next birthday, and as I get older, I become more and more convinced that our path always lies in offering praise and thanksgiving for whatever is coming our way, no matter what we may humanly think about it. This is easy to do in good times, but it is a matter of some persistence of discipline to train the mind not to shrink away from trouble we perceive coming at us. However, I encourage in everyone that patient tenacity that refuses to doubt the Creator, no matter what. Once we have very clear the fact that we are safely in the Creator's hands and heart, this becomes easier. But the work is never fully done, for we fail again and again to witness to the light, and this causes confusion in our patterns of destiny.

Session 32,
February 27, 1981

QUESTIONER: I have a question that I will throw in at this point from Jim. I will read it. The instrument's physical vehicle is now in the process of recovery from the ingestion of a chemical. She was ignorant of the opening that she was creating. How may the three of us present be more aware of how such openings may be created in our actions and our thoughts? Is it possible that we can make such openings innocently as we question in different areas during these sessions? And what can we do to protect ourselves from negative influences in general? Are there any rituals or meditations that we can do to protect ourselves?

RA: I am Ra. Although we are in sympathy with the great desire to be of service exemplified by the question, our answer is limited by the distortion of the Way of Confusion. We shall say some general things which may be of service in this area.

Firstly, when this instrument distorted its bodily complex towards low vital energy due to this occurrence, it was a recognizable substance which caused this. This was not a, shall we say, natural substance nor was the mind/body/spirit complex enough aware of its distortion towards physical weakness. The natural ways of, shall we say, everyday existence, in which the entity without the distortions caused by ingestion of strongly effective chemicals, may be seen to be of an always appropriate nature. There are no mistakes, including the action of this instrument.

Secondly, the means of protection against any negative or debilitating influence for those upon the positive path was demonstrated by this instrument to a very great degree. Consider, if you will, the potentials that this particular occurrence had for negative influences to enter the instrument. This instrument thought upon the Creator in its solitude and in actions with other-self, continually praised and gave thanksgiving to the Creator for the experiences it was having. This in turn allowed this particular self such energies as became a catalyst for an opening and strengthening of the other-self's ability to function in a more positively polarized state. Thus we see protection being very simple. Give thanksgiving for each moment. See the self and the other-self as Creator. Open the heart. Always know the light and praise it. This is all the protection necessary.

Fragment 20

Because Carla's physical energy level was always very low and constantly being drained by the arthritic condition and the persistent presence of some degree of pain, it became necessary for her to engage in daily exercise in order to maintain the function of each portion of her body. We found that the more distorted or low on energy she was, the greater was the need for this exercise. When her body was functioning most nearly normally, the exercise could be reduced in length until it also was normal. For Carla that was about one hour of rapid walking per day.

When Don queried about an experience that he had in 1964, the specificity of the answer was limited by Ra's desire to maintain Don's free will. Most events in our lives are a mystery in some degree or another. One way of looking at the process of evolution is to see it as the process of solving the mysteries all about us. All events are illusions or mysteries because each represents the One Creator in one disguise or another, offering us a greater or lesser opportunity to find love, joy, balance, and perfection in each moment. There is a spiritual strength that comes with unraveling such mysteries for one's self. It is not always a service for those with better-trained eyes to tell another what he does not yet see for himself, but which he has the capacity to learn to see. Thus Ra often invoked the Law of Free Will, also known as the Law of Confusion.

When I was a child, I danced and swam and rode horses. I loved exercise, especially when it was rhythmic. The exercise that was my lot to do during this time was, though very hard because I felt so tired, an energizing experience. Both Don and Jim helped me remember to get these periods in, and Jim made them easier still by joining me. It is always easier to do such things with a buddy! Don was not able to join me in these walks, as he had a painful condition of the feet brought on by working in tropical climes, and every step hurt. However, I witnessed, from time to time, a level of animal strength in Don that was miraculous. For instance, in 1977 Don and I went to join in a Mind Link held by Andrija Puharich. Gathered were a mixed bag of established psychics, all women, and other middle-aged supporters, and about an equal number of college-age kids who had identified themselves to Puharich as Wanderers. The kids loved soccer and played it when we weren't in session. Don joined in their first game. He did really well, impressing not only me but all the kids. They finally had to stop the game, red faced and panting. Donald was not even breathing heavily. Needless to say, the kids warmed up to Don quickly! But they never could get him to play again.

Session 34,
March 4, 1981

QUESTIONER: The instrument would like to know if two short exercise periods per day would be better for her than one long one.

RA: I am Ra. This is incorrect. The proper configuration of the physical complex exercising during the three-month period, wherein the instrument is vulnerable to physical complex distortion intensification, needs the strengthening of the physical complex. This may appropriately be seen to be one major period of the exercising, followed late in your diurnal cycle before the evening meditation by an exercise period approximately one-half the length of the first. This will be seen to be wearing upon the instrument. However, it will have the effect of strengthening the physical complex and lessening the vulnerability which might be taken advantage of.

QUESTIONER: Is it possible for you to tell me what I experienced, around 1964 I believe it was, when in meditation I became aware of what I considered a different density and different planet and seemed to experience moving onto that planet? Is it possible for you to tell me what experience that was?

RA: I am Ra. We see some harm in full disclosure due to infringement. We content ourselves with suggesting that this entity, which is not readily able to subject itself to the process of hypnotic regression instigated by others, nevertheless has had its opportunities for understanding of its beingness.

Fragment 21
Having only a faint but persistent idea that we had come to this planet in order to be of service to others was apparently a sufficient degree of the "penetrating of the forgetting process" that Don mentioned in Session 36, for we had little more than that with which to begin the Ra contact.

Any third-density entity apparently has a Higher Self or Oversoul that is at the mid-sixth-density level of being. In addition, the Wanderer who is a member of a social memory complex also has another complex of consciousness upon which to call for assistance, for each social memory complex also seems to have the equivalent of its own Oversoul, or what Ra calls a "mind/body/spirit complex totality."

The forgetting process, or the veil, is a term used often by our sources. The basic thought is that when we take on flesh and become a manifested entity on the earth plane, that flesh shuts our metaphysical senses. All that we knew before birth is hidden in the deeper mind, and we set out on our earthly pilgrimage with only our naked selves and our heartfelt desires. It is no wonder then that Wanderers have some difficulty waking up within the illusion we call consensus reality. There is always the fear, as one enters incarnation, that one will not awaken at all but be lost for the whole life experience. You who read this sentence are probably right in the midst of this awakening process, beginning more and more to identify with a new and larger concept of the self as an eternal and metaphysical being.

As we all awaken and develop our truer selves, we can help each other, and I encourage each Wanderer to find ways to support fellow pilgrims of the light. People will come your way. They may not seem to be very "aware," or they may seem quite aware but very confused or frightened. If the Creator put them in your way, then you are well equipped to aid them. Simply love and accept them.

This is much harder to do than to say. It involves first coming to love and accept yourself, forgiving yourself for the myriad imperfections and folly you find when gazing within. But all work is upon the self, speaking metaphysically. If you have trouble loving someone, look within for the place within self where you have rejected part of yourself, some slice of the dark side you'd rather not see or experience. As you work with this loving, accepting, and forgiving of the dark side of self, you are working on service to all the other selves coming your way. I think the key to this acceptance of self is to see that to be in flesh is to be very imperfect and confused. There is no way to be without error when in the context of the world. Yet, within us there is that self without the veil, with perfect memory of who we are and what we came to do. Once one is able to face one's wretched side, one becomes much more able to be transparent to that infinite love that comes not from us but through us, to bless all.

In this practice of loving, we have a wonderful source of strength and courage: the Higher Self. I call this self the Holy Spirit, because I am of the distortion called mystical Christianity. Other people refer to this Higher Self as inner guides, angelic beings, the higher nature, or simply Guidance. Whatever the term, this energy is quite dependable, always there, supporting and sustaining. One can practice becoming more aware of this energy, consciously opening to it within meditation, and calling upon it in times of challenge. I encourage each to see the self as an awakening being, with much support from the unseen forces. Lean into these sources of strength in silence and prayer. They will truly aid you.

Session 36,
March 10, 1981

QUESTIONER: I was wondering if qualification for contact with Ra might include penetrating this forgetting process. Is this correct?

RA: I am Ra. This is quite correct.

QUESTIONER: Otherwise the Law of Confusion would prohibit this? Is this correct?

RA: This is correct.

QUESTIONER: I was also wondering if three was the minimum number necessary for this type of working. Is this correct?

RA: I am Ra. For protection of this instrument, this is necessary as the minimum grouping and also as the most efficient number due to the exceptional harmony in this group. In other groups the number could be larger, but we have observed in this contact that the most efficient support is given by the individual mind/body/spirits present at this time.

QUESTIONER: I'm a little fuzzy on a point with respect to the Higher Self. We each, I am assuming, have an individual Higher Self at sixth-density positive level. Is this correct? Each of us in the room here; that is, the three of us?

RA: I am Ra. This shall be the last full question of this working. We shall attempt to aim for the intention of your query as we understand it. Please request any additional information.

Firstly, it is correct that each in this dwelling place has one Oversoul, as you may call it. However, due to the repeated harmonious interactions of this triad of entities, there may be seen to be a further harmonious interaction besides the three entities' Higher Selves; that is, each social memory complex has an Oversoul of a type which is difficult to describe to you in words. In this group there are two such social memory complex totalities blending their efforts with your Higher Selves at this time.

Fragment 22

In March 1981, we sent off the first ten sessions of the Ra contact to the Scott Meredith Literary Agency in New York City. We wanted to get the information out to as many people as we could, and we thought that a large literary agency could help us find a publisher. After considering the manuscript for about two weeks, Mr. Meredith was kind enough to write us a four-page, single-spaced letter thanking us for sending him the material and telling us why it had no chance in the marketplace. The heart of the letter may be summarized by the following quote:

"No entity that wreaks such havoc with the English language is going to ingratiate himself with the general reading public. This has all the denseness of *The New England Journal of Medicine*, or the *Journal of English and German Philology*, or a PhD dissertation on epistemology . . . and for another thing, the dialogue form gets pretty tedious after a while. It was all the rage in Athens for a while, I know, and its popularity continued all the way through the Neoclassic Renaissance, but it died out shortly afterwards, and I don't think that it's about to be revived."

Ra's final comment on the topic of how to make the information available brought a somewhat humorous end to our earnestness. A few days earlier we had been sitting around the kitchen table, wondering aloud what cosmic humor might be like, and Ra took this opportunity to give us an illustration. We would give the same basic advice to any group trying to disseminate information that it has collected so that it might be of service to others. Relax, and let the Law of Attraction work. Even if only one person is aided by the work, that is enough. At the very least, the benefit that the material provides to the group alone will become like unto a light that each in the group will radiate to all others met in the daily round of activities.

And since we had discovered for ourselves the necessity of pursuing nontransient information, Ra clearly states that that was a requirement for maintaining the contact, in contrast to Don's estimate of the kind of information that usually attracts the attention of the marketplace.

It was always a hope of Don's that we would be able to communicate to a large number of people. He felt a real urgency at getting the word out, and as the contact with Ra persisted, his concern deepened. It was like a breath of fresh air to find Ra counseling us to be content with our "reasonable effort." As we write these comments, the first book of The Law of One series has sold about 30,000 copies. Our mail this week included queries from Poland, Romania, Malaysia, and Japan, as well as the USA and Canada. I am sure that a little part of Don is sitting on my shoulder like the angel he is, content at last with his life's work and seeing it taken up by those who find it useful.

The concept of sacrifice as part of the beginning of contact is not new at all. The channel for Oahspe was told in a vision that he must live austerely for ten years before he could be of help, and he and a friend did just that, living monastically, waiting for the time of opportunity. When his decade of sacrifice was through, he was told to get a typewriter, new at the time. He did so. Over the next few years, he channeled the huge book, being put at the typewriter while he was asleep at night. He would awaken each morning to find his work lying by the machine. And Edgar Cayce had similar experiences with being told he needed to sacrifice in order to serve. In our case, Jim sacrificed his love of isolation and retreat from humankind; Don sacrificed his solitude with me, that happy and safe harbor we had made together. He let Jim into the very fabric of our lives, with never the first word of complaint. He also sacrificed himself by working in order to support us. I had the easiest sacrifice, that of myself as channel. The contact was hard on me, and I wasted away under the brilliant energy of Ra's vibration, losing two to three pounds per session. But I would gladly have died in this service, for during these sessions, Don was a happy man. This was the only time during which I knew him that he was not melancholy in his quiet way. To see him fulfilled and content was one of the greatest sources of pleasure in my whole life, for I knew that I'd been a part of that. It was worth every-thing, and I'd do it all again in a heartbeat, even the extremities of grief that we all felt as Donald sickened and perished, and I came closer and closer to death through the years following Don's suicide. My part of sacrifice has been turned into joy and satisfaction, and I know Don and Jim feel the same.

That reviewer at the agency was quite right to view the language of Ra as technical. It represents the most balanced attempt I have ever read at creating a vocabulary for talking about metaphysical issues with neutral emotional words. It may be stilted at first read, but one always knows what Ra is trying to say, a real achievement in such subjects.

Session 37,
March 12, 1981

QUESTIONER: Is Ra familiar with the results of our efforts today to publish the first book that we did?

RA: I am Ra. This is correct.

QUESTIONER: I don't know if you can comment on the difficulty that we will have in making the Law of One available to those who would require it and want it. It is not something that is easy to disseminate to those who want it at this time. I am sure that there are many, especially the Wanderers, who want this information, but we will have to do something else in order to get it into their hands in the way of added material, I am afraid. Is it possible for you to comment on this?

RA: I am Ra. It is possible.

QUESTIONER: Will you comment on it?

RA: I am Ra. We shall. Firstly, the choosing of this group to do some work to serve others was of an intensive nature. Each present sacrificed much for no tangible result. Each may search its heart for the type of sacrifice, knowing that the material sacrifices are the least; the intensive commitment to blending into an harmonious group at the apex of sacrifice.

Under these conditions, we found your vibration. We observed your vibration. It will not be seen often. We do not wish to puff up the pride, but we shall not chaffer with the circumstances necessary for our particular contact. Thus you have received and we willingly undertake the honor/duty of continuing to offer transmissions of concepts which are, to the best of our abilities, precise in nature and grounded in the attempt to unify many of those things that concern you.

Secondly, the use you make of these transmissions is completely at your discretion. We suggest the flowing of the natural intuitive senses and a minimum of the distortion towards concern. We are content, as we have said, to be able to aid in the evolution of one of your peoples. Whatever effort you make cannot disappoint us, for that number already exceeds one.

QUESTIONER: I have been very hesitant to ask certain questions for fear that they would be regarded, as I regard them, as questions of unimportance or of too great a specificity and thereby reduce our contact with you. In order to disseminate some of the information that I consider to be of great importance—that is, the nontransient type of information, information having to do with the evolution of mind, body, and spirit, it seems almost necessary in our society to include information that is of little value simply because that is how our society works, how the system of distribution appraises that which is offered for distribution. Will you comment on this problem that I have?

RA: I am Ra. We comment as follows: It is quite precisely correct that the level and purity of this contact is dependent upon the level and purity of information sought. Thusly, the continued request for specific information from this particular source is deleterious to the substance of your purpose. Moreover, as we scanned your mind to grasp your situation as regards the typescript of some of our words, we found that you had been criticized for the type of language construction used to convey data. Due to our orientation with regard to data, even the most specifically answered question would be worded by our group in such a way as to maximize the accuracy of the nuances of the answer. This, however, mitigates against what your critic desires in the way of simple, lucid prose. More than this we cannot say. These are our observations of your situation. What you wish to do is completely your decision, and we remain at your service in whatever way we may be without breaking the Way of Confusion.

QUESTIONER: We will attempt to work around these problems in the dissemination of the Law of One. It will take some careful work to do this. I personally will not cease while still incarnate to disseminate this. It will be necessary to write a book, probably about UFOs, because the Law of One is connected with the phenomenon. It's connected with all phenomena, but this seems to be the easiest entry for dissemination. I plan firstly to use the UFO in the advertising sense, as it was meant by the Confederation as an entry into an explanation of the process of evolution that is going on on this planet, and how the rest of the Confederation has been involved in a more understandable way, shall I say, for the population that will read the book. We will use the Ra material in undistorted form, just as it has been recorded here in various places throughout the book, to amplify and clarify what we are saying in the book. This is the only way that I can see right now to create enough dissemination for the people who would like to have the Law of One for them to be able to get it. I could just print up the material that we have off of the tape recorder and publish it, but we wouldn't be able to disseminate it very well because of distribution problems. Will you comment on my second idea of doing a general book on UFOs, including the material from the Law of One?

RA: I am Ra. We shall comment. We hope that your Ra plans materialize. This is a cosmic joke. You were asking for such an example of humor, and we feel this is a rather appropriate nexus in which one may be inserted. Continue with your intentions to the best of your natures and abilities. What more can be done, my friends?

Fragment 23

Serving as the instrument for the Ra contact was very wearing on Carla. She would lose between two and three pounds per session, and the psychic-greeting component of the contact often intensified her arthritic distortions to the point that her functioning on all levels was severely curtailed. Thus, Don and I had hoped that one or the other of us could take her place from time to time in order to give her rest, but neither of us was properly prepared for this service. So rest was obtained by spacing the sessions out over a greater period of time, and we all contented ourselves with the fact that there was a price to be paid for being able to offer this kind of service, and Carla would have to bear the brunt of that price.

I cannot express the amount of pleasure I felt at being able to serve in this way. To see Donald happy and inspired was a satisfaction of the heart that struck to the depths of my being. I adored Don and wished to make him comfortable and happy. But he was not comfortable in this world and so often felt painfully lonely and isolated, although this was never mentioned, nor did he show it in any way. For some reason, his pain and loneliness were always utterly apparent to me and called forth my deepest sympathy and desire to nurture. The days of the Ra contact were golden indeed. I would have died quite gladly doing one last session, and rather expected to, and embraced that freely, but Don's death came first. So I remain! The years since his death have opened to me a wonderful path of service, as readers write in, and I have become counselor and friend to so many all over the world. It is as though I received a second life, for truly when Donald died, the Carla that was, was gone. He had taken a 25-year-old and molded her to his needs, with my willing aid. I became truly his creature. When I woke up from that life, 16 years later, I was neither that 25-year-old nor Don's. I really had to start from scratch to discover my current self.

Session 38,
March 13, 1981

QUESTIONER: Will you tell us if there would be any hope or any purpose in either Jim or me taking the instrument's place as instrument by attempting the trance work ourselves?

RA: I am Ra. This information is on the borderline of infringement upon free will. We shall, however, assume your desire to constitute permission to speak slightly beyond limits set by Confederation guidelines, shall we say.

At this space/time nexus, neither the one known as Don nor the one known as Jim is available for this working. The one known as Don, by, shall we say, practicing the mechanics of contact and service to others by means of the channeling, as you call it, would in a certain length of your time become able to do this working. The one known as Jim would find it difficult to become a channel of this type without more practice also over a longer period of time. Then we should have to experiment with the harmonics developed by this practice. This is true in both cases.

Fragment 24

The difficulties in recovering physical energy that Carla experienced as a result of the two experiences with LSD continued to shorten sessions and keep her condition somewhat fragile. We again saw not only the powerful effects of this chemical agent—which we do not recommend to anyone—but the even more powerful effects of unwise choices made by those who wish above all else to be of service to others. As time and experience with the Ra contact accumulated, we became increasingly aware that the honor of providing this kind of service brought with it the need for just as much responsibility for providing the service with as much purity and harmony as one was capable of producing in every facet of the life experience. What was learned needed to be put to use in the daily life, or difficulties would result in the life pattern that were the means by which the subconscious mind would provide the opportunity to regain the balance and harmony that had been lost. These difficulties could then also be intensified by Orion crusaders in the form of psychic greetings designed to stop the contact with Ra.

We also discovered that every person who incarnates brings with him or her certain avenues, preferences, or ways of nurturing its inner beingness. This inner beingness is that which is the true enabler and ennobler of our daily lives. When we would ask Ra how best to aid the instrument, we would often get more-specific suggestions according to the situation, but we would always be reminded of those qualities that were Carla's ways of nurturing her inner beingness.

Data from the Ra contact indicates that I never had much actual physical energy at all, which fits with my own personal, subjective sense of myself as one who runs on spiritual and mental energy, and as one physically lazy. I call it laziness because I have such a hard time making myself do physical work, unless it is walking and wandering, dancing or swimming, rhythmic activities I love. Even as a young child I was easily able to sit and read, or sit and imagine, for hours. So the sessions we were doing completely exhausted my actual innate physical energy quite quickly. To this very day, I think that since then I have always run on nerve alone, and the simple joy of being alive, which I have in abundance.

Don and Jim both were very upright persons of marked integrity and character, which helped tremendously, as the process of psychic greeting could work only on our inherent distortions. They loved each other and treated each other with great respect, and did their utmost to care for me. They were wonderful in making sure that all was done as well as possible to make me more comfortable. I also had the advantage of being a straight-arrow kind of soul all my life. So the negative energy could only intensify my many physical "problems." Thus the sessions were extremely wearing, but I gloried in them nevertheless, for seeing Don's pleasure in the talks with Ra was more than enough payment to me. I was and am careless of life force if by giving it I can see another live more fully.

I should note that I see the purity that Ra speaks of in myself not as a shining virtue or as a personal achievement, but rather as a gift of nature. I cannot remember a time when I was other than completely involved in the passion of my life: that life itself. I saw myself as a child of God and wanted my life to be a gift to that deity. I was drawn to virtue as others are to gambling or drugs. This inexplicable condition still prevails—my hopes for this life remain simply the giving of all I have to the Creator. What this purity is not is celibacy or retreat from the workings of the world. I have always followed my relationships and based my life around them, trusted my passion, and had an earthy, even vulgar side. I simply find life a wonder and a joy, and all the limitation, mess, loss, and pain in this world have not changed my mind on that.

Session 39,
March 16, 1981

QUESTIONER: The instrument was wondering if the fragile feeling she has now is the result of the chemical ingestion of about six weeks ago.

RA: I am Ra. This is correct. This instrument is now undergoing the most intensive period of physical complex debilitation/distortion due to the doubling effects of the two ingestions. This instrument may expect this extremity to proceed for a period of fifteen to twenty of your diurnal cycles. The weakness distortions will then begin to lift; however, not as rapidly as we first thought due to this instrument's weakness distortions. This instrument is very fortunate in having a support group which impresses upon it the caution necessary as regards these sessions at this time. This instrument is capable of almost instantaneously clearing the mental/emotional complex and the spiritual complex for the purity this working requires, but this instrument's distortion towards fidelity to service does not function to its best use of judgment regarding the weakness distortions of the physical complex. Thus we appreciate your assistance at space/times such as that in your most recent decision-making not to have a working. This was the appropriate decision, and the guidance given this instrument was helpful.

QUESTIONER: Is there anything that the instrument can do in addition to what she is attempting to do to help her condition get better faster? I know that she hasn't been able to exercise because of her foot problem for the last couple of days, but we are hoping to get back to that. Is there anything else that she could do?

RA: I am Ra. As we have implied, the negative entities are moving all stops out to undermine this instrument at this time. This is the cause of the aforementioned problem with the pedal digit. It is fortunate that this instrument shall be greatly involved in the worship of the One Infinite Creator through the vibratory complexes of sacred song during this period. The more active physical existence, both in the movements of exercise and in the sexual sense, are helpful. However, the requirement of this instrument's distortions toward what you would call ethics have an effect upon this latter activity. Again, it is fortunate that this instrument has the opportunities for loving social intercourse, which are of some substantial benefit. Basically, in your third-density continuum, this is a matter of time.

QUESTIONER: From your reading of the instrument's condition, can you approximate how often and the length of workings we should plan on in future workings?

RA: I am Ra. This query borders upon infringement. The information given sets up fairly followable guidelines. However, we are aware that not only can each of you not read this instrument's aura and so see conditions of the physical complex, but also the instrument itself has considerable difficulty penetrating the precise distortion condition of its physical complex due to its constant dependence upon its will to serve. Therefore, we believe we are not infringing if we indicate that one working each alternate diurnal period in the matinal hours is most appropriate, with the possibility of a shorter working upon the free matinal period if deemed appropriate. This is so not only during this period but in general.

Fragment 25

Almost everyone on the path of consciously seeking the truth has had some kind of mystical experience that may or may not make much sense to the person. Most such experiences remain unfathomable to our conscious minds and accomplish their work in an unseen and incomprehensible fashion. Being inhabitants of the third density, with the great veil of forgetting drawn over our ability to see and to truly know, we must content ourselves with the fact that we only make the barest beginnings upon understanding in this illusion. But we may also rest assured that there are no mistakes, and that the events of our lives, whether ordinary or extraordinary, fall into the appropriate place at the appropriate time.

Don had several experiences of altered consciousness that were permanently etched into his mind. The initiation he spoke of here was received in 1968, while we were in meditation together. He suddenly found himself in a world where the colors were living. He said these colors made our earthly hues look like black-and-white photos. They were three-dimensional. He saw living waters, and a golden sunrise streaming over the sky. He could open his eyes and he was in his chair, then close them again and see the other world. This state lasted about half an hour. The other event that is notable, to me, was a night he was meditating and found his arm moving rapidly up and down from elbow to fingers as his arm rested upon the chair arm. A blue light began to emanate from his lower arm, and he was forever grateful that he had company who saw his arm turning blue and glowing. Later transmissions indicated that the UFO entities were winding his battery!

Session 42,
March 22, 1981

QUESTIONER: I had one experience in meditation which I spoke of before which was very profound, approximately twenty years ago, a little less. What disciplines would be most applicable to create this situation and this type of experience?

RA: I am Ra. Your experience would best be approached from the ceremonial magical stance. However, the Wanderer or adept shall have the far-greater potential for this type of experience, which, as you have undoubtedly analyzed to be the case, is one of an archetypal nature, one belonging to the roots of cosmic consciousness.

QUESTIONER: Was that in any way related to the Golden Dawn in ceremonial magic?

RA: I am Ra. The relationship was congruency.

QUESTIONER: Then in attempting to reproduce this experience, would I then best follow the practices for the Order of the Golden Dawn in reproducing this?

RA: I am Ra. To attempt to reproduce an initiatory experience is to move, shall we say, backwards. However, the practice of this form of service to others is appropriate in your case, working with your associates. It is not well for positively polarized entities to work singly. The reasons for this are obvious.

QUESTIONER. Then this experience was a form of initiation? Is this correct?

RA: I am Ra. Yes.

Fragment 26

(Entire session)

Session 44 was removed from Book II because it is almost entirely a maintenance session. In querying as to how best to revitalize Carla's physical vehicle and aid the contact with Ra in general, we did, however, discover a couple of fundamental principles that we found useful thereafter.

In the first answer, we found that a strong desire to be of service is not enough when it is uninformed by wisdom. Carla, and our entire group as well, suffered in the first months of the Ra contact from an overactive desire to be of service through having more sessions with Ra than was helpful for the contact over the long run. Scheduling so many sessions in such a short period of time was overly draining on Carla's physical energy and would mean that the total number of sessions that was possible during her incarnation was probably being reduced.

The second principle that we found of interest was the power of dedication. If Carla dedicated herself to having a session with Ra, she would expend an amount of energy equal to a full day's work—even if the session did not occur. Thus, it was most important that her dedication be informed by wisdom, if not her own then that of the support group's. Thus, for any person, it is the will that drives the dedication, all thoughts, words, and actions depending therefrom. As one points the will, one's desires become manifest. It is important, therefore, that one use the will carefully.

My body has always been fragile. Born with birth defects, laid low by rheumatic fever at the age of 2 years and kidney failure at ages 13 and 15, I have since worked with an increasing amount of rheumatoid arthritis and other rheumatoid diseases. By 1981, when the contact with Ra began, I had had several operations on my wrists and finger joints and was experiencing rheumatoid changes in virtually every joint in my body, the neck and back being the worst hit after the hands. I had worked as a librarian, a job I loved, and as a researcher and writer for Don, but 1976 was the last year I was able to manage a typewriter, and by 1981 I was on Social Security disability and having grave problems physically, both organic and rheumatoid. I was in pain constantly. I tolerated this without much remark and tried to appear well; indeed, I felt healthy. But the body was a weak one. And I think that the trance state was difficult, because without my being able to move my body around, it simply lay in one position during the sessions. This meant that the bad joints were liable to become far more painful, especially in those joints of back, neck, and wrist that were severely damaged. I would wake up in a world of hurt. There did not seem to be a way to avoid this, and it was easy for me to be discouraged at my imperfect physical vehicle. I felt as though I were letting the group down when Ra said they had to limit the session length, and always tried my hardest to maximize my time in trance.

Donald and Jim never reproached me even the first time and were endlessly patient in working with my limitations. However, I cried many a tear of frustration, for I wished so much to be able to continue with this channeling of Ra. It was fortunate for the contact that Jim and I were lovers, for apparently all the physical energy I had to give, after the first few sessions, was the energy transferred during lovemaking. How does a person called "pure" have a lover? Purely, of course. I tried celibacy for about two years when Don and I first got together. I found it extremely difficult and unsatisfying as a life choice. After talking this over with Donald, we agreed that I would take a lover if I wished. As he was gone fully half of the time flying for Eastern Air Lines, I was able to be completely discreet. He never saw the lover, who never saw him. When Jim began coming to meditations regularly, I had once again been celibate for about four years, not having anyone I felt good about to be a lover and friend. Jim was the answer to a maiden's prayers, being extremely fond of his solitude most of the time, but a marvelous companion and an amazing lover when he was in the mood. He wanted nothing from me in the everyday sense of having a constant companion. Don wanted only that companionship. The two men fitted into my life like puzzle pieces, just so. It was, for the time it lasted, a seamless and wonderful threesome of those who truly and entirely wished to serve.

I pondered Ra's words about martyrdom for some time and eventually decided that I should take a vacation, the first one I had taken since 1971. Jim and I went to the seashore, and I rested and felt great healing. I see this as the first step I took away from the forces of death and toward an embrace of continued life. I wish that Don could also have done this, but it was not in him.

I think Ra's comments on how to treat psychic greeting are very wise. To look on these experiences of being "attacked" as less than vitally important was to invite their prolongation. When faced and given full consideration, without fear, just being with these energies and loving them, seeing them as the dark side of oneself, the greetings were simply experiences to have and to ponder, working toward acceptance of the full self. Jesus suggested that we not resist evil, and I think this is part of what He meant—to embrace the greeting as coming from the self, and as loved by the self, was to draw its teeth and neutralize its venom.

Donald had a long-standing interest in ritual magic, one that predated my arrival in his life. He was fascinated with the thought that somehow he could help me by dealing with the negative entities that were offering greetings. It has always been an uneasy thought that he, as he once discussed *with Jim, might have tried to make a pact with the entity that was so persistently greeting me, to give himself instead of me.*

Session 44 (in total),
March 28, 1981

RA: I am Ra. I greet you in the love and in the light of the One Infinite Creator. We communicate now.

QUESTIONER: The instrument had some question as to her vitality. We were having some difficulty in appraising it. Is it possible for you to comment on this?

RA: I am Ra. We scan this instrument and find that we may be of service without infringement due to this instrument's decision to abide by the most careful appraisal possible rather than the most desired.

We have been surprised that we have been able to maintain contact on a regular basis during this most intense period of negatively influenced interference. Sexual-energy transfers have at some workings given this instrument additional vital resources upon which to draw. However, this is not so at this working, and, therefore the will of the instrument drives its bodily complex. This instrument has no judgment about this service. The faculty of will, while recognized as most central and valuable, could in this application cause serious distortion in the bodily complex of the instrument. May we note that martyrdom is not necessarily helpful. We ask this instrument to examine these thoughts, judge, and discriminate the possible truth of them, and if they be deemed true, we suggest this instrument release the power of judgment to the support group, whose interests are balanced far more than this instrument's. Allow decisions to be made without expectation or attachment to the outcome. Our hopes, may we say, for long-term contact through this instrument depend upon its maturing ability to be of service to other-selves by accepting their help and thus remaining a viable instrument.

May we thank the questioner for allowing us to speak to this point, for we were aware of the distortions incumbent upon one whose will to serve is not regulated by knowledge of limitations of bodily complex distortion.

QUESTIONER: Could you please terminate this contact as soon as necessary, since we are not aware of the vitality of the instrument at this time?

RA: I am Ra. In your way of speaking, our hands are, to a certain extent, tied. This instrument has called upon inner reserves which are dearly bought. Therefore, we have the honor/duty of using this energy to the best of our ability. When it becomes low, we shall most certainly, as always, express the need for ending the working. The only way of avoiding this sharing of service at whatever cost is to refrain from the working. It is a dilemma.

QUESTIONER: Can you tell me what the tone was that I heard in my left ear when you started your communication?

RA: I am Ra. This was a negatively oriented signal.

QUESTIONER: Can you tell me how I would hear a positively oriented signal?

RA: I am Ra. Two types there are of positive signal. First, in the right-ear location the signal indicates a sign that you are being given some unworded message saying, "Listen. Take heed." The other positive sign is the tone above the head, which is a balanced confirmation of a thought.

QUESTIONER: Are there any other negatively oriented signals that I get?

RA: I am Ra. This is correct. You are able to receive thought-forms, word-forms, and visions. However, you seem able to discriminate.

QUESTIONER: Is there a reason that I am open to these signals of a negative nature?

RA: I am Ra. Are you not all things?

QUESTIONER: I think that it might be a good idea if we terminated the contact at this time to allow the instrument to gain more of the necessary energy before continuing these sessions. This is my decision at this time. I would very much like to continue the contact, but it seems to me, although I can't tell the instrument's level, that the instrument should not use up any more energy.

RA: I am Ra. We are responding to an unasked query. However, it is most salient and therefore we beg your forgiveness for this infringement. The energy has been lost to the instrument, dedicated to this purpose only. You may do as you will, but this is the nature of the instrument's preparation for contact and is the sole reason we may use it.

QUESTIONER: I am not sure if I fully understood you. Could you say that in a little different way? Could you explain more completely?

RA: I am Ra. Each of you in this working has consciously dedicated the existence now being experienced to service to others. This instrument has refined this dedication through long experience with the channeling, as you term it, of Confederation philosophy, as you may say. Thus when we first contacted this instrument, it had offered its beingness, not only to service to other-selves but service by communication of this nature. As this contact has developed, this dedication of beingness has become quite specific. Thus, once the vital energy is dedicated by the instrument to our communications, even if the working did not occur, this vital energy would be lost to the day-by-day experience of the instrument. Thus we indicated the importance of the instrument's releasing of the will from the process of determining the times of working, for if the instrument desires contact, the energy is gathered and thus lost for ordinary or mundane purposes.

QUESTIONER: In that case, since her energy is already lost, we might as well continue with this session, and we should very carefully monitor the instrument and be the sole judge of when the sessions should occur. Am I correct?

RA: I am Ra. This is profoundly correct. This instrument's determination to continue contact during this period has already extended the low-energy period.

QUESTIONER: This is very revealing to us. Thank you. Each of us gets signals and dreams. I have been aware of clairaudient communication at least once in waking up. Can you suggest a method whereby we might be able, shall I say, to nullify the influence of that which we don't want of a negative source?

RA: I am Ra. There are various methods. We shall offer the most available or simple. To share the difficult contact with the other-selves associated with this working and to meditate in love for these senders of images and light for self and other-selves is the most available means of nullifying the effects of such occurrences. To downgrade these experiences by the use of intellect or the disciplines of will is to invite the prolonging of the effects. Far better, then, to share in trust such experiences and join hearts and souls in love and light with compassion for the sender and armor for the self.

QUESTIONER: Can you tell me the source of the instrument's dream this morning as soon as she woke up?

RA: I am Ra. The feeling of the dream, shall we say, was Orion influenced. The clothing of the dream revealing more the instrument's unconscious associative patterns of symbolism.

QUESTIONER: In meditation a number of years ago, my arm started to glow and to move rapidly involuntarily. What was that?

RA: I am Ra. The phenomenon was an analogy made available to you from your Higher Self. The analogy was that the being that you were was living in a way not understood by, shall we say, physicists, scientists, or doctors.

QUESTIONER: What I am trying to get at in this session is if there are any practices that we might be able to do to best revitalize the instrument, for it is going to be necessary to do all we can in order to maintain our contact. Can you tell us what we can do to increase the instrument's vitality for these contacts?

RA: I am Ra. Your experience was a function of your ability to contact intelligent infinity. Therefore, it does not have a direct bearing upon this instrument's vital energy.

We have spoken before of those things which aid this instrument in the vital energy: the sensitivity to beauty, to the singing of sacred music, to the meditation and worship, to the sharing of self with self in freely given love either in social or sexual intercourse. These things work quite directly upon the vitality. This instrument has a distortion towards appreciation of variety of experiences. This, in a less direct way, aids vitality.

QUESTIONER: I was looking at a diagram of the advancement of magical practices, starting from Malkuth and ending at Kether. I was wondering if these corresponded to the colors or the densities, with Malkuth as one, Yesod as two, Hod and Netzach being three, Tiphareth four, and so on. Is this correct?

RA: I am Ra. This is basically incorrect, although you are upon the correct track of thinking. Each of these stations has a complex number and shading of energy centers, as well as some part in various balances; the lower, the middle, the high, and the total balance. Thus there are complex colors or rays and complex charges, if you will, in each station.

QUESTIONER: Does the left-hand path of this represent the service-to-self path and the right-hand path the service to others?

RA: I am Ra. This will be the last full query of this working.

This is incorrect. These stations are relationships. Each path has these relationships offered. The intent of the practitioner in working with these powerful concepts determines the polarity of the working. The tools are the tools.

QUESTIONER: As an ending question, I will just ask if it is possible for the Ipsissimus then to have either positive or negative polarity, or must he be neither?

RA: I am Ra. We shall respond to the meaning of this term in a specialized sense. The Ipsissimus is one who has mastered the Tree of Life and has used this mastery for negative polarization.

Is there any brief query which we may respond to as we take leave of this instrument?

QUESTIONER: I am sorry that we got a little off the track today. I think that the most important thing that we accomplished was discovering how to better regulate the instrument's sessions, and I would hope that you would bear with me for my inability to select questions properly at times. Sometimes I probe into areas to see if it is a direction in which we might go, and, once entering, am then able to determine whether or not to continue in that direction.

Other than that, all I would like to ask is if there is anything that we can do to make the instrument more comfortable or to improve the contact?

RA: I am Ra. There are no mistakes. Be at rest, my friend. Each of you is most conscientious. All is well. I leave you in the love and the light of the One Infinite Creator. Go forth, therefore, rejoicing in the power and in the peace of the One Infinite Creator. I am Ra. Adonai.

Fragment 27
(Entire session)

Session 45 was also a maintenance session with a few other minor areas of investigation included. The sessions were at their shortest at this time while Carla was regaining her vital energy level. At the end of the session, Ra found the need to end the session somewhat prematurely. The fellows who delivered our water for our cistern had shown up and failed to read our notes on the door, which said that we were not available and that silence was required for the experiment in which we were engaged. Thus they proceeded to knock loudly on every door that they could find, including the door to the Ra session room. Needless to say, we blocked our driveway after that experience so that we would not again be disturbed by visitors while we were having a session with Ra.

This must have been a hilarious situation. I am sorry I missed it. We were so very careful in preparing our place of working, getting the various preparations done with care and grace, then my going off to sleep while Don and Jim walked the circle of One. And then, the exquisitely careful choice of questions, listening for Ra's very soft, very uninflected words—altogether a delicate operation. And then to have loud noises and the hurrying emotions behind them—I can just see the two men going quietly ballistic!

It is hard to read the constant reports of my failing energies, even now, because I remember so well the feelings of frustration and anger that I experienced as I offered myself, poor as I was, for contact. Inside, I felt a strength and power of self that was much different from my physical state, and I wondered why I had chosen such a limited physical body. Why had I not given myself a totally healthy body so I could be a better worker for the Light? And yet I knew, at least intellectually and consciously, that all is perfect, that this was the very best configuration of mind and body and energy balance, that this was precisely where I needed to be. Were I not a mystic and able to access that part of me that is pure faith, I would have been tempted to give up.

In the time since Don's death and the end of the Ra contact, I have come to much more of a peace with this issue, seeing clearly the way my limitations worked to refine me, to hone my sense of purpose and make ever more substantial those joys of spirit that informed my awareness. I see them still at work and can embrace now that fragility, which has given me such fruits of consciousness and hollowed me out so well. It is the empty instrument that is able to offer the purest substance through it, and it is limitation and loss that have refined and hollowed me and given me that transparency of spirit that moves into simple joy. I am so very glad to see each new day—I cannot express it, and this is a gift given through suffering. So often, as we look at spiritual gifts, that is true: the gaining of them can be seen to involve trag-edy and pain. Yet, as we experience those depths of sorrow, we also find ourselves more able to move into joy in the everyday things that are so right and so precious.

Session 45 (in total), April 6, 1981

RA: I am Ra. I greet you in the love and in the light of the One Infinite Creator. We communicate now.

QUESTIONER: Could you give us an estimate of the instrument's physical condition now that she is rested?

RA: I am Ra. This instrument's condition as regards the bodily complex is extremely poor. This instrument is not rested. However, this instrument was eager for our contact.

QUESTIONER: Did the period of abstinence from contact help the instrument's physical condition?

RA: I am Ra. This is correct. The probability of this instrument's development of what you would call disease either of the pulmonary nature or the renal nature was quite significant at our previous contact. You have averted a possible serious physical malfunction of this instrument's bodily complex. It is to be noted that your prayerful support was helpful, as was this instrument's unflagging determination to accept that which was best in the long run and thus maintain the exercises recommended without undue impatience. It is to be further noted that those things which aid this instrument are in some ways contra-dictory and require balance. Thus this instrument is aided by rest but also by diversions of an active nature. This makes it more difficult to aid this instrument. However, once this is known, the balancing may be more easily accomplished.

QUESTIONER: Can you tell me if a large percentage of the Wanderers here now are those of Ra?

RA. I am Ra. I can.

QUESTIONER: Are they?

RA: I am Ra. A significant portion of sixth-density Wanderers are those of our social memory complex. Another large portion consists of those who aided those in South America; another portion, those aiding Atlantis. All are sixth density and all brother and sister groups due to the unified feeling that as we had been aided by shapes such as the pyramid, so we could aid your peoples.

QUESTIONER: Can you say if any of the three of us are of Ra or any of the other groups?

RA: I am Ra. Yes.

QUESTIONER: Can you say which of us are of which group?

RA: I am Ra. No.

QUESTIONER: Are all of us of one of the groups that you mentioned?

RA: I am Ra. We shall go to the limits of our attempts to refrain from infringement. Two are a sixth-density origin, one a fifth-density harvestable to sixth but choosing to return as a Wanderer due to a loving association between teacher and student. Thus you three form a greatly cohesive group.

QUESTIONER: Can you explain the right and left ear tone and what I call touch contact that I continually get?

RA: I am Ra. This has been covered previously. Please ask for specific further details.

QUESTIONER: I get what I consider to be tickling in my right and my left ear at different times. Is this any different as far as meaning goes from the tone that I get in my right and left ear?

RA: I am Ra. No.

QUESTIONER: Why is the left ear of the service-to-self contact, and the right, service to others?

RA: I am Ra. The nature of your physical vehicle is that there is a magnetic field positive and negative in complex patterns about the shells of your vehicle. The left portion of the head region of most entities is, upon the time/space continuum level, of a negative polarity.

QUESTIONER: Can you tell me what is the purpose or philosophy behind the fourth-, fifth-, and sixth-density positive and negative social memory complexes?

RA: I am Ra. The basic purpose of a social memory complex is that of evolution. Beyond a certain point, the evolution of spirit is quite dependent upon the understanding of self and other-self as Creator. This constitutes the basis for social complexes. When brought to maturity, they become social memory complexes. The fourth density and sixth density find these quite necessary. The fifth positive uses social memory in attaining wisdom, though this is done individually. In fifth negative, much is done without aid of others. This is the last query, as this instrument needs to be protected from depletion. Are there brief queries before we close?

QUESTIONER: I just need to know if there is anything that we can do to make the instrument more comfortable or to improve the contact.

RA: I am Ra. All is well, my brothers. [Loud rapping at the door. Water truckers!]

QUESTIONER: What did you say?

RA: I am Ra. All is well, my brothers. I leave you now in the love and in the light of the One Infinite Creator. Go forth, then, rejoicing in the power and the peace of the One Infinite Creator. Adonai.

Fragment 28

In querying about how best to aid two of our cats as they were about to be put under anesthetic at the veterinarian's, and how to reduce any negative influences that might have sought an inroad while the cats were being operated on, we discovered that when the investment of a second-density being has been successful, that second-density being attracts to it the spirit complex. And the presence of the spirit complex makes that being vulnerable to the same psychic-greeting process that any third-density entity may experience, given the appropriate circumstances. The ritual sentences mentioned are taken from the Book of Common Prayer of the Episcopal Church.

When I was a young woman of 17, I thought I wanted a life full of children and home. But life never offered me that. Instead, I was drawn to follow a life of devotion, to Don and to the Creator. Instead of children, I have had the joy of being friend and/or counselor to many courageous and seeking souls. And cats!! Plenty of cats! I cannot remember being without a cat my whole life long! They delight me, and their company is always a pleasure. We relate to them as children, and they soak up a lot of my maternal feelings!

Gandalf was an exceptionally devoted cat. He loved our laps and would retrieve for Don, catching the peppermint candy wrappers that Don tossed and bringing them to deposit in Don's shoe. When he became old and full of years, he was more than ever devoted, and even after he could no longer walk, if I forgot to carry him with me, he would scrape along the floor little by little to come nearer again. Needless to say, we did not forget him often. And he still lives in loving memories.

Session 46,
April 15, 1981

QUESTIONER: The one question that is bothering us, which I got in meditation, may be an inappropriate question, but I feel it is my duty to ask it because it is central to the instrument's mental condition and ours. It has to do with the two cats which we were going to have worked upon today for teeth cleaning and for the removal of the small growth from Gandalf's leg. I got the impression that there might be an inroad there for the Orion group, and I was primarily concerned if there was anything that we could do for protection for these two cats. It may be out of line for me to ask this question, but I feel it my duty to ask it. Would you please give me any information that you can on that subject?

RA: I am Ra. The entity, mind/body/spirit complex, Gandalf, being harvestable third density, is open to the same type of psychic attack to which you yourselves are vulnerable. Therefore, through the mechanism of images and dreams, it is potentially possible for negative concepts to be offered to this mind/body/spirit complex, thus having possible deleterious results. The entity, Fairchild, though harvestable through investment, does not have the vulnerability to attack in as great amount due to a lack of the mind complex activity in the distortion of conscious devotion.

For protection of these entities, we might indicate two possibilities. Firstly, the meditation putting on the armor of light. Secondly, the repetition of short ritual sentences known to this instrument from the establishment which distorts spiritual oneness for this instrument. This instrument's knowledge will suffice. This will aid due to the alerting of many discarnate entities also aware of these ritual sentences.

The meditation is appropriate at the time of the activity on behalf of these entities. The ritual may be repeated with efficacy from this time until the safe return, at convenient intervals.

QUESTIONER: I am not familiar with the ritual sentences. If the instrument is familiar, you need not answer this, but which sentences do you mean?

[*Silence. No response from Ra.*]

QUESTIONER: I assume that the instrument is familiar with them then?

RA: I am Ra. This is correct.

QUESTIONER: Can you tell me something of the little growth on Gandalf's leg, and if it is of danger to him?

RA: I am Ra. The cause of such growths has been previously discussed. The danger to the physical body complex is slight, given the lack of repeated stimulus to anger.

Fragment 29

The spiritual transfer of energy is apparently possible for Carla in any sexual energy transfer. It happens without any particular effort on her part and seems due, primarily, to her nature as one who considers all of her actions, first, in the light of how she may be of service to another. This kind of spiritual energy transfer, however, is possible for anyone to achieve through a conscious mental dedication of the shared sexual intercourse for the purpose of achieving such a transfer. With that dedication consciously made, the male will transfer the physical energy, which he has in abundance, to the female and refresh her, and the female will transfer the mental/emotional and spiritual energies, which she has in abundance, and inspire the male. The kinds of energy transferred by each biological sex are determined by the nature that is unique to each. The biological male tends to express the male principle of that quality that reaches. The biological female tends to express the female principle of that quality that awaits the reaching. The orgasm is the point at which the transfer takes place, although well-mated partners do not necessarily need to experience the orgasm in order to achieve the transfer.

Since these sessions were recorded, I have continued to study the sexual part of red-ray activity, with the hope of finding ways to share the beauty and joy I have found in my sexuality with other people who wish to move into the experience of sacramental sex. More and more, I am convinced that we all have the ability to move into this vibratory level, where intercourse becomes ever more deeply a Holy Eucharist of red ray. I think that this orgasmic energy is pure love, and that as we experience this ecstasy, we are simply knowing the creator's vibration at rest. I suspect that the universe dwells in a state of orgasm, a timeless ecstasy. So much of our culture's training is bent on blunting the power of passion, so that social strictures may be observed, that the spontaneity of the act itself is lost. And the constant bombardment of sexual images in commercials and advertisements of every kind sharpen the desire for more and more: more partners, more unorthodox experiences, more thrills, more novelty.

In contrast to this, there is the red-ray part of self and its natural functions, natural and right and, like all other natural functions, something to fulfill in privacy, and with an eye to grace and purity of form in the doing. Once a man has found the wisdom to fix his desire upon Woman, the Goddess, as incarnate in his mate, and the woman has opened her heart to Man, as incarnate in her mate, there is laid the stage for an ever-deeper practice of this glorious natural sharing of energy. It has been a blessing to me, certainly, as I apparently ran out of energy some years ago—but am still alive and kicking! Thanks in no small part to the truly fine natural functions of one James McCarty, a man most lovingly sensitive to the Goddess within.

Session 48,
April 22, 1981

QUESTIONER: I have a question from the instrument that I will read. "You have suggested several times that sexual energy transfers aid the instrument's vital energy and this contact. It seems that this is not true for all people; that the sexual circuitry and the spiritual circuitry are not the same. Is this instrument an anomaly, or is the positive effect of sexual activity on spiritual energy normal for all third-density beings?"

RA: I am Ra. This instrument, though not anomalous, is somewhat less distorted towards the separation of mind, body, and spirit than many of your third-density entities. The energies of sexual transfer would, if run through the undeveloped spiritual electrical or magnetic complex which you call circuitry, effectually blow out that particular circuit. Contrarily, the full spiritual energies run through bodily complex circuitry will also adversely affect the undeveloped circuit of the bodily complex. Some there are, such as this instrument, who have not in the particular incarnation chosen at any time to express sexual energy through the bodily circuitry. Thus, from the beginning of such an entity's experience, the body and spirit express together in any sexual action. Therefore, to transfer sexual energy for this instrument is to transfer spiritually as well as physically. This instrument's magnetic field, if scrutinized by one sensitive, will show these unusual configurations. This is not unique to one entity but is common to a reasonable number of entities who, having lost the desire for orange- and yellow-ray sexual experiences, have strengthened the combined circuitry of spirit, mind, and body to express the totality of beingness in each action. It is for this reason also that the social intercourse and companionship is very beneficial to this instrument, it being sensitive to the more subtle energy transfers.

Fragment 30

I was the one of the three of us most interested in querying about my own experiences. Having once also been a conspiracy buff, this may be understandable as the result of an over-active and over-dramatic curiosity. Questions about Carla were always of a maintenance nature, trying to figure out the best way to keep her physical vehicle running smoothly or at least running in some cases, and Don seldom queried about himself at all. The following comments by Ra amplify the sacramental function that sexual intercourse can fulfill in one's journey of seeking the truth. With the proper balance of mind and body, uniquely determined for each entity, the orgasm can serve as a kind of triggering mechanism that activates the spirit complex and serves as a kind of shuttle, and which then can allow the entity to contact what Ra calls intelligent infinity.

The "pertinent information" concerning the frontal-lobe portion of the brain that Ra speaks of concerns the fact that no one knows for sure what that part of the brain is for. All of the qualities that make us human beings are accounted for in the rear five-eighths of the reptilian and mammalian brain. Pioneer thinkers studying this portion of the brain have posited the possibility that the frontal lobes are dormant in most people and may be activated by removing the various blockages in the lower energy centers that childhood experiences have placed there, in accordance with pre-incarnative choices of lessons for the incarnation. When these blockages have been removed—i.e., lessons have been learned—then the frontal lobes may in some degree be activated and a quantum leap in consciousness may be experienced for various lengths of time, usually quite short except in the cases of genuine yogis, saints, and mystics. This is the theory. However, Jim is still "looking forward," shall we say.

Jim's fascination, early on, about possible conspiracies of political, economic, and metaphysical nature was one he had in common with a large number of people interested in UFOs and UFO messages. Somehow, the mind that revolved around to the mystery of UFOs was also vulnerable to the sensational and elaborate theories that involved secret governmental and international corporate powers. When I first began to channel in 1974, such questions were very common. It took me several years of experience in channeling and watching how the group energy felt to me, to determine to my own satisfaction that asking questions about this sort of fear-based specific material was substantially detrimental to the tuning of the contact, and therefore to the virtue of the information received. In recent years, I allow and even welcome questions that may touch on specific issues for a questioner—but I also offer caveat that the answer will not be specific. I value highly the good contact we continue to be able to sustain, and guard its tuning carefully.

Jim's whole experience with frontal-lobe research was a life-changing thing. It seemed to be the thing that opened up for him the lifestyle of homesteader, certainly an unusually retiring and abstemious way of life, but one that suited Jim to a tee. So without understanding much of the research, I can see that it was very helpful to Jim. The man who created and promulgated this research, however, was a person increasingly devoted to specific questions, when his students began channeling. So I think Jim learned the hard way that any channel can be tainted when the questioning gets too specific and focuses on worldly things rather than eternal values.

Session 49,
April 27, 1981

QUESTIONER: I have a question here from Jim first. He says: "For the past nine years I have had what I call frontal-lobes experiences in the preconscious state of sleep when I wake up in the morning. They are a combination of pleasure and pressure which begins in the frontal lobes and spreads in pulses through the whole brain and feels like an orgasm in the brain. I have had over 200 of these experiences, and often they are accompanied by voices and visions, which seldom make much sense to me. What is the source of these frontal-lobes experiences?"

RA: I am Ra. We scan the questioner and find some pertinent information already available which regards the physiological disposition of this particular part of the brain. The experiences described and experienced are those distillations which may be experienced after a concentration of effort upon the opening of the gateway or indigo mind complex so that experience of a sacramental or violet ray may occur. These experiences are the beginnings of that which, as the body, the mind, and the spirit become integrated at the gateway or indigo level, may then yield not only the experience of joy but the comprehension of intelligent infinity which accompanies it. Thus the body complex orgasm and mind complex orgasm becoming integrated may then set forth the proper gateway for the spiritual complex integration and its use as a shuttle for the sacrament of the fully experienced presence of the One Infinite Creator. Thus there is much to which the questioner may look forward.

Fragment 31

When I was in the process of cutting trees with which to build my cabin in the woods of central Kentucky in the spring of 1973, I was quite unsure of how or if I would be able to survive alone in that remote environment. Though subdued most of the time, my nervousness about this whole project was obvious. One night, in my tent, I was awakened by the sound of a friend's dog eating dog food from its plastic bowl. I mentally heard the message that is spoken of in the following material and wrote it down by flashlight. It appears that each of us has at least three guides to aid us, and aid is usually given in a symbolic manner in order to give us clues that will stimulate our own thinking and seeking abilities rather than by laying out answers in a plain and unquestionable fashion.

I have experienced Jim's nervousness through our long association and found that his quickness and alertness are preternatural. The trait seems to be a mixed blessing, however, for if the objects he is manipulating have the temerity to be balky, the tension can escalate. I suppose virtues always have their shadows! I have come to find that level of trust with Jim where one accepts another without regard for anything but complete support, and would not change him to be one iota less fiery. That racehorse temperament is simply the shadow of so many wonderful traits that make him the extremely efficient and ever-resourceful good judge of men and situations that he is.

Session 50,
May 6, 1981

QUESTIONER: I have a question from Jim about an experience which he had when he first moved to his land, in which he was told, "The key to your survival comes indirect, through nervousness." The entity was Angelica. Could you give him information with respect to this?

RA: I am Ra. Yes.

QUESTIONER: Would you please do that?

RA: I am Ra. As we have noted, each mind/body/spirit complex has several guides available to it. The persona of two of these guides is the polarity of male and female. The third is androgynous and represents a more unified conceptualization faculty.

The guide speaking as sound vibration complex, Angelica, was the female polarized persona. The message may not be fully explicated due to the Law of Confusion. We may suggest that in order to progress, a state of some dissatisfaction will be present, thus giving the entity the stimulus for further seeking. This dissatisfaction, nervousness, or angst, if you will, is not of itself useful. Thus its use is indirect.

Fragment 32
We have omitted the name of the person contacted in this query in Session 53 because we still would not want to be part of reducing the polarity of those of Ra. We would, however, like to share the rest of the question and answer because it seems to us to be a good illustration of the general principles that extraterrestrials of the positive polarity utilize in their face-to-face encounters with the population of our planet.

In the spring of 1981 Don traveled by himself to Laramie, Wyoming, to give a talk on the Law of One at one of Leo Sprinkle's UFO contactee conferences. The cause of his sickness during that conference and the aid of a support group are interesting points gleaned from that experience. Again, we see the desire not to abridge free will paramount in Ra's answer. The answer was possible because Don had already reached the same general conclusion in his own thinking.

The last question and answer in this section give an interesting perspective on the phenomenon of ball lightning. When Carla was a small child, a ball of what looked to be lightning came in through the window, rolled around her crib, and left through the same window.

When Don was a young child, he had a similar experience.

It would seem that once any seeker dedicates herself to following the path toward the Creator that has opened before her awakening gaze, odd coincidences and events mount up rapidly. The silver flecks were first noticed by Andrija Puharich, as he and Uri Geller worked together. They might be strewn around a hotel room's rug, showing up overnight. After Don and I made contact with Puharich in 1974 and began working with him from time to time, I began getting them on my face and upper body. We got glitter of all the kinds we could find and compared them. The sparkles on my face were not the shape of any of the manufactured kinds. When the contact with those of Ra began, silver flecks started showing up much more frequently. This little phenomenon ended when Donald died in 1984. However, we do continue to be blessed frequently with Ra's other form of saying hello: the hawk. We actually have a family of hawks nesting in our trees for the second year! And often, when Jim and I are discussing something, we will get a hawk sighting just when we come to a decision. It always feels great to see this sign of Love.

Everyone will have his own set of these little signals that say "you are on the beam" or "perhaps not." As illogical as this sounds, we encourage you to note these coincidences when they begin to repeat. They are a definite form of communication with spirit energies that are benign and loving, as far as we can tell.

Our association with Leo Sprinkle is long standing. This courageous researcher became interested in UFO phenomena when asked to participate as hypnotist in the research being done on a UFO contactee. He worked with many such contactees through the years and eventually founded a research organization that holds a yearly Rocky Mountain Conference for UFO contactees. It is a good support group for these witnesses to the unusual. In 1975, we spent a hilarious weekend at a UFO convention held in Fort Smith, Arkansas, working on a movie together. (The movie, The Force Beyond, *turned out so badly that Don renamed it* The Farce Beyond!*) Leo was hypnotizing a UFO witness, Don and I were consultants on the script, and he obtained most of the psychics and witnesses that were in the film. When Leo did the actual hypnosis, things went wrong repeatedly with equipment and so forth, and it was midnight before we sat down to eat. I asked him how he was holding up. Completely deadpan, he dropped his head on the table in front of him as though pole-axed. It was a delightful moment after a long day.*

Since Don and I began talking about these experiences with light coming to greet us, seemingly, we have heard from many others to whom this has also occurred. It is a marvelous thing to ponder. Are these the bodies we shall use to experience a higher density? They are most fair and pure.

Session 53,
May 25, 1981

QUESTIONER: First I will ask if you could tell me the affiliation of the entities who contacted [name].

RA: I am Ra. This query is marginal. We will make the concession towards information with some loss of polarity due to free will being abridged. We request that questions of this nature be kept to a minimum.

The entities in this and some other vividly remembered cases are those who, feeling the need to plant Confederation imagery in such a way as not to abrogate free will, use the symbols of death, resurrection, love, and peace as a means of creating, upon the thought level, the time/space illusion of a systematic train of events which give the message of love and hope. This type of contact is chosen by careful consideration of Confederation members which are contacting an entity of like home vibration, if you will. This project then goes before the Council of Saturn and, if approved, is completed. The characteristics of this type of contact include the nonpainful nature of thoughts experienced and the message content which speaks not of doom but of the new dawning age.

QUESTIONER: It is not necessary that I include the information that you just gave in the book to accomplish my purpose. In order to save your polarity, shall we say, I can keep that as private material if you wish. Do you wish for me to keep it unpublished?

RA: I am Ra. That which we offer you is freely given and subject only to your discretion.

QUESTIONER: I thought you would say that. In that case, can you tell me anything of the "blue book" mentioned by [name] in that case?

RA: I am Ra. No.

QUESTIONER: Can you tell me why [name] has so many silver flecks on her?

RA: I am Ra. This is infringement. No.

QUESTIONER: Thank you. Can you tell me why I got sick during Carl Rushkey's talk?

RA: I am Ra. We scan your thoughts. They are correct, and therefore we do not infringe by confirming them. The space/time of your allotted speaking was drawing near, and you came under Orion attack due to the great desire of some positively oriented entities to become aware of the Law of One. This may be expected, especially when you are not in a group lending strength to each other.

QUESTIONER: Thank you. Can you comment on my and the instrument's, if she approves, so-called ball-of-lightning experiences as a child?

RA: I am Ra. This will be the last query of this working.
   You were being visited by your people to be wished well.

Fragment 33

When it becomes known to a seeker that there are negative entities of an unseen nature that may present one with psychic greetings that, in general, tend to intensify difficulties that the seeker has freely chosen, it is often easy for the seeker totally to blame the negative entities for difficulties that appear in the life pattern, rather than continuing to trace the line of responsibility to its source within the free-will choices of the self. I illustrated this trait in the following question.

   I had known very well from an early age that I had a well-exercised temper. In Ra's response to my question about that temper, it is interesting to see one possible source for such anger and the potential for balancing that such anger can provide. A future query in this same general area elicits another facet of this quality of anger.

When one feels she has a fault, it is very easy to focus on eliminating the fault. Yet, Ra encourages us not to erase faults but to balance them. I think this to be a key concept. All of us dwelling in this veil of flesh have biases and opinions that seem distorted to some degree. Of course, if one has a fault that involves infringing on the free will of another, then the fault does need to be addressed by eliminating that behavior. One does not find ways to balance thieving or murder. But Jim's anger, my eternal vagueness and forgetfulness, all of people's little quirks, can be seen to be energies that need balancing, rather than removal. One tries to behave completely without error, yet errors occur. This should not be an excuse for the self to judge the self, but rather a chance for the self to offer love and support to the self, while gently bringing the behavior into balance. Unless we get this principle solidly under our metaphysical belts, we will be self-judgmental people who are petty in complaint and grudging with praise, not just for the self, but for others.

Session 59,
June 25, 1981

QUESTIONER: I have a question from Jim, and it states: "I think that I have penetrated my lifelong mystery of my anger at making mistakes. I think that I have always been aware subconsciously of my ability to master new learning, but my desire to successfully complete my work on Earth has been energized by the Orion group into irrational and destructive anger when I fail. Could you comment on this observation?

RA: I am Ra. We would suggest that as this entity is aware of its position as a Wanderer, it may also consider what pre-incarnative decisions it undertook to make regarding the personal or self-oriented portion of the choosing to be here at this particular time/space. This entity is aware, as stated, that it has great potential, but potential for what? This is the pre-incarnative question. The work of sixth density is to unify wisdom and compassion. This entity abounds in wisdom. The compassion it is desirous of balancing has, as its antithesis, lack of compassion. In the more conscious being, this expresses or manifests itself as lack of compassion for self. We feel this is the sum of suggested concepts for thought which we may offer at this time without infringement.

Fragment 34 ....

The first two questions in this portion of Session 60 touch upon Carla's tendency toward martyrdom in general terms; that is, in the case of the Ra contact Carla's desire to be of service in this contact was strong enough that she would open herself completely to the contact until there was no vital energy left for her own ease of transition back to the waking state. Ra's suggestion in this regard was that if she were to reserve some vital energy, it would be possible that the contact could continue over a longer period of time. Ra recognized that her basic incarnational lesson was to generate as much compassion as possible and was the root of the unreserved opening to the contact, but Ra also suggested that a little addition of wisdom in the reserving some small amount of vital energy might enhance her service.

In fact, our entire group was then in the process of exercising more caution regarding the frequency of sessions. We had begun to travel the martyr's path in having sessions too frequently and giving of the self—of the instrument—until there was nothing left. As we continued to hold sessions when she was not in good shape, it was also suggested to us by Ra that overly to stress caution in scheduling sessions further apart and in resting Carla was as deleterious to retaining the contact as our martyring behavior was at the beginning of the sessions. In having the sessions, in distributing the material to others, and in living the daily life in general, we found that there is a basic kind of dedication to serving others that is helpful. But when that dedication becomes focused on a strong desire that a specific outcome be the result of any effort to serve others, then one is distorting the service with preconceived ideas. "Not my will, but Thy will" is the attitude offering the most-efficient service.

And once again we see the beneficial role that a physical limitation can play in one's incarnation. In this case, Carla's arthritis is seen to be the means by which she pre-incarnatively determined to focus her attention, not on the usual activities of the world but on the inner life, the life of meditation and contemplation that her physical limitation offered her. This same limitation has also been used to carry out other pre-incarnatively chosen lessons, as mentioned by Ra in the last two responses. Such pre-incarnatively chosen limitations confound many healers, who have the opinion that no disease is ever necessary. However, it seems that some people choose lessons that will utilize the entire incarnation and not just a portion of it. Thus, the distortions needed to present the opportunities for these kinds of lessons are not meant to yield to healing efforts.

It may seem as though I have had a life ruled by disease and limitation. In actuality, that just isn't so. At one time, when Donald had died and I had not yet fully decided to survive him, my condition worsened to the point where I had to stay horizontal all the time. But even then, I was able to make letter tapes and to channel, until the very end of that dark period, the month or so before going to the hospital in January 1992. And I can honestly say that even in that extremity, I wanted to stay.

Today, I simply do not think very much about my aches and pains, and I don't think other people notice anything out of the ordinary about me. I don't appear ill and do not act that way either, so people just assume I am healthy. Having done everything I could to better my condition, and failed to make any dent by any means, I have concluded that the symptoms of pain that I experience are not signal, but noise. This is the basic pain management theory I learned in rehab that fateful year of 1992. Something that has no message is a useless thing, no matter how irritating. I was riding one of those electric buggies airline employees use to transport the elderly and feeble, and remarked on the constant bee-baw, bee-baw, bee-baw as the cart wended its way through the pedestrian traffic in the huge corridor. The driver said she didn't even notice it any more, she was so used to it. Exactly.

I don't do this perfectly: I complain at least daily to my mate, who has iden-
tified listening to the daily report as a service to the weary! It really helps
to gripe a bit. As long as the griper doesn't take it too seriously.

I know this is not easy, and I spent months during that period thinking
that I might not make the cut! It is difficult to face pain, especially ancient,
blade-keen pain that has crippled, and to work through the crystallizations
that kept the arms down and the back separated from the neck. What saved
me was love. I have a real passion for cooking. I love to play with tastes, to
mix herbs and spices and all the kinds of food there are. The fact that the
result of this playtime is meals that people enjoy is icing on the cake! I'd been
banned from the kitchen twelve years ago. After thorough testing to be sure
I would not harm my condition, I was OK'd to take up cooking again. I loved
being in the kitchen, to the point where I would just hang on to the stove
and cook long past the point where I would have given up if I'd just been
sitting or standing and doing nothing. And then there was the love I had for
Jesus—I promised Him that I would get better, and give praise and thanks-
giving and glory to His holy Name. Which I do, frequently! Between the two,
a miracle occurred for me, given by Love to love for Love's sake. And I pray
to be able to share my story of being a Wanderer and one who wishes to
serve, with all those who are awakening to their spiritual identity at this
time.

Yes, I am still limited by my physical restrictions. I have spent literally
years refining a schedule that I can live with, that has the most things in it
that I want in my life, without over-stressing my frail body. At this point,
Jim and I have things worked out very well, and I have been fortunate to
escape difficulty this last year or so. It is a first! I just take things at the
speed I know is safe for me.

Needless to say, when this contact was ongoing, I had no such concept
of caution. I adored Don—he wanted this contact more than anything I'd
ever seen him go after; during this time he was actually a happy man. These
were golden moments for me: I had had but one goal for a long time from
1968 onward, and that was to make a real home, both physical and meta-
physical, for Don. I knew he was comforted by being with me, so I felt I
always helped. But this state he was in was unique. Here was my star-
crossed love, peaceful and completely satisfied with his life for the first and
only time I ever saw. I couldn't wait to do the next session, just so I could
wake up to see him grinning with delight.

It is fairly easy to see from the questions he was asking that Don felt
my best chance for healing lay in mental work along the lines of his Church
of Christ Scientist mother's faith. He was accustomed, when a family
member got a cold or illness, to calling the practitioner, who would spend
time in prayer and meditation, affirming the perfection of whatever seemed
to be imperfect. This method of thinking is extremely valuable, and I do want

to give credit to this marvelous practice of affirming perfection. For that is the over-riding truth—behind all of this seeming imperfection there is utter perfection beyond telling or measure. I have sensed and felt it but have never been able to bring back words. However, I believe those experiences to be true.

As to the idea of my pre-incarnatively choosing the limitations and the lesson of loving without expectation of a return, both of these topics had been covered in a past-life regression done by Larry Allison in 1975, and I felt sure that this was the case. It rang true with that depth of resonance I have come to associate with personal truth. I felt and feel fortunate to be alive, and if I have to pay some dues, that's OK. I'm glad to be at the party! When I do die to this world, I hope that I will be satisfied I've done all I can—and I don't feel that way yet. One thing I know I still have ahead is to write some sort of witness to those truths that have been shared with me at dear cost. When I have written all I know about the devotional life lived in the midst of it all, then I will be fairly satisfied that I have served my part. But we never really know what the sum of service is, do we? I don't presume to think that I know all that is slated for me to experience. And am satisfied to let it surprise me.

Session 60,
July 1, 1981

QUESTIONER: It is my opinion that the best way for the instrument to improve her condition is through periods of meditation followed by periods of contemplation with respect to the condition and its improvement. Could you tell me if I am correct, and expand on this?

RA: I am Ra. Meditation and contemplation are never untoward activities. However, this activity will in all probability, in our opinion, not significantly alter the predispositions of this instrument which cause the fundamental distortions which we, as well as you, have found disconcerting.

QUESTIONER: Can you tell me the best approach for altering, to a more acceptable condition, the distortions that the instrument is experiencing?

RA: I am Ra. There is some small amount of work which the instrument may do concerning its pre-incarnative decisions regarding service to the Infinite Creator in this experience. However, the decision to open without reservation to the offering of self when service is perceived is such a fundamental choice that it is not open to significant alteration, nor would we wish to interfere with the balancing process which is taking place with this particular entity. The wisdom and compassion being so balanced by this recapitulation of fourth density is helpful to this particular mind/body/spirit complex. It is not an entity much given to quibbling with the purity with which it carries out that which it feels it is best to do. We may say this due to the instrument's knowledge of its self, which is clear upon this point. However, this very discussion may give rise to a slightly less fully unstopped dedication to service in any one working, so that the service may be continued over a greater period of your space/time.

QUESTIONER: You are saying, then, that the physical distortions that the instrument experiences are part of a balancing process? Is this correct?

RA: I am Ra. This is incorrect. The physical distortions are a result of the instrument's not accepting fully the limitations placed prior to incarnation upon the activities of the entity once it had begun the working. The distortions caused by this working, which are inevitable given the plan chosen by this entity, are limitation and to a degree consonant with the amount of vital and physical energy expended, weariness, due to that which is the equivalent in this instrument of many, many hours of harsh physical labor.

This is why we suggested the instrument's thoughts dwelling upon the possibility of its suggesting to its Higher Self the possibility of some slight reservation of energy at a working. This instrument at this time is quite open until all resources are quite exhausted. This is well if desired. However, it will, shall we say, shorten the number of workings in what you may call the long run.

QUESTIONER: Will spreading the workings out over greater intervals of time so that we have more time between workings help?

RA: I am Ra. This you have already done. It is not helpful to your group to become unbalanced by concern for one portion of the work above another. If this instrument is, in your judgment, capable, and if the support group is functioning well, if all is harmonious and if the questions to be asked have been considered well, the working is well begun. To overly stress the condition of the instrument is as deleterious to the efficiency of this contact as the antithetical behavior was in your past.

QUESTIONER: Aside from the workings, I am concerned about the physical distortions of the instrument in the area of her hands and arms. Is there a, shall we say, mental exercise or something else that the instrument could work on to help to alleviate the extreme problems that she has at this time with her hands, etc.?

RA: I am Ra. Yes.

QUESTIONER: Would this be an exercise of meditation and contemplation upon the alleviation of these problems?

RA: I am Ra. No.

QUESTIONER: What would she do then, in order to alleviate these problems?

RA: I am Ra. As we have said, this instrument, feeling that it lacked compassion to balance wisdom, chose an incarnative experience whereby it was of necessity placed in situations of accepting self in the absence of other-selves' acceptance and the acceptance of other-self without expecting a return or energy transfer. This is not an easy program for an incarnation but was deemed proper by this entity. This entity therefore must needs meditate and consciously, moment by moment, accept the self in its limitations, which have been placed for the very purpose of bringing this entity to the precise tuning we are using. Further, having learned to radiate acceptance and love without expecting return, this entity now must balance this by learning to accept the gifts of love and acceptance of others which this instrument feels some discomfort in accepting. These two balanced workings will aid this entity in the release from the distortion called pain. The limitations are, to a great extent, fixed.

QUESTIONER: Is the fact that the instrument was already consciously aware of this the reason that the first distortion was not in force in making it impossible for you to communicate this to us?

RA: I am Ra. This is not only correct for this entity, which has been consciously aware of these learn/teachings for some of your years, but also true of each of the support group. The possibility of some of this information being offered was not there until this session.

Fragment 35

Carla's arthritis began just after her kidneys failed when she was thirteen years old. In her childhood she had the very strong desire to be of service to others, but after many difficult experiences as a child unable to fit well anywhere, she felt so sure that she would never be able to really be of service that by the age of thirteen she prayed that she might die. When her kidney failure six months later provided her with an avenue for such an exit from the incarnation, her near-death experience was of the nature where she was told that she could go on if she chose to, but that her work was not done. She immediately chose to return to this life, now feeling that there was indeed service to be provided, and the juvenile rheumatoid arthritis set in immediately.

You can also see here how the efforts of negative entities intensified the choice to die that she had made of free will, but by that same free will there was no force that could hinder her return to service once she had made that choice.

The concept of limitation, especially in the form of physical disease, being a benign thing can be disturbing to think upon at first. I asked myself why in heaven's name would I choose this particular condition? For it is as cunning in how it limits me as it could be. Although the rheumatoid disease has altered each joint in my body, it has focused on my hands, wrists, and shoulders and back. I simply cannot do anything physical for too long a period, including typing at this very computer's keyboard. I cannot pick up heavy things or do heavy cleaning around the house. In general, I must watch how long I work at anything, for I cannot do a good day's work and expect to rise the next day feeling well. I simply must write a lot of rest into the schedule. Any time I do overstep these unseen limitations, I reap the reward of having lots of quiet time while I recuperate.

Through the years, therefore, I have become very able to live in a world that is retired to the point of being a hermit's way. Even in the depths of illness, in the early '90s, I was still given work to do, in the channeling and in correspondence with a wide variety of students, counselees, and friends. My voice, because it hurt to produce a tone, was faint, but my thoughts still flew with wings, and there was immense satisfaction in continuing to serve.

It has always been difficult for me to take things lightly. I am always the one so intensely riveted on whatever I am doing that there's no possibility of my being "cool." Forget it! So Ra's telling me I needed to reserve energy for myself during sessions did not sit well. However, given the way I was physically wasting away, I realized I would have to learn how to do that. I have come to appreciate this lesson greatly and so pass the advice on to each who sees himself in these words. It is a worthwhile thing to preserve the physical shell; indeed, it is the kind of loving act that teaches as it aids.

Session 63,
July 18, 1981

QUESTIONER: Was the original problem with the kidneys some twenty-five years ago caused by psychic attack?

RA: I am Ra. This is only partially correct. There were psychic-attack components to the death of this body at that space/time. However, the guiding vibratory complex in this event was the will of the instrument. This instrument desired to leave this plane of existence, as it did not feel it could be of service.

QUESTIONER: You are saying then that the instrument itself created the kidney problem at that time?

RA: I am Ra. The instrument's desire to leave this density lowered the defenses of an already predisposed weak body complex, and an allergic reaction was so intensified as to cause the complications which distorted the body complex towards unviability. The will of the instrument, when it found that there was indeed work to be done in service, was again the guiding factor or complex of vibratory patterns which kept the body complex from surrendering to dissolution of the ties which cause the vitality of life.

Fragment 36
The following material returns to the realm of transient information in general—and a portion of the conspiracy theory specifically—as an outgrowth of our querying about prophesies, earth changes, probable futures, and their effect on seeking truth. You will notice that we didn't linger long here this time.

I think it is important, in the context of this little volume of fragments we kept out of the first four volumes of The Law of One, *that we look straight and hard at the tendency of UFO researchers and people in general to see conspiracies and treachery behind every bush and gossip item. When I first started reading in this area, in the late sixties, there were prophets claiming a near future in which war, catastrophe, and desolation would reign. In the years since, nothing has changed but the dates. Always this great trouble is seen to be coming a couple of years from now, and the call is to put all else aside except for preparing for this time of trial. I have known people of sound judgment who have basement walls lined with freeze-dried food, proof against disaster. Let's call it the bomb shelter syndrome.*

The thing I wish to emphasize is that these thoughts do harm to the innocent future. They take present energy away from the immediate happenings of the day, and sap it with chronic fear and fear-based planning. Disasters do occur, indubitably. And when they do come, we can hope simply to meet them with some grace. In that day, it will be the people who have learned to live from a loving heart that will be able to help the most, not the people who have barricaded themselves into a mindset based on fear.

Session 65,
August 8, 1981

QUESTIONER: Are you saying then that this possible condition of war would be much more greatly spread across the surface of the globe than anything we have experienced in the past, and therefore touch a larger percentage of the population in this form of catalyst?

RA: I am Ra. This is correct. There are those now experimenting with one of the major weapons of this scenario; that is, the so-called psychotronic group of devices which are being experimentally used to cause such alterations in wind and weather as will result in eventual famine. If this program is not countered and proves experimentally satisfactory, the methods in this scenario would be made public. There would then be what those whom you call Russians hope to be a bloodless invasion of their personnel in this and every land deemed valuable. However, the peoples of your culture have little propensity for bloodless surrender.

Fragment 37
There were no great tricks or elaborate rituals employed to aid Carla in maintaining her physical health and her ability to serve as the instrument for this contact. Good foods, reasonable exercise, and a healthy and happy attitude are techniques that are within most people's reach.

It was not very much fun to be so scrutinized for estimation of my energy level in this way. I have always had tons of mental, emotional, and spiritual energy, but low physical energy. In fact I would say my life has been lived mainly on nerve. To me, life has always seemed a marvelous celebration, a party of sun and moon and earth and sky, birdsong and green leaves, and people of every sort and kind, doing various amazing things. This joy in life is a pure gift, and it has made my life a dream of love. It was no surprise to

*me when Ra spoke of my low energy! And I doubt any athlete worked harder
to keep in shape than I did during this time.*

Session 66,
August 12, 1981

QUESTIONER: Would you give me an indication of the instrument's
condition?

RA: I am Ra. The vital energies are somewhat depleted at this time, but
not seriously so. The physical energy level is extremely low. Otherwise,
it is as previously stated.

QUESTIONER: Is there anything that we can do, staying within the
first distortion, to seek aid from the Confederation in order to alleviate
the instrument's physical problems?

RA: I am Ra. No.

QUESTIONER: Can you tell me the most appropriate method in
attempting to alleviate the instrument's physical problems?

RA: I am Ra. The basic material has been covered before concerning
the nurturing of this instrument. We recapitulate: the exercise according to ability, not to exceed appropriate parameters, the nutrition, the
social intercourse with companions, the sexual activity in green ray or
above, and in general, the sharing of the distortions of this group's
individual experiences in an helpful, loving manner.

These things are being accomplished with what we consider great
harmony, given the density in which you dance. The specific attention
and activities, with which those with physical complex distortions may
alleviate these distortions, are known to this instrument.

Finally, it is well for this instrument to continue the practices it
has lately begun.

QUESTIONER: Which practices are those?

RA: I am Ra. These practices concern exercises which we have outlined
previously. We may say that the variety of experiences which this entity
seeks is helpful, as we have said before, but as this instrument works
in these practices the distortion seems less mandatory.

Fragment 38

In the first question, Don is asking Ra how we could resolve the seeming paradox of being able to serve various portions of the same Creator, some of which rejoiced at our service and some of which wished nothing less than to remove the instrument and the contact from the third density (i.e., our fifth-density, negative friend). We removed the sentence that you see in brackets because we did not wish for overattention to be given to our personalities. We include it now because it might be helpful for those who have the feeling that they may be here from elsewhere to know that there is a kind of momentum of serving others that adds its support to the individual's desire to learn and to serve well.

Those who have read *The Crucifixion of Esmerelda Sweetwater* will recognize the last query of this section. This book was written by Don and Carla in 1968, when they first got together and formed L/L Research. It was their first project and was unusual in that it seemed to be seen first and then recorded as a story. And it was also unusual in the fact that it seemed to anticipate many of the experiences that Don and Carla, and later I, would share in their work together.

Into this first work of ours was poured all the love we had for each other and for the ideals and concerns of a purer, higher way, a way of love undefiled by any hint of the heaviness of earth. We were smitten with each other; it was a wonderful time. Mind you, Don was never verbal, but this time held our short-lived intimate physical relationship, which I treasure, and our time of that nearly trembling joy one has when one is in love. The story seemed to tell itself, and we saw the characters so clearly they might have been telling us the story over our shoulder. The only part of the book that was in error was the ending. The character that rather resembled me on a perfect day was killed off by the bad guys at the end of the book. In real life, my frail body was stronger than Don's, due, I think, to my gifts of faith and élan vital. Don was never the least bit at home on this earth. He lived his life very defended and isolated, except for me and a very few close friends and relations. One thing is sure: his gifts have been well shared in the body of work that comprises the material Ra shared with us. His questions were marvels of sense and always game to head in a new direction. The romance ended badly, in the sense that Don has entered a larger life, and I have been left to become a whole different person than the one he groomed and appreciated. But the work has not ended at all and will not until the world no longer has any need of our material.

Session 67,
August 15, 1981

QUESTIONER: Then how could we solve this paradox? [The sentence of personal material that was removed from Ra's answer is inserted in this paragraph, which may be found on p. 122 of Book III.]

RA: I am Ra. Consider, if you will, that you have no ability not to serve the Creator, since all is the Creator. In your individual growth patterns appear the basic third-density choice. [Further, there are overlaid memories of the positive polarizations of your home density.] Thus, your particular orientation is strongly polarized towards service to others and has attained wisdom as well as compassion.

QUESTIONER: Are you familiar with a book that the instrument and I wrote approximately twelve years ago, called *The Crucifixion of Esmerelda Sweetwater*, in particular the banishing ritual that we used to bring the entities to Earth?

RA: I am Ra. This is correct.

QUESTIONER: Were there any incorrectnesses in our writing with respect to the way this was performed?

RA: I am Ra. The incorrectnesses occurred only due to the difficulty an author would have in describing the length of training necessary to enable the ones known in that particular writing as Theodore and Pablo in the necessary disciplines.

QUESTIONER: It has seemed to me that that book has somehow, in its entirety, been a link to many of those whom we have met since we wrote it, and to many of the activities we have experienced. Is this correct?

RA: I am Ra. This is quite so.

Fragment 39

In seeking advice from Ra on caring for Carla's condition and in scheduling sessions, we again found that Ra constantly guarded our free will by providing loosely formed guidelines that offered us direction but required that we continually exercise our ability and duty to make the decisions ourselves. Thus was the contact a function of our free will by the fact that information was given only in response to questions, that the kind of information was determined by the nature of our seeking being formed into such and such a question, and by the actual scheduling or timing of sessions. So it is necessary for each seeker of truth to decide what to seek, how to seek, and when to seek. Not everyone speaks so directly to Ra, but everyone speaks with the One Creator in one form or another. If the seeking is strong enough, any portion of the Creator can teach you all that you wish to know. It is the seeking that determines the finding.

The last two questions and answers refer to a most unusual phenomenon that we discovered was a possibility in Session 68; that is, the misplacement of the mind/body/spirit complex of the instrument, under certain unprotected conditions, by the fifth-density, negative entity that monitored our Ra sessions. This possibility was unusual enough, but to add to its extraordinary nature is the fact that Don and Carla wrote about an identical situation in *The Crucifixion of Esmerelda Sweetwater* thirteen years earlier. The ending of the book was not seen as was the remainder of the book, and it had to be written in the usual way. Now this all makes sense to us, for it seems that the ending of that book was a symbolic description of Don's death in November 1984.

Have you ever been put on the spot by someone asking how you were? Usually, the civil greeting "How are you?" is a meaningless murmur indicating respect and awareness of presence, rather than a true request for information. The last thing wanted is a laundry list of woes and ailments. So I was not accustomed to being so in touch with myself that I could tell my exact condition. When one is in pain all the time, as I have been for a long time now, the stimulus eventually becomes dulled and ignored simply because it is telling one nothing useful. When one has done all one can, one is far better off simply getting on with the life that is offered. This may sound extreme, but I know just how many chronic-pain patients there are out there, quietly dealing with life, usually very well indeed. So the last thing I would wish is to be constantly checking to see my energy level. My reaction, at that time and at this one, is "Ya gotta be kidding!" I cannot remember ever having physical energy. Mental, emotional, spiritual energy, oh YES! Tons of that I have, and a heart full of joy to be here, whatever my limitations. But I run on nerve alone, in my own perception. So this concern, while genuine and necessary, was a challenge to me. I really wanted to do sessions so much, also, which biased my response.

The matter of The Crucifixion of Esmerelda Sweetwater *playing itself out in real life is to me a fascinating example of the liquidity and permeability of the supposed boundaries of space and time. We saw that story as if it were a movie running in our heads. We wrote it never knowing it had to do with us in the future. It was most unsettling when the more tragic parts of the book played themselves out with horrid accuracy. Life humbles one again and again, bringing us all to our knees and revealing self to self in utter fidelity. As always when I think on Don's death, I am warmed by the perfection of his opening to love and his nobility, as I am chilled by his absence from my side. One can do little except offer it all up to the Creator in thanksgiving and praise.*

Session 68,
August 18, 1981

QUESTIONER: Could you first please give me an indication of the instrument's condition?

RA: I am Ra. This instrument's physical energies are depleted completely. The remainder is as previously stated.

QUESTIONER: With the physical energies completely depleted, should I continue with the session? I'm not sure exactly what that means.

RA: I am Ra. We have available transferred energy which is due to the service offered by two of this group, and, therefore we are able to continue. Were it not for this transferred energy, the instrument, whose will is strong, would have depleted its vital energies by willing the available resources. Thus if there is no transfer of energy, and if the instrument seems depleted to the extent it now is, it is well to refrain from using the instrument. If there is energy transferred, this service may be accepted without damage to the distortion of normal vital energy.

We may note that the physical energy has been exhausted, not due to the distortion toward pain, although this is great at this space/time, but primarily due to the cumulative effects of continual experience of this distortion.

QUESTIONER: Would you recommend a greater rest period between the end of this work period and the next work period? Would that help the instrument?

RA: I am Ra. We might suggest, as always, that the support group watch the instrument with care and make the decision based upon observation. It is not within our capacity to specifically recommend a future decision. We would note that our previous recommendation of one working on alternate diurnal periods did not take into account the fragility of the instrument, and thus we would ask your forgiveness for this suggestion.

At this nexus, our distortion is towards a flexible scheduling of workings based upon, as we said, the support group's decisions concerning the instrument. We would again note that there is a fine line between the care of the instrument for continued use which we find acceptable and the proper understanding, if you will excuse this misnomer, of the entire group's need to work in service.

Thus, if the instrument's condition is truly marginal, by all means let more rest occur between workings. However, if there is desire for the working and the instrument is at all able in your careful opinion, it is, shall we say, a well-done action for this group to work. We cannot be more precise, for this contact is a function of your free will.

QUESTIONER: We have been speaking almost precisely of a portion of the Esmerelda Sweetwater book which we wrote, having to do with the character Trostrick's misplacement of the space girl's mind/body/spirit complex. What is the significance of that work which we did with respect to our lives? It has been confusing to me for some time as to how it meshes in. Can you tell me that?

RA: I am Ra. We scan each and find we may speak.

QUESTIONER: Would you please do so now?

RA: I am Ra. We confirm the following, which is already, shall we say, supposed or hypothesized.

When the commitment was made between two of this group to work for the betterment of the planetary sphere, this commitment activated a possibility/probability vortex of some strength. The experience of generating this volume was unusual in that it was visualized as if watching the moving picture.

Time had become available in its present-moment form. The scenario of the volume went smoothly until the ending of the volume. You could not end the volume, and the ending was not visualized as the entire body of the material but was written or authored.

This is due to the action of free will in all of the creation. However, the volume contains a view of significant events, both symbolically and specifically, which you saw under the influence of the magnetic attraction which was released when the commitment was made and full memory of the dedication of this, what you may call, mission restored.

Fragment 40

The time/space or metaphysical portion of ourselves is not apparent to any of us most of the time, yet it is the place or realm of our truer being. This is true for anyone. It is the essence from which that which we know of as our conscious selves manifests as a portion of our true selves. Our space/time, physical selves are a reflection or shadow of our true selves, which those who have eyes that can see behind illusion see when they behold our time/space beingness. It was this metaphysical self that Ra observed when first considering our group as a potential group for contact.

Don, Jim, and I had a common interest in spiritual community before we ever got together. When we did join households at Christmas in 1980, we consciously joined together as a light group. We wanted to live a spiritually directed life with each other and serve as we might. Much was sacrificed for this joining, on both Jim's and Don's parts, for they were both loners, fond of their own company and not much fond of society, although they were both excellent hosts when guests did come by. But the sacrifices were gladly made, and we felt very blessed to be together. When the Ra contact began three weeks later, we felt very happy that we had gone ahead on faith and joined forces.

What we had together was that clear, pure, unmuddied love and fellowship that stems from there being no fear between us, or needs that were not met. For a golden few months and years, this remained so. I have long felt that Don's decline and death were the result of his becoming fearful that I might leave him for Jim. I would never have done such a thing and had no idea he was concerned. But I believe that this fear, which he never expressed, and which I knew nothing of, led to his woeful last months, in which he suffered so greatly.

Session 71,
September 18, 1981

QUESTIONER: When you say you searched for this group, what do you mean? What was your process of search? I ask this question to understand more the illusion of time and space.

RA: I am Ra. Consider the process of one who sees the spectrograph of some complex of elements. It is a complex paint sample, let us say, for ease of description. We of Ra knew the needed elements for communication which had any chance of enduring. We compared our color chip to many individuals and groups over a long span of your time. Your spectrograph matches our sample.

In response to your desire to see the relationship betwixt space/ time and time/space, may we say that we conducted this search in time/ space, for in this illusion, one may quite readily see entities as vibratory complexes and groups as harmonics within vibratory complexes.

Fragment 41

In Session 75 we were trying to help Carla through her upcoming hand operation in a local hospital. When the Ra contact began, the pre-incarnatively chosen arthritic limitations set in more strongly than ever, and Carla's desire to do things for others with hands that were meant to be restricted from mundane work brought more and more pain and damage to the arthritic joints—thus necessitating the operation for short-term repair. The length or success of the surgical repairs would depend upon Carla's growing ability to accept the limitations that she placed upon herself before the incarnation, in order that her focus might move inward and prepare her for the possibility of becoming a channel. Her ability to accept these limitations delayed the next surgery for four years.

Since she had been a Christian mystic from birth, certain prayers of her Episcopalian church, and the communion service in particular, were felt by Ra to be of aid to her. The Banishing Ritual of the Lesser Pentagram, which we had been using for some time to purify our place of working for the Ra contact, was suggested for her hospital room and the operating room. The greatest protective and healing device, however, was seen to be love, whether manifest or unspoken, for all any ritual such as prayer, communion, or the Banishing Ritual of the Lesser Pentagram actually does is alert positively polarized, discarnate entities so that they may provide that quality that we call love from their quarters, for whatever the purpose might be. Each of us may also provide that same love as a function of our truly caring for another. As we learn the lessons of love within this third-density illusion, we are also learning the basics of healing and protection.

There are surprises in this material, even after all these years. It was not until this moment (writing in 1997) that Jim and I realized we did not follow one of Ra's suggestions during that hospital experience. Jim, Don, and I vibrated the Banishing Ritual twice a day; Jim and I both remember that. Neither of us can recall reading the Mass in any form. We just missed it. Imagine wasting Ra's advice! I know we did not do that on purpose. After sixteen years, all we can say is that refrain of bozos everywhere . . . oops!

As to the hand-holding when I meditated, this was a practice that began after a particularly discomfiting experience during one of our public meditation sessions. These were completely separate from the sessions with Ra. Any and all could come and check us out. I did not go into trance at these sessions as I did with Ra sessions, but channeled from a very light trance state. However, during the question-and-answer period, someone asked a question that I had no earthly idea about, and I thought to myself, "I wish I were channeling Ra." Immediately I began to leave my body, which was absolutely NOT to be done, according to Ra. The source that I was channeling, Latwii, simply kept me channeling—probably pure nonsense—but it sufficed to keep me in the body. After that, someone, usually Jim, always held my hand during sessions. To this day, Jim holds my hand as we meditate during our morning offering, and at all meditation sessions we offer. Better safe than sorry is the cliché that covers this.

I remember with great affection the utter fidelity of love and concern that Don and Jim showed me during this time. It was very hard for Don especially to see me in pain. But he did not flinch or draw away but rather tried ceaselessly to protect and aid me. The same could be said of Jim, but I think it was light-years harder for Don to bear this than Jim. Jim is a simple, straightforward person. To him, what is, is. I remember asking him once if all he was going to say in this life was "yup, nope, or maybe." "Yup," he replied. Then, after considering, he said, "Nope . . ." Then more consideration, and he finally settled on, "Maybe!" To Don my pain was his pain, for we were truly one being in that ineffable sense that is beyond space and time. The pain, severe though it was, did not overly distress me, but it foundered Don. His level of concern was profound.

Through the years since this channeling, I have more and more come to appreciate Ra's suggestion that I fully accept my limitations. After my miraculous rehabilitation in 1992, I found myself out of the wheelchair and vertical for the first time in many years. A year ago, I was able to give the downstairs hospital bed back to Medicare (I still find one helpful at night, for sleeping). When I first started to rebuild a "vertical" life, I was full of ideas as to what I might accomplish. I tried going back to school to get myself current in my old field of library service. I tried to take a job. I volunteered at church, far beyond my actual capacity to serve. And this took its toll, as I collected injuries, a broken ankle, sprained knees, and two more hand operations. Finally, about a year ago, I managed to pare down my work to the point where I allowed much rest time within the schedule of the day. I've tinkered with this schedule, finding ways to harmonize my efforts with Jim's, finding how to nurture myself, finding what priorities my life really has. I am hopeful that I have at this point realized these set limits to effort, and have begun to cooperate with my destiny.

I fully respect my pre-incarnative choice to take on these uncomfortable limitations. The experience has hollowed me out and made me an ever better channel. I continue to rejoice as I see little bits of my ego fall away. My prayer *these days is "Lord, show me Thy ways." There is much work left for me, a true idiot. But I exult in being upon the King's Highway.*

Session 75,
October 31, 1981

QUESTIONER: Could you first please give me the condition of the instrument?

RA: I am Ra. It is as previously stated, with some slight lessening of the reserve of vital energy due to mental/emotional distortions regarding what you call the future.

QUESTIONER: I felt that this session was advisable before the instrument has her hospital experience. She wished to ask a few questions, if possible, about that.

First, is there anything that the instrument or we might do to improve the hospital experience or to aid the instrument in any way with respect to this?

RA: I am Ra. Yes. There are ways of aiding the mental/emotional state of this entity, with the notation that this is so only for this entity or one of like distortions. There is also a general thing which may be accomplished to improve the location which is called the hospital.

The first aiding has to do with the vibration of the ritual with which this entity is most familiar, and which this entity has long used to distort its perception of the One Infinite Creator. This is an helpful thing at any point in the diurnal period but is especially helpful as your sun body removes itself from your local sight.

The general improvement of the place where the performance of the ritual of the purification is to be performed is known. We may note that the distortion towards love, as you call this spiritual/emotional complex which is felt by each for this entity, will be of aid whether this is expressed or unmanifest, as there is no protection greater than love.

QUESTIONER: Do you mean that it would be valuable to perform the Banishing Ritual of the Lesser Pentagram in the room in which she will be occupying in the hospital?

RA: I am Ra. This is correct.

QUESTIONER: I was wondering about the operating room. That might be very difficult. Would it be helpful there?

RA: I am Ra. This is correct. We may note that it is always helpful. Therefore, it is not easy to posit a query to which you would not receive the answer which we offer. This does not indicate that it is essential to purify a place. The power of visualization may aid in your support where you cannot intrude in your physical form.

QUESTIONER: I see the way to do this as a visualization of the operating room and a visualization of the three of us performing the banishing ritual in the room as we perform it at another location. Is this the correct procedure?

RA: I am Ra. This is one correct method of achieving your desired configuration.

QUESTIONER: Is there a better method than that?

RA: I am Ra. There are better methods for those more practiced. For this group, this method is well.

QUESTIONER: I would assume those more practiced would leave their physical bodies and, in the other body, enter the room and practice the ritual. Is this what you mean?

RA: I am Ra. This is correct.

QUESTIONER: The instrument would like to know if she can meditate in the hospital without someone holding her hand. Would this be a safe practice?

RA: I am Ra. We might suggest that the instrument may pray with safety but only meditate with another entity's tactile protection.

QUESTIONER: The instrument would like to know what she can do to improve the condition of her back, as she feels it will be a problem for the operation.

RA: I am Ra. As we scan the physical complex, we find several factors contributing to one general distortion experienced by the instrument. Two of these distortions have been diagnosed; one has not; nor will the entity be willing to accept the chemicals sufficient to cause cessation of this distortion you call pain.

In general we may say that the sole modality addressing itself specifically to all three contributing distortions, which is not now being used, is that of the warmed water, which is moved with gentle force repeatedly against the entire physical complex while the physical vehicle is seated. This would be of some aid if practiced daily after the exercise period.

QUESTIONER: Did the exercise of the fire performed before the session help the instrument?

RA: I am Ra. There was some slight physical aid to the instrument. This will enlarge itself as the practitioner learns/teaches its healing art. Further, there is distortion in the mental/emotional complex which feeds the vital energy towards comfort, due to support which tends to build up the level of vital energy, as this entity is a sensitive instrument.

QUESTIONER: Was the exercise of the fire properly done?

RA: I am Ra. The baton is well visualized. The conductor will learn to hear the entire score of the great music of its art.

QUESTIONER: I assume that if this can be fully accomplished, that exercise will result in total healing of the distortions of the instrument to such an extent that operations would be unnecessary. Is this correct?

RA: I am Ra. No.

QUESTIONER: What else is necessary, the instrument's acceptance?

RA: I am Ra. This is correct. The case with this instrument being delicate, since it must totally accept much which the limitations it now experiences cause to occur involuntarily. This is a pre-incarnative choice.

Fragment 42

Ra mentioned a number of times that impatience is one of the most frequent catalysts with which the seeker must work. When a general outline of the path of evolution is seen, it is often too enticing to resist jumping ahead of one's actual place upon the path and making quickly for the goal. This was the case for me as I queried about the steps of accepting the self that I had discovered in my own seeking. Ra's suggestion to carefully place the foundation of one's house before hanging the roof seems sound. It brings to mind the old saying "There is never time enough to do a thing right the first time, but there is always time enough to do it over."

Note also how any thought and action, when carefully scrutinized, can lead one to the basic distortions or lessons that one is working on. Thus, any portion of the life experience can be seen as a holographic miniature of the entire incarnational plan for an entity, as layer upon layer of meaning is discovered behind the smallest surface of things. As we discovered in Book IV, this is not because the events in our world are naturally filled with layers of meanings—though this is also true—but because we subconsciously color the events in our lives in the way that we have pre-incarnatively decided will provide us with the opportunities to learn what we wish to learn. That's why different people see the same catalyst in different ways—often wildly varying. As we work with these colorations/distortions/reactions in a conscious manner, we begin to accept ourselves for having them because we begin to see the purpose behind them. This acceptance draws to us the balancing attitudes for our distortion, so that our viewpoint expands and we are able to accept and love another part of the Creator that was previously not accepted and loved. Love, then, is the potential product of any distortion.

The course of spiritual seeking is often unclear, and seekers are always looking hopefully for some single point of clarity to hold against the universe as yardstick. Certainly, the remembrance of Love Itself suffices in this wise. But this remembrance comes slowly when we are caught up in our reactions. We each have these hooks that catch us up, and there is some time that passes before we are reoriented. We wish we were more alert! But we are not always attentive, no matter how abreast of things we hope to be. I like Ra's insistence that we continue to catch ourselves in the act, rather than swinging around in a supposed shortcut that keeps us from seeing into why we got caught. It is a real breakthrough for me every time I see myself GETTING caught. This moment reveals to us that inner distortion we've been looking for! Once we can see the mechanism, we can far more effectually work on its release. I think the goal here is not to be without error, but to see our errors more clearly. We are human: we will err. It is impossible not to. But we can, slowly, learn ourselves well enough to do the erring during inner processes, rather than upon the outer world stage. Perhaps, one day, all the "buttons" from childhood and other traumas might become released, and we be clear. And perhaps not. I don't think this matters nearly as much as how much we have loved.

Session 82,
March 27, 1982

QUESTIONER: Jim has a personal question that is not to be published. He asks, "It seems that my balancing work has shifted from more-peripheral concerns such as patience/impatience, to learning to open myself in unconditional love, to accepting my self as whole and perfect, and then to accepting my self as the Creator. If this is a normal progression of focus for balancing, wouldn't it be more efficient once this is discovered for a person to work on the acceptance of the self as Creator rather than work peripherally on the secondary and tertiary results of not accepting the self?"

RA: I am Ra. The term "efficiency" has misleading connotations. In the context of doing work in the disciplines of the personality, in order to be of more full efficiency in the central acceptance of the self, it is first quite necessary to know the distortions of the self which the entity is accepting. Each thought and action needs must then be scrutinized for the precise foundation of the distortions of any reactions. This process shall lead to the more central task of acceptance. However, the architrave must be in place before the structure is builded.

Fragment 43

The first portion of Session 84 is mostly nuts-and-bolts maintenance of the instrument. Her primary exercise each day was one hour of brisk walking, and when her feet began to suffer injury, we tried alternating two different kinds of shoes, hoping that each would aid one portion of the injury without aggravating another portion.

Don also asked Ra about information concerning earth changes, which Andrija Puharich had received from one of his sources. Instead of responding directly to the query and risking infringing upon the free will of Dr. Puharich, Ra chose to speak to the subject of earth changes as representative of one of two choices that a person may make in the search for truth.

Between that response and the last question and answer that you see was a portion of information concerning a person's encounter with a UFO, which Ra asked us to keep private. The question and answer that you do see is in reference to this same

UFO contact and reveals the general way in which many face-to-face encounters between our third-density population and extraterrestrial entities occur. What is actually remembered by the third-density entity is a product of its expectations and what its subconscious mind fashions as an acceptable story that will allow the entity to continue functioning without losing its mental balance. This is the nature of the positive contact in which the third-density entity is being awakened to seek more clearly the nature of not only the UFO encounter but the life pattern as well. Negative contacts, however, utilize the concepts of fear and doom to further separate and confuse the Earth population.

My poor feet! Rheumatoid disease is notorious for its depredations upon one's extremities, and perhaps my hands, feet, and neck have suffered the worst from its progression. Thirteen operations on my hands and six on my feet have staved off total dysfunction, but the old digits are not what they once were. During these sessions, they suffered far more than normal, because when I was in trance, I did not move at all. Those of Ra did not know how to make my body move very well, and so whatever aches and pains I had became rapidly very hard to bear. It was easy for me to be discouraged. I can remember asking the Creator, with some asperity, what It had in mind when it gave me these gifts! How inconvenient! Especially in terms of this contact, which we all knew was special, I tended to feel that I had let down the side by these sore joints taking time away from the sessions in length. Feeling unworthy in the first place, I felt sheepish that I was, by these distortions, lessening the content of each working. At this latter day, however, I have ceased to rail against whatever comes my way. I am just glad to be here. And if I can still channel, fine. But I think all of us have one main job, and that is just to be who we are, living in an open-hearted love of the Creator and His creation.

Ra's zinger of an answer to Puharich's question about coming earth changes is worth pondering in depth. The answer concerning the person's remembrance of a close encounter of the third kind, being on board a craft, is also pithy. We really have a great deal to do with how we experience events of an archetypal nature, and this bleeds through into the everyday. So much of what we receive from the world is set by what we give to it. Ra's comments are provocative in suggesting how we can view that ineffable thing called sanity.

Session 84,
April 14, 1982

QUESTIONER: What disease in particular were you speaking of and what would be its cause?

RA: I am Ra. One disease, as you call this distortion, is that of the arthritis and the lupus erythematosus. The cause of this complex of distortions is, at base, pre-incarnative. We refrain from determining the other distortion potential at this space/time due to our desire to maintain the free will of this group. Affirmations may yet cause this difficulty to resolve itself. Therefore, we simply encourage the general care with the diet with the instructions about allergy, as you call this quite complex distortion of the mind and body complexes.

QUESTIONER: Could you make any suggestions about the instrument's feet or how they got in the bad shape that they are in, and if alternating the shoes would help?

RA: I am Ra. The distortion referred to above—that is, the complex of juvenile rheumatoid arthritis and lupus erythematosus—acts in such a way as to cause various portions of the body complex to become distorted in the way in which the instrument's pedal appendages are now distorted.

We may suggest care in resumption of the exercise, but determination as well. The alternation of footwear shall prove efficacious. The undergarment for the feet, which you call the anklet, should be of a softer and finer material than is now being used, and should, if possible, conform more to the outline of those appendages upon which it is placed. This should provide a more efficient aid to the cushioning of these appendages.

We may further suggest that the same immersion in the waters which is helpful to the general distortion is, in general, helpful to this specific distortion as well. However, the injury which has been sustained in the metatarsal region of the right pedal appendage should be further treated for some period of your space/time by the prudent application of the ice to the arch of the right foot for brief periods, followed always by immersion in the warm water.

QUESTIONER: I am sure that we are getting into a problem area with the first distortion here, with a difficulty with a bit of transient material, but I have questions from a couple of people that I would like to ask. The first one especially is of no lasting value. Andrija Puharich asks about the coming physical changes, specifically this summer. Is there anything that we could relay to him about that?

RA: I am Ra. We may confirm the good intention of the source of this entity's puzzles and suggest that it is a grand choice that each may make to, by desire, collect the details of the day or, by desire, seek the keys to unknowing.

QUESTIONER: I can't help but be interested in the fact that this other entity to whom we were previously referring reported being taken on board a craft. Could you tell me something about that?

RA: I am Ra. The nature of contact is such that in order for the deep portion of the trunk of the tree of mind affected to be able to accept the contact, some symbology which may rise to the conscious mind is necessary as a framework for the explanation of the fruits of the contact. In such cases the entity's own expectations fashion the tale which shall be most acceptable to that entity, and in the dream state, or a trance state in which visions may be produced, this seeming memory is fed into the higher levels of the so-called subconscious and the lower levels of the conscious. From this point the story may surface as any memory and cause the instrument to function without losing balance or sanity.

Fragment 44

The gift of a crystal that has been charged by a friend is a very special gift. Apparently, it is also the kind of gift that creates a special connection between the one who gives it and the one who receives it, and because of this connection it would seem that a special care needs to be exercised both by the one who would give and the one who would receive such a crystal as a gift.

People like myself, who are sensitive to energy flow, often find that they simply cannot ignore certain crystals. I do not wear them at all, having found that their energy can disturb me, make me edgy. In these latter days of crystal technology, it is not surprising that crystals can be seen to have power. It is their magnetization by the people who have them, or give them, that makes them unique beyond their structure's singularity. They need to be handled with care, I think. I have been told many stories of the effects, good and bad, of such magnetized stones.

If you receive one or are drawn to one, be sure to cleanse it in salt water overnight, and then magnetize it for your own use by holding it during meditation and asking silently that it be blessed for service.

Session 88,
May 29, 1982

QUESTIONER: Is the small crystal that the instrument uses upon her during the session of any benefit or detriment?

RA: I am Ra. This crystal is beneficial as long as he who has charged it is functioning in a positively oriented manner.

QUESTIONER: Who charged the crystal?

RA: I am Ra. This crystal was charged for use by this instrument by the one known as Neil.

QUESTIONER: It would be an abridgment of the first distortion for you to tell us if he is still functioning in a positive manner, would it not?

RA: I am Ra. We perceive you have replied to your own query.

Fragment 45

The first few questions and responses in this session are more of the nuts-and-bolts maintenance that we constantly found ourselves having to deal with in keeping up both with Carla's arthritic flare-ups of pain and our fifth-density, negative friend's accentuating of these difficulties.

Toward the beginning of Session 92 in Book IV of *The Law of One*, one of Ra's responses was "There is the need for the instrument to choose the manner of its beingness. It has the distortion, as we have noted, towards the martyrdom. This can be evaluated and choices made only by the entity." And at the end of that same session, Ra added, "The instrument, itself, might ponder some earlier words and consider their implications. We say this because the continued calling upon vital energies, if allowed to proceed to the end of the vital energy, will end this contact. There is not the need for continued calling upon these energies. The instrument must find the key to this riddle or face a growing loss of this particular service at this particular space/time nexus." The last part of the personal material from Session 94 consists of a query from Carla upon which she pondered long, concerning the riddle that Ra had presented in Session 92. The riddle was Ra's way of maintaining Carla's free will and at the same time giving her a direction for thought that might enhance both her own growth and the service of the contact to others.

As time went on, we fiddled around more and more with clothing and such, trying to maximize my comfort and the length of sessions. I was warmly clothed, all in white, with the white comforter placed so it did not drag down the arms, and then my hands were gloved, and the kind of tubing used to vent washer/dryers went over both hands up to about the elbow, to keep the weight of the cover off them completely. It was a job just getting dressed for the sessions. It seems almost funny when one looks back on it, that we kept on with such perseverance. But at the time, there was only one thought among us three, and that was to continue this contact and learn all we could. I think if it happened again, I'd do the same thing again: give my utmost. And I imagine Jim would say the same. Without question, Don was also absolutely single-minded about pursuing the questioning with Ra. He felt that this was the culmination of his life's work. If we were somewhat wearied and even battered by the conditions we had to work in, that was acceptable. And we did indeed all feel the weariness.

I appreciate the point those of Ra make concerning my gift of faith. It has been true for as long as I can remember that I have enjoyed that attitude of faith and hope. It may well be why I am alive today, while Don is a soldier fallen in the spiritual battle. Don was a person of infinite dignity, intelligence, and ethical purity, but always a somewhat melancholy man under the mask of polite courtesy, efficiency, and professorial charm that he wore to meet the world. Much has been given me in this life in the way of gifts, but this is surely the most precious.

Doesn't Ra offer a marvelous perspective to the myopic spiritual eye, in suggesting that I was only looking at what still needed doing, rather than giving thanks for what had come around already? I have often taken their advice and pondered the merits of judging as the stern critic that would have everything just so. Life is messy, and often things are very much untidy, and that needs to be released, forgiven, and accepted.

And Ra's final thought is truly a jewel. What, after all, is all our striving in the end, including this contact and all human thought, but a vain and empty folly? We cannot move from illusion to truth in this body, on this plane of existence. So where is our truest and central service? Not in the doing but in the being, in allowing the true self, that open-hearted lover of all things in creation, to share its essence with the world, and to allow the love and light of the Infinite One to pass through it and radiate into the planetary consciousness. That is our true geste, all of us who have come here at this time to be of service: being, living a devotional and devoted life.

Session 94,
August 26, 1982

QUESTIONER: I have questions here from the instrument. The first one is "Is our fifth-density friend responsible for the instrument's extreme distortion towards pain during and just after sessions?"

RA: I am Ra. Yes.

QUESTIONER: Is there anything that we can do that we are not doing to remedy this situation, so that the instrument does not experience this pain, or as much pain?

RA: I am Ra. There is little that can be done due to a complex of preexisting distortions. The distortions are triple in the source.

There is the, shall we say, less than adequate work of your chirurgeons which allows for various distortions in the left wrist area.

There is the distortion called systemic lupus erythematosus which causes the musculature of the lower left and right arms to allow for distortions in the normal, shall we say, configuration of both.

Lastly, there is the nerve damage, more especially to the left, but in both appendages from the thoracic outlet.

In the course of the waking behavior, the instrument can respond to the various signals which ring the tocsin of pain, thus alerting the mind complex, which in turn moves the physical complex in many and subtle configurations which relieve the various distortions. Your friend greets these distortions, as has been stated before, immediately prior to the beginning of the working. However, during the working the instrument is not with its yellow-ray chemical vehicle, and thusly the many small movements which could most effectively aid in the decrease of these distortions are not possible. Ra must carefully examine the mental configurations of the mind complex in order to make even the grossest manipulation. It is not our skill to use a yellow-ray vehicle.

The weight of the cover has some deleterious effect upon these distortions in some cases, and thus we mentioned that there was a small thing which could be done; that is, the framing of that which lifted the coverlet from the body slightly. In order to compensate for loss of warmth, the wearing of material warming the manual appendages would then be indicated.

QUESTIONER: I immediately think of the instrument wearing long underwear under the robe that it now wears, and an extremely light, white cover. Would this be satisfactory?

RA: I am Ra. Due to this instrument's lack of radiant physical energy, the heavier cover is suggested.

QUESTIONER: In your statement, at the beginning of it, you said "less than adequate work of" and then there was a word that I didn't understand at all. Are you familiar with the word that I am trying to understand?

RA: I am Ra. No.

QUESTIONER: Then we'll have to wait until we transcribe the material. I assume that our fifth-density, negative friend doesn't cause these distortions all of the time, because he wishes to emphasize the fact that the instrument is going to be distorted only if she attempts one of these service-to-others workings and, therefore, attempts to stifle the workings. Is this correct?

RA: I am Ra. This is partially correct. The incorrect portion is this: The entity of which you speak has found its puissance[1] less than adequate to mount a continuous assault upon this instrument's physical vehicle and has, shall we say, chosen the more effective of the space/time nexi of this instrument's experience for its service.

QUESTIONER: Could you tell me why I have felt so tired on several recent occasions?

RA: I am Ra. This has been covered in previous material.

The contact which you now experience costs a certain amount of the energy which each of the group brought into manifestation in the present incarnation. Although the brunt of this cost falls upon the instrument, it is caparisoned by pre-incarnative design with the light and gladsome armor of faith and will to a far more conscious extent than most mind/body/spirit complexes are able to enjoy without much training and initiation.

Those of the support group also offer the essence of will and faith in service to others, supporting the instrument as it releases itself completely in the service of the One Creator. Therefore, each of the support group also experiences a weariness of the spirit which is indistinguishable from physical-energy deficit, except that if each experiments with this weariness, each shall discover the physical energy in its usual distortion.

QUESTIONER: Thank you. I didn't mean to go over previous material. I should have phrased my question more carefully. That is what I expected. I was trying to get a confirmation of my suspicion. I suspected that. I will try to be more careful in questioning.

The second question from the instrument says, "While on vacation I uncovered a lot about myself not consciously known before. It seems to me that I have coasted a lot on the spiritual gifts given at birth, and never have spent any time getting to know my human self which seems to be a child, immature and irrational. Is this so?"

RA: I am Ra. This is partially correct.

QUESTIONER: Then she says, "If this is so, this seems to be part of the riddle about the manner of my beingness that Ra spoke of. I fear that if I do not work successfully on my human distortions, I shall be responsible for losing the contact. Yet, also Ra suggests the over-dedication to any outcome is unwise. Could Ra comment on these thoughts?"

RA: I am Ra. We comment in general first upon the query about the contact which indicates once again that the instrument views the mind/body/spirit complex with jaundiced eye. Each mind/body/spirit complex that is seeking shall almost certainly have the immature and irrational behaviors. It is also the case that this entity, as well as almost all seekers, has done substantial work within the framework of the incarnative experience and has indeed developed maturity and rationality. That this instrument should fail to see that which has been accomplished and see only that which remains to be accomplished may well be noted. Indeed, any seeker discovering in itself this complex of mental and mental/emotional distortions shall ponder the possible nonefficacy of judgment.

As we approach the second portion of the query, we view the possibility of infringement upon free will. However, we believe we may make reply within the boundaries of the Law of Confusion.

This particular instrument was not trained, nor did it study, nor worked it at any discipline in order to contact Ra. We were able, as we have said many times, to contact this group using this instrument because of the purity of this instrument's dedication to the service of the One Infinite Creator and also because of the great amount of harmony and acceptance enjoyed each by each within the group, this situation making it possible for the support group to function without significant distortion.

We are humble messengers. How can any thought be taken by an instrument as to the will of the Creator? We thank this group that we may speak through it, but the future is mazed. We cannot know whether our geste may, after one final working, be complete. Can the instrument, then, think for a moment that it shall cease in the service of the One Infinite Creator? We ask the instrument to ponder these queries and observations.

Fragment 46

Don's job as a pilot for Eastern Airlines saw him based in Atlanta.

Commuting to and from Atlanta became more and more wearing on him and reduced the amount of time available for Ra sessions, due to his absence and due to the time needed for him to recover from his weariness when he was home. Thus, in the fall of 1982 we found a house near the airport in Atlanta that we thought we would move to, so Don's commuting time would be reduced. It had previously been inhabited by people who had trafficked in illegal drugs and who had apparently had numerous disharmonious experiences within the dwelling that was to become our new home. These unfortunate experiences by the former tenants had apparently attracted elementals and lower astral entities into the house, which Carla was somewhat able to perceive.

She wanted very much to move into the house because it would have greatly helped Don to be that close to his work. She wanted to buy new carpeting to replace the soiled one, or, failing that, to begin scrubbing the carpet to cleanse the house of the undesirable presences, but the limitations of our budget and her arthritis made that impossible. Thus a blue-ray blockage of communication occurred that, two days later while she was on her daily walk, was entered by our fifth-density, negative friend and enhanced in the magical sense until she was unable to breathe for about thirty seconds. This was symbolic of her inability to talk to Don about what the house needed. Keeping calm during the distress saw her through it, and talking to Don about the house cleared the blockage.

The queries about the malfunctioning tape recorder refer to strange sounds that came from it a few days later, when Carla was trying to record some of her singing to send to a friend.

The last portion of this session returns to the subject of the house next to the airport in Atlanta that was to become our new home. In our personal and fallible opinions, it is from this point that the difficulties that eventually led to Don's death may be traced. When we returned to our home in Louisville from looking at the new home-to-be in Atlanta, we had just walked in the front door when, all of the sudden, a hawk with a wing span of at least 4 feet landed outside our kitchen window, remained for a few moments, and then flew off over the treetops. Carla and I took the appearance of the hawk as a sign confirming the desirability of the house in Atlanta as our new home. Don, however, was not sure that the hawk was a good sign, and he began to doubt whether we should move to the house after all.

I cannot tell you just how sorry I was that the Atlanta "farm" they were talking about here did not work out as a dwelling place for us. In it, Don was just 3 miles from the airport. It was a very nice place, although peculiar

123

in that the house simply ended with no wall between it and the adjoining horse barn. It was less expensive to rent than the place we had in Louisville, it was a milder climate, and there was room for Jim to stretch out and have his own place, and Don and me to do likewise. What foiled it was an attitude of Don's that was deeply characteristic and, I imagine, stemmed from growing up in the Depression. He did not want to spend the money to get the place really clean. The dirtiness of the place was everywhere; it had been neglected for some time, dusted and vacuumed occasionally, but any spills were left as they fell, and there was the slight patina of ground-in dirt that only good soap would get, and much hard scrubbing. The most logical solution to me was simply to replace the floor covering throughout the dirtied area. Barring that, hiring a good cleaning agency with professional equipment would have sufficed. Don wished to do neither of these things.

When the hawk flew, and Don took it as a bad omen, that was it. There was no more to discuss, as far as Don was concerned. At that point, as Jim has said, there was a definite shift in Don's peace of mind. He was more concerned about having enough energy to work as a pilot than ever, and yet everything seemed to be too much trouble. When we tried to buy the Louisville house from its owner, there was a $5,000.00 dispute that the owner and Donald developed that put the quietus on that deal. So we had to move somewhere, as the owner of the Louisville property was selling it out from under us. Don eventually OK'd a lovely and pricey house on Lake Lanier, about 40 bad miles from the airport. What we hadn't realized was that Atlanta traffic is terrible; after the Olympics were held there, the whole nation became aware of that. And Don had to drive from the extreme north of the traffic tangle to the extreme south, where the airport lay. He spent more time getting there from the lake house than he had done from Louisville, since all he had to do in Louisville was take a short drive to the airport and commute for an hour to Atlanta. The driving from the lake was always an hour and a half to two hours, because of the traffic. There simply seemed no relief and no solution at that house. And so began a difficult experience for all three of us, who somehow had no safe place to be.

If Donald had been normal, he would have been talking a good deal about his various fears. But Don was Don, a wonderful, wise, charming, funny, and truly great man, but a unique man who had from an early age pretended he had no preferences and was only an observer. After his death I found out that he was developing real fears about losing me to Jim. But to me he said nothing, following his usual practice of behaving as though he had no preferences. So I was utterly confused. I figured he was just upset about having the right place, and spent countless hours poring over newspaper ads trying to find him a place he felt good about, but to no avail. From this point on, we were never at peace. And little by little, I realized at a deep level that something serious was going wrong with Don. He began acting *very unlike himself, being unwilling to leave my presence to the point of listening to my music rehearsals, watching me exercise, sleeping in my room; all things the usual Don would scorn. I did not take these things as positive, for I truly loved the irascible and indifferent Don and longed to have him back.*

I was grieving for Donald for months while he was still alive, for he quickly changed to the point that neither I nor he himself could recognize him. This was a time of the most profound distress for Don and for me. Jim was deeply concerned about both of us but was pretty stable. Both Don and I went rather quickly beyond the bounds of normalcy. I suffered a breakdown. I asked for and got help from family, friends, and therapists. So I walked through my nervous breakdown, continuing to function at a basic level. Don suffered a breakdown also, but his came with a real break from reality, and he was in a place where it seemed no one, most of all I, could help him.

Session 96,
September 9, 1982

QUESTIONER: Could you tell me the cause of the lessening of the physical and vital energies?

RA: I am Ra. We found the need of examining the mental configurations of the instrument before framing an answer, due to our reluctance to infringe upon its free will. Those concepts relating to the spiritual contemplation of personal catalyst have been appreciated by the entity, so we may proceed.

This entity has an habitual attitude which is singular; that is, when there is some necessity for action, the entity is accustomed to analyzing the catalyst in terms of service and determining a course. There was a most unusual variation in this configuration of attitude when this instrument beheld the dwelling which is to be inhabited by this group. The instrument perceived those elementals and beings of astral character of which we have spoken. The instrument desired to be of service by achieving the domicile in question but found its instincts reacting to the unwelcome presences. The division of mind configuration was increased by the continuing catalyst of lack of control. Had this entity been able to physically begin cleansing the dwelling, the, shall we say, opening would not have occurred.

Although this entity attempted clear communication upon this matter, and although each in the support group did likewise, the amount of blue-ray work necessary to uncover and grasp the nature of the catalyst was not affected. Therefore, there was an opening quite rare for this mind/body/spirit complex, and into this opening the one which greets you moved and performed what may be considered to be the most potent of its purely magical manifestations to this present nexus, as you know time.

It is well that this instrument is not distorted towards what you may call hysteria, for the potential of this working was such that had the instrument allowed fear to become greater than the will to persevere when it could not breathe, each attempt at respiration would have been even more nearly impossible until the suffocation occurred which was desired by the one which greets you in its own way. Thus the entity would have passed from this incarnation.

QUESTIONER: Does this threat, shall I say, still exist, and, if so, is there something that we can do to alleviate it?

RA: I am Ra. This threat no longer exists, if you wish to phrase this greeting in this manner. The communication which was affected by the scribe and then by the questioner did close the opening and enable the instrument to begin assimilating the catalyst it had received.

QUESTIONER: Was the unusual sound on the instrument's tape recorder that occurred while she was trying to record her singing a greeting from our fifth-density, negative associate?

RA: I am Ra. No. Rather it was a greeting from a malfunctioning electronic machine.

QUESTIONER: There was no catalyst for that machine to malfunction from any of the negative entities then. Is that right? It was only a function of the random malfunction of the machine. Am I correct?

RA: I am Ra. No.

QUESTIONER: What was the origin of this malfunction?

RA: I am Ra. There are two difficulties with the machine. Firstly, this instrument has a strong effect upon electromagnetic and electronic machines and instruments, and likely, if continued use of these is desired, should request that another handle the machines. Also, there was some difficulty from physical interference due to the material you call tape catching upon adjoining, what you would call, buttons when the "play" button, as you call it, is depressed.

QUESTIONER: How is Ra able to know all of this information? This is somewhat of an unimportant question, but it is just amazing to me that Ra is able to know all of these trivial things. What do you do, move in time/space and inspect the problem, or what?

RA: I am Ra. Your former supposition is correct; your latter, unintelligible to us.

QUESTIONER: You mean that you move in time/space and inspect the situation to determine the problem. Is that correct?

RA: I am Ra. This is so.

QUESTIONER: Was there a significance with respect to the hawk that landed the other day just outside the kitchen window?

RA: I am Ra. This is correct. We may note that we find it interesting that queries offered to us are often already known. We assume that our confirmation is appreciated.

QUESTIONER: This seems to be connected with the concept of the bird being messengers in the tarot, and this was a demonstration of this concept. I was wondering about the mechanics, you might say, of this type of message. I assume that the hawk was a messenger, and I assume that as I thought of the possible meaning of this with respect to our activities, I was, in the state of free will, getting a message in the appearance of this very unusual bird, unusual, I say, in that it came so close. I would be very interested to know the origin of the message. Would Ra comment on this, please?

RA: I am Ra. No.

QUESTIONER: I was afraid that you would say that. Am I correct in assuming that this is the same type of communication as depicted in Card Number Three of the Catalyst of the Mind?

RA: I am Ra. We may not comment due to the Law of Confusion. There is an acceptable degree of confirmation of items known, but when the recognized subjective sigil[2] is waved and the message not clear, then it is that we must remain silent.

Fragment 47

After more thought on the subject of the hawk, Don again queried Ra about its significance. Since Ra did not wish to infringe upon Don's free will by clearly explaining the meaning of the hawk—and thus making Don's decision to move or not move to the house for him—the most Ra could do was speak in an indirect sense, in a kind of riddle that required that Don, and each of us, make our own determinations. The extreme desire on the part of any positive entities such as Ra to maintain the free will of each person on our third-density planet is due to the fact that if an entity such as Ra gives information that could change one's future choices, that entity, then, has not only taught the third-density being but has learned for it. By learning for it, it has removed the spiritual strength that comes to one who struggles and finally learns for him/herself. In the larger view, this is not seen as a service but as a disservice. Because of Don's doubt about the appropriateness of the house in Atlanta as our next home, we did not move to that house but remained in Louisville for another year. It was the fall of 1983 before we finally found another house in the Atlanta area and moved there. By that time, Don's weariness had increased to the critical point, and he had begun worrying more and more about whether he was even going to have a job since Eastern Airlines was rapidly failing financially.

Ah, to be able to read aright the little hints that the Creator always seems to be offering us! Both Jim and I thought the hawk was simply a confirmation of that location. But Don was the boss and he really felt unsure, to the point that he left, for a time, the idea of moving completely and tried to purchase the house we were renting. As I mentioned, the difference of about 4 percent of the house's cost was in dispute, and Donald did not see his way clear to giving the rather greedy owner an extra bonus for having us over the barrel of "buy or move." So in the end, we were forced to move somewhere, either in Louisville or Atlanta. It was a fateful move, attended from the beginning by struggles and problems. The sad tale of our demise as a group able to contact Ra was beginning.

Session 97,
September 15, 1982

QUESTIONER: I've been doing some consideration of the appearance of the hawk and have made this analysis of the bird in Card Number Three. The bird is a message from the Higher Self, and the position of the wings on Card Three, one pointing toward the female, indicates that it is a message to the female acting as catalyst for the mind. The position of the downward wing indicates that the message is of a negative nature or of a nature indicating the inappropriateness of certain mental activity or plans. Would Ra comment on that?

RA: I am Ra. No.

QUESTIONER: Is the reason for this lack of comment the first distortion?

RA: I am Ra. This is correct.

QUESTIONER: I have analyzed the hawk that I saw immediately after returning from the house in Atlanta as a message, probably from my Higher Self, indicating that the plan of moving was not the best or not too appropriate, since, without the hawk, we would have continued as planned with no added catalyst. This single catalyst of a remarkable nature then, logically, from my point of view, could only mean that there was a message as to the inappropriateness of the plan for some reason yet to be discovered. Would Ra comment on that?

RA: I am Ra. We tread as close as possible to the Law of Confusion in suggesting that not all winged creatures have an archetypical meaning. We might suggest that the noticing of shared subjectively notable phenomena is common when, in another incarnational experience, work significant to the service of increased polarity has been shared. These subjectively interesting shared phenomena then act as a means of communication, the nature of which cannot be discussed by those outside of the shared incarnational experience without the interference with the free will of each entity involved in the complex of subjectively meaningful events.

QUESTIONER: Can Ra tell us the source of the unusual odor in this room this morning?

RA: I am Ra. There are two components to this odor. One is, as has been surmised, the decomposing physical vehicle of one of your second-density rodentia. The second is an elemental which is attempting to take up residence within the putrefying remains of this small creature.

The cleansing of the room and the burning of the incense has discouraged the elemental. The process of decomposition shall, in a short period of your space/time, remove the less than harmonious sensations provided for the nose.

QUESTIONER: I find myself presently in a difficult position of decision, primarily because of the appearance of the aforementioned hawk upon our return from Atlanta. The only objective of any value at all is the work that we are doing, which includes not only the contact but communication and dissemination of this material to those who might request it. Since a move was connected with that, and since the hawk was, to me, obviously a function of that process, I am presently in a quandary with respect to the optimal situation, since I have not yet definitely decided on the significance of the hawk or the advantages or the efficaciousness of the move and do not want to create any process which is basically irreversible if it is going to result in a lack of our ability to be of service to those who would seek that which we are able to manifest in our efforts. Would Ra comment on that situation?

RA: I am Ra. The questioner presumes much, and to comment is an infringement upon its free will. We may suggest the pondering of our previous comments regarding the winged creatures of which you speak. We repeat that any place of working, properly prepared by this group, is acceptable to Ra. The discrimination of choice is yours.

Fragment 48

Session 98 is presented in total here. Our experiences were beginning to become a little more unusual and difficult at this point in our lives. We had difficulty agreeing on how to proceed concerning the house near the airport in Atlanta, and this is the difficulty of blue-ray blockage that Ra speaks of in the very long response to Carla's compound question. Since our difficulties were freely chosen by us, they were fair game for our negative companion of fifth density to intensify.

In querying about how once again to aid our longtime pet and companion, Gandalf, in another tumor-removal operation, we found that second-density creatures are also subject to causing cancer by creating unresolved anger within themselves—the same process that applies for third-density beings.

And, finally, we found when one constructs the artifacts, clothing, or structures with which one accomplishes service-to-others work, there is a great investment of love and magical potential that may result from such homemade and heart-made artifacts.

As we prepare this personal material for publication, I am sitting at the computer and am very tempted to rub my eyes, because the gardening I did earlier placed me in one of many environments to which I'm allergic. I think these allergies are often a complaint of Wanderers and have to do at least partially with the mismatch of vibrations between this earth world and the world of origin. Often the more uncomplaining the Wanderer, the more the body shall act out the difficulties we may have emotionally and mentally with the vibrations here. Certainly this is true of myself. I do see the psychosomatic nature of these allergies and by long practice have developed a fair resistance to them, which allows me to do some of the too many things I enjoy, whether it be patting the cats or pulling henbit out of the ivy. Or eating one of many foods, or dusting, or getting the mold out of something I find at church on one of my housekeeping forays. I doubt I could duck these no matter what my attitude, but I hope they are as little a part of my awareness as possible, and feel that the attitude really is key.

What it shows me is just how carefully balanced we are, as we come into incarnation here. I was given just these distortions, largely in order that I would have plenty of forced time to become more contemplative. It may seem that I am a thoroughgoing mystic, and certainly during many years of forced stillness, I have always found a depth of faith and a joy that illumined my life from within. It is almost as though the adversity of illness or limitation is a teacher, taking you out of the old ways of doing and introducing you to the contemplative life. I have wanted to be here every day of my life, with the exception of some sorry time during early puberty when I lost all faith and decided if I couldn't be of help to anyone, I might as well go on. Which my body obligingly did not six months later, throwing itself into kidney failure brought on by an allergic reaction. And the allergies are there because of the mismatch in vibratory complexes. See how neatly this works. Such is catalyst. It's a wonderful world.

As I got up from the sickbed at last during 1992, I vowed not to lose this love of stillness. But I also love to do, busy bee that I am. Of course I love to help L/L Research with correspondence and writing and channeling, and my church and singing. These are like the footers for the building I live in, real pillars of renewing spirit within. But there's more. I love the company of women and go out of my way to have that gal's night out in my schedule. I love to cook and do as much as I can cram in, and an extension of that is that I take a morning each week to go through the parish where I worship in community and just go around straightening, washing out, putting away, and making ready, especially in the church kitchen but really all over the building. It is a joy being a servant in the Lord's house! And I could continue till you were exhausted of any possible interest. There are so many good things to do, so many needs I hear and wish to respond to. Too many to accomplish, sadly. The plight of the nineties: no time!

What this is all in aid of is simply to demonstrate how deeply bred in the bone my love of helpful activity is. Activity at whatever level I can accomplish it is inevitable. It is part of who I am, and some would say that is a born martyr. Perhaps this is somewhat true. I only know we live and then we are gone, and while I am here, I want to respond as deeply as I can. This means I am always pushing the envelope, and always prey to psychic greeting. I have not ceased being greeted. It is just that I deal with it, as does Jim, with respect, in acknowledging it, and discipline, in allowing it to pass quickly without judgment, knowing the negative essence behind it as part of myself that I love. Acceptance and forgiveness simply move the situation forward, and the crises pass. This is hard-won wisdom. I encourage any groups who get into a situation where psychic greeting is occurring to study the ways of forgiveness and acceptance of this seemingly opposing energy. In claiming the higher truth that all is one, we place ourselves in that finer, fuller light, and the difficulties ease away as we simply persevere in living without fear of these greetings. For those who might be interested, I do have a chapter on psychic greeting and psychic self-defense in my Channeling Handbook. The essence of that advice: fear not, and lean on prayer and keeping the self aligned in open-hearted love.

My recovery from the bad throat infection discussed above was accomplished by a six-week course of antibiotics taken with lots of buttermilk, not a substance I enjoy. It did, however, work.

Gandalf was a very special little person. Given to me by an old friend in 1968, he was a kitten when Donald and I began our life together. He adored Don and would play retriever with him, repeatedly fetching the peppermint candy wrappers Don would tie in a little bow-tie and throw, and putting them in Don's shoes, which were always off if he was at home. His devotion was intense. If we were sitting, he was almost always upon one of us. Don loved to walk around with Gandalf hanging over his shoulder, and I can still see them clearly, doing their daily tour of the rooms of our apartment. Gandalf expressed such love! As he became quite old, he got both arthritis and cancer, but until the moment he died, he was fiercely determined to be here and as close to us as possible. I feel that he has now reincarnated in our beautiful cat "Mo," who expresses much the same energy. I am thankful we have had more time with this soul, who is certainly harvestable to third density.

Session 98 (in total),
September 24, 1982

RA: I am Ra. I greet you in the love and in the light of the One Infinite Creator. We communicate now.

QUESTIONER: Could you first please give me the condition of the instrument?

RA: I am Ra. The physical-energy deficit has somewhat increased. The vital energy distortions are somewhat improved.

QUESTIONER: We eliminated our meditation prior to the session. Would Ra comment on that?

RA: I am Ra. The purpose of preparation for a working is the purification of each entity involved with the working. The removal of a portion of this preparation has a value determined by the purity of each which takes part in the working has achieved without that particular aid.

QUESTIONER: I had just taken a wild guess that possibly it was during that meditation prior to the working that was used by our fifth-density, negative friend to create the allergic reactions and other reactions in the instrument. Was I correct in that assumption, or was I incorrect?

RA: I am Ra. This entity greets the instrument as close to the working in your space/time continuum as is practicable. The elimination of that preparation caused the fifth-density entity to greet this instrument at this juncture of decision not to meditate. The greeting does not take what you would call a noticeable amount of your time.

QUESTIONER: Was the greeting as effective as it would have been if meditation had been done?

RA: I am Ra. Yes.

QUESTIONER: I have a question from the instrument. It states: "Could Ra tell us what factors are allowing our fifth-density, negative companion to be able to continue greeting the instrument in the throat area, as well as with other unusual sensations such as dizziness, the smelling of orange blossoms, the feeling of stepping on imaginary creatures, and what can be done to lessen these greetings? Also, why do the greetings occur on walks?"

RA: I am Ra. There are various portions of the query. We shall attempt answer to each. We tread close to the Law of Confusion, saved only by the awareness that given lack of information, this instrument would, nonetheless, continue to offer its service.

The working of your fifth-density companion which still affects the instrument was, as we have stated, a potent working. The totality of those biases which offer to the instrument opportunities for increased vital and physical strength, shall we say, were touched by the working. The blue-ray difficulties were not entirely at an end after the first asking. Again, this group experienced blockage rare for the group; that is, the blue-ray blockage of unclear communication. By this means the efficacy of the working was reinforced.

The potential of this working is significant. The physical exercising, the sacred music, the varieties of experience, and indeed simple social intercourse are jeopardized by a working which attempts to close the throat and the mouth. It is to be noted that there is also the potential for the loss of this contact.

We suggest that the instrument's allergies create a continuous means whereby the distortion created by the magical working may be continued. As we have stated, it shall be necessary, in order to remove the working, to completely remove the distortion within the throat area caused by this working. The continuous aggravation of allergic reactions makes this challenging.

The orange blossom is the odor which you may associate with the social memory complex of fifth-density positive, which is known to you as sound vibration Latwii. This entity was with the instrument as requested by the instrument. The odor was perceived due to the quite sensitive nature of the instrument, due, again, to its, shall we say, acme in the eighteen-day cycle.

The sensation of stepping upon the small animal and killing it was a greeting from your fifth-density, negative companion also made possible by the above circumstance.

As to the removal of the effects of the magical working, we may make two suggestions, one immediate and one general. Firstly, within the body of knowledge which those healers known among your peoples as medical doctors have is the use of harsh chemical substances which you call medicine. These substances almost invariably cause far more changes than are intended in the mind/body/spirit complex. However, in this instance the steroids or, alternately, the antibiotic family might be useful in the complete removal of the difficulty within which the working is still able to thrive. Of course, the allergies would persist after this course of medicine were ended, but the effects of the working would no longer come into play.

The one you call Jerome might well be of aid in this somewhat unorthodox medical situation. As allergies are quite misunderstood by your orthodox healers, it would be inappropriate to subject the instrument to the services of your medical doctors, which find the amelioration of allergic effects to be connected with the intake of these same toxins in milder form. This, shall we say, treats the symptom. However, the changes offered to the body complex are quite inadvisable. The allergy may be seen to be the rejection upon a deep level of the mind complex of the environment of the mind/body/spirit complex. Thus the allergy may be seen in its pure form as the mental/emotional distortion of the deeper self.

The more general recommendation lies with one which does not wish to be identified. There is a code name prayer wheel. We suggest ten treatments from this healer and further suggest a clear reading and subsequent following upon the part of the instrument of the priorities of allergy, especially to your foodstuffs.

Lastly, the effects of the working become apparent upon the walking when the body complex has begun to exert itself to the point of increased respiration. Also a contributing factor is the number of your second-density substances to which this instrument is allergic.

QUESTIONER: Thank you. The second question is "Our oldest cat, Gandalf, has a growth near his spine. Is there anything that makes the surgical removal of this growth less appropriate than the surgical removal of the growth that we had performed a year ago last April, and would the most appropriate action on our part to aid his recovery be the visualization of light surrounding him during the surgery and the repeating of ritual phrases periodically while he is at the veterinarians?"

RA: I am Ra. No. There is no greater cause for caution than previously, and, yes, the phrases of which you speak shall aid the entity. Although this entity is, in body complex, old and therefore liable to danger from what you call your anesthetic, its mental, emotional, and spiritual distortions are such that it is strongly motivated to recover that it might once again rejoin the loved one. Keep in mind that this entity is harvestable third density.

QUESTIONER: Would you explain why you said "Keep in mind that this entity is harvestable third density" and tell me if you have any other specific recommendations with respect to the proposed operation on the growth?

RA: I am Ra. We stated this in order to elucidate our use of the term "spirit complex" as applied to what might be considered a second-density entity. The implications are that this entity shall have far more cause to abide and heal that it may seek the presence of the loved ones.

QUESTIONER: Is there any additional recommendation that Ra could make with respect to the proposed operation?

RA: I am Ra. No.

QUESTIONER: I was wondering if I was correct in my assumption for the reason for the growth was a state of anger in the cat Gandalf, because of the addition of the newer cats in his environment. Was I correct?

RA: I am Ra. The original cause of what you call cancer was the distortion caused by this event. The proximate cause of this growth is the nature of the distortion of the body cells which you call cancer.

QUESTIONER: Are there any other cancerous growths at this time in Gandalf?

RA: I am Ra. Yes.

QUESTIONER: Can we alleviate those and, if so, how and where are they?

RA: I am Ra. None can be alleviated at this space/time nexus. One is located within the juncture of the right hip. Another which is very small is near the organ you call the liver. There are also small cell distortions under the, we may call it, arm, to distinguish the upper appendages, on both sides.

QUESTIONER: Is there anything that we can do to alleviate these problems that are other than surgical to help Gandalf?

RA: I am Ra. Continue in praise and thanksgiving, asking for the removal of these distortions. There are two possible outcomes. Firstly, the entity shall dwell with you in contentment until its physical vehicle holds it no more due to distortions caused by the cancerous cells. Secondly, the life path may become that which allows the healing. We do not infringe upon free will by examining this life path, although we may note the preponderance of life paths which use some distortion such as this to leave the physical body, which in this case is the orange-ray body.

QUESTIONER: Does the cat Fairchild have any of these same type of problems?

RA: I am Ra. Not at this space/time nexus.

QUESTIONER: Was it necessary for the cat Gandalf to be a mind/body/

spirit complex and harvestable third density to have the anger result in cancer?

RA: I am Ra. No.

QUESTIONER: Then any mind/body complex can develop cancer. Is this correct?

RA: I am Ra. This is correct.

At this time we would break our routine by making an observation. We observe the following coincidence. Firstly, the congestion of this instrument's throat due to the flow of mucous caused by energized allergic reaction has, at this point, become such that we may safely predict the probability/possibility vortex approaching certainty that within one-half of an hour we shall need to depart from this working. Secondly, as we noted above, the sound vibration made by one of your sound vibration recording devices was audible to us. If this group desires, it may choose to have sessions which are brought to an ending soon after this sound vibration occurs. This decision would ensure the minimal distortions within the instrument towards the discomfort/comfort within the throat until the effects of the magical working of your fifth-density companion have been removed.

QUESTIONER: That is perfectly fine with us. That noise occurs at the forty-five-minute time period, since the tapes are forty-five minutes on a side. I would just ask as the final question, then, if the new table that Jim has built for the appurtenances is satisfactory to hold them, since it will give us more room to walk around the bed, and is it better to leave it in its natural condition, or is it better to coat it with linseed oil, varnish, or paint?

RA: I am Ra. We view this appurtenance. It sings with joy. The pine vibrates in praise. Much investment of this working in wood has been done. It is acceptable. We may suggest it be left either as it is or rubbed with the oil, which also is easily magnetized and holds the proffered vibration to a profound extent.

QUESTIONER: I was wondering if this would be an appropriate time to end since the tape recorder clicked some time ago.

RA: I am Ra. This is a matter for your discrimination. The instrument remains open to our use, although, as we have noted, the physical distortions begin to mount.

QUESTIONER: Then we had better close to protect the instrument's physical energy, and I will ask if there is anything that we can do to improve the contact or to make the instrument more comfortable?

RA: I am Ra. All is well. We find your concerns appropriate.

We leave you in the love and in the light of the One Infinite Creator. Go forth, therefore, rejoicing in the power and in the peace of the One. Adonai.

Fragment 49

Most people would probably not have described the feeling of not quite being whole and in harmony that our group experienced during the fall of 1982 as true disharmony. Yet, as one moves further along the path of seeking light and begins to stand closer to it, as we were privileged to do in the Ra contact, even the smallest of lapses of harmony, when left unresolved, can become targets of opportunity for those such as our friend of negative polarity to intensify. These psychic greetings can become great opportunities to heal those lapses of harmony and to move even further and faster upon the evolutionary journey, because what such a negative entity is actually doing when it intensifies one's disharmonious choices is pointing out to you weak points that you might have missed in your own conscious seeking. But one must take quick and thorough action in order to unravel these distortions in one's beingness or further confusion and difficulty may ensue, again due to, first, your original free-will choice; second, the intensification of that choice by the negative entity; and, third, by lack of attention on your part in finally resolving the distortion and balancing it. Fortunately, most people do not have to deal with the magical abilities of a fifth-density entity but with the lesser abilities of the fourth-density minions, who are usually quite effective on their own.

Thus as Carla was finally getting rid of the effects of the intensification of her blue-ray blockage concerning renting and then cleaning the house next to the airport in Atlanta, I began to notice an increase in my pre-incarnatively chosen distortion of anger/frustration. Notice the fundamental principle in Ra's first sentence in response to my question. All of our distortions and thus all of our learning are the result of the limitation of the viewpoint. We limit our points of view consciously or unconsciously, pre-incarnatively or during the incarnation, in order to gain a certain bias that may then draw unto it the opposite bias and offer us the opportunity for balance. By being able to see each bias as an opportunity for the Creator to know Itself and for us to know ourselves as the Creator, we more and more become able to accept ourselves. We become able to find love and acceptance not only in ourselves but in others who share our characteristics, and our viewpoint is widened by our efforts to learn and to serve. Such growth is not possible without biases or distortions, and these biases and distortions are not possible without the choice to limit the viewpoint in one way or another. So we determine what lessons and services we shall attempt during any incarnation by the way in which we limit our viewpoint.

Another interesting point to note here is that whatever one's basic nature is, whether it be love, wisdom, power, or some blend of these three, one does well to express that nature in a regularized fashion. So does one become a channel for it, not by holding on to it but by giving it away.

Again, we see another purpose of anger or the opportunity that it might present to one expressing it. Being the polar opposite of love, it may attract that love and compassion to the person feeling it. Remorse and sorrow often attract love and compassion to a positive seeker who has experienced a great deal of anger. Anger may also be seen as the negative expression of power; that is, destruction and separation, with the positive side being construction and unification. So it is not necessary to repress or overcome qualities in our being that seem negative and hurtful, but, rather, to see them as potentials for achieving balance. When these negative qualities are followed to their source, they can enable the seeker to take advantage of the opportunities for knowing the self, the Creator, and the creation as portions of a complete unity. Ra's last sentence underscores this point.

I have thought that this particular fragment is perhaps the best example in this current volume of why Ra can be so helpful. We three humans were doing our level best to stay totally harmonized in movement and rhythm, but we often erred, as do all of us, no matter what, if not today then tomorrow. This is the human estate. Working on this catalyst between us with an intensity born of wishing to remain clear enough to contact Ra, we developed questions for Ra, trying to get more of a bead on what our distortions were, and how to approach seating these incoming catalysts. But no question, however cleverly phrased, could expect to garner a piece of advice like "as in all distortions, the source is the limit of the viewpoint." In terms of the old saw about a choice between giving a man a fish and giving him a pole and teaching him fishing, Ra always went for the fishing pole, plus bait. And all without infringement on free will: an impressive task, and appreciated by us. We pored over these little comments a lot. They really did help us focus.

I've already talked about the buttermilk/penicillin cure. The principle Ra followed in OK'ing my wearing of a little cross in sessions seems very telling for a lot of questions we have about whether we should do something or not. They said it wasn't the greatest in terms of what complications it would cause, but it was OK because it was a symbol that strengthened me in a real way. This concept of balance and the strength of being as flowing into a pattern that is read as metaphysical rather than physical is a real help to people who want to be less allergic or depressed or whatever: do what feels right, letting the mystical meaning have as much importance as the physical. Find the balance.

Ra's advice to Jim struck home both to Jim and to Don and me. After we read this, we decided to encourage Jim to take the afternoon for solitude. He really enjoyed, and still enjoys, this routine, going out into the gardens for whatever needs doing after lunch and finishing up at eventide with a bath. I am often out there with him, but I do leave him in solitude unless I have a gardening question. To watch Jim work is to understand the power and purpose of ritual and magic.

My dear Mick (I call him that to distinguish him from my brother and also from my first husband, both named Jim) still has an amazingly bright and fiery temper. I stand in awe, quite literally, and watch it sweep through him like a tornado. He has, through the years, found ways to behave less angrily, but that core imbalance for him runs very deep, rather like my wanting to do too much. Some things about all of us are far from smart, but when you try to eradicate them, they just snicker! Nope—we're part of the package, they seem to say. I have worked my way through the substantial catalyst this has been for me, and give Mick thanks for such excellent catalyst. I have never been hurt physically, mind you. This is a solo act. I now simply observe and accept. I know it only seems that way. I affirm perfection. That is what I have learned to do so far, both to my own humanity and other people's. Meanwhile, he has had to learn to tend me rather like a shepherd, walking along and picking up the things I drip behind me as I go absent-mindedly on. No one gets away free!

I can only say that meditation and a daily offering each day as a beginning help for me. They are the basis of my day, and I think Jim would also say that. So I encourage any who might have had trouble doing that to try again. This time, adapt the practice to your life. It is a routine that has served us well. Perhaps that is too much for you, but you see how to build a time for you and the Creator to meet. You can't just remake your life around a newly discovered devotional or mystic aspect of yourself; you have to practice a rule of life that gives you time to do your necessaries. I think that one quick drink is a powerful thing. So please try again, if you have given up. For those who want to read about meditation, I recommend Joel Goldsmith's little book, The Art of Meditation.

Session 99,
November 18, 1982

QUESTIONER: What are the foodstuffs that are creating this allergic reaction?

RA: I am Ra. That which you call the buttermilk, though appropriately used in the healing work undertaken for the throat and chest areas, is the substance to which the entity has allergy.

QUESTIONER: The instrument asked if she could keep the small gold cross on while she is in one of these sessions. Will that cause any distortion in these workings?

RA: I am Ra. We scan the mental distortions of the instrument. Although the presence of the metallic substance is, in general, not recommended, in this instance, as we find those distortions weakening the mental/emotional complex of the instrument due to its empathic distortions, the figure is specifically recommended for use by this instrument. We would request that should any strengthening be done to the chain, as we find intended by this instrument, the strengthening links which symbolize eternity to this instrument be as high in purity or higher than the remainder of the device.

In this nexus that which this device represents to this instrument is a much-needed strengthener of the mental/emotional patterns which have been much disrupted from the usual configuration of distortions.

QUESTIONER: Is there anything further that needs to be done by or for the instrument to remove the magical working, or any of its after-effects, in her throat area by our fifth-density, negative companion?

RA: I am Ra. No.

QUESTIONER: Finally, I have a question from Jim, stating: "For the last two weeks I have often found myself on the edge of anger and frustration, have had a nearly constant dull pain in the area of my indigo-ray center, and have felt quite drained of energy. Would Ra comment on the source of these experiences and any thoughts or actions that might alleviate them?"

RA: I am Ra. As in all distortions, the source is the limit of the viewpoint. We may, without serious infringement, suggest three courses of behavior which shall operate upon the distortion expressed.

Firstly, it would be well for the scribe to engage, if not daily then as nearly so as possible, in a solitary strenuous activity which brings this entity to the true physical weariness. Further, although any activity may suffice, an activity chosen for its intended service to the harmony of the group would be quite efficacious.

The second activity is some of your space/time and time/space taken by the entity, directly or as nearly so as possible to the strenuous activity, for solitary contemplation.

Thirdly, the enthusiastic pursuit of the balancing and silent meditations cannot be deleted from the list of helpful activities for this entity.

We may note that the great forte of the scribe is summed in the inadequate sound vibration complex power. The flow of power, just as the flow of love or wisdom, is enabled not by the chary[3] conserver of its use but by the constant user. The physical manifestation of power being either constructive or destructive strenuous activity, the power-filled entity must needs exercise that manifestation. This entity experiences a distortion in the direction of an excess of stored energy. It is well to know the self and to guard and use those attributes which the self has provided for its learning and its service.

Fragment 50

In the material from Session 100, note how the limit of the viewpoint changes the nature of the answer. Carla's tendency toward martyrdom, seen from the time/space or metaphysical point of view, is quite helpful in her own evolutionary process. But that same tendency, seen from the space/time or physical point of view, is seen as a tendency that may present difficulties for the services that one wishes to offer during the incarnation.

I had a very hard time with the "swirling waters" from the start; immersed in that high tub, just big enough to fold myself into, I had to tolerate levels up around my mouth in order for the water to beat on my upper back and neck, which were where the worst of the joints of my spine were. All the claustrophobia I had ever felt was squared by this exercise. It was as much an act of will and faith as a physical practice. I did find it very comforting. At the time, I was so small, wearing preteen sizes and weighing around 80–85, that I had to wear a weight to hold myself down on the floor of the specially made tub; otherwise I floated around. I would have no such trouble now, as change of life has rendered me a larger and more mature-looking being. Jim says I used to be a little angel and now I am a cherub. So I could probably endure this better now. But I find that Jim's massages are the best thing. Water is wonderful, but the healing power of touch cannot be over-rated.

Shortly after we acquired this therapy tub, I was struck with a sudden and dramatic frenzy of fear. I bolted out of the tub and found myself cowering on the back of one of the sofas, growling at Jim and Don. At the time I thought it was a psychic greeting, but later Ra confirmed that Don and I had just made a deleterious and complete unity/exchange of our mental and emotional natures, and I was experiencing for the first time the degree of alienation and real fear with which he saw this quarrelsome world. He really, really had trouble living on this earth, although one would never have known it from gazing at him. Don was always infinitely cool. But beneath that calm surface was a really difficult and challenging amount of imbalance. How he managed to live here as long as he did is perhaps beyond me to know.

Session 100,
November 29, 1982

QUESTIONER: The instrument asks if there is some problem with the swirling waters, since she feels very dizzy after each application. Could Ra comment on that, please?

RA: I am Ra. Yes.

QUESTIONER: Would Ra please comment?

RA: I am Ra. As has been previously noted, the instrument has the propensity for attempting to exceed its limits. If one considers the metaphysical or time/space aspect of an incarnation, this is a fortunate and efficient use of catalyst, as the will is constantly being strengthened, and, further, if the limitations are exceeded in the service of others, the polarization is also most efficient.

However, we perceive the query to speak to the space/time portion of incarnational experience and in that framework would again ask the instrument to consider the value of martyrdom. The instrument may examine its range of reactions to this swirling waters. It will discover a correlation between it and other activity. When the so-called aerobic exercise is pursued no less than three of your hours, and preferably five of your hours, should pass betwixt it and the swirling waters. When the walking has been accomplished, a period of no less than, we believe, forty of your minutes must needs transpire before the swirling waters, and preferably twice that amount of your space/time.

It is true that some greeting has encouraged the dizziness felt by the instrument. However, its source is largely the determination of the instrument to remain immersed in swirling waters past the period of space/time it may abide therein without exceeding its physical limits.

Fragment 51

In Session 101 I got an excellent opportunity to work on my anger/ frustration distortion again. This time, however, it was not pointed only at myself. This "negative wisdom" was pointed at Don over a period of two days when it was time to have Books II and III reprinted. Don wanted to put all of the books—I, II, and III—into one book instead. It didn't matter that that was impossible due to lack of money to do it the way Don wanted to do it—typeset and hardback. What mattered was that I allowed a disharmony to result that went unresolved for two days. This became an excellent opportunity for our friend of negative fifth density to magnify the difficulty, and the means by which this was done proved to be quite interesting, especially to me, when I developed a rare kidney disease. It was called lipoid nephritis or minimal change syndrome, and soon I had gained about 30 pounds of water weight as a result of it. The last sentence in the first paragraph of Ra's response seems to us to be the key concept in this particular incident. The last two sentences in that response are interesting in their general application to all seekers.

You will note toward the middle of this session that another house in Atlanta is mentioned as a possible location for our group. We were still hoping to get closer to Don's work so that there would be less strain on him in getting to his job. Later, we found a third house, which will be mentioned in Session 105, and it was this house that we eventually moved to in November 1983.

The next-to-the-last question concerns another instrument who had reported difficulties with her body swelling much as mine had done. Don asked if there were any way that we could give her information about her condition, since we had just talked to her on the phone to compare the swelling in the ranks of our two groups. The first paragraph of Ra's response lays out the general principle that affects all individuals and groups doing work of a more intensive service-to-others nature. The second paragraph of Ra's response refers to the situation in which that particular instrument worked, but the general application of those concepts is obvious.

The combination of healing approaches found my condition in remission within six months.

I wish you could have seen the look on Dr. Stewart Graves's face when that worthy reviewed Ra's diagnosis. He carefully looked up the known causes of Jim's variety of kidney disease and found that insect bites and the allergic reaction to them were a rarely found but duly noted cause of the condition. In the absence of any other possible cause, it was recorded an allergic reaction. Oddly, when I experienced kidney failure as a teenager, allergic reaction was also the doctor's best guess as to cause.

By this time, it may seem to you that psychic greetings were really occupying our time. You would be right. As Jim and Ra both say, it is easier to be noticed when you're standing in a spotlight. Metaphysically, the contact with those of Ra was a blinding cynosure. Although we continued to be obscure and completely anonymous in any earthly sense, we had become very noticeable to "the loyal opposition."

To my mind, the fatal weakness of our group was its humanity, in dealing with threeness. Although in fact our consciously known energies were in perfect harmony and agreement, there were human distortions from below the level of conscious control that allowed a wedge to be driven in between Don and me, so he lost faith in "us." When he began experiencing this profound depression, which seemed to over-take him at a crawling, yet inexorable pace, his utter disdain for any opinion but his own did not stand him in good stead. This was the beginning of a pattern that in the end turned fatal and ended my beloved companion's life, and dear Ra's contact with our group.

Does this constitute a suggestion that a group should not work unless the energies are two by two, and only couples can join in? Not specifically, I do not think, but it is certainly something to ponder. Could we have done better? After years of the Joycean "agenbite of inwit," I still do not think we could have. Our behavior was at all times a true manifestation of ourselves. In no wise did either Jim or myself ever even think to change the relationship with each other, or with Donald. And Don had ever kept his own counsel, and there was no hope that he would come to me or Jim and tell us what worries he had in his mind and heart.

Further, when any group works and lives together, regardless of whether the number is paired or singles are mixed in, there will always be human error in the manifested life of each, and to the extent that people's distortions and fears have a dynamic, there will be misunderstandings and confusion, pulling back and apart from total trust. So it behooves all those working with the light, hoping to be a positive influence on the planetary consciousness, to communicate at once those fears and doubts that might pile up inside. If we had ever been able to talk with total openness, Don and I, I think I could have set his mind at ease. But Don would not have been himself if he had done so. Nor would I have been myself if I had somehow known Don was doubting my fidelity. Being within my self, I cannot imagine, either then or now, anyone thinking that I would be disloyal or untrue to any agreement. I have never done that in this incarnation.

Ultimately, one looks at such a pickle as we got into, and knows its utter perfection and inevitability. I have and will always think of Don, my B.C., every hour of every day, and his suffering is ever before me. But I no longer feel the keen sorrow that laid me low for the first few years after his death. All is well, nothing is lost. And I can feel the sun on my face this day, without the urge I used to have to stay in the shade and mourn my losses. Time has restored my broken spirit and let my being flow sweetly and rhythmically again. And Donald is right here, within. Interestingly enough, we often get mail saying that Don has helped them, either with something from his work or in an actual visitation. Don's great generosity of spirit, freed from the constrictive hold he had on it when alive, has over-flowed into timelessness, and I think his service will continue as long as there are those who need his special brand of wisdom and depth of soul.

Ra's statement that the source of catalyst is the self, especially the higher self, is profound, I think. We always relate to the pain of new catalyst by relating to the other person as bringer of catalyst. In doing so, we forget that the other is ourselves. Not LIKE ourselves, but our very hearts and souls. In this way of seeing, we can look at the fullness of tragedy in Don's and my illness and his death as the Creator serving the creator with exactly the catalyst needed for the utmost polarization in consciousness and the greatest growth of spirit. In opening his heart, Don fell ill and died, in the tradition of lost love and desperate romance that has moved us since the beginning of history. And that death was an utter giving away of self. It was as though Don finished everything else he wished to do in life and then took on the personal reason he had come to earth's physical plane: the opening of his heart. He was so very wise—and with the sacrifice of self in the most brutal, literal sense, that wisdom was balanced fully with compassion and open-hearted love.

As for me, I cannot fault the path that stubbornly sent my soul to batter against the walls of self until I at last began struggling to express wisdom as well as love in my life. Such were our gifts to each other; such are the currents between us all.

Since Ra gave us the cleansing ritual referred to in this session, I've seen it used several times by those who have come to

L/L Research, and in every case it seems to have been quite useful. I think that doing some sort of cleansing of a new place is a good metaphysical habit, for people do leave behind the thought-forms' traces imprinted on the aura of the places they have been, especially those they've stayed in for considerable time. And even when the vibrations are basically good, they might not harmonize completely with your own. So it is good to magnetize the place for your own uses, even if all you do is burn sage or say a prayer of dedication. The world of spirit has much to do with us, though we cannot in most ways know or see such influence. Offering that part of things respect is wise.

Session 101 (in total), December 21, 1982

RA: I am Ra. I greet you in the love and in the light of the One Infinite Creator. We communicate now.

QUESTIONER: Could you first please give me the condition of the instrument?

RA: I am Ra. All energy levels of the instrument are somewhat diminished due to the distortions of physical pain and recent mental/emotional catalyst. However, the energy levels appear to be very liable to be improved in what you call your immediate future.

QUESTIONER: Thank you. What has caused the swelling in Jim's body, and what can be done to heal it?

RA: I am Ra. For the answer to this query we must begin with the consideration of the serpent, signifying wisdom. This symbol has the value of the ease of viewing the two faces of the one who is wise. Positive wisdom adorns the brow indicating indigo-ray work. Negative wisdom, by which we intend to signify expressions which effectually separate the self from the other-self, may be symbolized by poison of the fangs. To use that which a mind/body/spirit complex has gained of wisdom for the uses of separation is to invite the fatal bite of that wisdom's darker side.

The entity has a mental/emotional tendency, which has been lessening in distortion for some of your space/time, towards negative wisdom. The entity's being already aware of this causes us not to dwell upon this point but merely to specifically draw the boundaries of the metaphysical background for the energizing of a series of bites from one of your second-density species. In this case the bite was no more than that of one of the arachnids, sometimes called the wood spider. However, it is possible that were enough work done to test the origin of the pathology of the entity, it is within possibility/probability limits that the testing would show the bite of the cottonmouth rather than the bite of the common wood spider.

The energizing took its place within the lymphatic system of the entity's yellow-ray, physical body. Therefore, the working continues. There is increasing strain upon the spleen, the suprarenal glands, the renal complex, and some possibility/probability of difficulty with the liver. Further, the lymphatic difficulties have begun to strain the entity's bronchial system. This is some general information upon what is to be noted as a somewhat efficient working.

The removal of these distortions has several portions. Firstly, it is well to seek the good offices of the one known as Stuart so that harsh chemical means may be taken to reawaken the histaminic reflexes of the entity and to aid in the removal of edema.

Secondly, we suggest that which has already begun; that is, the request of the one known now to this group as Bob that this entity may focus its aid upon the metaphysical connections with the yellow-ray body.

Thirdly, the entity must take note of its physical vehicle's need for potassium. The ingesting of the fruit of the banana palm is recommended.

Fourthly, the link between the swelling of contumely[4] and the apparent present situation is helpful. As always, the support of the harmonious group is an aid, as is meditation. It is to be noted that this entity requires some discipline in the meditation which the others of the group do not find necessary in the same manner. Therefore, the entity may continue with its forms of meditation, knowing that each in the group supports it entirely although the instinct to share in the discipline is not always present. Each entity has its ways of viewing and learning from the illusion, and each processes catalyst using unique circuitry. Thus, all need not be the same to be equal in will and faith.

QUESTIONER: Thank you. I will make a statement about the way I see the action in this instance and would request Ra's comment on it. I see the present situation as the Creator knowing Itself by using the concept of polarization. We seem to accentuate or to produce catalyst to increase the desired polarization, whether the desired mechanism be random, through what we call the Higher Self, or through utilizing the services of an oppositely polarized entity acting upon us. All of these seem to produce the same effect, which is more intense polarization in the desired direction once that direction has been definitely chosen. I see the catalyst of the second-density insect bite being a function of either or any of the sources of which I have spoken, from random to the Higher Self or polarized services of negative entities who monitor our activities, all of which have roughly the same ultimate effect. Would Ra comment on my observation?

RA: I am Ra. We find your observations unexceptional and, in the large, correct.

QUESTIONER: In this particular case, which avenue was the one that produced the catalyst of the bite?

RA: I am Ra. The nature of catalyst is such that there is only one source, for the catalyst and experience are further attempts at specificity in dealing with the architecture of the unconscious mind of the self. Therefore, in an incarnational experience, the self as Creator, especially the Higher Self, is the base from which catalyst stands to offer its service to the mind, body, or spirit.

In the sense which we feel you intend, the source was the fifth-density, negative friend which had noted the gradual falling away of the inharmonious patterns of the distortion called anger/frustration in the entity. The insect was easily led to an attack, and the physical vehicle, which had long-standing allergies and sensitivities, was also easily led into the mechanisms of the failure of the lymphatic function and the greatly diminished ability of the immune system to remove from the yellow-ray body that which distorted it.

QUESTIONER: Something occurred to me. I am going to make a guess that my illness over the past week was a function of an action by my Higher Self to eliminate the possibility of a residence in the proximity of a large number of bees that I observed. Would Ra comment on my statement?

RA: I am Ra. We can comment, not upon the questioner's physical distortions but upon the indubitable truth of second-density hive creatures; that is, that a hive mentality as a whole can be influenced by one strong metaphysical impulse. Both the instrument and the scribe have the capacity for great distortions toward nonviability, given such an attack by a great number of the stinging insects.

QUESTIONER: Are the thought-form parameters and the general parameters of the 893 Oakdale Road address in Atlanta such that no cleansing would be necessary, if Ra has this information?

RA: I am Ra. No.

QUESTIONER: Would cleansing of the nature suggested for the other house just south of the airport in Atlanta be advisable for the 893 Oakdale Road address?

RA: I am Ra. We note that any residence, whether previously benign, as is the one of which you speak, or previously of malignant character, needs the basic cleansing of the salt, water, and broom. The benign nature of the aforementioned domicile is such that the cleansing could be done in two portions; that is, no egress or entrance through any but one opening for one cleansing. Then egress and entrance from all other places while the remaining portal is properly sealed. The placing of salt may be done at the place which is not being sealed during the first of the cleansings, and the salt may be requested to act as seal and yet allow the passage of gentle spirits such as yourselves. We suggest that you speak to this substance and name each entity for which permission is needed in order to pass. Let no person pass without permission being asked of the salt. This is the case in the residence of which you speak.

QUESTIONER: Thank you. Could Ra give information on any way that we could give information to [name] as to how to alleviate her present condition of swelling?

RA: I am Ra. We may only suggest that the honor of propinquity to light carries with it the Law of Responsibility. The duty to refrain from contumely and discord in all things, which, when unresolved within, makes way for workings, lies before the instrument of which you speak. This entity may, if it is desired by the scribe, share our comments upon the working of the latter entity.

The entity which is given constant and unremitting approval by those surrounding it suffers from the loss of the mirroring effect of those which reflect truthfully rather than unquestioningly. This is not a suggestion to reinstate judgment but merely a suggestion for all those supporting instruments; that is, support, be harmonious, share in love, joy, and thanksgiving, but find love within truth, for each instrument benefits from this support more than from the total admiration which overcomes discrimination.

QUESTIONER: Thank you. That was the forty-five-minute signal, so I will ask if there is anything that we can do to make the instrument more comfortable or to improve the contact.

RA: I am Ra. We find that this instrument has used all the transferred energy and has been speaking using its vital-energy reserve. We do suggest using the transferred sexual energy to the total exclusion of vital reserves if possible.

The alignments are as they must be for all to continue well. We are grateful for the conscientiousness of the support group.

I am Ra. I leave this group glorying in the love and in the light of the One Infinite Creator. Go forth rejoicing, therefore, in the power and in the peace of the Creator. Adonai.

Fragment 52

And now, in Session 102, it was once again Carla's turn to experience another psychic greeting, which intensified a momentary lapse from harmony on her part. She was unable to accept a portion of my perception of our shared relationship for the period of about an hour or two, but that was long enough, due to her intense emotions during that time, for a potent working to be accomplished by our friend of negative polarity. Fortunately, most people will not have to worry about such instant and dramatic intensifications of disharmonious moments, since few people or groups attract the attention of fifth-density, negative entities. But the general principle is that one who is standing close to light experiences an honor that must be balanced by the responsibility of reflecting that light as harmoniously as possible, and this principle holds for all seekers. Failure to live up to that responsibility simply brings one another more intensive opportunity to do so until it is done, or until one steps away from the light.

In the third paragraph of Ra's second response, we find the key concept or attitude for dealing with any such psychic greetings, or any difficulties in general, that one may face in the life patterns. Further into the session, Ra gives the basic criteria for the unblocking of the yellow-ray energy center, the one with which Carla was working in this situation. Surgery was avoided, and the spasming condition of Carla's abdominal region was brought under control over a period of about two years. A potent working, that one!

Ah, humanity! Jim's and my discord was about that age-old dynamic between men and women: monogamy. Who was it that wrote the little ditty "Hogamus, higgimus, men are polygamous; Higgimus, hogamus, dames are monogamous"? Ogden Nash? Dorothy Parker? At any rate, this is true, or tends to be. Jim asked for an open relationship several times in our early days together. Being most honestly more a friend than a BOY-friend, being linked to me primarily by our work together rather than any romantic interest, he naturally responded to the many lovely women who came his way. In this same circumstance, it never occurred to me to seek a further relationship. I was totally satisfied to have Don as my companion and mate and had long since left off blaming him for wanting to be celibate, and also was perfectly happy with Jim's and my friendship and intimate life together. How we do stir up confusion with our desires! Yet to desire is most proper.

I think much of learning in life is involved with the right use of will and desire.

One of the major healings of my life occurred with the removal of about half my descending colon in 1992. This cleared out much old and dead matter and enabled me to do corresponding work within myself at the metaphysical level. There was much to release, and I felt wonderful to be able to do that. The psyche and the soma, soul and body, are inextricably intertwined, and pain to one will be reflected in the other. However, when the body alone is harmed, the mind is much freer to revision the trauma than when it is the mind and emotions that are injured. If such damage is not addressed and respected, it can move ever deeper into the body's health, unbalancing and undermining it.

After that surgery, with its attendant metaphysical work, I had released all I could of the whole tragedy of Don's death and my life, so diminished without his company. And so I became finally able to move on into new life. I was sent home with a new diet, following closely Ra's suggestions. Every look into my GI system showed ulcers, and given my thirty-year use of cortisone, this is not remarkable. The diet was called "low sediment," and on it were the well-cooked meats, veggies and fruits, sugars, and fats that Ra had recommended, but not on it were the usual health foods—whole grains, nuts, berries, uncooked fruits and vegetables. I think one could almost characterize it as the UN-health diet! Yet, it has worked, thank the Lord, for five years so far, and I am most grateful. I think I share with many people who have chronic disease that feeling of living on the razor's edge. I have to be careful, as mistakes are costly. I do miss salads especially but have no argument with the destiny that has allowed me these years of life I almost did not have.

One note about "Bob": he was an amazing help in one area: my feelings of suicidal nature. After Don's death, and especially after I found out what Don had been thinking, I felt totally guilty for not being able to see his fears and allay them. I felt as though it was all my fault. The penalty, I felt strongly, should be death. I was quite unwilling to take my own life. Knowing how it had affected me when Don died, I knew I could never do that to those I love. Which left me hanging between life and death. Through the years from 1984 to 1992, the forces of death circled ever closer until finally I could look death in the eye and find the faith to affirm life and love and healing. The part prayer had in this was substantial to say the least. And Bob's prayers were especially powerful to save. He told me of these suicidal vibrations long before I could do much besides drown in sorrow, and helped me through those pangs of self-knowledge and self-judgment that were so unbalanced. And he was joined by so many others. I had the sensation of being upheld in love, safe and sound, during the whole of the 1991–92 experience, which involved four trips to the hospital, critically ill and quite foundered, my GI tract closed tight.

We have lost touch with Bob, in case you would wish us to give his name and direction. He let us know he had retired from active healing and wished to spend his time now in deep prayer on the planetary level. Our thanks and blessings, wherever you are, dear Bob.

It was not easy to find Arthur Schoen. Ra had pronounced his last name "Shane," but there was not an M.D. of any type by that name. Finally we hit upon the German spelling—although if the name had been pronounced correctly, it would be "shourn," more or less. But this IS America, so of course the name was Americanized. We actually did go see this man but left before he could treat me, as he and Donald did not see eye to eye. This is no surprise, for Don wanted him to read Ra's diagnosis, and the doctor did not really feel comfortable consulting with a discarnate entity.

Ra's suggestion to "link hands and walk towards the sun" is good counsel indeed. Had we been able to dwell in praise and thanksgiving, much would have been altered. But things were as they were. From this remove of time, I see and give praise and thanks for every moment we had together. Whatever it has cost, it was and is worth it all.

Session 102 (in total), March 22, 1983

RA: I am Ra. I greet you in the love and in the light of the One Infinite Creator. We communicate now.

QUESTIONER: Would you first please give me the condition of the instrument?

RA: I am Ra. The physical-energy deficit of this entity is the most substantial across which we have come. The mental and mental/emotional distortions are near to balance, and the vital energy of the instrument, as a whole, is distorted towards health or strength/weakness due to the will of the instrument.

QUESTIONER: Will Ra please tell us what caused the pain and cramping in the instrument's stomach, and what could be done to heal it?

RA: In order to observe the cause of physical distortions towards illness, one must look to the energy center which is blocked. In this situation, the blockage being yellow ray, the experience has had the characteristics of that region of the chemical body. The so-called lacuna in the wind-written armor of light and love was closed and not only repaired but much improved. However, the distortions energized during this momentary lapse from free energy flow are serious and shall be continuing for, in all possibility/probability vortices, some of your space/time, for a predisposition to spasticity in the transverse colon has been energized. There is also preexisting weakness in pancreatic functions, especially that link with the hypothalamus. There is also the preexisting damage to portions of the liver. These lacks or distortions manifest in that portion of the system directly proceeding from the jejunum. Further, there is some irritation closer to the duodenum which causes the instrument to fail in assimilating foodstuffs. This is an allopathically caused irritation.

The diet is of central import. We can go no further in observing the system of the entity, as a full discussion of those distortions towards various weakness/strengths which contribute to the present difficulty begins with the lips and ends with the anus. We may note that the instrument has remained centered upon the Creator at a percentage exceeding 90. This is the key. Continue in thanksgiving and gratitude for all things.

There are stronger antispasmodic drugs which the one not known to this instrument, but known as Arthur, may aid by the offering. The recommendation to do this, being as it is that which does not retain or remove life and does further remove from the instrument its opportunities for study in this situation, needs must be withheld. We are not in a position to recommend treatment at this space/time beyond the watching of the types of foodstuffs ingested.

QUESTIONER: Thank you. I'm not sure that I understood everything that you said. The last name of this Arthur, and where he is located? Can you give me that information?

RA: I am Ra. We can.

QUESTIONER: Will you please do that?

RA: I am Ra. The entity, sound vibration Arthur, has a surname Schoen and is of your locality.

QUESTIONER: What foods should the instrument eliminate in her diet in order to alleviate these painful attacks?

RA: The information gained from the one known as Bob is that which is to be recommended. Further, all foodstuffs are to be cooked so that those things which are ingested be soft and easily macerated. There is a complex addiction, due to long-standing eating habits, to your sugars.

It is to be recommended that, therefore, this sugar be given in its more concentrated form in your time of late afternoon, as you term it, with the ingestion of the sugared libation approximately one to two of your hours after the evening meal. It is further suggested that since this instrument has been using sugars for carbohydrates that a small amount of carbohydrates, low in sugar, be ingested approximately one to two of your hours before the sleeping period.

QUESTIONER: As I understand what you say, the instrument is to have no sugar until late in the afternoon. Is that correct?

RA: I am Ra. No.

QUESTIONER: I didn't fully understand what you meant about when she should have the sugar. Could you clear that up, please?

RA: I am Ra. The concentrated sugar—that is, the dessert, the ice cream, the cookie—should be ingested at that time. Small amounts of the fructose, maple, or raw honey may be ingested periodically for, as we have said, the chemistry of this yellow-ray body is such that the sugar is being used by blood enzymes as would carbohydrates in a less distorted yellow-ray, physical vehicle.

QUESTIONER: I'm sorry that I am so slow at picking up precisely what we are getting at here. I want to be sure that we get this right, so I'll probably ask a few more stupid questions. Was the spasm that caused the extreme pain a spasm of the ileum?

RA: I am Ra. Partially. The transverse colon also spasmed, as did the ducts to the liver in its lower portion. There were also muscle spasms from the bronchial coverings down through the pelvis and from shoulder blades to hips. These sympathetic spasms are a symptom of the exhaustion of the entity's physical vehicle.

QUESTIONER: Then the opening for these spasms was originally made by the yellow-ray blockage but are triggered by the foodstuff that has to do with the ingestion of sugar. Am I correct?

RA: I am Ra. You are partially correct.

QUESTIONER: Then what else causes the spasms?

RA: I am Ra. We speak of two types of cause. The first or proximate cause was a meal with too much oil and too large a burden of under-cooked vegetable material. The sugar of the dessert and the few sips of your coffee mixture also were not helpful. The second cause—and this shall be stated clearly—is the energizing of any preexisting condition in order to keep this group from functioning by means of removing the instrument from the ranks of those able to work with those of Ra.

QUESTIONER: Now, there are two areas that the instrument can look to for curing this problem. I understand that the yellow-ray blockage problem has been completely repaired, shall I say. If this is not correct, could you make suggestions on that, please?

RA: I am Ra. Each entity must, in order to completely unblock yellow ray, love all which are in relationship to it, with hope only of the other selves' joy, peace, and comfort.

QUESTIONER: The second thing that the instrument must do to effect this cure is to be careful of diet, which includes all that Ra has just stated and that which Bob recommends from his readings. There seem to be so many different things that can cause this spasm. I was wondering if there were a general approach to food. Could Ra recommend those foods that the instrument could eat that would have no chance of causing a spasm? Could Ra do that?

RA: I am Ra. No.

QUESTIONER: Is that because of the first distortion?

RA: I am Ra. No.

QUESTIONER: Why cannot Ra do that?

RA: I am Ra. There are no foods which this instrument can take with total confidence that no spasm shall occur. The spasming portions of the vehicle have become sensitized through great distortions towards that which you call pain.

QUESTIONER: Is there a group of foods that is most likely to not cause the spasming, or any foods that Ra could name that would be highly likely not to cause spasms?

RA: I am Ra. Yes.

QUESTIONER: Could Ra please state which foods are highly probable to not cause the spasming?

RA: I am Ra. The liquids not containing carbonation, the well-cooked vegetable which is most light and soft, the well-cooked grains, the nonfatted meat such as the fish. You may note that some recommended foodstuffs overlap allergies and sensitivities due to the juvenile rheumatoid arthritic distortions. Further, although sugar such as is in your sweetened desserts represents a potential, we may suggest that it be included at this period for aforementioned reasons.

QUESTIONER: Would Ra please estimate the length of time in our time periods for the probability of this problem, if we follow these curative measures, for this problem to continue with extreme severity?

RA: I am Ra. One of your moon's revolutions has a good possibility/ probability vortex of seeing either the worsening of the spastic condition so that surgery becomes indicated, or the bettering of the situation so that the diet continues be watched but the spasms be removed. The housing of the working is within the infection within the duodenum, the stomach, the jejunum, the ileum, the transverse colon, and portions of the liver. This shall be somewhat difficult to remove and constitutes perhaps the most efficient working to date. We may suggest, again, that the one known as Bob may be of aid. The one known as Stuart could, if it wished, discover the infection which is only marginally detectable, but may prefer not to do so. In this case it would be well to request physical aid from an allopathic specialist, such as that which has been mentioned.

QUESTIONER: Do you mean by that Arthur Schoen?

RA: I am Ra. That is correct.

QUESTIONER: You mentioned the possibility of surgery. What would be the surgery to be done, specifically?

RA: I am Ra. The body cannot long bear the extreme acidity which is the environment of such spasms, and will develop the holes or ulcerations which then do appear upon the allopathic testings and suggest to the chirurgeon that which is to be excised.

QUESTIONER: In other words, would this be the removal of a duodenic ulcer that would be performed?

RA: I am Ra. If the ulceration occurs, it shall be past the jejunum and most likely include the ileum and upper portions of the transverse colon.

May we ask for one more query of normal length, as this entity, though filled with enough transferred energy, has the most fragile framework through which we may channel this and our energies.

QUESTIONER: Obviously we would like not to get to the point of surgery. The only other alternative that comes to mind other than the diet and the instrument's mental work is healing through a healer, and I would like Ra's recommendation with respect to a nonallopathic-type healer, and any recommendations that Ra could make for either Jim or myself to act in that capacity or anyone else that Ra could recommend so that we wouldn't have to go through a surgical operation if it seems to become necessary. If we could begin working on one of these other approaches right away, I think it would be highly recommended. Would Ra comment on that, please?

RA: I am Ra. We salute the opening of compassion circuitry in the questioner but note that that which is being experienced by this group is being experienced within an healing atmosphere. The healing hands of each have limited use when the distortion has so many metaphysical layers and mixtures. Therefore, look not to a healing but to the joy of companionship, for each is strong and has its feet set upon the way. The moon casts its shadows. What shall you see? Link hands and walk towards the sun. In this instance this is the greatest healing. For the physical vehicle we can suggest far less than you had hoped.

QUESTIONER: Is there anything that we can do to improve the contact or make the instrument more comfortable?

RA: I am Ra. All is well. Find love and thanksgiving together, and each shall support each. The alignments are conscientious.

We are known to you as Ra. We leave you in the love and in the light of the One Infinite Creator. Go forth, then, merry and glad in His power and peace. Adonai.

Fragment 53

The information in Session 103 concerns the continued spasming condition of Carla's abdominal region. Large amounts of pain accompanied the spasming and caused her to be less and less able to function in any manner of service at all. Thus she felt useless, and her natural joy became reduced and was the focus for this series of questions. Further, Carla had decided to stop buying clothes for a year, because she felt that she had devoted too much time and attention to a transient part of her life and wished to break that habit, and this decision added to her loss of joy.

By June 1983, Don and Luther, our lessor and the owner of the house in which we had lived for all of the Ra sessions, were locked in a Mexican standoff. Because Luther raised the asking price an arbitrary $5,000.00 in the middle of negotiations, and because Don was absolute in his refusal to buy the house without Luther's adhering to his original price, all bets were off. At this point, I was just trying to get Don's deposit out of escrow. Luther would not release it after we agreed not to buy the house. He felt it should be his, regardless. Luther was not a great help. Eventually, I was to agree, long after Don's death, to give him over half the escrow amount. It really didn't seem to matter what was fair. There was more confusion because our lawyer for the purchase of the house did not do his paperwork. I did not want to go to court, feeling that Don would not have done so. Nothing would resolve; everything felt like we were moving in molasses. This was the sort of baffling energy that seemed to have over-taken us. Nothing seemed to work well, me included. Don was feeling poor, too, though in a vague and generalized way rather than anything acute. Jim alone was regaining health every day.

I was concerned about Don without knowing why, really. At this stage of his mental illness, it was very subtle. He simply felt very low and was very prone to think and plan for the worst-case scenario. While he, all his life, was always rigorously careful and cautious in his dealings, a change of address was in order, and his normal response was not this slow. We had to move. But month by month, looking constantly both here and in Atlanta, we could find nothing that Don was pleased with. I would target this point as the time period within which I was becoming aware that something was really wrong. As was always our pattern, I responded to the feelings of concern by asking for help and communicating. Don responded to the same with an increase of reserve. He could be firm about only one thing: that nothing we were looking at was the right place.

In this atmosphere, we were all uneasy, unsettled. I tend to get busy when I get worried. I was busy. All the records were in order. I went on my walks and did my time in the whirlpool and tried to remain hopeful. I felt constantly a bit irritated with Don, because I could never figure out why he rejected every single house we found in the listings or saw from the street. He seemed to be dragging his feet for no reason. Don was never one to share in his motives for doing things. He just said no, much as Nancy Reagan suggested later. It wasn't a solution for either environment. This is the first place I can think back and say, HERE I was feeling both of us losing ground, Don and myself.

I was heavily dependent upon him. I had been raised a most independent person, and I had to learn to let go of everything except what Don needed from me. And Don had needed all my choices to be made around him. He wanted me to be at home and right there, a person he could count on to be loving and willing to do whatever he decided. He never really consulted me, and it sounds very chauvinistic, but he did not mean this personally. He simply consulted no one. He never had. And his view on women was so bad that I could only look better! I quickly formed the opinion that when I stopped getting interference for an idea, that idea was the right one. It took me at least the first six years of our relationship to figure out that no matter what, I should never take a job that took me away from him, even as far as my desk. He even stopped me from working on our projects, many times, when he was at home. "When I am off, you are off," he would say. So I had pretty much given over my decisions to him. It is to be noted that I was aware of the unhealthy tinge of this relationship. However, it was and remains my opinion that this was the absolute best Don could do in the way of having a relationship. And that was good enough for me. Where Don was concerned, I was ready to do whatever he needed. Period.

And at this point, with my health compromised and aiming for more sessions, I was not "allowed" to do much except follow my regimen and try to keep my weight above 80. I was wholeheartedly into this model for living, for what mattered most to me from the first was to see Donald really happy, as only the contact with Ra made him. So our every effort was toward that goal: just to have one more session.

However, what had always before gone hand in hand with my dependency was his willingness to steer our course; indeed, his insistence upon that. I was glad to give this leadership over to him, and to do what he said. He was far wiser than I was or ever could be. When he stopped giving orders and indeed seemed not to know what to do, I was quite lost. My mode was to find out what he wanted, and do it. But with the question of moving, we entered an arena where I could not succeed. No house, no apartment, was acceptable. I do not find it at all odd that I had "lost my joy." I was totally bewildered. My sense of reality had been compromised.

The comments about clothing address a facet of my personality of which I am not proud but do own: I absolutely love to wear a new dress or pair of socks or whatever else might catch my fancy. My childhood had been very low on pretty clothing, as our family finances were tight. My mother and I, when I was grown and her career as a psychologist had begun, had a standing date on Saturday for lunch and shopping, which we kept faithfully until her death in 1991. I would find wonderful things with her, as she was a champion shopper, looking through great masses of sales racks with the patience of an archaeologist, sifting for good labels and just the right bargain. To this day, when I can, I love to go bargain-hunting and just thrill to be able to wear something new.

I kept my promise to myself and did not buy clothes for myself for a whole year. However, I cheated, in that I bought things for Momma, and she bought things for me. I kept the letter of the promise anyway!

Session 103 (in total), June 10, 1983

QUESTIONER: The instrument asks the question why she lost her joy in the recent past. Could Ra comment on that?

RA: I am Ra. The instrument made a free-will decision not to address the physical catalyst, causing great pain by means of the allopathically prescribed chemical compound which the instrument was sure would be efficacious due to its reliance upon the suggestions of Ra. Thus the catalyst was given in a more complete form. The outer service to others became nearly impossible, causing the entity to experience once again the choice of the martyr; that is, to put value in a fatal action and die, or to put value on consciousness of the creation of the One Creator and, thereby, live. The instrument, through will, chose the latter path. However, the mind and mental/emotional distortions did not give the support to this decision necessary to maintain the state of unity which this entity nominally experiences and has experienced since its incarnation's beginnings.

Since this catalyst has been accepted, the work begun to remove distortions blocking indigo ray might well be continued apace.

QUESTIONER: Could Ra recommend work appropriate for removing indigo-ray blockage?

RA: I am Ra. We cannot recommend for the general situation, for in each case the distortional vortex is unique. In this particular nexus, the more appropriate working is in the mental and mental/emotional powers of analysis and observation. When the strongest and least distorted complex is set in support, then the less strong portions of the complex shall be strengthened. This entity has long worked with this catalyst. However, this is the first occasion wherein the drugs to dull the pain that sharpens the catalyst have been refused.

QUESTIONER: Can Ra recommend anything that the instrument can do or that we can do to improve any of the energies of the instrument?

RA: I am Ra. This is previously covered material. We have outlined the path the instrument may take in thought.

QUESTIONER: I didn't mean to cover previously covered material. I was hoping to add to this anything that we could do to specifically focus on at this time, the best possible thing that we or the instrument could do to improve these energies, the salient activity.

RA: I am Ra. Before responding, we ask your vigilance during pain flares, as the channel is acceptable but is being distorted periodically by the severe physical distortions of the yellow-ray chemical body of the instrument.

Those salient items for the support group are praise and thanksgiving in harmony. These the group has accomplished with such a degree of acceptability that we cavil not at the harmony of the group. As to the instrument, the journey from worth in action to worth *in esse* is arduous. The entity has denied itself in order to be free of that which it calls addiction. This sort of martyrdom, and here we speak of the small but symbolically great sacrifice of the clothing, causes the entity to frame a selfhood in poorness which feeds unworthiness unless the poverty is seen to be true richness. In other words, good works for the wrong reasons cause confusion and distortion. We encourage the instrument to value itself and to see that its true requirements are valued by the self. We suggest contemplation of true richness of being.

Fragment 54

Ra made a point in Session 104 that seems to us to be one of the central principles that govern our evolution through the third density. It was in reference to the amount of exercise that would be most appropriate for Carla when her body was near normal and when it was weakened by one distortion or another. Ra suggested that it should be exercised more when weakened by distortion because "It is the way of distortion that in order to balance a distortion one must accentuate it."

In the next response, Ra refers to the use of gifts with which one has entered the incarnation as a kind of "Use it or lose it" proposition.

When Book I of *The Law of One* was being published by the Donning Company under the title of *The Ra Material*, we were asked to write an introduction. In one portion of that introduction, Carla was writing about the concept of reincarnation. When we got the galley proofs back from the Donning Company, we noticed that a sentence that we had not written had somehow appeared in what we had written. It was truly "subjectively interesting."

Ra's eloquent closing was in response to a series of queries concerning our oldest cat, Gandalf, who then was going blind and losing weight, apparently in preparation for death. We have considered leaving this material out, once again, because it has little general application, but we have left it in because Ra's desire not to infringe upon our free will is notable and well illustrated here.

When people try to improve their living habits, they always go for diet and exercise as being the first things to change. I think these changes have a mental and emotional benefit as well as a physical one, in that it feels as good for the mind as the body to be doing something when there is a concern. The concern for me, by all three of us, seemed never ending. I don't watch soap operas; they move too slowly for me to keep an interest. But certainly at this point we were living in one. I was steadily losing weight, even eating more than I ever had. So the focus was on diet and exercise. I think we all felt better because we were trying to work on the problems actively. It did, however, seem to take up so much time! Much of the days seemed spent on maintenance. We all were stressed by the situation.

I always have loved my childhood summers spent dancing at the Noyes Rhythm Foundation's camp in Portland, Connecticut. It exists still today and is a wonderful place altogether, one I cannot recommend highly enough, for you can live in a tent, dance on a sprung wood floor to classical piano music in an open pavilion with greenswards and forest about in an absolutely unspoiled environment. The teachers still follow Florence Fleming Noyes's original method of instruction, which posits that all things have their own rhythm, so one may dance a starfish or a star, a bear or a horse, or a blade of grass. It teaches that all things are alive, and that they are all one consciousness. It is very like the Isadora Duncan style of dancing, but with a much-elevated philosophy driving the technique. You can be a beginner and still have a wonderful time. I certainly did, and I measured the exercises I was doing at that time with the yardstick of the dance. (These days the Noyes Rhythm Foundation offers a Senior and a Junior Camp/ School. For more information about this wonderful dance system and the spirits that dance and camp there, write to Shepherd's Nine Summer Creative Arts Center, Noyes School of Rhythm Foundation, 245 Penfield Hill Road, Portland, CT 06480.) The walking came up short! But I was faithful and kept up with the routine. Jim usually was kind enough to walk with me, which motivated me greatly.

I see here, for the first time, really, that Ra was echoing Don's request of me, which always was to take more time just to sit. I am an avid reader and have always loved to toss myself headlong into a romance or science fiction or fantasy novel. To this day it is not unusual for me to read a book a day. Ah, if only the books were "good literature!" —but NO! I love to read just for fun and winkle away to adventure land. As time has passed, I have more and more found the time to rest in silence but still tend to read too much.

The stomach problems were to plague me for some years; indeed, still. But things were greatly aided in 1988, when my doctor finally figured out that my gall bladder was infected. Ever since 1982, they had been reading the picture of my gall bladder as showing some sludge—not an operable problem. However, in actuality it was simply infected, and not working at all. Until the sick organ was removed, I was to suffer greatly. And four years later, in 1992, I had the second cleansing operation, when half my colon was removed. These days, I still deal with discomfort throughout the GI tract, but it is not beyond management, and most days I can do well and just put such aches and pains out of my mind. When the sessions were going on in 1983, however, I was in sorry shape. The stress of knowing things weren't right with Don was undoubtedly a factor here.

One can note the way Ra moved fluidly between the psyche and the soma in working with illness. They linked the severity of the pain to work in consciousness, which I was pursuing as intensively as I could, but to slow avail. When one has felt unworthy for a long time, one is slow to learn self-respect of the deep and lasting kind. I was embarking on a life lesson, which was all about learning to be wise and live. Don was also embarking upon a journey, a much-darker one. He was learning how to love completely and die.

Meanwhile our beloved cat, Gandalf, was getting old and creaky. How he loved us! He wanted only to be on us, or beside us, always. His devotion never let up, even when, in Georgia some months later, we had to lift him to the food and sandbox, as he could no longer walk. He would move heaven and earth just to be with us, and I got in the habit of carrying him with me so he would not have to walk on his sore paws.

It may seem like Donald spent a lot of time on this kitty, but you have to remember how much like a child such a special pet is. We had no children; being celibate, he wasn't likely to sire a family. But we did have Gandalf and Fairchild. They meant a great deal to us, as our cats still do to Jim and me.

Notice how the tuning started drifting as Don persisted in trying to get specific information from Ra. It is abuse of a well-tuned channel to ask for specific information, I think. And notice how Ra's suggestions for bettering a situation always begin with rejoicing in, giving thanks for and praising the situation, whatever it is. To Ra's way of thinking, when the attitude

with which you met the moment was praise and thanksgiving, you'd be best
prepared to meet it well. Simple advice, hard to follow, but worth it.

Session 104 (in total),
July 27, 1983

RA: I am Ra. We greet you in the love and in the light of the One Infinite
Creator. We communicate now.

QUESTIONER: Could you first please give me the condition of the
instrument?

RA: I am Ra. The readings are somewhat less distorted towards physical
bankruptcy and vital-energy loss than at the previous asking. There is
still considerable bias in these readings.

QUESTIONER: The instrument would like to know what is the optimum amount of aerobics, walking, and whirlpool exercises for the best
condition at this time.

RA: I am Ra. We shall answer in two ways. Firstly, to speak to the general case which pertains to this instrument in varying degree. Each
form of exercise is well accomplished approximately three to four times
per your week. The amount of exercise, all quantified as one sum, is
approximately one hour per diurnal period.

We now answer in a second way, distorted in this response to the
duple conditions of yellow-ray, physical difficulty and mind complex
distortion. The swirling waters then must needs be viewed as being
appropriate four to five of your times per week. The walking and the
exercising as much as is desired by the entity. The total of all these
should in no case exceed ninety minutes per diurnal period.

The yellow-ray, physical body has been experiencing that which is
called lupoid changes in much tissue of muscle and some of the organs
as well.

The exercise regains the wasting physical muscular strength. In
some ways the walking is the more appropriate exercise due to the
proximity of the entity to second-density creatures, particularly your
trees. However, the habitation you enjoy does not offer such opportunity and instead offers the proximity to creations of mind/body/spirit
complexes. This does not feed the mental/emotional needs of this
entity, although it produces the same physical result. The exercise ful-
fills more of the mental/emotional need due to the entity's fondness

for rhythmic expressions of the body, such as those found in athletic endeavors derivative of the artifact system which is known among your peoples as the dance.

We suggest the support group encourage any exercise except that which exceeds the time limit, which is already far beyond the physical limitations of this body complex. It is the way of distortion that in order to balance a distortion one must accentuate it. Thusly, the over-wearing of the body may, if correctly motivated, produce a lack of deficit at which juncture the lesser exercise limitations should be put into practice.

QUESTIONER: The instrument has determined that the unwise use of her will is its use without the joy and faith components and constitutes martyrdom. Would Ra comment on that, please?

RA: I am Ra. We are pleased that the entity has pondered that which has been given. We would comment as follows. It is salubrious for the instrument to have knowledge which is less distorted towards martyrdom and which is rich in promise. The entity which is strong to think shall either be strong to act or that which it has shall be removed. Thus manifestation of knowledge is an area to be examined by the instrument.

We would further note that balancing, which in this entity's case is best accomplished in analysis and manifestation seated with the contemplation of silence, may be strengthened by manifested silence and lack of routine activity. We may go no further than this recommendation of regularized leisure, and desire that the entity discover the fundamental truths of these distortions as it will.

QUESTIONER: Is there anything further that we can do to help the instrument's stomach and back-spasming problem?

RA: I am Ra. The greatest aid is already being given to the fullest. The encouragement of the instrument to refrain from the oil-fried nature of foodstuffs in its intake is helpful. Cheerful harmony is helpful. The spasms must subside as a function of the entity's indigo-ray work and, to some extent, the recommendations made in response to a previous query. The definitive refraining from over-stepping the already swollen boundaries of physical limitation is recommended. The infection remains and the symptoms are now far less medicable, the entity having chosen the catalyst.

QUESTIONER: Can you tell us what is wrong with our cat's, Gandalf's eyes?

RA: I am Ra. The one known as Gandalf nears the end of its incarnation. Its eyesight dims and the aqueous membrane becomes tough. This is not a comfortable circumstance but is one which causes the entity no true discomfort.

QUESTIONER: Is there anything that we can do to alleviate this situation?

RA: I am Ra. There is a course of therapy which would aid the situation. However, we do not recommend it as the condition is more benign than the treatment.

QUESTIONER: I don't understand. Could you explain what you meant?

RA: I am Ra. A doctor of the allopathic tradition would give you the drops for the eyes. The cat would find the experience of being confined while the drops were given more distorted than the discomfort it now feels but is able to largely ignore.

QUESTIONER: Can the cat see at all?

RA: I am Ra. Yes.

QUESTIONER: Does it seem that the cat will lose all of its vision in the very near future, or is the cat very near death?

RA: I am Ra. The one known as Gandalf will not lose eyesight or life on most possibility/probability vortices for three of your seasons, approximately.

QUESTIONER: I feel very bad about the condition of the cat and really would like to help it. Can Ra suggest anything that we can do to help out Gandalf?

RA: I am Ra. Yes.

QUESTIONER: What would that be?

RA: I am Ra. Firstly, we would suggest that possibility/probability vortices include those in which the entity known as Gandalf has a lengthier incarnation. Secondly, we would suggest that this entity goes to a graduation if it desires. Otherwise, it may choose to reincarnate to be with those companions it has loved. Thirdly, the entity known to you as

Betty has the means of making the entity more distorted towards comfort/discomfort.

QUESTIONER: Could you tell me who you mean by Betty? I'm not sure that I know who you mean by Betty. And what Betty would do?

RA: I am Ra. The one known as Carla has this information.

QUESTIONER: I'm concerned about the possibility of moving. If we did move, it would make it very difficult for Gandalf to find his way around a new place if he can't see. Does he see enough to be able to find his way around a new environment?

RA: I am Ra. The vision is less than adequate but is nearly accommodated by a keen sense of smell and of hearing. The companions and the furnishings being familiar, a new milieu would be reasonably expected to be satisfactorily acceptable within a short period of your space/time.

QUESTIONER: Could we administer the drops that you spoke of that would help his eyesight so that he wouldn't be confined? Is there any way that we could do that?

RA: I am Ra. It is unlikely.

QUESTIONER: There's nothing that we can do? Is there any other possibility of using any techniques to help his eyesight?

RA: I am Ra. No.

QUESTIONER: Is this loss of eyesight . . . What is the metaphysical reason for the loss of eyesight? What brought it about?

RA: I am Ra. In this case the metaphysical component is tiny. This is the condign catalyst of old age.

QUESTIONER: Would the drops that you spoke of that would aid the eyesight . . . How much would they aid the eyesight if they were administered?

RA: I am Ra. Over a period of applications the eyesight would improve somewhat, perhaps 20, perhaps 30 percent. The eye region would feel less tight. Balanced against this is rapidly increasing stiffness of motion so that the holding in a still position is necessarily quite uncomfortable.

QUESTIONER: Then Ra thinks that the benefit derived from these drops would not be worth the cat's discomfort. This would probably . . . Is there any way that the cat could be given anesthetic and the drops put into the eyes so that the cat was not aware of them?

RA: I am Ra. The harm done by putting the allopathic anesthetic into the body complex of this harvestable entity far overshadows the stillness accruing therefrom which would allow administration of medicaments.

QUESTIONER: I'm sorry to belabor this subject so much, but I was really hoping to come up with something to help Gandalf. I assume then that Ra has suggested that we leave things as they are. How many applications of drops would be necessary to get some help for the eyes, roughly?

RA: Approximately forty to sixty.

QUESTIONER: Each day, or something like that?

RA: I am Ra. Please expel breath over this instrument's breast. [This was done as directed.]

QUESTIONER: Is that satisfactory?

RA: I am Ra. Yes.

QUESTIONER: I had asked if the drops should be administered once per diurnal period. Is that correct?

RA: I am Ra. This depends upon the allopathic physician from whom you receive them.

QUESTIONER: What is the name of the drops?

RA: I am Ra. We have a difficulty. Therefore, we shall refrain from answering this query.

QUESTIONER: I am sorry to belabor this point. I am very concerned about the cat, and I understand that Ra recommends that we do not use the drops and we won't. I just wanted to know what it was that we weren't doing that would help the eyesight, and I apologize for bela-boring this point. I'll close just by asking Ra if there is any further recommendation that he could make with respect to this cat.

RA: I am Ra. Rejoice in its companionship.

QUESTIONER: When we got our introduction back from our publisher on the book which originally was called *The Law of One*, in the intro-duction Carla had been speaking on reincarnation, and there was this sentence added: "For although originally part of Jesus' teachings they were censored from all subsequent editions by the Empress." Would Ra please comment on the source of that being placed in our introduction?

RA: I am Ra. This follows the way of subjectively interesting happen-ings, conditions, circumstances, or coincidences.

We would suggest one more full query at this time.

QUESTIONER: Prior to the veiling process there was, I am assuming, no archetypical plan for the evolutionary process. It was totally left up to the free will of the mind/body/spirits to evolve in any way that they desired. Is this correct?

RA: I am Ra. No.

I am Ra. We leave you in appreciation of the circumstances of the great illusion in which you now choose to play the pipe and timbrel and move in rhythm. We are also players upon a stage. The stage changes. The acts ring down. The lights come up once again. And throughout the grand illusion and the following and the following, there is the undergirding majesty of the One Infinite Creator. All is well. Nothing is lost. Go forth rejoicing in the love and the light, the peace, and the power of the One Infinite Creator. I am Ra. Adonai.

Fragment 55

After a good deal of searching, we finally did find a house north of Atlanta to which we were about to move in November 1983. We decided to query Ra about the metaphysical cleansing needs of this new dwelling before moving there, and that was the purpose of this session. As Jim was giving Carla her presession massage, he noted reddened welts, symmetrical in nature, on both sides of her back. They were similar to the welting that had covered her body when her kidneys failed at age thirteen from glomerulo nephritis. Apparently, if Carla had chosen to meet difficulties in completing our lease agreement with our landlord by allowing a feeling of separation from him to occur or had allowed this same feeling of separation to grow for Don as he hemmed and hawed about what house to choose in Atlanta, that allowing of separation of self from other-self could have been energized by our negative friend until her self was separated from her physical vehicle, and her incarnation would have been at its end. She had to deal with our landlord, who had numerous requirements for our leaving that he felt justified in making, and with Don's mental condition, which was beginning to show further signs of the long-term stress to mind and body that commuting and worrying about his job had brought about. Strikes and bankruptcy were continually threatening Eastern Airlines, and, though he knew it would be easier to get to work from his base in Atlanta, he had great difficulty in even looking at houses in Atlanta, much less choosing one, because of his lifelong love of Louisville and the comfort and beauty of our home as we had known it together. But our home was up for sale, and we had to move somewhere.

My first trip with the 24-foot U-Haul truck saw me lost in the mountains of northern Georgia. Many curves and turns later, I found our new home in the countryside around Lake Lanier. It was midnight when I saw the house for the first time—Don and Carla had picked it out—and I immediately began searching in the darkness for each window and doorway to perform the ritual of cleansing with salt and blessed water. It was an inauspicious beginning to an unusual experience there.

A small beginning is made near the end of this session to query again on the archetypical mind, and Ra's comment at the end of this session is a key part of the mystery of Don's illness and his death.

By the time Don accepted the house we moved into, he was in a settled state of disorientation, something unknown before this time. I, too, was quite at low ebb. Dimly grasping that I needed to be exquisitely correct in all ethical dealings, and willing to go to almost any lengths to remain in the light, I did manage to keep the anger and vast irritation I felt with our landlord out of my actual dealings with him. We packed up the kitties and Don flew us down to Atlanta. Friends drove our cars down, another friend drove the second rental van, and we piled into a huge and glamorous—and decidedly nonwinterized—lakefront house in Cumming, Georgia. As if warning us that this trip was going to be dicey, Jim's first attempt to take the van to Georgia found him fetched up, barely 60 miles from Louisville, with a broken truck. We disregarded this event and pressed on.

The whole five months that we were there was like a sitcom, overlaid with bizarre situations. Cumming was the county seat of Forsythe County, a place notorious for its prejudice against any race but Caucasian. On a Saturday, one could drive through the little town and see Ku Klux Klan members in regalia, except for their head masks and hats, handing out brochures at the stop lights. Grandmothers, children, all ages, and both sexes wore these sad little costumes and waved racial hatred around as though it were cotton candy. I had planned to join the Robert Shaw Chorale, but when I sang my piece, there was a misunderstanding, and the judges thought I had sung a wrong note. So I did not get accepted, something I had not even thought of. I had been singing all my life, and I was a competent chorus member. But I was out. Instead, needing to sing, I found a little group in the Cumming area and plodded along while I was there with Irish folk songs and the like, fun to sing but not the marvelous prayer experience I had always found classical sacred choral singing to offer. I planned to sing, on Sundays, at the cathedral there, St. Philip's, and had made every arrangement to do so. But they would not let me start singing until after Christmas, a practice the church had been forced to adopt after people tried to drop in for Christmas and not sing the rest of the year. Meanwhile, I found a mission church five minutes from our house, which had no choir whatever. So I stayed in tiny All Saints' mission and sang the old Anglican hymns during Eucharist. Every expectation was baffled. Nothing worked out as envisioned.

The worst of it was that Don had more, not less, to do in order to arrive at work. He had to run the whole gamut of paralyzing traffic from far north of Atlanta to south of it, where the airport was. And the weather seemed fated to make things harder. It was extremely cold in Georgia that winter, and when icing conditions were there, as was the case several times, there was absolutely no way to drive anywhere. I can remember Don having to stay in a motel he managed to slide into the parking lot of, unable to reach either home or work. Christmas Eve found me singing two services at All Saints' while Jim and Don bailed water from burst pipes. By the time the New Year came, the wet carpets had begun to become moldy, and both Don and I were allergic to mold and mildew. As luxurious as the house was for fun on the lake in summer, it was nothing short of a disaster as far as winter living went. I got ulcers on my toes because they were so cold—the floor was never warmer than 50 degrees, ever.

Since all this was wrong with the house, we immediately began looking again for another house, both in Atlanta and back in Louisville. We never had one settled day in Georgia, and, pretty as the state was, I cannot say I would wish to be there again. Until Don found the house we now live in, in March, we were in a constant restless perch, having no real order to things. Our belongings remained boxed, our feelings fragile. I was the one who dealt with the new landlord, which was not a picnic. Don was very insistent that we move immediately for the whole time there, so even though we did stay in that one place for five months, the landlord and I had to talk at least weekly so that he could be apprised of our latest plans—none of which worked out. Finally, in March, he asked us to leave, so that his family could use the house themselves that summer. It was at that juncture that Don flew to Louisville by himself over a weekend, found this lovely and venerable old bungalow in which we still live, and agreed to buy it.

Buying a house was something Don had always felt was unwise for himself to do. And as soon as he had done it, he began to regret it. For Jim and me, this was most difficult to bear, as we had unwisely let ourselves hope that we would come to this little exurb and really settle in and just live as we had before. But Don remained convinced that we must move, again, while always turning down any possible place we found to look at. When I found a house twenty thousand dollars cheaper, with a duplex design that would give Don and me a full home plus an apartment for Jim, and Don turned that down too, I realized that something was really wrong. Things were in a fine pickle.

In this atmosphere, it was faintly off-balance even to try to pursue the work and questioning about the archetypical mind that we had begun, but persist we did, cleansing the new working room daily and hoping for the day when we could have another session with those of Ra. I remember feelings of great hope and faith welling up within me as this period spent itself, and wonderings about what in the world was happening with Don. None of us knew anything to do except persevere, and follow Ra's suggestion to meet all with praise and thanks. Or try!

Session 105 (in total), October 19, 1983

RA: I am Ra. I greet you, my friends, in the love and in the light of the One Infinite Creator. We communicate now.

QUESTIONER: Could you first please give me the condition of the instrument?

RA: I am Ra. The vital energies of this instrument are in a much more biased state than the previous asking, with the faculties of will and faith having regained their prominent place in this entity's existence and balance. The physical deficit continues.

QUESTIONER: I am sorry that we have to ask so many maintenance questions. We seem to be in a confused condition now with respect to our abilities to continue in the direction that we wish to with respect to the archetypical mind.

I would like to ask what caused the symmetrical welts on the instrument's back, and is there anything further that we can do to heal the instrument and her condition, including these welts?

RA: I am Ra. The welting is a symptom of that which has been a prolonged psychic greeting. The opportunity for this entity to experience massive allergic reaction from streptococcal and staphylococcal viruses has been offered in hopes that this entity would wish to leave the incarnation. The previous occurrence of this state of the mind complex, which occurred upon, in your time-numbering system, the ninth month, the twelfth day, of your present planetary solar revolution, caught your fifth-density companion unprepared. The entity is now prepared.

There have been two instances wherein this entity could have started the reaction since the first opportunity was missed. Firstly, the opportunity to separate self from other-self in connection with the choosing of a house. Secondly, the possible vision of self separated from other-self in regard to the dissolving of mundane bonds concerning the leaving of this dwelling. Both opportunities were met by this entity with a refusal to separate self from other-self, with further work also upon the indigo-ray level concerning the avoidance of martyrdom while maintaining unity in love.

Thusly, this instrument has had its immunal defenses breached and its lymphatic system involved in the invasion of these viri. You may see some merit in a purging of the instrument's yellow-ray, chemical body in order to more quickly aid the weakened body complex in its attempt to remove these substances. Techniques include therapeutic enemas or colonics, the sauna once or twice in a day, and the use of vigorous rubbing of the integument for the period of approximately seven of your diurnal periods.

We speak not of diet, not because it might not aid but because this entity ingests small quantities of any substance and is already avoiding certain substances, notably fresh milk and oil.

QUESTIONER: Is there any particular place that the integument should be vigorously rubbed?

RA: I am Ra. No.

QUESTIONER: Could you please tell me what caused Jim's kidney problem to return, and what can be done to heal it?

RA: I am Ra. The entity, Jim, determined that it would cleanse itself and thus would spend time/space and space/time in pursuit and contemplation of perfection. The dedication to this working was intensified until the mind/body/spirit complex rang in harmony with this intention. The entity did not grasp the literal way in which metaphysical intentions are translated by the body complex of one working in utter unity of purpose. The entity began the period of prayer, fasting, penitence, and rejoicing. The body complex, which was not yet fully recovered from the nephrotic syndrome, began to systematically cleanse each organ, sending all the detritus that was not perfect through kidneys which were not given enough liquid to dilute the toxins being released. The toxins stayed with the body complex and reactivated a purely physical illness. There is no metaphysical portion in this relapse.

The healing is taking place in manifestation of an affirmation of body complex health, which, barring untoward circumstance, shall be completely efficacious.

QUESTIONER: Is any consideration of the appropriateness of the house at Lake Lanier which we intend to move to or special preparation other than that planned advisable?

RA: I am Ra. We believe you have queried obliquely. Please requery.

QUESTIONER: We plan to cleanse the property at the Lake Lanier location, using the techniques prescribed by Ra having to do with using the salt for thirty-six hours, etc. I would like to know if this is sufficient or if there is any salient problem with respect to moving to that house that Ra could advise upon at this time, please.

RA: I am Ra. The cleansing of the dwelling of which you speak need be only three nights and two days. This dwelling is benign. The techniques are acceptable. We find three areas in which use of garlic as previously described would be beneficial. Firstly, the bunk-bed room, below the top sleeping pallet. Secondly, the exterior of the dwelling facing the road and centering about the small rocks approximately two-thirds of the length of the dwelling from the driveway side.

Thirdly, there is the matter of the boathouse. We suggest weekly cleansings of that area with garlic, the cut onions, and the walking of a light-filled perimeter. The garlic and onion, renewed weekly, should remain permanently hung, suspended from string or wire between workings.

QUESTIONER: Just so that I don't make a mistake in interpreting your directions with respect to the second area outside the house, could you give me a distance and magnetic compass heading from the exact center of the dwelling to that position?

RA: I am Ra. We may only be approximate but would suggest a distance of 37 feet, a magnetic heading of 84 to 92 degrees.

QUESTIONER: I know that it is unimportant for our purposes, and from the philosophical point of view I don't want to do anything to upset the Law of Confusion, so don't feel that it is necessary to answer this, but I was wondering what condition created the necessity for such continual cleansing of the boathouse?

RA: I am Ra. The intent is to create a perimeter within which the apiary denizens will not find it necessary to sting and indeed will not find it promising to inhabit.

QUESTIONER: Are you speaking of bees or wasps or creatures of that type?

RA: I am Ra. That is so.

QUESTIONER: Are Jim's plans and ritual for the deconsecrating of this dwelling sufficient, or should something be added or changed?

RA: I am Ra. No change is necessary. The points necessary to be included in consecration or deconsecration of the place are covered. We may suggest that each second-density, woody plant which you have invested during your tenancy within this dwelling be thanked and blessed.

QUESTIONER: Is there any other suggestion that Ra could make with respect to any part of this move that is planned, and will it—will we have any problems at all in contacting Ra in the new dwelling, and if so, will Ra tell us about those and what we could do to alleviate any problems in contacting Ra in the new dwelling?

RA: I am Ra. We weigh this answer carefully, for it comes close to abrogation of free will, but find the proximity acceptable due to this instrument's determination to be of service to the One Infinite Creator regardless of personal circumstances.

Any physical aid upon the part of the instrument in the packing and unpacking will activate those allergic reactions lying dormant for the most part at this time. This entity is allergic to those items which are unavoidable in transitions within your third-density illusion; that is, dust, mildew, etc. The one known as Bob will be of aid in this regard. The scribe should take care also to imbibe a doubled quantity of liquids in order that any allergically caused toxins may be flushed from the body complex.

There is no difficulty in resuming contact through this tuned instrument with the social memory complex, Ra, in the chosen dwelling, or, indeed, in any place whatsoever once physical and metaphysical cleansing has been accomplished.

QUESTIONER: I have come to the conclusion that the meaning of the hawk that we had about a year ago when we started to move the first time had to do with the nonbenign nature of the house, in the metaphysical sense, which I had picked. If it would not interfere with the Law of Confusion, I think that it would be philosophically interesting to know if I am correct with respect to that.

RA: I am Ra. What bird comes to affirm for Ra? What bird would be chosen to warn? We ask the questioner to ponder these queries.

QUESTIONER: We have been, you might say, experimentally determining a lot of things about the body, the next portion of the tarot, and have been experiencing some of the feedback effects, you might say, between the mind and the body. From everything that we have done so far with respect to these effects, the great value of the third-density, yellow-ray body at this time is as a device that feeds back catalyst to create the polarization, I would say. I would ask Ra if initially, when they were designed for third-density experience, the mind/body/spirits—not the mind/body/spirit complexes—had as the major use of the yellow-ray body the feeding back of catalyst, and if not, what was the purpose of the yellow-ray body?

RA: I am Ra. The description which began your query is suitable for the function of the mind/body/spirit or the mind/body/spirit complex. The position in creation of physical manifestation changed not one whit when the veil of forgetting was dropped.

QUESTIONER: Then the yellow-ray body, from the very beginning, was designed as what Ra has called an athanor for the mind, a device to accelerate the evolution of the mind. Is this correct?

RA: I am Ra. It is perhaps more accurate to note that the yellow-ray, physical vehicle is a necessity, without which the mind/body/spirit complex cannot pursue evolution at any pace.

QUESTIONER: Then you are saying that the evolution of that portion of the individual that is not yellow ray is not possible without the clothing at intervals in the yellow-ray body. Is this correct?

RA: I am Ra. No.

QUESTIONER: Would you clear up my thinking on that? I didn't quite understand your statement.

RA: I am Ra. Each mind/body/spirit or mind/body/spirit complex has an existence simultaneous with that of creation. It is not dependent upon any physical vehicle. However, in order to evolve, change, learn, and manifest the Creator, the physical vehicles appropriate to each density are necessary. Your query implied that physical vehicles accelerated growth. The more accurate description is that they permit growth.

QUESTIONER: As an example I would like to take the distortion of a disease or bodily malfunction prior to the veil and compare it to that after the veil. Let us assume that the conditions that Jim experienced with respect to his kidney malfunction had been an experience that occurred prior to the veil. Would this experience have occurred prior to the veil? Would it have been different? And if so, how?

RA: I am Ra. The anger of separation is impossible without the veil. The lack of awareness of the body's need for liquid is unlikely without the veil. The decision to contemplate perfection in discipline is quite improbable without the veil.

QUESTIONER: I would like to examine a sample, shall we say, bodily distortion prior to the veil and how it would affect the mind. Could Ra give an example of that, please?

RA: I am Ra. This general area has been covered. We shall recapitulate here.

The patterns of illness, diseases, and death are a benignant demesne[5] within the plan of incarnational experience. As such, some healing would occur by decision of mind/body/spirits, and incarnations were experienced with the normal ending of illness to death, accepted as such since without the veil it is clear that the mind/body/spirit continues. Thusly, the experiences, both good and bad, or joyful and sad, of the mind/body/spirit before veiling would be pale, without vibrancy or the keen edge of interest that such brings in the postveiling mind/body/spirit complex.

QUESTIONER: At the end of an incarnation, before veiling, did the entity appear physically to have aged like entities at the end of their incarnation in our present illusion? Did the Significator look like that?

RA: I am Ra. The Significator of Mind, Body, or Spirit is a portion of the archetypical mind and looks as each envisions such to appear. The body of mind/body/spirits before veiling showed all the signs of aging which acquaint you now with the process leading to the removal from third-density incarnation of the mind/body/spirit complex. It is well to recall that the difference betwixt mind/body/spirits and mind/body/spirit complexes is a forgetting within the deeper mind. Physical appearances and surface and instinctual activities are much the same.

QUESTIONER: Then I was wondering what was the root reason for the change in appearance that we see as the aging process. I am trying to uncover the basic philosophical premise here, but I may be shooting in the dark and not questioning on it correctly. I am trying to get at the reason behind the design in this change in appearance, when it seems to me that it would be just as possible for the mind/body/spirit or mind/body/spirit complex to look the same throughout an incarnation. Could Ra explain the reason for this change?

RA: I am Ra. When the discipline of the personality has led the mind/body/spirit complex into the fifth and especially the sixth level of study, it is no longer necessary to build destruction of the physical vehicle into its design, for the spirit complex is so experienced as a shuttle that it is aware when the appropriate degree of intensity of learning and increment of lesson have been achieved. Within third density, not to build into the physical vehicle its ending would be counterproductive to the mind/body/spirit complexes therein residing, for within the illusion it seems more lovely to be within the illusion than to drop the garment which has carried the mind/body/spirit complex and move on.

QUESTIONER: I see, then, that it is, shall we say, when an individual reaches a very old age it becomes apparent to him in third density that he is worn out. Therefore, be is not attached to this vehicle as firmly as he would be with a good-looking, well-functioning one.

After the veil, the body is definitely an athanor for the mind. Prior to the veiling, did the body serve as an athanor for the mind at all?

RA: I am Ra. Yes.

You may ask one more full query.

QUESTIONER: I believe that I should ask if there is anything that we can do to make the instrument more comfortable or to improve the contact, since in the last session I was not able to get that question in.

RA: I am Ra. We find the weariness of the group well balanced by its harmony. That weariness shall continue in any future circumstance during your incarnations. Therefore, look you to your love and thanksgiving for each other and join always in fellowship, correcting each broken strand of that affection with patience, comfort, and quietness. We find all meticulously observed in the alignments and give you these words only as reminder. All that can be done for the instrument seems done with an whole heart, and the instrument itself is working in the indigo ray with perseverance.

We have previously mentioned some temporary measures for the instrument. If these are adopted, additional liquids shall be imbibed by the instrument and by the questioner, whose bond with the instrument is such that each difficulty for one is the same in sympathy for the other.

I am Ra. I leave you rejoicing merrily in the love and the light, the power, and the peace of the One Infinite Creator. Adonai.

Fragment 56

We lived in the house on Lake Lanier for five months—from November 1983 until April 1984—before deciding that that experiment had been a failure. We were able to have only one session with Ra during that time because Don's physical condition was worsening, and his worry was increasing his mental distortions as well. Most of the time, Carla's physical condition was also below the level necessary to safely attempt contact with Ra. In January 1984, Don's condition became so bad that he was forced to call in sick for the first time in his nineteen years with Eastern Airlines. He would fly only a few more trips before his death that November.

However, as we were about to move back to Louisville, Don was able to gin himself up to be in good-enough condition for a Ra session, so we could ask about the metaphysical cleansing needs of our new home as well as ask about Don's and Carla's difficulties. Ra's reference to Carla's "inappropriate use of compassion" concerns her response to Don's continued worrying about his job, his health, and the continuance of our work. One afternoon while, Don was sharing his worries, Carla simply told him that she would take over those worries for him, and he could do what she usually did: relax, have a good time, and be carefree. Don innocently agreed. The bond of unity between Don and Carla was apparently of such a nature that this simple agreement resulted in a deleterious transfer of energy between them. This occurred at a time when both were apparently under-going an internal process of transformation that is usually called initiation.

We can assume that our friend of negative fifth density found targets of opportunities within these combined experiences of initiation and the negative energy transfer and was able to increase their intensity. The mystery-filled nature of the cumulative situation becomes more evident here, as we do not know why Carla survived and Don didn't. We can only remind ourselves of Ra's parting words after this last session, when Ra suggested, "the nature of all manifestation to be illusory and functional only insofar as the entity turns from shape and shadow to the One."

At the time of this session, I had gone through every kind of alarm and concern you could possibly imagine. Don had stopped eating, more or less. He was acting extremely unlike himself, and while I had not yet realized he was psychotic and not entirely in our usual reality, I was disturbed and scared by these changes. Don's entire pattern of previous behavior had trained me to respond to his wishes. Don picked our meal times, our movie dates; he liked and received total control over my life. Call me dependent and you'd be right. However, it was the only way Don could bear the intimacy of a live-in relationship. I could object and be heard; I could suggest and sometimes get lucky, but on the whole, Don was an old-fashioned man who liked me to be at home, period. I awaited his fancy. Meanwhile, I read or did quiet desk work.

Suddenly, he was always asking me what I had to do next, and then driving me, a chore that hurt his piles and that he usually left to Jim (I was at that point no longer driving; it hurt too much). He simply sat while I went to church, to exercise class, to the folksong rehearsals. Even though Jim was swamped with things to do for L/L business, for the landlord, who had him dig a root cellar out of red-orange clay, and for the house, Don began to try hard to stay in and eat at home every night, also a radical departure from his usual wont. Jim was off-balance—I think that's as far as his humor was affected. He was puzzled. But I was in full nervous collapse.

I feel that B.C. and I really did merge into one mind, one person, in that "inappropriate" transfer between us, triggered by my suggestion to switch roles, and his agreement. Between us, we had a simple dynamic: he was wise and I was loving. Actually, we shared much ground, but our deeper natures were quite polarized between wisdom and love. In that transfer, Don received the extreme sensitivity with which I receive all sense impression, and the fully expressing and open nature of my heart. And I received in full strength the stark terror that lived behind Don's calm and oh-so-blue eyes, tempered by his firm and very solid grasp on the big picture.

I have come to feel that in the time from this session, which was done two weeks before we left Atlanta, thankfully to return to the blessed hills of Kentucky, until B.C.'s death in November of that year, Don was able to complete an entire incarnational course of how to open his heart. I cannot express how much agony and suffering he sustained in this time. The concrete walls that were so very strong and had protected him always, fell away as if they were never there, and he felt everything. And how he loved! He could not watch television, even the sitcoms, because there was too much suffering. He, the lifelong observer by actual oath, cried at the Mary Tyler Moore Show. And when he was in the same room with me, he tried, over and over, to explain to me just how bad the situation was. This one thought was uppermost in his mind, always. The sheer horror of what he was feeling wiped him fairly clean of most other emotion, and he was unable to remain collected for long around me.

Meanwhile, I was utterly and damnably unaware of Don's fears that I preferred Jim. When Don began snatching me to him and kissing me, not knowing his strength, he hurt me, cracked a rib, split the skin of my lips against my teeth, left bruises, even, when he was in hospital in May, put me into the hospital with him, with sciatic nerve pain, which I'd gotten having to stay in an uncomfortable chair for several hours (to Don, this was the only chair that was not bugged). I became frightened of Don. I began waking up in the morning to find Don sitting beside me, waiting patiently for me to awaken. When he had said, "Good morning," he simply began telling me how bad everything was. No matter how I attempted to get him to relax, take it easy, do what the professionals had said about exercise and medication, and trust in time to heal—all of which I tried to retail to him, with absolutely no success, he was utterly sure nothing could get better, ever. For him, reality really began to slip away, to the point where I was afraid to ride with him. My nerves broke under this most difficult strain. I was completely downcast, for I could not find Don, and all I could think was that I didn't have him to go to—I had to keep together by myself on behalf of me AND L/L Research, because Don was no longer with us. He seemed a different person altogether. The color of his eyes even changed from deep, brilliant sky blue to navy. I'd been doing his paperwork for a long time. I knew that Don had slightly more than two years of built-up sick time with the airlines, and had interacted with everyone who had to be notified of his illness. Everyone, to a man, wanted nothing more than that Don take all that time, if that's what it took, to get it together again. The crises in his head were not real to me, or to Jim. Only he had the awful sense of impending economic doom. Don made a comfortable salary. His expenses for all three of us and the kitties cost him about half his check, usually, each month. But Don lost all hope, and truly that being that he became was living in hell.

And how can I look at that and say that it is all part of a perfect pattern? Only by having been given the grace to see it, finally, after many years of gazing at the riveting scenes in memory, probing them and working with them over the days, months, and years since Don died. Fifteen years have passed, and that gives a much-clearer perspective. In accepting at last the importance of the open and giving heart to balance wisdom, Don completed the personal lesson he intended to learn. Opening his heart killed his body, but truly he was rejoicing not a day after he was gone from the physical illusion, for he appeared to me several times joyful and laughing and telling me all was well. And I, my nerves permanently less than they were before the Ra contact and Don's death, have embarked upon that balancing of the compassion I have been given and earned in this next lesson, which began the day Don died.

When I woke the morning after Don's suicide, I expected my hair to be completely white. There was no outer change. But I began a completely new life at this point. Until November 1990, I spent my time in self-judgment almost entirely. I had found out about Don's suspicions of me and felt that he had enlarged these fears until he'd killed himself over them. It was my fault, not because I was guilty of any sort of infidelity, but because I should have guessed what he was thinking, and reassured him. But this never occurred to me, in my foolish pride. I just assumed that he would KNOW that I, that paragon of virtue, would never break an agreement. I really have a continuing problem with pride, because I do try to be exact in my ethics. I got completely blindsided with Don's illness.

It was further confusing that every doctor, social worker, and friend suggested the same thing—that Jim and I needed to let him alone, not to try to bribe him to do things, because he was going to have to make the decision to get well himself, and we would only lengthen the process if we fussed. Looking back, how I wish I had had the vision to say "NUTS" to that and just stay with him no matter what. And yet, as I tried my best to do just that, vowing to stay if it killed me, my body simply went dumb on me, and I woke up one morning pretty out of touch with reality. From March onward, my beloved Don was in full and fast decline, and I was walking through a complete nervous breakdown.

The allergies that had Don so worried about the Hobbs Park house were on his mind because of the lake house's unhappy brush with being flooded by burst pipes that frigid Christmas Eve. The damp had penetrated deep into the thick wall-to-wall carpeting in the hallway and rendered about half the house unlivable for me and Don. When we arrived here, we found a dry basement, or rather a basement with a sump pump and no unusual drainage problems. The humidity was fine, and the place was, indeed, a very angelic-feeling place, one that Jim and I have come to love deeply. It was Don's last work in the world, to pick out this place. As always, he did a fantastic job. It has been a privilege to be able to abide here, where my Donald was alive, where he suffered and died, and where he loved me so well. Jim and I have turned to this lovely little bungalow and its modest yard and have made more and more of it into gardens. We are still working for Don! That gives us both great comfort. Whatever we do, it is only the continuation of that which he so wonderfully began with his sharp mind and wide and thoughtful nature.

It has been a dark-hued experience for me, complete with literally years of suicidal feelings and self-condemnation. Yet, through this catalyst, I have learned to love myself, really to love and care for my self without trying to justify or defend. And this is not so much an advance in loving as it is an advance in wisdom—for one learns to love the mistakes only through wisdom. While I shall definitely never come vaguely close to being as wise as Don, I can feel the gifts he left with me. My intelligence has a persistence and clarity I feel are his gifts to me. And I see it as my remaining personal lesson to follow the pattern of devotion and love through every day and hour of the rest of this earthly life. I live now for both of us, as he died for both of us. And I feel the peace that comes with cooperation with one's destiny.

Session 106 (in total),
March 15, 1984

RA: I am Ra. I greet you in the love and in the light of the One Infinite Creator. We communicate now.

QUESTIONER: Could you first please give me the condition of the instrument?

RA: I am Ra. The parameters of this instrument are marginal, both physically and mental/emotionally. The vital energy of this entity is biased towards strength/weakness.

QUESTIONER: What would the instrument do to make the marginal condition much better?

RA: I am Ra. The instrument is proceeding through a portion of the incarnational experience during which the potential for mortal distortion of the left renal system is great. Less important, but adding to the marginality of distortion towards viability, are severe allergic reactions and the energizing of this and other distortions towards weakness/strength. The mental/emotional complex is engaged in what may best be termed inappropriate compassion.

QUESTIONER: Would Ra recommend the steps which we might take to alleviate or reverse the conditions of which you just spoke?

RA: I am Ra. We can do this. The renal distortions are subject to affirmations. The entity, at present, beginning what may be called initiation, is releasing toxins, and, therefore, larger amounts of liquids to aid in the dilution of these toxins is helpful. The allergies are already being largely controlled by affirmation and the near-constant aid of the healer known as Bob. Further aid may be achieved by the relocation of dwelling and future vigilance against humidity exceeding the healthful amount in the atmosphere breathed.

The mental/emotional distortions are somewhat less easily lessened. However, the questioner and instrument together shall find it possible to do such a working.

QUESTIONER: How serious or critical is this renal problem? Is drinking liquids the only thing she can do for that, or is there something else?

RA: I am Ra. Note the interrelationship of mind and body complexes. This is one example of such interweaving of the design of catalyst and experience. The period of renal delicacy is serious, but only potentially. Should the instrument desire to leave this incarnational experience, the natural and nonenergized opportunity to do so has been in-built, just as the period during which the same entity did, in fact, leave the incarnational experience and then return by choice was inlaid.

However, the desire to leave and be no more a portion of this particular experiential nexus can and has been energized. This is a point for the instrument to ponder and an appropriate point for the support group to be watchful in regards to care for the instrument. So are mind and body plaited up as the tresses of hair of a maiden.

The nature of this entity is gay and sociable, so that it is fed by those things we have mentioned previously: the varieties of experience with other-selves and other locations and events being helpful, as well as the experience of worship and the singing, especially of sacred music. This entity chose to enter a worshipful situation with a martyr's role when first in this geographical location. Therefore, the feeding by worship has taken place only partially. Similarly the musical activities, though enjoyable and therefore of a feeding nature, have not included the aspect of praise to the Creator.

The instrument is in a state of relative hunger for those spiritual homes which it gave up when it felt a call to martyrdom and turned from the planned worship at the location you call the Cathedral of St. Philip. This too shall be healed gradually due to the proposed alteration in location of this group.

QUESTIONER: Then as I understand it, the best thing for us to do is to advise the instrument to drink more liquid. I think water would be best. We will, of course, move. We could move her out of here immediately— tomorrow, say—if necessary. Would this be considerably better than waiting two to three weeks for the allergies and everything else?

RA: I am Ra. Such decisions are a matter for free-will choice. Be aware of the strength of the group harmony.

QUESTIONER: Is there anything, with respect to the present spiritual or metaphysical condition or physical condition of this Hobbs Park Road house, that Ra could tell us about that would be deleterious to the instrument's health?

RA: I am Ra. We may speak to this subject only to note that there are mechanical electrical devices which control humidity. The basement level is one location, the nature of which is much like that which you have experienced at the basement level of your previous domicile. Less humid conditions would remove the opportunity for the growth of those spores to which the instrument has sensitivity. The upper portions of the domicile are almost, in every case, at acceptable levels of humidity.

QUESTIONER: How about the metaphysical quality of the house? Could Ra appraise that, please?

RA: I am Ra. This location is greatly distorted. We find an acceptable description of this location's quality to elude us without recourse to hackneyed words. Forgive our limitations of expression. The domicile and its rear aspect, especially, is blessed, and angelic presences have been invoked for some of your time past.

QUESTIONER: I'm not sure that I understand what Ra means by that. I'm not sure if the place is metaphysically extremely good or extremely negative. Could Ra clear that up, please?

RA: I am Ra. We intended to stress the metaphysical excellence of the proposed location. The emblements of such preparation may well be appreciated by this group.

QUESTIONER: Would the cleansing by salt and water be necessary for this location, then? Or would it be recommended?

RA: I am Ra. There is the recommended metaphysical cleansing as in any relocation. No matter how fine the instrument, the tuning still is recommended between each concert or working.

QUESTIONER: If the instrument stays out of the basement, do you think that the humidity and the physical conditions will be good for the instrument, then? Is that correct?

RA: I am Ra. No.

QUESTIONER: We must do something about the humidity in the whole house, then, to make it good for the instrument. Is that correct?

RA: I am Ra. Yes.

QUESTIONER: I want to come back to a couple of points here, but I want to get in a question about myself. It seems to be critical at this point. Could Ra tell me what is physically wrong with me, what's causing it, and what I could do to alleviate it?

RA: I am Ra. The questioner is one also in the midst of further initiation. During this space/time, the possibility for mental/emotional distortion approaching that which causes the entity to become dysfunctional is marked. Further, the yellow-ray, chemical vehicle of the questioner is aging and has more difficulty in the absorption of needed minerals such as iron and other substances such as papain, potassium, and calcium.

At the same time, the body of yellow ray begins to have more difficulty eliminating trace elements such as aluminum. The energizing effect has occurred in the colon of the questioner, and the distortions in that area are increasingly substantial. Lastly, there is a small area of infection in the mouth of the questioner which needs attention.

QUESTIONER: Could Ra recommend what I should do to improve my state of health?

RA: I am Ra. We tread most close to the Law of Confusion in this instance but feel the appropriateness of speaking due to potentially fatal results for the instrument. We pause to give the questioner and the scribe a few moments of space/time to aid us by stepping away from those distortions which cause us to invoke the Law of Confusion. This would be helpful.

[*A few moments' pause*]

I am Ra. We appreciate your attempts. Even confusion on your behalves is helpful. The questioner has, in the recent past, allowed a complete transfer of mental/emotional pain from the questioner to the instrument. The key to this deleterious working was when the instrument said words to the effect of the meaning that it would be the questioner and be the strong one. The questioner could be as the instrument, small and foolish. The questioner, in full ignorance of the firm intent of the instrument and not grasping the possibility of any such energy transfer, agreed.

These two entities have been as one for a timeless period and have manifested this in your space/time. Thusly, the deleterious working occurred. By agreement in care and caution, it may be undone. We urge the attention to thanksgiving and harmony on the part of the questioner. We may affirm the previous recommendation in general of the skills and the purity of intention of the one known as Bob, and may note the sympathetic illness which has occurred due to the instrument's sensitivities.

Lastly, we may note that to the one known as Peter, several aspects of the distortions experienced by the questioner, the instrument, and the scribe may be quite apparent and rather simply traduced to lesser distortions.

QUESTIONER: What is Peter's last name? I am not familiar with who he is.

RA: I am Ra. The name by which this entity chooses to be known is Inman.

QUESTIONER: Does Ra think that surgery in my case would be of any help?

RA: I am Ra. We assume you speak of the colonic indisposition and its potential aid by your chirurgeons. Is this correct?

QUESTIONER: Yes.

RA: Again, I am Ra. Please blow across the face and heart of the instrument.

[This was done as directed.]

RA: I am Ra. We shall continue. The atmosphere has been meticulously prepared. However, there are those elements which cause difficulty to the instrument, the neurasthenia of the right side of the face being added to other arthritically energized pain flares.

Such an operation would be of aid in the event that the entity chose this physical cleansing as an event which collaborated with changes in the mental, mental/emotional, and physical orientations of the entity. Without the latter choice, the distortion would recur.

QUESTIONER: Now, going back to summarizing what we can do for the instrument is through praise and thanksgiving. Is that all that we can do, other than advising her to drink a considerable amount of liquid and moving her into a better atmosphere? Am I correct on that?

RA: I am Ra. We examine the statement and find two items missing, one important relative to the other. The chief addition is the grasping of the entity's nature. The less important is, for little it may seem to be, perhaps helpful; that is, the entity absorbs much medication and finds it useful to feed itself when these substances are ingested. The substitution of substances such as fruit juice for the cookie is recommended, and, further, the ingestion of substances containing sucrose which are not liquid is not recommended within four of your hours before the sleeping period.

QUESTIONER: With my experience with the dehumidifiers, I think that it will probably be impossible to lower the humidity in that house much. We can try that, and probably if we do move in there, we will have to move out very shortly.

Is there anything else that needs to be done to complete the healing of Jim's kidney problem?

RA: I am Ra. If it be realized that the condition shall linger in potential for some months after the surcease of all medication, then care will be taken and all will continue well.

We may note that, for the purposes you intend, the location, Hobbs Park Road, whether humid or arid, is uncharacteristically well suited. The aggravated present distortions of the instrument having abated due to lack of acute catalyst, the condition of the location about which the assumption was made is extremely beneficial.

QUESTIONER: Then you are saying that the effect of the humidity—we will try to get it as low as possible—is a relatively minor consideration when all of the other factors of the Hobbs Park Road address are taken into consideration? Is this correct?

RA: I am Ra. Yes.

QUESTIONER: I am quite concerned about the instrument's health at this point. I must ask if there is anything I have failed to consider with respect to the health of the instrument. Is there anything at all that we can do for her to improve her condition other than that which has already been recommended?

RA: I am Ra. All is most wholeheartedly oriented for support here. Perceive the group as here, a location in time/space. Within this true home, keep the light touch. Laugh together and find joy in and with each other. All else is most fully accomplished or planned for accomplishment.

QUESTIONER: Is it as efficacious to cleanse the house with salt and water after we move in as it is before we move in?

RA: I am Ra. In this case it is not an urgent metaphysical concern as timing would be in a less benign and happy atmosphere. One notes the relative simplicity of accomplishing such prior to occupancy. This is unimportant except as regards the catalyst with which you wish to deal.

QUESTIONER: Can you tell me what the instrument's difficulty was with her last whirlpool?

RA: I am Ra. The instrument took on the mental/emotional nature and distortion complex of the questioner, as we have previously noted. The instrument has been taking whirling waters at temperatures which are too hot and at rates of vibration which, when compounded by the heat of the swirling waters, bring about the state of light shock, as you would call the distortion. The mind complex has inadequate oxygen in this distorted state and is weakened.

In this state the instrument, having the questioner's distortion without the questioner's strength of the distortion one might liken to the wearing of armor, began to enter into an acute psychotic episode. When the state of shock was past, the symptoms disappeared. The potential remains as the empathic identity has not been relinquished, and both the questioner and the instrument live as entities in a portion of the mental/emotional complex of the instrument.

May we ask for one more full query at this working and remind the instrument that it is appropriate to reserve some small portion of energy before a working?

QUESTIONER: I would just ask if there is anything that we can do to make the instrument more comfortable or to help her and to improve the contact, and what would be the soonest that Ra would recommend the next contact? I would certainly appreciate the return of the golden hawk. It gave me great comfort.

RA: I am Ra. You have complete freedom to schedule workings.

We suggest the nature of all manifestation to be illusory and functional only insofar as the entity turns from shape and shadow to the One.

I am Ra. We leave you, my friends, in the love and in the glorious light of the One Infinite Creator. Go forth, then, rejoicing in the power and in the peace of the One Infinite Creator. Adonai.

EPILOGUE

After we moved back to Louisville, the mental/emotional dysfunction that Ra spoke of concerning Don occurred. Don was noted all his life for being very cool and extremely wise, emotionally unmoved by events that caused others to fall apart. His observations and advice always proved to be correct. Now, as this dysfunction worsened, Don saw himself intensely affected by even the smallest stimuli. His worrying deepened to depression, and he sought healing counsel from every available source, yet nothing worked, and he resigned himself to a death that he saw quickly approaching.

After seven months of this mental, emotional, and physical deterioration, he became unable to sleep or to eat solid foods. By November he had lost one-third of his body weight and was experiencing intense pain. He refused further hospitalization, which we saw as the last hope for his survival. The thought of having him put into the hospital against his will was abhorrent to us, but we decided to do it and to hope for a miracle, knowing of no other possible way to save Don's life at that point.

When the police came to serve the warrant, a five-and-one-half-hour standoff resulted. Don was convinced his death was imminent, and he did not want to die in a mental hospital. When tear gas was used to bring Don out of the house, he walked out of the back door and shot himself once through the brain. He died instantly.

After his death, Carla saw him three times in waking visions, and he assured us that all was well and that all had occurred appropriately—even if it made no sense at all to us.

So we give praise and thanksgiving for Don's life, for his death, and for our work together.

Though this book is a more personal portion of that work, we hope that you can see that the principles underlying our experiences are the same ones that underlie yours. Though expressions may vary widely, the purpose is the same: that the many portions of the One may know themselves and the One as One. Or, as Ra put it:

"We leave you in appreciation of the circumstance of the great illusion in which you now choose to play the pipe and timbrel and move in rhythm. We are also players upon a stage. The stage changes. The acts ring down. The lights come up once again. And throughout the grand illusion and the following and the following, there is the undergirding majesty of the One Infinite Creator. All is well. Nothing is lost. Go forth rejoicing in the love and the light, the peace, and the power of the One Infinite Creator. I am Ra. Adonai." (from Session 104)

Jim and I have wished to open this personal material for those who feel they might find it useful, because we see in our experiences a good example of the kind of stress that working in the light will produce. The more full of enlightenment the channeling received, the more enlightened the patterns of living and talking need to be. In the case of Don, Jim, and me, all of our outer behavior was correct, and it was not to be held against Don that he didn't become a talker when he got sick. He had never taken another's advice, and he did not want mine or Jim's, then, anymore than usual. And so the tendency Don had of being paranoid bloomed until he was sure I was no longer his love. For him the world without me was unacceptable.

Looking deeper at the timing here, it is crucial that it be seen that I was at this point weighing in at around 84 pounds, at 5 feet, 4 inches. Each session was extremely hard, and yet I never flagged in my desire to continue. I was perfectly willing to die in the process of gaining these sessions' contents. Don was very worried that I would indeed die, and fussed over me continually. There was some mechanism within him that persisted in trying to figure out how to substitute himself for me in taking the brunt of the contact. He spoke about it from time to time, and I always discouraged that line of thinking. But he did just that, in the end. His death ended the contact with those of Ra, and we have never been tempted to take it up again, as we are following Ra's own advice not to do that except with the three of us.

I want to express to each reader the profound feeling of peace that has come to me in the healing of my present incarnation. There will always be that part of me that wishes I could have either been able to save Don or to die with him. I think that is one valid way I could have gone. Then he and I would be a vastly romantic, and quite dead, part of L/L history. But this is not the lesson that was mine. Mine was the lesson concerning wisdom. Ra put it to me quite bluntly when he asked what my time was for going to Jerusalem. He was asking me whether I wanted to martyr myself. This was in the context of questions Don asked concerning the possibility of more-frequent sessions. My response to that was to go on my first vacation in eleven years. Don and I had adventures, NOT vacations!

Don's lesson when our energies and mental distortions were exchanged and merged by our talk in Georgia was concerning the complete opening of his heart. By remaining an observer, he had not yet succeeded in unblocking that great heart of his. In his illness, he truly thought that he was dying that I might be well and live peacefully. There is no more utter devotion and sacrifice than the giving of one's life. It does not matter, in this context, that he was dead wrong. He never lost me, far from it. He lost himself. In his moment of death, he was completely open of heart, and uncaring of the pain of living or of leaving. Of course I have many and conflicting emotions about this. But always I am absolute in my faith that Don's ending was as noble as his life as a whole. To me, he is beyond words. I just adore that soul.

My lesson was the opposite: that of adding wisdom to completely open love. My heart chakra is usually quite unblocked, but my sense of limits has long been shaky. The mind-meld we shared at that time left me with a choice of dying for Don's sake or living for his work, for L/L Research, and all we had done and been together. I did exactly what I had to do to stay in this world. It was touch and go for me for a long time; long after Don's death I was working the energy of death through my own mind, body, and spirit. Through the years, I plumbed the depths of despair, anger (how dare he doubt me!), grief, and sorrow. I faced my own physical death and knew that the crux had come, and the joy of living was still strong within me. This was during the difficult days around Christmas of 1991. I have never been in that much extremity before, not even when my kidneys failed. But my love felt never stronger. I felt as though all was being burned away, and I welcomed that. In the heat of that pain, I felt cleansing and completion. From that time, it was as if a whole new strength had poured into my frail body. As I have achieved a rise from wheelchair and hospital bed, I have felt more and more joy-filled and at the same time transparent. This is a new life I am experiencing, in a new and much replenished body. Indeed, at the age of 54, I feel a grounding and balance that are solid and healthy. I am glad to be here and feel that have entered into the working out of the second pattern that my divided life offers. I bless Don's and my sad tale. And I bless all that has occurred. We loved; we were human. It seems as though we often erred. We did not, for we truly loved. And though I shall always feel orphaned by his absence from my side, I embrace the wonderful things that are now mine to treasure. Jim and I are fueled constantly by the blessing of being able to carry on Don's work.

Any group that stays together and works harmoniously while being of service to the light will begin to attract psychic greeting of the sorts we experienced. In this crucible, every fault and vanity, however small, is a weapon against the self. Ethical perception needs to remain very alert and cogent of issues and values being tossed around. This is a matter of life and death. L/L Research is a special and wonderful place, and not unlike many other lighthouses other wanderers and seekers have lit. Many, many others are awakening now and wishing to become ever more able to be channels for light. And it is a wondrous ministry, to be there as a metaphysical or spiritual home for wanderers and outsiders everywhere. We hope this helps you and your group to stay in full communication, to refuse to offer each other less than joy and faith, no matter what! And never, NEVER to make a deal with the loyal opposition!

We at L/L Research continue to keep our doors open for regular meetings, and many visitors come through our doors, through the snail mail and email, and as our books continue to be spread around, those who are aware of Ra's ideas are all over the globe. Our email address is contact@llresearch. org, *our website is* www.llresearch.org, *and our snail-mail address is* L/L Research, PO Box 5195, Louisville, Kentucky 40255-5195. *We answer each piece of mail and are always glad to hear from readers old and new. Our hearts are eternally grateful for each other, for Don, for those of Ra and the contact they shared with us. Blessings to all who read this book.*

L/L Research
Carla L. Rueckert
Jim McCarty

Louisville, Kentucky
December 20, 1997

ENDNOTES

1. puissance: The power to accomplish or achieve; potency [< OF]
2. sigil: A seal or signet; a mark or sign supposed to exercise occult power. [< L *siggilum* seal]
3. chary: Cautious, careful, wary; fastidious; particular; sparing, frugal; stingy [<OE *cearig* sorrowful, sad < *cearu* care]
4. contumely: Insulting rudeness in speech or manner; scornful insolence; an insult, or an insulting act [<OF *contumelie* < L *contumelia* reproach]
5. demesne: In feudal law, lands held in one's own power; a manor house and the adjoining lands in the immediate use and occupation of the owner of the estate; the grounds belonging to any residence, or any landed estate; any region over which sovereignty is exercised; domain. [< AF *demeyne*, OF *demeine*, *demaine*. *Doublet of domain.*]

INDEX

ABOUT THE AUTHORS

DON ELKINS was born in Louisville, Kentucky, in 1930. He held a BS and MS in mechanical engineering from the University of Louisville, as well as an MS in general engineering from Speed Scientific School. He was professor of physics and engineering at the University of Louisville for twelve years from 1953 to 1965. In 1965 he left his tenured position and became a Boeing 727 pilot for a major airline to devote himself more fully to UFO and paranormal research. He also served with distinction in the US Army as a master sergeant during the Korean War.

Don Elkins began his research into the paranormal in 1955. In 1962, Don started an experiment in channeling, using the protocols he had learned from a contactee group in Detroit, Michigan. That experiment blossomed into a channeling practice that led eventually to the Law of One material 19 years later. Don passed away on November 7, 1984.

CARLA L. RUECKERT (McCarty) was born in 1943 in Lake Forest, Illinois. She completed undergraduate studies in English literature at the University of Louisville in 1966 and earned her master's degree in library service in 1971.

Carla became partners with Don in 1968. In 1970, they formed L/L Research. In 1974, she began channeling and continued in that effort until she was stopped in 2011 by a spinal fusion surgery. During four of those thirty-seven years of channeling (1981–1984), Carla served as the instrument for the Law of One material.

In 1987, she married Jim McCarty, and together they continued the mission of L/L Research. Carla passed into larger life on April 1, 2015.

JAMES MCCARTY was born in 1947 in Kearney, Nebraska. After receiving an undergraduate degrees from the University of Nebraska at Kearney and a master of science in early childhood education from the University of Florida, Jim moved to a piece of wilderness in Marion County, Kentucky, in 1974 to build his own log cabin in the woods, and to develop a self-sufficient lifestyle. For the next six years, he was in almost complete retreat.

He founded the Rock Creek Research and Development Laboratories in 1977 to further his teaching efforts. After experimenting, Jim decided that he preferred the methods and directions he had found in studying with L/L Research in 1978. In 1980, he joined his research with Don's and Carla's.

Jim and Carla were married in 1987. Jim has a wide L/L correspondence and creates wonderful gardens and stonework. He enjoys beauty, nature, dance, and silence.

NOTE: The Ra contact continued until session number 106. There are five volumes total in The Law of One series, Book I–Book V. There is also other material available from our research group on our archive website, www.llresearch.org.

You may reach us by email at contact@llresearch.org, or by mail at: L/L Research, P.O. Box 5195, Louisville, KY 40255-0195

NOTES

NOTES